BUSINESS ETHICS

FIFTH EDITION

BUSINESS ETHICS

RICHARD T. DE GEORGE

University of Kansas

PRENTICE HALL
Upper Saddle River, New Jersey 07458

Library of Congress Cataloging-in-Publication Data
DE GEORGE, RICHARD T.
    BUSINESS ETHICS / RICHARD T. DE GEORGE.—5th ed.
    p.   cm.
    Includes bibliographical references and index.
    ISBN 0-13-079772-3 (alk. paper)
    1. Business ethics.   2. Business ethics—Case studies.   I. Title.
HF5387.D38 1999
174'.4—dc21   98-42973

Editorial director: *Charlyce Jones Owen*
Acquisitions editor: *Karita France*
Assistant editor: *Emsal Hasan*
Production editor: *Edie Riker*
Cover art director: *Jayne Conte*
Cover design: *Bruce Kenselaar*
Cover image: *Ron Lowery/Tony Stone Images*
Buyer: *Tricia Kenny*
Marketing manager: *Isle Wolfe*
Editorial assistant: *Jennifer Ackerman*

This book was set in 10/12 Palatino by East End Publishing Services
and was printed and bound by Courier Companies, Inc. The cover was
printed by Phoenix Color Corp.

© 1999, 1995, 1990, 1986, 1982 by Prentice Hall, Inc.
Simon & Schuster / A Viacom Company
Upper Saddle River, New Jersey 07458

Printed in the United States of America

10 9 8 7 6 5 4 3 2 1

ISBN   0-13-079772-3

Prentice Hall International (UK) Limited, *London*
Prentice Hall of Australia Pty. Limited, *Sydney*
Prentice Hall Canada, Inc., *Toronto*
Prentice Hall Hispanoamericana, S.A., *Mexico*
Prentice Hall of India Private Limited, *New Delhi*
Prentice Hall of Japan, Inc., *Tokyo*
Simon & Schuster Asia Pte. Ltd., *Singapore*
Editora Prentice Hall do Brasil, Ltda., *Rio de Janeiro*

CONTENTS

MORAL ISSUES IN INTERNATIONAL BUSINESS

PREFACE

In the many years since the first edition of this book appeared courses in business ethics have become firmly established in colleges, business schools, and MBA programs. Such courses took root in the post-Watergate era and were nurtured by successive exposés involving bribes and kickbacks, illegal political contributions, airplane disasters, and the sale of defective tires, automobiles, and other products. Consumerism, the cry for increased governmental control, and a changing attitude of large numbers of people toward business and its social responsibility have made questions of business ethics topics of general and current concern. Business ethics is no longer considered a contradiction in terms and most large corporations have taken measures to incorporate at least some of the trappings of ethics into their structures.

This book is an attempt to cover the field in a systematic and reasonably comprehensive way. It deals first with the techniques of moral reasoning and argumentation that are needed to analyze moral issues in business. It then raises basic questions about the morality of economic systems, especially that of the United States. It next discusses a variety of current and pressing moral issues in business from worker's rights to legitimate computer use. Because business has changed, this edition attempts to mirror the ethical issues raised by those changes, foremost of which are ethical questions that stem from information technology and the globalization of business.

This is not simply a book in general ethics that takes its examples from the business world. Ethics as a discipline has a long and venerable history. But students do not need to know that history, nor do they need to know the large number of disputed questions with which that discipline abounds, in order to engage in moral thinking. Moral issues are pressing, and people must grapple with them using the best tools available at the time. I try, therefore, to introduce the student to as much of the technical aspect of ethics as is necessary in order to approach moral issues intelligently and to take part in the ongoing debate about the morality of certain social and business practices. The aim of my initial chapters is a practical one, and to achieve this end I necessarily ignore or pass over lightly some of the theoretical issues on which much of contemporary professional ethical thought is focused. Students, I assume, come to classes in business ethics with a good deal of moral baggage. They are not nonmoral beings who must be made moral but rather moral beings who can be helped to think through moral issues and to argue cogently and effectively for their moral views. The present edition highlights how to apply the standard ethical approaches in analyzing issues, problems, and cases.

The traditional approach to ethics is an individualistic one. Our notions of morality, moral worth, and moral praise and blame have grown up primarily from consideration of the human person as a moral agent. We know what it means to call a person moral or his actions morally praiseworthy. The present edition adds the dimension of virtue and character to the discussion, two concepts that have taken on increasing importance in recent years. Yet economic systems do not act in a way comparable to the way human individuals act; and corporations and nations act only figuratively and through the agency of human intermediaries. Moral language must be used with care and caution when applied outside of the realm of human individuals and their actions. Special problems arise when considering the morality of corporations, nations, and people—problems that concern the meaning of moral terms, and problems that must be faced and clarified if we are to be clear about our moral judgments in these areas.

I assume that there is little need to argue that murder is wrong, that stealing and lying are in general wrong, or that discrimination on the basis of sex, race, or creed is immoral in business as in other areas of life. There is no need therefore for a course in business ethics to arrive at or justify those conclusions. But many of the questions of business ethics that involve reverse discrimination, truth in advertising, whistle blowing, and disclosure, among others, are not clear-cut. They require careful analysis and a weighing of appropriate facts and applicable principles in order to arrive at justifiable answers. Our society is clearer on some of these issues than on others. I have tried to present the complexities of each problem and to weigh the opposing views on an issue. When I have taken sides, I have given my reasons for doing so; if an argument is inconclusive I have indicated where and why. On broad social issues no argument will be the final one, and my hope is that students using this text will, by reading it, be encouraged and emboldened to help continue and advance the public debate on these issues.

I do not think it is sufficient simply to identify moral problems in business, to determine what actions are right and wrong, and to demand that people be moral heroes in doing what is required of them. If practices are immoral and if people are faced with the obligation of sacrificing their jobs and their security to fulfill their moral obligations, then those practices should be changed. I therefore attempt not only to discuss what is morally required of a person in a firm—a worker, a manager, a member of the board of directors—but also what structures are conducive to a person's accepting moral responsibility and fulfilling his or her moral obligations. How firms can be reorganized so as to preclude the necessity for whistle blowing is as pressing (if not more pressing) a question as asking when a person is morally obliged to blow the whistle.

Business is a social activity and, like all social activity, could not function unless certain moral prerequisites were fulfilled. Recent experience in some of the states of the former Soviet Union has demonstrated this clearly. An analysis of needed prerequisites and of the social and business structures conducive to morality form, I believe, an important and frequently neglected aspect of business ethics. At each stage of investigation, therefore, I raise and attempt to answer not only the question of whether a particular practice is moral or immoral but also the question of what alternative can and should be pursued with respect to immoral practices. The morality of individuals should not be separated from the morality of business procedures and institutions, and in what follows I handle them together to the extent possible.

I start each chapter with a case or two that raises an issue pertinent to the contents of that particular chapter. I have also incorporated in a number of chapters actual and fictitious case studies to illustrate specific principles, to exemplify ways of analyzing moral problems, and to contrast varying approaches to an issue. For those who wish additional cases, the daily newspaper carries ample materials for analysis and current, specific, timely examples of moral issues in business.

Although I have written this book so that it develops a total view through successive chapters, each chapter can be studied apart from the others. Those who wish to omit the analysis of some issues and concentrate on a selected few can do so without a loss of intelligibility. Those wishing to read further on a topic will find suggestions in the footnotes and references to material on both sides of controversial questions.

Each chapter is followed by study questions that highlight the contents of the chapter and can be taken as a guide to the chapter. The questions also contain one or two cases or brief issues not explicitly covered in the chapter, that may be used for discussion, reflection, or written paper assignments.

Each successive edition of this book has attempted to take into account the significant research that has appeared in the intervening years as well as the pertinent developments in business and society. The present edition of this book continues to do so. In addition to cases and footnotes, all the chapters have been updated, and many have been significantly revised. The chapter order has been slightly changed, and I deal with conceptual issues of corporations and responsibility in a separate chapter. I have added material on information technology and I have expanded the discussion of issues in international business. Despite these changes, the book's aim, approach, and theme remain the same. American business can be made more moral. This book is an attempt to help its readers think about how this goal might be accomplished.

I would like to thank the following reviewers for their helpful comments regarding this edition: Robert L. Cunningham, University of San Francisco; Richard L. Wilson, Towson State University; Sally A. Dresdow, University of Wisconsin at Green Bay; and Joy K. Benson, University of Illinois at Spring-filed.

R. T. De George

INTRODUCTION

1

>─┤◆├─◯─┤◆├─┤─<

ETHICS AND BUSINESS

Johnson & Johnson and the Tylenol Case

On September 30, 1982, three people in the Chicago area died from cyanide introduced into their Extra-Strength Tylenol capsules. The link between the deaths and the capsules was made with remarkable speed, and authorities notified Johnson & Johnson, the manufacturers of Tylenol. As the number of deaths grew—the final total was seven—the firm faced a crisis and potential disaster. Tylenol, a leading pain-reliever, was Johnson & Johnson's single largest brand, accounting for 7.4 percent of its revenue and 17 to 18 percent of the corporation's income.[1]

The small number of executives involved in deciding how to respond did not know whether the cyanide had been introduced into the Tylenol bottles during the manufacturing process or later; whether the deaths that had already been reported were just the first of an indefinitely large number; or whether the deaths would be limited to Chicago or extend to other cities. The U.S. Food and Drug Administration had issued a warning not to take Tylenol, but the government had not ordered the company to take any specific action. Perhaps the deaths would be local, and the number would not go beyond seven. Perhaps the authorities would not demand a recall. Perhaps a temporary cessation of sales until the cause could be determined would be sufficient to contain the harm to the public. Against these unknowns were the cer-

---

[1] Details on the Tylenol case come from the *Chicago Tribune* and the *New York Times*, October 1–10, 1982; and *Business Week*, October 18, 1982.

tainties that a recall would involve a loss of up to $100 million; that the loss was not covered by insurance; that news of a recall would so damage the product that the company executives had no assurance Tylenol would ever be able to regain public confidence and the 37 percent market share it then held; that the news and loss would surely result in a dramatic drop in the company's stock (it in fact went down 15 percent in the first week of October); and that the competition in the analgesic market was fierce and certainly their competitors would try to make Tylenol's loss their gain. These were certainties; the rest was guesswork and speculation.

How should a company decide what to do in such a situation? Aren't the health of the company and the interests of the shareholders management's first priority? Aren't these best served by using caution, by adopting a wait and see approach, by denying the deaths were the fault of the company and by claiming they were due either to a saboteur or to a perhaps demented criminal? Shouldn't business decisions be based on facts and finances?

>─┼─◄►─●─◄►─┼─◄

For many, the answers are yes. Yet we know that when faced with the fact of seven deaths and the possibility of more, Johnson & Johnson ordered an immediate recall of all Tylenol bottles. The company put the safety of the public first, as the company's Credo says it should.[2] The certain damage to the firm, though tragic and unwelcome, came second.

The incident has grown into legend, and the reaction of Johnson & Johnson has become a textbook study in how to respond to a tragedy. Not only was the decision hailed as the proper one from an ethical point of view, but also the company handled the aftermath of the tragedy in a skillful manner. The company was open in supplying the public with information, and within 18 months won back 96 percent of its former market share. It did in fact lose $100 million, and the worth of its stock did fall.

James Burke, the chairman and CEO of Johnson & Johnson, who was praised in retrospect for his action, has commented both that the action was in fact the only one to take, given the company's Credo, and that he found it surprising that people would expect anything less than such action from his company.

Yet he knows full well that not every company would have acted as Johnson & Johnson did, even if that was the ethically correct action to take. Despite its example, a few years later when a customer found a chip of ceramic in a jar of Gerber baby food, Gerber reacted by denying any culpability and resisted a recall[3]—as have a number of automobile companies when faced with complaints of unsafe vehicles.

---

[2] The first item of the Johnson & Johnson Credo reads: We believe our first responsibility is to the doctors, nurses, and patients, to mothers, and all others who use our products and services.

[3] Patricia Strnad, "Gerber Ignores 'Tylenol Textbook'," *Advertising Age*, 57 (March 10, 1986), p. 3.

Are companies ethically liable for their actions? Should the public hold them to ethical standards? Or should we simply expect them to obey the law and to govern themselves by business, economic, and market considerations?

The American people have for a long time been ambivalent in their response, and despite a growing consensus that ethics has a role to play in business, the public view of business is still expressed in what can be called the *Myth of Amoral Business.*

The Myth of Amoral Business

The Myth of Amoral Business expresses a popular, widespread view of American business. Like most myths, it has several variations. Many people believe the myth, or somewhat believe it. It expresses a partial truth at the same time that it conceals a good deal of reality.

The myth describes how many American businesses and many American businessmen and -women perceive themselves and are perceived by others: Business is concerned primarily with profit. To earn a profit, a business produces goods or provides services and engages in buying and selling. According to the myth, however, businesses and people in business are not explicitly concerned with ethics. They are not unethical or *immoral*; rather, they are *amoral* insofar as they feel that ethical considerations are inappropriate in business. After all, business is business. They are opposed to moralizing. They dislike being preached to by moralists, and they are very reluctant to throw stones at the glass houses of even their fiercest competitors. Ethical language, the myth continues, is simply not the language of business.

Most people in business do not act unethically or maliciously. They think of themselves, in both their private and their business lives, as ethical people. They simply feel that business is not expected to be concerned with ethics. Even when a firm acts according to an ethical principle, it rarely boasts about it in ethical terms or even presents its action as ethical. In this respect Johnson & Johnson was typical, even though the media acclaimed its action as exemplary.

One of the interesting variations on the theme is that because many businesses are not explicitly concerned with ethics, some of them act unethically. One need only think of the many unsavory scandals that make newspaper headlines—accounts of bribery, misrepresentation, white-collar crime, kickbacks, unsafe products, and insider manipulation of markets. The 1980s were full of such accounts, and Michael Milken and Ivan Boesky[4] became examples of how not to act, just as the Johnson & Johnson case became an example of how to act. Equally well known are the damage that some industries have wreaked on the environment, the harm done to some towns where the local plant has closed, and the prevalent disregard for the common good. Accord-

---

[4] For details of these cases, see James B. Stewart, "Scenes from a Scandal: The Secret World of Michael Milken and Ivan Boesky," *Wall Street Journal,* October 2, 1991, p. B1, and Karen W. Arenson, "How Wall Street Bred Ivan Boesky," *New York Times,* November 26, 1986, p. 8F.

ing to the myth, businesses act unethically not because of a desire to do evil, but simply because they want to make a profit and therefore disregard some of the consequences of their actions.

The Myth of Amoral Business represents not only the way many people in and out of the business world perceive business but also the way many would like to continue to perceive business. It is much easier to deal with dollars and cents than to deal with value judgments. It is more comfortable to discuss a problem in terms of a bottom line that represents profit or loss than one that does not. It is easier not only for those in business but also for those not in business to judge a firm by its financial status or by the products it produces. The bottom line is what concerns investors and what directly affects the workers in a company. The end product is all that concerns most consumers.

As with most popularly held myths, the Myth of Amoral Business captures a popular truth. Yet it also conceals a good deal of real life. This book and the general topic of business ethics concern what for a long time was concealed or ignored and has only lately been surfacing for discussion and action. Scandals, environmental issues, and energy problems have all helped the reality surface now and then, but no new Myth of Moral Business has resulted. For despite some progress made by business in developing ethical codes or instituting ethics training programs, most people do not yet believe that business has made ethics a primary concern and an overriding value in its business decisions.

What, then, is the hidden reality: What is the true relation of ethics and business, which is only slowly emerging? What are the indications of its emergence?

Take the last question first. The breakdown of the Myth of Amoral Business has been signaled in three fairly obvious ways: by the reporting of scandals and the concomitant public reaction to these reports; by the formation of popular groups such as the environmentalists and the consumerists; and by the concern of business in ethics, as expressed in conferences, magazine and newspaper articles, and by the burgeoning of corporate codes of ethical conduct and of ethics programs.

How do the reporting of scandals in business and the popular reaction to them signal a breakdown of the myth? By way of a reply, consider what the myth implies, if it is taken seriously. If it is true that business is viewed as amoral, that it is not expected to behave according to ethical rules, and that it is expected to do whatever is necessary in order to increase its profit, then there would be no indignation, shock, or uproar when a business acted unethically. The uncovering of bribes and kickbacks would not be news. Revelations about unsafe products and white-collar crime would be routine—expected and unexceptional. The fact that such events *do* make news, that they *do* cause public reaction, that they *do* adversely affect a company's image, and that they *do* cause scandal is an indication that the Myth of Amoral Business is not unambiguously accepted.

The hidden reality, now emerging, is that it is no longer true that anything goes. Many people now expect companies to act morally, at least in certain instances and within certain limits. Contemporary reactions provide evidence that, if the myth does describe the way things are, many people think that things should be otherwise, that is, that business should behave ethically. At least two groups—the environmentalists and the consumerists—articulate their demands and try to force businesses to consider values other than those that are reducible to sales figures and ledger sheets. The issues raised by these groups are not stated in terms of dollars and cents but in terms of other values, such as the beauty of the land, the preservation of certain species of animals and fish, and the right of people to adequate information about the goods they purchase. These demands have a new dimension, which has forced even those firms reacting negatively to the environmentalists and consumerists to consider the claims that these groups and others are making. If the Myth of Amoral Business were the whole story, the environmental and consumer movements would make no sense, and business would not respond to them. Because the movements do make sense and because business does respond, the myth is only part of the story.

The reaction of business to these movements has been significant. Sometimes the reaction has been one of annoyance and puzzlement. Some businesses have tried to ignore the claims made in the name of the environment, consumers, and ethics and have acted in conformity to the Myth of Amoral Business. Others have seen that ignoring demands will not make them go away. Another reaction has been for companies to seek counsel and to share their perplexity about how to respond to the increasing public demands. A result has been the convening of a surprising number of conferences, meetings, and symposia, sponsored by business or attended by those in business. The theme is most frequently related to values, to questions of business ethics, and to ways of handling what has become known as the *social audit.* Business is not structured to handle questions of values and ethics, and its managers have usually not been trained in business schools to do so. Experience has supplied even less training along these lines. Hence, many businesses have faced a new dilemma. They are now beginning to feel they should respond to demands involving social values and should take ethical issues into account in their deliberations, but they do not know how to do so. Nonetheless, conferences, meetings, new ethical codes, and the emergence of what are called corporate ethics officers in business prove that the Myth of Amoral Business is slowly waning.

The American Business Value System

The Myth of Amoral Business in part reflects, and in part ignores, the fact that American business is embedded in American society and shares its values.[5] The myth focuses on the rugged individualism emphasized in a free-

---

[5] For another a discussion of the American business value system, see Gerald F. Cavanagh, *American Business Values,* 3rd ed. (Upper Saddle River, N.J.: Prentice Hall, 1990).

enterprise approach to business, on the negative aspects of competition, and on the pragmatism characteristic of the American approach to abstractions. It recognizes that *freedom* is necessary to the system. But the line between freedom and license in business is not always sharp.

The American business system is often described as a free-enterprise system. In contrast with socialism, American business claims to be free from government ownership and domination. It is, of course, not totally free of government intervention, or of government support and protection. But freedom *is* a value that forms an important basis for business activity in the United States.

On the positive side, freedom in American business extends not only to the owners and managers of business but also to the employees and consumers. Those who defend the free-enterprise system against critics typically emphasize the value of individual freedom as opposed to planned, directed, state-owned, and state-dominated economies. The argument in defense of free enterprise trades heavily on the maturity, intelligence, and responsibility of those operating within the economic system. The value of free enterprise, though taken to be self-evident by Americans, is not so perceived by all people. Our system assumes that all persons wish for their own good and know better than anyone else what they want. The system allows all adult persons to make their own decisions, to follow their own ways of life, and, within the limits set by the rights of others, to choose the values they wish to pursue. This freedom tends to mask the common values held by most people and to promote a wide tolerance of different life-styles and ways of acting. The Myth of Amoral Business reflects this tolerance.

The system presupposes the value to each of us of entering into transactions of our own choosing, of pursuing our own good, and of satisfying our individual needs and desires. Because all of us differ to some extent in what we want and need, we are all free to use our own resources to obtain what we want. Some spend comparatively more on housing than others, some spend more on food, and some spend more on clothing, transportation, or entertainment.

The possibility of acting freely puts a premium on the social and geographic mobility of individuals, as well as on the mobility of money and resources. The freedom of the manager to hire and fire is matched by the freedom of workers to choose their kind of work, and, within limits, their employer. Freedom, however, carries with it the risk of failure and frequently tends to favor the business more than the individual employee or job applicant.

Those who enter the marketplace carry on transactions with an eye toward advancing their own good. The system itself holds promise of producing goods in great abundance, of allowing people to satisfy their needs and wants, and of providing them with a higher standard of living than was in previous centuries imagined possible. If freedom is central to free enterprise, however, the value of *profit, money,* and *goods* cannot and should not be overlooked. The free-enterprise system places a premium on profit because it is for profit that profit-making enterprises are established. Together with the desire for profit goes the desire for goods and for the kind of life that money can buy. The desire for a good life and the value placed on a good life are not unique to the free-enterprise system, but they are central values in it. These values do not necessarily lead to the overemphasis on possessions and on materialistic values that many of its critics claim, but a tendency in that direction certainly exists. The Myth of Amoral Business frequently focuses on the desire for profit rather than on the freedom to choose one's good. Both are part of the system.

Even to characterize the system as one of free enterprise, however, is to accept a somewhat idealized view of it because the freedom has always existed within the limits imposed by a political framework. In that context, freedom in business is limited by two traditional values that have been held as ideals—the values of *fairness* and of *equal opportunity*. The notion of fairness is a typically American value; business transactions are expected to be fair. Both sides enter a transaction in order to achieve their own good, and both achieve this if the transaction is fair. Fairness, in turn, assumes the additional values of honesty and of truthfulness on the part of those who take part in the transaction. Fairness is, of course, not always realized, but it does exist as an ideal. Similarly, there is a tacit assumption that talented people who are willing to work can advance and succeed. The ideal of equal opportunity thus forms a backdrop against which reality is measured.

Competition at all levels makes the free-enterprise system work. It operates on all levels. The laws of supply and demand regulate the cost of goods and the allocation of resources. Consumers vote with their dollars for the products of their choice, selecting from competing brands. There is competition among makers of goods, who compete for workers; there is competition among workers for better jobs, more pay, and more rapid advancement. The Myth of Amoral Business assumes that the competition is not only fierce but also cutthroat. In fact, competition involves both benefits and costs and is only sometimes, not always, ruthless.

Although everyone expects to benefit from the system, inequality is built into it. Some will succeed in a competition, and others will fair less well. Wealth is an attractive impetus for people to develop their creative, productive powers, but differential reward is part of the system. There is also a premium on risk taking: Those who take the greatest risks are offered the prospect of the greatest reward, and also the possibility of failure. The system does not prevent failure; it requires it. Competition weeds out the weak and the less productive, the overly cautious and the less skillful.

Two other values of the American business system are *pragmatism* and *efficiency*. Pragmatism evaluates reality in terms of results. The pragmatic approach of Americans emphasizes the practical over the theoretical; it distrusts abstractions and looks continually for results. Pragmatism coheres well with efficiency—a value that is identified with American business and a value that it embraces. Fair competition rewards the most efficient—those able to produce, at a lower price, commodities of a quality equal to or better than a competitor's. As machines multiply the productive output of human labor, and as microchips replace machines, more goods of a better quality can be produced more quickly and frequently at a lower cost. Efficiency enables businesses to increase their productive capacities and to receive the greatest return for the energy expended. The efficiency of the machine, the advances made possible by technology, and American ingenuity and genius for organization have enabled Americans to produce the wealth and achieve the standard of living that we collectively enjoy.

Those who believe the Myth of Amoral Business tend to ignore some of the vices of the American business system. Inadequately restrained freedom in the marketplace tempts some to seek their own goals at the expense of other people. Greed often blinds people to the requirements of fairness. Many people succumb to the temptation to win by whatever means available, fair or not. We know the history of the robber barons and of the many holders of power and wealth who exploited those who had neither. We also know that many transactions into which people enter are not fair and free but are forced and manipulated. Competition, moreover, leaves behind many who cannot compete, as well as those who fail. How are they to be cared for?

Some commentators characterize the American system as materialistic and morally soft. They claim America's wealth has undermined the industry and thrift exemplified in the Protestant work ethic and replaced it with profligacy and the desire for the easy life. The reverse side of efficiency and rapid development is extravagance and the waste created by built-in obsolescence. Products are not made to last as long as possible because to do so would undercut the continuing need to replace them and so the need for continuing production. Short-term considerations—reflected in quarterly reports by corporations—dominate long-term ones. The optimism characteristic of American society is reflected in the belief that things will always get better, that the abundance we enjoy will continue into the foreseeable future, and that the long run will take care of itself if we take care of the short run. But we buy such optimism at a price, and the "future," when it comes, is not always as good as we had hoped.

The American business value system is, consequently, a mixture of good and bad. Should freedom be emphasized more than security, or competition more than equality? How can we limit the negative aspects of some values and check the undesired consequences of pursuing others? Is the value system changing? Are some of the values—for instance, those based on abundance—obsolete? Many people ask these questions, as our society struggles with the realities of limited resources, a growing demand for economic as well as political equality, increasing pressures from foreign competition, the aging of many of our industries, and the pollution of the air, water, and land. Which values are morally justifiable? And is the system of free enterprise itself morally justifiable? If so, under what conditions? Business ethics studies these issues.

The Relation of Business and Morality

Business and morality are related in a number of significant ways that are ignored by the Myth of Amoral Business. Some of these relationships are obvious—so obvious that we take them for granted and hence tend to ignore them. Others are subtle—so subtle that, again, we tend to ignore them. But whether obvious or subtle, they are part of our daily lives and experience. We can illuminate them, focus on them, and bring them into the open, thus articulating the relationship of business and morality. We shall consider five aspects, under the following headings: the Moral Background of Business, the Foundations of Property, the Business of Business, Business and the Law, and the Changing Mandate for Business.

The Moral Background of Business

Business is an important part of contemporary society. It involves all of us, in one way or another. We all purchase goods that we need for survival and comfort. We all rely on the availability of electricity and gasoline. We buy food, clothing, and services. People supply these for us. Manufacturers make goods that we need and want. Other people transport them to stores, where others sell them to consumers. Business is not something separate from society or imposed on it—it is an integral part of society. Morality consists of rules of human behavior and specifies that certain actions are wrong or immoral and that others are right or moral. We can take the moral point of view to evaluate human action. Some actions, such as murder, are recognized as being immoral. Others, such as helping one's neighbor, are generally considered moral. Still others, such as tying one's shoe, are, at least in the abstract, morally indifferent. These latter actions assume moral character only in particular circumstances—for instance, when used purposefully to annoy someone or to cause someone harm. Any action can be viewed from a moral perspective. Hence, it is difficult to imagine what people mean when they say that morality and business do not mix or are antithetical.

Because business activity is human activity, it can be evaluated from the moral point of view, just as any other human activity can be so evaluated. The relationship of business to morality goes even deeper than this. Business, like most other social activities, presupposes a background of morality and would be impossible without it. For instance, employers expect their employees not to steal from the firm; parties to a contract each expect the other to honor an agreement; those who buy a product expect it to be as advertised, when they take it home and unpack it. People who work with others expect their co-workers generally to tell the truth, to respect rather than to assault them, and to do the job for which they are paid. In most cases, these expectations are met. If everyone involved in business—buyers, sellers, producers, management, workers, and consumers—acted immorally or even amorally (i.e., without concern for whether their actions were moral or immoral), business would soon grind to a halt. Morality is the oil as well as the glue of society and, therefore, of business. It is only against the background of morality that immorality can be not only possible but also profitable. Lying would not succeed if most people were not truthful and did not tend to believe others. A breach of trust requires a background of trust. Most businesses do not operate according to the dictum "let the buyer beware." Businesses generally value their reputation. We therefore do not really live in a "dog-eat-dog" business world; such a world would be intolerable.

People, of course, do act immorally in business, just as they do in other spheres of life. There are numerous cases of fraud, misrepresentation, and inflated business accounts, but there is no proof that people are more immoral in their business lives than in their private lives. The structures of business are no more prone to immorality than the structures of government, family, education, or religion, nor are large, impersonal businesses either more or less moral or immoral than small, individually owned businesses.

The point that the actions of people in business are subject to moral rules is probably so obvious as to be generally forgotten. Most adults do not need to be told that lying and stealing are wrong or that murder is wrong. These are wrong whether done in or out of business. It is because the ordinary person does not need to be told that these things are wrong that they form part of the background of business. In other words, this is an assumption made by those in business. Consequently, the proposition that business and morality do not mix cannot be convincingly maintained. The point of business ethics is not necessarily to change anyone's moral convictions but to build on them.

The Foundations of Property

Private property is a cornerstone of capitalism and of the free-enterprise system, and socially owned property is the cornerstone of socialist economic systems. But what is property? What makes property private? By what right do I call property mine? These are not economic questions. Legally, property is defined in terms of rights. If something is mine, I have the right to use it, to destroy it, to sell it, or to protect it from another person taking it or using it. But rights may be moral as well as legal. The question of property can therefore be put in terms of morality as well as legality. In order to produce, human beings need raw materials with which to work. Who then owns nature? John Locke, the British philosopher whose theory influenced the American Founding Fathers, argued that every man is allowed to use what nature provides. He may make it his own if he can use it and if other people have as much, and as good, remaining for their use as well. The initial partition of the earth is a fact. Some people own the diamond mines, others the oil fields, and still others the iron and coal mines. By what right do certain people assert the exclusive claim to the earth's resources simply because they were fortunate enough to have been born in the country where the resources existed? Do some people have a right to resources and the riches they bring, whereas others, who happen to inhabit barren land without resources, are doomed to poverty and starvation? Can one argue plausibly that the resources of the world are for the benefit of all people and not just for the lucky few? The less developed countries of the world are asking Americans these questions. Eight percent of humankind uses 40 percent of the earth's natural resources; the other 92 percent ask what right they have to do so.

Similar questions are raised within the United States. Can we justify the wealth and opulence of a few together with the poverty of large numbers of others? Those who claim that we cannot do so demand the transfer of wealth from those who have wealth to those who do not. The transfer of some wealth in the United States is achieved primarily through taxation. Taxation, therefore, is a means of transferring property—namely money—from one person or group to another. By what right is this done? The answer requires not only legal reasoning but also moral reasoning and argument.

The Business of Business

A famous cliché maintains that "the business of business is business." The business of business is not government, charity, or social welfare—nor, as the cliché implies, is it morality. But what does "the business of business is business" mean? Who is to decide what it means? To get some perspective on the question, we must look beyond any particular society. What we find is this: What is considered to be business and its business varies from society to society. In Japan, the business of large corporations is not only to produce goods but also to care for the firm's employees—in effect, to guarantee them lifetime employment. Paternalism is thus part of the business of business in Japan, in a way that it is not in the United States. In the former Soviet Union, private ownership of the means of production—that is, of companies and factories— was prohibited by law. There were factories, offices, stores, and goods, but business there was a state affair, not a private affair. What constitutes business varies from society to society. Defining business per se and its proper concern is a social question, one that must be answered in a social context.

In the United States, the mandate to business was initially rather simple. People wanted goods to be as plentiful, as good, and as cheap as possible. Those interested in producing them were given relatively free rein under competitive conditions. Some businesses succeeded and grew; others failed. As problems developed, regulations were introduced by law. These laws regulated working conditions, protected children, prevented monopolistic practices, and preserved the environment. The regulations frequently represented the moral concerns of the American people. The business of business was, and is, decided by the people of each society. Neither the practices to be tolerated nor the determinations of what is acceptable to a society are eternal givens. To some extent, the mandate to business also sets the limits to its proper activity and to what is not socially tolerable. The limits are not set by business or by those who run business, even though some of them act as if they were. The limits and demands imposed on business by society are frequently moral ones. A business may ignore the moral demands of an individual, but it can hardly ignore the moral demands of a whole society because it is both part of that society and dependent on it, even though it serves society.

There is increasing evidence that the mandate to business in the United States is changing and that businesses are increasingly expected to weigh more than financial factors in their actions. What constitutes the business of business, in fact, is itself a moral decision and one that is socially made and implemented. Insofar as business is part of society, it rightfully has a voice in arriving at the social determination of what its business is. To do so effectively, it must be able to enter into the moral social discourse that is debating its future. Business ethics helps to clarify some of the issues and provides the techniques for effectively entering into the debate.

Business and the Law

Business is a social enterprise whose mandate and limits are set by society. The limits are often moral, but they are also frequently written into law. The history of the development of business in America is an interesting one, as is the history of the relationships of business and morality, and business and law. In the early days of our history most American businesses were small. The Protestant work ethic was a strong influence providing both motivation and justification for the businessman's activity. According to this ethic, the good and the hardworking were blessed with riches; the lazy and incompetent suffered. Rugged individualism was both an ingredient in the work ethic and a secular moral value.

In contemporary society the work ethic has changed to some extent. Society, through welfare, attempts to take care of some of the poor and needy. Small businesses have largely given way to giant corporations. The large firms are owned by stockholders and are run by managers who are paid wages—but very handsome wages. Hired managers run the companies not for themselves but for the stockholders. They manage the company not necessarily as they choose, but to some extent as they must. They are subject to a board of directors. They cannot impose their own morality on company policy and therefore must run it in a somewhat neutral way.

The dissociation of management from ownership took place at the same time that laws regulating business proliferated. As a result, it was natural, for those who were managing firms, to feel that what society and the stockholders of their company required of them was compliance with the law. If they complied with the law, they fulfilled their social obligations. As a result, they began to feel that morality was personal, that it varied from person to person and from group to group, and that all that could be expected of the managers of business, as well as of business itself, was fulfillment of the law. The law prohibits theft, enforces contracts, sets limits to advertising, and reinforces many moral norms. Equating what is required of business with what is required by law became a convenient and easy norm to adopt. It made clear one's duty and limited what one had to consider. It provided a convenient rationale for ignoring moral demands and for living by the Myth of Amoral Business.

This view fails to consider carefully the relation of law and morality.[6]

- Many laws prohibit immoral practices; immoral practices, for the most part, are socially harmful practices. Some, such as murder, stealing, and perjury, are so harmful that to moral sanction is added the sanction of law. Hence, one way to argue that a law should be passed is to argue that the conduct the law is to govern is immoral and seriously harmful to society. For instance, racial discrimination was immoral before it was made illegal.
- Law is for the most part reactive. There is a lag between practices that society discovers are harmful and legislation being drafted and passed to render it illegal.
- Not all laws are morally defensible. Laws requiring racial segregation and discrimination are a case in point. To abide by the law in practicing discrimination was, in fact, to act immorally. It is dangerous to equate law with what one is morally, as well as legally, required to do because this denies the possibility of arguing, from a moral point of view, that either a law should be passed or a bad law repealed.
- Not everything that is immoral can be made illegal. Although, for instance, it is immoral to lie, this does not mean that all lying should be made illegal. Such a law would be unenforceable, nor would it be worth the time and effort to try to enforce it to any considerable extent. Yet it does not follow—even for those in businesses who claim that they are bound only by law—that it would be right for businesspeople to lie whenever they feel like it, either to those within the company or to those with whom they do business. In most cases it would be considered bad business as well as immoral.

The retreat to law as the sole norm by which to guide business is in part a reflection of the fact that most managers do not know how to handle many moral issues in business. Having equated morality with personal opinion, they understandably find it difficult to defend their moral judgments in objective terms. A correct perception of the status of morality and a knowledge of the techniques of moral argumentation are necessary to handle moral values and moral issues in business. Part of the task of business ethics is to supply the appropriate perception and knowledge.

---

[6] On the relation of ethics and law, see David Lyons, *Ethics and the Rule of Law* (Cambridge: Cambridge University Press, 1984). Christopher D. Stone's, *Where the Law Ends* (Prospect Heights, Ill.: Waveland Press, 1991, reissue), is an excellent study of the relation of law and morality to the corporation.

The Changing Mandate for Business

The social mandate to business is not only given in law. The general mandate to provide a plentiful supply of high-quality goods at a cheap price is in fact also a social mandate. It arises from the need of the general public and is expressed in many ways. Today the mandate to business is more complex. Demands are made on it from many quarters. Businesses have responded to some and not to others. Frequently, they do not know how to evaluate conflicting demands. (We have already noted the retreat to law on the part of some firms.) Some businesses choose to ignore the background of morality with which, and in which, they operate.

The retreat to law, together with a disclaimer concerning moral demands, is frequently a reflection neither of bad will nor of a desire to be immoral. Rather, it often reflects the lack of internal structures within a firm to consider and weigh moral as well as financial considerations, as well as a lack of confidence in the ability of those within a firm to engage in public, moral reasoning. Even those firms that are exemplary from a moral point of view are reluctant to defend their positions in moral terms.

This is in part another reflection of the Myth of Amoral Business. The economic system is thought by some to be value-free: Each person within it seeks his or her own good; and buyers contract with sellers to the mutual benefit of both. The marketplace thus becomes the neutral ground of common activity, and the general good is achieved without its being intended by anyone. This view, which is a simplified form of how the free-enterprise system is sometimes presented, does not correspond to the way any economic system works. But it is certainly clear that it corresponds even less today to the economic system of the United States than it did in the nineteenth century.

The nation and the world have come to see that there are limits to available natural resources, that industrialization has been purchased at a considerable price, and that the ecosystem is so delicately balanced that each change we produce in it triggers other, sometimes deleterious changes, which we do not necessarily intend. As a result, we now collectively know that many of our actions involve value judgments. For instance, do we want more electricity? If so, are we willing to risk the dangers involved in nuclear reactors? When oil is scarce, we know that we must sometimes choose between having gas for our cars and fuel for heating our homes. If we want a strong military force, we cannot have it unless we raise, through taxes, the money required to support it.

Individuals in business can no longer act as they choose. Government regulations, decisions, and guidelines temper the moves of the marketplace. In addition, corporations are asked, if not forced, to consider the impact of their decisions and actions on the environment, the public, and the common good. Air and water are no longer resources to be freely used. No manufacturer today can ignore the safety of workers and consumers of products. Most businesses, however, are not structured to handle moral demands or to weigh values in nonmonetary terms. How can they do this? They can do so by considering what structures promote moral responsibility and facilitate the weighing of moral and other values, topics that are appropriately raised in business ethics.

Business Ethics and Ethics

Thus far we have referred to business ethics, but we have not seen what it is in any detail. The term is used in several different senses, only two of which we shall pursue here. The first of these is business ethics as a movement, and the second is business ethics as part of the general field of ethics.

Business Ethics as a Movement

Ethics has always been a part of business, and to speak of ethics in business is neither new nor any different from speaking of ethics in any other area of human endeavor. Nonetheless, what we can refer to as the business ethics movement is of relatively recent vintage. In the period prior to 1960 there were certainly discussions of ethics in business, for example, of the right of workers to a just wage and to decent conditions of employment, of truth in advertising, and of honesty in business dealings. In the United States the 1960s saw the rise of social issues in business. The 1960s witnessed the emergence of a counterculture, the divisive Vietnam War, the growth of ecological, pollution, and nuclear and toxic waste problems, and protests against the so-called military-industrial complex. Joined to all these developments was the rise of consumerism and the growing strength of the consumer movement. Business came under attack for lacking social consciousness and for harming society in myriad ways. Business schools responded by instituting social issues courses in which the charges against business and possible answers and remedies were considered. Business initially reacted defensively and then sought to make changes necessary to offset the attacks.

The 1970s saw the rise of the business ethics movement. The student- and consumer-group demands of the 1960s spread to the larger population. Business initially reacted to the increasing public concern by holding conferences sponsored by groups such as the National Chamber of Commerce. Other conferences were initiated by universities, often bringing together businesspeople with academics in business schools, philosophy and religion departments, law schools, and other specialists. The term *business ethics* was modeled after the term *medical ethics,* which had been adopted a decade or so earlier by people interested in ethical issues in medicine. The Myth of Amoral Business was still strong, and many treated the very notion of business ethics as a contradiction in terms. Nonetheless, courses in the area were gradually introduced, textbooks were written, professional societies and journals were formed, and the subject became established in colleges and universities. The interaction of those working in this area with businesspeople and groups continued. The media took notice, and individual companies took tentative steps in the direction of developing ethical corporate codes, instituting in-house ethics programs, and becoming increasingly sensitive to charges of unethical conduct.

By the 1980s activity in the business ethics area had become significant enough to be called a movement.[7] By the end of that decade the number of Fortune Five Hundred companies that had adopted corporate ethical codes, that had ethical hotlines on which employees could register ethical concerns, that had established ethics committees at the board of directors level, or that had launched ethics training programs had become impressive indeed. By the 1990s the government had also entered the act. A number of judges had already mandated corporatewide ethics training in companies that had federal contracts and been found guilty of fraud or of overcharging the government.

In 1991 the U.S. Congress enacted Federal Sentencing Guidelines applicable to corporations found guilty of breaking a wide variety of laws. A significant provision of the Guidelines was the opportunity it gave companies to receive reduced fines if they could show they had taken steps to develop an "efficient program to prevent and detect violations of law."[8] Such a program includes establishing standards and procedures to be followed by employees, assigning a high-level official to oversee the program, taking steps to communicate its standards, taking steps to monitor and audit compliance, enforcing the standards through disciplinary mechanisms, and taking steps to modify its program after an offense is detected. Although the emphasis in the law is on legal compliance, this has served as an impetus for many corporations to go beyond the letter of the law and seek to establish an ethical climate that would lessen any tendency among their employees to break the law. One result has been the emergence of corporate ethics officers, part of whose job is to oversee the ethics programs of the corporation. Business ethics has thus become part of the business landscape.

The business ethics movement is thus a social phenomenon with academic, business, social, and governmental aspects. As a social phenomenon it should not be ignored. Yet the movement remains ambiguous from an ethical point of view and is not without its critics. Has the movement made businesses more ethical? Has business coopted the movement and turned it to its own purposes? Does training in business ethics teach and motivate employees to be ethical in evaluating the activities of the firm for which they work, or does it simply encourage them to refrain from stealing and in other ways act-

---

[7] For details of the developments and bibliographical information, see Richard T. De George, "The Status of Business Ethics: Past and Future," *Journal of Business Ethics*, 6 (1987), pp. 201–211. Three book-length bibliographies are available: Donald G. Jones et al., *A Bibliography of Business Ethics, 1971-1975; 1976-1980; 1981-1985*, 3 vols. (Charlottesville: University Press of Virginia, 1977, 1982, 1986). A number of journals carry articles on business ethics, and several are dedicated to business ethics, including *Journal of Business Ethics*, 1, 1982-   ; *Business Ethics Quarterly*, 1, 1991-   ; and *Business and Professional Ethics Journal*, 1, 1981-   .

[8] *United States Sentencing Commission Guidelines Manual*, United States Sentencing Commission, November 1, 1993, Chapter 8, p. 337.

ing contrary to the firm's interests? Has the movement led to the adoption of the trappings of ethics, with little or no change in corporate actions? These are crucial questions to which there are as yet no clear and definitive answers.[9] Yet the movement has made it possible and respectable to raise these questions publicly and have them discussed seriously both in and out of business. That in itself is a gain over conditions prior to the rise of the movement.

Business Ethics as a Part of Ethics

Business ethics is not a separate ethics that constrains business in a way that other human and social endeavors are not constrained. Nor does it permit business to do what one is not allowed to do in other areas of life. It is part of the general field of ethics and only within that wider sphere can it be properly understood.

Ethics studies morality. *Morality is a term used to cover those practices and activities that are considered importantly right and wrong; the rules that govern those activities; and the values that are embedded, fostered, or pursued by those activities and practices.* The morality of a society is related to its mores, or the customs that a society or group accepts as being right and wrong, as well as those laws of a society that add legal prohibitions and sanctions to many activities considered to be immoral. Hence, ethics presupposes the existence of morality, as well as the existence of moral people who judge right from wrong and generally act in accordance with norms they accept and to which they and the rest of society hold others. Without an accepted morality there would be no stable society in which business or any other positive, productive activity could be carried out in relative peace and security.

Ordinary moral experience encompasses our moral beliefs, judgments, and feelings, all of which we express in moral language. Moral judgments include evaluations of people or actions or institutions as good or bad, right or wrong, just or unjust, fair or unfair, and so on. They also express emotions, typically negative emotions toward wrong actions and positive emotions toward right actions. Moral language also includes praise and blame, shame and pride, and the whole range of virtues. Often moral language is stated in imperative form; sometimes it states prohibitions. In general morality covers all human actions, some of which are morally permitted, some of which are either morally required or morally prohibited, and some of which are beyond one's duty and so especially praiseworthy. The latter are often referred to as

---

[9] See Kenneth Labich, "The New Crisis in Business Ethics," *Fortune*, 125 (April 20, 1992), pp. 167–176; James M. Gustafson, "The Booming Business of Business Ethics," *Business and Society Review*, 81 (Spring 1992), pp. 84–86; Warner Woodworth, "Remoralization of Management," *Executive Excellence*, 9 (September 1990), pp. 5–7; and Richard T. De George, "Will Success Spoil Business Ethics?" in R. Edward Freeman (Ed.), *Business Ethics: The State of the Art* (New York: Oxford University Press, 1991), pp. 42–56.

moral ideals. All of this applies no matter what the society, or what its particular moral judgments are.

In its most general sense *ethics is a systematic attempt to make sense of our individual and social moral experience, in such a way as to determine the rules that ought to govern human conduct, the values worth pursuing, and the character traits deserving development in life.* The attempt is systematic and therefore goes beyond what reflective people tend to do in daily life in making sense of their moral experience, organizing it, and attempting to make it coherent and unified. If one approaches ethics through revelation—for instance, through the Bible or through religious teachings—we can speak of theological or religious ethics. If—as we shall do—one approaches ethics prescinding from revelation and religious belief, and using only arguments based on reasons applied to nonreligious human experience, we can speak of *philosophical ethics.* Insofar as it attempts to ascertain what rules and values *ought* to be followed and pursued, philosophical ethics can be distinguished from anthropology, psychology, and sociology. Those disciplines *describe* how people behave, but they usually do not *prescribe* how they ought to behave. Ethics concerns itself with human conduct, taken here to mean human activity that is done knowingly and, to a large extent, willingly. It does not concern itself with automatic responses, or with, for example, actions done in one's sleep or under hypnosis. To the extent that ethics is concerned with how people *ought* to act, it has a critical dimension. Given any set of practices, any rules, or any actions one can appropriately ask: Is it ethical? Simply because something is an accepted course of behavior or simply because something is enacted into law does not make it ethically justifiable. Some behavior may be accepted and still be morally wrong, just as something may be an enforceable statute and be morally wrong.

Despite the accuracy and usefulness of this definition of ethics as the study of morality, the term *ethics* is used in a variety of ways by different people. Sometimes *ethics* is synonymous with *morality;* for example, an action that is morally right is called an ethical one. We referred earlier to the work ethic, because that is the common phrase, though we could have called it the work morality. Codes of moral conduct adopted by professions are frequently called ethical codes. Although, philosophically speaking, business ethics is a branch of general ethics, some people interpret the phrase *business ethics* to mean business morality. They interpret this either descriptively—that is, as the morality followed in business—or normatively, as the morality that ought to be followed. We cannot legislate the use of terms, so it is wise to be conscious of divergent uses.

Those engaged in ethics as a branch of philosophy perform analysis and synthesis. There are three related phases of ethical study, which are commonly known as descriptive ethics, normative ethics, and metaethics. The three constitute what is sometimes called general, as opposed to special, ethics.

1. *Descriptive ethics* is closely related to anthropology, sociology, and psychology and leans heavily on them.

- It consists of studying and describing the morality of a people, culture, or society.
- It compares and contrasts different moral systems, codes, practices, beliefs, principles, and values.
- It provides basic material that normative ethics must account for, and it provides a touchstone of the considered morality of a people or society with which the normative theory must more or less coalesce.

Although normative ethics is critical, it starts from the assumption that most of the moral rules, norms, and values that a society holds, and that are detailed in descriptive ethics, are justifiable. Yet a society may hold incompatible norms, it may unjustifiably restrict the scope of its rules so as to exclude protection for slaves or women or foreigners, and it may hold values that it fails to implement or that it undermines in practice. The task of normative ethics is to remedy these and other possible defects. Typically, as people grow up in a society, they learn which actions that society considers right and which it considers wrong. These judgments are internalized, so that people tend automatically or intuitively to know that this action—telling the truth—is right and that one—killing someone—is wrong. However, when pressed, people are often unable to provide any further justification for their judgments of what is right and wrong other than that they "feel" they are correct in making those judgments, or that is what "everyone" says.

2. *Normative ethics* builds on the whole that descriptive ethics provides and attempts to supply and justify a coherent moral system based on it. Typically, it seeks to uncover, develop, and justify the basic moral principle or principles, or the basic moral values, of a moral system found in a given society, and more generally and ideally in human society as a whole. The task of normative ethics is threefold:

- It attempts to form into a related whole the various norms, rules, and values of a society's morality. It tries to render these as consistent and coherent as possible, with perhaps some hierarchical arrangement of norms.
- It attempts to find the basic principles from which the particular norms can be derived.
- It attempts, in a variety of ways, to justify the basic principle of morality.

Because normative ethics is a systematic attempt to explain and justify the morality of a society or of society in general, such attempts are called "ethical theories."

If the basic principle is powerful enough, it should provide the means for deriving the set of consistent norms accepted by a society, as well as for making explicit norms that were previously held only implicitly. The theory should also provide a procedure by which conflicting norms can be adjudicated and particular cases decided. A moral theory interacts dynamically with the norms of a society in that both remain open to correction. A moral theory that resulted in injunctions to murder, steal, lie, or commit other actions a society considered immoral would be properly suspect. It is difficult to imagine why a society would accept or adopt such a theory. In general, a society is more certain of the bulk of its traditional norms of morality than it is of any theory of morality. Exceptions are possible, however. For instance, a society may undergo a conversion and adopt a religion along with that religion's moral code. But this is not the general rule.

3. *Metaethics,* the third portion of general ethics, is closely related to normative ethics.

- Metaethics is the study of normative ethics, and, to some extent, both normative and descriptive ethics involve some metaethical activity. It is sometimes called *analytical ethics* because it is concerned with analysis. Metaethics deals with the meaning of moral terms. It asks, for instance, what the terms *good* and *bad* mean in the moral sense and what *moral responsibility, moral obligation,* and other similar phrases mean. Meaning, of course, is closely related to linguistic usage. Some people think meaning is identical with such usage. To say what *good* means may be distinct from saying what things or actions are good. The former is generally considered a metaethical concern, the latter a normative ethical concern.
- Metaethics studies the logic of moral reasoning. The analysis of moral reasoning involves clarifying and evaluating presuppositions and investigating the validity of moral arguments. A famous, and still not completely resolved, metaethical dispute concerns the question of whether a moral ought or duty can be derived logically from a statement of what is, exclusive of normative premises. For instance, from the fact that people typically wish to live rather than die, can we infer a right to life or an injunction against murdering them? From the fact that people pursue pleasure, can we conclude that it is ethically right or good to pursue pleasure? If we cannot derive how we should act from facts about how we do act, can we derive them from any set of facts, or do we need values or preferences or rules? If we do, why should we act in accordance with these? What is the basis or rationale for prescribing how we should act? The general answer to that question is metaethical. A particular theory that in fact presents a basis or rationale is a normative theory.

General ethical theory provides a careful and systematic approach to morality, one that finds parallels in ordinary life and discourse. It develops and analyzes the kinds of moral arguments that are used in ordinary language and in everyday life, in newspapers and magazines, and in books and articles on moral problems. Hence, it is a practical discipline with practical import. Like science, ethics constitutes a continuing social endeavor. It is not a completed discipline, but a developing one in which there are a number of disputed issues. The presence of these disputes, however, does not indicate that there is no agreement, nor does it indicate that ethics has produced no usable results. Some results are negative: Certain theories that were initially plausible have been shown to be mistaken, and some popular approaches to morality have proved untenable. The last word has yet to be written, but this is to be expected of an ongoing enterprise. Mastery of ethical theory, however, provides the necessary tools to engage intelligently in personal and social analysis of moral issues.

Special ethics applies general ethics (which, as we have said, includes descriptive, normative, and metaethics) first to solving particular problems and second to investigating the morality of specialized areas of human endeavor.

The first of these is sometimes called casuistry. *Casuistry* is the art of solving difficult moral problems, cases, or dilemmas through the careful application of moral principles. Casuistry uses the principles and norms that have been developed and justified in general ethics. It is an important art or skill, but one that has sometimes been held in low repute. It can easily degenerate into the technique of seeing how close one can come to the line that separates a moral from an immoral action. Moral people, its critics maintain, are more interested in pursuing a moral course of action than in seeing how they can minimally fulfill what is morally demanded. The attempt to determine the latter has frequently led to all-too-subtle rationalizations of questionable actions.

The second area of special ethics involves the application of general ethics to specialized fields. This yields business ethics, medical ethics, engineering ethics, professional ethics, and so on. Business ethics obviously deals with business. We shall take business to include any and all economic transactions between individuals, between individuals and profit-making organizations, and between profit-making organizations and other such organizations. It will include the various activities carried on in producing, selling, and buying goods and services for profit. This definition is broad enough to include the business activities of people in the professions and therefore encompasses part of what is considered *professional ethics*. The delimitation of these domains, however, is not at all sharp, and great precision in delimiting them is not necessary.

Business ethics as a field is defined by the interaction of ethics and business. Business ethics is as national, international, or global as business itself, and no arbitrary geographical boundaries limit it.

- If we consider business ethics in the American context, its major focus on the macro-level is the moral evaluation of the economic system of American free enterprise, and of possible alternatives to and modifications of it.
- A second level of moral analysis—and to date, the level of greatest attention—is the study of business within the American free-enterprise system. Since corporations are a prominent feature of this system, they have

attracted the most concern. But unions, small businesses, consumerism, and the vast variety of business practices within the system are all appropriate objects of moral evaluation. Within the economic system and the corporations and businesses are individuals who invest in, run, work for, buy from, and are in many ways affected by them.

- The moral evaluation of individuals and of their actions in economic and business transactions forms a third level of investigation. The field of business ethics embraces these three levels in their interconnections, as well as treating them as discrete areas of investigation. A corporation can be only as ethical as the people who own, manage, and work for it; but its structure, organization and practices can be more or less conducive to ethical activity, which can in turn be reinforced or impeded by the larger system of which it is a part.
- Finally, because business is becoming more and more international and global, a fourth level of analysis is international, and it considers the actions of American and other multinational corporations, as well as conditions of trade; the distribution of goods and jobs; the use, abuse, and depletion of natural resources; and the role of business in global warming, destruction of the tropical rain forests, and other activities that vitally affect humankind as a whole.

Business ethics typically involves five kinds of activities. The first is the applying of general ethical principles to particular cases or practices in business. Deciding whether the actions involved are immoral or morally justifiable is important. But the analysis of cases does not end there. Solving cases frequently involves the development, as well as the application, of special rather than general moral principles, which can nonetheless be made universal. Cases involving unethical activity sometimes suggest issues that need attention, clarification, and discussion. Such cases also challenge us to consider imaginatively how we can prevent similar cases from arising in the future, and to develop suggestions that business, if it wishes to act ethically, might implement, or that government, if necessary, might adopt. Some questions are: What changes in organization, managerial techniques, social structures, programs, or approaches are required? And would moral imagination, care in assessing future development, or changes in attitude help preclude moral dilemmas? Business ethics, however, involves more than just applying moral principles to business.

The second kind of activity is metaethical. We shall investigate, for instance, whether moral terms that are generally used to describe individuals and the actions they perform can also be applied to organizations, corporations, businesses, and other collective entities. For instance, are corporations artifacts to be controlled, or moral or quasi-moral entities with rights, or do they have some other status? Do they have consciences in the same way individuals do? Does moral language appropriately apply to them, and if so, does it apply in the same way as it does to individuals? The answers to these questions are not supplied by general ethical theory, which traditionally has been concerned with the actions of human individuals. The meaning of *responsibility* must be changed if it is to be appropriately applied to corporations as well as to human persons. The analysis of this type of problem in business ethics cannot take place in abstraction from general ethical theory. There is a reciprocal relation between business ethics and general ethics. But those involved in business ethics often engage in metaethical inquiries that their work demands and that general theory does not provide.

A third activity of business ethics is the analysis of the presuppositions of business—both moral presuppositions and presuppositions from a moral point of view. Because business operates within an economic system, part of the proper task of business ethics is to raise questions about the morality of economic systems in general and about the morality of specific, for example, the American, economic systems in particular. In evaluating structures of business, we must also analyze the meaning and justification of such nonmoral terms as *property, exploitation, competition,* and the presuppositions and uses of cost-benefit analyses, accounting procedures, and so on.

Fourth, those in business ethics are sometimes led by embedded problems to go beyond the field of ethics into other areas of philosophy and into other domains of knowledge, such as economics or organization theory. But when they go beyond their own areas, they usually do so to resolve some problem in business ethics or to investigate in some other area what appeared, initially, to be a problem in business ethics. This activity becomes especially important in dealing with macro-moral issues, such as whether rich countries have any moral obligations to poor countries, or multinational corporations to host countries. Here our ordinary moral intuitions are less clear than they are in our personal dealings with individuals. Hence, there is a special need to sort out the issues carefully, to see which are moral and which are not, and to clarify the language and the level of moral discourse. Sometimes the task concerns reducing moral problems to managerial, organizational, or economic problems, or vice versa.

The fifth activity in which business ethics is typically involved is describing morally praiseworthy and exemplary actions, of either individuals in business or particular firms. Business ethics initially developed in reaction to scandals, and the cases that aroused public indignation were those that violated fundamental norms of human decency. Business ethics, however, is involved not only in the negative task of trying to clarify what actions are wrong, but also of presenting moral ideals to which businesspeople and corporations can rise. Just as society provides moral exemplars, heroes, saints, and others on whom we can model our lives and behavior, so there are moral exemplars in the business world who can serve as examples to others and set a goal toward which others might aspire.

Business ethics can help people approach moral problems in business more systematically and with better tools than they might otherwise use. It can help them to see issues they might typically ignore. It can also impel them to make changes they might otherwise not be moved to make.[10] But business ethics will not, in and of itself, make anyone moral. Business ethics, as is true of ethics in general, presupposes that those who study it already are moral beings, that they know right from wrong, and that they wish to be even better, more thoughtful, more informed moral beings. Business ethics will not change business practices unless those engaged in the practices that need moral change wish to change them. Business ethics can produce arguments showing that a practice is immoral, but obviously, only those in a position to implement the changes will be able to bring them about. Business ethics is a field with practical import, but it is up to those who study it to put what they learn into practice.

The Case of the Collapsed Mine

The following fictitious case illustrates the sorts of questions that might arise in business ethics and various ways to approach these questions. Consider the case of the collapsed mine shaft. In a town in West Virginia, miners were digging coal in a tunnel thousands of feet below the surface. Some gas buildup had been detected during the two preceding days, and the director of safety had reported it to the mine manager. The buildup was sufficiently serious to have temporarily stopped operations until it was cleared. The manager of the mine decided that the buildup was only marginally dangerous, that he had coal orders to fill, that he could not afford to close down the mine, and that he would take the chance that the gas would dissipate before it exploded. He told the director of safety not to say anything about the danger. Two days later, the gas exploded. One section of the tunnel collapsed, killing three miners and trapping eight others in a pocket. The rest managed to escape.

The explosion was one of great force, and the extent of the tunnel's collapse was considerable. The cost of reaching the men in time to save their lives would amount to several million dollars. The problem facing the manager was whether the expenditure of such a large sum was worth it. What, after all, was a human life worth? Who should make the decision, and how should it be made? Did the manager owe more to the stockholders of the corporation or to the trapped workers? Should he use the slower, safer, cheaper way of reaching them and save a large sum of money, or the faster, more dangerous, more expensive way, and possibly save their lives?

He decided on the latter way and asked for volunteers. Two dozen men volunteered. After three days, the operation proved to be more difficult than anyone had anticipated. There had been two more explosions, and three of those involved in the rescue operation had already been killed. In the meantime, telephone contact had been made with the trapped men, who had been fortunate enough to find a telephone line that was still functioning. They were

---

[10] For a discussion of the value of business ethics courses, see Thomas R. Piper, Mary C. Gentile, and Sharon Daloz Parks, *Can Ethics Be Taught?* (Boston: Harvard Business School, 1993).

starving. Having previously read about a similar case, they decided that the only way for them to survive long enough for any of them to be saved was to draw lots, and kill and eat the one who drew the shortest straw. They felt it was their duty that at least some of them be found alive; otherwise, the three who had died rescuing them would have died in vain.

After twenty days, seven men were finally rescued, alive; they had cannibalized their fellow miner. The director of safety, who had detected the gas before the explosion, informed the newspapers of his report. The manager was charged with criminal negligence, but before giving up his position, he fired the director of safety. The mine eventually resumed operation.

There are many issues in the foregoing account. The tools for resolving them are part of what we shall develop in later chapters.

Consider the director of safety. Did he, before the accident, fulfill his moral obligation when he obeyed the manager, instead of making known to the miners, to the manager's superior, or to the public the fact that the mine was unsafe? Did he have a moral obligation, after the explosion and rescue, to make known the fact that the manager knew the mine was unsafe? Should he have gone to the board of directors of the company with the story, or to someone else within the company rather than to the newspapers? All these questions are part of the phenomenon of worker responsibility. To whom are workers responsible, and for what? Do their moral obligations end when they do what they are told? Going public with inside information such as the director of safety had is commonly known as "blowing the whistle" on the company. Frequently, those who blow the whistle are fired, just as the director of safety was. The whole phenomenon of whistle blowing raises serious questions about the structure of companies in which employees find it necessary to take such drastic action and possibly suffer the loss of their jobs. Was the manager justified in firing the director of safety?

The manager is, of course, the villain of the story. He sent the miners into a situation he knew was dangerous. But, he might argue, he did it for the good of the company. He had contracts to fulfill and an obligation to the owners of the company to show a profit. He made a bad decision. But every manager has to take risks. It just turned out that he was unlucky. Does such a defense sound plausible? Does a manager have an obligation to workers as well as to the owners of a company? Who should take precedence, and under what conditions does one group or the other become more important? Who is to decide this, and how?

The manager decided to try to save the trapped miners, even though it would cost the company more than taking the slower route. Did he have the right to spend more of the company's money in this way? How does one evaluate human life in comparison with expenditure of money? It sounds moral to say that human life is beyond all monetary value, and in a sense it is. But there are limits to what society and the people in it will, can, and should spend to save lives. The way to decide, however, does not seem to be to equate the value of people's lives with the amount of income they would produce in their remaining years, if they were to live to a statistically average age, minus the resources they would use up in that period. Then how does one decide? How do and should people weigh human lives against monetary expenditure? When building roads, designing automobiles, or making many other products, there is a trade-off between the maximum safety one builds into the product and the cost of the product. Extremely safe cars cost more to build than relatively safe cars. We can express the difference in terms of the number of people likely to die driving the relatively safe ones as opposed to those likely to die while driving the extremely safe ones. Should such decisions be made by manufacturers, consumers, government, or some other group?

The manager asked for volunteers for the rescue work. Three of these volunteers died. Was the manager responsible for their deaths in the same sense that he was responsible for the deaths of the three miners who died in the first mine explosion? Was the company responsible for their deaths in either case? Do companies have obligations to their employees and their employees' families, in circumstances such as these, or are the obligations only those of the managers? If the manager had warned the workers that the level of gas was dangerous, and if they had decided that they wanted their pay for that day and would work anyway, would the manager have been responsible for their deaths? Is it moral for people to take dangerous jobs simply to earn money? Is a system that impels people to take such jobs for money a moral system? To what extent is a company morally obliged to protect its workers and to prevent them from taking chances?

The manager was charged with criminal negligence under the law. Was the company responsible for anything? Should the company have been sued by the families of the dead workers? If the company were sued and paid damages to the families, the money would come from the company profits and hence from the profits of the shareholders. Is it fair that the shareholders be penalized for an incident with which they had nothing to do? How is responsibility shared or distributed in a company? And can companies be morally responsible for what is done in their name? Are only human beings moral agents, and is it a mistake to use moral language with respect to companies, corporations, and businesses?

The decision of the trapped miners to cast lots to determine who would be killed and eaten raises a number of moral issues. Because this case is not an ordinary one, our moral intuitions can provide no ready answer as to whether their decision was morally justifiable. The question of how to think about such an issue raises another question: How are moral problems to be resolved? And this emphasizes the need for a moral theory by which we can decide unusual cases. A number of principles seem to conflict: the obligation not to kill; the consideration that it is better that one person, rather than eight, die; the fact, noted by the miners, that three persons had already died trying to rescue them. The issue here is not necessarily relevant to business ethics; it has been posed because it involves a moral difficulty that requires some technique of moral argument to solve.

In the narration of the case, we are not told what happened to either the manager or the director of safety. Frequently, the sequel to such cases is surprising. The managers often get off free and are ultimately rewarded for their concern for the company's interest, but the whistle blower is often blackballed throughout the industry. The immorality of such an outcome seems obvious: Justice does not always triumph. What can be done to see that justice triumphs more often? This is a question that involves restructuring the system.

Business ethics is sometimes seen as conservative and is used as a defense of the status quo. Sometimes it is seen as an attack on the status quo, and then it is viewed as radical. Ideally, it should be neither. It should strive for objectivity. Where there are immoral practices, structures, and actions, business ethics should be able to show that these actions are immoral, and why. But it should also be able to supply the techniques with which the practices and structures that are moral can be defended as such. The aim of business ethics is neither defense of the status quo nor its radical change. Rather, it should serve to remedy those aspects or structures that need change, and it should protect those that are moral. It is not a panacea. It can secure change only if those in power take the appropriate action. But unless some attention is paid to business ethics, the moral debate about practices and principles central to our society will be conducted poorly.

Study Questions

1. Was Johnson & Johnson ethically obliged to recall Tylenol immediately, as it did? Would it have been ethically permissible for it to wait until it was surer about what was happening, or to recall the product only from the Chicago area until there was evidence of tampering with the product in some other part of the country? In each case, give reasons for your answer.

2. What is the Myth of Amoral Business? To what extent is it true? false? Does it represent a view that you have encountered? If so, indicate how.

3. What are some of the moral values presupposed by business? Could business be carried on if they were not presupposed? Explain.

4. Who decides what the business of business is? Is this decision implicit or explicit? Explain.

5. If business operates within the law, does it thereby operate morally? Why or why not?

6. Define *ethics*; *morality*; *descriptive ethics*; *normative ethics*; *metaethics*; *casuistry*; *business ethics*.

7. Explain how the ethics of an individual's actions within a corporation are affected by the ethics of the corporation and by the fact that the corporation operates within the system of American free enterprise.

8. Are there metaethical issues in business ethics? If so, what are some? If not, why are there none?

9. Is it proper to judge business ethics by whether it produces changes in American business? Why or why not?

10. In the case of the collapsed mine did the manager act unethically in any way? Explain the reason for your answer.

11. If, in the case of the collapsed mine, one could guess that eight or more of those who volunteered might have been killed in trying to save the seven trapped men, would it have been ethically permissible to ask for volunteers? Why or why not?

MORAL
REASONING
IN BUSINESS

2

>–┼‹›•○•‹›┼‑<

CONVENTIONAL
MORALITY AND
ETHICAL RELATIVISM

Purchasing Abroad: A Case Study

Mary Thompson is the vice-president and head of the strategic planning division of an American-based multinational. She long believed in the slogan "When in Rome, do as the Romans do," but in recent years she has been forced to rethink that position. In 1990, when the company considered opening a manufacturing branch in South Africa, it finally decided against the move because of the then-existing apartheid laws, which mandated racial segregation and discrimination against blacks. She is now faced with three somewhat similar situations—or were they similar? First, the company has the opportunity to contract at an excellent price for fabric woven in China. However, she has reports that the fabric probably came from factories employing forced labor.[1] A second opportunity is to buy clothing manufactured in Pakistan.[2] Again, however, she has reports that her sources are using child labor,

---

[1] For reports on the use of forced labor in China, see "The Last Gulag," *Newsweek*, September 23, 1991, pp. 26–28; Hongda Harry Wu, *Laogai: The Chinese Gulag* (Boulder, Colo.: Westview Press, 1992); and A. M. Rosenthal, "Sixteen Million Slaves," *New York Times*, June 19, 1992, p. A15. For descriptions of slave or forced labor in a variety of countries, see "Slavery," *Newsweek*, May 4, 1992, pp. 30–39.

[2] For six views on a case study dealing with child labor, see Martha Nichols, "Third-World Families at Work: Child Labor or Child Care?," *Harvard Business Review*, 71, January–February 1993, pp. 12–23. According to the International Labor Office, child labor is a growing problem. See "Danger: Children at Work," *The Futurist*, 27, January–February 1993, pp. 42–43; and "Slavery: By Any Other Name," *The Economist*, 314, January 6, 1990, p. 42.

usually girls under 14 years of age. Her third opportunity is to open a plant in Saudi Arabia. In this situation, she is warned that for the operation to be successful, women should not be placed in executive positions because they would not be taken seriously by those with whom they had to deal.[3] Should she use American values and American views as a guide to what is right and wrong, or should she simply get the best products she can at the best price and not worry about how or by whom they are produced? After all, who is she to impose her views of what is ethical and what is not on others?

>─┼─◁▷─○─◁▷─┼─◁

Many people in business, as well as in other areas of life, feel that morality is personal, that each person has his or her own moral views, and that no one should force such views on others. According to this position, each person is entitled to his or her own moral opinion. All members of a society must abide by the law, but beyond that, each is to be guided only by individual conscience. Many people hold a similar position with respect to different countries and cultures. Each, they maintain, has its own views of what is moral and immoral. No one country or culture is better than the other. If someone is doing business in a different culture, then that person should adopt the local ways. If bribery is the common practice in a given society, then it is proper to engage in bribery in that country. It is arrogant, they say, to think that the morality of one's own country is better than that of another country, or to think the morality of one's own country is binding when doing business in another country.

This view is a popular form of moral and ethical relativism. It is a popular position and deserves careful attention. Is morality simply a matter of individual choice? Is it culturally determined? Is the claim defensible that there is a universal morality, applicable to all people and all times? This chapter will deal with these questions.

The Levels of Moral Development

The late American psychologist Lawrence Kohlberg did extensive work on moral development and then generalized the findings based on his studies.[4] The results of his investigations coincide with what many people experience in their own moral development, and therefore his position, at least in its

---

[3] For more on this issue, see Soraya Altorki, *Women in Saudi Arabia* (New York: Columbia University Press, 1986); and Philip R. Harris and Dorothy L. Harris, "Women Managers and Professionals Abroad," *Journal of Managerial Psychology*, 3 (1988), pp. i–ii.

[4] For a short presentation of the levels of moral development, see Lawrence Kohlberg, "The Claim to Moral Adequacy of a Highest Stage of Moral Judgment," *Journal of Philosophy*, 70 (1973), pp. 630–646. For a fuller development, see Lawrence Kohlberg, *The Psychology of Moral Development: The Nature and Validity of Moral Stages*, 2 vols. (New York: Harper & Row, 1984).

broad general outlines, is widely accepted.[5] Kohlberg identifies three major levels in the moral development of an individual. Not everyone advances to the third level; and no one operates only on the third level. Most people operate sometimes on one level and sometimes on another. Yet the levels of development are characteristic of the moral development of individuals and serve as handy classificatory devices.

Kohlberg not only identifies three levels but also subdivides each of the levels into two stages. He calls Level I the *preconventional level.* As infants start to grow up, they go through a phase of development that is not yet moral. In the first stage of the first level of their moral development, they react to punishment. Toddlers do not have any sense of moral right and wrong, but they soon learn that if they write on the living room wall with a crayon they will get scolded or otherwise punished. What keeps them from writing on the wall is their desire to avoid a scolding, or whatever other punishment they have come to associate with the action. The second stage of this level reflects their desire to receive a reward. Here they seek the praise of their parents. They act so as to maximize their pleasure, though of course they do so unwittingly. This reaction to punishment and reward teaches children that certain behavior is undesirable and other behavior is permissible. Children thereby learn what to do and what not do to. But they do not yet understand that they are obeying rules or performing an action *because* it is right; they do not yet have a developed sense of what morality means.

All of us to some extent react to pleasure and pain and reward and punishment. Hence, all of us sometimes act on the preconventional level.

Kohlberg calls the second level of moral development, or Level II, the *conventional level.* The morality practiced here is the morality of conventional role-conformity. He calls the first stage of Level II "Good Boy/Nice Girl Morality." In this stage, a person reacts to the expectations of parents or peers. We conform to the norms learned at home, in school, or in church. The motivation for action is more subtle than in Level I—we come to understand what moral norms and rules are. We learn how a good boy or a good girl is supposed to act. The norms we get from our family, school, and peers may not all coincide. They will probably coincide more in a homogeneous society than in a less homogeneous one; they will also tend to coincide more closely in a traditional society than in a dynamic one. But in all cases, the morality we accept is a morality that we learn from others. We learn what is expected of us in our role as a devoted child, as an adolescent, and as a student. Conventional role-conformity in its first stage is a reaction to peers, parents, or other similar per-

---

[5] Nonetheless, Kohlberg has his critics. The best known is Carol Gilligan, who in *In a Different Voice: Psychological Theory and Women's Development* (Cambridge, Mass.: Harvard University Press, 1982), claims that girls develop differently from boys and that women put more emphasis on relationships, caring, and responsibility for others rather than on principles of justice, abstract rules, or an impartial point of view. For our purposes, their differences are less important than their agreement that there is moral development and that both men and women reach a conventional stage and can go beyond it to a critical stage.

sons or groups. In its second stage, it usually develops into conformity with the laws of one's society. Kohlberg calls it the "law and order" stage. The individual becomes acculturated; he or she understands what a good citizen is supposed to be and do and lives in accordance with the role he or she has in society and with the conventional rules that govern that role.

Most adults live at the level of conformity morality. Some, probably many, never get beyond this level. All of us spend a good part of our lives on this level. Murder is wrong, lying is wrong, stealing is wrong. Why? Because everyone knows those actions are wrong. And, though, as we have said, it is impractical to have laws against all lying, lying in important circumstances is illegal (e.g., perjury), and both murder and theft are against the law.

Many adults never reach the third level of moral development, but some do. The third level will be of most interest to us. Kohlberg calls Level III the *postconventional, autonomous,* or *principled level.* This is the level of self-accepted moral principles. At this level, we accept moral principles not because society says they are right and acceptable, but because we know what it means to say that principles are right, and we understand what makes them right. The first stage of Level III is that of contract and individual rights. We speak of, and understand, morality based on the rights of individuals and on agreements made between consenting adults. At the final and highest stage of Level III, we are able to give a rational defense of the moral principles that guide our actions. Moral agents are conscious of the moral law and act in accordance with it, not because of reward or punishment, and not because others say they should but because they understand why the moral law is binding on them. Individuals accept the principles as their own, not as a foreign constraint imposed by others.

The third level is the most interesting to us, because at this level we raise questions about the justification of the moral norms we hold. Most people simply accept the morality of their society. But it is possible to ask: Is what my society holds to be right *really* right? Might the people of my society be mistaken? Why should I accept what my parents told me is right or wrong, or why should I accept what legislators tell me is right and wrong? How do they know? They certainly cannot *make* actions right or wrong; or, if they can, so can I. If none of us can, then there must be reasons why some actions are right and others are wrong, other than because people classify them in this way. What are those reasons?

These are the questions that ethics seeks to answer, and it is at this third level that ethical theory operates. Of course, what conventional morality holds to be immoral may well be immoral. The difference between Levels II and III is not necessarily their content; rather, the difference lies in their reasons for considering actions to be right or wrong.

Kohlberg's description of the levels of development helps us to understand a good deal about business ethics. We noted earlier that people in business frequently claim that they are bound only by the law and not by moral norms, which they see as personal. Most people like to operate at the second level of morality, so it is not surprising that most businesses operate at this level, too. Certainly some business practices are held to be moral and proper, and others are held to be improper. It is possible simply to accept these conventional norms. But it is also possible to ask whether these norms should be held, whether some of them may in fact be improper, and whether there are other activities in which businesses *should* engage but do not.

Thus, at one time in the United States large numbers of people in the South accepted slavery. Now, most people think that slavery is immoral. Was it always immoral? We might answer that slavery was moral according to the conventional morality that was held in the South at that time. But if one were to operate on Kohlberg's third level, slavery would be seen to have been immoral then as well as now. Actually, many did argue that it was immoral, despite the fact that it was part of conventional morality.

Subjective and Objective Morality

When we speak of morality, we refer to our judgments of right and wrong, good and bad. Three characteristics are usually associated with such judgments.

- First, moral judgments about the rightness or wrongness of an action are held to be universally applicable. If an action is right for me, it is also right for anyone else in the same circumstances. If it is wrong for you, it is also wrong for anyone else similarly placed. Something of the notion of universality is captured in the injunction "do unto others as you would have them do unto you." The moral rule against murder says it is wrong for anyone to murder someone else. It is universal because it applies to everyone.
- Second, moral judgments are important. They are so important, in fact, that they override other considerations. We are morally bound to do what we sometimes may not want to do. For instance, it is wrong to steal, even when we would like to steal. If we say that it is our moral duty to perform an action, that means we have an obligation to do it, and this can only be overridden by a stronger moral consideration. Convenience, personal gain, and even legal requirements fall before moral obligations.
- Third, moral praise can properly accompany the doing of morally right actions, and moral blame can properly accompany acting immorally. If we say that someone in a business transaction acted immorally, this means that, from a moral point of view, it is appropriate for us to blame that person. For instance, if taking bribes is immoral, then those involved in bribery deserve moral blame or censure.

The vocabulary of morality is rich, and it is applied to a variety of objects in a number of ways. We can make clear our meanings if we keep separate the various uses of the terms. We call individual persons moral or immoral; we call actions moral or immoral; and we call economic systems, social institutions, and business practices moral or immoral. We do not mean the same thing in each of these cases, though each has something to do with conformity, or lack of conformity, to the moral law or to morality.

When we speak of persons being moral or immoral, we may mean at least three different things. It is not always clear which meaning an individual has in mind when describing someone as being moral. In one sense, a person may be considered moral if he habitually acts in accordance with his conscience. We may speak of him as more or less moral, depending on how frequently, within tolerable levels, he acts contrary to his conscience. What we mean is that he tries to do what he thinks is right. Here, sincerity is the keynote of morality. Although each of us knows our own conscience, we do not know the conscience of others, and so we cannot be sure when they are acting in accordance with their beliefs.

In another sense, if we hold that certain actions are immoral, then we might call someone a moral person if he acts in conformity with the moral law, if he does what the moral law requires, or if he does not do what the moral law forbids.

The third sense in which we mean moral is a combination of the other two. We may reserve the term *moral* to describe only individuals who act in conformity with the moral law and do so because they know what that law requires. They act in accordance with their conscience, which is correct in its judgments of right and wrong. The meaning of moral in this third sense is the one to which a moral individual aspires. He knows that he should do the right thing and that he should act in accordance with what his conscience dictates. Only then is his action fully praiseworthy, from a moral standpoint. But none of us can be sure we know, in all situations, what is right. We are all fallible. Hence, we can only try to determine, as carefully as possible, what is right, and so act. We can follow our conscience and hope that our efforts to form a correct conscience have been successful.

The distinction between what we believe to be right and what is actually right is an important one. We can make the distinction by referring to *subjectively* right (and wrong) and *objectively* right (and wrong) actions. What we are judging now, from a moral point of view, is actions, not persons. An action is subjectively right if a person believes that the action is moral. An action is objectively right if the action is in conformity with the moral law.

If I believe that telling the truth is right, and it is right, then telling the truth is both subjectively and objectively right. An action may be subjectively right and objectively wrong. If I am mistaken about the morality of bribery, for instance, I may believe it to be moral for me to take a bribe, even though it is actually (objectively) immoral. Conversely, an action can be subjectively wrong and objectively right. This again involves a mistake on my part about the morality of the action. Suppose that in taking candy from a box I think that I am stealing; in fact, however, the candy is part of a display and is there for anyone who wants to take it. I did not objectively steal, even if I thought I was stealing. Finally, an action may be both subjectively and objectively wrong; for instance, when I believe bribery to be wrong, and, in fact, it is immoral.

One of the pitfalls in the study of morality is that we typically operate on two levels: the first-person level, in which we wish both to judge the action and to act in accordance with our conscience; and the third-person level, in which we wish to judge the actions of others from an objective point of view but do not wish to know, or cannot know, the subjective state of the one performing the action.

Because people are reluctant to judge the internal state of others, sometimes they refuse to judge the actions of others. The two judgments, however, can be kept distinct. We can judge the crimes of Hitler without knowing whether or not he *thought* he was doing something morally right when he performed, or ordered others to perform, immoral acts. Attitudes and intentions constitute a part of what is properly the object of moral evaluation. However, many actions can be considered in their own right, in abstraction from the intent of the agent, and can be evaluated from a moral point of view. This is how we usually judge such actions as stealing, bribery, murder, lying, and so on. Obviously, when we speak of an economic system as being moral or immoral, or of business practices as being immoral, we are also judging them without reference to whether those involved in them believe them to be moral.

Some people adopt a moral tolerance toward others for these reasons: Because we are fallible in our moral judgments; because we sometimes believe an action to be right when it is objectively wrong; because people disagree in their moral judgments; and because, in a pluralistic society, the norms of conventional morality are sometimes not clear. They not only refuse to judge others but also refuse to judge their own actions. Because they cannot give reasons for actions being right or wrong, they often take this position: "There is no objective morality," or "morality is purely subjective." They consider themselves to be personally moral when they act as they believe they should. (But others may act differently and still be moral, if they believe they are acting morally.) This position confuses subjective guilt and blame with objective guilt and blame. Pushed to its conclusion, it denies the objectivity of moral judgments; it claims that whatever anyone considers to be moral is thereby moral. It therefore abandons the universal characteristic of morality. When made explicit, this position is known as *ethical relativism.*

Descriptive Relativism

Anthropologists and sociologists have documented the fact that people in different cultures, as well as people within a given culture, hold divergent moral views on particular issues. The ancient Greeks believed that infanticide was not immoral, although we believe that it is. Some members of our society believe that abortion is immoral, and others believe that it is morally permissible. These differences are examples of transcultural and intracultural relativism. We should, however, distinguish what is often called cultural relativism which is descriptive, from ethical relativism, which is a normative position. Both positions can be applied to individuals as well as to particular societies.[6]

Given the fact that a practice is held to be moral in one society at one time and wrong at another time or in another society, and given the fact that people within a society in a given time differ in their moral views, we can draw no conclusions about cultures or about a society, except that the differences just described do exist. Consider a class of twenty third-graders who have been given a long addition problem. Suppose that each child in the class comes up with a different answer to the problem. Because of our knowledge of mathematics, we can say that no more than one of the children has the right answer. (Of course, none of them may have the right answer.) But we would be mistaken if, on the basis of the reported differences, we concluded that there was no right answer to the problem.

Anthropology and sociology supply data to be considered and explained. Starting with the differences between societies concerning what is viewed as moral, we can appropriately ask about the extent of the disagreement and about the bases for the disagreement. Actually, it may be more interesting to inquire about the extent of the agreement rather than the disagreement, for surely the agreements as well as the disagreements deserve consideration and explanation.

Differing views regarding the morality of a given action or practice may be the result of a number of factors. Two societies may basically and ultimately disagree on moral principles, but the disagreement may also be on many other levels. For instance, two societies may adhere to this basic principle: What helps the society flourish is moral, and what hinders it is immoral. But if one society lives in a warm climate and has an abundance of water, it will have a different view of clothing and of the use of water than a society that lives in a very cold climate and has little water. A country with many men and few women will probably not look on monogamy in the same way as a society with an approximately equal number of men and women. Differing conditions, therefore, provide a reason for holding differing actions to be moral or immoral. A society's factual beliefs also affect what it holds to be moral or immoral. A society that believes in volcano gods that demand human sacrifice will consider this practice to be moral—one that is demanded by higher authority and therefore necessary for the preservation of the society. A society that does not believe in volcano gods will not consider the practice to

---

[6] W. G. Sumner, an anthropologist, in *Folkways* (Boston: Ginn & Co., 1907), presents the case for cultural relativism. E. Westermarck argues for ethical relativism based on cultural relativism in *Ethical Relativity* (New York: Harcourt Brace, 1932). The anthropologist M. Ginsberg, in *Essays in Sociology and Social Philosophy*, vol. 1 *On the Diversity of Morals* (New York: Macmillan, 1957), argues that anthropological relativism does not entail ethical relativism.

be either necessary or morally justifiable. Factual beliefs are an important ingredient in the morality of any society, and differences in the beliefs about facts lead to differences in what is considered moral or immoral.

Some societies believe what is false. To some extent, this is probably true of all societies. However, most societies are aware that they obtain more and more factual knowledge as they develop and progress. Just as a society may be mistaken about facts, so it may be mistaken about some of its moral judgments. From history, we know that members of a society frequently believe that one or more of the moral beliefs of that society are erroneous. There is no reason, in principle, why members of another society cannot make and defend similar claims about a society other than their own.

Descriptive transcultural relativism describes the differences between cultures. In some cases, the differences are such that the terms *right* and *wrong* or *better* and *worse* are not applicable to the differences noted. All cultures have a language, and some languages are more complex than others. But it makes little sense to say that one language is, in some absolute sense, better than another. Similarly, many aspects of one culture will differ from aspects of another, but the two can be equally good.

Many people dispute the accuracy of anthropological reports of the morality of primitive tribes and foreign cultures, because they consider that what the anthropologist describes as a society's morality may be simply an imposition of his or her own categories of morality, resulting in faulty interpretations of unfamiliar practices. Yet there are clear cases: The ancient Greeks, as we have already noted, believed that infanticide was morally permissible, and we do not. And, once again: In the South, before the Civil War, many people thought slavery was morally permissible, whereas many in the North held it to be immoral. Do the differences in beliefs show that morality is relative? Does descriptive cultural relativism imply normative ethical relativism?

Normative Ethical Relativism

Normative ethical relativism claims that when any two cultures or any two people hold different moral views of an action, both can be right. Thus, an action may be right for one person or society, and the same action, taken in the same way, may be wrong for another person or society, and yet the two persons or societies are equally correct. What exactly is meant by these claims? A first form involves saying that neither of two conflicting moral judgments is right and neither is wrong because moral judgments are not right or wrong—they are simply statements of opinion or of feeling. The defense of this form of relativism usually depends on a metaethical view of moral language and the logic of moral discourse. A second form holds that judgments of right and wrong are culturally determined and that transcultural judgments make no more sense in questions of morality than they do in judgments about whether one language is better than another. Those who maintain this position claim that cultural relativism is applicable in the area of morality as in other cultural areas, and they defend normative ethical relativism on anthropological grounds. A third form claims that we should not say that either of two competing judgments is right or wrong because we have no way of deciding which is which. One may be right and the other wrong; but because we have no way of proving this, it is better, more prudent, and more cautious not to claim either is right or wrong.[7]

These forms of relativism deserve some attention because they bear directly on such questions as which morality businesspeople in a foreign country should follow—their own or that of the country in which they are conducting their business. Whose morality are they to follow? The various forms of moral relativism all hold that there is a close connection between the fact of moral diversity and the claim that there are many moralities, each equally valid or good. The connecting link between cultural relativism and normative ethical relativism is a theory or view about morality.

The obvious forms of normative ethical relativism, however, do not stand up well to analysis. Consider the first view, that moral judgments are neither true nor false, neither right nor wrong, because they are simply statements of feeling or emotion. From this position a number of consequences follow that do not cohere well with the moral experience of most people. One of the results of adopting this view is that a moral judgment about an action— the judgment that stealing is immoral, for examples—is not a judgment about stealing at all. It is simply the expression of one's feeling about stealing. Suppose *A* feels negatively about *B*'s taking his wallet and *A* says that *B*'s taking *A*'s wallet is immoral. *B* replies that *B* feels no guilt about taking *A*'s wallet; therefore, according to *B*, his action is moral. If both are simply reporting or expressing their feelings, then each is speaking about himself. If each is speaking about himself, they are not speaking about the *action* of *B* taking *A*'s wallet. That they have different reactions is perfectly possible and involves no disagreement between them. Hence, they each express their emotions, and if the emotions happen to differ, they differ. Nor does it change matters to say that when someone makes a moral judgment he not only expresses his emotions or feelings, he also adds that others should feel as he does. For once again, different people have different emotions. Each can feel that others

[7] A. J. Ayer in Chapter VI of *Language, Truth and Logic,* 2nd ed. (New York: Dover Publications, 1946), presents the logical positivist attack on moral language as literally meaningless. He is answered by Brand Blanshard in Chapter V, "Subjectivism," of *Reason and Goodness* (New York: Macmillan, 1961). Two other refutations of ethical relativism are Chapters 1 and 2 of W. T. Stace, *The Concepts of Morals* (New York: Macmillan, 1937); and Carl Wellman, "The Ethical Implications of Cultural Relativity," in *Journal of Philosophy,* 60 (1963), pp. 169–184. For a defense of a subtle version of ethical relativism, see Gilbert Harman, "Moral Relativism Defended," *The Philosophical Review,* 1975, pp. 3–22. An interesting discussion of levels of moral argument is R. M. Hare's *Moral Thinking* (Oxford: Clarendon Press, 1981). A useful collection of articles is contained in Michael Krausz and Jack W. Meiland; Eds., *Relativism: Cognitive and Moral* (Notre Dame, Ind.: University of Notre Dame Press, 1982).

should feel as he does. It may be said that each is simply saying something about himself and neither of them is judging the action.

A second consequence is that we can never disagree with anyone about the morality of an action. If a moral judgment is simply a statement about myself, my reactions, or my expression of my emotions, when someone expresses his or her emotions and they happen to differ from mine, we appropriately say that we have different emotions or are expressing differing emotions. But emotions are not true or false; therefore, because we are making no claims of truth or falsehood, no claims of right or wrong, we are not disagreeing with each other.

A third consequence is that, in this view, people can never be mistaken in their moral judgments. This is so because if someone feels negatively about an action today and feels positively about the same action tomorrow, then he or she will have had, or expressed, different emotions. But expressing one emotion today is not incompatible with expressing a different one tomorrow. In neither case does the individual make a factual statement or claim, so there is nothing to be right or wrong about, and hence no way to be mistaken.

A fourth consequence is that people can change the morality of an action by expressing a different emotion concerning it. If a moral judgment is only the report of an emotion or the expression of an emotion, then by changing his or her emotion a person changes the morality of the action.

These four consequences of normative ethical relativism do not correspond well with the moral experience of most people, because people do make judgments about actions—at least that is what they intend to do. They do find that, in some cases, they disagree with others about the morality of an action. People do change their minds, and they often conclude that they were mistaken in the past in judging an action to be right, whereas today they know it is wrong. And they do not think they can change the morality of an action simply by changing their emotions or by expressing different emotions. What reason do they have for giving up these common-sense beliefs that form part of their experience? So far, we have not been given any reason that is strong enough to overcome our ordinary experience. What we have been given is a theory of what moral judgments supposedly are. But why accept that theory? We certainly do express our moral feelings when we make moral judgments. We do wish people to have feelings similar to ours when we express our emotions relative to an action. But that is not all we do. We also judge the action, disagree with those who judge it differently, and so on.

Consider next the view of the defender of normative ethical relativism who argues that judgments of right and wrong are culturally determined. The claim may be that one society holds some act to be right, whereas another society holds a similar act to be wrong because the circumstances in which the act is performed make the acts different. What appears to be brutality in one society may appear as kindness in another. For instance, a society where it is the custom to have the aged leave the society, to die alone, might appear heartless to someone from a society where the moral thing to do is to care for the aged, keeping them alive as long as possible and by whatever means possible. Both actions might be construed as showing respect for the aged, although the respect is shown in very different ways. In this instance, however, we do not have normative ethical relativism; we simply have differing instantiations, on the level of practice, of a similar higher moral norm, which is shared by both societies.

Another interpretation of normative ethical relativism might be to maintain that what each society means by the term *moral* is that the action is held to be right in that society. *Moral* then means, "is approved by this society." In this case it would follow that no two societies disagree on the morality of an action, for what each means by the term *moral* is different. By judging an action to be moral, a member of society *A* is reporting that the people of his or her society believe it to be moral. By judging the same action to be *immoral*, a member of society *B* is reporting that the members of his or her society believe it to be immoral. Each report can be correct. A consequence of this view is that no two societies can disagree on the morality of an action. All anyone can do is report what one's own society thinks about the action. A second consequence is that no member of the society can disagree with his or her society about the morality of an action. According to this view, when we say that an action is immoral, we are really only saying that our society *believes* it to be immoral. And if this society actually believes the action to be moral, then we are simply mistaken when asserting what the society does not believe. Yet it is a fact of moral life that people do sometimes disagree in some instances with what the other members of the society believe regarding moral matters, and societies do disagree with one another on moral matters. Hence, once again there is more reason for denying the doctrine of normative ethical relativism than there is for holding it.

Some cultural differences are matters of taste, which offer no basis for deciding that one is right and another wrong—nor is there any need to do so. For instance, if one culture likes boiled food and another dislikes it, each can have its own way, without harm. If one person likes chocolate ice cream and another strongly dislikes chocolate but likes vanilla ice cream, we are not tempted to say one is right and the other is wrong. Cultural and individual differences exist. There is usually no claim of truth or falsehood and no basis, or need, to decide one is right and the other wrong. Why is this not so in the moral realm?

The argument from moral experience claims that we do judge actions to be moral or immoral and that in making these judgment we are saying something about the actions and not just something about ourselves. The argument also claims that people do disagree on moral issues. Because they believe they are making statements that are true or false, right or wrong, they are not satisfied if they are told that they are *not* doing this. Their protest is not sufficient to show that they are correct in their assertion. However, more is needed to show them that they are mistaken than simply someone's theory asserting the contrary.

A closer look at what many people think they are doing when they make moral judgments will show us, in part, why moral disputes occur. For instance, when making the judgment that murder is immoral, the ordinary person means that the act of murder is immoral for everyone. He is not making the judgment that it is immoral only for himself and that others, if they feel differently, may be acting morally if they kill him arbitrarily. He is claiming that the action is immoral for everyone. Nor is he restricting his judgment only to the members of his society. Murder is immoral in his own country and in other countries as well, whether or not the people of that country realize or admit it. In making his moral judgment, therefore, he is making a claim about the nature of an action, and it is a claim with universal import. This is what he means by saying murder is immoral: That no one should do it, and that it is wrong for anyone to do it.

A society may morally judge the actions of only its own members because it ignores all other societies, or because it considers all other people barbarians and not worthy of respect. The domain of a society may be restricted because of that society's beliefs about other people. But when a moral judgment is made in such a society, the judgment still has universal import because it applies to all those within the moral community. If one's view of the moral community includes all human beings, then the moral judgment of an action is made in the name of all. If, in addition, one's moral community includes animals, then the judgments also apply to them.

Yet it does not follow that because people make universal moral judgments they do so correctly. Nor does it follow that simply because people disagree in their moral judgments it is therefore possible to determine which one is correct.

The third interpretation of ethical relativism states that we should not say that disagreements on moral issues are right or wrong because no one can show that he himself is right and someone else wrong. There is no way of deciding such disputed issues. According to this view, it is arrogant to claim that one is right and another wrong in moral disputes. At best, we can discuss our differences to determine whether they rest on differing facts. If this is the case, then we can try to determine which facts are correct. We can also try to find out if we have different beliefs. Once again, we can try to adjudicate our differences. If we finally find, however, that we agree on the facts and have the same nonmoral beliefs but still differ on the morality of an action, according to this view, there is then no way to show that one of us is right and the other wrong. The view implies that moral principles are not right or wrong and cannot be rationally defended; yet moral principles frequently have been given rational defense, and disagreements on moral issues are argued in rational as well as in emotional terms. It is worthwhile to look at these debates, but we should be clear about what can and what cannot be claimed for them.

If the arguments presented here against normative ethical relativism are valid, what follows? What follows is not a complete moral system, and we do not claim that somewhere there is a complete moral system, waiting to be found. The fact is that moral judgments are judgments that can and should be defended, but that the arguments given are sometimes good and sometimes not so good. If we are faced with contradictory judgments about an action, only one of them can be right. The way to determine which one is right is to see which judgment is best supported by the facts and by the arguments presented in its defense. We may eventually arrive at high-level, abstract, moral principles. If they clash, we will then have to decide which of the alternative principles or approaches has been best defended. Upon investigation, we may conclude that no theory that has been investigated is completely defensible or completely satisfactory. In that case, more work is necessary. The conclusion that there can be no satisfactory theory is not a valid conclusion based on the evidence. We do not conclude that there is no satisfactory unified theory of physics simply because we have not yet found one. In both cases the appropriate response is to continue the search, to continue to make improvements, and to continue to use what we presently have available, despite the deficiencies.

Moral Absolutism

One alternative to ethical relativism is *moral absolutism.* A moral absolutist holds that there are eternal moral values and eternal moral principles that are always and everywhere applicable. There are different versions of absolutism. Some absolutists, for instance, hold that the most general principle of morality is absolute but that, as it is applied in differing circumstances, certain lower-level norms may vary. Other, more extreme, absolutists claim that all moral norms are everywhere and always the same. Between the two positions is a third position, which holds that the most general principle of morality is everywhere and always the same and that the moral norms are everywhere and always the same, but that these norms have exceptions, which are also everywhere and always the same.

There is a difference between holding that the principles of morality are universal and eternal and holding that one knows with certainty what the principles are. A person might maintain that there are eternal moral principles without being able to produce them. Instead, he might produce various approximations of those principles, which he is willing and ready to modify when he sees they are not exact in their formulation.

There is an alternative to absolutism, however, which does not fall into the category of relativism. This position claims that morality is not eternal. Rather, it is an attempt by human beings to adopt principles to govern human society and the lives of those within society, principles that will help people live together and abide by rules that all of them, in their reasonable and objective moments, would accept. Unlike the absolutist, someone holding this position need not claim that some final, ultimate, eternal moral principle exists somewhere—for instance, in the mind of God. He need only claim that the idea of such a principle forms an ideal toward which ethics strives. He is then content to examine the various moral principles that have been suggested during the history of humankind, and the various ethical theories that human beings have produced. He can see which ones stand up best to rational scrutiny, which ones are most helpful to him, and which ones correspond most closely to the value he perceives. This is not only an individual endeavor, but also a collective one, for we can build on the accomplishments of others as well as on their mistakes. We shall follow this alternative in the succeeding chapters. No claim to infallibility or privileged eternal knowledge shall be made. Rather, we shall explain the most successful traditional approaches to morality and the types of moral arguments currently used in our society.

Moral Pluralism

American society is diverse, a combination of various cultures and traditions. It is heterogeneous in composition, with many ethnic and racial groups. Dynamic and changing, it is pluralistic in many ways, not only culturally but also, to some extent, morally.

We can distinguish four levels of moral pluralism: radical moral pluralism, the pluralism of moral principles, the pluralism of moral practices, and the pluralism of self-realization. *Radical moral pluralism* describes that state of affairs in which people hold mutually irreconcilable views about morality, such as what the terms *right* and *wrong* mean, and which actions are right or wrong. People who hold such radically divergent views, however, do not form a society. To be a society, a group must accept certain fundamental practices and principles. At a basic level, for instance, there must be general agreement that life is worth living, that the lives of the members of the society should be respected, or that people will respect existing differences to the extent that they do not interfere with each other. If some people do not care whether they live or die and also believe it is their moral duty to kill others, it may not be possible to convince them they are mistaken. But people with such a view cannot form a society. To the extent that society and morality go together, the morality of a society must be a shared morality, not a radically pluralistic set of opposing moralities. Yet a society may be morally pluralistic on the other three levels.

A plurality of moral principles within a society does not necessarily mean irreconcilable diversity. Pluralism on the level of moral principles is compatible with social agreement on the morality of many basic practices. Such agreement does not necessarily involve agreement on the moral principles that different people use to evaluate practices. The vast majority of the members of our society, for instance, agree that murder is wrong. Some members of our society operate only at the level of conventional morality and do not ask why murder is wrong. Some may believe it is wrong because the God in whom they believe forbids such acts; others because it violates human dignity; still others because murder has serious consequences for society as a whole; and so on. Each of these involves a different moral principle. These different principles are compatible with similarity of moral judgments.[8]

On the level of specific actions, we encounter a variety of moral opinions about some of them. This pluralism regarding moral practices may stem from differences of moral principles, but it may also stem from differences of fact or of perception of facts, differences of circumstances, or differences in the weighing of relevant values. Even when there is basic agreement on principles, not all moral issues are clear. In a changing, dynamic, developing society there is certainly room for moral disagreement, even if there is unanimous agreement that what helps the society to survive is moral. New practices might be seen by conservatives as threatening the society's survival, and the same practice might be championed by others as the necessary means for survival. Pluralism of practices, however, is compatible with areas of agreement, and this is usually the case.

The fourth level of moral pluralism is that of self-realization. As long as the members of a society abide by the basic moral norms, they are allowed, in such a pluralistic society, to choose freely their other values and their lifestyles. This constitutes a kind of moral pluralism because self-development and fulfillment, according to some views, are moral matters. A society that allows divergence of self-development within the basic moral framework tolerates a great many differences that would not be allowed (or found) in a homogeneous society.

Pluralism and American Business

Moral pluralism of the second, third, and fourth kinds is found in the United States. These varieties of pluralism do not imply normative ethical relativism, and in fact they presuppose a wide common background of moral practices. The diversity of moral practices that we encounter is often so striking that we forget the similarities: Respect for human beings, respect for truth, and respect for the property of others are all commonplaces found in America, making business possible. Despite our moral pluralism, we have adopted laws to enforce common moral norms, to define proper areas of toleration, and to provide adjudicatory functions in cases of moral disputes on socially important issues.

Hence, the question some people raise when speaking of morality in business: "Whose morality should I follow?" is a misleading question, as if everyone's morality is different from everyone else's. Ultimately, I must follow my conscience, and in this sense the morality I follow is mine. As a morality, however, it makes claims that are universal. Even though we are a pluralistic soci-

---

[8] An influential discussion of the pluralism in American ethical thinking and a defense of a virtue-based approach to ethics is contained in Alasdair McIntyre, *After Virtue* (Notre Dame, Ind.: University of Notre Dame Press, 1981).

ety, we share a large core of commonly held values and norms. If we did not, we could not be a functioning society. These shared norms form the common morality of the society. They are yours, mine, and ours and we hold them as applicable to everyone. They cohere with and underpin our laws, our everyday customs, and our political system. In areas of serious difference (which I described as the third level of moral pluralism), the clash of moral values within our society is decided by public debate and perhaps by legislation. Moral arguments are raised and countered until clarity emerges or until a way of resolving the problem, while recognizing differences, is worked out. Such disputes, even when they capture headlines and dominate public concern, take place against a background of accepted norms and institutions. In fact, without such common norms and institutions the disputes could not arise or be carried on as they are. It is not true, therefore, that when faced with moral claims against me or against my business practices I can dismiss them as being your moral views and not mine. Because moral norms have a universal dimension, they are appropriately applied to the actions of others, who can be called upon to justify their actions or suffer the moral opprobrium of others.

Pluralism and International Business

The pluralism found in American society pales when compared with the pluralism found worldwide. Certainly, the moral codes and views held in each country of the world share some basic similarities. In every country, for example, the murder of members of the society is prohibited; otherwise no society would long exist. In all of them, lying and deceiving others are immoral; otherwise there would be no secure social interaction. There is also respect for property, however defined; if this were not so, no one would be able to count on having what is needed to live. Yet the way in which the nations of the world form an international or global society is at best a tenuous one. National sovereignty limits the extent to which any nation wishes to abide by a tribunal higher than itself. For instance, on the international level, law cannot always play the same mediating and adjudicating role it does in the United States because there is no generally acknowledged body to enforce such law. The differences that divide nations are much more profound than the differences that divide members of the same society. The notion of a common morality for everyone in the world—pluralistic in nature but providing a basic framework within which all can work—is a goal still to be achieved, not a present reality. Societies are in sufficient agreement, however, to allow business to be carried on internationally. There remain a host of unresolved problems. The moral intuitions, feelings, and beliefs of most people have been primarily focused and formed within their own society and on the level of personal morality. Their views on the international level of obligation among nations are less well formed, partly because people in general have not given it much thought. Therefore, we find few ready answers to questions on this level. Nonetheless, we can give some answers.

First, the injunction "When in Rome, do as the Romans do" has limited applicability. When one drives a car in England, one had better drive on the left, because that is the rule of the road in England. One clearly should observe local etiquette and other such customs in countries other than one's own. To this extent, when in Rome one should indeed do as the Romans do. It is equally clear, however, that if a business operates in a country in which slavery or bondage or apartheid is legal or widely practiced, this gives no one the license to do likewise. We can and should draw the line between local practices and customs that are morally indifferent—such as which side of the road you drive on in a country—and others that are immoral or that we clearly perceive to be immoral, such as engaging in slavery. No individual and no company can ethically justify engaging in practices the individual or company believes are immoral or unethical. A person of integrity and a company of integrity not only have principles but live by them. Hence, the answer to the question "Whose ethics do I follow?" on the international level, just as on the national level, must be: my own. Yet on the international level, just as on the national level, this does not imply that my ethics are individual only, that they make no universal claims, or that they are not widely shared.

There is a difference, however, between saying that American companies of integrity abroad must abide by the moral norms they hold and saying that American companies should impose their ways of doing business on the rest of the world—or that American norms and American standards are the only ethically or morally justifiable ones. The one claim in no way implies or justifies the others. There are many ethically justifiable ways of doing business, and there are many standards that are ethically justifiable. American standards are not the only justifiable ones. But while many are justifiable, some—such as slavery—are not justifiable, even if commonly practiced in some country. And it is these that are precluded.

What, then, of the Mary Thompson example with which this chapter began? Her company has already acknowledged that it should not and would not follow the South African apartheid laws. Similarly, it is clear that it should not engage in slavery or promote or abet it. Hence, it cannot ethically produce products made by slave or forced labor, nor should it purchase them, since that at least indirectly promotes and supports the practice. The length to which the company should go in determining whether the products it receives are in fact made by forced labor brings up a more complicated question, but not one that can be simply ignored. The issue of child labor is more complex. In the United States, even though we prohibit child labor and require schooling up to a certain grade, children do chores around the house or take small odd jobs, like delivering newspapers. In agrarian societies children typically work on the farm, the level of mandatory schooling varies from society to society, and other factors make this issue somewhat different from slavery or forced labor. In some societies, however, there is little difference between the two. The obligation is to determine the actual conditions and the alternatives, and in the light of the best information to make an informed decision. Any use of child labor that is stultifying and that impedes normal growth, development, and education is equivalent to forced labor, and on that basis it is not morally justifiable. The issue of the fair, equitable, and equal treatment of women is again a complicated one. But whatever the local custom, Mary Thompson's company cannot legitimately engage in any practice that discriminates against women or that violates their right to fair and equal treatment. Exactly how this prohibition translates into practice in different countries depends in part on the situation in each of those countries. In the former Soviet Union women worked in coal mines; in the United States they do not. It does not automatically follow that women are better treated or that their rights are better respected in one of these countries than in the other.

Approaches to Ethical Theory

In describing the plurality of moral principles, we saw that though people may all agree that murder is immoral, they may arrive at that judgment on the basis of different moral principles. Ethical theories attempt to systematize ordinary moral judgments, and to establish and defend basic moral principles.

Most moral judgments in business, as in other areas of life, are made on the basis of such generally accepted rules as "Do no harm" "Do not kill," or "Tell the truth." Why then do we need ethical theory? Why are not these rules sufficient?

The answer is a threefold one. First, although the general rules are frequently sufficient, they are not always so. How are we to decide cases in which the moral intuitions of people differ, in which two or more general moral rules seem to conflict, in which following a general moral rule seems to lead to an immoral action, or in which a generally accepted rule or practice is challenged? New practices arise constantly in business for which our moral rules do not clearly give us answers. How are we to evaluate these practices? In any of these cases it would be helpful if we had some way of deciding which rules apply and which rules are moral and which are not. Ethical theory provides these answers by explaining why actions are right or wrong and by providing a decision procedure for resolving difficult or controverted cases. Someone who knows ethical theory can engage in moral reasoning as outlined by the theory. This is useful for an individual in resolving difficult moral issues that the individual may face. Thus, one reason for studying ethical theory is to help moral individuals clarify to themselves what their moral values are and think through difficult issues in an orderly way.

Second, knowing some of the standard methods of moral reasoning makes it possible for an individual who does make moral decisions to explain and justify them to others. If a business executive hires or fires or promotes certain individuals and is challenged as to the justice or fairness of his or her decision, that executive is called upon to justify the action. Simply saying that we believe the action is fair is not enough. We must present reasons or arguments in defense of our decision. To do so means to engage in moral reasoning, and armed with ethical theory we can do so effectively. Knowledge of the standard techniques of moral argumentation also enables us to take part in corporate discussions or public policy discussions in an intelligent way, with knowledge of how to present and evaluate moral arguments.

Third, even though conventional morality is the starting point for ethical theory and is generally accepted, it may not always be correct. How are we to determine this if all we have are the norms and rules of conventional morality? To evaluate conventional morality we must have another point of view, one that allows us to explain why the parts of conventional morality that we accept should be accepted, while allowing us to question or show why other parts of it need rejection or revision. Ethical theory provides this point of view. Ethical theory, to this extent, is *critical* rather than conventional. The relation of conventional morality and ethical theory is an interactive one. Ethical theory attempts to justify conventional morality, in turn corrects conventional morality, and is then evaluated in terms of how well it explains the resulting whole. This ongoing interrelation of conventional morality and ethical theory continues until we either reach at least a temporary point of equilibrium or until we are forced to act on the basis of the best insight that our theory, however defective or incomplete, permits.

The search for a completely satisfactory ethical theory is a never-ending one. There is no theory on which all people or all philosophers agree. Nonetheless, we need not describe here the many different ethical systems that have been developed in the history of philosophy. Through the centuries, two basic approaches to moral reasoning have prevailed. One approach argues on the basis of ends. This approach to ethical reasoning is called a *teleological* approach, the most prominent version of which is consequentialism. The latter states that whether an action is right or wrong depends on the consequences of that action. A common form of consequentialist ethics, one that is very strongly represented in our society is *utilitarianism,* a theory we shall examine in the next chapter.

The second basic approach is called the *deontological* approach. This states that duty is the basic moral category and that duty is independent of consequences. An action is right if it has certain characteristics or is of a certain kind, and wrong if it has other characteristics or is of another kind. The traditional Judeo-Christian approach to morality is deontological. The German philosopher Immanuel Kant (1724–1804) gave a classical philosophical statement of the deontological approach, which is currently influential in our society. Most of the discussion on questions of business ethics, as well as on questions of social ethics (e.g., welfare or the morality of governmental practices or of laws) is conducted by people who use—knowingly or unknowingly—a utilitarian, a Judeo-Christian, or a Kantian approach to ethics. Included in the deontological approach is a consideration of the meaning, content, and justification of both justice and rights. And judgments about fairness or justice, as well as claims involving rights—whether they be human rights, workers' rights, or the civil rights of women and minorities—are undeniably pervasive in American society.

Philosophers and others who wish to be consistent often attempt to use only one of the ethical approaches to questions. Those interested in ethics as a theoretical pursuit attempt to construct their approach so that it can handle difficulties and objections, and can be defended and rationally justified. Those who are willing to mix their approaches are sometimes called *ethical pluralists*. They hold one primary approach or set of principles but join them with another approach or set of principles. One charge often brought against utilitarianism, for instance, is that it cannot provide a satisfactory account of justice. Hence, some philosophers join a deontological notion of justice to their utilitarian ethical views. The mixing of approaches has advantages. It also obviously has disadvantages, because the pluralist needs some way to decide when to use one principle rather than another.

While philosophers argue, both they and the other members of society must act. In the absence of definitive ethical theories, we make do with the best we have. In our society, the moral arguments are basically of the types previously named. We therefore need to be familiar with them, to know how to employ them, and to be conscious of their strengths and weaknesses. To a large extent, our country is ethically inarticulate. The members of our society make moral judgments and hold moral values, but most are poorly trained in the art of defending their moral views, and they fail to use moral reasoning in a focused way when debating public policy, social issues, and business practices. The art of moral reasoning is an important part of business ethics.

Two other aspects of moral experience deserve some attention before we turn to ethical theory: moral virtue and moral ideals. A growing number of philosophers emphasize that morality involves more than moral rules and moral reasoning, and they are certainly correct. Morality also involves virtue, which has to do with an individual's character, and the type of actions that emanate from that character. What is moral in a given situation, they argue, is not only what conventional morality or moral rules, however justified, require, but also what the mature person with a good moral character would see as appropriate. This may often be more than what moral rules require— which is sometimes referred to as the moral minimum. There is no doubt that moral actions come from moral persons; that moral character is important; and that virtues, such as honesty, truthfulness, and moral courage, are traits that should be promoted and developed. But these claims are consistent with the claims that people ought not to lie, steal, murder, or cheat. To focus on the rules as if they were all that is important in morality is as much a mistake as to hold that there are no rules. The training of character is an important part of moral education, as is the teaching of moral reasoning.

The status of ideals in morality is often overlooked, and ideals are sometimes confused with moral obligations or what is morally required. Moral ideals present a goal towards which people—and arguably businesses—

should strive, even though they are not morally at fault for not achieving them. From a moral point of view, to ignore moral ideals is still to be less than one can and should be. Moral saints and moral heroes go beyond what is strictly demanded of them. We all know that we fall short of what we can be, from a moral point of view. Yet, important though moral ideals are, it is a mistake to treat them as moral obligations. In many instances in private life as well as in business, we can speak of actions that "it would be good" to do, which we are not obliged to do. The sphere of the morally praiseworthy is broader than the sphere of the morally obligatory. In judging others and in judging business firms, we should be careful not to fault them for not achieving moral ideals, as opposed to holding them accountable for doing what is morally required and avoiding what is morally prohibited.

The notions of virtue, character, and ideals are all important. They apply with special clarity to individuals. How, if at all, virtue, character, and ideals should be applied to corporations or economic systems are disputed issues, as is the question of whether business is to be judged only by the criterion of whether it fulfills the moral minimum or whether it should go beyond that minimum.

What is not disputed is that we can take part effectively and intelligently in these and similar discussions only if we know the standard techniques of moral reasoning that people in our society typically use, either implicitly or explicitly.

Study Questions

1. In the three decisions Mary Thompson faces, how should she go about making her decisions? What additional facts, if any, does she need? What decisions would you make in her place, and how would you defend those decisions?

2. Lawrence Kohlberg identifies three major levels in the moral development of an individual. He subdivides each level into two stages. Name and describe the three levels and the two stages within each level. Do his stages correspond with your own moral experience? If not, in what ways does your experience differ from his generalizations?

3. At which level do philosophical analysis and reflection take place? Why is that level higher than the other levels?

4. What are the three characteristics usually associated with moral judgments? Can you think of a moral judgment that does not have these three characteristics?

5. In what three senses might we take the judgment that someone is a moral person? Can we use the same three senses with respect to our evaluations of ourselves?

6. What does it mean to say that an action is subjectively right? objectively right? Might an action be subjectively right and objectively right at the

same time? Explain. Might it be objectively right and subjectively wrong at the same time? Give an original example of each type of case.

7. Define and distinguish: descriptive transcultural relativism and normative ethical relativism.

8. Differing views in different cultures about the morality of an action may be the result of a number of factors. State some of those factors and show how each might lead to differing moral judgments.

9. What follows from the view that moral judgments are neither true nor false? Are those consequences consistent with the moral experience of most people? What conclusions can you draw from this?

10. What are the consequences of holding that "moral" means "is approved by this society"? Are these consequences consistent with the moral experience of most people? What conclusion can you draw from this?

11. Do the above considerations show that normative ethical relativism, understood in the above ways, is probably false? Why or why not?

12. Define moral absolutism. Must one be either a moral absolutist or relativist? If not, what other option is there?

13. Distinguish four levels of moral pluralism and explain what each consists of.

14. How does moral or ethical pluralism in the United States differ from ethical or moral pluralism on the international or global level? How does this affect how businesses should behave abroad as opposed to how they should behave in the United States?

15. Why should one study ethical theory?

16. What is the relation of conventional morality and ethical theory?

17. What is a teleological approach to ethical reasoning? a deontological approach? Define each and distinguish them.

18. Is the Judeo-Christian approach to ethical reasoning teleological or deontological? the Kantian approach? the utilitarian approach?

19. What are the advantages of knowing ethical theory?

3

>─┤◆⟩──◯──⟨◆├─◄

UTILITY
AND
UTILITARIANISM

An Airplane Manufacturing Case

An airplane manufacturer has spent a great deal of money developing a new airplane. The company badly needs cash because it is financially overextended. If it does not get some large orders soon, it will have to close down part of its operation. Doing that will put several thousand workers out of jobs. The result will be disastrous not only for the workers but also for the town in which they live. The president of the company has been trying to interest the government of a foreign country in a large purchase. He learns that one of the key governmental ministers in charge of making the final decision is heavily in debt because of gambling. He quietly contacts that minister and offers him $1 million in cash if he awards the contract for five planes to his firm. The money is paid and the contract is awarded. The president argues that his action is justifiable because the business, the workers' jobs, and the town were all saved; the minister was able to pay his debts; and the foreign country received the planes it needed. The good produced, he argues, is greater than any harm done by the payment to the minister. Is he correct?

Utilitarianism

Businesses seek to make a profit. They engage in accounting and attempt to have their income exceed their costs. This is a rational procedure, one we all understand, for it is a procedure we all use in our own lives. For instance, a family has an income, and it sets limits on what it can spend. The members of

56

a family need a great many different kinds of goods. People also want things that they do not absolutely need. Typically, a family apportions its funds to take care of immediate needs first and then decides how to allocate the remainder, taking into account both present and long-range needs and desires. A budget helps a family plan the wise use of its money. Although it is difficult to weigh the desirability of a music lesson as opposed to a movie, and to weigh that against one's desire for new clothes or a vacation, we know that people make these comparisons and choices. We also know that occasionally people forgo earning more money in order to have more leisure time or more time to devote to members of their family. Although we can put a price tag on many things that we desire, we cannot calculate the value of all of them in terms of money.

This common practice of calculating what we want, balancing our wishes with our resources, and comparing present versus long-range desires forms the basis of the utilitarian approach to ethics. *Utilitarianism is an ethical theory that holds that an action is right if it produces, or if it tends to produce, the greatest amount of good for the greatest number of people affected by the action. Otherwise the action is wrong.*[1]

Utilitarianism does not force on us something foreign to our ordinary rational way of acting. It systematizes and makes explicit what its defenders believe most of us do in our moral thinking, as well as in much of our other thinking. It is reasonable for rational beings, who are able to foresee the consequences of their actions, to choose those actions that produce more good than those that produce less good, other things being equal. Businesses traditionally reduce *good* to money and calculate costs and benefits in monetary terms. Because the aim of a business is to make money, those actions that tend to help it make money are considered good and those that tend to make it lose money are considered bad. A rationally operated company tries to maximize its good and minimize its bad so that when income and costs are balanced out, there is a profit. The bottom line of the ledger sheet, which shows a profit or a loss, is the final accounting in which business is traditionally interested.

This cost-benefit analysis is a form of utility calculation. People in business theory use utility curves to plot the results of various actions, choosing those that maximize whatever it is that they wish to achieve. This utility

---

[1] The classical statements of utilitarianism are found in Jeremy Bentham, *An Introduction to the Principles of Morals and Legislation* (Oxford: Clarendon Press, first published in 1789); and John Stuart Mill's *Utilitarianism,* first published in three parts in 1861. A useful edition of Mill's work, Samuel Gorovitz (Ed.), together with twenty-eight critical essays and a selected bibliography, is *Utilitarianism, with Critical Essays* (Indianapolis, Ind.: Bobbs-Merrill Co., 1971). Two important later developments of the theory are Henry Sidgwick's *The Methods of Ethics* (London: Macmillan, 1874); and G. E. Moore's *Ethics* (London: Oxford University Press, 1912). Richard B. Brandt presents a contemporary defense of utilitarianism in "Toward a Credible Form of Utilitarianism," in H. N. Castaneda and G. Nakhnikian (Eds.), *Morality and the Language of Conduct* (Detroit: Wayne State University Press, 1963), pp. 107-140, as does R. M. Hare in *Moral Thinking* (Oxford: Clarendon Press, 1981).

approach is not foreign to most people. It is widely used in many forms of general decision making and can be applied to moral issues as well as to strictly business issues. A defense of utilitarianism as an ethical theory is that it describes what rational people actually do in making moral decisions. It explicitly formulates for them the procedures they intuitively and spontaneously use in moral reasoning. The theory renders explicit what is implicit in the ordinary moral reasoning and argumentation that we ourselves use; we see it displayed in newspapers, we read it in discussions of public policy and in the opinions of the Supreme Court, and we encounter it in debates with our friends on moral issues.

There is a significant difference, however, between utilitarianism and a utility analysis as used by business. When a firm uses a utility, or a cost-benefit analysis, it weighs the good and the bad consequences of performing a certain action (usually in monetary terms) as it relates to *itself*. A utilitarian analysis, as an ethical analysis, weighs the good and bad results of an action on *everyone* affected by it.

Utilitarianism adopts a teleological approach to ethics and claims that actions are to be judged by their consequences. According to this view, actions are not good or bad in themselves. Actions take on moral value only when considered in conjunction with the effects that follow upon them. Actions by themselves have no intrinsic value. They are simply means to attain that which has value. But what has value? To answer this question we must distinguish what has value as a means towards something else and what has value in and of itself. A few examples might help.

Businesses seek to make a profit. But what is the point of having money? Is there anything intrinsically valuable in the pieces of paper that we use as money? The paper in itself is not intrinsically valuable, but it can be used to buy goods that we want. It is valuable as a means to an end. The more money we have, the more goods we can buy. But are goods valuable in themselves? Food, shelter, books, and clothing are, in turn, only a means to satisfy our needs and wants. The stopping point in this progression seems to be ourselves and others. People are the centers of value, and what satisfies their needs is what they consider valuable. Basically, then, it is human satisfaction that is valuable in itself; money and goods are means to produce this satisfaction. Dissatisfaction, harm, pain, or unhappiness are examples of disvalue.

According to utilitarianism, we should evaluate an action by looking at its consequences, weighing the good effects against the bad effects on all the people affected by it. If the good outweighs the bad, it tends to be a good action; if the bad outweighs the good, it tends to be a bad action.

When we try to state what utilitarianism is and we try to use it, we encounter a number of complications. These have been discussed at length in the philosophical literature, but we need note only a few here. One question that surfaces immediately is: How can we calculate consequences that are radically different one from another? In a business calculation everything is typically reduced to dollars and cents. This makes calculation relatively easy. But how are we to evaluate actions from a moral point of view? Is there some least common denominator in terms of which we can and do calculate? A number of answers to this question have been proposed. One, which is called *hedonistic utilitarianism,* holds that the basic human values are pleasure and pain (sometimes defined simply as the absence of pleasure). According to this view, everything that people desire, want, or need can be reduced in one way or another to pleasure or pain. Hence, the calculation, though not easy, is possible because we are dealing with units of the same kind.

The advantage of this approach has been challenged by those who claim that not all intrinsically valuable goods can be reduced to uniform pleasure and pain. What is intrinsically valuable, they maintain, is not simply pleasures—which may differ in quality as well as quantity—but happiness. This second view is called *eudaimonistic utilitarianism,* since the basic value in terms of which the calculation is made is happiness, not pleasure.

A third approach is called *ideal utilitarianism.* This position maintains that what has to be calculated is not pleasure or happiness but all intrinsically valuable human goods, which include friendship, knowledge, and a host of other goods valuable in themselves.

The differences among these utilitarians are subtle; there are interesting and strong arguments on all sides. We need not settle the dispute here because the debate does not actually call into doubt whether such things as knowledge, beauty, or friendship are valuable; rather, it questions whether they are valuable for their own sake or for their role in producing pleasure or happiness. Most calculations will come out the same, whether we use the ideal utilitarian approach, which allows a plurality of intrinsic values; or the hedonistic approach, which reduces all values ultimately to pleasure; or the eudaimonistic utilitarian approach, which reduces them to happiness. The hedonistic calculation may seem to be more straightforward than the others because we deal with the same units—that is, pleasure and pain. But the problem of trying to reduce the multiplicity of goods and values to pleasure and pain is not an easy one. How do we decide the amount of pleasure we receive from drinking our favorite beverage when thirsty, compared with the amount of pleasure we receive from learning a new theorem in geometry, or reading an exciting novel, or giving a gift to a friend? Whether we face the problem of comparison as we weigh the various goods and values, or whether we face it in attempting to reduce each to a common denominator of pleasure, face it we must. Thus, the dispute about the differing approaches to the interpretation of good in the utilitarian formula, though interesting, is not as crucial in deciding actual cases as it may seem.

Several assumptions of utilitarianism should be made explicit. In carrying out the calculation of good and bad consequences of an action, the utilitarian rule tells us to consider all the persons affected by the action. The assumption is that our good counts for no more than anyone else's good, and no one else's good counts for more than ours. The approach is neither egoistic nor altruistic—it is universalistic. The defense of this approach is that it captures the essence of what we actually do when we make moral judgments. Moral judgments are judgments that we make concerning actions, and we believe that the actions are right, not only for ourselves but also for anyone else similarly situated. From the moral point of view, which is impartial, my good counts no more than anyone else's, nor does anyone else's good count more than mine. All persons are equal, and each person's good is as important and worthwhile as each other person's good. Thus, our moral calculation is a calculation made from an impersonal point of view. It should come out the same whether made by me or by you, or by any other rational person adopting an objective point of view. What is weighed is the good or bad resulting to each person affected by an action. This is an objective state of affairs. Although pleasure, happiness, or other goods may be subjectively experienced, the experiences are considered and weighed objectively, with each given its due.

Jeremy Bentham (1748-1832), who was a hedonistic utilitarian, argued that in attempting to evaluate the pleasure or pain produced by an action there are various aspects of the pleasure and pain that we should consider.[2] We can generalize his analysis to any value or good we are taking into account. We should consider the intensity, duration, certainty or uncertainty, propinquity or remoteness, fecundity, and purity of the value in question for each person affected. A more intense pleasure, for instance, might have to be weighed against a less intense but longer lasting pain. In making our calculation, we give greater weight to the pleasure or other value we are more certain of attaining, and less weight to less certain values. Similarly, we weigh differently those goods we will get immediately and those we will acquire at a more distant time. Frequently, we are willing to undergo immediate discomfort and unpleasantness because we know these are necessary in order to achieve something worthwhile in the future, which makes the present unpleasantness worth suffering through. *Fecundity* refers to whether the action will produce more of the same kind of value we achieve in the first instance. The pleasure we get from learning a new skill, for instance, may be followed by other instances of pleasure as we utilize that skill. If a value is followed by its opposite, then it is *impure*. For instance, the pleasure of the final glass of beer that makes one intoxicated is frequently followed by the pain of being sick or having a hangover.

In each case we consider the good and the bad produced by an action in the first instance, and also in later instances, for those most directly affected by the action. We sum this up and then we consider all the others who will be affected less directly by the action. The number of others may be very large, but the intensity of the effect quite small. The good and the bad done to all these people must be totaled.

Many of our actions affect society as a whole. When I break a contract, I affect not only myself and the person with whom I made the contract; I also

---

[2] Bentham, *An Introduction to the Principles of Morals and Legislation.*

affect a great many other people—for instance, all those who hear about it. Many will be more cautious in making contracts, not only with me but also with others. Some will worry more than they otherwise would have. Still others may refuse to make contracts for fear of their partner's breaking the contract, as I did. All these are real consequences and must be included in the calculation. After considering all the persons affected, we sum up the good and the bad. We then add this, together with the calculation we made concerning the effects on those more directly affected by the action. The final result of our calculation determines the morality of the action. If the action produces more good than bad, then it tends to be a morally right action.

But our calculation is not yet over, for the utilitarian principle tells us that in order for the action to be right, it must produce the greatest good for the greatest number of those affected by it. To know whether the action produces the greatest good, we need to compare it with alternative actions. In some cases the comparison will be simply with the opposite action. If we are considering the morality of breaking a contract, we should calculate the effects of breaking it; but we should also ask what the alternative action is. In this case it is not breaking the contract. Hence, we should sum up the results of that alternative in a way comparable to the way we did the first sum. When we compare the two, the morally right action is that which produces the greater net amount of good.

We can add several dimensions to the calculation. For purposes of determining whether a certain kind of action is moral or immoral, we need only calculate the action and its opposite. If the action in general produces more good than harm, whereas its opposite produces more harm than good, then the action is generally a moral action. If more than one action and its opposite are available to us, we can calculate the results of all the alternatives. A stringent application of utilitarianism would lead to the conclusion that, among all the alternatives, the action that produces the greatest amount of good is the moral action in the situation in question.

A less stringent interpretation of utilitarianism would simply require that I choose one of the actions that tends to produce more good than harm but would not require that I always choose only the best action among good actions. In any interpretation of utilitarianism, if two actions produce equal net amounts of good, then, from a moral point of view, they are equally moral, and we may do either. If we have only two alternatives, and both of them produce more bad than good, then we are morally obliged to do the one that produces the least bad. We thereby choose the lesser of two evils.

Act and Rule Utilitarianism

Two versions of utilitarianism are compatible with the utilitarian principle just stated. They are known as act utilitarianism and rule utilitarianism. *Act utilitarianism* holds that each individual action, in all its concreteness and in all its detail, is what should be subjected to the utilitarian test. When faced with the temptation to break a contract, we are always concerned with a particular contract in a particular set of circumstances. To determine the morality of the action we should calculate the effects of breaking this particular contract. The effects will be, in part, similar to those of breaking any contract, but they will be somewhat different. If we believe that what is true of breaking contracts in general will not be true in this case, we should investigate the effects.

When faced with the temptation to break a contract, we may know that the bad consequences will outweigh the good ones. This is based on our knowledge of what the results of breaking contracts are, and also on our knowledge that this case has no special qualities such that the consequences might be different from other cases. The act utilitarian knows that the vast majority of past cases of breaking contracts have resulted in more bad than good. Hence, we arrive at a rule of thumb about the morality of breaking contracts. The rule of thumb, however, is a generalization about past instances, and some particular future instance may prove an exception to the rule. In that particular case, the act utilitarian claims, breaking the contract is morally permissible.

Those who defend rule utilitarianism object to the act utilitarian approach. *Rule utilitarians* hold that utility applies appropriately to classes of actions rather than to given individual actions. Thus, by looking at the general consequences of breaking contracts in the past, we can determine that breaking contracts is immoral. It is immoral because the bad consequences outweigh the good consequences. We therefore arrive at a rule stating that it is morally wrong to violate contracts. By a similar analysis a rule utilitarian determines that people should not lie, steal, or murder. Each of these injunctions is the result of having observed the consequences of those acts as performed in the past, together with an assumption that the consequences in the future will be similar.

Why favor the rule utilitarian rather than the act utilitarian approach? The answer is that we cannot know all the consequences of a particular act, nor can we know in advance, and with certainty, many of the specific consequences of such an act. Always present in act utilitarianism is the temptation to think that the instance we are considering will be the exception to the rule. If we are the primary beneficiaries of breaking a particular contract, we may tend to discount the harm done to others; we diminish its seriousness and guess that the consequences will not be as serious for them as they usually are for those affected by broken contracts. And if finding out is what will cause others to be reluctant to make contracts, we will be inclined to assume that no one will find out. We will be tempted to project what we would like to have happen because we cannot know what will happen. The rule utilitarian maintains, therefore, that more harm is done by breaking a moral rule than any good that can supposedly be achieved by doing so. The rule utilitarian approach does not require guesswork as to what will happen. The history of humankind provides the sourcebook. If we wish to see the results of murder, lying, stealing, or breaking contracts, we can easily recall the consequences in many past cases. We know that most criminals think they will get away with their crime. We also know that many, if not most, do not; and we know that even some of those who are not caught suffer pangs of conscience. We need not be prophets to foresee that the consequences of certain kinds of actions are on the whole bad rather than good. We can learn from human experience why people have come to hold the general moral rules they do.

Rule utilitarianism provides a technique for determining the moral value of actions—both those on which society has already made a moral determination and those on which it has not. It encourages us to determine whether conditions have changed to such an extent that what was once immoral because it produced more bad than good is now moral because, in changed circumstances, the action produces more good than bad. It also enables us to see whether we have been mistaken in our past calculation concerning certain practices. If we miscalculated as a society, we can now recalculate and correct our past error. By making explicit the utilitarian principle that we implicitly used before, we have the means to check our prior moral judgments, challenge those that are mistaken, and evaluate actions, the moral values of which change because of new circumstances.

In our own society there are a number of disputed moral questions. In part, the disputes hinge on consequences, which are foreseen as likely by one group and denied as likely by another. To some extent business faces questions that are truly new, and we have no easy way to determine the real consequences of these questions. We have seen that both act and rule utilitarianism are used to decide the morality of actions. They may also be used to decide the morality of laws, social practices, social structures, political systems, and economic systems. For instance, does the adoption of free enterprise produce more good than bad? Compared with socialism, does it produce more total good than bad? The answer is not easy to determine because the consequences are so complex; there is no way of knowing what the consequences of adopting a new economic system really will be. The adoption of an economic system is not like the performance of particular acts that are very similar to one another, acts for which we have an abundance of information as to the consequences.

When dealing with legislation, utilitarian arguments are frequently used. A moral political system is one that produces an abundance of good over bad for the members of the society. A policy is morally justified if it produces more good than bad, and it is optimally justified if it produces more good than any other alternative would. But because we cannot know that we have considered all the alternatives, and because we cannot know what all the consequences of any alternative will be, we cannot have certainty on the morality of policies. Sometimes we can foresee that they will produce more harm than good, and we can attack them on moral grounds. In some instances we think they will produce more good, and only after they are implemented do we find that we are mistaken. In still other instances, we may choose what appears to be the better alternative, only to find out that it may not be better, but we may decide that sticking with it will produce more good than trying to start all over. These are all part of our ordinary experience, and utilitarians are not surprised that they are. For, they claim, utilitarianism is simply the result of making explicit the ways in which we ordinarily think and argue about policies, laws, and actions.

Because some immoral actions seem at times to produce more good than bad, utilitarians promote penal legislation. A thief who sometimes gets away with his action may come to believe that theft produces more good consequences than bad. If, however, theft is made illegal, and if the penalty is serious, then the fear that accompanies stealing is increased; therefore, the pain from stealing is made greater than the pleasure. One purpose of legislation, according to this view, is to attach legal sanctions to crimes so that any calculation of the consequences of committing a crime will obviously not be to the advantage of the perpetrator. Society protects itself by passing laws against those acts that tend to harm society and the people in it. By imposing sanctions, society reinforces the bad effects of those actions for the one who commits them.

The application of this approach to business activities is no different from its application to actions in general. If we adopt the utilitarian perspective, we can evaluate certain business practices on the basis of their consequences. If they tend to produce more bad than good, they are immoral. If the harm done to society by these practices is sufficiently serious, then legislation might be passed, subjecting the action to legal as well as moral sanctions. To be effective, the sanctions must outweigh the good that the perpetrator of the action hopes to gain. For example, the usual punishment imposed on a corporation for breaking a law is a fine. If the fine is to serve as a deterrent, the amount of the fine should be greater than the amount the company would gain by performing the action. Law is used to protect the members of society when moral means do not suffice. The justification for such law is often utilitarian, just as the evaluation of the action is. Law can provide an incentive to act morally for those who would not otherwise do so.

Utilitarians also consider moral and other nonlegal *sanctions* in their calculations. If an action does more harm than good to society, the members of society can impose various sanctions on the wrongdoer, short of legal measures. Consumers can boycott a firm, refusing to purchase its goods, in order to pressure the firm to stop some unethical practice. If a merchant overcharges, people can stop patronizing him and spread the word to others to do the same. They can stop speaking to him, exclude him from various social activities, chastise him, vent their moral indignation on him, and so on. These sanctions should be expected by those who perform certain actions. The reason for imposing them is to prevent people from performing the actions to which the sanctions are attached.

Some people claim that act utilitarianism, properly applied, is reducible to rule utilitarianism. The argument hinges on the broad consequences of adopting the act utilitarian approach. If an action that violates a rule can be justified by act utilitarianism, it tends to do damage to the good of having the rule. Without rules, many people will no longer know how a moral individual will act or should act. From an act utilitarian point of view, this is a negative consequence, one that should always be taken into account in any calculation. And this consequence will tend to outweigh the marginally good consequences of supposedly justifiable violations of a rule. The argument goes like this: In the vast majority of cases, if not demonstrably in all cases, the person who adopts the act utilitarian approach will end up justifying the same thing as the person who adopts the rule utilitarian approach. If we use the act utilitarian approach, we must be scrupulously certain that we are not giving ourselves any undue advantage; that the results we calculate are not simply wishful thinking; and that we consider all the results of the action, including the effect that it will have on society. To be morally justifiable, moreover, the results must be such that the action is right not only for me but also for anyone in similar circumstances. If the results are such, then we already have the basis for generalizing an exception to the rule or for changing the rule to include the exception, which results in a slightly different rule. Hence, the result is equivalent to adopting a rule utilitarian approach.

Objections to Utilitarianism

One of the classic statements of utilitarianism was given by John Stuart Mill (1806-1873) in his work *Utilitarianism* in which he answers a number of arguments against utilitarianism. One objection claims that utilitarianism is ungodly because it proposes utility, rather than the Bible or God, as a basis for moral judgments. Mill's reply was, in some ways, a charming one. He indicated that because God was benevolent and loved His creatures, He would wish them to be happy. Hence, what He commands are those actions that tend to produce the greatest amount of good or happiness for the greatest number. What He forbids are those actions that tend to produce more harm than good or happiness. Thus, Mill argued, the actions commanded and forbidden by utilitarianism are the same as the actions commanded and forbidden by God. The advantage of adopting utilitarianism is that we have a technique for deciding moral questions on which we have no direct information from God. Even the Ten Commandments require interpretation. Utilitarianism gives us the tool necessary for deciding those acts of killing (e.g., self-defense) that are compatible with the commandment "Thou shall not kill," and those that are not.

A second objection frequently brought against utilitarianism is that no one has the time to calculate all the consequences of an action beforehand. This is frequently true. But utilitarianism does not require that we actually calculate all the consequences before we act, any more than the religious person must reread the Bible before he acts. As we saw with rule utilitarianism, we have the history of humankind on which to build. We know that murder is wrong, and we need not calculate the results of murder every time we get angry at someone. We know that the bad results of murder outweigh the good. This is obvious and is a part of our general knowledge. But if we are ever questioned as to why murder is wrong, or if we ever seriously want to consider whether murder is wrong, we have in utilitarianism the means for arriving at a decision about the morality of murder, together with knowledge of why it is wrong. This also holds regarding other actions. If ever we are uncertain about the morality of an action, we know how to think about resolving the issue. We are not always in a moral quandary. But when we are faced with very difficult moral choices, we should stop and consider the consequences, weigh them, and arrive at the best possible conclusion. Moreover, the calculation is usually a fairly simple one. For instance, when lying *seems* advantageous, we focus on the advantage to ourselves and play down the harm done in the long run either to ourselves or to others. We can resist the temptation to lie by quickly producing a more accurate calculation of the consequences, which means using a rule utilitarian approach, in which the disadvantages are more clearly set out.

A third objection to utilitarianism is that we cannot know the full results of any action, nor can we accurately weigh the different kinds of good and evil that result. The calculation is artificial and not practical.

The reply to the first part of the objection is twofold. First, as we have already seen, in judging most actions we have the benefit of knowing the consequences of similar actions done in the past. Second, we can frequently foresee a large number of possible, if not actual, consequences; among these are some consequences so important that they dominate the calculation. This observation also applies to the second part of the objection. For instance, the utilitarian approach does not require mathematically precise calculations; it is not possible to get mathematical precision in most calculations dealing with the morality of actions. In the more standard cases the consequences are sufficiently obvious; the good or the bad predominates so clearly that great precision is not necessary. In difficult cases, where the calculation is not clear, we cannot be sure we are correct in our moral assessment, and we should be ready to revise it if we find our calculation is mistaken. This is not a defect of the theory but a statement of the human condition and the nature of morality. To those who claim that we cannot compare different values and weigh them, we can simply reply that all of us make such calculations every day; we weigh present against future good and one value against another, all the time. The claim that it cannot be done is false and is contrary to our ordinary experience.

A fourth objection concerns the interpretation to be given to the utilitarian principle itself. The principle claims that an action is right if it tends to produce the greatest good for the greatest number of persons affected by it. But, the objection goes, the formulation is ambiguous. Are we to put our emphasis on the greatest aggregate of good, or are we to concern ourselves with the good of the greatest number? Suppose, for instance, we had to choose between two cases. Action *A* results in 1,000 units of good for 100 people and 10 units of good for 9,900 people. Action *B* results in 19.9 units of good for each of the 10,000 people. In both cases we have a total of 199,000 units of good. If the resulting good at issue is the standard of living of a community, utilitarianism would have us conclude that there is no moral difference between the two cases. A society in which a few live at a very prosperous level and the many live at a very much lower level is no better than another society in which all the people live at a level almost twice as high as the latter group in the first community. To the critics, such a result seems clearly mistaken. To make the case even stronger, we can add one unit of good to the privileged group in the first society; because that society now has more good than its alternative, action *A* is morally better than action *B*. This, the objection continues, runs counter to our moral intuitions. Nor can we remedy the situation by putting the emphasis on the number of people rather than on the greatest good, because the problem will still remain.

The utilitarian counter to the objection takes two forms, usually offered jointly. The first is that the objection, though theoretically possible, is in real life implausible. The case is fabricated, the product of a philosopher's imagination; the case cannot be filled out in any concrete, historical detail. If one ever had such a choice, we should choose what produces good for more people rather than maximizing the greater good of a small number, because this choice maximizes good in the long run. This fact has to be added to the calculation. The foregoing case trades on an obvious discrepancy between the few and the many, and this discrepancy has negative consequences that the calculation does not take into account. The case seems to work because it is manipulated in such a way that the bad consequences, which result from the great discrepancy between the two groups, are not fully considered. If our moral intuitions tell us the calculation is mistaken, this is an indication that we have miscalculated and that we are ignoring some negative component in the case. Once this has been said, the utilitarian is then content to claim that there may well be cases in which equal good is produced by two different actions, and that in such a case one may choose either alternative. This was made clear earlier, in the explanation of utilitarianism. Hence, this observation is not a criticism of the position; it is a result that the utilitarian accepts.

Utilitarianism and Justice

Even if the utilitarian's answers to the previous objections are accepted, some critics claim that the theory cannot account for justice and, in some instances, runs counter to it. The claim is not a new one because it was raised and answered by Mill in *Utilitarianism*. Nonetheless, the criticism has persisted and remains a live issue today. The typical argument is as follows: Suppose we consider a small town in the western United States during the nineteenth century. Law and order are newly established. Jim James is caught with a stolen horse and accused of being a horse thief. He claims he bought it from a passing stranger. The penalty for stealing horses is hanging. The judge in the town, unbeknownst to anyone, happened to have been passing by and actually witnessed the purchase. He was hidden by trees and was therefore not seen by

Jim. The judge, it turns out, was in the vicinity only because he was buying some illegal whiskey. The town is outraged by the horse theft and wants an example made of Jim. If the judge comes forward as a witness, he will have to say what he was doing out in the woods; he will then be dismissed by the town, another judge will not be available for some time, and the town will suffer. In addition, the people of the town are so convinced that Jim is guilty that they will probably hang him anyway. Innocent people may well be killed in trying to prevent this outcome. Taking all this into account, the judge decides it is better for him not to come forward with his information. He should condemn Jim and have him hanged. Jim will be killed no matter what. And more harm than good will come to the town if the judge tries to defend Jim.

The utilitarian calculation, its critics maintain, would result in saying that the right thing to do is to condemn an innocent man. But condemning an innocent man is obviously unjust. Hence, it might be said that utilitarianism results in saying that to do what is obviously unjust is the morally right thing to do. The conclusion is that utilitarianism cannot be an accurate account of morality, nor can it be an appropriate way to make moral judgments.

In its generalized form the argument maintains that justice does not depend on consequences. Justice consists in giving each person his or her due or treating people equitably. Such considerations do not depend on consequences. It is unjust to condemn an innocent person regardless of whether doing so produces better consequences than not doing so. Because consequences are irrelevant, justice is not based on utility, and utilitarianism is therefore inadequate as a foundation of justice.

The objection has not convinced all utilitarians. The standard reply is that in the foregoing example, or in any other situation like it, the objection is plausible only because not all the results are considered. The case does not end with the hanging. We must consider the consciences of the judge and of the people of the town. What will the reaction be when the truth is discovered? What happens to the notion of justice if the judge continues to try to guess the consequences in each case that comes before him? When we consider all these effects, then we see that, in the long run, more harm than good is done by condemning an innocent man than by not condemning him. We must consider the results of this practice, not those of some isolated, hypothetical action whose results are arbitrarily cut off at a convenient point for the objector.

Many critics have not been satisfied by the reply, nor have they been convinced by attempts to give a utilitarian account of justice. As a result, some people have advocated using two conjoint principles in moral evaluation: the principle of utility and the principle of justice. In most cases the principle of utility will take precedence, but in those cases in which the principle seems to go against justice, then the principle of justice takes precedence. The justification for this approach is itself utilitarian—namely, that it produces the best results or the greatest amount of good on the whole.

Despite the debate between the utilitarians and their opponents on the issue of justice, *in most cases* both sides will agree on which actions are just. If a case involves condemning an innocent man, most utilitarians will admit that such an action is morally wrong and will show how such an action is not in fact required by utilitarianism. For practical purposes, this observation is important. It indicates that whether or not utilitarianism can be so formulated as to give an adequate theoretical account of justice, both sides can frequently agree on which actions are just. Because, from the practical point of view, we are interested in rendering moral decisions about cases, we can do so without having to resolve fully the theoretical issue. It is only when the two approaches—the utilitarian and the deontological—actually result in divergent moral judgments that we will have to choose between them. But if such cases exist, they can be treated separately, as special cases. In most instances, the utilitarian and the deontological approaches to justice, as well as to the moral evaluation of actions and practices, will result in similar moral judgments. This conclusion should not be surprising because both utilitarianism and deontological theories are attempts to systematize and provide the reasoned ground for our moral judgments. Both have as their starting points the large number of actions that we agree are morally right and those that we agree are morally wrong.

Applying Utilitarianism

Having seen the arguments in favor of utilitarianism and the answers to some objections, we can now draw the various threads of the descriptions of the technique together and review the method of carrying out a utilitarian analysis.

The first step is to specify, clearly, the action that we wish to consider. Identifying the action is not always easy. We should avoid the temptation to characterize the action too quickly as being one that has the connotations of either morality or immorality. If an analysis is required it is because the morality of the action is unknown, or questioned, or challenged. In a complex situation, clarifying which action is to be analyzed is an essential first step. The action, once determined, is best described in morally neutral language. For example, the phrase "killing human beings" is a neutral description, compared with "murdering human beings." The latter phrase characterizes the killing as unjustifiable. And the addition of the term *self-defense* to either phrase characterizes the act as being justifiable.

How specific do we have to be in characterizing the action? Act utilitarianism, as we explained, demands that we guess all the consequences of a particular act—something we cannot possibly do with any degree of accuracy. Rule utilitarianism asks us to consider the general consequences of the kind of act in question, and this is usually possible because of the accumulated store of social information concerning kinds of actions. The action should be described not as unique, but as capable of being subsumed under a general rule.

Now to the second step. Having once clarified the act we wish to evaluate, we must carefully specify all those affected by the action. There is often a strong temptation to ignore some of those affected and to ignore, as well, the general effects of the action on society. Someone who is tempted to falsify a record, for instance, might consider only his or her personal gain versus the harm done to other persons immediately affected by the falsification. Those immediately affected must certainly be considered, but rarely are the agent and victim the only ones affected. This might be the case on a desert island inhabited by only two people who would never leave it. But morality, as a social practice, is not properly tested in this way. Acts are usually performed in social contexts, and it is these acts with which we are most concerned in business ethics. Even those who are remotely affected, including business and society as a whole, should be specified, and they must all be considered in the evaluation of an action.

The third step is to formulate carefully and objectively the good and bad consequences for all those persons who would be affected. The calculation need not proceed immediately to a detailed examination of the good and bad for each individual. At this point, we should look for the salient features. Is there a dominant consideration? Are certain consequences so serious that we do not need to carry out a detailed analysis of all the consequences? Suppose, for example that someone is causing us difficulty in business and we wish that person were out of the way, so we consider killing that person. We should not need to weigh all the consequences of killing him. We know that the practice of eliminating annoying people by killing them does an overwhelming amount of harm, not only to those killed but to society as well. A brief moment's reflection tells us the action is wrong—and the harm done is a dominant consideration. To entertain the possibility of some instance being an exception to this consideration would require very extraordinary circumstances. Unless we had such extraordinary circumstances—as in the case of self-defense—we need not calculate further. However, if we wished to prove to someone that killing a competitor is immoral, we could carry out the calculation. It is very clear that we do not have to review similar cases each time. Were we to pursue the morality of the action further, we need to consider only briefly whether the good done us or our company can possibly justify the harm done to the individual killed and to society—remembering that if it is right for us, it will be right for all others to kill their competitors (including us!). The answer is clearly that the action is immoral.

In more complicated cases, however, we shall have to consider all the good and bad consequences of the action under consideration, starting with the consequences for those principally affected. But even in these cases we should look for both the dominant aspects of the case and the outstanding consequences. These will help to guide us in our analysis.

There is sometimes disagreement about the consequences of some actions. There are also possible disagreements about the dominant considerations in a case and whether they are in fact overridden by other consequences. The application of utilitarianism is not an automatic procedure. It requires thought, analysis, and serious, impartial consideration of facts and consequences. When utilitarians argue among themselves about unclear cases, the arguments sometimes hinge on the description of the action, the facts, and the consequences; sometimes on the choice of the dominant consideration; and sometimes on the relative weight given to some important conflicting factors.

We have already seen that we cannot expect mathematical precision. Talk of relative weights, and of summing up good and bad and comparing them, is appropriate only on a gross level. We can make approximations, and we should make these as explicit as we can. We know how to weigh the pain of going to a dentist against the pain of a toothache, and how to weigh the future pain of not going, and the future pleasure of a fixed tooth. That is a simple model of what the calculation is like. If we are making the analysis for ourselves, we must try to be objective; but we probably do not have to convince ourselves of the objectivity of our analysis. If we are using the method to convince others of the morality or immorality of an action, we should state, as clearly as possible, not only our evaluations but also why we make them as we do.

Once we have determined all the good and all the bad results for those primarily affected by the action, we compare the results. If the bad is overwhelming, further calculation may not be necessary. But even if the good is overwhelming, we should consider the results of the rule's being generally followed. This may be the dominant consideration. Whether or not it is, the good and the bad of adopting the rule is added to the good or bad results for those primarily affected; this is then summed. If the calculation produces overwhelming good or bad, further calculation may not be necessary. If the calculation is close, then we should consider, in as much detail as is reasonable, those indirectly affected by the action. The analysis gets wider and wider and more and more detailed, depending on how close the good and bad are, how far-reaching the action is, and what other considerations seem appropriate. Reasonableness is the guide as to when to end the calculation.

Once we have summed all the good and bad, having considered the consequences for all those affected by an action, we know whether that kind of action is morally good or bad. If it produces more harm than good, it is in general immoral. If it produces more good than harm, it is in general moral. But one more step is required.

We must now ask about the action as it takes place in the given context. What are the other choices, given this context? Is the choice simply to do the action or not to do it? Is it to kill my competitor or not to kill him? If that is the only question, then, in normal circumstances, we know what to do. Killing is wrong because it produces more harm than good. Not killing is morally right because it produces more good than harm. Hence, we should not kill our competitor.

Frequently, however, our choices are more complex, and we are faced not only with giving in or not giving in to an immoral temptation but also with a number of alternative actions. If the choice is not simply doing x or not doing x, then we can and should evaluate the various alternatives in the same way that we did the original action. The action that produces the most good is the best one. Morally, we are not allowed to choose an act that produces more bad than good, if we have the alternative of choosing one that produces more good than bad. As we saw earlier, if faced with a choice between two actions, x and y, both of which produce more bad than good, we should choose the lesser of two evils. But often, if we use our moral imagination, we may find that there is another alternative, z, and this z produces more good, or less bad, than the alternatives we originally considered. Utilitarianism encourages us to look for these other, better alternatives, because it encourages us to choose the best action available. The temptation to limit one's choices, to consider too few alternatives, or to entertain false dilemmas frequently obscures the fact that, correctly applied, the utilitarian technique does not preclude moral imagination; it demands it.

The steps of the method can be summed up as in Figure 3-1.

Figure 3-1

STEPS OF A UTILITARIAN ANALYSIS

1. Accurately state the action to be evaluated.

2. Identify all those who are directly and indirectly affected by the action.

3. Consider whether there is some dominant, obvious consideration that carries such importance as to outweigh other considerations.

4. Specify all the pertinent good and bad consequences of the action for those directly affected, as far into the future as appears appropriate, and imaginatively consider various possible outcomes and the likelihood of their occurring.

5. Weigh the total good results against the total bad results, considering quantity, duration, propinquity or remoteness, fecundity, and purity for each value (kind of good and kind of bad), and the relative importance of these values.

6. Carry out a similar analysis, if necessary, for those indirectly affected, as well as for society as a whole.

7. Sum up all the good and bad consequences. If the action produces more good than bad, the action is morally right; if it produces more bad than good, it is morally wrong.

8. Consider, imaginatively, whether there are various alternatives other than simply doing or not doing the action, and carry out a similar analysis for each of the other alternative actions.

9. Compare the results of the various actions. The action that produces the most good (or the least bad, if none produces more good than bad) among those available is the morally proper action to perform.

Utilitarianism and Bribery

Most people in the United States readily acknowledge that bribery is immoral. Yet bribery in business is an interesting kind of action to examine from a utilitarian point of view, because those who engage in bribery frequently justify their actions based on something similar to utilitarian grounds.

Consider the case of the airplane manufacturer with which we began this chapter. When justifying his action, the president of the firm pointed out all the benefits that resulted from the bribe: An important government official was much better off financially than he would be otherwise, the government purchased planes that were of good design and workmanship, the airplane company got the contract and stayed in business, and the workers at the plant did not lose their jobs. The town in which they live also benefited. The president therefore concluded that the results were, on the whole, positive. The only negative aspect was that an action that some people would not approve of took place. He claimed that overall his actions produced more good than harm.

The argument appears to be a utilitarian one in that it seeks to evaluate the results of the action, weighs the good against the bad, and argues that the good outweighs the bad. The alternative would have been not to give the bribe. But if it had not been given, then the contract might not have been awarded. If it had not been awarded, then all of the bad consequences indicated would have taken place. No good would have been achieved, and the result would clearly have been worse.

The argument may sound plausible. Nevertheless, we believe that bribery is immoral. Is it that utilitarianism does not work in this case? The reply is that it works, but it has not been properly used here. The foregoing account is obviously a one-sided version of the situation. It describes the thinking of the president of the company, his point of view, and his concerns, which, here, are not the same as the moral point of view. The moral point of view is objective and considers all the consequences of an action for all the people affected by it. We must therefore take into consideration much more than what we have so far. We must broaden the picture, look more closely at the effects on the people already mentioned, and then open our vision to those whom we have so far ignored.

Our first step is to state precisely what we wish to evaluate. The president used a truncated *act utilitarian* approach. Try to state the rule that he is implicitly advocating. Is it that all firms should be allowed to bribe government officials when they have the opportunity to do so? The president puts great emphasis on the negative consequences of not getting the contract; therefore, perhaps the rule is that only firms in financial difficulty should be allowed to bribe government officials. If the company is in financial difficulty as the result of poor management, perhaps the rule is that only poorly managed companies should be permitted to bribe government officials. None of these rules sounds plausible. The dominant consideration in evaluating all of them is the harm done to the *system* of doing business, to the notion of fair competition, to the equality of opportunity assumed in business, to the other competing firms and their employees, and to the integrity of government officials. If the action is clearly described as a rule for all firms similarly placed, we immediately see that we do not need a detailed analysis.

Even if we accept the president's approach, however, a full examination of the consequences of his action will show the action to be morally unjustifiable. First, what are the consequences of the bribe for the public official? The only consequence we have considered so far is that he gets the money he needs and gives a contract to the company in question. What are the chances that the bribe will be discovered, and what will the consequences be if it is discovered? Bribery is illegal. If the public official's action is discovered, he would in all likelihood be charged with a felony, lose his job, and, if convicted, be heavily fined and/or go to jail. Will his life be better? If he is not found out, he may be blackmailed. He may also be tempted to live beyond his means and end up in a similar situation again. He will have to explain where he got the money to his wife, and perhaps to others. He will not report it on his income tax and will thus be liable for not reporting income. We can continue to consider what might happen to him and try to evaluate how likely these things are to occur, how seriously they will affect him, and so on.

The good done to the workers, plant, and town have to be given their due weight. But the story does not mention competing firms. What is their situation? Will their workers be out of jobs? Will their towns be depressed? Consider the president of the company. How will he manage to pay $1 million? Where will it come from? How will he pay it without its being recorded and reported to the Internal Revenue Service and to the company auditors? For this project to succeed, it is clear that the president will have to break more laws than the law against bribery. All of his actions will have their effects. If his actions are found out, he will be held liable, may lose his job, and may be imprisoned.

Consider next the effects on the general public. The government official is spending their money. If he is not buying the best equipment at the best price he can get, then he is misusing public funds and hence harming the taxpayers. If the airplanes he contracted for were the ones he would have purchased anyway, then what was the point of the bribe? But even if he would have placed the order with that firm without a bribe, the $1 million he received had to come from somewhere. Either it was added to the cost of the planes he purchased and thereby came from the taxpayers, or it came from the company's profits and thereby came from the shareholders. In either case the money was taken from those who had legitimate claim to it, and they will be negatively affected to that extent.

The bribe also had an effect on the general system of bidding, on the practice of competition, and on the integrity of those engaged in these practices. Once bribery is an accepted way of doing business, people will no longer get the best value for their money. Does the good done to the person who receives the bribe and to the person who gives it outweigh the possible harm done to them if they are caught? What about the certain harm done to those who must pay more, or who receive less profit, and to the system as a whole?

If we doubt whether the practice of bribery does more harm than good, we need only consider why it is not carried on openly. Why is the giving of a bribe not considered a legitimate part of doing business? The obvious reason is that a few people benefit from the practice but at the expense of a great many other people, including society and business in general.

The argument is a utilitarian one. We did not attempt any exact quantitative evaluation of good and bad results. But in our reasoning we did consider consequences for all those involved, and we avoided arbitrarily cutting off the consequences to be considered.

The president's account did not consider all those affected by the action. He ended his investigation of the consequences at the point most suitable to him. Obviously, the use of the utilitarian calculation does not provide an automatic guarantee of morality. To produce a morally justifiable result, it must be used by someone who truly wishes to find out what is right and who impartially takes into account the immediate and future consequences for all concerned.

Someone might object that we omitted some important considerations in our analysis. If we have overlooked something important, then we should take that into account and see whether considering what we omitted changes the final outcome. In questions of public policy and public morality, the debate among utilitarians frequently takes place in just this way. Opposing sides may point to omitted considerations, such as the further consequences of an act, or they may argue that insufficient weight is given to one of the consequences discussed, or that a supposedly unlikely outcome can very likely occur.

The mid-1970s witnessed major international scandals concerning bribes, kickbacks, and illegal campaign contributions, both in the United States and abroad. Lockheed Corporation, among others, was involved in giving $12.5 million in bribes and commissions in connection with the sale of $430 million worth of TriStar planes to All Nippon Airways. Carl Kotchian, who later defended his payments in an article in the *Saturday Review*,[3] was forced to resign from his position after the news of the payoffs broke. Defenders of the payments claimed that the practice was not only common in Japan but was also expected. Nonetheless, the news rocked Japan even more than it did the United States. The prime minister of Japan, Kakuei Tanaka, and four others were forced to resign from the government and were brought to trial. Legislation attempting to control bribery was proposed both in the United States and Japan, and some of it passed. The results of the bribery were far-reaching.

---

[3] Carl A. Kotchian, "The Payoff: Lockheed's 70-Day Mission to Tokyo," *Saturday Review,* July 9, 1977, pp. 7-12. For more material on this case, see Neil H. Jacoby, Peter Nehemkis, and Richard Eells, *Bribery and Extortion in World Business* (London: Collier Macmillan Publishers Ltd., 1977); and Robert Shaplen, "Annals of Crime: The Lockheed Incident," *The New Yorker,* 53 (January 23, 1978), pp. 48-50; (January 30, 1978), pp. 74-91.

But the Lockheed case was not a simple one. Lockheed did not offer a bribe; rather, the Japanese negotiator demanded it. Are those who accede to bribery as guilty as those who demand bribes? Do the same moral obligations exist in dealing with a corrupt government as in dealing with an honest one? If the people of a country tolerate bribery among their officials, do they in effect consent to the system? If the paying of such commissions is the *sine qua non* of doing business with the government, is it morally justifiable? These are complex questions, the answers to which are not deducible from the general claim that bribery is immoral. Some attempts have been made to control bribery by such legislation as the U. S. Foreign Corrupt Practices Act, which prohibits U. S. companies from paying bribes to foreign government officials. Other forms of payment made abroad sometimes approach extortion and are not under the control of American laws. How should American companies react? Some, such as Gulf Oil, having once been stung, decided not to make any such payments. To the surprise of many, Gulf's new policy did not decrease its sales or lead to the threatened nationalization of its plants. Many fears were unfounded, and we have learned that the people of some nations have less tolerance for questionable practices than was thought. Firms in many countries have attempted to bring order into the international marketplace by demanding that companies compete on the merit of their products rather than of their skill at secret payments. All these facts must be taken into account in a utilitarian approach to the questions we have raised and left unanswered.

Utilitarianism, far from being a self-serving approach to moral issues, demands careful, objective, impartial evaluation of consequences. It is a widely used—but often misused—approach to moral evaluation. A powerful tool of moral reasoning, it is a technique well worth mastering.

Study Questions

1. In the case with which the chapter begins, did the airplane manufacturer use a utilitarian analysis to justify his action? Develop a utilitarian analysis of that case.

2. Define utilitarianism. Do you find utilitarianism a plausible approach in deciding the morality of an action? Why or why not?

3. Distinguish hedonistic utilitarianism, eudaimonsitic utilitarianism; and ideal utilitarianism. Which type do you consider most useful? Why?

4. With respect to weighing values, what aspects of values should we consider? What is meant by intensity, duration, certainty, propinquity, fecundity, and purity? Give an example showing how you can compare these aspects of values.

5. Distinguish act from rule utilitarianism, and define each. Which is preferable? Why?

6. State and answer four objections raised against utilitarianism.

7. Does following a utilitarian calculation sometimes lead to unjust actions? Why or why not? If yes, give an example. If no, how do you reply to those who claim it does?

8. What are the steps in carrying out a utilitarian calculation to determine the morality of an action? Illustrate the steps in evaluating a moral issue of your own choosing.

9. What is meant by a "dominant consideration" in a utilitarian calculation? What is its significance?

10. According to rule utilitarianism, can we say that bribery is immoral? Why or why not? Can we say the same thing if we use act utilitarianism? Why or why not?

11. Distinguish bribery from extortion, from what are called "facilitating payments," and from tipping. Carry out a rule utilitarian analysis of these three practices similar to the analysis of bribery done in this chapter.

12. Should there be a law against bribery? Answer this question using a rule utilitarian approach. (*Note:* In doing this, you should evaluate the consequences of this type of *law.*)

13. How would a utilitarian respond to the claims of the relativist? To the Myth of Amoral Business?

14. Are there any moral actions that are not valued for their utility? If there are any that appear to be exceptions to the utilitarian view, how would a utilitarian account for them?

4

>-·-‹›-·-O-·-‹›-·-‹

MORAL DUTY, RIGHTS, AND JUSTICE

The Johnson Controls Case

Although the Johnson Controls case was decided by the U.S. Supreme Court, it continues to raise a number of ethical issues.[1] Central to the case are various claims about rights, which deontologists claim do not depend on consequences.

Manufacturers of batteries have known for some time that their manufacturing process, which involves considerable exposure to lead, can cause harm to a fetus. As a result, in the name of fetal protection, a number of such manufacturers prohibited women from working under conditions in which they would be exposed to lead. In doing so, they claimed the right of the fetus not to be harmed; the right of the company to protect itself against damage from legal suits either from women whose fetus was injured due to their working conditions or from the child, who after birth, might sue the company for harm done to it during its fetal development; and the right of the company to set conditions of employment. Since a company could not be certain when a woman might be pregnant, it avoided the problem by excluding all women from that type of work. Johnson Controls, a battery manufacturer, followed

---

[1] *International Union, UAW v. Johnson Controls, Inc.*, 111 S. Ct. 1196 (1991).

this policy until June 1977, when it adopted a new policy. It acknowledged that it could not protect the unborn children in this way without simultaneously violating the women's rights to equal opportunity, as guaranteed under the Civil Rights Act of 1964. Under its new policy, the company advised women of the danger to an unborn child while she was exposed to lead and required her to sign a statement relieving the company of responsibility.

After eight of its employees became pregnant and registered blood lead levels higher than those considered safe by the Occupational Safety and Health Administration for a worker planning to have children, the company in 1982 once again revised its policy, this time excluding women from jobs that exposed them to lead, unless they could medically document their inability to bear children. As a result of the new policy, one worker, Mary Craig, chose to be sterilized rather than lose her job, and another, Elsie Nason, a 50-year-old divorcee, was transferred to a lower paying job. They and others formed a class-action suit charging that the Johnson Controls' Fetal Protection Policy violated the rights of women and constituted discrimination on the basis of sex—a nonjob-related criterion for working on the batteries. They argued that the women were responsible for the safety of their fetuses and that if properly warned of the dangers to which they were being exposed, it was up to them to decide whether or not to work under the conditions to which they were exposed. Of the eight pregnancies reported by female workers from 1977 to 1983, none of the babies had any abnormalities or birth defects.

Although the United States District Court ruled in favor of Johnson Controls, and although its judgment was affirmed by the Court of Appeals, that judgment was overturned by the Supreme Court, which held that the Johnson Controls' policy was a violation of the Civil Rights Act. Three of the Supreme Court justices in part dissented from that decision, stating that "The Court's narrow interpretation . . . means that an employer cannot exclude even *pregnant* women from an environment highly toxic to their fetuses. It is foolish to think that Congress intended such a result."

>-⊷-◆-○-◆-⊷-≺

Our task here is not to decide what Congress intended or whether the Johnson Controls' policy violates the Civil Rights Act. Rather, our question is, leaving aside the specifics of the law, what are the obligations of a manufacturer, if any, with respect to fetal protection? Does a fetus have rights, and if so are they the concern exclusively of the woman bearing the fetus or of others as well? Does a company have the right to protect itself against possible suit by an employee or later by a child who was harmed as a fetus due to the employment conditions of the mother? Is the right not to be discriminated against except for bona fide occupational qualification an absolute one, or may it be overridden by other rights? How does one weigh conflicting rights? May rights be overridden by consequences?

Deontological Approaches to Ethics

In general, the deontological approach to ethics denies the utilitarian claim that the morality of an action depends on its consequences. Deontologists maintain that actions are morally right or wrong independent of their consequences. Moral rightness and wrongness are basic and ultimate moral terms. They do not depend on good and the production of, or the failure to produce, good. One's duty is to do what is morally right and to avoid what is morally wrong, regardless of the consequences of so doing.

The deontological position is a commonly held one, with a long history. In contemporary American society it is associated both with the Judeo-Christian tradition and with a philosophical tradition that goes back to the Greek Stoic philosophers. It includes the formalistic theory of the eighteenth-century German philosopher Immanuel Kant, as well as the theories of many contemporaries who present moral arguments in terms of justice and rights.

Judeo-Christian Morality

The Judeo-Christian tradition has nurtured the morality of the West for centuries and that of our country since its inception. It is still an extremely potent force. Judeo-Christian morality includes not only a body of moral rules but also a view of what it means to be a human being and to have a set of values. These moral rules, the view of human beings, and their values have, to a large degree, been absorbed into the secular life of the West in general and of the United States in particular. The morality taught in the pulpits is fairly close to the conventional morality found in our society.

Those aspects of the Judeo-Christian moral heritage that refer explicitly to religion and one's duty to God can be distinguished from other aspects of morality, those that involve one's relations to other people. Primarily the latter have been taken over by Western society—absorbed, and to a large extent secularized.

The Ten Commandments, or at least the last seven, are still widely held to sum up what, morally, we should do (e.g., honor thy father and mother) or not do (e.g., thou shalt not kill). To these are joined the injunction to love your neighbor, together with all that it implies. The other virtues follow. Because the morality of the Judeo-Christian tradition rested for so many centuries on a foundation of faith, there was great fear that, as religious faith diminished, immorality would increase. However, what has tended to happen is that, as religious faith diminished, the virtues and commands that it had sustained found different underpinnings, both secular and philosophical. We have already seen how utilitarians have been quite ready to accept and explain the content of religious morality using the utilitarian approach. Philosophical deontologists have also provided a secular foundation for the content of religious moral norms and virtues.

A Christian *theological* ethics, or theory of morality, is based on theology and hence on the acceptance of divine revelation. There are two dominant positions in this approach. One holds that *divine inspiration* took place not only in ages past through the prophets of the Old Testament, Christ, and the authors of the New Testament, but that it also continues even now and is available to all believers. According to this view, conscience is God's word, and those who are in tune with Him know what is right and what is wrong. Viewed as an ethical theory, it claims that what is right and what is wrong are determined by God, and that He communicates knowledge of right and wrong directly to His followers. The second position holds that God determined what is right and what is wrong, that He revealed it through His prophets, Christ, and the authors of the New Testament, but that this revelation requires interpretation. In some Christian religions the interpretation is performed by each individual; in others it is performed by either the church collectively or by special persons in the church who speak authoritatively about the morality of actions.

According to these interpretations, morality ultimately rests on God and is held because of revelation. Though members of our society frequently guide their lives by such an ethics, a religiously based moral argument is frequently discounted by those not practicing the same faith as the person who puts forth the argument. Because the argument has as a central feature belief in God and in a certain kind of revelation, those who do not believe in God or who believe in a different kind of revelation are not logically compelled by such an argument. A believer quoting the Koran might have little influence on someone who does not accept the Koran as a guide to morality.

Ever since the ancient Greeks, some people have asked whether an action is right because God says it is, or whether God says an action is morally right because it is morally right. In the former case, God could make murder, theft, or lying moral if He chose to do so. In the latter case, He could not. God knows those actions are morally wrong, and He helps us know this through His revelation. But the rightness or wrongness of the actions is not subject to His whim. Because He made us in a certain way, the moral rules by which we should live have been built into our nature as human beings. Ultimately, they depend on God; but we need not constantly ask or wonder whether He has changed His mind, and whether what He once said was immoral is today moral.

Three points should be made clear. First, if we believe that we know, through direct divine intervention, which actions are right and which are wrong, then we have no need of a philosophical ethical theory, unless we wish to defend our moral judgments to those who disagree with us or to those who do not believe in God's direct intervention.

Second, those of us who do not believe in God's direct personal moral communication to each person must interpret the Ten Commandments and the injunction to love our neighbor. What specific actions do these prescriptions and proscriptions command or forbid? Is killing in self-defense a justifiable form of killing? Is killing in defense of our property defensible? Both actions are forms of killing. The Commandment "Thou shalt not kill" does not come with any exceptions built into it. How, if at all, do we justify exceptions? The rules by which we arrive at and justify exceptions make up part of a theory of morality and are therefore part of an ethical system. If these rules are defended only on the basis of scripture, then the defenses are designed for the religious believer.

The third point is that what is demanded by a religious-based morality might also be justifiable on nonreligious grounds. The content of religious morality might be acceptable, at least in large part, to nonreligious people. Both they and religious believers might find philosophical grounds adequate to support at least the portion of morality that is not specifically religious. Many in the history of philosophy have defended this position, including such a major figure as Thomas Aquinas (1225–1274). Both Mill and Kant thought they were supplying a philosophical ethical theory that could support the content of a Christian morality.

Churches have been effective in inculcating moral norms and in teaching and preaching morality in the marketplace as well as in other areas of life. They have emphasized the development of virtue and of a virtuous character and have provided their members with role models. They have also developed and preached religious ideals, and ideals of virtue to which the faithful could, and should, aspire. Individual people engaged in business may of course be religious, and their religious convictions may govern the practices in which they engage. Moral individuals who live up to their religious and moral values in their business lives help make and keep business and their practices moral. Nonetheless, moral defenses of business practices are not usually made in religious terms to those not practicing one's own religion, nor are most public-policy questions that involve business argued convincingly only in religious terms. If arguments are intended to be convincing to large segments of the population, they are, characteristically, put in such terms that the premises are acceptable to all human beings, and not only to believers.

The Ten Commandments and the commandment to love our neighbor are deontological in form: They are commandments to do certain actions and to refrain from others. The commands do not instruct us to look at the consequences of the actions before deciding whether they are right. Hence, they command without concern for consequences. Whether they could be derived by looking at consequences, as utilitarians maintain, is another issue. The present point is that the form they have is not consequentialist but deontological.

Reason, Duty, and the Moral Law

The standard deontological approach in contemporary philosophical ethical theory received its classic formulation in the writings of Immanuel Kant.[2] Both the contemporary deontological approach and Kant's are compatible with the Ten Commandments. But why should we obey these commands? Why should we do what our parents, peers, or society tell us to do? It may be that God, our parents, our peers, and our society inform us correctly about the right thing to do. But the reason that the actions are right is not because our parents, for example, command them. Morality and moral obligation cannot be imposed on us by others; we are the only ones who can impose such obligations on ourselves. If we are moral, we impose a certain way of acting on ourselves because we understand what it means to be a moral being, and we understand what sorts of actions are appropriate for such a being. For someone in the Kantian tradition, to be moral is the same as being rational. Just as no one can force us to be rational, no one can force us to be moral. In this view, if we choose to be rational, we also choose to be moral. No reason can be given as to why we should be rational prior to our deciding to be so; to give reasons, to ask for them, or to be convinced by them are all rational activities and so presuppose the acceptance of reason. If we wish to see more clearly what it means to be moral, and what morality demands, we must analyze closely what it means to be rational and what the implications of being rational are for our actions. Because morality consists in acting rationally, it applies only to rational beings. The source of morality is to be found in ourselves and in our reason, not in anything external to us. Reason is the same in each of us; therefore what is rational and moral is the same for all of us. According to this view, we act morally when we knowingly choose to act in the way reason demands. The statement of what reason demands in the realm of action is the moral law. By analyzing reason as applied to action, which we can call practical reason, we find the key to morality.

The deontological tradition holds that what makes an action right is not the sum of its consequences but the fact that it conforms to the moral law. The Kantian test of conformity to the moral law which an action must pass is a formal one. An action is morally right if it has a certain *form*; it is morally wrong if it does not have that form. The moral law at its highest and most general level states the form that an action must have to be moral. But the moral law at this level, or the highest principle of morality, does not state what content an action must have to be a right action. It states only the form the action must have. Such an approach is therefore called a *formalist ethical approach*.

---

[2] Kant's position is most accessibly presented in his *Foundations of the Metaphysics of Morals*. An excellent edition, which also contains nine critical essays, is Robert Paul Wolff (Ed.), *Foundations of the Metaphysics of Morals, with Critical Essays* (Indianapolis, Ind.: Bobbs-Merrill Co., 1969). A well-known book-length commentary is H. J. Paton's *The Categorical Imperative* (Chicago: University of Chicago Press, 1948).

What is the form an action must have to be moral? How can we state the moral law? The answer lies in the nature of reason. Because being moral is the same as acting rationally, we can determine the moral law by analyzing the nature of reason itself, by analyzing rational activity, and by analyzing what it means to be a rational being.

Consider what we know about reason by examining the reasoning we engage in when we do mathematics. Take the simple process of adding two plus two and getting four. Two plus two do not equal four because our teachers said so. Two plus two equal four independently of our teachers. Two plus two equal four for everyone—for all rational beings—even if they do not know it and even if they add two plus two and get a number other than four. If we uncover the foundations of mathematics, we come to understand why two plus two equal four. But even without such an understanding we know that two plus two equal four for everyone, and that the validity of this addition does not depend on our experiencing two things and two other things equaling four things, but on the self-consistency of the mathematical operation.

Because the moral law is the statement of the form of a rational action, we should make explicit some of those characteristics that are central to reason. One of these is *consistency*. Moral actions must not be self-contradictory, and, to the extent that we have a system of morality, moral actions must not contradict one another. A second characteristic is *universality*. Because reason is the same for all, what is rational for me is rational for everyone else, and what is rational for anyone else is rational for me. A third characteristic of reason, which we found exemplified in mathematics and which we also find characterizing the moral law, is that it is *a priori*, or not based on experience. The moral law applies to experience, but it is not derived from it, nor is its truth dependent on experience. This is why the morality of an action does not depend on consequences.

Because the moral law is a law, it issues a command or states an imperative—something that must be done. The imperative is an unconditioned one. It states what everyone is to do because it is a command of reason. Following the somewhat technical terminology of Kant, the moral law commands *categorically*, not hypothetically. A hypothetical imperative states that an action should be done if, or on the hypothesis that, one wishes to achieve a certain end. Thus, "If you wish to do well in school, study!" is a hypothetical imperative. Not everyone is required to go to school, and not everyone is required to study. The moral law, however, is not stated in hypothetical form. It is not something we can choose to follow or not, depending on whether we wish to achieve this or that end. We are bound by the injunction to be moral no matter what else we wish to do. The moral law binds unconditionally. Kant called the statement of the moral law, or of the supreme principle of morality, the *Categorical Imperative*. We noted that the Ten Commandments are also stated in categorical form. "Thou shalt not kill" states a moral norm or principle, applicable to all and binding on all unconditionally. But it is an imperative with content. Therefore, it is, according to the formalist approach, not the highest moral principle; it is a principle, an imperative, a norm that is *a* moral principle because it is in accord with the moral law, but it is not *the* principle of morality. It is a *second-order* or *second-level principle*. The highest moral principle—the Categorical Imperative—states the *form* moral actions have and provides the criteria against which we can test whether an action or a second-order principle is moral. Kant gave three formulations of the Categorical Imperative. These state three aspects of it, or three formal conditions that an action must have if it is to be a moral action.

For an action to a moral action, (1) it must be amenable to being made consistently universal; (2) it must respect rational beings as ends in themselves; and (3) it must stem from, and respect, the autonomy of rational beings. These three formal conditions are all derivable from an analysis of reason and of what it means to be a rational being.

Consistency in Universalization

Actions, strictly speaking, are specific, intentional bodily movements that human beings do in a context and for a purpose. An action itself, therefore, is individual and not universal. It is what it is. Similarly, an action cannot contradict another action. We can, however, speak of a description of an action, of a rule or principle of action, or of the maxim of an action. It is the rule, principle, or maxim of an action that we test when we wish to determine whether an action is moral. The *maxim* of an action is a careful statement or description of its essential features. If the maxim is put in imperative form, it is a rule of action. The content of the rule can be considered a second-order principle of action telling us what we ought to do or not do.

The a priori products of reason are universal and self-consistent. If an action is to be a moral action, it must have a rational form. This means that the rule, principle, or maxim of the action must be capable of being consistently universalized. If an action is moral for me, it must be moral for everyone. We are all commanded to do what is morally right; therefore, any action we are all commanded to do must be such that in doing it, none of us interferes with or prevents others from doing it. An action that does not have this form is an immoral action.

It is important to note that in asking whether the action can be consistently universalized we are not asking, as we would from a consequentialist point of view, what the results of everyone's doing that action would be. We need not suppose that everyone would do the action. In many instances people who act immorally trade on the fact that not everyone does what they do. We are inquiring whether the rule, principle, or maxim of the action is internally consistent when made universal. Since the test is a logical or conceptual one, it does not depend on the factual question of whether everyone does or would do the action.

Let us consider some examples to see how we can test the morality of an action. Is murder wrong? Is lying wrong? Murder is the killing of a human being without a justifying reason. Defining it in this way, of course, characterizes it as unjustifiable from the start. So let us consider instead the action of killing, in anger, another human being. Stated as a rule it would read: "Kill others whenever you are angry at them." Can this rule be made consistently universal? The test is whether there is internal consistency within the rule when applied to everyone. Because it is likely that everyone gets angry at someone at some time, and because it is likely that everyone has had someone angry at him at some time, if everyone followed the rule we would kill each other off. If we all followed this rule, none of us would be alive to continue following it. The rule, therefore, when made universal, leads to its own demise and therein lies its inconsistency. On the other hand, consider the action of respecting human life. The rule reads: "Respect human life." If the rule were made universal, everyone would respect everyone else's life. The rule is consistent, for we can all go on respecting human life indefinitely. Following the rule does not lead to the rule's demise.

Now consider lying. The rule is: "Lie!" Can it be made universal, consistently? The answer is that it cannot. If everyone lied, then no one would believe anyone else. But if no one believed anyone else, the possibility of lying would disappear. Hence, lying cannot be made consistently universal. "Tell the truth!" however, is a rule everyone can always follow. If we all tell the truth, we can all believe one another. We can go on telling the truth indefinitely. There is no inconsistency in the rule when made universal. Hence, it is a moral rule.

The formulation of the Categorical Imperative that Kant gave concerning this condition of consistent universalization was, "Act only according to that maxim by which you can at the same time will that it should become a universal law."[3]

Respect for Rational Beings

A rational being can understand the need for consistency in action. A rational being is also conscious of being a person, an entity who is valuable in himself or herself, and a being that is an *end in itself.* Because of this a rational being is worthwhile, has dignity, and is worthy of respect. Hence, each person should be treated by every person as an end, with respect and dignity.

We all use objects for our own purposes, as means to our own ends. We also use people as a means to an end when, for instance, they serve us in a store or restaurant, or when we hire them to do what we want done. But even when we treat people as means we should not forget that they always remain ends. Thus, Kant formulated a second version of the Categorical Imperative: "Act so that you treat humanity, whether in your own person or in that of another, always as an end and never as a means only."[4]

---

[3] Kant, *Foundations of the Metaphysics of Morals*, p. 44.
[4] Ibid, p. 54.

This formulation of the Categorical Imperative, according to Kant, is simply a different statement of the supreme moral law contained in the first formulation. Consequently, it commands and forbids the same actions as the first formulation. Consider the two actions we examined earlier. If we kill people in anger, or to get them out of our way, we clearly do not treat them with respect. We use them exclusively as means to what we want and not as ends in themselves. When we lie to them we intend to deceive them. We are denying that as rational beings they deserve the truth, and we are attempting to achieve our own ends at their expense. We treat them as the means to get what we want, including the avoidance of unpleasantness or punishment. Lying, theft, and murder all involve treating people only as means, not as ends, and therefore we do not treat them with the respect they deserve as rational beings.

The kind of treatment that rational beings deserve, as ends in themselves, is sometimes put in terms of rights. People thus have the right to life, and this right imposes obligations on others not to take their life and, in certain conditions, to help them preserve it. A person's right to his or her property imposes the obligation on others not to take that property. This approach to rights maintains that people have rights because of the kinds of beings they are, and denies that rights are dependent on consequences.

Autonomy

Because being moral is the same as acting rationally, morality is not imposed on persons from the outside. It is part of their nature. They recognize the moral law insofar as they recognize that they are rational beings and belong to the kingdom of beings who are ends in themselves. The moral law is self-imposed and self-recognized. This position does not deny either that people act immorally or that many people act only on the level of conventional morality. When they act in conformity with conventional morality, they may act in conformity with what the moral law commands. But to have true personal moral worth, their actions should not only conform with the moral law; their actions should also be done with consciousness of the moral law and of the fact that they are obeying it.

Three aspects of morality are captured in the notion of autonomy: freedom, the self-imposition of the moral law, and the universal acceptability of the moral law.

Rational beings are the only entities that can be full-fledged members of the moral community because morality requires the possibility both of conceiving and understanding the moral law, and of knowingly and willingly acting in accordance with it. Animals are not moral beings because they fail in both these respects. They are not able to conceive of the moral law, and they are not able to choose whether to act in accordance with it. Animals act from instinct and in reaction to immediate sensations. Human beings are able to inhibit and control their instincts, passions, and drives, and are able to examine their actions before performing them. Their reason enables them to do so. The ability to so act carries with it the obligation to do so, and constitutes the *freedom* of the rational being. Nonrational entities that act only instinctively and in response to present stimuli are not free. They are determined by their instincts and stimuli. The ability to override instincts and stimuli constitutes the freedom of the human being. This freedom, which we can call the *rational freedom of self-determination*, becomes moral freedom when we choose to act in accordance with the moral law. This moral freedom can be called the *rational freedom of self-perfection*. The first type of freedom is a human being's ability to choose to act morally or immorally. But people act morally only when they act in accordance with the demands of reason. When acting in this way, they exercise their moral freedom, and, from the moral point of view, perfect themselves.

The second aspect of autonomy emphasizes the fact that moral beings give themselves the moral law. As ends in themselves, moral beings are not subservient to anyone else. They each determine the moral law for themselves in accordance with reason. They impose it on themselves and accept its demands for themselves. This is simply a function of the rational being's freedom and of his dignity as an end in himself. But though each person gives himself the moral law, he cannot prescribe anything he wants. He is bound by reason and its demands. Because reason is the same for all rational beings, we each give ourselves the same moral law. The Categorical Imperative is the same for all of us, though imposed by each of us and recognized by each of us for ourselves. Kant's third formulation of the Categorical Imperative is "Act only so that the will through its maxims could regard itself at the same time as universally lawgiving."[5]

The third aspect of autonomy, the universal acceptability of the moral law, is a function of the fact that moral beings give themselves the moral law. This aspect provides a third test of moral rules or principles. If we wish to see whether a rule, principle, or maxim is moral, we should ask if what the rule commands would be acceptable to all rational beings acting rationally. Hence, in considering murder, lying, theft, and so on, we must consider the action not only from the point of view of the agent of the action but also from the point of view of the receiver—that is, the person who is murdered, lied to, or stolen from. Rational beings will all see that they do not want murder, lying, and theft to be universal laws applied to themselves as well as to others. They do not want to be murdered, lied to, or stolen from. It is not simply a matter, however, of their own good being violated, though it is also that. As rational beings, they also accept limitations on what they permit themselves to do, for they understand that they live in a community. They see the necessity of restricting their own actions, just as they expect others to restrict theirs. The test of the morality of a rule is not whether people in fact accept it. The test is

---

[5] Ibid., p. 59.

whether all rational beings, thinking rationally, should accept it regardless of whether they were the agents or the receivers of the actions.

Application of the Moral Law

The Categorical Imperative, or the ultimate principle of morality, according to the dominant deontological position, requires that any second-order moral rule or maxim must be capable of being consistently universalized, must respect the dignity of persons, and must be acceptable to rational beings. Any action ruled out by one of these criteria should be ruled out by the other two. But sometimes one rather than another of the tests is clearer and leads more obviously to a moral evaluation. In testing whether the maxim of an action is moral, therefore, it is prudent to apply all three tests. *If the maxim passes all three tests, it is moral; if it fails any one of the three, it is immoral.*

There are two difficulties in attempting to apply this test to actions. One involves determining the level of generality of the rule on which we are acting; the second involves a clash between the actions that two second-order moral rules command.

The Level of Generality

Consider once again the case of the airplane manufacturer who wishes to save his company and feels that in order to do so he must bribe a potential foreign purchaser. What is the rule on which he is acting? We might consider the rule to be "Bribe!" If we attempt to universalize the rule involved, we quickly see that it is self-contradictory. If bribery were made a universal rule, it would no longer be bribery but a universal way of doing business. Bribery only works with a background of nonbribery, for it is a way of gaining special advantage. If everyone always gained advantage in this way, the advantage would no longer be special. Universal bribery is self-contradictory. Hence, bribery is immoral. Bribery also fails the second and third tests. It fails the second test because in bribing we implicitly, if not explicitly, do not care what happens to other people over whom we get special advantage. We do not treat these people as ends in themselves or as worthy of respect but only as a means to achieve the end we desire. Bribery also fails the third test because if we thought carefully about it, we would not want bribery to be a universal law. If it were a universal law, we would often be disadvantaged when other people paid bribes and received special advantage over us. Hence, bribery fails all three tests. However, one failure is enough to make clear its immoral status.

The airplane manufacturer, however, might protest that he was not acting on the rule, "Bribe!" He would not advocate everyone always bribing everyone else. Rather, he advocates bribery only in certain select circumstances. The rule might be "Bribe only when necessary to keep your company from going bankrupt!" Hence, the test of universality requires only that all companies threatened with bankruptcy engage in bribery, not that all companies do so. Because the other companies do not engage in bribery, they form the necessary background for the bribery to be successful. But consider this rule more carefully. Would rational beings accept this rule as reasonable? Would everyone agree that a company facing bankruptcy should act in this way? Why should a company that is so managed as to be facing bankruptcy be allowed to gain special advantage? No company competing with other companies is likely to accept such a rule, nor are the people of a society, who will eventually pay for the bribe in higher prices. The rule clearly fails the third test, and hence is immoral.

The point of the airplane manufacturer, however, is partially correct. We can construe the maxim of actions more or less broadly. When we considered the injunction "Kill other human beings!" we saw that it could not be made universal without contradiction. But does this mean that self-defense is immoral? Most people would argue that it is not. The rule of self-defense is "Kill an unjust attacker if that is the only way you can defend innocent life, whether your own person or that of another!" This can be made universal. It respects innocent life above that of our unjust attacker and, upon rational consideration, would be accepted by everyone. It is an exception, therefore, to the general injunction "Do not kill!" The injunction we should ultimately test is the injunction not to kill, together with all its exceptions. That would be a full statement of the rule concerning killing. It is sufficient, however, to test portions of it when considering particular cases. It is not always easy to state accurately the maxim of an action or to test it. It is also not always easy to be completely honest with ourselves in stating the rule on which we are really acting. We are frequently tempted to fabricate a maxim that will allow us to do what we wish, rather than stating the maxim or principle on which we are actually acting.

The Clash of Moral Rules

The Categorical Imperative, or the supreme principle of morality, in itself involves no conflict, and principles or maxims of actions that are in accord with it can each be made universal without contradiction. But there are circumstances in which two second-order moral rules or principles, each of which is self-consistent, clash. Such clashes pose a moral dilemma. If we cannot follow either of the rules without violating the other rule, we necessarily violate one of them. We do what we should not do. Are we, in such cases, forced to do what is immoral? We cannot have a moral obligation to do what is immoral. This would be a contradiction, for we would have the moral obligation to do, and to refrain from doing, the action. How can we escape the dilemma?

Suppose that in a slaveholding society we are hiding a runaway slave. The slaveholder comes to the door and asks if we are hiding the slave. Should we lie and oppose the immoral institution of slavery? Or should we tell the truth and cooperate in that immoral institution?

In attempting to resolve this and similar cases, we should first make sure that we are really facing a dilemma. Is there some third way of acting by which we can avoid performing any action that violates the Categorical Imperative? Could we, in response to the question, not answer but faint instead? Would fainting preclude the necessity of answering the question and still protect the slave? If it would not solve the problem, and no other strategy would, then we must face the dilemma head-on and attempt to resolve it.

There are two standard ways of resolving such dilemmas, both of which should produce the same outcome. One is to construct the maxim of our action in such a way that it allows for the exception needed in the resolution of the given case. Just as we construct the rule allowing a person to kill as a last resort in the case of self-defense, we can attempt to construct a universal rule about lying which includes certain exceptions, and, in particular, an exception that fits this case. But how do we know we should seek an exception to the prohibition against lying rather than an exception to the prohibition against slavery? Unless the answer is obvious, we can attempt to construct rules allowing an exception to each rule. We then ask which action can be made universal, which respects human beings, which would be universally acceptable to rational beings. Because the answer is not always clear, arguments must be given. For instance, someone might argue that the slaveholder has no right to knowledge of where his slave is because slavery is immoral. Hence, in not giving him the information he requests, we are not denying him anything he rightfully deserves as a person. We are thus not denying him respect and so are not treating him only as a means. This line of reasoning claims that, although the statement made to the slaveholder is false, it is not a lie because it does not violate anyone's legitimate right to information. Hence, we in effect reconstrue what lying is and the immoral aspect of making false statements. Another line of reasoning admits that the false statement is a lie but argues that it is permissible because all rational persons would accept as a rule the telling of a lie when necessary to protect someone against the unjust violations of human freedom that slavery involves.

A second approach to a clash of second-order rules views each of the moral rules as a prima facie moral rule. A *prima facie rule is one that is in general binding.*[6] If in a given case only one prima facie moral rules applies, that states our actual duty. But when several prima facie moral rules apply, and when we cannot fulfill all of them, then they cannot all be morally binding. Our actual moral duty in such a case is to obey that prima facie moral rule that is appropriate in the given case. How are we to decide which prima facie duty is our *actual* moral duty? One answer, defended by some philosophers, is that when

---

[6] See W.D. Ross, *The Right and the Good* (Oxford: Clarendon Press, 1930).

we carefully compare conflicting duties we come to see which takes precedence. However, reasons can and usually should be given as to why one rule takes precedence over another. These reasons constitute the justification for breaking a prima facie moral rule. In doing so we are not acting immorally, because prima facie rules do not express absolute moral obligations.

In the example of our hiding the runaway slave we are faced with two prima facie moral rules. One is "Do not lie." The other is "Do not engage in or abet slavery." Each rule is one we should follow. But if they conflict, and if we cannot follow both, then we must decide which one takes precedence in this case. The one that takes precedence states our actual moral duty. In weighing the two rules we can argue that slavery is a greater evil and does more violence to the respect due to human beings than does lying. Hence, using the criterion of respect for persons in evaluating both rules, we see that our obligation to prevent someone from being a slave is greater than our obligation not to lie to a slaveholder seeking his slave.

If we use the notion of prima facie obligations, we can incorporate much of utilitarianism into a deontological ethical position. The command, "Produce the greatest amount of good for the greatest number of people affected by an action" can be considered a prima facie moral obligation. It states a rule or principle that can be universalized, that respects people as ends, and that can be rationally accepted by all. However, from a deontological point of view, this rule or principle is not the highest moral principle. Hence, if what it commands comes into conflict with some other moral rule (e.g., that of justice), it might have to give way. This approach will not satisfy utilitarians, because they argue that utilitarianism states the highest moral principle. Yet this approach does satisfy many people who feel that utilitarianism states a moral principle, but admit that there are others as well.

When moral principles clash, it is often difficult to decide which takes precedence. In these cases both individuals and society should very carefully and objectively consider the various arguments in support of opposing positions. When a clear decision is not available and we are forced to act, we should act on the basis of the strongest arguments available.

The Ten Commandments can be considered prima facie moral obligations. They and other prima facie moral obligations can also be considered second-order moral rules. Once established, second-order moral rules can be, and most frequently are, used to solve particular cases. Hence, one need not apply the Categorical Imperative on every occasion. But we can do so, and if we ever have reason to doubt the validity of second-order moral rules we can submit them to the tests required by the Categorical Imperative. It is in this sense the Categorical Imperative supplies the basic criterion of morality, even though in ordinary life we tend to solve moral problems by using second-order moral principles or rules.

We can sum up this approach to moral decision making in five steps, as in Figure 4-1.

STEPS OF A DUTY-BASED ANALYSIS

1. Accurately state the action to be evaluated, being careful not to specify it too narrowly.

2. Can the action be subsumed under some generally acknowledged (prima facie) substantive duty, such as not to kill, lie, or steal?

   a. If so, and there is only one such duty, that duty applies.

   b. If there are actions about which there is doubt, go to step 3.

   c. If the action falls under more than one of these, go to step 5, or describe the action as a universalizable exception and go to step 3.

3. Submit the action to the three tests:

   a. Can the action be performed by everyone without any contradiction developing to prevent its continued performance? If no, the action is immoral. If yes,

   b. Does the action respect people as ends and not as means only? If no, the action is immoral. If yes,

   c. Is the action such that all rational people, whether on the giving or receiving end of the action, would will all people to so act? If no, the action is immoral. If yes, the action is prima facie moral.

4. If the action is prima facie moral, does it conflict or seem to conflict with other general prima facie duties, such that both cannot be fulfilled together? If no, then the morality of the action is decided. If yes, go to step 5.

5. Consider arguments in defense of and against each of the prima facie duties being the actual duty in the case in question. The one with the strongest argument in its favor is the actual duty.

Figure 4-1

Imperfect Duties, Special Obligations, and Moral Ideals

Universal second-order or second-level prima facie duties, we saw, are in general binding, in the sense that they state our actual obligation providing they are not overridden by some more important duty. Negative duties preclude our doing what they forbid. Thus, we may not kill or steal or bribe, since all of those are prohibited by the moral law. We can call such duties *perfect duties* because they clearly prescribe both the action that is forbidden and those to whom they pertain (namely, everyone). There are some duties, however, that cannot be specified with the same precision or may not bind with the same rigor. These are called *imperfect duties*. In some cases the object of the action in question is indeterminate; in others the degree to which the rule must be fulfilled is indeterminate. Some actions are indeterminate in both respects.

An example of the first kind is the duty to help those in need. The obligation to help those in need satisfies all three tests of the Categorical Imperative. First, the obligation to help others is self-consistent since we can all help each other indefinitely. Aiding others is in no way self-contradictory. Second, the action of acknowledging that others are worthy of receiving help treats them as ends in themselves. In helping others we do not use them as means only. Third, we would all wish to be helped when in need, and so, when thinking rationally, we would all wish that those able to do so would help us. In this sense we would wish the rule of mutual help to be universal. Because the rule satisfies all three tests, it is a moral rule. But the rule specifies neither exactly whom we should help nor the degree to which we must help. Because so many people in the world are in need, and because each of us has only limited resources, it is evident that no one can help everyone in need. For this reason, the command to help those in need is a limited or an imperfect duty. It is imperfect because the degree to which we are obliged by this universal rule depends on our ability to help others and because we are not obliged to help all others but only some others. The rule thus allows us a certain amount of freedom in fulfilling it.

The limits on our obligation to help others come from two sources. One is from the general rule that we are morally obligated to do only that of which we are capable. The general rule, in its Kantian formulation, is "Ought implies can." We are only obliged to do what we can do. Hence, if we are unable to help others for whatever reason—lack of resources, lack of opportunity, lack of means—we are excused from the obligation. Second, when we can help others, we are not required to help them if doing so causes or threatens us with an amount of harm equal to the aid we might give the needy. I am obliged to help someone who is drowning if I can do so without endangering my own life. I am not obliged to do so if I cannot or if my attempt puts me in equal danger of drowning.

It is difficult to specify imperfect duties with precision. Hence, there is frequently some dispute about the extent to which we are obliged by them and about the exact time or conditions under which we are obliged. For instance, the extent of our obligation to help the poor depends at least in part on our own affluence. The well-to-do have more of an obligation to help the poor than do those who are less well off themselves. We are not obliged to become impoverished from giving to the poor. Moreover, since no one can help everyone, choosing those whom we might help again depends in part on a variety of circumstances. Since there are more needy people than any individual person can help, we satisfy our obligation to help the needy by helping any of them to the extent that we can. Our general obligation to help the needy does not oblige us to help some particular needy person, unless we have some special obligation with respect to that person. In this respect the imperfect rule is indeterminate.

The indeterminateness of imperfect duties has a positive side and serves a positive function in morality. The negative perfect duties set the moral minimum below which no one may morally go. The imperfect duties, because they are not restricted, provide a positive call to go beyond the minimum. For instance, although we all have a moral obligation to help the poor, we recognize that some people do much more in this regard than anyone believes they are morally obliged to do. Although they have no obligation to impoverish themselves, some of the recognized saints in human history have done just that. Similarly, although we are not obliged to endanger our own lives in order to save the lives of others, those who do so are considered moral heroes. They go beyond the call of duty.

While it is clear that perfect duties bind in business just as in any other aspect of life, there is a good deal of controversy about whether imperfect duties apply in business and, if so, the extent to which they apply. Clearly, neither people in business nor firms can justifiably murder, steal from, or cheat others. But how much must an individual in business or a firm contribute to the poor or help others? In a competitive situation people tend not to help their competitor compete, and one business has no obligation to help a competing business survive. A business that is barely making ends meet has no more obligation to help the poor than do individuals in similar circumstances. Does a business that is making a reasonable profit and is financially healthy have any obligation to donate to charity or to sponsor social programs? Since the managers of corporations most often do not own the corporation, is it morally permissible for them to use corporate money for philanthropic purposes? While we might praise an individual who sold all he or she had to give to the poor, we would not praise a manager who, in order to give to the poor, drove a firm to bankruptcy and thus harmed the shareholders. And even if we acknowledge that firms have the imperfect duty to help the needy or to help society, the degree to which they must do so, the time at which they must do so, and the recipients of that aid all remain indeterminate. To the extent that it is up to the firms to decide how to fulfill their imperfect duties, it is difficult to fault any firm for not doing so, at least in the short run.

Special Obligations

As human beings, we all have the same moral general obligations. In addition, we can have a large variety of special moral obligations. These are general or universal not in the sense that they apply to all persons, but in the sense that they apply to all persons similarly placed. Some of these are obligations that we can avoid. For instance, we all have the general obligation to keep our promises, but unless we make a promise, we are not obliged in any particular way. And if we do make a promise, we are only obliged in the particular way that we promised.

We can divide special obligations into a great many kinds; three are of particular importance. One type is those obligations that come from special relations. A second is those obligations that come from particular actions we perform. A third is those obligations that come from the particular roles we occupy.

Obligations that arise because of special relations, for instance, are familial obligations. Husbands and wives have special obligations—to provide love, fidelity, and care—to each other that they do not have to other people. One can avoid such obligations by avoiding the relationship of marriage. Parents have special obligations with respect to their children that they do not have to other children. In general, parents are obliged to raise and care for their children, providing them with food, shelter, clothing, love, and education to the extent that they are able. One can avoid the obligations of parenthood by not having children. However, children have obligations with respect to their parents and siblings, despite the fact that they did not choose their parents or their siblings. Other obligations similarly come from one's relations to others and may include obligations that come from friendship, love, religion, proximity, shared work, citizenship, or other relationships. For instance, we may be obliged to help those to whom we are related in a way we are not obliged to help others, or we may be obliged to help them first, if we are in a position in which we are forced to choose between their need and the need of those to whom we are not related in any special way.

We have already seen a special obligation we may have because of a particular action we have taken. If we promise to do something for another, then we are in general obliged to do so. If we borrow money and promise to repay it, then we are morally obliged to repay the money as promised. Although by not making promises we can avoid such obligations as those involved in promising, we cannot avoid all special obligations in this way. For instance, we have the obligation to make good the damage we do to others, even if we did not intend to do that damage. If, while driving our car, we hit another car, we are obliged to make good the damage we do to that car, even though we did not intend to hit the car or damage it. Similarly, a firm that harms others must make good that harm. We may also incur obligations of gratitude when people do us a special favor, or go out of their way to help us when we are in need. Hence, obligations of promises, reparations, and gratitude are special obligations.

Obligations that come from roles are especially important in business. Those who accept jobs take on certain roles and are obliged to do those legitimate activities that their role within an organization demands and for which they are paid. The president of a firm has different obligations from the janitor, but each has the responsibility to fulfill the obligations that go with the positions they occupy. Clearly, people occupy a great variety of roles. The president of the United States takes on obligations that the rest of us do not have. They are obligations that go with the position or role of president. If the role we occupy is one that we occupy voluntarily, then we voluntarily take on the obligations that go with that role. Professions carry with them special obligations that members of that profession take on, both individually and collectively. Special obligations do not replace general moral obligations that all people have, but are additional moral obligations that people have because of their relations, actions, or roles or positions. Delineation of the special moral obligations that go with accepting and occupying roles in a firm or in a profession makes up a part of what is called business ethics and professional ethics.

Moral Ideals

Moral ideals and counsels of perfection are goals towards which we can strive. We deserve moral blame when we fail to fulfill our moral obligations. We do not deserve moral blame for failing to go beyond our moral duty, but we deserve no special moral praise either. We deserve moral praise for going beyond our moral duty towards moral ideals. The same is true of counsels of perfection. No human being can be perfect. Hence, we cannot be obliged to be perfect. But we can attempt to do more than simply fulfill our duty. For instance, we can strive to fulfill our potential to the greatest extent possible. How we do this depends on our talent and abilities, as well as on our circumstances.

The notion of moral ideals is important in any ethical theory if we are to make sense of the fact that we recognize some people as doing more than is required and of being moral saints or heroes. Most people recognize in their own lives that they can do more than they are minimally required to do in the way of self-sacrifice, helping others, and giving of their time and their selves— all of which are considered good and moral things to do. Yet we do not fault ourselves or others for falling short of what we could do in these ways.

The degree to which *individuals* in a firm can strive toward implementing moral ideals and can do more than is minimally required by moral rules is at least arguably greater than the degree to which publicly owned *firms* may go. The reason is that the resources of a firm belong to the shareholders, and their use by management for purposes of fulfilling not the moral minimum but some higher moral ideal usually needs some business-related (and not simply moral) justification, if not approval by the shareholders. Nonetheless, this line of reasoning does not imply that individuals and firms in business are not bound at all by imperfect duties or that ideals have no place in business ethics.

Some businesses do go well beyond what is morally demanded and strive towards achieving ideals, whether these are stated in terms of pursuing excellence in their product line or of committing themselves to a no-layoff policy with respect to their employees or of freely choosing to locate in a decaying inner city to help revitalize it. Each of these ideals goes beyond the moral minimum, and companies that act in such ways tend to stand out from the rest, just as do individuals who go well beyond what is morally required.[7] In both cases they become models or examples for others to emulate or follow.

Rights and Justice

Deontologists claim that rights and justice are not derivable from a utilitarian calculation and that they do not depend on weighing the consequences of actions. Giving people what they deserve or what is their due may not be the best use of resources, from the point of view of utility. However, this fact does not lessen their right to what they deserve or change the justice of giving them what they deserve.

Rights

Many social issues and business ethics topics are discussed in terms of rights.[8] *Moral rights are important, normative, justifiable claims or entitlements.* The right to life (or the right not to be killed by others) is a justifiable claim, based on our status as rational beings, worthy of respect, and ends-in-ourselves. Does our status as rational beings confer other rights on us? What are these, and how can they be defended? In the Declaration of Independence the American Founding Fathers spoke of the natural rights of life, liberty, and the pursuit of happiness. The British philosopher John Locke (1632-1704) had earlier spoken of the natural right to property. Today we speak of human rights, rather than natural rights. Some of these are rights vis-à-vis government, some vis-à-vis other people. Legal rights are rooted in law and protected by it. In a just society, moral and legal rights overlap to a considerable degree. Moral rights are rooted in morality and in the nature of the members of the moral community. They can be seen as applications of the second version of the Categorical Imperative, which stresses that human beings are ends in themselves, worthy of respect, and are always to be treated as such. Rights are specifications of important ways human beings are to be treated.

Whether rights can be successfully defended by a utilitarian approach is debated. But whether or not they can, an important aspect of "rights talk" is that basic human rights cannot be overridden simply by considerations of utility. A right can be overridden only by another or by other, more basic rights. The purpose of designating certain claims as human rights is to underline their importance so that they will not be treated merely as one more claim among all those that might enter into a case. If we acknowledge the human right to life, for instance, we are precluded from considering whether to mur-

---

[7] The Business Enterprise Trust, for example, gives annual awards in recognition of both firms and employees who set an example by their outstanding actions in the business world.

[8] For a survey of the literature on rights, see Rex Martin and James Nickel, "Recent Work on the Concept of Rights," *American Philosophical Quarterly,* 19 (1980), pp. 165-180. An important contemporary statement of rights is given by Ronald Dworkin in *Taking Rights Seriously* (Cambridge, Mass.: Harvard University Press, 1978).

der someone so as to produce more good for others. Similarly, if we have a right not to be discriminated against, it would be improper to argue that discrimination against someone produced more good than nondiscrimination and therefore was morally justified. (It is doubtful whether in real life we could ever successfully argue for either murder or discrimination on utilitarian grounds.) Both utilitarians and nonutilitarians acknowledge rights as important claims that should be respected, even if they ground the claims differently.

Rights are sometimes divided into negative and positive. *Negative rights* require others to forbear acting in certain ways and to allow the bearer of the right to act without impediment. The right to life precludes others from killing the bearer of the right. The right to freedom of speech precludes others from preventing one from speaking in the normal circumstances in which speech is appropriate. Negative rights protect an individual from interference both by the government and by other people. *Positive rights,* on the other hand, require either the government or other individuals to provide the bearer of the right with certain positive goods or opportunities. Economic rights are frequently positive rights. The right to subsistence requires not only that the state and others not prevent us from getting what is necessary for subsistence, but also that the state or others provide what is necessary for subsistence if we are unable to do so for ourselves. The right to education requires not only that children not be prevented from going to school, but also that they be provided with schooling by their society. The line between positive and negative rights is not always clear. The state may, for instance, have to take positive measures to protect the negative right of its citizens to life. Because the right to life entails the positive right to subsistence, this is considered by some the right to life in its positive form. Nonetheless, as long as it is not pushed too far or made to bear too much weight, the distinction of positive and negative rights can serve some useful purposes.

Moral rights also carry with them moral obligations. Our right to life, negatively interpreted, for instance, imposes the obligation on all others (including government) not to kill us, and it imposes the positive obligation on government to provide adequate protection against others killing us. It also imposes on others and government the obligation, if necessary and possible, to help keep us alive if we are unable to provide the necessities of life for ourselves. But before we can claim such help, we have the obligation to do what we can to support ourselves. It is only when we are unable to do so that others have the obligation to help us. Thus, our rights impose obligations not only on others to respect our rights but also, at least with respect to economic rights, on us to take appropriate actions and to do what we can for ourselves.

Just as we can speak of obligations being prima facie obligations, so we can speak of human rights as being prima facie. Just as one prima facie obligation may conflict with another and may be overridden, so one prima facie right may conflict with another prima facie right and may be overridden. The right to life of an unjust attacker, for instance, may be overridden by the right to life of the innocent victim, if killing the aggressor is the only way the victim can save his or her own life. In general the right to life is more important than the right to property and, in a conflict, takes precedence. Although it is possible to argue persuasively that some rights are more basic than others, it is not always possible to rank rights or to see clearly which rights take precedence over which other rights in specific cases. Where there is conflict of rights, only careful analysis of the particular case and careful moral argumentation can help us decide.

In the case presented in Victor Hugo's *Les Miserables* Jean Valjean steals a loaf of bread because he is starving and that is the only way he can survive. Was he justified in doing so? The case involves a conflict of rights: the baker's right to his property and Valjean's right to life. Which is to take precedence? How does one argue using rights?

In this case both the right to property and the right to life are widely accepted as moral or human rights. People typically invoke these rights and do not need to justify them, although if pressed, we could derive them from the respect due everyone as ends in themselves (the second version of the Categorical Imperative). Given the two rights, which one takes precedence? Clearly, the right to life is the more important of the two because without life there is no one to need property. But saying that is not enough to justify taking someone else's loaf of bread. For the right to life to take precedence over the right to property in this particular case, we must show that in fact Valjean could not have survived without taking the bread and that the baker was not in a similar situation of needing the bread for survival. If the latter were the case, the baker's right to life would offset Valjean's. Since the baker was not in Valjean's position, that consideration can be put aside. The key question then becomes: Was stealing the bread the only alternative left Valjean? Was there no possible way for him to work to earn either food or the money with which to buy it? Could he have gone to the local church and received food? Were there any public facilities that provided food? If there were any other option, his taking the bread violates the baker's right to property and is stealing. But if there were in fact no other alternatives, and if he would die unless he took the bread, then his right to life overrides the baker's right to property.

The conditions necessary for one right to override another in this case are very stringent, and appropriately so. It is very difficult to override moral or human rights because they are justifiable claims. Part of the purpose of calling them rights is to identify them as important claims that cannot be easily overridden. The point of the story of Jean Valjean is not so much to justify his taking the bread as it is to condemn as unjust a society that makes it impossible for people to exercise their positive right to life by taking part in some activity by which they can sustain their lives. In any decent society that respects people as ends in themselves people are not forced to the extreme alternative of either starving to death or stealing in order to live, while others are well off.

Moral or human rights are not the only kind of rights. Civil rights are legal rights, but typically they apply to citizens and not to all human beings.

The right to vote in the United States, for instance, is a civil right held by citizens of the United States. Some other civil rights, guaranteed by law to citizens, such as the right to freedom of religion, are also human rights. Some workers' rights are moral rights, some are both moral and civil, others are only civil, and still others are neither moral nor civil but granted by one's place of employment. Just as we can speak of special moral obligations that result from our relations, actions, or positions, so we can speak of special rights that come from our relations, actions, or positions. The president and other high-level officers of a corporation, for instance, by virtue of their position, might be given the right to purchase a certain number of the corporation's stock at a favorable price. Such a right is not granted to every employee of the corporation, nor can lower ranking employees of the corporation make a justifiable claim in this respect. But if it is the corporation's policy to grant this right to anyone holding a certain position, then anyone holding such a position can claim that right on the basis of their moral right to equal treatment. Not all special rights are moral rights in any sense—only those are that can be justified on moral grounds.

The language of rights is frequently abused. People have claimed a wide variety of rights. All privileges are not necessarily rights, although they are sometimes called rights. Whether the claim in question can be justified is the crucial question. The way moral rights are justified is by presenting moral arguments of the kind we have seen in this and the preceding chapter.

Justice

Justice, in one of its most general formulations, consists of giving each person his or her due, treating equals equally, and unequals unequally. There are various ways of construing what each person is due, however. Individuals might be given what they are due according to their work, their ability, their merit, their need, and so on. Each criterion might be appropriate for certain purposes and in certain conditions. When the male head of a household was the typical wage earner in society, it was generally considered just to pay him more than a single male or a female for the same work. The rationale was that the male head of the household had more mouths to feed and therefore needed more money. But as the social structure changed and women entered the work force in greater numbers, the just thing to do became to pay people equally for equal work, regardless of their personal obligations to support a family.

There are different kinds of justice. *Compensatory justice* consists in compensating someone for a past injustice or making good some harm he or she has suffered in the past. *Retributive justice* concerns punishment due a lawbreaker or evil-doer. *Procedural justice* is a term used to designate fair-decision procedures, practices, or agreements. *Commutative justice* refers to justice in transactions. *Distributive justice* involves the distribution of benefits and burdens, usually by the state.

Since commutative justice refers to justice in transactions or exchanges, it is of great importance in business. Commutative justice demands that equals be exchanged for equals. Thus goods should be sold for what they are worth. To charge more than they are worth is to gouge the customer and is unjust. For instance, unless regulated or controlled in some way, monopolies, a state of affairs in which there is only one seller, tend to put the seller in a position in which he can take advantage of the need of the buyer and charge considerably more than the product or good or service is worth. Hence unregulated monopolies tend to lead to injustice in the marketplace. Commutative justice calls for just or fair prices, based on the worth of whatever it is that is being sold or exchanged. Yet what something is worth is not always easy to determine and different people from different perspectives might evaluate it differently. In general an exchange or transaction is just or fair if both parties to the transaction

- have access to all the pertinent information about the transaction;
- enter it freely and without any coercion;
- benefit from the transaction.

Competition among suppliers is one way to help prevent coercion and to encourage suppliers to sell at a fair price rather than simply at the highest price the market will bear. If labor or labor power are considered similar to commodities that are bought and sold, then commutative justice governs wages and whether or not a wage is just or fair.

While commutative justice is central to business transactions, distributive justice is central to governmental actions. If a society, composed of people who hold different religious beliefs and who espouse somewhat different moral positions, is to be stable, the government of that society must be perceived by its citizens as acting justly towards all of them. But how can it be so perceived if its members have different and competing views of what justice demands?

The contemporary American philosopher John Rawls[9] has formulated an influential theory of distributive justice, which attempts to answer this question. The technique by which he defends it is Kantian in its approach and might be seen as a way of applying the third version of the Categorical Imperative. He attempts to arrive at principles of distributive justice that are acceptable to all rational persons. The principles would thus be universal, would respect all persons and would be rationally acceptable to all. In order to find

---

[9] John Rawls, *A Theory of Justice* (Cambridge, Mass.: Harvard University Press, 1971). For a succinct, early presentation of his position, see his "Justice as Fairness," *The Philosophical Review*, 57 (1958), pp. 525-533. A collection of critical essays is Norman Daniels (Ed.), *Reading Rawls* (New York: Basic Books, 1975). Rawls's position is frequently contrasted to the libertarian position developed by Robert Nozick, *Anarchy, State, and Utopia* (New York: Basic Books, 1974), which also contains an extended critique of Rawls.

such principles, he suggests we perform a thought experiment. Let us imagine that all people are behind a "veil of ignorance." Behind that veil we would know that we are rational human beings and that we value our own good. But we would not know whether we are rich or poor, members of the upper or lower class, talented or untalented, handicapped or physically and mentally fit, white or black, or a member of some other race, male or female, and so on. This is the question we are to ask ourselves: What principles would we call just or fair if we did not know what place we would have in society? This technique is useful if we wish to achieve objectivity in our moral judgments. It is a technique that we can generalize beyond the way Rawls uses it. It can help us apply the Kantian test of autonomous acceptability to any principle or rule we wish to consider. To determine our answer, however, we must, for those behind the veil of ignorance, sometimes build in more knowledge than Rawls allows in his consideration of the basic principles of justice.

Consider a medical school that wishes to increase the number of minorities it admits. Would it be fair or just to use a dual set of criteria, one for white males and another, less stringent one, for minorities? Let us place all the students interested in entering medical school behind a veil of ignorance, such that they do not know their race or their ability. They know that more applicants wish to enter medical school than there are places and that therefore some method is necessary to decide whom to admit. All would want equal treatment and equal access. They could all accept a system that admitted applicants on the basis of grade point average, MCAT scores, and other stated criteria, providing those in turn were considered fair. If the school previously admitted 100 new students, would candidates behind the veil of ignorance agree to setting aside ten out of a hundred places for minority candidates? Since behind the veil of ignorance no candidate knows what race he or she belongs to, they would have to ask themselves that question from the point of view of each of the different races. If a candidate were to emerge from behind the veil of ignorance and be a member of a minority race, they would have a better chance than otherwise. Hence, from a self-interested point of view they would have no objection to the plan. But if when emerging from behind the veil they happened to be white, then their chance of getting accepted would be reduced by 10 places. Hence, they would have a reason to reject the plan. Since the candidates behind the veil of ignorance do not know whether they will be white or a member of a minority race, and since they assume they will be in the least advantaged position, they would reject the plan. Thus, the plan is not just.

If it is true that the criteria used are not fair to all and that the tests or other criteria are skewed in favor of whites, then those criteria are not just. But correcting them with a system that is also not just is not a proper solution. A fair or just solution is one that all would agree to behind the veil of ignorance.

In essence then, the technique tells us that a practice or program is fair to all affected parties if all parties, considering it rationally and objectively, would agree to it. The veil of ignorance helps us obtain the objectivity required. If the medical school had added 10 places to the entering class and reserved those for minority students, would that be just? We would again have to go behind the veil of ignorance to decide. In this case, since the position of white applicants would be no worse than it was before, and since the position of minority candidates would be better than it was, if one did not know whether the student was white or black, this would be a more advantageous system. Hence, this system, unlike the other, can be defended as just, using this technique.

Although the technique can be used in considering many issues of justice, Rawls uses it specifically to arrive at the basis for distributive justice. Rawls argues that, behind the veil of ignorance, people would agree to two specific principles of distributive justice that they can use in establishing a just constitution. In their simplest formulation in *A Theory of Justice*, Rawls states the two principles as follows:

- First: Each person is to have equal right to the most extensive basic liberty compatible with similar liberty for others.
- Second: Social and economic inequalities are to be arranged so that they are both (a) reasonably expected to be to everyone's advantage and (b) attached to positions and offices open to all.[10]

The first principle guarantees the equal liberty of each person, at a maximal level compatible with the same liberty for everyone else. Individuals want as much freedom as possible to achieve their ends; freedom is a function of rationality, and respect for it is respect for persons. Each person under this rule is to be treated equally. Hence, the first principle fulfills the requirements of the moral law, is morally justifiable, and would be accepted by all rational people. In the political realm, this principle guarantees each person equal political freedom, protection by law, and equal treatment before the law.

The second principle is more controversial. The second part of this principle requires equality of opportunity and access to positions and offices. This is generally accepted. The first part allows for inequalities of wealth and income, influence and prestige. But it claims that such inequalities are acceptable to all only if the least advantaged group is better off as a result of them. For instance, consider the choice between two societies: in Society *A*, all members of the society have a standard of living of 100; in Society *B*, the standard of living of the members of the society varies, ranging from 150 to 200. It would be rational for everyone to choose Society *B*. Although all are not equal in that society—some live better than others—all are better off than in Society *A*. Though the second part of the principle demands equal opportunity, the first part allows for inequalities of success, providing all are better off because of it. The justification for capitalism is sometimes framed in this way. Because

---

[10] Rawls, *A Theory of Justice*, p. 60.

all are free to compete, some fare better than others, but the competition increases productivity, raising everyone's standard of living. Hence, all are better off than they would otherwise be.

The second principle is attacked both by those who claim that the condition is too strong and by those who claim it is too weak. Those who hold the principle is too strong say that as long as there is equal opportunity, there is no injustice in some benefiting from their skill, work, and ingenuity, or from the risks they take. They deserve more than others, and their benefit need not be conditioned by its also producing benefit for the least advantaged group in society. Those who claim the principle is too weak argue that the inequalities allowed may be so great as to be obviously unjust. The principle, they argue, allows the very, very rich to get very much richer as long as the very, very poor get only a little less poor. This, they claim, is unacceptable.

Rawls's principles are meant to be used to determine just basic structures of society. They can also be used to judge whether existing societies are fundamentally just. As principles of distributive justice they do not apply to other kinds of justice. Yet we can use the technique Rawls used to seek principles for those other kinds of justice as well.

Exactly which principles or practices people would agree to behind the veil of ignorance can be, and is, disputed. But there are some principles rational people would agree to, and using the behind-a-veil-of-ignorance technique is useful for choosing principles with detachment and objectivity.

Consider discrimination. If we are faced with the question of whether discrimination in hiring is just, we can step behind a veil of ignorance and ask: If we did not know whether we would be male or female, black or white, would we prefer a system in which there was discrimination on the basis of gender and race or in which there was none? The strategy is as follows: If we were to be assigned our place in society by our worst enemy, would we pick the one or the other system? The point does not hinge on whether we are gamblers and risk-takers; it is whether we would all accept the chosen system or structure as just, prior to knowing which place we occupied in it. If all rational people would accept the system or practice, then it would be just. Clearly, however, if we did not know what sex or race we would belong to, we would not want a system that might discriminate against us. We would prefer one in which there was no discrimination. Hence, a system that involves gender or racial discrimination is unjust. A society in which discrimination is allowed or enforced is unjust in that regard.

In this case, because the issue involves the basic structures of society, if we accepted Rawls's two principles we could also apply them directly, and we would get the same answer. Discrimination violates the second principle of justice. The least advantaged in this case are those who are discriminated against. Since we are the ones who may well be the object of the discrimination, we can see that we would not be advantaged in any way by being discriminated against, nor would we be better off because there is discrimination. We are obviously worse off. Nor are positions open to all. They are closed to those discriminated against. Hence, discrimination, which involves unequal treatment, cannot be justified by the second principle of justice, and discrimination is unjust.

Because Rawls's two principles of justice do not handle all questions of justice, we should not expect more from them than they can supply. The principles, for instance, won't help us decide what constitutes a fair wage, nor what is fair or just with respect to the internal structures of a corporation. A corporation is different from society as such, and treating employees fairly, for instance, does not necessarily mean granting them all the most extensive liberty. Nor does justice necessarily require that inequalities within the firm be handled as they are with respect to society as a whole. Nonetheless, Rawls's theory does suggest an approach to, and provides a framework for, a fruitful social discussion of the justice of economic systems, of various social institutions and of social practices, and the veil of ingorance provides a technique for thinking about a number of issues involving questions of justice or fairness.

We can summarize the general application of rights and justice in Figure 4-2.

Duty (or moral obligation), rights, and justice are common terms that people use in discussing the rightness and wrongness of actions, policies, and economic systems. They are powerful terms, and their use involves powerful claims. Like any moral claims they require justification. Understanding how judgments using these terms can be defended makes it possible for us to take part intelligently and effectively in the discussions about them in our homes, our workplaces, and our public life. Without such understanding we are reduced to simply asserting what we believe in the hope that others might agree with us. Passionate statements of our beliefs do not equal and rarely are an adequate substitute for an articulated defense of them. Mastery of the techniques of moral argumentation—both deontological and utilitarian—provides the key to taking part in the ongoing discussion of ethical issues, including ethical issues in business.

Study Questions

1. Do you think the 1982 Johnson Controls' fetal protection policy was morally justified? Why or why not? Could it be defended on utilitarian grounds? Is there any way for Johnson Controls both to protect fetuses and not violate the right of women to have access to the same jobs as men in the production of its batteries? If so, how?

2. What is a deontological approach to ethics? Do a deontological approach and a utilitarian approach to an issue necessarily yield different results?

3. Are Judeo-Christian ethics deontological or teleological?

4. What is the difference between a theologically based ethics and a philosophically based one? Do they necessarily differ in content? Can you give an example in which they might lead to opposite moral judgments on an action?

```
┌─────────────────────────────────────────────────────────────────────┐
│                                                                       │
│              STEPS OF APPLYING RIGHTS AND JUSTICE                      │
│                                                                       │
│   1. State clearly the moral issue to be resolved and whether it involves claims │
│      of justice or rights.                                            │
│                                                                       │
│   2. In some cases both sorts of consideration are present. If so, can you either │
│      translate the moral norm expressed in rights terms into justice terms or │
│      vice versa? If you can, do so.                                   │
│                                                                       │
│   3. If rights are the dominant consideration, then determine about each right: │
│                                                                       │
│      a. Is it widely accepted and acknowledged as a right? If not, how can it be │
│         defended?                                                     │
│                                                                       │
│      b. Who holds the right and against whom is it exercised in this case? │
│                                                                       │
│      c. What obligation does it impose on the one against whom it is exer- │
│         cised?                                                         │
│                                                                       │
│      d. Is there more than one right present in the case, and if so do they con- │
│         flict?                                                         │
│                                                                       │
│   4. If the rights conflict, determine which is most important and should take │
│      precedence in this case, presenting the reasons for that precedence. │
│                                                                       │
│   5. Having determined the dominant right in the case, is there any reason to │
│      think it might be overridden by other considerations? If so, consider them. │
│      If not, apply the right in question.                             │
│                                                                       │
│   6. If justice is the dominant consideration, determine which kind of justice is │
│      pertinent.                                                        │
│                                                                       │
│   7. If distributive justice or questions about the ordering of society or law are │
│      in question, apply Rawls's two principles.                       │
│                                                                       │
│   8. If other types of justice are at issue, go behind an imaginary veil of igno- │
│      rance and ask whether all affected parties, if they did not know whether │
│      they were on the giving or receiving end of the action (or transaction or │
│      practice) if they were adequately informed with the appropriate informa- │
│      tion, and if they were thinking as rational people, would view the proposed │
│      action as acceptable. If so, the action is thus far just. If not, it is not just. │
│                                                                       │
│   9. Determine whether there are other considerations, consequences, or cir- │
│      cumstances that mitigate or change the application of that judgment. If so, │
│      settle these to determine whether the action is just. If there are none, the │
│      previous conclusion stands.                                      │
│                                                                       │
└─────────────────────────────────────────────────────────────────────┘
```

Figure 4-2

5. According to the Kantian tradition, what is the relation of reason and morality?

6. Why is the Kantian approach to ethics called formal?

7. What are three characteristics of the moral law insofar as it is the statement of the form of a rational action?

8. What is a categorical imperative? a hypothetical imperative?

9. What are the three Kantian formulations, in Kant's words, of the Categorical Imperative? Restate them in your own words.

10. What does it mean to say moral actions or rules are universalizable? Does this mean that everyone will in fact do the action in question? Explain.

11. How do immoral actions violate respect for persons?

12. What does autonomy mean with respect to morality?

13. How can one test whether an action is moral by using the Categorical Imperative? Illustrate by using an original example.

14. What is a prima facie moral rule? What is the relation between a prima facie obligation and an actual obligation in a given situation?

15. Distinguish perfect from imperfect duties and give an example of each.

16. Distinguish three kinds of special obligations and give an example of each.

17. What function do moral ideals play in morality? Explain.

18. What is a moral right? Give an example of one.

19. How are moral rights justified?

20. When moral rights clash, how does one decide between them?

21. What is the relation of moral rights and moral obligations?

22. Distinguish compensatory justice from retributive justice and from distributive justice. With which do Rawls's principles primarily deal?

23. What does Rawls mean by a veil of ignorance? What purpose does it serve? Illustrate how the technique might be used in solving an issue of justice.

24. State accurately Rawls's two principles of justice. How can they be applied? Illustrate by applying them to a case of your choosing.

5

>—:—‹›—•○•—‹›—:—‹

Moral Responsibility, Virtue, and Moral Reasoning

The Love Canal Case

In the 1890s William J. Love decided to build a canal in the area of Niagara Falls to help provide energy for a city he planned.[1] The project was never completed, but a trench 10 blocks long dug out of clay remained as testimony to the effort. In the 1940s Hooker Electrochemical Company (now Hooker Chemical and Plastics Corporation and part of Occidental Petroleum Company) started legally using the canal to dispose of drums of toxic waste and buried about 22,000 tons of such waste by 1952. Various federal government agencies also dumped chemicals into the canal. The Niagara Falls Board of Education became interested in the land and wished to purchase it from Hooker. According to the company's executive vice-president, Bruce D. Davis, "We did not want to sell them the land."[2] But when the board threatened legal action to have the land condemned, Hooker sold the land for $1, warning the board and stating in the deed of sale that toxic waste was buried there and that the land should be used only as a park and not for a school or housing. Nonetheless, the board proceeded to build a school on the land, transferring title to the city of Niagara Falls, and sold what it did not need to a developer. The school was built, as were houses and roads, evidently without much con-

---

[1] For details of the case, see *Business Week,* August 28, 1978, p. 32; *New York Times Magazine,* January 21, 1979, pp. 23 ff; *Christian Science Monitor,* August 17, 1990, p. 7; *New York Times,* May 15, 1990, pp. B1, 4; and Peter Neushul, "Love Canal: A Historical Review," *Mid-America,* 69 (October 1987), pp. 125-138.

[2] *Business Week,* p. 32.

cern for the buried waste. The walls of the canal were punctured by city workers for sewer lines, and some of the protective topsoil placed by Hooker to seal
the waste was removed during the grading process to provide access to the
school. In the 1970s after heavy rains, evidence showed that the drums had
leaked. Chemical ooze sprang up in the school yard and seeped through home
basements and up sump pumps. The number of deaths in the area increased,
and the number of cases of cancer and birth defects was abnormally high. In
1978 the government declared the area unsafe. Two hundred houses were
demolished. On May 21, 1980, President Carter declared a state of emergency
at Love Canal and 2,500 people were relocated. The state and federal governments spent $150 million in cleaning up the area and additional millions in
buying up the houses that were destroyed. Representatives of Occidental continued to claim that they had no control over the development of the land
since Hooker sold it, that Hooker did not hide the fact that toxic chemicals
were buried there, that Hooker only sold the land when in effect forced to by
the Board of Education, and that Hooker warned against building on the site.

In August 1990 the Environmental Protection Agency declared much of
the area around the canal habitable, and people started buying houses there.
Despite some individual settlements, suits were still pending, including one in
the New York courts to decide whether Occidental should be held liable for
the cleanup costs. In 1998 Occidental agreed to pay $250,000 to the city to be
used for parks, and the case was finally settled.

With knowledge of this much of the case, do you hold Hooker Electrochemical Company (and/or Occidental Petroleum) morally responsible for
the ill effects of the waste Hooker buried? Should either be held liable for the
costs? If, as Hooker claimed, it warned the Board of Education about the dangers of the waste and sold the land reluctantly and under legal duress, were
the city and the Board of Education, which built the school and resold some of
the land, responsible for the harm done to the people adversely affected?

In order to discuss the case, the facts are crucial. In addition, we must clarify
what we mean by responsibility and liability and how these are imputed or
ascribed.

Moral Responsibility

Responsibility and obligation are closely related. In general, we have an obligation or a duty to fulfill our responsibilities, and we are responsible for fulfilling our obligations. Yet duty and responsibility are not the same.

There are many kinds of responsibility. Parents are responsible for their
children—for raising them, feeding them, and caring for them. Hence, we
speak of parental responsibility. There are responsibilities of citizenship—the

responsibility that goes with public office and positions of trust. Certain responsibilities also go with one's job and with one's place in an organization. Some of these responsibilities are legal responsibilities, and some are moral responsibilities; some are both, some are neither.

In a general sense each of us is responsible for all of his or her actions.[3] For instance, if I drop and break a friend's expensive vase, I am responsible for having broken it. If, while I am driving a car, a child suddenly dashes out in front of me and I hit him before I can apply the brake, I am responsible for having hit him. In neither case may I be morally responsible; yet if someone asks who broke the vase or who hit the child, the answer is that I am responsible. In what sense am I responsible? I am *causally responsible* in each case. I was the cause of the broken vase, and I was the cause of the injured child.

Causal responsibility is an ingredient in both moral and legal responsibility. The causal chain sometimes is a long one. If I give a command and a number of people transmit that command until it is finally carried out, both the ones who carry out the action and I (the one issuing the command) are responsible for it, though each is responsible in a different way in the causal chain. Usually, we are most concerned with the proximate cause in the chain, with the person doing the action in question. Yet, especially in questions of agency, the originator of the chain also bears responsibility for the action.

For an action to be a moral action it must be done knowingly and willingly. For instance, though I am causally responsible for things I do in my sleep, I am not morally responsible for them. Actions I do in my sleep are neither moral nor immoral. When we say that I am *morally responsible* for an action, then, we mean

- that I did the action (i.e., I am the cause of the result of the action)
- that I did the action knowingly and
- that I did the action willingly.

Instead of saying that I did the action knowingly and willingly, we might say that I did it intentionally. The important point is that I was not forced to do it, that I had a choice, that I knew what I was doing, and that I did it deliberately. I can also be morally responsible for *failing* to do what I was morally obliged to do; but here too my failure must be intentional. A person who assumes his or her responsibilities is frequently called a responsible person, and such people are said to act responsibly. There are degrees of knowledge and degrees of deliberation; there are, accordingly, degrees of moral responsibility also.

---

[3]There is a large literature on responsibility. Two useful collections of articles are John M. Fischer (Ed.), *Moral Responsibility* (Ithaca, N.Y.: Cornell University Press, 1986), and Ferdinand Schoeman (Ed.), *Responsibility, Character, and the Emotions* (Cambridge: Cambridge University Press, 1987).

Excusing Conditions

Moral responsibility may be lessened or mitigated in a number of ways. The conditions that diminish moral responsibility are known as *excusing conditions*. These conditions provide the reasons for lessening or canceling moral responsibility, and they are related in one way or another to the conditions necessary for a moral action. Excusing conditions fall into one of three categories: those conditions that preclude the possibility of the action, those conditions that preclude or diminish the required knowledge, and those conditions that preclude or diminish the required freedom.

Conditions Precluding the Possibility of Action

To be morally obligatory, an action must be possible. We do not have an obligation to do what is impossible. Similarly, we cannot be morally responsible for doing what is impossible. We are relieved of moral responsibility in those cases in which we cannot do what is demanded of us. The impossibility of doing an action may be a function of the type of action in question, of particular circumstances, or of lack of ability. We are excused from moral responsibility if (a) the action in question is an impossible one to perform, (b) we do not have the ability required in the given case, (c) the opportunity for our performing the action is absent, or (d) the circumstances are beyond our control. For instance, assuming that I had been driving carefully, with due attention and observing the speed limit (i.e., assuming that I had been driving responsibly), I am not morally responsible for running over the child who darts in front of my car if it was impossible for me to stop the car before hitting him. If I do not know how to swim, I cannot be morally responsible for letting someone drown if the only way I could possibly have saved him was by swimming out to him. Nor, if I knew how to swim, could I have the moral responsibility for saving him if I were not at the scene of the drowning and if there was no reason why I should have been there. Similarly, if, as I swam out to him, he was attacked and killed by a shark, that is a circumstance beyond my control, and it excuses me from moral responsibility for his death. These are just four examples of excusing conditions related to the possibility of performing the action.

Conditions Precluding or Diminishing Required Knowledge

Because knowledge and will are necessary for moral actions, moral responsibility is lessened or removed when these aspects are less than fully present or when they are entirely absent. With respect to knowledge, we can distinguish two excusing conditions: (a) *excusable ignorance* and (b) *invincible ignorance*. Both are failures of knowledge. We are morally responsible for our actions and for the consequences of the things we do. But we cannot possibly know all the consequences of our actions. Which ones are we morally responsible for?

We are morally responsible for the immediate and obvious consequences of our actions, as well as for the other reasonably foreseeable consequences of them. Our lack of knowledge may be either about the circumstances giving rise to a particular responsibility or about the consequences of our actions. Lack of knowledge is excusable if through no fault of our own we did not know the circumstances or the consequences. Ignorance, however, does not excuse us from moral responsibility if we could have and should have known of the circumstances or consequences. A common test of whether ignorance is *excusable* is whether the average person of goodwill would have known the circumstances or considered the possibility of the consequences in question. *Invincible* ignorance, or ignorance that we cannot overcome and for which we have no blame, is an excusing condition because we cannot be expected to know what it is impossible for us to know. Before people knew that asbestos was a health hazard, those who installed it in houses could not know, given the state of knowledge at the time, that it was dangerous; hence, they were not morally responsible for the then-unforeseeable harmful consequences of its use. Once knowledge of the harmfulness of asbestos emerged, those who continued to use it until it became illegal to do so could not claim excusable ignorance, since they could have and should have known of the harm it would cause.

Is everyone who was involved in the production of the atom bomb responsible for it and for the uses to which it has been and might be put? The atom bomb was developed in the United States in such a way that many people did not know what they were working on. Different people were responsible for working on different portions of its development, frequently without any knowledge of the nature of the project as a whole. Many people working in laboratories were responsible for only particular portions of the bomb. They were told that their work was secret and that they would not know the type of end product to which their work was contributing. In many cases they had assurances that what they were working on would help the United States win World War II. Though we can say they were partially responsible for producing the atom bomb in a causal sense, they were not responsible in a moral sense. Adequate knowledge was lacking, and its absence was morally acceptable. What about the leaders of the project? Should we hold the scientists who developed the atom bomb responsible for its use? Could they reasonably have foreseen the uses to which it would be put? They certainly knew that once developed it could be used to destroy both cities and the people in them. Assume that during World War II use of the bomb might have been legitimate. But suppose tomorrow some country that has developed the bomb uses it to attack and destroy a neighboring country, or uses it as a means of extortion. Were the scientists who originally developed the bomb responsible for its immoral use by others later on? Could they and should they have foreseen such uses? These questions are not easy to answer. Many scientists have pondered their moral responsibility in this area. We can say that those who were ignorant of the nature of the project are free of moral responsibility for its production. We can also say with some confidence that no one could have foreseen all the uses to which the development of atom bombs would be put. The moral responsibility for the use of these weapons in immoral ways is much greater for those who decide to use them immorally than for those who originally developed them. We do not hold those who invented gunpowder morally responsible for all the harm that has been done with it, most of which they could not possibly have imagined. The degree of moral responsibility is a function of our knowledge, and an absence of knowledge may diminish or remove our moral responsibility.

Conditions Precluding or Diminishing Required Freedom

The third set of excusing conditions has to do with impairments or impediments to our freely choosing the action in question. We can distinguish four: (a) the absence of alternatives, (b) lack of control, (c) external coercion, and (d) internal coercion.

(a) If there is only one possible action that I can perform, and there are really no other alternatives, not even that of nonperformance of the action, I cannot be said to have chosen the action, though I may or may not consent to it. By extension, if there is no reasonable alternative to the action that I perform, then my moral responsibility for it is lessened.

(b) Lack of control extends to a number of different kinds of cases. In some instances, it removes all moral responsibility; in others, it diminishes it. For instance, actions that I do in my sleep are actions over which I have no control and for which I am not morally responsible. Similarly, if I faint, and in the process knock over a lamp, which starts a fire, I am not morally responsible for starting the fire.

(c) External coercion or compulsion either diminishes moral responsibility or removes it, depending on the coercion and the alternatives. If I am a bank teller and a bank robber puts a gun to my head and tells me to hand over the money in my cash drawer, I give him the money under compulsion, and I am not morally responsible for giving away the bank's money. There are various more subtle kinds of compulsion, however, which pose difficult problems. Suppose my boss tells me to falsify a report and also tells me that unless I do so, I shall be fired. Suppose, further, that I am deeply in debt because of the illness of my wife, and that I am unlikely to be able to find another job that pays as well as this one. Because of the coercion applied by my superior, am I morally relieved of my responsibility not to falsify documents? The details of the case must be examined more fully before we can answer the question satisfactorily. But even with this sketchy information, if I do sign, as commanded, I am less morally guilty than if I had falsified the documents without any outside compulsion. External compulsion may involve the use of physical force, the threat of death or violence to one's self or to others, or the threat, or use, of other kinds of pressures. Not all such pressures constitute excusing conditions. The kind and degree of external compulsion must be carefully considered, and the criterion of what the ordinary reasonable person of goodwill would expect and demand of himself or herself is the best we sometimes have to work with.

(d) Internal compulsions can be divided into two kinds. One is the clinically abnormal, and the other is the normal. Let us suppose that a kleptomaniac is forced to steal because of some inner compulsion over which he has no control. If he is actually forced to steal, and has no choice, he is not morally responsible for his action. Other abnormal psychological conditions that drive a person to do what he does diminish his responsibility. Normal people are also sometimes overcome by passions that they say they cannot, or could not, control, such as sorrow or rage, lust or hate. Each person is morally obliged to control his passions and dominate them. But possibly there are cases in which, through no fault of the person in question, passions dominate him and lead him to perform some immoral action. Such internal compulsion provides an excusing condition and mitigates the agent's moral responsibility. The law also recognizes such conditions as excusing to some extent; for instance, a murder of passion is treated as a less serious crime than a premeditated murder.

Excusing conditions supply reasonable ways for lessening or precluding moral responsibility. But they must be used with care if we wish to assess accurately our own and others' moral responsibility. For instance, if I drive recklessly and I run over a child, does the fact that I was drunk lessen my moral responsibility for hitting the child? If I got drunk knowingly and willingly, the answer is no. For, although in my drunken state I had less control over the car than I would have had otherwise, and although, in a sense, I could not help hitting the child, I should have foreseen, when I decided to both drink and drive, that one of the possible consequences might be such an accident. I am morally responsible for the foreseeable results of my actions. How far people are expected to foresee the results of their actions in business, and to foresee the use to which their products might be put, is not always an easy question to answer. Many engineers and scientists have, appropriately, worried about the possible bad uses to which their research, discoveries, and inventions might be put. They are responsible for the products they create, even though they will not control the uses to which they are put. The problem of how much moral responsibility a manufacturer has for the use to which his product is put is a similar question. If a handgun is used to kill a shopkeeper during a robbery, the gunman is responsible for the death. Are the person who sold him the gun, the company that manufactured the gun, and the person who designed the gun also responsible? How far back do we go in the causal chain? What about the steel company that provided the metal to the gun maker, and the iron ore company that provided the iron to the steel maker? Obviously, the further back we go, the more remote the cause and the less likely that the person could have reasonably foreseen a particular consequence or could reasonably be held responsible. The drug thalidomide caused a large number of birth deformities, and many parents sued the manufacturer.

We assume that the doctors who prescribed the drug did so in ignorance of the drug's bad consequences; the druggists who sold it and the women who took it were also ignorant of them. If they acted in invincible ignorance, they are absolved of moral blame. Whether the drug company could have and should have known of the bad effects is a question we cannot answer without detailed investigation, even though the company was liable for the effects of the drug.

The doctrine of excusing conditions is used by some people in a way that removes moral responsibility entirely for certain immoral acts, or entirely removes moral responsibility from everyone. In defense of those accused of murder, for instance, some argue that anyone who commits a murder must be at least temporarily insane. They are not responsible for their actions because they did not know what they were doing, or they had no control over their actions. Others, who believe that people are completely determined in all their actions, sometimes argue that all of us act from internal compulsions, and, because of the nature of these compulsions, we never really choose between actions. According to this view, we are compelled to do whatever actions we perform; our feeling of choice is an illusion; and we are truly compelled to do whatever we do, just as the kleptomaniac is compelled to steal. Such a view does not take adequate account of our common human experience and of our ability to distinguish between acts of the kleptomaniac and acts of purposeful stealing. Such distinctions are sufficient to sort out different kinds of cases, varying degrees of consent and knowledge, and hence, varying degrees of moral responsibility.

Liability and Accountability

Moral responsibility is closely connected to several other concepts besides duty and obligation, possibility, knowledge, freedom, and choice. These include liability, accountability, agency, praise, blame, intention, pride, shame, remorse, conscience, and character. *Liability* for one's actions means that one can rightly be made to pay for the adverse effects of one's actions on others. Automobile liability insurance for drivers, for instance, is intended to cover the costs of damage to other persons or property. We are liable for such payments as long as we are causally responsible for the damage. If we accidentally run into another car, we do not do so intentionally, yet we are liable for the damage we do. Liability, therefore, does not necessarily involve moral responsibility for the action. We may be morally (as well as legally) liable to make good the damage we do to others, even if we are not morally responsible for the action. In many cases, however, the excusing conditions that apply to moral responsibility also apply to moral liability. We may be liable to punishment, blame, or censure for an action we do knowingly and willingly, but not for similar consequences that we produce unwittingly or accidentally.

Legal liability can be fitted into a similar pattern of analysis with respect to individuals. Businesses, however, are often bound by laws of strict liability. *Strict liability means that no excusing conditions are accepted or applicable.* For instance, several people recently died of food poisoning. The cause was botulism that developed in cans of seafood that had tiny holes in the can covers. The packer did not intend to poison anyone, and no one intentionally punctured the can covers. Yet, under rules of strict liability, the packer was held legally liable and was successfully sued for damages by the relatives of those killed. Corporations are formed, among other reasons, to limit the liability of owners or shareholders to the amount represented by their shares. The personal assets of the shareholders are not liable to seizure. The extent to which strict liability should be applied to corporations for damage done by misuse of their products is a controversial topic. Should the manufacturer of a single-control shower faucet be liable if someone turns on only the hot water and gets scalded? The Fifth U.S. Court of Appeals upheld a jury's affirmative answer, even though this seems counter to common sense. The debate about liability concerns where the line should be drawn when assigning strict liability.

Accountability is the obligation of giving (or of being prepared, if called upon to give) an account of our actions. The account should explain the reasonableness, appropriateness, correctness, legality, or morality of the action. Accountability might be moral or legal. We are accountable for our actions and the consequences thereof. We are accountable to ourselves, and we are properly accountable to others for actions that affect them. An agent acting for others is also accountable for the actions, and failures to act, with respect to the domain covered by his or her agency. Financial accounting is one familiar way in which an agent justifies or accounts for his or her actions with respect to a business.

Moral accountability consists in being prepared to render a moral account of an action done either for ourselves or as agents for others. We appropriately give an account of those things for which we are responsible. A moral account of our actions is not always given explicitly in moral terms. For instance, we might give an account in financial terms, through a financial report in which we list income and expenditures (which we justify if called on to do so). The report is an account of our handling of the funds, on the assumption that it is accurate, contains all income and expenditures, and balances properly.

Within a firm or organization, moral accountability may be structured or unstructured. Organizational accountability is frequently structured hierarchically, with those below accountable to those above, but not vice versa. Moral accountability is not determined only by organizational structure, however. Each person is morally accountable to those whom his or her actions affect and only rarely will a person be called to account, for most actions fall within an acceptable range. They need no special justification because they form part of the large class of generally acceptable actions.

We are morally responsible in the sense of being liable, and in the sense of being accountable for our actions and failures to act. Broadly speaking, we are morally responsible for all our actions; more narrowly, we are responsible for fulfilling our obligations. We are responsible to ourselves, because we are rational agents and follow the moral law. Hence, we appropriately hold ourselves morally responsible, and if we wish to be moral we appropriately *assume* (in the sense of accept) moral responsibility. We may also take on particular moral responsibilities as a result of contracts, agreements, special relationships, or prior commitments, or when we occupy certain positions. If we act immorally, we appropriately feel *moral guilt*. When we act immorally we do not act in accordance with our true ends, and, appropriately, we feel *moral shame*. *Moral remorse* is the feeling of sorrow for our immoral actions, together with an intention not to perform similar actions in the future. These emotions result from self-evaluation, whether or not prompted by the evaluation of others.

Because we all belong to the moral community, we can also *ascribe* moral responsibility to others; we hold them morally liable and appropriately demand a moral accounting of their actions insofar as they affect us, the organization or group to which we jointly belong, or society as a whole. Although we can ascribe moral responsibility, it may not be assumed by the one to whom we ascribe it, and he or she may not agree to render an account. We can ascribe moral praise and blame for the actions of others and attempt to induce moral guilt, shame, or remorse.

Conscience is the ability to reason about the morality of an action, together with a set of values, feelings, and dispositions to do or to avoid doing certain actions. Conscience is something that every rational being has, insofar as he or she is rational. But we can act against our conscience and stifle it, just as we can act in accordance with it. Though we give ourselves the moral law, we are all fallible, and so conscience must be informed, developed, trained, and corrected. We are morally obliged to act in accordance with our conscience; but we are equally obliged to develop an objectively correct conscience.

Failure to fulfill one's responsibilities sometimes leads not only to blame, shame, and remorse but also to punishment. We are liable to punishment if we do certain actions and are not able to provide any sufficient excusing conditions. The threat of punishment is a means of motivating people to act morally and responsibly, and to accept their responsibility. Yet justice demands that punishment be meted out only to those responsible for the actions in question. The innocent, or those not responsible for actions, should not be punished for them. Those who are more responsible deserve more punishment than those who are less responsible. Diminished responsibility because of excusing conditions rightfully diminishes the severity of the punishment appropriate for an action.

Agent and Role Moral Responsibility

We saw earlier that the causal chain in an action may sometimes be a long one. If one person acts for another person, we can often correctly say that the second person is acting as an agent for the first person. We can, accordingly, speak of *agent responsibility.* Such responsibility is frequently found in business; it is often complex, and it raises a number of special types of problems.

Consider first the simple case of agency, in which one person acts for another. A lawyer draws up a contract for a client. He acts as agent for the client and does what the client wants done but is unable to do himself. The lawyer draws up the kind of contract the client wants, with the provisions he desires. The client is morally responsible for the contents of the contract, because they represent his desires. The lawyer is simply an agent for the client. But the lawyer has a moral responsibility for his actions, which he cannot dismiss simply because he acts as an agent for another. He cannot morally do what is immoral simply because he acts for another.

In a large organization the chain of agency frequently involves many people who are hierarchically related to one another. This raises problems of moral responsibility, both for those at the top and for those lower down the chain.

Suppose the president of a corporation tells his vice-president that costs have to be cut in a certain division of the corporation. He does not say how or where the cuts are to be made; he leaves that up to the vice-president. The vice-president, in turn, decides that the cuts have to come from a certain section of his operation and tells the manager below him that certain cuts have to be made. This continues until finally, at the end of the line, corners are cut, endangering people's lives. Those near the end of the line feel that they are forced to do what they do. They have received their orders, and the options open to them are limited. They may not have wanted to cut the corners that they cut; they feel that the responsibility for their actions belongs to those above them. They did not initiate the action or the practice; they are just following orders. The president of the company does not see the specific results of the order he gave to the vice-president because he is far removed from its concrete implementation. He feels that those below him should be given the authority to make decisions, and, as long as they perform well, he does not feel he should second-guess them. He did not intend to cause the particular dangers to which people at the receiving end might be exposed. He did not intend that anything immoral or unjust take place. Those at the bottom claim they had no other choice and were simply following orders; they did not initiate the policy and so are not responsible for its effects. Hence, at both ends of the chain, the people involved feel that the actions are actions for which they are not morally responsible.

The absence of the *feeling* of moral responsibility, however, does not indicate an absence of moral responsibility. The delegation of authority to carry out a command or policy does not relieve the delegator of the moral responsibility for how the command or policy is carried out. We are morally responsible both for our actions and for the foreseeable consequences thereof. The diminished feeling of moral responsibility is psychologically understandable, but it is not therefore excusing. Similarly, those near the bottom of the chain may find themselves forced to do what they, on their own, would not choose to do. They may wish to deny moral responsibility for their actions and feel that they are not morally responsible for them. Yet they remain moral agents and so cannot deny moral responsibility for their actions.

Agent moral responsibility, especially in large organizations, poses a variety of problems, some of which we shall investigate in later chapters.

Closely related to agent moral responsibility, and often overlapping it, is *role responsibility*. Role responsibility is usually a corollary of assuming a certain position, function, or role in society or in an organization, or by becoming a member of a certain profession, class, or group that assumes special obligations. Not everyone has the obligations of a parent, but when individuals become parents they take on the obligations of that position or role. They are responsible for their children in a way that others are not. Similarly, when one assumes a position in a firm, that person takes on the responsibility of performing the functions and tasks of that position. The president of a corporation takes on the responsibility of acting as president of the firm. Managers take on the responsibility of doing the job for which they were hired, as do all other workers. In each case one is expected to subordinate one's own desires and wishes to the requirements of the role that one fills. An individual in a position within a corporation should properly distinguish between his responsibility and that of the corporation. He should distinguish between his goals and those of the corporation; and he should not inappropriately substitute the one for the other. Typically, a firm generates rules that are to govern the tasks done by the various members of the firm and that outline one's function and tasks within the firm. The more specific and inclusive the set of rules, the less discretion employees have in their work. In general, we can say that a person fulfills his moral obligations to his employer by following the rules and carrying out the tasks that go with his role or position. In doing so he acts impersonally, in the sense that he does what is prescribed by the position, or what he is ordered to do by those above him. "I followed the rules," or, "I did what I was told," are perfectly acceptable defenses for someone called to account for his actions in a rule-governed position, unless the rule requires one to act immorally or if one is commanded to do what is immoral. For although each person has the moral obligation to fulfill the tasks for which he is hired, the assumption must be that the task is not itself immoral. Those who establish roles or give orders are morally responsible for the tasks assigned each role or position and for the orders they give. But this does not excuse those who hold roles from the immorality of actions they commit in fulfilling those roles.

Members of a profession and of certain groups (e.g., religious groups) frequently take on special moral obligations of the profession or group. Because of the special training and knowledge a doctor has, for example, a doctor has a greater obligation to help the injured in an emergency than does the ordinary person. As a member of a profession with a role in society, moreover, the doctor shares in the responsibility of the medical profession to care for the health of the members of the society and to help see that the other members of the medical profession, and the profession as a whole, live up to their responsibilities. When professionals such as doctors, lawyers, or engineers accept roles in organizations, they carry with them their professional role responsibility in addition to their role responsibility within the firm. Such dual-role responsibility should pose no moral problems because role responsibilities are always subordinate to general moral responsibility. We can never justifiably do in a role what is immoral. But not all of our responsibilities in a role are moral responsibilities, and loyalty to one's role in a firm may conflict with one's loyalty to one's profession, or to one's role as a family member. If there is a clash of moral responsibilities, it must be resolved in the same way that clashes of comparable prima facie obligations are resolved.

Virtue

Until now we have focused primarily on actions and their evaluation, and we have seen how to use standard techniques of moral reasoning to determine which actions are ethically permissible, which are prohibited, and which are mandatory. We noted earlier that moral discourse and evaluation are not limited to actions. We speak not only of good and bad, right and wrong, moral and immoral actions, but also of good and bad, moral and immoral people. We have also seen that by extension we speak of good and bad, moral and immoral corporations, formal organizations, social and economic systems, and countries. What is the relation of our analysis of actions to evaluations of people and of character?

Persons—Virtues

In recent years a number of philosophers have argued for a virtue-based moral theory, in addition to or instead of the deontological and utilitarian approaches we have seen so far.[4] They typically harken back to and take their inspiration from the ancient Greek philosopher Aristotle.[5] Whatever position one takes on that debate, it remains a fact that people do meaningfully evaluate actions, and that there are many actions—such as murder, stealing, and lying—that are prima facie wrong. Yet there is a good deal to learn from an Aristotelian approach to ethics that we can add to what we have already seen.

Aristotle's analysis of the moral life emphasizes the importance of judgment, of virtue and of character. Each deserves a closer look.

Although actions can be characterized as in general or prima facie right or wrong, good or bad, moral or immoral, situations are often complex and

---

[4] See, for instance, Alasdair MacIntyre, *After Virtue* (Notre Dame: University of Notre Dame Press, 1981).

[5] Aristotle, *Nicomachean Ethics,* translated by Terence Irwin (Indianapolis: Hackett Publishing Company, 1985).

there are often borderline cases. Murder is wrong, but is this particular instance of killing murder or self-defense or involuntary homicide or should it be characterized in some other way? There are no general rules that we can apply to tell us the correct characterization. Borderline cases are borderline because the general rule may or may not apply. In such cases a decision must be made. Yet the decision should not be arbitrary. There should be some good reason for making it, and the decision should be defensible to others. The art of making good or sound decisions involves the exercise of judgment. Sound judgment comes from careful deliberation, experience, and a well-developed moral sense. One must be sensitive to moral nuances and weigh competing moral claims. Some people's moral judgment is better than that of others. Yet everyone who faces moral problems must make moral judgments to the best of their ability. Those who emphasize virtue argue that moral rules do not solve real moral problems because they must always be applied, and any application requires judgment, which cannot be automatic, and which requires a virtuous person to make the judgment correctly.[6]

What then is virtue, and what constitutes a virtuous person? Aristotle's theory of virtue has been extremely influential in answering these questions, even though societies differ somewhat on the traits they value as virtues. He starts with the notion of goodness with respect to some end. For instance, what makes a person a good flute player is the ability to play the flute well. That is an excellence in the performance of a specific kind of activity. Similarly, what makes a good person is one who excels in the activity of leading a truly human life. The characteristics that make for living such a life are what he calls the virtues.

Aristotle divided virtues into two basic kinds, which he called the intellectual virtues and the moral virtues. The intellectual virtues, the highest of which was wisdom, resulted from the proper functioning of the higher or intellectual aspects of human beings. Since human beings are, for Aristotle, rational animals, what distinguishes them from other animals is their reason. Hence, the proper functioning of reason constitutes the highest excellence human beings can achieve, and, for him, wisdom is the highest virtue.

The moral virtues, on the other hand, come about from the proper control by reason of the bodily appetites and inclinations. These appetites and inclinations are natural, and to that extent they are normal and appropriate for human beings. Yet they must be controlled, because if they are not they can lead to excess to the detriment of the individual or of others in the society. The proper control of the passions and appetites typically consists in neither repressing them completely nor in allowing them free reign. Rather one should seek the mean between extremes. Thus, although we all have a natural inclination to eat and drink, we should control both by reason. The happy

---

[6] See, Edmund L. Pincoffs, *Quandries and Virtues* (Lawrence: University Press of Kansas, 1986).

mean with respect to eating is to avoid gluttony on the one hand, and to avoid starving oneself on the other. With respect to intoxicating drinks, the mean is between drunkenness and abstemiousness. In the face of danger, courage is the mean between foolhardiness and cowardice. In each case, although we seek the mean between the extremes, which are vices, we exercise prudence in recognizing our inclinations and when necessary dragging ourselves further away from the extreme to which we are prone.

To the general moral virtues, moreover, we can add the characteristics that make for excellence in any human endeavor for the virtues proper to that endeavor. For Aristotle, moreover, we are not only rational beings but also social beings, and our end of happiness or fulfillment or of excellence is always found within the context of our society. The virtues are not only individual ways of achieving excellence and happiness as human beings, but they are always socially beneficial as well, and as such are socially recognized. The virtues are skills of excellence in the art of living in society with others.

We are not born virtuous. We become virtuous by practice. Only when our actions become habitual and we have the disposition to exercise the proper mean do we have the virtue in question. In the face of temptation to act as we ought not, the virtuous person has his or her habitual way of acting to fall back on to resist the temptation. The honest person is habitually honest and can resist the temptation to steal when it arises, even if he will profit from the dishonesty without fear of being caught.

These dispositions, when viewed collectively, are sometimes called *character*. The character of a person is the sum of his or her virtues and vices. A person who habitually tends to act as he morally should has a good character. If he resists strong temptation, he has a strong character. If he habitually acts immorally, he has a morally bad character. If despite good intentions he frequently succumbs to temptation, he has a weak character. Because character is formed by conscious actions, in general people are morally responsible for their characters as well as for their individual actions.

This account of virtue and of what constitutes a virtuous person is not at odds with an account of what makes actions right or wrong, or with claiming that actions are right or wrong because of certain reasons. An honest person is one who habitually refrains from stealing; a truthful one is one who habitually refrains from lying; a person of moral integrity is one who habitually does what he or she believes is right. The moral evaluation of persons is not the same as the moral evaluation of actions. But they are related. Good people are good because they do what they ought. If they stole and cheated and murdered, they would not be good or virtuous people.

For Aristotle, good or virtuous people do not simply emerge or develop on their own. Children must be raised and taught what virtue is from virtuous people. They are taught by example, by stories, by moral models; they are raised in a tradition and presented with heroes, historical or mythical; they need a society in which the virtues are held in esteem, and in which virtuous persons respected and looked up to. Aristotle described his society and the virtues of that society.

Although Aristotle's fourth-century B.C. city-state of Athens is not the society in which we live, much of what Aristotle wrote about ethics and virtue is applicable to societies today. And, the virtue theorist claims, this tends to be forgotten if we put our emphasis exclusively on rules and laws. We tend to gravitate towards a legalistic approach to ethical thinking, instead of seeing it as simply a way of leading excellent human lives and thereby fulfilling our potential as human beings and achieving the happiness that comes from such excellence and fulfillment. To the extent that it is forgotten, society and the individuals in it will be diminished.

A somewhat similar position is taken by those who argue that the standard approaches to ethics, which put emphasis on rules and impartiality, are defective because they fail to account for the virtue or disposition of caring, or for close relationships, or for the moral obligation to be partial, rather than impartial, to one's family and close friends.[7] To the extent that these have been ignored, the criticism is well taken. It is widely acknowledged that justice is appropriately at times tempered with mercy; and surely everyone knows that we do and should treat members of our families and our close friends differently from the way we treat strangers. Within the family justice has a place, in that the members should treat each other fairly and with respect. But love is or should be the dominant consideration and motivator. We can universalize this to a general rule. Yet love is not guided by rules. The sacrifices that members of a family make for one another go beyond rules and strict obligations. That parents give preference to their children rather than to children they do not know is expected. It is because this is a commonplace that in cases where justice is required those with close ties to another are not considered objective judges. In a family business nepotism or favoritism for the members of one's family is expected; in a publicly owned firm, nepotism is usually considered inappropriate because it undermines the fairness to all that is the expected norm.

None of this implies that we cannot or should not evaluate actions from a moral point of view, although it does caution us that such evaluation does not constitute all of morality.

Systems and Organizations—Responsibility and Virtue

Some authors have recently applied the Aristotlean approach of virtue to business.[8] They tend to emphasize the need for the virtues in business and develop the notion of business as a human endeavor in which people ought to

---

[7] See Carol Gilligan, *In A Different Voice: Psychological Theory and Women's Development* (Cambridge: Harvard University Press, 1982); and Nel Noddings, *Caring: A Feminine Approach to Ethics and Moral Education* (Berkeley: University of California Press, 1984).

[8] See, among others, Robert C. Solomon, *Ethics and Excellence: Cooperation and Integrity in Business* (New York: Oxford University Press, 1992); and Thomas V. Morris, *If Aristotle Ran General Motors* (New York: Henry Holt & Co., 1997).

find fulfillment. Corporations are where many people spend most of their adult life. If they are to achieve happiness and develop as full human beings, they should be able to do so at work as well as in other areas of their lives. Personal integrity, moreover, requires that they not compartmentalize their lives but that they live the values in which they believe and that they exercise the virtues of human life in all the aspects of their lives. Furthermore, as we have seen, Aristotle emphasized the social nature of the virtues. This refers not only to the societal context as a whole but it can also be interpreted as referring to what is commonly called corporate culture. Just as society reinforces and helps individuals develop the virtues, so can and should corporate cultures. To the extent that they do not, they fall short of the excellence they can achieve and they can be faulted. The virtue approach to business is a valuable reminder that business is part of human life and so part of moral life.

Whether we speak in Aristotelian or Kantian or other terms, the language of ethics and morality has human beings as its primary referent. It is human beings who are moral or immoral, it is human beings who act ethically or unethically, and it is human beings who are virtuous or vicious. Nonetheless, we use moral terms to describe economic and political systems, we use them to characterize corporations and other organizations, and we use them to evaluate their actions. As we use these terms, however, we should be conscious of the fact that many of the terms cannot and so do not mean the same thing when applied to persons and when applied to systems or organizations. People are ends in themselves; societies and organizations are not. People have human rights; societies and organizations, since they are not human beings, do not have human rights. Moral responsibility for human beings requires that they act knowingly and willingly. The attribution of knowledge and will to society or to organizations obviously must be interpreted differently from what they mean for individual human persons.

We shall examine the moral status of economic systems and of corporations in later chapters. But there are two observations we can make at this stage. The first is that people are the center of ethics, and the ethical analysis of systems and organizations will always in the end hinge on how people are affected. The second is that while systems and organizations are created by people, each individual is born into an already existing society that contains an economic, political, and social system, and a variety of organizations, all of which affect the individual.

To the question of whether we need moral laws and moral social and business structures or whether we need moral people, the answer is that we need both. Structures and laws that are immoral encourage people to act immorally, while structures and laws that are moral encourage people to act morally. A good, in the sense of moral, society or organization or business is good because of both its good structures and the good people who make it up. Moral people are needed to create and sustain moral structures. The two reinforce each other. Yet clearly if structures are immoral or if they reinforce and reward unethical activity, then they can only be changed by people who recognize them as such and have the power, ability, and will to change them. In this sense ethical people are necessary for ethical societies, organizations and corporations.

Applying Moral Reasoning

We are both responsible for our actions and responsible and accountable to others for what we do that affects them. Whether we evaluate our own actions, whether others evaluate our actions, or whether we evaluate the actions of others, the techniques of moral evaluation are the same. Although it is true that we know our own motives in a way that others do not, insofar as our actions are public, they are open to public evaluation. Although it is also true that we should develop and exercise the various virtues, we develop them by acting appropriately. Part of that involves knowing which actions are in general right and which are wrong, and acting accordingly.

Actions—Solving Moral Problems

Some people prefer to use a deontological approach to the ethical evaluation of actions, others prefer a utilitarian approach, and still others use both. Whatever basic approach we choose, we must understand both if we are to take part intelligently in discussions of ethical issues in business as well in other areas of life, if we wish to evaluate and perhaps refute those with whom we disagree, and if we wish to justify the positions we hold.

Philosophers disagree about the ultimate satisfactory foundation for ethics, and about whether there is one. Yet, despite many claims to the contrary, there is no conclusive argument that either deontological or utilitarian approaches to ethics are irremediably defective. Moreover, we can fruitfully distinguish the dispute about which is most fundamental from the usefulness of the methods each espouses. Thus, even if utilitarianism is not the ultimate ethical principle, that does not mean that utilitarian reasoning has no place in ethical thinking. The same can be said of Kant's categorical imperative. The argument against using both utilitarian and deontological approaches together is that in some cases they tend to yield differing results. When this is so, it is claimed, one must know how to choose between them and hence which takes precedence over the other. Giving preference to one approach over another is one way to resolve the difficulty. But some who use both approaches deny that one or the other approach must always take precedence, and they are content to resolve such disputes, if and when they arise, on the basis of the best arguments given in that particular case. Sometimes one approach may win out as most reasonable and appropriate, sometimes the other, and sometimes there may simply be no clear way to decide.

In spite of differences and unresolved fundamental problems, the philosophical debates have yielded more than some critics realize. Both deontological and utilitarian approaches to moral issues have been developed and honed, partially as a result of controversies about them, so as to provide powerful and widely used techniques of moral argumentation. The debates in business ethics—whether on the level of individual action, corporate practice, or public policy—that take place on the job, in the newspapers, and in the business, philosophical, and popular literature are couched primarily in terms of consequences (or utility), rights, justice, and duty. The philosophical debates on ethical theory have sharpened the conceptual tools that people in general use in those debates, have made us aware of the pitfalls and shortcomings of each approach, and have helped clarify some of the issues involved, for instance, in addressing questions related to discrimination. Moreover, all ethical theories start from widely accepted moral beliefs about which actions are right and which wrong; and to the extent that different philosophical approaches have justified such beliefs and second-order moral rules, the rules become that much more secure.

For most practical issues of business ethics, we need not resolve all the philosophical disputes between the utilitarians and the deontologists. Despite the fact that the approaches differ, in the great majority of cases either method, if carefully, subtly, and conscientiously applied, will produce the same moral conclusions with respect to the morality of the practice or act.

How, then, are we to solve practical moral problems in business? The answer is that we must use all the techniques of moral analysis and argumentation at our command. In attempting to solve any case, we must first get the facts of the case clear and try to ascertain all the relevant facts. If we cannot get all the relevant facts, then we must see what plausible assumptions we can make about the missing facts and acknowledge that these are assumptions. Any conclusions we reach in such a case will be conditional. That is, the conclusions will be sound only if the assumptions are correct.

Once we have the facts straight, we should try to ascertain as clearly as possible what the moral issue or problem is. If there are several moral issues, we should try to sort them out, distinguishing clearly which is central and which secondary or more peripheral. Whenever possible, it is best to try to solve one issue at a time.

We should then ask ourselves which moral rules seem to apply. If the case is fairly obvious (for example, if it involves stealing, lying, falsification of information, or directly harming others), then the direct application of ordinary moral values will probably suffice. Our response may be intuitive. If we are careful to make sure that our response is justified and that we have no reason to believe that the given case constitutes a valid exception to the general rule, the question may be thus directly answered. If the issue cannot be easily and directly resolved, we must decide which more detailed ethical approach is most appropriate.

Sometimes the issues or problems are initially stated in terms of consequences, justice, rights, or duty, and the very statement of the problem or case suggests the approach to take. If actual or threatened harm is involved and we are dealing with harmful consequences, we are almost naturally led to ask what the possible positive consequences are that we should consider. Nonetheless, before carrying out a utilitarian analysis, we should also ask whether anyone's rights are being threatened or violated and whether there is an issue of justice involved. If dealing with a case that seems to involve rights, we can still appropriately ask whether there are also consequences that have to be taken into account. Sometimes one approach is easier to apply than another, or yields clearer results. Some people prefer one approach to another. There is no procedure or algorithm that we can automatically apply and rest assured that it will produce a satisfactory solution. Solving moral issues requires a certain amount of practical common sense, some informed judgment, goodwill, and the application of the variety of techniques of moral analysis and argumentation that we have at our disposal.

After due consideration, if the case seems to be most amenable to a utilitarian approach, then that is how to proceed. We proceed similarly with respect to the various deontological approaches. After we have used whichever approach we apply in the given case, it is helpful to ask ourselves whether someone carefully and objectively using other approaches would come out with a different solution. If so, can we give persuasive reasons for our solution being preferable? Very frequently, as we have already stated, different approaches will yield the same moral judgments. When different approaches lead to different moral evaluations or to conflicting judgments, care should be taken to review the accuracy and completeness of each analysis. If the conclusions still diverge, we must ultimately decide on the basis of which argument is stronger or clearer, and which result coheres better with our other moral judgments. If forced to act, we should do so with the realization that we may be mistaken.

In addition to standard techniques, sometimes, in attempting to solve a moral issue, we can try to argue by analogy. Is this case like some other case in which the solution is clear? If so, what are the relevant differences? How much difference do they make, and how do we handle them? If the issue is complex, we might try seeing how we would solve a similar but somewhat less complicated case. Does that solution throw light on how to argue in the present case? Imagination is a necessary ingredient in solving cases. We should avoid settling too quickly on what seems to be an insoluble dilemma. Rather than accepting the situation as posing a dilemma, see if approaching the case imaginatively produces solutions. Often, going beyond the obvious alternatives means simply talking to those whom we perhaps mistakenly assume will act a certain way or will refuse to listen to reasonable alternatives.

In approaching problems in business we should remember that issues arise on three levels—the individual, the corporate, and the national or systemic. Sometimes a solution to what seems like an individual's dilemma is to be sought on the corporate level, or vice versa. We should also remember that moral rules provide a moral minimum. Is the question we are asking one that involves not a moral minimum but a moral ideal? If so, how much is actually required, how much is permitted, and how much is morally precluded?

STEPS OF A GENERAL MORAL ANALYSIS

1. Get all the facts about the case.

2. Determine the ethical issue or issues to be resolved.

3. Use your moral imagination to consider the possible alternatives.

4. Determine all those affected by the action who should be considered in your analysis.

5. Determine whether the action you are now contemplating is morally required or whether it constitutes an ideal toward which you aspire. If the latter, the action is good but not required.

6. If required, in the most promising alternative(s) does some clear prima facie obligation apply, such as don't kill or steal or lie? If so, apply it.

7. Is there still an ethical issue? If no, act appropriately. If yes, go to step 8.

8. If there are two or more prima facie obligations that apply and they conflict, does one clearly take preference? If so, act on it. If not, go to step 9.

9. Does the case or practice or issue lend itself more clearly and obviously to a utilitarian analysis or to a deontological approach of duties, rights, or justice? Use the approach that applies most clearly or obviously.

10. After using that approach, determine whether considerations of consequences, duty, justice, or rights that were not used in 9 are pertinent and should be added to the analysis. If yes, do so.

11. Consider how someone who disagreed with your analysis might argue for the opposite moral conclusion. Note that the objection might be made using a different approach from the one you used in Step 9. Adjust your conclusion if you discover some error or oversight in your previous analysis; otherwise, reply to the objection and show why the objector's analysis is mistaken or deficient.

12. Is the action you have now arrived at one that lives up to your sense of moral integrity, that exemplifies moral virtue, and that would be chosen by someone whom you consider a moral model? If no, reconsider until you find an alternative that does.

13. Determine whether you would be comfortable if your acting as you presently contemplate were made public. If not, determine why and how to reconcile the discomfort with the analysis. If you would be comfortable, act accordingly.

Figure 5-1

Once we have arrived at our moral judgment and decided how we should act, we can ask ourselves how comfortable we are with the judgment and the decision. Do they cohere with our other values and beliefs, with our conception of the good moral life, and our view of the virtues? How comfortable would we be if we described the action we are taking to our friends or family, or if our taking that action were printed in the newspaper? Our reactions to such questions are not the ultimate test of the morality of our actions, but sometimes they are a good place both to start and to end. If we are considering acting contrary to our moral feelings or intuitions, we should be clear why, and we should be careful that we are not rationalizing improper behavior.

We can sum up the steps of a general moral analysis in Figure 5-1. (p. 129)

The process of moral reasoning is a continuous individual and social endeavor, applicable to business as to all other spheres of life. Many of the ethical issues in business are complicated, bear careful consideration, and are not easily resolved. The remaining chapters in this book will describe and illustrate ethical reasoning. Sometimes one technique will be used, sometimes another, and sometimes several. The intent of the chapters is not to force conclusions or to champion a particular ethical approach or point of view, but to represent some of the standard arguments relevant to the issues that are discussed and to demonstrate ethical reasoning in practice.

Study Questions

1. In the Love Canal case, distinguish the various kinds of responsibility involved and present your analysis of who bears which kind of responsibility and the extent of that responsibility.
2. What is causal responsibility? moral responsibility? Give examples of each, showing the difference between them.
3. What in general are excusing conditions? Into what three categories do they fall? Why are they excusing?
4. What is meant by excusable ignorance? invincible ignorance? Give an original example of each.
5. What is liability? strict liability? accountability? moral accountability?
6. What is meant by agent responsibility? Who has agent responsibility, and how does one get this kind of responsibility?
7. Can moral responsibility be delegated? Why or why not?
8. What is role responsibility? Give an example of such responsibility. How does one get such responsibility?
9. What is the role of judgment in making moral decisions?
10. What is a virtue?
11. Distinguish intellectual virtues from moral virtues.
12. What is the doctrine of the mean?
13. What is meant by character?
14. What is the difference between using moral language with respect to people and with respect to corporations?
15. Can a business be said to have a moral character, to be virtuous, or to be held to a moral ideal beyond the moral minimum prescribed by moral

rules? Explain both what you mean by your answer and the reasons for your answer.

16. What are the steps of a general moral analysis of an action?

17. You are a section manager with sixty employees under you. You do not consider any of them below average. Some have been with the firm a long time. Others are recent hires, either women or minority employees hired in an attempt to rectify past discriminatory hiring practices. You have just received a directive that due to financial difficulties you (and all other section managers) must cut your section by 10 percent. How do you go about deciding a morally justifiable way to implement this directive?

MORAL ISSUES
IN BUSINESS

6

>-·-‹›-·-O-·-‹›-·-‹

JUSTICE AND ECONOMIC SYSTEMS

The Case of the Two Slaveholders

Consider the case of two neighboring slaveholders in the American South before the Civil War. The first slaveholder, Jack Good, treats his slaves reasonably well. He knows them by name, provides them with adequate shelter, and does not beat them unless they break the rules he sets. Although he works them hard, they have some leisure time. None of his slaves has ever attempted to run away. On the whole, they consider themselves lucky to have Mr. Good as their owner. The second slaveholder, Simon L., is very different. He gives his slaves swill to eat, does not worry about their shelter, and makes them work sixteen hours a day. He is capricious in his dealings with them, arbitrary in the punishment he metes out, and surly in his attitude towards them. He is not above beating them for the slightest infringement of his rules. He relentlessly pursues his runaway slaves and makes an example of them with the severest of floggings.

Of the two slaveholders, which is the more moral?

>-·-‹›-·-O-·-‹›-·-‹

The temptation to call the first slaveholder the more moral is a strong one, because clearly he is kinder, fairer, and more just in his dealings with his slaves. By contrast, Simon L. is cruel in his punishments and unfair in his dealing with his slaves. Within the system of slavery, we can and do make judgments of fairness and justice, and making such judgments is intelligible and makes sense.

Nonetheless, to call either slaveholder moral has an odd ring to it. If holding slaves is immoral (that is, if it is wrong to own other human beings and hence to fail to recognize them as ends in themselves), then there is a fundamental injustice in the practice. A slaveholder's treating his slaves kindly is better than his treating them unkindly, but such treatment does not justify, or make up for, his engaging in slavery. Both slaveholders are involved in an immoral practice, even if one is kinder than another. Perhaps neither of the slaveholders believes slavery is immoral. That may be true. But their believing slavery is morally permissible does not make it objectively right. It is immoral whether or not, subjectively speaking, they believe it is.

Now, we can approach our own society in a similar way. Consider two employers. One discriminates against women and blacks, does not care about the safety of his employees, pays them subsistence wages, and replaces them as they wear out, just as he would replace his machines. The other employer does not discriminate, introduces safety devices where possible, pays his employees well above the subsistence level, and has a retirement plan. Which of the two is more moral? The answer is obvious and simple. But we can ask the question that we do not often ask: Are the employers in our system comparable to the slaveholders in the slave system? Is something wrong with the economic system in the United States today, just as there was something wrong with the economic system in the Southern United States before the Civil War? The fact that most of us do not feel that there is anything wrong with the wage system or with the economic system in general says something about us, although it does not necessarily say anything about the morality of the system in which we live. But is our system moral? We struggle with the questions of whether reverse discrimination is the proper way to make up for past discrimination, whether whistle blowing is morally defensible, and whether advertising aimed at small children takes unfair advantage of them, but are we questioning the morality of practices within a system when we should be questioning the system itself? Is the system basically just?

Moral Evaluation of Economic Systems

Usually we speak of people or of actions being moral or immoral. Can we also describe an economic system as immoral? The answer seems to be clearly yes, because the overwhelming majority of Americans—as well as most other people—would readily admit that slavery is immoral. And slavery constitutes an economic system. Yet we would do well to look a little more closely at the question and at our answer.

In characterizing the system of slavery as immoral, we use the term *slavery* in two different senses. In the first sense we mean the practice of slavery. This defines a relation between people and a way of treating people. We can analyze both the relation and the actions that follow as a result of the relation. In the second sense, by slavery we mean that economic system in which the slave relation is the fundamental productive relation. Because it is fundamental, we characterize the system by that relation. The system would not be that particular system if that relation were not present in a fundamental, constitutive way. If, for instance, we had an economic system that was basically capitalist or socialist, but a few people within the system had slaves, we could say that the practice of slavery was immoral. But that would not mean that the system within which it was found was immoral, because slavery was not a fundamental or defining relation of the system.

We can evaluate the economic system of slavery in two different ways. One involves evaluating the morality of the fundamental economic relation on which it is built, and by extension analyzing the actions that follow as a result of that relation. This is a *structural analysis*. It involves looking at the basic structures and practices of the system, because the system is defined by its structures and practices. These are necessarily seen as relations among people, and as practices that involve transactions among people. Are these fair and just?

The second way of evaluating economic systems is an *end-state* approach. It involves looking at what the system as a whole does to the people affected by it. Does the system help them fulfill themselves and realize their potential as moral beings? Does adoption of the system produce a kind of human society that exemplifies or fulfills the moral aspirations of human beings? Both the structural and the end-state evaluations may be made from either the utilitarian or the deontological point of view.

Consider the economic system of slavery. We define it as a system in which the fundamental productive relation is the owning of one human being, the slave, by another, the master. The slave works for the master and produces the basic goods needed by the society. These include the food that the members of the society eat, the clothes they wear, the utensils they use, the tools they employ, the buildings they inhabit, and whatever else is necessary for their way of life. The masters may produce art, literature, philosophy, or other human products that typically require leisure and time for reflection. The slave not only works for the master but also belongs to the master, as property belongs to a property-owner. The slave, insofar as he is a slave, is not considered a person with rights, or worthy of moral consideration. He or she is an object to be used, much as animals are objects to be used. The primary function of slaves is work, even if slaves may not be used for work but for other purposes, just as the primary function of work animals is work, though some may be kept as pets, for breeding, or for other purposes.

As we have described it, this fundamental productive relation may be defined and circumscribed by law. But it is the economic, not the legal relation that is the center of our concern. We can look at the moral quality of the relation itself. We can also morally evaluate the actions that usually follow as a result of the relation.

First, let us consider the moral quality of the relation itself. Is it a moral relation? The obvious answer, from the deontological point of view, is clearly that it is not. The relation denies that the slave is an end in himself, worthy of respect. The maxim implied in the relation—namely, "Treat human beings who have the status of slaves as possessions"—is in direct opposition to the second formulation of the Categorical Imperative, which requires that we treat all rational beings as ends in themselves, not only as means. If we were to go behind a veil of ignorance, not knowing whether we would end up as a slave or as a master when we emerged, and if we wished to protect ourselves in case we were assigned our place by our worst enemy, would we choose a slave society or one in which all were free? Clearly, we would choose the latter. Slavery violates the first principle of justice, as developed by John Rawls, and hence, according to that criterion, it is unjust. A utilitarian approach would require that we examine the results of actions, and not only relations. Yet even from the utilitarian point of view it does not take much imagination to realize that the status of the slaves is such as to cause them great harm, regardless of how well they are treated.[1] They will necessarily suffer loss of dignity in their status as slaves—a loss for which they cannot be compensated, even by kind treatment. Because a slave society is one in which the slaves dominate numerically, the pain they suffer as a result of their status is enormous, and clearly greater than the pleasure or good of the slaveholders. In general, therefore, the relation in itself has a tendency to produce, in those affected by it, more harm than good.

Second, let us consider the actions that follow as a result of the slave relation. Are they moral or immoral? The answer, of course, depends on which actions we choose to evaluate. The productive work of the slave is not immoral, nor, necessarily, is the giving of commands by the master. But work and giving commands are not peculiar to slavery. Are there actions that follow from slavery as such? We need not deny that slaves might be treated kindly by masters. But if in all ways they were treated by masters as masters treat free persons, then we would not in fact have the practice of slavery. The actions we must morally evaluate are those in which masters treat their slaves as property, as animals, as beings who are not ends in themselves. The analysis from both the deontological point of view and the utilitarian point of view would parallel the ones we just gave, except that the utilitarian analysis would include actions, the results of which we could evaluate. And the results would be similar. The conclusions we can draw are that the practice of slavery is immoral and that an economic system that is dependent on the practice of slavery is inherently immoral. It cannot be made moral without changing the fundamental practice of the slavery on which it is based. A slave system might be more tolerable to the slaves in one society than in another, and one master might be kinder to his slaves than another, but neither of these considerations changes the moral character of slavery.

The results are similar if we take an end-state approach to slavery. The deontological evaluation will not differ significantly from the previous analy-

---

[1] For a good discussion of the immorality of slavery from a utilitarian point of view, see R. M. Hare, "What Is Wrong with Slavery," *Philosophy and Public Affairs,* 8 (1979), pp. 103-121.

sis. Slavery will still exist, and because that is the central ingredient in the system, the system remains immoral. But might slavery be only prima facie immoral? Might it be unjust but preferable to the other real alternatives? From the utilitarian perspective, might it not be possible that the results of adopting slavery are actually better than adopting some other system?

Suppose that as a result of a worldwide nuclear war the population of the world is decimated. The great majority of those who survive have been affected by radiation poisoning of a type that affects their brains, making them dull-witted and devoid of initiative. There are a few lucky people who were shielded by lead walls in bank vaults or who were deep underground. When they emerge and assess the situation they realize that if the human race is to survive, they must reproduce. Meanwhile, they cannot handle all of their needs. But the masses can be corralled and forced to work. In being so forced, they will each be better off than they would otherwise be, because the alternative is that they would die. By being forced to work, they will both keep themselves alive and keep alive those who have the capacity to develop the human race again. Hence, the fortunate few institute what we call slavery. They argue that all the people in the society will be better off with slavery than any of them would be without it; the alternative is death for all. Therefore, though slavery is prima facie immoral, when compared with the even worse alternative of the extinction of humankind and the dreadful suffering those who die would go through, it is the lesser of two evils and so morally justifiable.

What are we to say of the argument? The first reply is that it is a flight of fancy—a philosopher's puzzle, not a real state of affairs. Morality, we can insist, is concerned with real alternatives. We have little basis for judging what might be right or wrong in the conditions described, which are far beyond our ordinary experience. But we need not stop with this reply. Take the example on its merits: It states that the people affected by the radiation are dull-witted and without initiative, and if left alone would die. How dull-witted are they? Can they think enough to consider consequences? Are they rational and able to decide between alternatives? Do they have a desire to live, and do they see life as worthwhile? How can we explain the fact that they can be forced to work under slavery but not otherwise? How can the claim be defended that there is really no other alternative? Who decided that? The example makes too many vague and dubious claims. It concludes, if all the claims are admitted, that slavery, though prima facie immoral, is the least of the possible evils and therefore morally justifiable. Given our knowledge of human history, it is difficult to believe that there are really no other alternatives; that the few who become the masters do so for the good of all; and that the slaves are better off than they would be if some other means of impelling them to action were employed. Nor is there much reason to think that the system of slavery, once adopted, would not tend to degenerate, that people would be treated worse instead of better, and that, as the practice continued, the masters would be more and more reluctant to give up slavery. Because it is speculative, we cannot settle the argument. But we should not be forced to admit more than is plausible.

History might provide a better example. We know that, as a great many societies emerged from primitive tribal conditions, they developed slavery. The great pillars of Western civilization, Greece and Rome, were built on slavery. If slavery was historically necessary for us to emerge to the state of society in which each person is free, was not ancient slavery justified by its necessity, as well as by its results?

It is very difficult to settle counterfactual issues. How can we know what other alternative to slavery was available in early Greece and Rome, and what would have happened had slavery not developed? To say that slavery was a reality in ancient societies is not to say that it was unthinkable that there be ancient society without slavery. To claim it was historically necessary is to make an ambiguous claim. Certainly it was not logically necessary. It may have developed because of a natural inclination on the part of some people to dominate, or because of the weakness of others in comparison with the strength of the few, or because of the desire for luxury or ease on the part of those who would be masters, or for any number of other reasons. None of these is a justification for slavery, although in a sense they provide an explanation of why and how it arose. Historical necessity, if it is taken to mean simply that whatever happened historically happened necessarily, renders everything moral. More accurately, it renders everything morally neutral— because if everything that happened happened necessarily, then one of the conditions for morality is denied, namely, the possibility of choosing freely. If Hitler's murder of millions of Jews in our century was historically necessary simply because it happened, then we can justify anything. The result would be that there is no basis for evaluating anything, and all we can do is state what happened.

The other historical rationale is to claim that slavery was necessary, but only up to a certain time; thereafter, it was no longer necessary and should have been given up. According to this argument, slavery in the United States was not necessary. Humankind had found ways to organize society productively without slavery. It was an anachronism, which was finally uprooted by the Civil War. But ancient slavery, the argument contends, was a step on the road to feudalism, which in turn led to the development of the world as we know it. We could not have developed our productive capacities unless we had gone through the stage of slavery. Hence, it was justifiable then, even though it is not justifiable now.

Even if this argument is taken to be a type of utilitarian argument, it still remains questionable. The central issue is whether there was no real alternative to ancient slavery. How that claim can be substantiated is the crux of the issue. We can concede that *if* there actually was no better alternative, then slavery was justifiable as the least bad of bad alternatives; but this is different from accepting the claim that actually there was no alternative available.

Whatever our conclusion about ancient slavery, we can be certain that in today's world slavery is immoral. Clearly, there are alternatives, and there is no justification for choosing an immoral system when moral systems are available.

We can generalize on the basis of our analysis, however. Because we have been able to argue conclusively that slavery is immoral, and that today it is an immoral alternative, we have shown that it is possible, at least in the case of slavery, to give a moral evaluation of an economic system. We have seen how the question of the morality of economic systems can in general be approached and how specific arguments can be advanced. What of contemporary systems?

Moral Evaluation of Contemporary Systems

In considering slavery we discussed an economically homogeneous economic system, characterized by the dominant productive relation of master and slave. We did not investigate the kind of political system to which it was joined. The political system of the Greek city-states was different from that of the Roman Empire, and both systems were different from the political system of ancient Egypt. But whatever the political system, it could not make up for the immorality of slavery, nor was there any way that slavery could be changed internally so as to be moral and still be slavery.

The moral status of contemporary economic systems is not so easily settled. It is tempting to think simplistically about capitalism. But we should remember the differences between nineteenth-century capitalism in England and capitalism as it exists in the United States today. If we consider contemporary capitalism, we should consider its structure not only in the United States but also in other countries, such as Japan and South Africa. In the latter case until recently it was joined with apartheid, a radical form of racial segregation and discrimination; in the former two it is not. In Japan, capitalism is joined with a kind of paternalism absent from its American counterpart. All socialistic systems are not identical either. Socialism in China is closely linked with a centralized and dominant Communist party. In England, socialism was mixed with a democratic form of government. Capitalism and socialism in each case are changed to some extent by the kinds of political systems and structures within which they operate. Moreover, pure capitalism and pure socialism do not exist in any country. Every country has something of a mixed economic system, though some can be characterized as more clearly capitalistic and others as more clearly socialistic.

Because apartheid was present in South Africa but not in the United States, it was not a constituent of capitalism. It was something added to capitalism, an ingredient in a particular kind of capitalism. Socialism in the USSR, under Stalin, existed together with totalitarianism, but socialism in England was not totalitarian. Hence, totalitarianism is not a necessary part of socialism. Though economic and political systems are intertwined, we can distinguish them to a considerable degree for purposes of analysis. The way in which any specific contemporary economic system actually works, however, cannot realistically be separated from a consideration of the political and legal systems with which it is found. Some of the moral deficiencies of an economic system, for instance, might be compensated for by the political system. Conversely, the political system might interfere in an immoral way with the workings of the economic system.

For purposes of analysis, let us briefly consider capitalism and socialism as economic systems, floating free from any particular political system. The analytic technique useful for this purpose is the construction of a model. We can develop a model of capitalism and a model of socialism, and we can then investigate the models to determine their necessary components. Once we have isolated the necessary components, we can evaluate them from a moral point of view. If we find any structural immoral elements, then we can see if we can change those elements and still retain a system that we wish to call capitalism. If we do not find any structurally immoral elements, we can see if adoption of the system would result in an end-state product we would describe as either moral or morally neutral. We can do the same with socialism. The conclusions we reach as a result of this analysis will pertain only to the model. Then we need to see to what degree, if any, the model is actually instantiated in any really existing society. Obviously, we are interested in models that bear some relation to existing societies. To the extent that we find the model defective or deficient from a moral point of view, we should see whether it can be made moral while retaining its basic structure. If this is not possible, then the system is inherently immoral. If we find such a system in a particular country, the appropriate approach is to replace the system with a moral one. Whether that can be done while retaining the existing form of government is a question we cannot decide without investigating particular cases. Such replacement frequently involves a drastic and dramatic social change, usually called a revolution, whether it be violent or peaceful.

Economic Models and Games

Some people consider economics a kind of game. By pursuing the analogy to games, we can see some of its strengths and weaknesses. Consider chess. To play chess you need a chess board and a number of pieces of a certain kind. The pieces can be considered to constitute two sides or two armies. Each side has a king and a queen, two knights, two bishops, two rooks, and eight pawns. Is the game fair? One obvious reply is that it is fair because both sides have the same number and kind of pieces, and both sides are bound by the same rules. But this is evaluating the fairness of the game from the point of view of the players. What if we looked at it from the point of view of a pawn? Think of the pawn standing in front of the queen. In the game, the queen can make many different kinds of moves, but the pawn moves one square at a time. Is that fair? The reply is that it is inappropriate to look at the game of chess from the point of view of the pieces. If you want to play chess, then you must follow the rules of the game. Fairness consists in following the rules, not in changing the possible moves.

If you prefer equality, you might prefer the game called Chinese checkers. In it all sides have the same number of marbles. All the marbles are of equal value, and all can make the same moves. Therefore, there is equality among the marbles as well as fairness for the players.

Consider now the game of economics. In one system we have slaves and masters. In another we have rich owners of industry and factory workers. In another we have commissars and workers. If each one of these is considered a type of game, with its own rules, we can describe how each operates. If each, taken as a whole, were considered a model, we could describe it in detail. We could talk of the place and role of each person in the economy. We could describe how prices rise and fall; how supply meets or fails to meet demand, and what this does to prices; what happens when taxes are increased, when the money supply is diminished, or when interest rates are raised; and how full employment might be achieved. We could describe all this with some precision, in our model, and possibly we could predict with some certainty the reactions of certain parts of the economy to certain actions in other parts of it.

According to this approach, economics is not something we evaluate morally. It is a game. Chinese checkers is one game and chess another. But it is silly to try to say that one is more moral than another. The rules are different; the players are different. Chess is more complicated and interesting because of the different kinds of pieces and moves allowable. Chinese checkers is less complicated; all the pieces are equal, and playing the game is comparatively dull. Some people prefer chess because of the skill it requires; others prefer Chinese checkers because of its simplicity. Similarly, some people feel that a free-enterprise system is more challenging and interesting than a system of radical equality. From an economic point of view, different systems can be described; the laws or rules governing the variables within the systems can be detailed. Each can be modeled. But models are not moral or immoral, just as most games are neither moral nor immoral.

Though economics might be considered a game, economic systems when actually implemented are not games. Frequently, economics is studied as if it had nothing to do with people, as if it was simply the study of abstract concepts, such as supply and demand, money, price, and profits. Ultimately, however, economic systems are ways in which people are related. Their relations are mediated by money and commodities, by prices and wages, by supply and demand. And all of these relations, in the end, are descriptions of how people interact. Their lives are shaped and seriously affected by the system in which they find themselves, and by the rules according to which that system operates. Hence, economic systems are not, ultimately, morally neutral; they should be closely examined from a moral point of view. A chess piece is not a person. But a soldier fighting for a king is a moral being, an end in himself, and not simply a pawn to be used. We can therefore plausibly evaluate an economic system by an end-state evaluation, as well as by an analysis of the fairness, justice, or morality of its structures and operative rules. What is interesting in the analogy with games, however, is that we consider them fair when all players start out equally and abide by the same rules. We allow one to win and the others to lose. In fact, that is the object of the game. Do we feel the same about the game of life? Should all start out the same and abide by the same rules? If they do, is it right that some win and some lose?

A Capitalist Model

A model may not correspond to any social reality. A model of capitalism may also not correspond to any economy existing in a society. But a model can help us get conceptual clarity on some issues.

Capitalism, in its long history, has gone through a number of phases and stages. What is called classical capitalism is a model that is frequently both attacked and defended. It does not exist in its pure form anywhere in the world today and may never have represented an actual economy, yet its main features are commonly used and understood.

Most economic systems produce and exchange commodities, use money as a medium of exchange, and pay labor. What are the specific defining features of the model of classical capitalism? We shall consider three that are necessary to it. Although each of the three features may be found in other kinds of economic systems, it is the combination of the three that makes the model different from other models. The three are an available accumulation of industrial capital, private ownership of the means of production, and a free-market system.

Available Accumulation of Industrial Capital

Capitalism derives its name from the fact that it is a system based on accumulated industrial capital. In a barter economy there is no accumulation of capital. Goods are exchanged for goods of equal value; there is no residue. Capital, which we can think of in terms of large amounts of money that can be put into the production of goods, must be accumulated. Before capitalism, kings might accumulate fortunes, but they did not usually use their fortunes for the production of goods. Merchants and tradesmen might accumulate some wealth (though rarely in very large quantities) but usually did not use their wealth for the production of goods.

Several features that correlate closely with its historical development are built into our model of capitalism. The accumulation of large amounts of wealth available for productive purposes is one such feature. Large sums of money alone, however, are not enough. We must also have industrialization. Capitalism did not exist prior to the industrial revolution. Hence, industrialization on a large scale is a necessary element of our model.

Neither the availability of wealth for productive purposes nor large-scale industrialization is unique to capitalism. Any large, modern society, whatever its economic system, needs both of these. But inherent in industrialization are certain problems, one of which is pollution. Industrialization involves the use of machines, which in case of accidents can be dangerous. Also, machines wear out, become obsolete, and need replacing. Industrialization typically demands a large degree of division of labor. Some of the work required in using machines efficiently is routine and dull; some requires great specialization and training. All of these aspects and functions of industrialization are not peculiar to capitalism. Any industrial society faces these potential problems and difficulties. But industrialization also has definite advantages, the greatest being that it multiplies human productive capacity and so makes possible a much larger amount of goods than would otherwise be the case.

The model of classical capitalism includes industrialization and capital. It does not question where capital comes from or how it was developed. Because the model is not a historical account but an analytic tool, the presence of capital is given, a prerequisite of a capitalist model. The same is true of models of other contemporary economic systems, which include capital and industrialization. Where did the capital present in that system come from?

The question of how capital was initially accumulated, as well as the question of how it is increased within a system, raises moral considerations. Although from a moral point of view we can examine the transactions within the model of the system, we cannot examine the process of the antecedent capital formation and accumulation if the presence of such capital is assumed by the model, and if such formation and accumulation are not part of the model.

Private Ownership of the Means of Production

The distinguishing characteristic of capitalism is sometimes said to be private ownership of the means of production. This is a distinguishing feature, however, only when joined with the first and third components of the model. In a slaveholding society or in a feudal society there may also be private ownership of the means of production. The characteristic feature of capitalism is that there is private ownership of the means of large industrial production.

Private ownership of the means of production should not be confused with private ownership of property. Personal property, for instance, might be privately owned in a socialist economy. Personal property is owned by an individual and is not generally used for the production of commodities, though personally owned tools may be so used. But personally owned tools are not the dominant type of productive instrument in capitalism. In speaking of private ownership of the means of production we mean private ownership of factories, plants, corporations and businesses, transportation and communication facilities, raw materials, and large, commercially farmed tracts of land.

Private ownership in this model is opposed to social or state ownership. There are a number of difficulties that we can avoid by clearly defining the components of our model. Some people claim that there is a variant called *state capitalism*, in which the state carries on all the functions generally attributed to private owners in a nonstate capitalist system. For our purposes, state capitalism is a different model. In our model, ownership by the state is not private ownership; private ownership is contrasted with state ownership. Private ownership is also contrasted with social ownership, but private ownership is not to be contrasted with public ownership. A firm may be owned outright by an individual or by a small group of individuals. Such ownership is private ownership. A firm may, however, be owned by many people, each of whom owns a small portion of it, represented by shares of stock in the firm. The owners of the stock may be individuals or perhaps other firms, or they may be groups investing pension-plan money, or the like. Such firms, whose stock is publicly sold and held, are publicly owned. But because the public members hold their shares privately, such firms are also private property. Social ownership, for our purposes, would mean ownership by members of the society in general, insofar as they are members of the society. Cooperatives, or firms owned by the workers, are for our purposes privately owned, but, because of the second ingredient of private ownership, they are marginal cases; they do not represent the dominant mode of ownership.

The second ingredient of private ownership characteristic of capitalism is that not everyone owns the means of production. The majority of people in our model of capitalism do not individually own the means of production that they use; they are employed by others and work for wages. Wages are the dominant source of income for the vast majority in our capitalist model. Workers sell their labor in order to earn money to keep themselves and their families alive, and to buy whatever else they wish with their disposable income.

Private property in our model is compatible with both private and professional management of firms. A firm that is privately owned may be run by those who own it. They may both own and manage the company or business, whatever it may be. The owners, however, may hire professional managers to run their businesses. The separation of ownership from management raises special problems for moral consideration. But in looking at the model in general, we need make no hard and fast decision on this issue. If, for analytic purposes, it would be helpful to distinguish the two cases, we could simply use two models. In one of them, ownership and management would go together; in the other, they would be separate. Our model is a third alternative and includes both of the others.

Private ownership of the means of production raises several moral issues. One is whether private ownership of the means of production is itself moral. By what right, some ask, do some people, either individually or collectively, claim the right to natural resources? The world is the home of all humankind. Its goods—coal, iron, copper, oil, and other resources—should be available to all and used for the good of all. Is it fair for certain people, simply because they or their forebears happened to have settled in an area, to claim the exclusive right to the resources of that area? Such questions form one part of the moral analysis of private property.

A second group of questions regarding private property concerns the social nature of knowledge and culture. Each people inherit a store of knowledge—knowledge of how to make iron and glass, or how to make engines and tools, and so on. Industry depends on a large store of accumulated information and know-how, inventions and discoveries that no individual owns because they have been socially developed. The modes of production are also social. No individual produces cars by himself or with knowledge he individually developed. Private ownership uses for private profit what society has developed. The knowledge, techniques, and processes are all social. By what right are they individually appropriated and used for individual rather than for social good?

A third group of questions relates to the workers in our model. In our capitalist model, the vast majority of people do not own the means of production, and they earn their living by working for others. Their livelihood is dependent on others. By what right do some have such power of life and death over others? The workers work for a wage. What constitutes a fair or a just wage? What constitutes exploitation? If goods are exchanged at their real value, does profit for the owner of private property come from stealing from the workers by not paying them their due? How is the owner-worker relation to be construed? We have already seen that the slave-master relation is immoral. What is the moral status of the owner-worker relation?

A Free-Market System

The third characteristic of our capitalist model is a free, competitive market system. A market-type system can be shared with other types of economic models. In our model, the free-market system is the dominant type operative within the system.

A free market is one that is not controlled either by government or by any small group of individuals. In a free market, government does not

- set the price of goods
- set wages
- control production.

Absence of government control and intervention is matched by absence of control by any small group. This rules out unregulated monopolies (exclusive ownership or control of supply) and monopsonies (exclusive control of demand, i.e., only one buyer).

Prices and wages in our model are determined by the mechanism of the market. They are a result of supply and demand. Skilled labor, if it is in short supply, will bring higher wages than if it is not in short supply. In general, unskilled labor will be in greater supply than skilled labor, and skilled labor will be paid more. Prices are also determined by supply and demand.

A second necessary component of our model is *competition*. Free competition involves the possibility of any who so choose to enter into the market structure as buyers or sellers. Access is not artificially limited by any power, government, or group. Free competition is driven in part by the profit motive.

Competition encourages many people to produce products in great demand, because there is a ready market for such products. Buyers prefer to pay less rather than more for goods of the same quality; therefore, competition encourages efficiency among producers, and competition encourages competing firms to lower their prices to acquire a larger share of the market.

Third, in order to try to achieve greater returns on investment, perhaps by taking more risk, resources must be free to move within the system to whichever portion of it someone believes will bring the greatest return. This is true of natural resources, capital, and labor. Workers are free to move to whatever employment they choose and to seek to earn as much as they can.

The free-market system, in our model, can claim several virtues. It promotes efficiency—the efficient production and use of resources. Even more importantly, it values freedom. Each individual within the system makes free choices in each transaction into which he or she enters. Competition tends to lower the cost of goods to consumers, who decide what will be produced by how they spend their money. The market responds by not producing what is not sold and by producing what is in demand. As demand changes, the market mechanism responds by encouraging the appropriate changes in the allocation of capital and resources. Workers are free to negotiate the conditions of their employment and the kind of work they will do. If the conditions under which each individual transaction takes place are fair, then each party freely enters into such a transaction to achieve his or her own good and ends. All benefit thereby.

Many moral issues arise in considering a free-market system. Each transaction entered into must be fair and free. What constitutes fairness? And to be free, what are the prerequisites of a transaction? One condition of fairness is that both sides have all the appropriate knowledge. Only if both parties know what they are doing can they properly evaluate the transaction. Is the doctrine of *caveat emptor* (let the buyer beware) a part of our system? Does freedom involve the possibility of one party taking advantage of the other party, or of one party gaining advantage of another party? If fairness is built into the system, then only fair transactions are allowed in the system. But efficiency or initiative, the willingness to take risks, or some other quality may well give one party an advantage over another. Can a worker be said to enter into a wage contract freely if, other than starving, he or she has no alternative but to accept the wages offered? Do consumers, acting as individuals, enter into transactions on an equal footing with large corporations?

In addition to questions about the fairness and freedom of transactions, some people ask what, from a moral perspective, competition does to people. Does it treat them as ends in themselves? Does it undermine their inclination to be helpful? Does it divide them into opposing classes and groups? Does it impede social cooperation? Does competition make people selfish, self-serving, mean, and inconsiderate of others?

Are there natural tendencies of the market that push it toward monopoly or that encourage people to attempt to gain unfair advantage in order to improve their chances for success? If there are such forces, can they be remedied within the system, or must they be handled by other forces—for instance, by the political and legal system with which the model is joined?

Capitalism and Government

The structural components of capitalism and the end-state produced in a capitalist society can be morally evaluated, but to attempt to do so in a vacuum would be unrealistic. For capitalism is always found embedded in some cultural and political setting. The basis for determining the legitimate relations of business and government from an ethical point of view is contained in the end of government and business and in the conditions necessary for both to be morally justified. Yet the limits that morality sets for the business-government relation are loose enough to allow a great variety of different types of governments, operating in rich and poor societies, with educated or uneducated populations and with a variety of different kinds of enterprises. We cannot fruitfully speak of the relation of business enterprises and government in the abstract because there are too many variables that must be taken into account in discussing this relation. Yet historically, there have been at least six types of relations between government and capitalism, which produce six variants of our basic model of capitalism. In any given society a mix of several types may be present. Looking at each of the six separately will help us gain some clarity on the relations.

1. The first is the model of laissez-faire capitalism. It is the version of the basic model of capitalism that was defended by nineteenth-century liberals. Today it is defended in the United States by libertarians and by some anarchists of the right.[2] According to this view, the proper function of government is to preserve the peace (and hence protect business from external and internal threats) and to adjudicate disputes among those engaged in business transactions. These are the only morally legitimate activities of government. Neither taxation nor any kind of regulation of business by government is morally justified. The resulting model assumes that, in Adam Smith's terms, some "invisible hand" will make individual transactions, done for the purpose of private gain, benefit society as a whole more than any attempt to directly benefit society could. It also assumes, if it is to be morally justified, that competing enterprises will act morally and that where they do not the mechanism of the market will act as a corrective.

The model, however, fails to take into adequate account the good of society as a whole, opposed simply to the good of those who enter into economic transactions. There is much evidence as well against the two foregoing assumptions. Hence, if a system based on this version of the model is to be morally justifiable, it must adequately address the issues of how those mem-

---

[2] For defenses of this type, see Murray Rothbard, *For a New Liberty*, 3rd ed.(San Francisco: Fox & Wilkes, 1985); and Robert Nozick, *Anarchy, State, and Utopia* (New York: Basic Books, 1974).

bers of society who cannot take part in business activities will receive at least the essentials for their survival and well-being and how business activities can be kept fair and honest despite the temptations and tendencies toward profitable, unfair practices.

2. The second model depicts government as the protector of capitalists at the expense of the other members of society. Under this version of the model, if government is not actually run by the capitalist class, it is run by their representatives for the benefit of the capitalist class. The function of government in this view is to protect the vested interests of the owners of the means of production against the members of the working class. Government protects profits, regulates what labor is allowed and not allowed to do, taxes enterprises at a lower rate than workers, guarantees profits through subsidies and contracts, and does whatever else is necessary for the benefit of business. In some instances the members of government are the entrepreneurs. Whether or not this is the case, the aim of government is to foster the interests of business—frequently big business—at the expense of the rest of society.

Marxist critics claim that this is the true relation of government and business under capitalism, despite attempts by both groups to camouflage the relation. If government in fact acts in the way described, its actions vis-à-vis business cannot be morally justified. The proper function of a legitimate government is to foster the interests of all the members of the society. To protect and promote some at the expense of others is a violation of its basic purpose.

This version of the model is undoubtedly implemented by some governments in some capitalist societies. In these cases the relation can be morally questioned. Anyone defending capitalism as morally justifiable must be able to show that this relation of government and business is not the dominant one in the society.

3. The third version of the model is one of governmental protectionism. According to this model, a proper function of government is to help business by protecting it from foreign competition through the imposition of quotas, import taxes, or other similar means. The function of government is also sometimes to help industries financially if they run into difficulties. From a moral point of view, the rationale for such government activity is that such industries benefit the society by producing goods and supplying jobs, or in other ways, such as making the country independent in time of war. It is therefore appropriate that government support such industries. Although the defense is plausible, such action is truly morally justifiable only if in fact the members of society do benefit by it and if they are not the victims of industries that are protected from competition for the benefit of those who own the industries. This answer, however, is made from the point of view of only the society whose industries are protected, and ignores the effect of such protection on other countries and peoples.

4. The fourth version of the model assigns to government a variety of different tasks vis-à-vis business, all of which are responsive to the general interests of the citizens. One is to make sure that competition is fair and that all businesses operate according to the same rules, established in law. In this version, government acts to define the rules of the capitalist system, and it acts as an umpire with respect to those engaged in the system. It also raises, by taxes, the money it needs to provide such common goods as roads and schools. In addition, government takes on the responsibility of caring for those in need who are unable to take part in economic activity and who are ignored by the classical economic model.

Each of these activities requires moral defense. They are all plausibly legitimate and widely accepted. The difficult question is to determine the extent to which actual governmental actions are in accordance with them in fact as well as in appearance.

5. In the fifth version of the model, government and business cooperate for the sake of both business and the society as a whole. The role of government is not one only of external umpire but also of internal helper. The best example of such a model is contemporary Japan. This model directly acknowledges the benefit of society as the proper moral end of both business and government, and the two work together to achieve that end. The model allows fierce competition within all industries and allows efficiency and innovation to operate. It allows businesses to fail as a result of competition. But government helps support successful large businesses, whose success it sees as being closely tied to the general welfare of the society as a whole. A proper function of government with respect to business in this model is to help successful businesses, especially in the area of foreign exports and competition. Such cooperation of business and government, if it truly leads to the benefit of all the people of society, is compatible with the legitimate aims of both government and business. Whether it is fair with respect to international competition depends on how that competition and the international system in which it operates are envisioned.

6. The sixth version of the model comes closest to socialism. It allows government to take over and run those industries that private enterprise cannot handle successfully, or industries in areas where competition would be inefficient, where economy of scale is important, or where compatibility of equipment is a necessity. Thus, frequently government will run the transportation system, often at a loss. It will operate the telephone and telegraph lines; sometimes it will run radio, television, and other communication networks, and so on. This is compatible with private industries of other kinds and is also compatible with government assuming, vis-à-vis those industries, any of the other approaches of the other versions of the model. There is no reason why a government's running an industry need be any more moral or immoral than private entrepreneurs doing so. What counts is how the running is done.

All six models illustrate possible and actual relations of government and business within a capitalist framework. In differing circumstances, exactly what a government justifiably allows or prohibits depends on a variety of factors. In a rich country, whose workers have a rather high standard of living and whose business enterprises are well established, a government might morally demand better working conditions in factories than is possible in a poor country with marginally profitable enterprises. This general principle applies in all cases: Government should protect the worker from injustice and exploitation. But how this is translated into actual practice depends on many specific aspects of the concrete social and economic situation. Once the basic safety of workers is ensured, it is appropriate to ask, for instance, whether requiring one more safety device will in the long run cause more benefit or more harm to society as a whole. The same is true with respect to consumers. There is much room for reasonable, moral people to disagree about exactly how much government regulation, and exactly what kind of regulation, is morally justified in a specific situation. Similarly, there is much room for reasonable, moral people to disagree about the proper relation of government and business, and many different kinds of relations may well be justifiable.

In 1991 the Soviet Union threw over its communist government, and the constituent states that had formed the union became independent. The story of the transition of the largest of those states, Russia, from socialism to something closer to free enterprise or capitalism is instructive. By 1998 although many of the largest enterprises were still government owned, and although land had not yet been privatized, many businesses had been privatized and the country was attempting to form a free market economy. One difficulty, however, was that the leaders of the country had introduced privatization and economic reform without first or simultaneously establishing the governmental mechanisms necessary for successful free enterprise. In all cases for capitalism to succeed, the minimal action required of government is that it enforce contracts, that it protect private property, and that it adjudicate disputes in the economic as in other realms. Russia was not prepared to do any of this during the period of transition.[3] One result was complaints about injustice or unfairness in the privatization of state industries. Another was claims that former government officials and plant managers were in special positions of privilege and were taking advantage of the transition to become rich through corrupt practices. A third was the growth of a criminal element, referred to as the "mafia," that engaged in extortion with respect to small, emerging businesses, under the guise of providing protection. All of this was justified by some commentators as simply a stage that capitalism historically went through and that countries establishing capitalism must also go through. The claim fails to acknowledge that societies can learn from one another and from history. Corruption and injustice are not necessary parts of a capitalist system, and both tend to undermine the proper working of such a system. A lesson that both history has taught and that the Russian experience has reinforced is that government has a necessary role to play in any capitalist model or system.

---

[3] For an account of the Russia's transition see Joseph R. Blasi, Maya Kroumova, Douglas Kruse, *Kremlin Capitalism: Privatizing the Russian Economy* (Ithaca and London: Cornell University Press, 1997).

A Socialist Model

There is no classical model of socialism as a purely economic system. Historically, we have a number of very diverse societies that have been, or are called, socialistic. To the extent that socialism involves government ownership, it is very difficult, if not impossible, to separate socialism as an economic system from socialism as a political system. At the same time, socialism should not be identified with or confused with communism. Communism, as an economic system, has never been achieved, though some countries, such as the former Soviet Union, claimed to have been developing such an economy. Communist governments in the Soviet Union and in much of Eastern Europe prior to 1989 had socialist-type economies. In those countries, socialism was closely linked with authoritarian types of governments, as it is today in China and Cuba. But the kind of socialism found in these countries is not the only kind of socialism, and it need not be so linked.[4]

A partial model of socialism which is restricted to socialism as an economic system could be characterized by three features, each of which parallels to some extent our model of capitalism. The three features are an industrial base, social ownership of the means of production, and centralized planning. This is only one of many models; it does not correspond to all socialist societies, but it does correspond in part to some of the more historically important ones.

An Industrial Base

Socialism as a modern phenomenon appears later on the historical scene than capitalism. In Marx's writings, socialism is the stage that follows the stage of capitalism. The French socialists of the nineteenth century saw it as an alternative to capitalism. It is possible to speak of socialism in an agricultural society, but the model we shall use restricts socialism to industrial societies. This means that the major form of production is industrial. All the problems of industrialization must therefore be faced by socialist economies as well as by capitalist ones. With industrialization come problems of waste and pollution, which must be handled. For some problems the solutions may be the same as under capitalism; for others, the solutions may be different. Worker dissatisfaction, tedium and boredom at work, and other problems resulting from the production process, from specialization and from the division of labor are problems that must be solved in socialist as well as capitalist economies.

Social Ownership of the Means of Production

Social ownership of the means of production is the most frequently mentioned characteristic of a socialist economy. Such social ownership does not deny pri-

---

[4] For instance, Michael Harrington's *Socialism: Past and Future* (New York: NAL—Dutton, 1992) is a contemporary defense of nonauthoritarian socialism.

vate ownership of personal goods; personal property is compatible with socialism. The form of social ownership in our model may be either state ownership or worker ownership. A model may be constructed with only state, or with only worker, ownership. Both are allowable in our model. Social ownership in the sense that the means of production are owned by all the people is not part of our model. The reason for excluding it is that there is (and has been) no socialist society to which such ownership is applicable. Neither is it clear what such ownership would mean, nor how it would function on a large scale that would be applicable to a whole society. State ownership involves control by the government. The government of the society may represent the people, and it may act in their name; but the government, even if legitimate, is not the people.

The relation of government to people is the central moral question of socialism. The government is the employer of all. Is it possible for the government to pay people less than the value they produce? Is it possible for the government to exploit people? Is it possible for government to be inequitable in its allocation of goods and to give preference to some at the expense of others? It is certainly possible for all these things to happen. Government ownership does not preclude them. Equality of opportunity is not necessarily guaranteed, nor will people's desires necessarily be fulfilled or weighed seriously. On the other hand, their desires may be weighed, their needs may be taken care of, and they may be treated fairly and equitably. There is no guarantee that government ownership will necessarily produce such a society, however, unless we build such virtues into the system. The difficulty with building these virtues into the model is that the model will not apply to an actual society unless the virtues are also present. Socialism as a model is frequently presented with such benefits built into it; our model, however, is neutral on this score.

Worker ownership is a relatively new phenomenon and is usually joined to some extent with government ownership. Worker ownership is comparable to co-ops. What makes them different is the total system or model in which they are found. If factories, for instance, are all owned by the workers, are they run competitively or not? Is competition between worker-owned factories to be considered a part of socialism or not? Because worker-owned factories are possible under capitalism, what would differentiate this portion of the socialist model from the capitalist model is that worker ownership would be the dominant form of ownership rather than a marginal one.

Centralized Planning

Centralized planning is a necessary part of our model of socialism, at least with respect to heavy industries, transportation, and communications. Total centralized planning is of course allowable under the model, but it is not a necessary component. Without centralized planning, at least in essential sectors, it would be difficult to distinguish the model of socialism from the model of capitalism. If worker-owned factories, for instance, were allowed to compete freely for resources, and in what and how they produced, they would not differ significantly in most respects from similar factories in the capitalist model.

Centralized planning involves government. It is the government that typically does the planning in a socialist society. The task might be done by some other group, but that group would in the final analysis be equivalent to a government. Its job is to allocate resources and to guide the production and allocation of resources and goods. Its ideal is to end the anarchy and wastefulness of the marketplace.

Centralized planning precludes free-market decisions of many types, though not of all types. The market might still be the indicator of what people want. Central planners can take into account such information as unfulfilled demand and a supply that exceeds demand. The point of centralized planning, however, is to replace competition. Hence, the competitive aspects of the market would not be allowed. For the system to work, the central planners obviously need an enormous amount of information, and they need it in time to use the information in making decisions about the allocation of resources and the goods to be produced and distributed. Planners need some way of knowing the needs of the people and of the society, some way of determining which goods and needs must be given preference over others. Typically, this involves a large government apparatus, usually of a bureaucratic nature.

Can government know all it needs to know successfully to operate such a system? The more centralized and encompassing the control, the more difficult it is to succeed. The fewer industries controlled, the more likely the success.

Comparison of Models and Systems

Although we have raised some of the moral issues involved in the capitalist and socialist models, we have not determined whether either one is (or both are) inherently immoral. If analysis revealed that there were structural elements in either model that were immoral, then the system depicted by the model would be immoral. To the extent that the model was instantiated in a society, people of that society would have to see what was necessary to remove the immorality, what other system might be adopted, and how the change might be best achieved.

We have not yet discussed how the economic models intertwine with political and legal systems. Do particular legal and political systems mitigate the negative tendencies of capitalism or of socialism? Do they interfere with the positive tendencies? Can the mix be modeled and morally evaluated? Specific cases, of course, require specific analyses.

In the abstract, the proponents of capitalism frequently enumerate the following values: It promotes individual freedom; it promotes and rewards initiative, innovation, and the taking of risks; and it results in the efficient production of multitudes of goods, increasing the productivity of society and so benefiting all members of the society. Capitalism is attacked for exploiting the workers, for producing false wants, for waste, and for allowing gross inequalities.

Champions of socialism emphasize equality, security, and the absence of exploitation. Gross inequalities of wealth and income are mitigated under socialism, though some differences in both still exist. Workers are guaranteed work, and all are guaranteed that their basic needs will be taken care of— food, shelter, medicine, clothing, education. The lack of exploitation is premised on the fact that no individual employs other individuals. The state is the major, if not the sole employer, and the state does not exploit its workers for profit, as private employers are tempted to do. The absence of complete equality, the difficulties of proper allocation of resources and markets, and the lower productivity on the whole, to the extent that they exist, are seen not as defects of the system but as remediable deficiencies.

During the twentieth century different countries opted for different models. The newly emerging countries of Africa frequently followed the model of socialism found in China, which is a primarily agricultural socialist model. Other countries followed the model of socialism in the Soviet Union. Others took Sweden as the socialist model to follow. Still others—for instance, Japan after World War II—followed something like the model of the United States. In each case the economic models were joined with a variety of political systems; they were adopted by people with a particular history and tradition, with particular natural resources, and with specific international friends and enemies. Though the moral problems in each case vary to some extent, some basic problems are common to all. Some of these are a function of the economic systems with which they operate.

Economic Systems and Justice

We cannot be moral and choose or espouse an inherently immoral economic system. But on the assumption that there is more than one economic system that is not inherently immoral, there is no moral imperative mandating that we choose one rather than another. If we assume, for the sake of an example, that neither the capitalist nor the socialist model presented is inherently immoral, the choice of one rather than the other involves a choice of certain values over others. The mixture of freedom, security, and risk is very different in the two models. Which is the best mixture, from a moral point of view? Because neither is immoral, either one, if it is freely chosen, is morally acceptable. Immoral practices might develop in either system, however. If they do develop, such practices should be avoided and if possible rooted out. Each society can improve and should attempt to do so. There is no one best society.

Yet any economic system as well as any political system should embody justice to a considerable degree. Distributive justice—that is, justice in the social allocation of benefits and burdens—is frequently thought to be the most important moral component of any economic system. Is justice a function of each system? Is there a capitalist conception of justice and a socialist conception of justice, each appropriate to the system? Is there an eternal, or system-neutral, conception of justice in terms of which we can evaluate any economic system?

In our earlier discussion of justice, we noted that it consists in giving each person his or her due, in treating equals equally and unequals unequally. We also saw that distributive justice could be formulated in a variety of ways.

In the capitalist system, justice demands equality of opportunity; it does not demand equality of results. The best way to tell who is the fastest runner is to have all runners compete under the same conditions. Someone will finish first, someone will finish last, and the others will finish somewhere in between. The capitalist system rewards some people who take risks and penalizes others. That is what risk-taking involves. The rewards are frequently proportional to the risk. Capitalism also rewards a number of other attributes—work, initiative, energy, intelligence, and similar qualities applied in the marketplace. Within the system, some may be lucky and others unlucky. But as long as there is equality of opportunity, and as long as rewards are sufficient to generate productive activity, justice has been served. If we need a formula, we might say that each is rewarded in accordance with his input into the economy. "From each as he wishes to participate, to each as his participation is successful," might be its slogan.

Justice in a socialist system consists not only in equality of opportunity; it also allows proportionality of differential rewards. It guarantees that all receive some reward, but it tends to limit the amount of the reward anyone may get. A common slogan used to describe socialism is, "From each according to his ability, to each according to his work." Lenin, among others, noted that this was not the social ideal. The social ideal that embodies justice is the slogan descriptive of communism, "From each according to his ability, to each according to his need."

We have already discussed John Rawls's suggestion that we choose our principles of justice behind the veil of ignorance. The two principles of justice thus derived, he claims, are compatible with both capitalism and socialism.

Obviously, a view of justice that demands equality of results will not be compatible with capitalism, nor will a view of justice that requires that differential rewards according to merit, work, or input be compatible with a system requiring equality of rewards. A variety of formulations of justice are possible and appropriate for various circumstances. For instance, in a race, it would be inappropriate to require that everyone be given first place. If we want a race, then the honor of first place should go to the one who wins. If we are not interested in seeing who is fastest, but we feel that other conditions should be taken into account, then we may assign handicaps, equalizing weight, size, training, or other differentials. But once these are established, we will still expect one person to win. Justice does not preclude our playing that game, nor does it require that when we play it we not reward the winner. However, it may, for a variety of reasons, require that we not award the winner certain kinds of prizes, prizes out of proportion to the fact that the race is a game or a sport. But the consideration of justice here is different from the consideration of justice when all the runners run under the same track conditions, or when some run with a handicap.

A similar approach can be taken with respect to justice in economic systems and the justice of economic systems. There is not just one notion of justice that is applicable; there are several different formulations, and one of them may be appropriate for one purpose and kind of activity and another for another kind of purpose and activity. Each formulation of justice may be taken as a prima facie formulation. If its application is appropriate, it should be applied. If two or more different approaches seem to apply, and if their application is mutually contradictory, then we must determine which arguments can be mustered in defense of each. What are the claimed injustices? How do they compare with the other claimed injustices? Is there some way to reconcile the differing claims? How are the claims supported? Which arguments prevail in the given case?

This solution may be unsatisfactory to some, those who claim to have the final, true, or applicable view of justice. But faced with competing claims, we can resolve the conflict in this instance only by trying to sort out the claims and arguments in support of them. We may not reach a solution with which everyone agrees, and the debate may not be settled. All this is true. But this does not mean that we should not continue to strive to achieve justice in our economic systems or that we should rest content that the view of justice we have is the last word on the topic. We should be constantly prepared to recognize injustice where we did not previously perceive it, and we should be ready, if the argument demands it, to reevaluate the justice of the economic system in which we find ourselves.

Study Questions

1. In which two ways can we evaluate the morality of an economic system?

2. What is meant by a structural analysis approach to evaluating economic systems? Illustrate the use of such an approach.

3. Why is an economic system based on slavery immoral? Is it immoral from both a structural analysis approach and an end-state approach? Evaluate the system using Rawls's two principles of justice.

4. Name some countries that have a capitalistic economic system. Do they all have similar political systems? How do the total systems differ from one another?

5. Name some countries that are (or were) primarily socialistic in their economic systems. Do they all have similar political systems? How do the total systems differ from one another?

6. How do some present-day socialist systems differ from the Soviet model?

7. Are models moral or immoral? Why or why not? Would a model of a slaveholding system be immoral?

8. What are three specific defining features of the model of classical capitalism? Show how the features are found in several different capitalist societies. Is there a capitalist society that does not have these three features?

9. Distinguish personal property from private property.

10. What is meant by a free market? Can a market be partially free?

11. What are three necessary components of a free-market?

12. How are prices determined in a free-market system? wages?

13. Is competition morally justifiable? Why or why not?

14. What are the minimal governmental actions necessary for capitalism to succeed?

15. What are three defining features of a socialist model? Show how the features are found in several different socialist societies. Is there a socialist society that does not have these three features?

16. What is meant by social ownership of the means of production?

17. Is centralized planning a necessary part of the model of socialism?

18. What are the values of capitalism, as put forth by its proponents?

19. What are the values of socialism, as put forth by its proponents?

20. Does justice operate similarly in capitalism and in socialism?

21. What different kinds and claims of justice do we find in economic systems?

22. By using Rawls's principles of justice, can capitalism be justified? can socialism? In each case develop the argument using Rawls's principles.

23. Is either the capitalist economic model or the socialist economic model preferable from a moral point of view?

7

AMERICAN CAPITALISM: MORAL OR IMMORAL?

The Case of Bill Gates

In 1980 William Gates III left Harvard before finishing his degree. What could one expect of a college dropout? By 1993 he was 37 years old, CEO of Microsoft, and had assets of $6.7 billion, most of which he made in a seven-year period.[1] By 1999 his Microsoft shares were worth over $50 billion. Microsoft was an infant company when in 1980 IBM chose it to develop the operating system for its new personal computer. The product, MS-DOS, still dominates operating systems for personal computers around the world. In addition, Microsoft developed Windows, Word, Excel, and Internet Explorer and is the world's leading software firm. In 1992 the company had 11,500 employees. Although Microsoft does not pay its employees as well as some competitors do, many workers get stock options. As a result, one analyst estimates that, owing to the worth of their stock, about one in five of Microsoft's workers are millionaires.

Bill Gates's meteoric rise to perhaps the richest person in America sounds like a Horatio Alger story and captures the allure of capitalism in America, where the rise from rags to riches has long been held out as the American dream. Gates earned his billions legally and, within the system, ethically. There have been some claims of antitrust violations, but as of 1998, no adverse judgments against the company.

---

[1] For details on Microsoft and Gates, see "The Billionaires List," *Fortune*, June 28, 1993, p. 45; Robert Levering and Milton Moskowitz, "Microsoft," *The 100 Best Companies to Work for in America* (New York: Doubleday, 1993), pp. 285-290; and James Wallace and Jim Erickson, *Hard Drive: Bill Gates and the Making of the Microsoft Empire* (New York: Wiley, 1992).

How does one earn an average of $2 billion a year? For some people, that raises a structural question about the system. Of course Bill Gates's salary plus bonus for 1996 was only $562,588—well below what many other top executives receive in the way of compensation. His extraordinary increase in wealth comes from the phenomenal growth in the worth of Microsoft stock, growth which anyone holding shares of Microsoft also enjoyed.

Is a system that allows some to accumulate such great wealth while so many live below the poverty line morally justifiable? That raises an end-state question about it.

⋗⊹⟨⟩⋅◯⋅⟨⟩⊹⟨

The most virulent attack on capitalism in general comes from Karl Marx, who claimed that the capitalist system necessarily involves exploitation of workers, which is the primary way successful businesspeople make a profit. His argument—a structural analysis—was fairly simple. Assume that on the whole products, goods, or commodities are exchanged for products, goods, or commodities of equal value. There may be special situations in which this is not the case (for instance, in a monopoly situation). Overall, however, there is no reason why in a free transaction one would exchange a commodity of greater value for one of lesser value. Now introduce money as the medium of exchange. Goods are still sold at their real value. Where then does profit come from? The traditional answer—that one adds a certain percentage of profit to one's cost to get the final price—won't do because, as Marx argues, what one gains in this way as a seller, one loses as a buyer. In general, then, goods sell for their real value, which is equal to the total labor time that goes into producing them (including, of course, the labor necessary to make the machines that produce the commodity, mine the ore necessary for the machines, and so on).

If all items were sold at their real value, there would be no profit. Hence, something must be sold at less than its real value. According to Marx, that something is human labor power. Because workers are forced to sell their labor power in order to live, they sell it at the best price they can get. But employers will not hire workers to whom they have to pay the equivalent of the value they produce. Why should they? They only employ workers if they can hire them at less than the value they produce. The difference between the value they produce and the value they get paid is profit. If you want to get rich, start a firm that will grow large. Only when it is large and employs many people will it be possible to earn large sums of money. If the cost of labor gets too high, move your production to a place where the cost of labor is less. The less you pay workers, the greater the profit when you sell the product. Marx's formula seems to fit the pattern of most companies.

Hence, a follower of Marx would comment that William Gates has had astounding success either because his product sells for more than it is worth—which is possible and is the basis for some competitors claiming the company almost holds a monopoly on the software based on MS-DOS—or because

Microsoft earns much more money from its products than it pays to its workers, who are the ones who add the value the product has. According to their analysis, there is nowhere else for profit to come from. Of course, much of Gates's money is in Microsoft stock (of which he owns 20.8 percent), but the stock price represents what the market believes it to be worth. Microsoft may, of course, treat its employees well, but that, on Marx's account, is beside the point, just as it is beside the point that a slaveholder treats his slaves well.

What are we to say about American capitalism?

The American Economic System

American capitalism, from its inception to the present day, has grown, developed, and changed. To reduce it to one of the models described in the last chapter would be a gross oversimplification. Although it continues to contain the general features of capitalism, its varying relations to government are central to the changes that have taken place in the development of American capitalism. The American economic system is closely tied to the political, cultural, and social system of the United States, and an adequate moral evaluation of it must take these relations into account. The American economic model we examine, therefore, must include government's action with respect to it.

Government intervention is part of the American economic system; therefore, a complete justification of the entire politico-economic system would involve a defense of the American system of government as being legitimate. For our purposes, however, a sufficient moral justification of government intervention is that it keeps the economic system internally fair, and that its intervention has as its end the protection and enhancement of the welfare of the people governed, while violating no basic rights and inflicting no unjustifiable injury. If government intervention benefits only the leaders of a country, only the official bureaucrats, or only the wealthy, or if it benefits these groups at the expense of the general population, it is not morally justifiable. A corrupt government that milks its own people for the enrichment of the leaders of the country might adopt either a capitalist or a socialist economic system. In either case the resultant politico-economic system can be morally condemned; but it would not follow that all capitalist or socialist systems are inherently immoral. In evaluating the morality of the American economic system we shall need to examine the structural components of the economic system, the legitimacy of government intervention, and the total effect of the system on the people in general. For the system to be morally justifiable it must contain no inherently immoral components, and the system—including the part played by government—must benefit the people as a whole as well as the individuals who carry on economic activities within it.

Because we hold that each human being is a person and as such has certain basic rights and is worthy of respect, there is no morally legitimate reason for treating those subject to government simply as a means to an end (the enrichment of the rulers), as slaves, or as objects. The legitimacy of government consists of the fact that the people accept the rule of government not because they are forced to do so by the government but because it is in their interest and welfare to do so. The proper end of government coincides with the reason for its acceptance by the people.

But, it might be objected, if free enterprise is the result of the legitimate activity of free citizens within a community, their activity has as *its* end the good of those who engage in it. Why must that activity benefit society as a whole? The answer is that business is possible only within a certain social context of institutions, agreements, understandings, shared values, and other social-background conditions. Those who engage in business activity must, of course, expect to benefit directly; otherwise they would not engage in such activity. A society can reasonably be expected to endorse, sanction, and support business as a private activity only if it in turn benefits from such activity; to do otherwise would be irrational. Society and all its members clearly need not benefit directly by each business transaction; but all its members must benefit somehow, either directly or indirectly, by the business structure. Otherwise it would be rational for the members of society to restructure economic activity so that they do benefit from it, because it is possible to do so. The typical benefit the society receives is the rising standard of living for all, even though typically some people benefit more than others. The point of including government within the economic system is to make sure that those who cannot compete successfully are nonetheless guaranteed protection of their rights as human beings, including their right to subsistence and provision of their basic needs.

The American economic system is sometimes called a free-enterprise system. Like the classical model of capitalism, free enterprise involves the absence of government ownership, control, regulation, and planning, and the freedom of individuals to enter into transactions of their own choosing. This freedom is significant from a moral point of view. The American version of free enterprise postulates maturity, intelligence, and responsibility on the part of those operating within the economic system. It assumes that each person wishes his own good and that each person knows, better than anyone else, what he wants. The system claims to respect each person as an autonomous adult and a responsible moral being when it allows him to make his own decisions and choose his own way of life. It further assumes that each person desires maximal freedom, and that as a competent, adult, and moral being, he or she deserves it, providing it is compatible with like freedom for all.

Adam Smith, in his classical defense of capitalism, claims that each person, in pursuing his own good, indirectly and unknowingly also promotes the public interest. The general good is better served in this way, he contends, than by any group directly attempting to promote the general welfare through some means of overall planning and control. American free enterprise adopts a modified version of this view.

Free enterprise, which prizes efficiency, nonetheless insists that the transactions between adults must be fair. Fairness can here be specified in procedural rather than substantive terms. *A transaction is fair if both parties to it—* usually the buyer and the seller—*engage in the transaction freely (without coercion), and if both parties have access to adequate and appropriate knowledge of the relevant aspects of the transaction.* An assumption is that neither party would take part in the transaction unless he or she benefited thereby. If one of the parties hides relevant information, misrepresents the transaction in some way, or intimidates the other party, then the transaction is not a fair one. In such transactions one party takes unfair advantage of the other. A transaction is not defined as fair only in terms of the value of the product or service that is transferred, because some people may value some product or service more than others do. If they are willing to buy a product at a higher price—providing they know what they are doing and are not coerced—the transaction is not unfair. This is the way the market works. Nonetheless, lack of coercion rules out as unfair situations in which one person's need for a basic good and another person's exclusive control over the needed good together with charging a price greatly in excess of what the market under ordinary conditions would yield are equivalent to making the transaction a forced one.

Relation of the American Government to the American Economic System

What is the relation of government to the system? The economic system can operate only in a broader social system of reasonable security and stability. Government has traditionally provided security and stability for the people of a country by arranging for the means of common defense, protecting the person and property of the members of a society from incursion by other members, enforcing contracts, and by facilitating conditions for the exchange of goods and services. Thus, a national government typically provides armed forces for the protection of the country, making the people secure from outside invasion. Through its laws, police force, court, and penal system, it protects individuals in the society in their person and property. People can thus feel secure in acquiring goods and feel safe in their use of them. A nation's laws and courts make possible and enforce legally binding contracts and make available acceptable procedures for the peaceful adjudication of disputes. The government also prints and mints money, the generally accepted medium of exchange, which facilitates transactions within the economic system.

The relation of government and the economic system in the United States, however, did not stop with these minimalist functions. At least five other needs arose, which the government sought to meet.

Development of a Welfare Safety Net

Even if the system of free enterprise works as its advocates argue it should, it rewards only those who contribute to the economy, and only in proportion to their contribution. It does not reward those who make no contribution to the economy. Those who cannot contribute are simply ignored, or left out of the activities of the marketplace. No one is forced to enter the marketplace, and those in the marketplace are not forced to consider those who do not enter it. But what does the free-enterprise system do for the sick, disabled, and incapacitated, those unable to take care of themselves, or those who fail disastrously? From the point of view of the classical economic model of capitalism, they are simply not considered. Yet, clearly, a nation should not ignore the plight of some of its citizens. They should not starve or die from lack of care simply because they cannot contribute to the economy. The other members of the society, from their largesse and kindness, might help such people through charity. But historically, such charity has been both inadequate and frequently demeaning. Hence, the government has been called upon, or has taken upon itself, to provide a safety net for everyone, and to help those unable to care for themselves. Has the governmental aid been administered wisely, and has the aid been sufficient? Have people taken undue advantage of the systems of welfare that government has set up? These and similar questions can be investigated, debated, and possibly answered. But it seems clear that a society has a moral obligation to prevent its members from starving and dying from lack of basic needs when the wherewithall to provide them is available. If free enterprise as a system does not consider those who do not contribute to the economy, society as a whole clearly must in some way make up for this deficiency; it acts immorally if it does not.

Provision of Common Goods

Government entered the marketplace to provide common goods that perhaps could not be (and in any event were not) provided adequately by the participants in the economic system. The United States highway system is an example of a type of common activity undertaken by the government. As in so many other areas, however, the United States government does not actually build the roads; it finances their building by private contractors. In the past, it assisted in the development of railroads, rather than building, owning, and operating them itself. It limited the liability of those who wanted to build nuclear power plants, enabling private producers to undertake a venture they felt involved too much risk to pursue otherwise. National, state, and local governments have provided public education, public parks, reservoirs, and dams. Government has sought to consider and protect the common good where it is threatened by the transactions of private individuals and firms.

Control of Economic Cycles

Capitalism historically suffers from cyclical crises. In the United States, the economic system has experienced periods of great expansion and productivity, followed by periods of recession and depression. The cyclical nature of capitalism seems to be part of its natural tendency. But the periods of decline and depression result in great pain and distress for many. As demand decreases, factories produce less. As they produce less, they need fewer workers; people are laid off and are unable to find work elsewhere. Unemployment grows, and with it comes misery for the unemployed and their families. Such a situation may be one that defenders of a capitalist system are willing to accept as part of the natural mechanisms of the market, which tends to be self-correcting. But such booms and busts take their toll on the members of a society, who clearly would prefer a system with more security and less drastic cycles. The United States government entered the economic realm both to alleviate the plight of the unemployed and to help set limits on the cycles through which the free market tends to go. It has attempted to keep the cycles from rising or falling too sharply. The task is complicated and is one that government has not yet mastered. But it attempts to do so through its fiscal and monetary policies, control of its spending, and similar devices. In fulfilling this function, government in America has become substantially involved in the economic system.

Correction of Unfair Tendencies and of Market Failures within the Free-Enterprise System

A premise of the free-enterprise system is that each party enters transactions freely and with access to adequate knowledge appropriate to each transaction. Several tendencies of American free enterprise, however, have historically tended to undermine the fairness of transactions. In each of these cases government has been called upon to regulate the conditions of the transaction, in an attempt to keep the transactions fair.

Antitrust legislation is one example of such an attempt. In any form of capitalism, capital tends to accumulate in the hands of a few who become rich and powerful. If they can successfully dominate an industry, they can prevent free entry into that industry and thereby set the conditions under which goods will be sold and persons hired. Such power clearly changes the conditions of a transaction; it is no longer a transaction between equals who freely enter into it for mutual gain. The one holding the monopoly is able to restrain trade and free enterprise in the area he or she dominates and is able to set the conditions for the transaction. The other member, if he or she wants the product, has no alternative but to enter into the transaction with the monopolist, on the latter's terms. If the former needs the product or the job to live, the transaction is not free. To prevent such a situation from occurring and to preserve the conditions of a free and fair market, antitrust laws make restraint of trade illegal.

Regulated industries, such as communications and the electric power industry, provide a second example. In many countries these industries are owned and operated by the government and are seen as a common good. In the United States, power companies are privately owned. It has been considered to be in the general interest not to have many small competing producers of electric power. Large producers of electricity in a given area, tied in with other producers, can achieve economies of scale and efficiency. Monopolies were allowed in this area. But the government regulated power companies, to prevent them from taking unfair advantage of their customers.

Government also operates in a third area—that of food and drugs. In many transactions a buyer can decide, upon inspection, whether he or she wishes to buy a product and whether or not to pay the price asked. But the ordinary person can hardly be expected to know the effects of many drugs (one would need a chemical laboratory of one's own in order to analyze a drug before taking it). Individuals are therefore at a great disadvantage when engaging in a transaction involving the purchase of pharmaceuticals. A transaction is fair only if both sides have adequate appropriate knowledge. Buyers can easily be taken advantage of, much to the detriment of their health. People have sought, therefore, to protect their interests and to guarantee the fairness of the transaction by having the government intervene. The government tests the effects of drugs, or forces drug firms to test the effects, and then regulates the sale of drugs. It also regulates the contents of food products, mandates clear labeling, and determines what other information the manufacturer must supply to the purchaser in order to make the transaction fair.

Taxation

The fifth type of government intervention in the system is a function of the four just mentioned and of similar activities. Through taxation, the government redistributes income, regulates business activity, and finances its own activities. It funnels money to the private sector through welfare-type programs and through contracts. It is also a giant employer in its own right, supporting vast numbers of people in the armed forces and in the large government bureaucracy required to run its many programs.

The free-enterprise model of American capitalism is not a static one. The intermingling of business and government has been justified, at various stages, in order to keep the conditions of the market's operation fair and just, to make up for deficiencies of the system, and to supplement the system. We can expect the continuing involvement of government in the economic realm, even though we cannot predict the exact nature of this involvement.

Taking all of this into account, what moral evaluation can we make of present-day American free enterprise? Is it inherently immoral? If not, does it contain any immoral aspects that can and should be remedied? We have already noted that many Marxists claim that capitalism is immoral, and we shall look at their charges first. A number of non-Marxists have also condemned capitalism and its American instantiation as being immoral, and we shall investigate their claims next. We shall then look at the positive defense of the American free-enterprise system. Finally, we shall consider, from several points of view, the moral alternatives to American capitalism as proposed by critics.

The Marxist Critique

With the demise of communism in Eastern Europe, many of the champions of capitalism have claimed that history has proven the superiority of capitalism over socialism and communism. The claim is an overstatement, since history has only shown that the totalitarian version of socialism that developed in the Soviet Union and that was forced on the Soviet Union's Eastern neighbors was not viable beyond a certain point. It may have been a useful way for an industrially backward country to develop quickly, but centralized planning failed to promote the initiative and innovation necessary for the next stage of development. However, even this does not show that the socialist ideal of equality for all, of absence of great discrepancies among people of a society, and that care for the benefit of all are not ideals to be sought and are preferable to their opposite.

Karl Marx analyzed nineteenth-century capitalism primarily as he found it in the England of his time.[2] Though Marx frequently uses the language of morality in describing the ills of capitalism, commentators disagree about whether he actually condemned capitalism from a moral point of view. Capitalism, for Marx, was a necessary stage of economic and social development, but a stage that was to be superseded by the higher stage of communism. Yet many of Marx's followers have put his condemnation of capitalism into moral form and have thus claimed that capitalism, in all its variations, is inherently immoral.

We shall examine three of the major claims of these Marxists: (1) Capitalism is inherently immoral because it cannot exist without robbing the worker of his due; (2) capitalism is inherently immoral because it necessarily involves the alienation of human beings; and (3) capitalism is inherently immoral at the present time because it protects the vested interest of the few and prevents the many from achieving a better, more just, more equitable society.

Exploitation of the Work Force

The first charge states that capitalism is based on exploitation of the worker—that is, not paying him what he truly deserves. Slavery, we have already seen, is inherently immoral. According to the Marxist critics, capitalism involves wage slavery. Capitalism cannot exist without exploiting the worker. Hence, there is no way of remedying this evil while preserving the system. Because capitalism is inherently immoral, it should be replaced by socialism, and eventually by full communism.

The basis for the claim of necessary exploitation is Marx's *labor theory of value*. We have already seen the heart of the claim in the analysis of Microsoft

---

[2] The classical attack on capitalism comes from Karl Marx, *Capital*, 3 vols. (Moscow: Foreign Languages Publishing House, 1959). For more recent attacks, see Richard C. Edwards, Michael Reich, and Thomas E. Weisskopf (Eds.), *The Capitalist System: A Radical Analysis of American Society*, 2nd ed. (Englewood Cliffs, N.J.: Prentice Hall, 1978).

with which this chapter began. What all commodities have in common is that they are the result of human labor, and it is in terms of the human labor necessary to produce them that we are able to equate the value of one commodity with another. The only commodity that is sold at less than its real value is human labor power. The difference between the value the workers produce and the amount they are paid is profit or, in Marxist terminology, *surplus value.* Because workers are forced to sell their labor power in order to live, the system involves a type of wage slavery. The only reason anyone has for hiring other people is to get more money by doing so. Hence, all employers exploit their workers or pay them less than they produce. The workers have the choice of being exploited by employer A or employer B. The system makes all employers exploiters and exploits all employees.

Because an employer makes his profit by paying his workers less than the value they produce, he will tend to increase his profit by paying them as little as possible. If he pays them by the day, he will wish them to work twelve rather than ten hours, and ten rather than eight hours. If he pays them by the hour, he will wish them to produce during that hour five rather than four objects, or four rather than three. As long as there is not enough work for everyone who wants it, there will be a buyer's market, and workers will have to work for lower wages than they would otherwise. It is in the interest of the owners of the means of production to have a surplus work force, or for there to be a pool of unemployed. A high unemployment rate, rather than a low one or no unemployment at all, is to their advantage. The workers, on the other hand, will seek to work shorter hours, or to work less hard during the hours they do work. They will also seek more pay rather than less, so that they can improve their standard of living. The war between management and labor stems from the fact that management wishes to pay as little as possible for labor in order to increase its profits, and labor wishes to receive as much as possible of what it deserves.

In the nineteenth century, Marx perceived certain trends in capitalism. He described the tendency of the owners to pay workers less and less, forcing women and even children to enter the labor force in order to help support their families. He described a growing army of the unemployed and foresaw more and more blatant exploitation, until the workers would finally be forced to seize the means of production, take over the factories, put an end to exploitation and capitalism, and form a new social order—communism (the first stage of which he termed *socialism*).

The scenario according to the Marxist script has not taken place. The workers united and formed unions, in part, ironically, because of the efforts of Marx. As a result, the workers were able to gain more pay, shorter hours, and better working conditions. The impetus for them to revolt and seize the factories diminished. Their interests became identified with the continuation of the system rather than with its overthrow. Later Marxists asked how this was possible and whether it meant that capitalism was no longer immoral.

Lenin gave an answer to both questions. According to him, the workers in the West were appeased by the increases they received in higher earnings and the goods they were able to buy with those earnings. Their standard of living rose, so that the American worker lived better than any other large population in human history. But, said Lenin, this does not mean that the worker is no longer exploited. He is still exploited, even if he does not realize it. Profit still comes from paying the worker less than the value he produces. But productive capacities have increased to such an extent that the worker can enjoy the fruits of productivity even while being exploited. Furthermore, the workers are no longer as grossly exploited as they were in the nineteenth century. This is not a result of the generosity of management; it is a result of capitalism's advance to the stage of imperialism. American corporations can pay their workers well because the corporations are able to exploit people in other countries, primarily in the underdeveloped countries of the world.

The upshot, for Marxists, is that capitalism still involves exploitation and therefore is still inherently immoral. The American workers are still exploited, even though they have achieved a high standard of living. They could be better off than they are. Part of the reason they enjoy the standard of living they do, moreover, is the fact that American companies are exploiting other peoples of the world. Capitalism, the Marxists claim, necessarily involves exploitation.

What are we to say of the claim? The claim depends on the validity of Marx's labor theory of value. This economic theory attempts to explain not only profit but also prices, wages, economic cycles, and the variety of economic phenomena with which economics deals. Most Western economists have not accepted Marx's version of the labor theory of value. It does not give due weight to knowledge, creativity, and initiative in the productive process, or to the place of invention and efficiency in expanding the economic pie that is to be divided. It fails to take into account the role of risk and the entrepreneur. It is inadequate as an analysis of contemporary American capitalism because that system is vastly different from the system Marx described. Through pension plans and insurance policies, American workers are in fact, to a considerable extent, the owners of the means of production. The workers are not oppressed. There may be some exploitation, but exploitation consists of paying the worker less than the productivity of a worker at the margin. It is not built into the system.

The claim that the worker deserves all the value he produces is neither obvious nor in accord with Marx's own ideal of just distribution, which requires that each give according to his ability and receive according to his need. Whatever notion of justice we use, moreover, the Marxist analysis of exploitation cannot be applied because, except in a very few cases, we cannot determine the exact value of what each worker produces.

Nor does the claim that American capitalism survives because it exploits the underdeveloped countries carry much weight. There was a time during which many European countries had colonies; however, this time has passed.

Moreover, the less developed countries did not sell the United States goods or raw materials at lower prices than they sold the same items to socialist countries. American firms also look to the less developed countries to supply large markets as well as resources, and this means that those in the less developed countries must have the disposable income to buy U.S. goods. Workers must therefore receive more than subsistence wages. American companies pay workers of a country with a lower standard of living than ours less than American companies pay American workers. Is this exploitation? The question is a complex one, involving comparisons of buying power, skill, and comparative wage structures. We shall examine it in a later chapter. We should note in passing, however, that American multinational corporations are sometimes criticized for paying workers more than the going rate in less developed countries. But the major point is that there are alternatives for less developed countries. They can refuse American industry, and they can deal with other countries if they think it is not to their advantage to deal with the United States.

The conclusion we can draw from this brief analysis is that there are plausible replies to the Marxist charge of exploitation. The replies have not satisfied the Marxists, nor have attempts at updating Marx's theory satisfied most Western economists. The attack is at least inconclusive, if not definitely false.

Alienation of the People

The second Marxist claim is that capitalism is inherently immoral because it alienates human beings. It does not treat them as ends in themselves; it separates them into antagonistic camps and sets one against another; it stultifies the workers; it involves domination of some by others; and it produces other negative effects on all those who live within the system.

Alienation is a negative term. It describes the state of a person who is wrongfully separated from something to which he should be united, or who is dominated by something of his own making. The state or condition of alienation may be a conscious one, as when a person feels alienated; but someone may be alienated without feeling so.

There are various kinds of alienation. People may feel alienated from their government. Government is something created by people to serve their needs. When they have no control over it, and when government dominates them instead of responding to them and serving them, they are alienated from it. Religious alienation might be described by a believer as being separation from God through sin; by an unbeliever, as man being dominated by the idea of God, a creature of man's own imaginative making. Marx claims, however, that basic to all the other kinds of alienation is economic alienation. He describes it as the alienation of workers from the product of their labor, from the productive process, and from other people.

Under the capitalistic system, Marx observes, objects come to dominate people. People are judged by what they have, not by what they are. People work and live for possessions. The possessions come to dominate them, rather than being objects that they use to satisfy their needs.

Under capitalism, Marx claims, work is typically stultifying, noncreative, and routine. Instead of expressing oneself through one's work and developing all the sides of one's personality, work limits, cramps, and dulls the worker. People live when they are not working, and when they are working they can hardly be said to be living. They look forward to their leisure time, weekends, vacations, and coffee breaks—times when they can be themselves. They are separated from their labor, which they have sold to their employer. They are alienated from their labor, which they must sell in order to live.

Finally, the capitalist system, built on competition, divides people from each other. Instead of all humankind living together in harmony and peace, capitalism pits workers against employers. It pits competitors against each other, just as it forces workers to compete against each other for jobs. Capitalism is built on the division of society into classes, the owners of the means of production on one side and the workers on the other. The society is divided, and the state, laws, courts, police, schools, churches, and media are all controlled by the ruling class. The ruling class uses all these social institutions to dominate the workers, keep them subservient, and ensure the continuation of the institution of private property. The workers are thus alienated in many aspects of their lives. The owners of the means of production also live in an alienated society; they are also evaluated in terms of what they have, and they are also separated from other people and dominated by what they have.

Marx maintained that capitalism necessarily produces alienation because it is a function of private property and of the division of labor. Alienation cannot be eliminated without eliminating private property, and that cannot be eliminated without at the same time eliminating capitalism. Therefore, capitalism is inherently immoral.

Defenders of capitalism have given various replies. One claim is that the picture Marx drew is a caricature of capitalist society. In America, they say, workers are freer than in any other society in the world. They have a strong voice in government, which frequently protects their rights and defends them against employers. Though there is still dull work to be done, automation has taken over much of it and has freed people to do more creative work. The dull work that is a function of manufacturing, moreover, is not peculiar to capitalism; it is present wherever there is industrialization. A second response points out that Marx's description of capitalist society as a society of class conflict may have been true of nineteenth-century England. The history of the United States, however, has been one of great class mobility. In fact, it is sometimes difficult for people to know to which class they belong. Classes are not obvious, and the division of people into proletariat and bourgeoisie is not clearly applicable to the people of the United States. Marx's description also ignores the spirit of cooperation that is present in many aspects of American life. The emphasis on goods undoubtedly characterizes many Americans. Yet even this emphasis has been somewhat tempered in recent times by concern for quality of life.

A third approach to the Marxist charge of alienation has been to see whether alienation has actually been eliminated in those countries that have done away with private property. The Soviet Union was the prime example of such a society. But clearly, the defenders of capitalism argue, during the reign of Stalin the Soviet people were more oppressed and alienated from their government than Americans have ever been. The claim that private property is the cause of alienation is therefore disproven.

There are other answers in defense of American capitalism; the ones we have given exemplify the line they take. The rebuttals have not convinced the Marxists; nevertheless they have a certain validity. Marx's description of the alienation of the worker in the nineteenth century is not an accurate picture of the worker in present-day America. There are, however, aspects of the Marxist attack that are valid. Many people in the United States complain that government is out of control and that they have no real say in how they are governed; others complain about the emphasis of Americans on material goods; and some speak in terms of alienation. Still, no one has produced an analysis that satisfactorily shows that these ills are inherent in contemporary American capitalism. Once again, then, the claimed inherent immorality of capitalism remains an open question.

Vested Interests

The third Marxist charge is that capitalism defends the vested interests of the few and prevents the vast productive forces of society from truly serving the masses. The natural tendency of the productive process is toward social ownership instead of private ownership of the means of production. Those in the capitalist class, however, defend their own position and interests by preventing the transformation from private ownership to social ownership. In so doing, they delay the inevitable and prevent the people from enjoying that satisfaction of their needs which, given the great resources and productive capacity of our country, is possible. According to this critique, capitalism may not always have been inherently immoral. But it is immoral now, because it prevents the development of a morally better stage of social development. This analysis can be given a utilitarian interpretation. Protecting the vested interests of the rich at the expense of the workers produces less good on the whole than would the adoption of socialism or communism.

The reply of the defender of capitalism is to deny that the American system protects the rich at the expense of the worker. It protects and benefits all in the society, even if some benefit more than others. The defender of the system then usually refers to socialism as it exists or has existed in the world, whether it is democratic socialism, such as existed in England, or communistic socialism, such as in the Soviet Union. Both are examples of highly productive societies. Yet neither society seems superior to American society, either morally or materially. Therefore, the reply continues, the claim that the American system prevents the development of a better society is a claim without adequate foundation. Moreover, the workers of the United States (the ones whom the Marxist critics say would benefit most by a change to socialism) show no signs of developing a Marxist revolution.

The third criticism of inherent immorality has therefore not been convincingly demonstrated. Capitalism may be inherently immoral, but the Marxists' attacks fail to prove this.

Non-Marxist Moral Critiques of American Capitalism

Though Marxists have tended to be the most vocal, systematic, and thorough critics of capitalism, they are not its only critics. The non-Marxist critics do not always speak with one voice, nor is it always clear whether the ills to which they point are inherent evils of capitalism or remediable byproducts. We will now consider three criticisms that are symptomatic of others: (1) Capitalism creates waste and false needs, (2) capitalism feeds the military-industrial complex at the expense of the general population, and (3) capitalism creates gross and unjust inequalities.

False Needs and Overproduction

The charge that American capitalism is wasteful takes a variety of forms. It is of course true that Americans have grown up with comparative abundance. We have large expanses of land, a wealth of natural resources, and a high standard of living. As a result of our competitive system, we have worried little about conservation of our natural resources, or about the resources that we could buy from the rest of the world. The waste is evident in many areas. Our use of energy and of gasoline is particularly profligate. We have extended our cities into suburb after suburb without providing adequate public transportation and then relied on large fuel-inefficient automobiles that rarely are fully occupied. We have tended to build obsolescence into most of our products. We have preferred disposable products to those with replaceable parts. The list is endless.

In many instances, the claim goes, we could have done much better. Our waste is a national disgrace.

The attack is in large part true. We are paying the price for mistakes we made in the past. But our past waste was not the result of capitalism, nor is waste a necessary ingredient in capitalism. For instance, many European countries with capitalist economies have not fallen prey to the vice of waste. Nor is it clear that centralized planning eliminates waste; that waste is frequently of a different kind. Duplication of effort is part of the price of competition. But with some justification, its defenders claim that, on the whole, competition is more efficient than centralized planning.

The second part of the criticism strikes at the creation of false needs. Entrepreneurs create a product (e.g., an electric toothbrush) for which there was not an antecedent need or desire. Through a high-powered advertising campaign the manufacturer convinces people that they need the product to clean their teeth. The result is that a false need is created and filled, consuming resources that could be better used for other products.

Defenders of the free-enterprise system have argued that the notion of false needs is an arbitrary one. Who is to decide what a real need is and what is a false need? Consumers, they claim, should decide for themselves how they want to spend their money. They are not forced to buy one product rather than another. Nor is it true that manufacturers can sell anything they make simply by advertising it. Many products fail to gain a market because consumers resist the ads and ignore the product. The attack assumes that someone knows best what the people of the country should have. The counterclaim is that the people should be free both to produce and purchase what they wish without direction from some group with supposedly privileged knowledge.

The criticism, whatever its validity, is not central enough to make the judgment that capitalism is inherently immoral. It may, however, indicate an area in need of control, attention, or reform.

The Military-Industrial Complex

Despite the end of the Cold War, the second critique, which attacks the military-industrial complex, continues in its various forms. One view claims that the government drains the people of the country through taxation in order to support industries that produce materials for war. Another view is that the system can in the long run exist only if it is periodically sustained by war and the destruction and need for rebuilding that war produces. If the latter were the case, then the charge of an inherently immoral element could be sustained. A third claims that the military-industrial complex controls the government and has taken power out of the hands of the people, if it did indeed ever reside there.

To such charges no easy answer is possible, but a few observations are in order. First, war did not start with the appearance of capitalism. It has existed since the beginning of recorded history. Capitalism is not the only root of war, if it is a root at all. Second, expenditure for war is not an exclusive characteristic of capitalism as found in the United States. The United States plausibly claims, moreover, that its major effort is in defense spending because of the threat posed by other countries. Each side has its hawks and its doves. Third, the United States does spend large sums on its military establishment, but it is not clear that its economy would topple if its defense budget were reallocated to peaceful pursuits. There is even reason to believe that the opposite might be the case. Finally, the claim that the people have no voice in the political process because of the military-industrial complex is an overstatement. They have less voice than many would like; however, they have some voice and have achieved some gains at the expense of the military-industrial complex, and there is no inherent reason why, within the system, they cannot make further strides in this direction. The trick is to preserve democracy and prevent a slide toward a dictatorship.

Inequalities Inherent in the System

The third attack charges that capitalism creates gross and unjust inequalities. The disparity between the very rich and the very poor in the United States is enormous. A small percentage of the population controls a large proportion of the nation's wealth and income. The tax structure that is supposed to tax the rich progressively is so full of loopholes that the tax burden is borne primarily by the middle class. Many of those with the largest incomes pay no tax or very little. No human being, the argument continues, is so much better than another that the vast discrepancy in income—$10 million a year, say, compared with $10,000—can be justified.

According to Rawls's principles of justice, differences in income are justifiable only if opportunities are open to all, and if the least advantaged group benefits by the difference. It is not clear that the least advantaged group does benefit by the large differences in income; nor is it clear that even if they did, the benefit they receive is in any way proportional to the benefit that the rich receive. The poor not only obtain little improvement in their material conditions, but by comparison with the luxury of the wealthy they suffer a loss of self-respect. To compound the difficulties, many of the wealthiest families of our country amassed their fortunes in questionable and unethical ways. The history of the robber barons describes a notorious period in American history.

The drive toward greater equalization of wealth and income has many supporters. The charge that the tax structure needs overhauling is widely argued. The claim that the discrepancy between the wealth of the very rich and the poverty of the very poor is excessive carries a good deal of weight. Yet the question remains whether all of this, though a result of capitalism, is a necessary feature of American capitalism. Differences in income are to be expected in a competitive system and in a system in which monetary reward is a prime incentive for creativity in production. Yet the overall system can reduce the differential between the highest and the lowest paid, or it can, through a different tax structure, equalize the two considerably more than it presently does. Such injustices can be handled within the system. The charge, therefore, does not necessarily require a change of system, although that is one way of achieving the equalization many seek.

The Moral Defense of the American Free-Enterprise System

Can a moral defense of the American version of capitalism be mounted?[3] Although none of its defenders would claim that it is morally perfect, all would argue that is not immoral. For those who believe the Myth of Amoral

---

[3] Among the defenses of the American system of capitalism are H. B. Acton, *The Morals of Markets; An Ethical Exploration* (London: Longman Group Ltd., 1971); and Robert Benne, *The Ethic of Democratic Capitalism* (Philadelphia: Fortress Press, 1981) (argued from a religious point of view). Michael Novak, *The Spirit of Democratic Capitalism* (New York: A Touchstone Book, 1982), presents a theological defense.

Business this suffices. Yet some defenders of free enterprise go further and claim that it is inherently moral; and a few even claim that it is the most moral of the available systems.

We have already shown some of the arguments in defense of American free enterprise, in the answers given to those who claim it is inherently immoral. A sketch of a positive defense is nonetheless in order. Typically, a defense of the American free-enterprise system includes (1) emphasis on its values, especially freedom and efficiency, (2) its historical record in the production and distribution of wealth, and (3) its preferability to actual socialist societies.

Freedom and Efficiency

Defenders of the American free-enterprise system place their greatest emphasis on the importance and value of human freedom, which they claim the system presupposes, develops, and enriches. From a moral point of view the importance of human freedom scarcely needs defense. Each person is an end in himself or herself and worthy of respect. The free-enterprise system starts by recognizing this and then attempts to give it substance. The system allows the greatest freedom of action and choice to each person, compatible with a like freedom for all. This is guaranteed not only in the legal and political system but effectively in the economic realm. Consumers are allowed to buy what they want and to vote for products with their purchases. Producers are allowed free entry into the marketplace, where they compete under conditions kept fair by government. Some fare better than others, but that is a morally acceptable result of competition. The system, they say, fulfills its moral obligation by providing a safety net for all and caring for those unable to care for themselves.

Political freedom, the defenders of free enterprise insist, is possible only when economic freedom is its concomitant. Without individual economic freedom government not only makes all the economic decisions but also makes them as it pleases. If the government controls both the economic and political realms, it has broad scope for unrestricted action. The concentration of power is more likely than otherwise to corrupt those who possess it. Political freedom is meaningful only when we can lead our lives as we ourselves determine—this is part of what political liberty means. Political freedom requires limiting the sphere of government intervention in our lives, as well as providing the freedom to vote or express our views on what government should do.

In terms of Rawls's theory of justice, the American free-enterprise system thus satisfies—at least in principle—the first principle of justice. All people within the system have the right to most extensive basic liberty compatible with similar liberty for others. Americans do not enjoy unlimited liberty; some restrictions on freedom are necessary so that everyone can live in peace and security. The claim is that all are equal before the law. All citizens enjoy the same basic rights and the same basic freedom. To the extent that this is not true, there are procedures to remedy the injustices, as the civil rights movement and the women's movement demonstrate.

Because recognition of human freedom is an essential ingredient in treating people morally, the free-enterprise system is morally based. It values and enhances all aspects of human freedom and it makes this the centerpiece of its moral justification.

This defense of freedom leads in turn to a moral justification of private property. Because human beings are by right and nature free, they are free to take the necessary means for their survival and development. This involves the proper use of the resources of the earth. Effective use, however, involves the right to exclude others from use, as well as the right to the produce that one derives from such use. But these claims to the right to exclusive use are what constitute the essential ingredient of private property. Hence, freedom and the human right to self-development yield the moral basis for private property.

The other value, efficiency, also has a moral defense. Efficiency involves the use of the resources of the earth, including human labor, in such a way as to be least wasteful and most productive. To the extent that we consider needless waste immoral because it deprives us or others of potential good, at least in the long run, efficiency is moral. Capitalism, its defenders claim, values and promotes efficiency. The American experience is less than perfect, and there are aspects of the economy and of everyday life where efficiency is not evident and waste clearly exists. But on the whole, the argument goes, the competitive process, which is embedded in American free enterprise, is in the long run more efficient in the allocation and use of goods than any other system. This is true, they say, because suppliers respond to demand. Unless the market is used to indicate demand, goods are produced or talents are valued by a central decision-making agency—usually government—with much less information and with much less accuracy than that provided by a free market.

The Production of Wealth

Even its critics will not deny that under capitalism humankind has made enormous strides in its ability to produce goods. With the introduction of the machine and the rise of the industrial age there has been a manifold increase in human productivity. The result was that many more of the goods necessary for life became available in great quantity and at prices that could be afforded by the masses. From the seventeenth to the twentieth centuries, the rise in the standard of living of Americans dwarfs that of any other period in history. The ordinary person has come to have and expect what not even the wealthiest persons of previous centuries had. Mass production has increased the goods available, both those necessary for life and those simply desired for the ease, comfort, or enjoyment they produce.

The dramatic development of the machine age, moreover, has continued up to the present. The industrial revolution has been matched by the technological developments of the second half of the twentieth century. Infant mortality has decreased, and life expectancy has increased. Health care has improved. The possibilities for universal education have been realized. People have more time for leisure and cultural development. The list of areas in which progress has been made, knowledge developed, and pain relieved is almost endless.

All this, its defenders claim, is the result of free enterprise. Historically, no one can deny that the productive forces of human beings were multiplied and developed through capitalism. Even Karl Marx acknowledges capitalism as a necessary stage in the development of the productive resources of humankind and evaluates it positively in that respect. Its defenders go further. Not only did capitalism help free humans from drudgery in the past; it also continues to help improve the standard of living today. Nor is it only the rich who profit from it: Even the poorest members of American society live incomparably better than a great many Americans just a few generations—not to mention centuries—ago. The quality and availability of safe drinking water, the conditions of sanitation, and the presence of roads are just a few of the common benefits that all enjoy and that help make for a higher standard of living.

From a moral point of view, we can evaluate the result of the U.S. economic system over time. It has unquestionably enhanced human life and welfare, not only for Americans but also for many people in other lands, through the export of its know-how and technology, its goods, and its example, as well as providing a refuge for people from a great many different lands. All this must certainly be to its moral credit. Moreover, its defenders claim, its positive contributions far outweigh its negative aspects and the undeniable negative side effects.

Hence, the American free-enterprise system satisfies Rawls's second principle of justice. Although inequalities exist, they tend to lead to benefits for all, and they are found in a system in which there is equal opportunity—at least in principle—for all. Whether all the inequalities are arranged so that all are advantaged by each of them is, of course, a matter of debate. Undoubtedly, not all are so arranged. But there is no obstacle in principle—as opposed to obstacles in fact—to changing those that are not.

If we take the case of Bill Gates with which this chapter began, he has reaped enormous wealth. In the process, however, he has provided employment through his firm, and his products have been enormously useful. This is in large part why the company has been so successful. His dramatic accumulation of personal wealth in a short period of time is exceptional. But it in no way shows that profit incentives do not help all in the end, and in this case it seems to support the claim that incentives help lead to products from which all in society in one way or another, and to a greater or lesser extent, benefit. If the claim is that this case exemplifies the discrepancy between rich and poor which harms society, then the system has the means—redistribution through taxation being the primary one—to help lessen the harm. In the case of Microsoft, where one of every five employees has become a millionaire, the charge of exploitation of the work force seems hardly applicable, since by owning shares many of the workers have shared in the company's success.

Preferability to Actual Socialist Systems

The third prong of the moral defense of American capitalism begins with the admission that it is not perfect. No system is. Every system can be improved, and the moral task of American free enterprise requires that its immoral aspects be constantly fought and that human welfare be further enhanced. Its defenders claim that the freedom inherent in the system makes it possible to reform it. Also, the checks and balances provided by the diffusion of power in a variety of hands makes it more likely that positive changes will be made than would be the case if power were centralized in government. If democracy is the worst system of government, except for all the other systems of government humans have known, then American free enterprise might be called the worst politico-economic system, except for all the other systems humans have known. Nor, claim its defenders, is there a better system waiting on the horizon.

Ever since the days of Marx, socialism has been touted as the next stage of human development and one that is morally preferable to capitalism. As a theory, socialism has a strong moral appeal. Who can deny that a society is desirable in which all live harmoniously together, in which each contributes what he can and gets what he needs, and in which wealth flows abundantly? This is what socialism preaches. But the defenders of American free enterprise ask us to compare the American system not with the ideal of socialism but with the real socialist societies that those who have fought revolutions in the name of socialism have produced. Socialism is no longer an ideal waiting to be fulfilled, say the defenders of free enterprise. We have over seventy years of the results of the great socialist experiments. Compare conditions in the United States with those of the former USSR or of the former socialist countries of Eastern Europe, or with China, or Cuba. The higher standard of living of the American people cannot be denied. But look further, at the political freedom enjoyed by the people of the United States in comparison with the people of any of those countries. Once again its defenders claim there is no comparison. In all the historical instances we have, socialism has brought with it enormous human suffering, and the lot of ordinary people is not demonstrably better than it would have been otherwise. The conclusion drawn is that the American system, despite its defects, is morally preferable to the models of socialism offered by twentieth-century examples. Furthermore, the experiences of the socialist countries give most Americans no incentive to follow the road the socialist countries took.

The people of the former Soviet Union and of the former socialist republics of Central and Eastern Europe threw off their communist governments in 1991 and 1989, respectively. Their experience is ample proof that the end-state to which those governments led was intolerable. The people of those countries have now turned towards capitalism. How much they will preserve from socialism is still an open question that will undoubtedly be answered differently in different countries. How successful they will be in developing viable and productive societies depends not on how closely they follow the American example but on how successfully they devise their own sociopolitical-economic system to fit their needs. Their experience is a positive deterrent for Americans to move down the socialist path those countries trod. The conclusion that most Americans have drawn is that the American free-enterprise system, although it is not perfect and can be improved, is the best alternative presently available to us. The risk involved in adopting any other system does not presently seem worth the price Americans would surely have to pay to try the experiment.

Nonsocialist Alternatives to Contemporary American Capitalism

If we admit that the system is not perfect and that socialism is not a real option for most people, the question then becomes what and how the American system should be changed. There are three approaches to changing the present American system championed by various groups. The three are not necessarily mutually exclusive. One is libertarianism, a movement of the right. A second is workers' democracy, a movement of the left. The third is piecemeal change, wherever and however possible, with no overall blueprint. The first two are in some ways compatible with the third. Both the libertarians and the proponents of workers' democracy complain about the power and influence of government. The libertarians seek to diminish the role of government in business. The defenders of workers' democracy—whether or not they call themselves socialists—seek to end the collusion of big business and government, and to bring democracy into the marketplace. In the American context, neither group seeks violent revolution; both pursue dramatic change within the system.

The Libertarian Alternative

The libertarians, as their name indicates, put great emphasis on liberty. They not only consider this the major virtue of the free-enterprise system, but they also believe that only a minimalist government is compatible with liberty. They therefore complain that government has entered the marketplace with its laws, regulations, and taxes to the detriment of the freedom of the American citizen and businessman.[4]

---

[4] For developments of this position, see Robert Nozick, *Anarchy, State, and Utopia* (New York: Basic Books, 1974), which is a libertarian defense. A more moderate view is Milton Friedman's *Capitalism and Freedom* (Chicago: University of Chicago Press, 1962), which is a vigorous defense of the relation between capitalism and freedom.

The attack takes several forms and involves not only a view of economics but also a view of government. The typical libertarian, although not an anarchist (someone who advocates the absence of government), is a minimalist concerning the role of government. The legitimate function of government, he maintains, is to protect people and property from foreign attack and internal violence, and to provide for the adjudication of disputes and the enforcement of contracts. Thus, armed forces, police, and a legal and penal system are allowable, but governmental activity beyond these is inappropriate.

In particular, libertarians attack the redistributive function of government. Government, according to this position, should neither tax people nor redistribute income through welfare and other similar programs. The attack on taxes is especially vociferous. Taxation by government, they claim, is theft. If someone at gunpoint stopped you in the street and forced you to hand over 25 percent of your earnings so that he could give it to the poor, you would certainly protest that you were being robbed. Government does the same thing in taxation. Moreover, the libertarians continue, government does not simply turn over to the poor the money it takes in taxes. It uses a significant percentage of what it takes in taxes simply to keep its own machinery and giant bureaucracy operating. Not only does government take money from all of us, but also it uses it in ways that many of us do not sanction. It wastes, squanders, and misspends enormous amounts. That it does so should come as no surprise. You and I are careful in how we spend our money because we have to make do on limited funds. Government spends not its own money, but yours and mine, and overspends with impunity—raising taxes if it needs more money, or printing or borrowing more. The resulting inflation further diminishes our real income, already cut by taxes.

The second strenuous attack by the libertarians is on government regulation of business. They see the capitalist system as one based on free competition. If allowed to operate as it could, they claim, there would be no need for government regulation. Competition would remedy the evils that government unsuccessfully and inefficiently tries to correct. Government has a penchant for overkill and overregulation, even when it operates with good intentions. Moreover, many regulations intended for big business slowly drive small businesses under. There are so many government regulations, and they are so complicated, that the small businessperson must spend more time and money than he or she can afford, just keeping track of them and fulfilling their reporting requirements. The government guarantees loans to giants such as Lockheed and Chrysler when they are faced with bankruptcy but provides no help for the small businessperson. The libertarians do not advocate that the government help small businesspersons; the government should stay out of the business sector entirely, helping neither big nor small business.

The libertarian view is based on the notion of the sanctity of private property. Private property belongs to an individual. If he has worked for it, he deserves to keep what he has earned. If he has taken risks, if he has been lucky, if he has worked especially hard, if he has been innovative, the market will reward him. The rewards he fairly receives rightfully belong to him; they do not belong to government. The truly needy will be taken care of through charity and insurance plans; the lazy and unworthy poor will be forced to change their ways or suffer the consequences of their own actions.

The libertarian view has, therefore, a moral thrust. It champions liberty as a moral virtue worthy of human beings. It faults government as acting immorally in view of taxation, welfare, and many of its other programs. It demands changes. Yet libertarians emphatically defend democracy in the political realm, just as they defend free enterprise in the economic realm.

The libertarian position has not received widespread support, but some of its claims have struck a responsive chord in a number of people. The contemporary American revolt against excessive taxation is one instance of this response. California's rebellion against unlimited property taxes has spread to other parts of the country. Rising inflation and an unreformed tax structure are leading more and more people to adopt the European practice of cutting their own taxes, gambling on not being caught.

Historically, business has not been libertarian. Businesses sought and received protection from government in the way of tariffs and limitations on certain types of imports. They argued that the United States had to be self-sufficient. Its industry had to be protected against the possibility that war might prevent imports. Farmers sought and received governmental support for the prices of their crops. They argued that such support was necessary if farming was to continue successfully. In these and other areas business accepted the protection and help of government. Libertarians maintain that business has paid the price in regulation.

Yet, to be consistent, the libertarian cannot complain if people choose to be governed in certain ways (e.g., if they vote for taxes and for government spending) and if they freely choose security over freedom. He claims, however, that government is not truly responsive to the people; that people have not freely chosen that government act as it does; and that those who do not choose certain practices should not be bound by them. The practical matter of how to accomplish the ends libertarianism proposes is yet to be resolved. As an alternative to the present system, it is at best an indicator, an arrow pointing in a possible direction of change. It is not a ready-made alternative, just waiting in the wings as a panacea for the problems and immorality of the present system.

Workers' Democracy

The other alternative to the present system goes under a variety of names.[5] It is sometimes called workers' democracy, sometimes socialism. But the kind of socialism advocated follows neither the Soviet model nor the British model,

---

[5] See Michael Harrington, *The Twilight of Capitalism* (New York: Simon & Schuster, 1976); and Robert L. Heilbroner, *Between Capitalism and Socialism* (New York: Vintage Books, 1970).

for the claim is not that government should take over and run industry. The advocates of these systems attack government as strongly as do the libertarians, but for different reasons.

Workers' democracy sees government as inextricably intertwined with big business. Our elected leaders do not necessarily or consciously aim at supporting business interests at the expense of the interests of the ordinary citizen, but the structures of society are such that the interests of government and the interests of business are most often the same. Government has an enormous budget. Because it does not own industry, the government spends a good deal in contracts, which it gives to private industry. America's interests abroad are predominantly business interests. We protect these interests in foreign countries and support them at home; we fight wars over natural resources in distant lands; and growing numbers of people move easily from the halls of government to the offices of big business, changing hats with little difficulty.

Capitalism has produced for the American worker a better life. American workers have more goods, comfort, and luxury than workers in any other part of the world and in any other period of history, but the American free-enterprise system has become more oppressive than liberating. Yet it can be liberated. True democracy is now possible, if we extend democracy to the economic realm and revivify it in the political realm.

Defenders of workers' democracy point out that many of the decisions made by the major corporations in America affect all of our lives more than the decisions made in Congress. We elect our representatives in Congress, but we have no say at all in what the board of directors of General Motors or Exxon or any other large corporation decides. The allocation of resources, the building and closing of plants, the creation and termination of jobs are all decisions that directly affect large numbers of people who have no voice in these decisions. Nor is government regulation the answer, because government is intertwined with big business.

The appropriate reply of the American people has been slow in coming. Consumer groups have grown up to protect their interests and to provide some sort of response to big business. Environmentalists have also organized to oppose business projects they consider harmful to the environment. Unions have, of course, represented workers vis-à-vis management and have fought for better wages and working conditions. But because they have been wed to their adversarial role with respect to management, they have not typically sought worker participation in management, worker control of the productive process, or workers' democracy. It seems unlikely that workers' democracy in the United States will be anything other than a peripheral movement for a long time to come.

Piecemeal Change

If the basic aim of libertarianism is the liberty of the businessman, the basic aim of workers' democracy is workers' control over their own destiny. In some ways the two positions are similar. Both want greater freedom for members of society than they have today. Both attack government and the interrelation of government and business. But the means they advocate are dramatically different from one another.

The worker in a workers' democracy would have a say in what is produced and how it is produced. The division between workers and manager would give way. The workers would share directly in the profits of the firm. The adversarial relation between employer and employee would be replaced by a cooperative effort of all those engaged in the same enterprise. An effective voice in business decisions would mean as much as an effective voice in government decisions. The democracy we have cherished in the political sector must be recouped and extended to the productive sector, in their view.

The separation of management from ownership has already taken place in most large firms. Managers are as truly employees as are assembly-line workers. Peter Drucker has written about the unseen revolution, in which workers, through union pension funds and insurance funds, are the largest owners of business.[6] Management works for them in their role as shareholders, and this relation should now be translated into fact. There should be an end to domination of the workers, their exploitation, and their alienation.

The movement toward workers' democracy has been slow in developing, although consumerism and environmentalism have grown rapidly. The demand for worker representation on boards of directors has been adopted in Germany, but such representation is rare in the United States. Ironically, the workers themselves have been slow to respond to the call for workers' democracy.

Both libertarianism and workers' democracy are straws in the wind. They are indicative of dissatisfaction with many aspects of big government and big business. They are rallying points for the expression of this dissatisfaction and for proposals for change. Both movements are wedded to change within the system, which may eventually lead to change of the system. They do not espouse violent revolution, or sudden, drastic change. Their gradualism is consistent with a piecemeal approach to the correction of the immoral practices within the system.

A small minority claims that the American system is free of immorality, is sufficiently just, and should not be tinkered with. But most people realize that we do not yet have a completely just society, that our structures can be improved, that the war on poverty has not yet been won, that we still have to solve the problems of the appropriate use of energy, and that we have barely begun to face the moral demands made on us by the poor and underdeveloped countries of the world.[7] Yet the consensus in the United States is that we

---

[6] Peter F. Drucker, *The Unseen Revolution* (New York: Harper & Row, Publishers, 1976).

[7] An interesting document that has caused a good deal of discussion is National Conference of Catholic Bishops, *Economic Justice for All: Pastoral Letter on Catholic Social Teaching and the U.S. Economy* (Washington, D.C.: U.S. Catholic Conference, 1986).

do not need another system. No other system is morally preferable, or waiting to be adopted. We can and should make the morally necessary changes in American capitalism, improve it, and work toward a yet unattained maximal mix of freedom and justice. The real alternative to our present American system does not consist in holistic change. What is most likely to succeed is piecemeal change: correcting ills where possible, outlawing immoral practices, and implementing structural changes that promote moral conduct. American capitalism can be made more moral than it is, and the task for all of us is to make the required changes where and how we can. One of the functions of business ethics is to scrutinize, from a moral point of view, the practices and structures within the American economic system, to identify immoral ones, and to propose preferable moral alternatives where possible.

Study Questions

1. Microsoft continually revises the system program MS-DOS. Based on those revisions, it then revises its application programs such as Word. It can make the latter changes before the revised system program is released to the public. Some competitors claim that this gives Microsoft an unfair advantage with respect to its application programs because other companies can revise their application programs only after a new version of MS-DOS has been released. Is their claim morally justified?

2. Is there anything immoral about an individual getting $1 billion a year from his or her business? Why or why not?

3. Does the model of capitalism described in Chapter 6 correspond to the economic system in the United States today? Why or why not? Is capitalism different from free enterprise?

4. Under what conditions is free enterprise morally defensible? Are these conditions met in the United States?

5. What constitutes a fair transaction? Defend the claim that these conditions make a transaction fair.

6. What are the traditional roles of government? Are these roles played by all governments or only by certain kinds of governments or only at certain times?

7. How does government deal with people who do not contribute to the economy? How should a government deal with them? Are there different categories of such people?

8. How does government enter the marketplace? Is its entry morally justifiable?

9. Why does government adopt fiscal and monetary policies?

10. How does government attempt to keep transactions in the marketplace fair? Is this a legitimate role for government? May a government morally favor, protect, or otherwise treat some firms differently from others?

11. Is taxation morally justifiable? If so, show how; if not, show why.

12. Present and evaluate the Marxist claim that capitalism is based on exploitation. What is meant by exploitation? the labor theory of value?

13. Define alienation. Present and evaluate the Marxist claim that capitalism alienates human beings. Is alienation peculiar to capitalism?

14. Present and evaluate the Marxist claim that capitalism prevents the productive forces of society from serving the masses.

15. Present and evaluate the claim that capitalism creates waste and false needs. If the claim is correct, does it show capitalism is inherently immoral? Why or why not?

16. Present and evaluate the claim that capitalism feeds the military-industrial complex at the expense of the general population. Does it do so less now that the Cold War is over?

17. Present and evaluate the claim that capitalism creates gross and unjust inequalities. Are all gross inequalities of wealth unjust? Why or why not?

18. Describe and evaluate the libertarian alternative to American corporate capitalism.

19. Present and evaluate the alternative of workers' democracy.

20. What is the alternative of piecemeal change? Is it compatible with either the libertarian or the model of workers' democracy?

21. Showing that attacks on the morality of the American free-enterprise system are not conclusive is not the same as showing that the system is morally justifiable. Sketch out the kind of argument that would be needed to show that the system is morally justifiable.

8

>–!–◆>–◦–‹◆–!–◃

CORPORATIONS
AND
MORALITY

The Case of Malden Mills

The fire, started perhaps by an exploding boiler, quickly enveloped one building, then spread to another, and then to a third. The main manufacturing
buildings of Malden Mills were reduced to rubble on the night of December
11, 1995.[1] Malden Mills had been founded in 1906 by Henry Feuerstein, the
grandfather of the present owner, Aaron Feuerstein. In 1956 the business had
been moved from Malden to Lawrence, Massachusetts. By 1995 most of the
other fabric companies in Lawrence had closed or moved South or abroad to
take advantage of cheaper labor costs. In the 1980s Malden Mills had gone
bankrupt when the market for the fake fur which it produced dried up. But in
addition to continuing its production of upholstery fabric and fleece it developed a new product, Polartec, and had made a successful recovery. Polartec is
a synthetic fleece, made from recycled plastic bottles, that is light, warm, and
resilient and used in sports- and outerware made by such companies as Eddie
Bauer, North Face, L. L. Bean, Patagonia, and Lands' End.

The night of the fire Aaron Feuerstein had been celebrating his seventi-
eth birthday, when he returned home to learn the news. He rushed to the
scene of the fire and with the help of the firefighters and some of his employees managed to save part of the one remaining production building. He was

---

[1] The fullest account of the fire and the immediate aftermath is presented by Bruce D. Butter-
field, "Test By Fire: The Story of Malden Mills," in four parts, *The Boston Globe*, September
8,9,10,11, 1998. See also Pater Michelmore, "One Boss in a Million," *Reader's Digest*, October 1996,
pp. 94-99.

determined to rebuild as soon as possible. His other options, pressed by some of his advisors, were to close down and retire on what he could get from insurance, or to rebuild elsewhere. Feuerstein rejected those options and decided, against the advice of some of his staff, that he would not only start rebuilding immediately, but that he would also give each worker a $275 Christmas bonus as planned and announce that he would continue to keep them all on the payroll for at least 30 days.

The plant was insured for $300 million. But the insurance company would not make payments until it had determined the cause of the fire and had concluded that it was not arson. Feuerstein needed the insurance money to rebuild, but he could not wait for it to come through. So he took out $100 million in loans, used his own money, and started the process immediately. His workers rallied around him. When the first thirty days were up, he guaranteed all his workers another thirty days wages, whether or not they worked. And he did this a third time as well. Their wages were among the highest in the industry, averaging $25.50 per hour. Within three months he had rebuilt the plants sufficiently so that he had not lost his major customers for Polartec and had most of his employees back to work. He was unable to reopen one upholstery division, however, and reluctantly had to let go 400 out of his 3,100 employees, 2,320 of whom were employed at the Lawrence location. Even then, however, he continued the health insurance for those 400 workers for an additional three months, opened a workers' center to help them, and gave them priority on call-back rights so they would be the first ones hired when he was able to take on new employees.

His treatment of his employees received national recognition. President Clinton invited him to sit next to the First Lady at his State of the Union Address. Newspapers carried Feuerstein's story. He was awarded honorary degrees by Yeshiva University and Boston University. An article in *Fortune* commented, "Malden Mills owner Aaron Feuerstein was both ridiculed and canonized when he kept his 1,000 employees on the payroll after a fire burned down his factory last Christmas. But now he's proving that treating workers well is just plain good business."[2]

It is not clear if the same thing would have been said about him if his business had failed instead of succeeding, even though his treatment of his workers would have been the same. Nor was it by any means certain for some time that he would succeed in his attempt to rebuild. By February the insurance company had paid only a $9 million advance. Paying his workers' salaries despite the fact he had no work for many of them to do cost him $13 million. In the first quarter following the fire Malden Mills posted a quarterly loss of $50 million. Feuerstein managed to keep his major Polartec customers, but he lost some of his customers for his upholstery line. Succeed he did, however. On June 6, 1997, the insurance company finally agreed to pay the full $300 million in fire damages. Rebuilding the plants with state-of-the-art equip-

---

[2] Thomas Teal, "Not a Fool, Not a Saint," *Fortune*, November 11, 1996, p. 201.

ment cost an additional $40 million. But the new factory was dedicated on September 16, 1997, and sales were up 40 percent since the time of the fire, with productivity up 25 percent. The last seventy of the terminated workers were rehired within months thereafter. In addition Malden Mills has enjoyed a publicity and advertising bonanza and has generated an inestimable amount of goodwill not only on the part of its workers but also of its customers and the general public.

Feuerstein claims he did what he had to do. He said that could not turn his back on either his employees or the city of Lawrence. His treatment of his employees has made them fiercely loyal to him and they worked enormously hard helping him to rebuild his plant in record time. Despite the fact that his decision to keep his employees on the payroll for ninety days after the fire, whether or not there was work for them, was controversial, it is now lauded as good business.

Was what Feuerstein did the right thing to do, as he claims, not only from a business point of view but also from an ethical point of view? Was it ethically mandatory or was it beyond what ethics demands? Would a publicly owned company have been able to make the same grand gesture and would the shareholders of the company and the Wall Street analysts have seen the move as enlightened business practice?

➤—┤◆➤—◆—◆┤—◄

Malden Mills is in many ways an exception to the way large firms operate. It is a privately held, not a public corporation, and it is run by its owner. Ethics applies to all business transactions and to all businesses, large and small. But the emphasis in most discussions of business ethics and the emphasis in this book is on corporations, and especially on larger corporations. The reasons are many. Small businesses typically tend to be run by their owners. They thus tend to reflect the ethics of the owners, who run the businesses the way they run their lives. If they have employees, the owner tends to know the employees, and the relation, although a business one, cannot help but be personal because it is face-to-face. One result is that most of the employer's actions with respect to the employees are reasonably transparent. Employees know the conditions under which they work, they know whether they are being treated fairly, and if they are not, they know who is to blame and to whom to complain. Similarly, transactions with customers tend to be transparent in the same way. Repeat customers demand that the business treat them fairly, or they will go elsewhere.

Corporations have a special status under American law in that they have limited liability. This is one reason for treating them differently, since the owners of stock in the company are only liable for the amount they have invested in stock. Their personal assets are not at stake. But the major reason for concentrating on large corporations is because they are typically impersonal, powerful, and capable of both great good and great harm. They are impersonal because they are typically run by managers hired by the shareholders to run the company. Because they are large, it is impossible for the top managers to know all the employees and there are usually various layers of management between the workers and the CEO of the company. Hence structures, rules, and operating procedures take the place of face-to-face management. The ethical tone of the corporation is set by upper management; but managers are also hired personnel, unlike the owner-managers who have a special and personal stake in their company.

Large corporations employ large numbers of people, who are dependent on the corporations. In turn, many of the towns in which the corporation's plants are located are similarly dependent on the corporation. Large-scale production of most products produces large-scale waste, often toxic. With great power goes great responsibility. And one of the tasks of business ethics is to help clarify those responsibilities to society, employees, stockholders, consumers, and all others affected by a corporation's actions.

The Moral Status of Corporations and Formal Organizations

The corporation is a special kind of entity. In 1819, Chief Justice Marshall, in *Dartmouth College v. Woodward,* defined it as follows: "A corporation is an artificial being, invisible, intangible, and existing only in contemplation of law. Being the mere creature of law, it possesses only those properties which the charter of creation confers upon it, either expressly, or as incidental to its very existence. These are such as are supposed best calculated to effect the object for which it was created." It can act, hold property, and be sued. A major aspect of corporations, and one of the primary reasons for which they are established, is that they have only limited liability. This shelters corporate shareholders or owners from personal liability. Those who invest in a corporation can lose only the amount of money they invest. Their personal assets cannot be attached.

Moral responsibility is usually both ascribed to and assumed by individuals. Does it make any sense to speak of the moral responsibility of nations, or corporations, and of other formal organizations?[3] If it does make sense to do so, do we mean the same thing by the term *moral responsibility* in these cases as we do when referring to human individuals?

If we start from ordinary usage, people clearly do refer to the actions of some nations as immoral; they speak of the moral responsibilities of rich nations vis-à-vis poor ones; they claim that corporations that sell unsafe or harmful products act immorally. Yet a strong position has been adopted by

---

[3] The contemporary discussion of the moral status of corporations and formal organizations began with John Ladd's "Morality and the Ideal of Rationality in Formal Organizations," *The Monist,* 54 (1970), pp. 488-516. An excellent collection of articles on the topic is Hugh Curtler (Ed.), *Shame, Responsibility and the Corporation* (New York: Haven Publishing Corp., 1986). See also Peter A. French, *Collective and Corporate Responsibility* (New York: Columbia University Press, 1984).

such people as Milton Friedman[4] and by such organizational theorists as Herbert Simon,[5] who seem to hold that corporations and other formal organizations are not moral entities. According to this view, they are legal beings, at best. They can be held legally liable, and they can be bound by laws, but only human beings are moral agents and only human beings have moral responsibility. Some people may speak as if corporations or businesses have moral obligations, but they are simply confused. Moreover, the view continues, when individuals work for a company, they act for the company and in the company's name. When so acting, their actions are part of the actions of the firm; hence, they should not be evaluated from a moral point of view. When they act contrary to the interests of the firm or when they break the law, steal from the company, or embezzle funds, then they act in their own right and are properly judged from a moral point of view. The conclusion is that businesses are not moral agents, have no moral responsibilities, and should not be morally evaluated.

Organizational View of the Corporation

This view, which I shall call the Organizational View, is a variant of the Myth of Amoral Business. It was developed in part as a reaction to a number of moral demands made by environmentalists and consumer groups concerning the social responsibility of business. Milton Friedman's reaction to such claims is to assert that the business of business is to make profits and that social reform, welfare, and the like are the proper concern not of business but of government.

The Organizational View has been widely attacked, yet it cannot be dismissed out of hand. It makes the valid point that organizations, corporations, and nations are not moral entities in the same sense as individual human beings. Therefore, if we are to consider them as moral agents, we must be careful how we use our terms and make clear what we mean by them.

Moral Person View of the Corporation

The argument against the claim that formal organizations are not moral beings is fairly simple. Morality governs the action of rational beings insofar as they affect other rational beings. Formal organizations—for instance, corporations—act. Ford Motor Company produces cars; it also builds factories, hires and fires people, pays them wages, pays taxes, recalls defective models, and so on. Not only do businesses act, they also act rationally according to a rational decision-making procedure. Because their rational actions affect people, these actions can be evaluated from a moral point of view. If it is immoral for an individual to discriminate, it is also immoral for a corporation to discriminate. If it is praiseworthy for an individual to give to charity, it is praiseworthy for a busi-

---

[4] Milton Friedman, "The Social Responsibility of Business Is to Increase Its Profits," *New York Times Magazine,* September 13, 1970.

[5] Herbert A. Simon, *Administrative Behavior,* 2nd ed. (New York: The Free Press, 1965).

ness to give to charity. If it is wrong for people to steal, it is wrong for businesses to steal. Actions can be morally evaluated whether done by an individual or by an entity such as a company, a corporation, or a nation. The alternative would be to say that although murder is wrong for individuals, it is not morally wrong for businesses, or that although exploitation of one person by another is morally wrong, exploitation of a person by a corporation is morally neutral. This is clearly unacceptable, because murder, stealing, exploitation, and lying are wrong whether done by a human being, a corporation, or a nation; the action is wrong whoever the perpetrator of the action is.

The dispute does not end here, however, for part of the point of the Organizational View is that formal organizations do not act. Neither do corporations, clubs, companies, or nations. People within them act, but the organization itself is nothing more than a formal structure. It does not do anything. People within it do whatever it is that gets done. Obviously, there is something correct about the assertion that only people act and that formal organizations do not act. Yet, as we noted previously, we often speak of firms and nations as acting. Who is correct? How do we decide?

Moral Actor View of the Corporation

The answer to both questions can be found through a closer analysis of our use of language. When we say, "Ford makes cars," we do not mean that the cars are made by magic; we know that no car will get made unless someone makes it. A great many people, using a variety of tools and machines, contribute to making a Ford car. Yet we can use the name *Ford* to mean all of the people and their relations and activities together. We know that there are workers and managers, a president of the firm, a board of directors, and shareholders. Yet without any knowledge of who does what within the firm, we can speak of Ford making cars. This is a perfectly understandable statement, made from outside the corporation and referring to it as a whole. If Ford recalls defective cars, someone must make the decision to recall them, and either the same person or other people must send out the notices. They act not in their own names but as employees or agents of the firm.

In our ordinary use of English it is proper and common to use the name of a firm to refer to all those associated with it, to refer to the products that those associated with it produce, or to refer to the entity that is liable to suit. Therefore, when we make a moral judgment about the actions of a firm or of a nation, we need not know who within the firm is the person or persons responsible. We can hold the firm as such responsible, from a moral as well as from a legal point of view. But granted that we can make moral judgments about the actions of a firm or nation, why should we? The answer can be found in what we wish to accomplish by such judgments. In making moral judgments about the actions we attribute to a firm or nation, we do many things. We express our emotions, evaluate an action, and encourage other people to react to the action as we do. In expressing our moral evaluation we either praise or blame. When we morally condemn an action, we might wish to encourage others to impose moral sanctions, or bring pressure to bear to rectify the wrong or to change the policy in question.

One method of doing this is a consumer boycott, such as the one that California migrant workers sponsored on lettuce at Safeway stores, or that the INFACT coalition sponsored against Nestlé.[6] A boycott attempts to bring pressure on a company to change what is seen as an immoral practice or policy. Those who call a boycott may not know who within the company is responsible for the questionable practices and may not care. A boycott may result in a cutback in production by the company, with a consequent laying off of workers who are not involved in setting policy or implementing it in any way. A boycott is called, however, not to lay off particular people but to change the company's policy. From the outside, it is a matter of indifference who is responsible for the practice and who carries it out. The intent is to identify the practice as immoral, to call it to people's attention, and to unite them to create moral pressure to stop the practice.

A similar analysis can be applied to nations. When the United States condemned the Iraqi invasion of Kuwait, spokesmen for the United States did the condemning. Although we say that Iraq invaded Kuwait, we obviously mean that Iraqi soldiers invaded it. We see them as agents receiving orders from the head of government. But the head of government does not himself physically invade. In some cases, we distinguish what the leaders of a country do from what the ordinary people do; in other cases, we do not. If one country blockades another, members of the armed forces of the one country prevent the exportation or importation of goods from or to the other country. One country may declare war on another and does so through its government; but war is not declared only against certain people in that country. Just as in talking about a business, the collective term serves many functions, and no nation acts unless people act for it.

The issue is not whether an action can correctly be attributed to a corporation (or formal organization or nation), or whether it should more appropriately be attributed to the person or people within the corporation who make the decisions in question and carry them out. Attribution of an action, and so of moral responsibility for that action, to a corporation is intelligible, and from a practical point of view may be effective. Nor is the issue one of deciding whether we should ascribe responsibility to *either* the corporation *or* to the individuals within it. There is no need to choose. We can ascribe responsibility to the corporation only; to the corporation, as well as one or more of the individuals within it; or only to an individual or individuals within the corporation.[7] To whom we ascribe responsibility depends on the facts of the particular case in question.

---

[6] For details on the Nestlé boycott, see Chapter 11.

[7] For discussions of collective responsibility, see Larry May, *The Morality of Groups* (Notre Dame, Ind.: University of Notre Dame Press, 1987); and Peter A. French (Ed.), *Individual and Collective Responsibility*, 2nd ed. (Rochester, VT: Schenkman Books, Inc., 1998).

The assumption of responsibility, however, must always be by individuals, whether they assume it for themselves or, by virtue of their position, for the corporation. Moral responsibility for a corporation's actions may be assumed by the members of the board of directors, the president, various levels of management, or by the workers. Each person may hold himself morally responsible for doing his job, and he may hold others morally responsible for doing theirs; or moral responsibility may be refused by some or all of them.

Moral charges made from the outside, and moral responsibility ascribed to a corporation or nation from the outside, may be rejected, rebutted, refuted, or ignored. This happens when no one within the corporation or nation accepts the responsibility ascribed to it.

Corporations are not human beings. The differences between human individuals and corporations, other formal organizations, and nations are significant from a moral point of view and from the point of view of moral responsibility. A corporation as such has no conscience, no feelings, no consciousness of its own.[8] It has a conscience only to the extent that those who make it up act for it in such a way as to evince something comparable to conscience. Because a corporation acts only through those who act for it, it is the latter who must assume moral responsibility for the corporation. It may not always be clear who within the corporation should assume this responsibility.

When harm is unjustly done to an individual by a firm, the firm has the moral obligation to make reparation to the individual. For example, it matters little whether the particular person who systematically paid women employees less than men for the same work is still with the firm. If the women deserve compensation for past injustice, the firm has the moral obligation to make it good. Someone who had nothing to do with perpetrating the past injustice but who is now employed by the firm may have the moral obligation to take action to make up for past wage discrimination. If a firm is morally responsible for wrongs done, it is morally obliged to make good those wrongs. But exactly who must do what within the firm can often only be appropriately decided by an analysis of individual cases.

We can and do use moral language with respect to the actions of businesses, formal organizations, and countries. But in any analysis, as we shift from individual human beings to organizational entities, we should be aware of the differences in meaning and application of the terms we use.

Insofar as corporations act intentionally, they can be held morally responsible for their actions. They are thus moral actors. But because corporations are not ends in themselves, they are not moral persons. Hence, we can morally evaluate the ends for which a corporation is established. Because corporations are not human beings, they cannot claim the moral rights of human beings—the right to life or continued existence, for example. The attempt to

---

[8] See Kenneth E. Goodpaster and John B. Matthews, Jr., "Can a Corporation Have a Conscience?," *Harvard Business Review*, 60 (January-February 1982), pp. 132-141.

attribute all the rights of human persons to corporations results from a confusion about the moral status of corporations.

Because the moral status of corporations is different from the moral status of human beings, the moral obligations of corporations are different from the moral obligations of human beings. The difference hinges on the fact that corporations are limited and organized for only certain purposes. The fact that a corporation does exist and has been established for certain purposes is no guarantee that it should exist or that its purposes are morally justifiable. But as long as the ends for which corporations are formed are not immoral, and as long as the means by which those ends are pursued are not immoral, corporations are not bound by a large range of moral rules that bind natural persons.

As is true of all other moral actors, corporations are bound not to harm others. This negative injunction is a major restraint on corporations. But the positive obligations of corporations depend on their ends, their particular situations, their legal status, and the sociopolitical environment in which they are organized and operate. Because corporations are not human persons, the injunction to produce the greatest amount of good applies differently to individual persons with a full range of activities open to them and to a corporation with very great restrictions on its purpose and its appropriate activities. Because corporations are not moral persons, it is doubtful whether we can expect them to act from moral motives. What we can expect is that they not do what is morally prohibited. We can praise them for doing what is in accord with the moral law, and blame them for what is a violation of it. Corporations lack the interiority characteristic of human individuals; therefore, their actions, not their motives, are the proper object of moral evaluation. Corporations are neither machines nor animals. They are organizations run by human beings and, as such, have a moral status that makes them amenable to moral evaluation, even though they are not moral persons per se.

Concept of the Corporation: Shareholder versus Stakeholder

The classical concept of the corporation presents the corporation as existing primarily to serve the shareholders. The corporation provides jobs and produces goods or services. But these are a means to the end of increasing shareholder wealth. There is no obligation on the part of a corporation to maximize the wealth of its shareholders. It could not have that obligation because it could not fulfill it. Yet some view the obligation of the managers of a corporation to attempt to achieve the greatest gains they can for the shareholders, within the boundaries of the law. They claim, therefore, that the managers of a corporation are hired and overseen by the board of directors of the corporation to enhance their wealth, and that they have a fiduciary obligation to the shareholders to attempt to do so to the best of their ability. According to this view the interests of the shareholders are paramount and come first over all other interests.

This view, however, is being challenged. The challenge is based on two different kinds of considerations. The first is that shareholders, although legally the owners, are very often simply speculators with no real interest in the long-range future of the company. Their interest is in the greatest immediate return on investment they can achieve, even if this leads to the ultimate long-range detriment of the company. As soon as the company's stock price starts going down, they will sell their stock and invest their money elsewhere. Running a company for such stockholders is in the long run detrimental to the existence of the corporation. In addition, there are a large number of owners of stock who have their holding through mutual funds or investment plans or insurance policies and who do not even know that they own the stock of a particular company. To say that the company should be run primarily, if not exclusively, for them seems at least a little odd.

The second consideration is that although stockholders of a corporation are technically the owners and have rights, including the right to have the company run well, there are other constituents who have a much stronger interest and involvement in the firm, and a much stronger stake in it and in its continuance and success. Hence this consideration argues for the view that instead of considering only shareholders in running the firm, one should consider all the stakeholders in the firm. A corporation is not run solely for the shareholders but for all the stakeholders. The employees of a firm clearly have a very strong stake in it. This is where they spend an important part of their lives. They devote their time and energy, their talents and creativity, their ideas and muscle to the corporation that pays them. Without them there would be no firm. They are surely as important to the firm as are the shareholders, and since they contribute not their money but themselves, they deserve respect and consideration in decisions taken by the firm that affect them.

The community in which a large corporation takes root is also directly affected by it and is in that sense a stakeholder in the corporation. Aaron Feuerstein understood that both the employees and the community relied on his corporation and he felt and expressed an obligation to them. Malden Mills was privately owned, so he had no other shareholders to whom he was accountable. But if his view was correct that his company had an obligation to the employees and the community, then the fact that the company was privately rather than publicly held is irrelevant. A public firm has the same obligations, or if one prefers, the owners of the firm have the same obligations, even though they may have little interest in or knowledge of the company of which they own a part. Their obligations are handled by management, just like the company's obligation to its customers, to its suppliers, and to the general public insofar as it is affected by the company's success or failure, for instance, in controlling its pollution.

This stakeholder view of the firm does not deny the obligation of the managers to provide as good a return as possible to the shareholders. But it realistically interprets this to mean the best returns possible in the long run, consistent with fulfilling its obligations as well to all the other stakeholders. Whether this means keeping all employees on the payroll for ninety days after a fire has destroyed the manufacturing plant in which they work may seem doubtful. But if what Aaron Feuerstein did was both morally correct and good business, then it would be the proper business decision for any company, private or public. Against this view, someone might argue, one difference is that Feuerstein took a chance and gambled with his own money. If managers of a publicly held company were to take a similar chance, they would be gambling not with their own money but with the money of their shareholders. Although this is correct, if the decision is both ethically proper and good business, top managers should be able to defend such a decision to the shareholders. Managers are paid to make decisions as best they can, weighing and balancing all their obligations to all their stakeholders. In the long run, keeping the loyalty of workers helps increase productivity, and satisfying customers helps increase sales and so profits.

Running a firm from the point of view of recognizing, considering, and treating all the stakeholders fairly involves a different view of the corporation from the traditional one of considering shareholder interests only or of holding those interests paramount. The stakeholder view of the corporation provides a different perspective of what the corporation is and how it should be run from the shareholder view. Yet the stakeholder view is not entirely new and is implicitly held by all those many managers who believe that the best and surest way to make a profit and to increase the value of the shares of a company is to develop a loyal and competent work force and to provide the best product for customers at the best and most competitive price. Companies that seek profits at the expense of their workers and customers rarely are able to generate that profit for very long.

All those to whom the corporation has any moral obligations are collectively referred to as stakeholders in the corporation. A *stakeholder analysis*[9] of an issue consists of weighing and balancing all of the competing moral demands on a firm by each of those who have a claim on it, in order to arrive at the firm's moral obligation in any particular case. The stakeholder approach has the strength of forcing us to consider carefully all the obligations involved, for instance, in a plant closing, instead of just looking at the closing from the point of view of profitability, and so from the point of view of the shareholders. The stakeholders in a plant closing include not only shareholders but also workers, suppliers, consumers, the local community, and possibly others. A stakeholder analysis, as we noted earlier, does not preclude the interests of the sharehold-

---

[9] For discussions of stakeholder analysis, see R. Edward Freeman, *Strategic Management: A Stakeholder Analysis* (Boston: Pittman, 1984); and Kenneth Goodpaster, "Business Ethics and Stakeholder Analysis," *Business Ethics Quarterly*, 1 (January 1991), pp. 53-72.

ers overriding the interests of the other stakeholders affected, but it ensures that all affected will be considered. Sometimes the rights of one set of stakeholders overrides the interests of the others; and sometimes the interests of that set of stakeholders is overridden by the interests or rights of another set. The stakeholder approach is compatible with utilitarian and deontological approaches, as well as with using second-order moral judgments. It simply requires that all those whose interests are involved get fair consideration.

Moral Responsibility within the Corporation

The general obligations of corporations stem from the nature of the corporation, of society, and of the implicit agreement between the two. The first is the obligation to "Do no harm." This is a general obligation binding on individuals and corporations alike. It is sometimes called the "moral minimum" that corporations must meet. The harm to be avoided is most clearly harm to people, who are to be treated with respect and as ends in themselves. This is a wide-ranging obligation that has ramifications for a company's operation. It influences the way corporations may treat their employees, the communities in which they are located, their customers, the general public, and the environment.

The second general obligation comes from the nature of the free-enterprise system in which the corporation is founded. The corporation depends on the integrity of the system and thus has the moral obligation not to undermine the freedom and the values of the system. This also has broad ramifications from the obligation not to engage in bribery to the obligation not to engage in monopolistic practices—both of which undermine the competitive system.

The third general obligation is to be fair in the transactions in which it engages. Fairness in transactions is essential for the system to continue. Without such fairness, transactions will tend not to take place, or not to be repeated. Those transactions that do take place will demand inefficient and unproductive transaction costs by each side in an attempt to reduce the expected injustice. The alternative of imposing transactions by force is bound to undermine continued transactions, as those who feel unjustly treated take what means they can to rectify the injustice or to stop it. Fairness covers a wide range of issues from just compensation, to truth in advertising, to providing the quality of goods or services that one represents oneself as providing.

The fourth general obligation is to live up to the contracts into which one enters freely. Contracts are the lifeblood of the free-enterprise system. In order to function effectively and efficiently parties must be able to count on the actions of other agents with whom they interact and they must be able to act, secure in the knowledge that their legitimate contractual obligations will be honored. Contract enforcement by law is a needed component of a free-enterprise system. But legal enforcement should reinforce and cannot replace the ethical observance of contracts. As with the other obligations, this one is also very broad, as broad as the range of issues over which contracts cover.

These four general obligations are derived from the system or free enterprise. They can also easily be defended as second-order ethical principles by both a utilitarian and a deontological approach. They are obligations that all corporations have. We shall see in forthcoming chapters the specific obligations they impose on corporations. Yet, as we have already noted, corporations only act through the agency of those who make it up, and even at this general level we can specify in more detail the obligations of the various parties that make up the corporation. We can refer to these as obligations within the corporation.

Corporations are the result of free agreements, even if most owners do not know what management does. They purchase stock, knowing that they will not have control and knowing that they will gain or lose, depending on how effectively management runs the corporation. They know that the corporation may be sued, they know it may make a profit or suffer losses, and they know in general how such things happen. Shareholders agree to invest money, and they understand what this means. The shareholders of the corporation are legally represented by the board of directors, whose job it is, among other things, to look out for the interests of the shareholders. The board of directors oversees management. Management has the task of organizing the corporation in such a way that it can effect its end, for example, make and market a product profitably.[10]

In a large corporation, responsibility for what the corporations does or fails to do falls ultimately on the board of directors. The board members are the legal overseers of management. *The members of the board are responsible to the shareholders* for the selection of honest, effective managers, and especially for the selection of the president of the corporation. They may also be responsible for choosing the executive vice-president and other vice-presidents. They are morally responsible for the tone of the corporation and for its major policies; they can set a moral tone or they can condone immoral practices. They can and should see that the company is managed honestly and that the interests of the shareholders are cared for instead of ignored by management.

Board members are also responsible for agreeing to major policy decisions and for the general well-being of the corporation. The members are morally responsible for the decisions they make, as well as for the decisions they should make but fail to make. To be effective in their roles as protectors of the interests of the shareholders and judges of the performance of management, they should be separate from management. Members of the board cannot be objective in their evaluation of management if they are also members of management. If the president and the chairman of the board are one and the same person, for instance, we can hardly expect the board to be as objective as

---

[10] For two critical discussions of moral responsibility within the corporation, see S. Prakash Sethi, Paul Steidlmeier, *Up Against the Corporate Wall*, 6th ed. (Upper Saddle River, N.J.: Prentice Hall, 1996); and Christopher D. Stone, *Where the Law Ends: The Social Control of Corporate Behavior* (Prospect Heights, Ill.: Waveland Press, 1991, reissue).

it should be in fulfilling its responsibility vis-à-vis management. Nor can we expect impartial evaluation of management if the board is composed of people appointed or recommended by management because of mutual ties. We can also not expect a board to be effective if it is not informed by management of what management is doing, if the board does not have access to all information about the firm it thinks necessary, and if its members do not have the time to investigate what should be investigated.

The increasing incidence of corporate takeovers raises special problems for boards of directors. Whatever the complications, the board is morally and legally responsible for the interests of the shareholders and must resist the temptation to act out of personal interest and advantage, which might be to the detriment of the shareholders.

Management is responsible to the board. It must inform the board of its actions, the decisions it makes or the decisions to be made, the financial condition of the firm, its successes and failures, and the like. Management is responsible, through the board, to the shareholders. It is responsible to the shareholders for managing the firm honestly and efficiently. Management is *not* morally responsible for maximizing profits, for increasing the worth of the company's stock, or for higher quarterly sales or profits. Although these are all reasonable goals toward which management may aim, shareholders have no right to any of these; if management acts as best it can within its proper moral and legal bounds, it cannot, strictly speaking, be faulted for not achieving them. If managers fail to produce as the board thinks they should, they may be fired or replaced. But that is different from their fulfilling or not fulfilling their moral obligations. Shareholders know that a corporation's stock may decrease as well as increase in value, and that profits may increase or decline. They should also know that profit maximization cannot morally override a firm's moral and legal obligations. Although shareholders may desire short-term profits, they have no right to them, and managers should manage for the long-term benefit of the firm as well as for short-term results.

Management is responsible for setting the moral tone of the firm. Unless those at the top insist on ethical conduct, unless they punish unethical conduct and reward ethical conduct, the corporation as a whole will tend to function without considering the moral dimensions of its actions.

Management is also responsible to the workers. It both hires them and provides for the conditions of work. In hiring workers it has the obligation to engage in what have become known as fair employment practices. These include following equitable guidelines and not discriminating on the basis of sex, race, religion, or other nonjob-related characteristics. Once a worker is hired, there is a continuing obligation of fairness in evaluation, promotion, and equitable treatment. These are moral matters, which may or may not be specified in contracts but are implied in the hiring of one person by another. It is not moral for management to ignore unsafe working conditions. For instance, it should not endanger workers by failing to provide screening from dangerous machines, where appropriate; by not supplying goggles for work where fragments may cause blindness; by not supplying adequate ventilation; and, in general, by ignoring the needs of workers as human beings.

Employers are not free to set any terms they wish as conditions of employment. They have a moral obligation to employees even if these are not spelled out in contracts or by government regulations. Government regulations, such as those imposed by the Occupational Safety and Health Act (OSHA), make explicit many of the conditions employers are morally as well as legally obliged to fulfill with respect to the safety and health of their employees. The OSHA regulations are sometimes inappropriate for certain firms, or are based on codes inappropriate to particular enterprises. Where inappropriate, the regulations can and should be changed. But if employers had lived up to the moral obligation to provide adequate conditions of safety and health for their employees, there would have been no need for OSHA regulations.

Workers, in turn, are responsible for doing the jobs for which they are hired. This obligation is captured in the dictum "a fair day's work for a fair day's pay." Failure to live up to this obligation is reasonable ground for discharge. From a moral point of view one's job can never legitimately involve either breaking the law or doing what is unethical, even if one is ordered to do so. But within the guidelines of one's job description, employees are expected to carry out their jobs as instructed by those above them. They are hired for specific tasks that they are expected to fulfill to the best of their ability—carefully, skillfully, and on time.

Corporations are responsible to their suppliers and competitors for fair treatment. Corporations deal with other firms as well as with the general public. They may buy raw or semifinished materials, parts, or a variety of supplies from others. In their dealings they are responsible for acting fairly, both in supplying and in receiving goods and services. If bidding is used, the bidding should be fair for all. If prices are agreed upon, they should be honored. If specifications are set, they should be met. If payment by a certain date is agreed upon, it should be adhered to. All this is fairly obvious, yet not always observed. The temptations for cutting corners, for cost-overruns, for manipulating bids, and for seeking and receiving preferential treatment are ever-present, and an ethical firm needs to guard constantly against them through a clearly stated and enforced company policy.

Fairness to one's competitors is also required. In a competitive situation no firm has any obligation to help a competing firm, and frequently competition involves gaining greater market share at a competitor's expense, hiring better workers and managers than one's competitor, charging less for similar products, producing better products, and the like. All of this is morally acceptable. If, as a result of fair competition, a competing firm goes out of business, the successful firm has no moral responsibility to the failing one. The key word, however, is *fair.* Fairness precludes lying about one's competitor or the competitor's products; it precludes stealing trade secrets, sabotage, or other direct intervention in the competitor's firm. Fairness in dealing with one's competitor also precludes colluding with competing firms, price fixing, manipulating markets, and in other ways acting to undermine fair competition at the public's expense.

The corporation is responsible to the consumer for its products. The goods produced should be reasonably safe. This means that the ordinary user is exposed to only a certain acceptable risk level that is known by the user, when using the product. For example, people do not expect to get shocked or electrocuted when they plug in an electrical appliance. They do not buy such appliances expecting to take that risk. A product that shocks or electrocutes them when plugged in is defective, causes harm to the consumer, and violates the contract involved in the purchase of the product. Goods must be as advertised or labeled, and the labeling should be adequate, so the buyer knows what he or she is buying. Because adequate knowledge is one of the ingredients of a fair transaction, it is the obligation of the manufacturer to inform the purchaser of those significant qualities that the purchaser cannot observe for himself or herself. For instance, the kind of material a garment is made of is pertinent, as is the horsepower of a vehicle. Also, goods should be reasonably durable; they should not fall apart on first use. Warranties should be clear and honored. The customer buys a product for a certain price. He should know what he is getting, and he has a moral right to have certain expectations fulfilled. Obviously, there are various grades of goods. Some are more expensive than others and may be correspondingly safer, more durable, more reliable, more attractive, and made of better quality components than cheaper products. For any transaction to be fair the consumer must have adequate information and his or her reasonable expectations must be fulfilled by a product, or there must be adequate notice that the ordinary expectation in the given case will not be fulfilled. Damaged goods can be sold if marked as damaged. "Seconds" may be sold as seconds, but to sell them as "first quality" is unethical.

These few examples do not exhaust the responsibilities of corporations to consumers. We have not questioned the morality of built-in obsolescence; of purposeful lack of standardization, which locks a consumer into a certain line of products; of failure to develop certain products; or of preventing the production of items that would benefit the consumer but hurt a particular industry or manufacturer. But we have illustrated enough of the moral responsibility of a corporation to consumers to indicate where its moral obligations in this area lie, and how they can be ascertained.

Finally, *the corporation is morally responsible for its actions to the general public or to society in general.* In particular, it has the moral obligation not to harm those whom its actions affect. We can group these obligations under three major headings. The first can be called its obligation not to harm the environment that it shares with its neighbors. It has the obligation not to pollute the air and water beyond socially acceptable levels and also to control its noise pollution. It is obliged to dispose of toxic and corrosive wastes so as not to endanger others. It must reclaim and restore the environment to a socially acceptable level, if its operation despoils the environment.

The second group of moral obligations to the general public concerns the general safety of those who live in an area affected by a company's plant. A company has no right to expose those people living near it to a health risk from possible explosion or radiation. Some jobs involve a high risk, and those who knowingly take this risk are paid accordingly. But a plant has no right to expose its neighbors, even its distant neighbors, to dangers without their consent. Similarly, a corporation has an obligation to the general public for the safety of its products. For instance, substandard tires endanger not only those who purchase them but also those whom the purchaser may kill or injure in an accident that the tires may cause.

The third set of responsibilities to the public concerns the location, the opening, and the closing of plants—especially in small communities and one-industry towns. These actions affect not only the corporation and its workers but also the communities in which the plants are located. Plant openings can affect a community positively or negatively, just as closings can. A corporation must consider, from a moral point of view, the impact of its actions on the community in these matters. This is not to say that plants can never morally be closed or opened. In both opening and closing a plant, a corporation has the obligation to minimize the harm, and so to consider a variety of strategies to achieve this end.

The opening of a plant may involve a large commitment on the part of the community in which it is located. The community, for example, may have to add sewer lines, increase its fire and police department staffs, and add to its social services personnel. Developers build houses for the increased employment the plant makes available. Businesses spring up to provide support services. Schools may be built to educate the children of the workers. The city or county begins to count on the increased tax base the plant represents. All of this results from the new plant. The corporation does not always ask that all this happen; but it at least expects that its workers will be provided housing and services in response to market demand.

The community may thus be said to provide indirect support to the plant. The corporation should, therefore, not ignore the community's contribution to its operation when it considers closing the plant. It may have no legal duty to consider the community with which it has been associated; but morally, it does have an obligation to consider the effects of its action and to minimize the harm its closing will cause the community.

If we ask who has the obligation to do all this, the answer is, the corporation. Management has the major role to play. Yet both the members of the board and the individual workers may find, on occasion, that they have the moral responsibility to take certain actions to satisfy the corporation's responsibility to the general public.

Since the corporation has responsibility to a great many constituencies, or stakeholders, it is not accurate to claim that a corporation owes allegiance only to the owners or shareholders of the firm. Nor is it appropriate from a moral point of view that the interests of the shareholders always take precedence over other interests. For instance, the moral obligations of the firm to ensure the safety of workers, the environment, and consumers properly take precedence over increasing profits.

A firm that wishes to operate morally will establish structures that encourage and facilitate ethical action on the part of all members of the firm. It will establish channels and procedures for accountability up, down, and laterally. It will develop input lines whereby employees, consumers, shareholders, and the public can make known their concerns, demands, and perceptions of the firm's legitimate responsibilities. Finally, it will develop appropriate mechanisms for anticipating and resolving ethical issues—whether the firm uses ombudsmen, ethical hot-lines, a corporate ethics office, an ethics committee, or other means for achieving those ends.

Morality and the Social Audit

In examining the moral responsibility of corporations, we noted the obligation not to harm. If pollution causes harm, then a corporation is morally required not to pollute. This obligation exists whether or not society explicitly demands it. But this obligation may also be expressed as a social demand, either through law or through public pressure of various kinds. Morality may not specify how a company has to control and prevent the harm it might do, whereas society may be explicit in this regard. Society may also demand more than morality does. Hence, although they often overlap, it is possible and useful to distinguish the moral obligations of a corporation from what have been called its "social obligations."

In one sense, a socially responsible corporation is one that abides by the law and so fulfills its legal obligations. This is analogous to the socially responsible individual who does likewise. But sometimes a "socially responsible individual" is one who not only obeys the law but also takes active part in social causes, social reform, and the political and civic life of society, and some people have come to use the phrase "corporate social responsibility" in an analogous sense. "Social responsibility," then, is ambiguous. Sometimes it goes beyond the legal obligations and refers to a corporation's responsibility to fulfill its social obligations. And sometimes it refers to the obligations themselves as imposed by society. Often, it refers to a corporation's concern for society or for the impact its actions make on society, whether or not its concern corresponds to society's demands.

Human beings are multifaceted individuals, but corporations are formed for limited ends and are structured for certain purposes. We have seen that although both humans and corporations are morally bound not to do harm, the amount of good they can be expected to produce varies. In particular, it is not clear that an appropriate end of every corporation is the improvement of the general welfare, except by its productive activity. This is true if by improvement one means that the corporation must engage in changing society directly, in changing the distribution of wealth within the society, or in improving the life of the inner cities, in addition to or instead of achieving its own ends. There is a difference, however, between claiming that a corporation does not have the moral obligation to engage in good works and social welfare—which are the proper province of individuals and of government—and claiming that it has no moral responsibility to society for what and how it produces, or how it treats its workers, its customers, and those affected by its actions.

In Chapter 1 we noted a changing mandate for business and saw not only that this is given in law but also that it arises from the general public and is expressed in many ways. Because the decisions of large corporations affect our society and the individuals in it in so many ways, it is no longer sufficient simply to demand that corporations provide a plentiful supply of high-quality goods at reasonable prices, despite the fact that some firms believe that merely doing this fulfills their moral responsibility. Concern for the ecosystem, worries about the limited supply of natural resources, and interest in the quality of employee life have all come to the fore. As we attempt to determine the nature of the changing mandate for business, however, we can distinguish three different sorts of claims or demands. They are not mutually exclusive and in fact overlap to a considerable extent.

Moral demands stem from the moral law. The obligations not to steal, not to cheat, not to lie are all examples. We must also treat people as ends in themselves and not harm them, and if we are in positions of authority within a corporation, we must see to it that working conditions are safe. Such moral obligations remain whether or not they are enacted into law and whether or not they are socially mandated. When companies do not adequately protect the safety of workers, sometimes a social mandate develops in the form of newspaper campaigns, protests at board meetings, calls for legislation, and the like. If firms react to such public demands, they can be said to be reacting to *social demands* that are also moral demands. If the legislature passes laws requiring certain standards of safety, then the social demands are spelled out as *legal demands* and corporations are forced to comply. We can distinguish moral demands, social but not legal demands, and legal demands, which are also of course social demands. Some social demands may be neither moral nor legal demands; and some social demands may be moral but not legal demands. Some social demands may be both moral and legal demands. Moreover, some demands may be couched in terms of social responsibility but may be only the demands, or statements of interest, of a small portion of society.

Moral obligations are sometimes correctly put forth as social obligations because they can and should be demanded by a moral society. Such moral demands as the obligation not to harm (e.g., in the case of pollution) may be handled in various ways by a society. What society demands of firms in this instance are actually social demands. They are morally justifiable both because they implement a moral demand and because society has the right to impose particular demands on corporations as a condition for doing business, providing the demands are in the interest of the common good.

Society may also impose on business certain demands that are not moral demands. Morality, for instance, requires that corporations be run honestly. But it does not require that a certain percentage of a board of directors be from outside the company. A corporation is not immoral if it has mostly internal board members (even though having a majority of outside members precludes some conflicts of interest). Yet there has been, over the past years, a growing *social* demand for changes in the composition of corporate boards. This has been expressed by petitions at board meetings, by motions at shareholder meetings, and by newspaper editorials and articles, among other means. As a result, by 1980 over 90 percent of *major* American corporations had a majority of outside board members, as compared to less than 66 percent in 1970. This is not required by U.S. law, although the New York Stock Exchange requires a majority of independent outside directors on audit committees of listed companies. In Germany, corporations are required by law to have a majority of outside directors. This does not necessarily mean that German boards are more moral than American boards, for there is no guarantee that outside directors make a board act more morally. But the fact that Germany has such a law shows that German society as such feels more strongly about the issue than does American society. Although moral demands are similar across national boundaries (e.g., all corporations have the moral obligation not to cause harm), social and legal demands may vary greatly.

Social demands may begin as demands made by one individual or by a small group. But not all such demands are social demands; only some of them express the interests of a major sector of society, and only some of those are independent moral obligations. Societies vary, for instance, in the safety they demand in automobiles or on the job. There are trade-offs of cost in most safety decisions. American society for a long time has demanded great safety in commercial airplanes, but for an equally long time has tolerated private automobiles that are less safe than the state of the art makes possible. Those who voiced demands for safer automobiles initially did not seem to speak for society, even though they were concerned with the social good. The American public has been slow in demanding the automobile safety that is technically possible but expensive. The social demand for greater safety is, however, increasing.

It is often difficult to distinguish between the vested interests of certain groups, which are presented as social demands, and the legitimate but not legally mandated demands of society. The growing literature on the social obligations of corporations includes a grab bag of obligations, some of them moral and some not. The social obligations that some people would like to have corporations undertake include taking care of the poor, rebuilding inner cities, fighting illicit drug traffic, giving to charity, endowing universities, and funding cultural programs. None of these is a moral obligation of corporations. People from a variety of quarters demand lower prices, increased profits, higher wages, more job security, more disclosure from corporations about their operations, and corporate programs to help solve the problems of poverty, discrimination, and urban blight. Some of these demands negate or contradict other demands. Which are moral, which are only social, and which are simply statements of vested interest? Businesses have frequently not known how to react to this plethora of demands, and some firms have decided to proceed with business as usual until forced to change by legislation. Some corporations have indicated they would like to comply with legitimate demands, if only they knew how. But, they complain, the demands are vague, sometimes at odds with one another, and no one except government spells them out clearly. Moreover, many indicate that they would modify their actions only if all their competitors also did so, for otherwise they would suffer a competitive disadvantage.

The term *social obligation* suggests that society requires the corporations to act in the specified way. The term also implies a threat—that unless corporations fulfill these obligations society will force them to do so through legislation, or possibly terminate their existence. The threat may be a real one. But as a society we should try to determine exactly what it is we are asking of corporations. We should clarify the issues: Which social demands are morally required; which are not morally required but are seen by the majority as appropriate; which might be nice for corporations to act on, if they are able; and which represent vested interests.

In the United States, the rebuilding of cities, caring for the poor, and the provision of welfare are social ends that traditionally have been socially implemented. Corporations may donate money to such projects if they choose. They would do so presumably to enhance their public image, to gain free publicity, or for some other such reason. The government encourages such donations by making many of them tax-exempt. But social welfare and social projects are appropriately the domain of government, not of business. Businesses are taxed, and such taxes may be used for social purposes. The purpose of the corporation, however, is profitable production and distribution, not social welfare. The manufacturing corporation is not structured to achieve social welfare. Moreover, there is great danger in expecting corporations to take upon themselves the production of public welfare, because they already have enormous power and are not answerable for its use to the general public. Politicians are elected by the public and are expected to have the common good as their end. We should not expect corporations to do what they are neither competent nor organized to do, but we should insist that they fulfill their *moral* obligations.

If as a society we decide that corporations should be forced to rebuild the inner city, should not be allowed to close down unprofitable plants, or should be made to train the hard-core unemployed, these demands should be thought through, discussed in the political forum, and then clearly legislated. They are controversial social demands and should not be confused with what is morally required.

Some corporations have begun issuing social audits[11] to inform the public as to where they stand on some social issues, and to explain their policies and their impact on society. Some people have suggested that social audits be made mandatory. However, we should keep in mind the distinctions we have already made between what is morally required and the meanings of the phrase *corporate social responsibility*. There is at present no consensus about what a social audit should contain, or how it should be constructed and presented. Greater clarity of purpose could be achieved if society were to impose on corporations not only a social audit but a moral audit as well, even though the content of the two audits would overlap. The social audit, in its broad sense, now includes charity and welfare (which are not moral obligations) and generally lacks any principles for determining what the audit properly includes and what it does not. Therefore, it is often either arbitrary or merely a self-serving public relations document. A moral audit would concern that portion of the social audit that can be generated from moral principles and listed as responses to moral obligations. The moral audit should be distinct from other aspects of a social audit, which would include charitable contributions and not morally demanded actions of interest to environmentalists, conservationists, or other groups.

Why should there be a moral audit, and how can it be implemented? Morality governs the interaction of rational agents. The actions of corporations affect people. The general public, as well as actual and potential investors, have the right to know the moral as well as the financial position and record of a corporation. The techniques of reporting the moral quotient of a corporation are similar to techniques for implementing the social audit; but the attempts thus far have been rudimentary. The government already requires reporting on injuries, pollution levels, handling of toxic waste, and other data pertinent to a moral audit; hence, much data are already available.

We have seen that corporations have the moral obligation not to harm people. This obligation is reasonably clear when it comes to many products. If pollution causes harm, then corporations are morally obliged not to pollute. This is a moral, not only a social obligation. It is a moral requirement, not a supererogatory act—that is, an act that is morally commendable but not required. How the corporation is to fulfill this obligation, however, is a social decision.

---

[11] Atlantic Richfield in 1980 was one of the first to do so *(Participation III: Atlantic Richfield and Society)*. An early book on the topic was R. A. Bauer and D. H. Fenn, Jr., *The Corporate Social Audit* (New York: Russell Sage Foundation, 1972). A number of organizations have conducted audits on their own, as a basis for rating companies, for example, Steven D. Lydenberg, Alice Tepper Marlin, Sean O'Brien Strub, and the Council on Economic Priorities, *Rating America's Corporate Conscience* (Reading, Mass.: Addison-Wesley Publishing Company, 1987); Amy L. Domini and Peter D. Kinder, *Ethical Investing* (Reading, Mass.: Addison-Wesley Publishing Company, 1986); and *Shopping for a Better World* (New York: Council on Economic Priorities, 1992). See also Meinolf Dierkes and Ariane Berthoin Antal, "Whither Corporate Social Reporting: Is It Time to Legislate?" *California Management Review*, 28 (Spring 1986), pp. 106-121.

The moral audit with respect to pollution would include information about emission levels, the levels allowed, and other pertinent information, on the basis of which someone could tell whether the corporation was or was not fulfilling its obligations with respect to pollution. Its accident record would indicate whether it was providing adequate safety protection for its employees; its recall record would indicate its quality control and the safety of its products; its legal suits and its out-of-court settlements would indicate how it fulfills some of its moral obligations with respect to its customers. For each category of moral responsibility, some method of reporting could be devised that would constitute an appropriate moral audit.

Corporations have moral obligations whether they wish to have them or not. Some firms attempt to fulfill these obligations; others are better at evading them. The free market allows consumers to cast their votes for a company by buying its product, and to cast votes against a company by not buying its product. If the moral audit were part of the public record of each company, people could take this into account when casting such votes. Routine moral audits would be extremely useful. The publication of such data would also be an incentive toward more morally responsible corporate activity.

People may, of course, buy a company's product if it is the best available, even if they know the company acts immorally. However, it is unlikely that they will ignore the immorality of a company if the immorality hurts them. But even that is possible. Defenders of a free market should have no reluctance about instituting a moral audit, for it would require a publicly owned firm to supply its potential customers and shareholders with information that they may appropriately wish to have before making their decisions about whether or not to deal with that firm.

In the first chapter of this book we examined the Myth of Amoral Business. The myth tends to obscure the moral obligations of corporations. The myth should be put to rest. Corporations *have* moral obligations, and they *can* and *should* be held morally accountable for fulfilling them. If such an audit were required of all large corporations, it would go a long way toward replacing the Myth of Amoral Business with a clear and open approach to corporate moral obligations.

Corporate Codes

Corporate codes have proliferated in recent years.[12] Many such codes aim to help employees act ethically by specifying or clarifying how general moral principles apply to the firm's kind of work or product. Despite the fact that

---

[12] For more on corporate codes, see Gary R. Weaver, "Corporate Codes of Ethics: Purpose, Process and Content Issues," *Business & Society*, 32, no. 1 (Spring 1993), pp. 44-58; Bodo B. Schlegelmilch and Jane E. Houston, "Corporate Codes of Ethics," *Management Decision*, 28, no. 7 (1990), pp. 38-43; George C.S. Benson, "Codes of Ethics," *Journal of Business Ethics*, 8 (May 1989), pp. 303-319; and *A Study of Corporate Ethical Policy Statements* (Dallas, Tex.: Foundation of the Southwestern Graduate School of Banking, 1980).

they are often called corporate ethical codes, none of them are *moral* codes, because no individual or group can make actions moral or immoral by fiat. Every code, therefore, can and should appropriately be evaluated from a moral point of view. Some corporate codes simply specify the legal requirements of which employees may not, but should, be aware. Some codes reflect specific concerns, such as bribery and illegal political contributions. Some firms have drawn up codes that serve as guidelines to what is accepted practice within the organization. Some companies feel that no gift from a supplier should be accepted, and others allow accepting gifts of up to $25 or $50. Some firms prohibit giving gifts to suppliers or customers. Others limit contributions to political parties, the purchase of stock from companies with which the firm does business, and other practices that may cause or give the appearance of causing conflict of interest.

Codes can nonetheless serve an important function and can help in resolving specific issues faced by members of a profession or by workers within a firm. If there is a company policy, for instance, about how large a gift can be accepted, then an employee knows not only that bribery is immoral and to be avoided, but also what his or her employer considers a bribe to be.

Even when intended to set moral standards, a typical defect of codes is that they give the worker no insight into how the code was formulated, what moral principles it exemplifies, or how to resolve issues of interpretation or of conflicts not covered by the code. The codes are usually promulgated by some board or committee of the profession or company in question; many seem like a form of the Ten Commandments. The Ten Commandments, however, purportedly came from God, Who many people thought and still do think has either the knowledge or the authority to dictate what is morally right and morally wrong. Are ethical committees or boards of directors similarly placed and gifted? Most people think not.

Although corporate codes cannot be expected to contain a detailed presentation of moral reasoning, they can make reference to general moral principles. The injunction to employees (found in one corporate code) to act in such a way that they would not be ashamed to have their actions exposed to the public—for instance, in the headlines of the local newspaper—is a step in the right direction. A code could appropriately and helpfully refer to the principles from which the code flows, to principles of justice and fairness. It could also refer to these moral principles: objectively weighing the consequences to all those affected by one's actions, respecting the rights of others, and the like.

An objection might be that this is asking too much of a code. It cannot and should not provide general moral principles because these are assumed to be held by everyone. People should learn these from their parents, ethics teachers, and churches, and not from their professional organizations or from their employers. There is some truth to such an objection. But unless the code is understood in terms of moral principles, it will tend simply to be the expression of rules learned by rote, or even worse, of ideals never to be attained. If the members of a profession are to internalize the rules of their profession, or if workers are to internalize the rules of their firm, they must understand how the rules are derived, and how they implement moral principles. Only in this way can those persons subject to a code use similar reasoning to cover situations of conflict, as well as those situations not handled explicitly by the code. Ideally, each member who is covered by a code should understand its moral principles, as well as the nature of his or her profession or firm. Rather than memorizing a code, each could then derive the same code by thinking clearly and objectively about the moral issues typically faced by those covered by the code.

Nonetheless, company codes have a certain usefulness. They are inadequate as guides to moral conduct or as guarantees that a profession or firm is serving the public and preventing its members from acting in a way detrimental to the public interest. But they are frequently better than nothing at all, and there are several advantages to developing them. First, the very exercise of doing so is in itself worthwhile, especially if it forces a large number of people in the firm to think through, in a fresh way, their mission and the important obligations they as a group and as individuals have to the firm, each other, their clients or customers, and society as a whole. Second, once adopted, a code can be used to generate continuing discussion and possible modification of the code. Third, it could help to inculcate in new employees at all levels the perspective of responsibility, the need to think in moral terms about their actions, and the importance of developing the virtues appropriate to their positions. Fourth, a code can be used as a document to which employees can refer when asked to do something contrary to it. Fifth, a code might be used to reassure both customers and the public of the fact that the firm adheres to moral principles, and to provide them with a touchstone against which they can measure the firm's actions.

At its best, a corporate code can not only guide the actions of employees on legal matters and conflicts of interests, but it can also enable workers and managers to evaluate in moral terms the *firm's* ends, practices, and actions, to be sure the *firm* measures up to the code. If management adheres to the code, the code can help develop a moral corporate ethos.

Corporate Culture and Moral Firms

In dealing with human individuals we speak of their moral character. Do firms, other formal organizations, and nations have moral character? Some people maintain that a firm that takes its moral responsibilities seriously, tries to be fair in dealing with its employees and customers, takes into consideration the effects of its actions, and so on, is correctly called a moral firm. It can be said to have a moral character, in a sense analogous to that used with respect to individuals. Its character is formed by its habitual actions in the past. It develops within it certain structures and patterns of acting. It molds those who join it into thinking and acting in certain ways. Tradition develops; pride in the policies of the firm takes root; and each member of the firm helps to form and to mold the others in the firm in conformance with its tradition. In this sense, then, a firm or a nation can be called moral or immoral, can be said to have a moral or an immoral character, and can be thought of as having, or as not having, a conscience. But the sense is only analogous; it is not identical with the meaning of these terms when used with respect to individual persons.

We can, however, properly speak of a *corporate culture,* and this may either foster or inhibit moral action on the part of its members. Corporate culture is analogous to the culture of a society, people, or nation. It includes the ambiance of the corporation, its values, beliefs, and practices; the relation of the people within the corporation to one another, and their feelings toward the firm; the history of the corporation; and the extent to which the present members identify with the history and tradition of the corporation in the past and present. Some firms have a strong corporate culture, unique and distinctive. Employees who join the firm are inculturated into it when hired by the firm. Such inculturation—which can take several years—may involve learning something of the firm's history, becoming familiar with its ideals and practices, and perhaps taking part in special activities of the firm. Some firms go so far as to have company songs; many have formal and informal meetings to discuss the firm's outlook, problems, or ideals. A company's culture may be consciously formed or may develop spontaneously. And part of a firm's culture may include a positive or a negative approach to moral issues and moral actions, both by individuals in the firm and by the firm itself, when dealing with employees, customers, and other firms.

Although a firm's corporate culture is established over time, it is both initially and continuously responsive, especially to direction from the top. Top management sets the tone that the rest of the firm follows. Those who do not agree with the tone and do not fit in usually do not stay long. It is possible for top management to insist on morality throughout the firm. It can expect moral conduct on the part of all its employees and establish a pattern—eventually a tradition—of moral action on the part of the firm and its officers. Not surprisingly, there is great loyalty and job satisfaction among employees who work for a firm that does not fire employees in times of cyclical downturns, and employees take pride in a firm that operates morally. Corporate excellence is not identical with corporate morality because competent management is also necessary. But it is doubtful that corporate excellence is compatible with corporate immorality, or with a corporate culture that condones or encourages its employees to act either immorally or amorally in their roles for the firm.

A moral firm, or a firm that acts with integrity, lives up to and fulfills its responsibilities. It helps its employees to act responsibly by clarifying their responsibilities, and it encourages them to assume their responsibilities. Only when all those within a firm assume appropriate moral responsibility can the full moral responsibility of a firm be met. Ultimately, moral responsibility, and morality itself, must be self-imposed and self-accepted.

Study Questions

1. Aaron Feuerstein defended his actions from both a utilitarian and a deontological point of view. Present a rule utilitarian analysis of Aaron Feuerstein's choices right after the fire occurred. Then present a deontological analysis.

2. Why does the field of business ethics focus on large corporations? Is this appropriate? Why or why not?

3. Can corporations and nations be held morally responsible? What is the Organizational View's answer? Are there defects with the Organizational View's answer? If so, what are they?

4. What is the Moral Person View of the corporation? Are there defects with it? If so, what are they?

5. What is the Moral Actor View of the corporation? Does it successfully capture the strengths and weaknesses of the other two views? If so, how? If not, why not?

6. In what sense, if any, can a corporation be said to have a conscience?

7. What is the point, if any, of using moral language with respect to and making moral judgments about corporations? Give an example of the use of such language.

8. What is the difference between ascribing moral responsibility to a corporation from the outside and assuming moral responsibility from within?

9. State the shareholder conception of the corporation.

10. What are some of the shortcomings of the shareholder view of the corporation?

11. What is the stakeholder view of the corporation?

12. Who are the stakeholders of a corporation? Which stakeholders' interests, if any, are more important than the others? Explain.

13. Show how a stakeholder view of the corporation is compatible with both a utilitarian and a deontological approach to the actions of a corporation considered from a moral point of view.

14. What are four general obligations of corporations?

15. What is the corporate "moral minimum"? Show how this general obligation can be established by a utilitarian analysis. By a deontological analysis.

16. What are the responsibilities of the board of directors of a corporation?

17. To whom is management responsible and for what?

18. What responsibility does a corporation have to its customers? to the general public? to society in general?

19. What are some means that a corporation that wishes to be moral might take in the way of structuring itself so that moral responsibility can be assigned and assumed?

20. Distinguish moral responsibility from social responsibility as they apply to corporations. Give examples in which they overlap, in which they are separate, and in which they conflict.

21. How are the responsibilities of individuals, corporations, and the economic system as a whole related, for example, with respect to harm to society?

22. What are corporate codes?

23. What useful functions might a corporate code serve?

24. What is corporate culture? What is its role in a company's morality?

25. You are a member of the board of directors of a large auto manufacturing firm. The chief engineer for safety claims that a new model being prepared for production carries a potential safety risk if hit from the rear. It could be corrected for about $10 per car. The car is not up to the "state of the art" exemplified by cars of comparable size produced by other manufacturers. The president of the company claims that the cost of making the car as safe as the competition's will cost more than the amount the company will have to pay if sued by families of those killed in accidents, and so he has authorized production. The chief engineer has gone over the president's head and has brought the issue to the board for a vote. You know that most of the board will support the president, and that if you oppose the president you will not be invited to serve another term on the board. What is your responsibility in this case, and what should you do?

9

>-•‹›-•O•-‹›•-‹

SAFETY, RISK, AND
ENVIRONMENTAL
PROTECTION

The McDonald's Polystyrene Case

Environmental consciousness has increased dramatically in the United States in the past fifteen years. More and more people are conscious of toxic wastes, of pollution, of the mountains of garbage that pour into landfills, of the depletion of forests. McDonald's, the largest restaurant chain in the world, presents a notable environmental case study.

For years McDonald's, like most other quick-food chains, used polystyrene containers—the famous Big Mac clamshell—for its hamburgers. This container was lightweight, did not absorb grease, and kept the hamburgers warm. McDonald's had chosen polystyrene over paperboard for these projects and had joined with others in a $16 million project to build seven polystyrene-recycling plants around the country. But by the end of 1990 it was to change its mind.[1] Because of its size and dominant position, McDonald's became the target of the Environmental Defense Fund, which claimed that making polystyrene packaging created toxic fumes, that it took up too much landfill, and that it took too long to biodegrade. In addition, a lobby called the Pro-Environment Packaging Council, funded by paper companies, started targeting schools with a campaign about the adverse impact of polystyrene products. McDonald's was soon faced with what *Forbes Magazine* called a "chil-

---

[1] Details of the case come from the sources noted below, as well as from *New York Times*, November 1, 1990, p. A1; November 2, 1990, p. A1; December 31, 1990, p. A3; and April 17, 1991, p. A14.

216

dren's crusade," which involved a Send-It-Back campaign, letters written by classes of children, and a threatened boycott.[2] On November 2, 1990, McDonald's announced that within sixty days it would phase out its polystyrene clams and replace them with coated paperboard.

The announcement was hailed as a victory for environmentalists and as a demonstration of the power of public opinion. Newspaper editorials across the country congratulated McDonald's for taking the leadership in environmental issues and put pressure on other chains to follow McDonald's lead.

Although no one spoke against the importance of environmental concern, several voices were raised, but scarcely heard, that questioned the soundness of McDonald's decision. Edward H. Rensi, head of McDonald's U.S. operations, who had long defended the clamshell boxes, said, "Although some scientific studies indicate that foam packaging is environmentally sound, our customers just don't feel good about it."[3] Jay Beyea, a scientist at the National Audubon Society, noted that the change would result in using a lot more paper and that "using a lot more paper means a lot more pollution."[4] It also means cutting a lot more trees. A study by the Stanford Research Institute concluded that there was no sound basis for claiming that using paper products was environmentally superior to using polystyrene or other such plastic-based materials.[5] Nor would the change affect the landfill problems, since such material accounts for only one-third of 1 percent of landfill waste by volume. Lynn Scarlett, vice-president of research at Reason Foundation, pointed out that manufacturing polystyrene clamshells used 30 percent less energy than paperboard and produced 40 percent less air pollution and 42 percent less water pollution.[6]

In the end, environmentalists had won—or had a certain wing, together with large paper interests, won? Public opinion had had its way. But who informed grade school children of the facts that led to their uncharacteristic assertiveness on this issue, and did they get the whole story? McDonald's move to paper products was probably a good business decision, given the circumstances and the pressure it was under. Was it the best environmental decision? Was it morally obliged to take the action it did?

>―◆>―O―<>―<

However one answers these questions, the McDonald's case shows that the public is concerned about the impact of business on the environment and on society. It illustrates the growing demand for corporations to be socially

---

[2] "McDonald's Caves In," *Forbes*, February 4, 1991, pp. 73-74.

[3] *Fortune*, June 3, 1991, p. 92.

[4] John Holusha, "Packaging and Public Image: McDonald's Fills a Big Order," *New York Times*, November 2, 1990, p. A1.

[5] Benjamin Zycher, "Self-Flagellation Among the Capitalists," *Regulation*, 14 (Winter 1991), pp. 25-26.

[6] Lynn Scarlett, "Make Your Environment Dirtier—Recycle," *Wall Street Journal*, January 14, 1991, p. A12.

responsible, it suggests that being socially responsible is good business, and it raises the question of whether there may be a difference between a corporation's social obligations and moral obligations.

Corporations, Products, and Services

We have seen that the reason a society allows corporations to exist is that it benefits thereby. Corporations produce goods and services needed by the society, and corporations supply employment for the members of the society. The typical reason for establishing a not-for-profit corporation is not to do good in some abstract sense, nor to help society in some altruistic sense, but to make money for those who start the corporation and for those who invest in it. It makes money by producing and selling goods and services. Nonetheless, the corporation is prevented legally and ethically from attaining its profits by harming its other stakeholders.

Since the primary function, other than making money, of a corporation is to produce a good or service, we can begin our ethical analysis with what is produced and how it is produced. A somewhat similar, although not identical, analysis applies to services.

Clearly it is unethical to provide a service of murderers for hire. Since it is also illegal to murder people, we can hardly imagine a group publicly incorporating for such a purpose. Thus, the service or product produced or projected for production can appropriately be subject to ethical as well as legal scrutiny. Most products and services produced by corporations are clearly ethically permissible. Obviously none are illegal; otherwise the corporation would not be legally incorporated within the same jurisdiction. But there are a few about which at least some groups or individuals have raised moral questions. The most prominent among these are the manufacture and distribution of cheap hand guns ("Saturday night specials"), cigarettes and other tobacco products, and alcoholic beverages, especially of the stronger variety. All three are legal in the United States and in many other countries of the world. It is not inconsistent for the production and sale of these goods to be unethical and for them to remain legal, because as we have seen, not everything that is unethical either necessarily must or even can be made illegal. Some would claim that the production of antipersonnel land mines and other implements of war, including the production of nuclear weapons, is unethical. In response, some others would reply that it is not the production of these goods that is unethical, but some uses to which they are put and their sale to certain people— minors, in the case of tobacco and alcohol, those with criminal records in the case of hand guns, and terrorists and rogue nations in the case of armaments.

We can certainly distinguish products, which in themselves are neither good nor bad, from harmful or unethical uses to which they might be put by some people. This sort of defense implies that there is a legitimate use to which they might also be put by others. From a utilitarian perspective, one might wish to inquire which use is likely to be most prominent, whether the harm produced by making the product available outweighs the benefits, and whether the harm can be adequately controlled through legislation, public disapproval and pressure, or other similar means. This is the way the debates on the products mentioned usually go. The freedom to produce and use products is assumed, unless great harm can be shown to result therefrom. Restrictions are applied to the extent necessary and practicable. Most countries have agreed to halt production of certain biological and chemical weapons, under conditions of supervision and inspection by agreed-upon international inspection teams and bodies. Under such conditions, it is unethical to engage in such production after agreeing not to. Whether it was unethical to engage in such production before the international agreement depends on whether the primary purpose was deterrence or possible first use. We need not settle these issues here, and they are the subject of continuing debate. Nonetheless, we can see that some goods and services should not be produced or provided, some are debated, some are arguably permissible although their distribution is appropriately limited, and most are clearly morally permissible, even if they might be misused or in other ways cause harm.

If this is the case, then the major ethical concern common to most production is not what is produced but how it is produced. The goods produced should be safe and not cause preventable, foreseeable harm; they should be produced in conditions that do not harm those engaged in the productive process; and they should be produced in such a way as to minimize any harm done to the environment.

Do No Harm

The injunction "Do no harm" is widely accepted as a prima facie second-order moral obligation binding on both individuals and corporations. Although the harm to be avoided is most clearly harm to people, the injunction is sometimes applied as well to preclude harm to animals and to the environment. The malicious, gratuitous, and unjustified imposition of pain or suffering on animals is morally repugnant, even to those who do not acknowledge that animals have rights. Harm to the environment at least indirectly harms people who are part of and depend on a clean, safe environment.

The principle that precludes harming others is the central principle governing the obligations of corporations with respect both to environmental protection and to worker and product safety.

The two sets of obligations have much in common. Since the obligation in both instances is to avoid harming others, each set requires that we clarify and specify the meaning of "harm" and the conditions under which the prima facie obligation might be overcome. Not only direct, but also indirect, harm is to be avoided, at least to the extent that it can reasonably be foreseen.

In both environmental protection and product and worker safety cases, there is often the possibility of people justifiably accepting some harm for greater good, and especially of accepting the *risk* of some possible harm for the attainment of some assured good. Hence, the ethical dimensions of both pollution control and product and worker safety involve risk assessment, and the moral evaluation of risk acceptance is essential in dealing with a corporation's obligations in these areas.

Safety and Acceptable Risk

While no one can reasonably insist that all products be made as safe as possible, regardless of expense, there are reasonable expectations of safety to which manufacturers can be held. An electrical product that gives people a shock every time they plug it in is not acceptable to the public, in part because the ordinary person knows that appliances can be produced that do not give people shocks. Companies have the obligation to make products at least as safe as the state of the art (an admittedly vague term) for that product permits and demands.

We can distinguish three different steps involved in the assessment of safety from an ethical point of view.[7]

- The first is determining how much safety is attainable and how to attain it in a given endeavor. This is technical knowledge that producers should have or obtain.
- The second is deciding how much safety is demanded with respect to a particular product or activity. This is a question of *acceptable* risk. It is not a technical question but a question of values and value comparisons. This question is rightly decided by those who will experience the risk— the end-user, the general public, or the government acting on behalf of the general public.
- The third step, once that determination is made, is ascertaining whether a particular instance of a product or activity comes up to the standards set by the public. As knowledge and techniques advance, we can expect that the level of acceptable risk will diminish. When automobiles were new and still experimental, only those willing to accept a certain amount of risk drove them. The risk had to be lowered before the ordinary person found it acceptable. The amount of risk the public accepts in driving automobiles is different from the amount of risk it tolerates in riding airplanes and that is different from the amount of risk the American public wants to assume in its space shuttle program.

Americans know they take some risk in driving an automobile, yet they do not expect brakes to fail, transmissions to jump gears on their own, gas

---

[7] Some good discussions of safety and risk are William W. Lowrance, *Of Acceptable Risk* (Los Altos, Calif.: William Kaufmann, 1976); Nicholas Rescher, *Risk* (New York: University Press of America, 1983); and K. S. Shrader-Frechette, *Risk and Rationality: Philosophical Foundations for Populist Reforms* (Berkeley: University of California Press, 1991).

pedals to stick, or cars to catch fire if left to idle for ten minutes. These are instances of legitimate expectations, even if not mandated by law. Americans expect they are taking almost no risk in entering hotels and high-rise buildings or in driving across bridges. They expect neither buildings nor bridges to collapse on or under them, except perhaps in a very severe earthquake—and even then, they expect a large margin of safety.

For people to rationally decide about risk, four conditions must be satisfied.

First, they must know that they are exposed to it. Just as people have a right not to be harmed, they have a right to know when they are being put at risk of harm. Hence, a manufacturing firm has the obligation to inform consumers of the harm they are or may be subjected to by using its products, if this is not evident. The obligation to inform people of risk of harm also obliges chemical and other manufacturers of dangerous or toxic substances to inform those near their production facilities of the potential risks those people face.

Second, people must know not only that they are at risk but also the nature and source of the risk to which they are exposed, if they are rationally to evaluate it. If the risk is from a product, they must know under what conditions the risk occurs. Without this knowledge they cannot know how to assess the risk and whether they wish to take it. If the risk is a constant one that comes from the ordinary use of a product—such as using a chain saw—then the user knows he or she must be very careful in using it. If the danger comes only under certain conditions, or when misusing the product, the consumer has the right to know this in order to decide whether to avoid the risk by not using the product or to take the risk with knowledge of the danger.

Third, in order to evaluate the risk the user must know both how great it is and how to deal with it—for instance, by avoiding it or minimizing it. If one buys tires rated for a maximum speed of 80 miles per hour, one can prevent a blowout by driving less than 80 miles per hour. If the chance of a blowout above 80 mph is one in ten and increases as the speed increases, driving faster than 80 with such tires would be foolhardy. If one knows both the risk and how to cope with it (e.g., by always driving slower than 80 miles per hour), it might be reasonable for someone to buy such tires. For the manufacturer not to warn customers of such a danger is to put them at risk without their knowing how to avoid it. This amounts to knowingly placing the customers in danger of harm.

Fourth, in order to rationally assess risk one must know what the alternatives are, if any. Those who wish to avoid the risk of flying in airplanes know that the alternatives are trains, motor vehicles, bicycles, animal transport, walking, and staying put. The risk one would assume in buying an unsafe automobile could be minimized by buying another that is somewhat safer. But driving any car invokes some risk, and that risk can be avoided only by not riding in a car. We can choose to avoid some risks; others are beyond our control and we learn to live with them, taking the precautions that we can to minimize the risk. Clearly, it would not be rational to accept great risk of personal injury when it could be easily avoided. It is rational to accept some risk if this is necessary to achieve a greatly desired end, but even then it is rational to attempt to minimize that risk to the extent possible.

Although we cannot give any simple or single answer to the question "How safe is safe?" at the least the criteria of rational risk acceptance and avoidance require that the potential users be informed of the risks they are taking. The manufacturer of products is morally responsible for producing products that are up to public expectations and to inform the public when this is not the case. Tires that will not withstand high speeds cannot ethically be sold as high-speed tires. The moral defect in knowingly selling products that are less safe than the ordinary buyer expects lies in the implicit deception such a transaction involves, and in the violation of an implicit contract or agreement with the public that those in business are expected to live up to. When defects are not obvious or a product is not up to the general level the public takes for granted in the products it uses, the risks should be clearly stated.

The level of acceptable risk should be determined by an informed public, and by its elected and appointed representatives. The solution of choice with respect to automotive safety, for instance, is a set of safety standards mandated by some agency such as the U.S. National Highway Traffic Safety Administration, provided that it is not controlled by the auto industry and that it truly acts in the interest of the public. Such an agency needs to be cognizant of the state of the engineering art, and of the technical aspects of the issues it decides. Mandated safety quotients might be developed that are attached to cars and other products so that the public knows what risks it is assuming, what alternatives there are, and how to protect itself from the risks it does assume. Beyond the mandated limits, producers may compete on the basis of additional safety features and reduced risks. The normal expectations would be that eventually such advances would become standard and the high levels of acceptable risk would be lowered.

We can apply a similar kind of analysis, for example, to the building of nuclear power plants.[8] Living next to such plants arguably involves some risk, and a community should know what that risk is before accepting it. Many communities are happy to accept the risk because such plants provide employment. Those who live somewhat further from the plant may be at some lesser degree of risk. Who has the right to stop such plants from being built, and under what conditions? The answer seems appropriately to be those who are put at risk, but the answer becomes much more complicated when the overwhelming majority want such a plant but a minority does not, or when those who want it are closer and those opposed to it further away. To resolve

---

[8] For two discussions of nuclear power plants, see K. S. Shrader-Frechette, *Nuclear Power and Public Policy: The Social and Ethical Problems of Fission Technology* (Boston: D. Reidel Publishing Company, 1980); and Bernard L. Cohen, *The Nuclear Energy Option: An Alternative for the 90s* (New York: Plenum Press, 1990).

these issues we need all the relevant information. Unfortunately, how we are to assess the risk of nuclear power plants is a much-debated issue, with some claiming the risk is less than that posed by alternatives such as power plants run by conventional fuels, and with others claiming that although the chance of a meltdown is slight, the harm done if that chance does occur is so great that the risk is not worth taking.

That is not the only difficulty. Nuclear power plants may help a great many people who are not at risk because they are far removed from the plant: How are their interests and needs to be weighed in opposition to those who would be put at risk? Although the obligation not to harm remains a paramount ethical consideration, the amount of risk people wish to take in exchange for benefits received is not only an ethical issue. What we typically use to settle such issues is the political process, which is not simply majority rule, but has built-in protection of people's rights.

The discussion of safety and risk analysis applies to products, to their production, and to environmental damage and pollution.

Product Safety and Corporate Liability

The approach we have taken to nuclear plants applies as well to product safety. Just as nuclear plants must not harm through leaks or malfunctions, so manufacturers must not harm through their products. The level of risk a society wishes to accept in using products can be set informally by the state of the art for the particular type of product, or, in more complicated matters, it can be set by government. In either case violations of such standards are unethical, even though they are illegal only in the latter case.[9]

We can illustrate the point with respect to automobiles. We all know that no car is totally safe. We also know that some cars are safer in some respects than others. A large car tends to be safer than a small one if they encounter each other in a head-on collision. A small car hitting a large truck in some cases is likely to come out the worse for the encounter. Mercedes Benz claims that it engineers its cars for safety; the consumer pays for the extra engineering that goes into its cars. It is unlikely that a small, inexpensive car can be made as safe as a larger, expensive car. If this is the case, then how safe must a car be to be "safe," and who is to decide?

Every car can be made safer than it is. Yet none of us wants to drive cars that weigh as much as army tanks, even if they would be safer than the cars we do drive. We are interested in getting many miles per gallon, paying what

---

[9] Concerning product safety, see Verne L. Roberts, "The Origins of Product Safety," *Journal of Product Liability,* 7 (1984), pp. 19-30; Harvey M. Sopolsky, *Consuming Fears: The Politics of Product Risks* (New York: Basic Books, 1986); John Kolb and Steven S. Ross, *Product Safety and Liability: A Desk Reference* (New York: McGraw-Hill, 1980); and Sharon Coffin, *Product Hazards: A Case History Guidebook* (Washington, D.C.: Washington Business Info, 1981). A well-known attack on auto safety is Ralph Nader, *Unsafe at Any Speed* (New York: Grossman, 1965). On the Ford Pinto case, see Lee P. Strobel, *Reckless Homicide? Ford's Pinto Trial* (South Bend, Ind.: And Books, 1980).

we can afford, and having certain comforts in our cars. Hence, any car manufacturer must make certain compromises, balancing weight, speed, cost, safety, comfort, and other factors.

A first approximation to the question of how safe a car should be is that it should come up to what engineers call the "state of the art." We do not expect cars to catch fire when hit from the rear at moderate speeds; we do not expect them to stall on the highway in a moderate rainfall; we do not expect the tires to blow out if we do 55 miles per hour. There are certain expectations that we have because cars have been engineered to fulfill those expectations. There is therefore an implicit contract between car makers and the American public according to which the safety standards routinely attainable by the state of the engineering art are expected to be in every comparably priced car. Before air bags became common and standard, they were often listed as an option. Now that they have become standard, it is their omission, rather than their inclusion, about which potential customers should be informed.

If a manufacturer makes a very inexpensive model car that does not come up to the state of the art with respect to safety, this is pertinent information the customer should know. If a car falls below the state of the art with respect to rear-end impact, then customers should be so informed. But it is unlikely that manufacturers of standard cars that fall below the state of the art will advertise this failing, unless the announcement is joined with a significant price reduction. If a customer willingly accepts somewhat more risk to save money, and if this is a result of an informed decision, the manufacturer cannot be faulted. Manufacturers can be faulted, however, if the risk is not a reasonable one for any informed driver to take or if they do not inform potential buyers of the added risk.

If a manufacturer knows of a defect that increases risk to the purchaser and neither corrects the defect nor informs the purchaser, then the manufacturer is open to a charge of *reckless negligence*. The manufacturer has a duty to its customers to protect their safety and it fails in its duty when it does not take sufficient care in its product design.

But whose responsibility is it to determine how safe "safe" is? Is it only up to the manufacturers and the purchasing public? In the United States the task of making that decision has also fallen on the National Highway Traffic Safety Administration (NHTSA), but since its establishment in 1966 it has not established many standards. In 1977 it set gas tank safety standards, and it has established rollover and side-impact standards among others. Its standards represent the amount of risk the public can expect and should be the result of some rational trade-off among the cost of achieving greater safety and the amount of safety achieved, the state of the art, and the desires of the public. Even without governmental standards, however, manufacturers are ethically responsible not to cause harm, and so they are ethically responsible for making their products as safe as the state of the art permits.

The general public does not expect ordinary automobiles to be as safe as commercial airplanes. We expect more redundant safety features in airplanes because of the greater risk of death or serious injury if some part fails while the plane is in the air. But we expect our cars to be reasonably safe, and engineering advances have helped make them safer and safer. When our reasonable expectations are not met, then public reaction of outrage is both predictable and justifiable.

What is true of automobile manufacturers can be generalized to all products—from small items such as can openers to large structures such as skyscrapers. The level of safety that we expect of small products is high, not because of the great damage they can usually do, but because of the ease with which they can be made safe. Electrical items usually have to come up to a safety level set by law. We all use electrical items everyday and simply assume that they are safe. The same is true of mechanical items. When safety is an issue to more than the individual user or to large numbers of people, then the degree of safety expected, and usually required by law, is very high.

When we walk into a building we expect it to be safe and expect that it will not collapse upon us. We are bolstered in this expectation by building codes and building inspectors whose job it is to ensure that the construction meets standards that guarantee the safety of occupants of the building. In the case of a very severe earthquake buildings sometimes collapse. Yet even here we expect that all has been done that can reasonably be done to offset this possibility, consistent with the knowledge available at the time the building was constructed. Structural failures due to faulty engineering or the use of substandard materials are usually the result of unethical conduct on the part of one or more persons, and the harm done can be placed at their feet.

Strict Liability

Manufacturers are responsible for the products they produce and are liable for the harm they do. With respect to consumer goods, consumers expect the products they buy to be as advertised and to perform within generally accepted expectations. They expect that the product will not break on its first use, that it will work, and that it will do what it was manufactured to do. If it does not, then the consumer has a legitimate complaint. Manufacturers usually warranty their products, and even when not explicitly warrantied, there is an implied warranty that the product is as represented and of at least average quality. If the product fails to perform as expected or if it breaks upon use or is otherwise defective, the warranty entitles the purchaser to repair or replacement of the product. This is part of what consumers have come to expect as a fair transaction with respect to the products they buy. They are not entitled, however, to compensation for incidental damage or harm—for instance the loss of time that exchanging the product involves, or the cost they may incur from not having been able to use the product at the time they needed it.

Harm caused by negligence, however, is another matter. In such cases compensatory justice demands that the purchaser be made whole and recompensed for any monetary loss as well as any harm suffered.

American law has gone further than compensatory justice demands and holds producers liable for harm they do even when they are not negligent. In discussing responsibility, we saw that legally corporations can be held liable for harm done by their products even if they did not know about defects or anticipate the harm. Several years ago a number of elderly people died from eating canned fish. The covers of the tins containing the food had developed very small holes through which air entered, leading to the growth of bacteria, which proved fatal. In a legal suit the food manufacturer was found legally liable under the doctrine of strict liability for the harm done.

Is the doctrine of strict liability morally justifiable, or does it punish companies unfairly for customer misuses of their products and for conditions beyond their control? The doctrine of strict liability does not assess blame, and is different from finding a company negligent, or culpable of not taking sufficient care in producing its products, or of failing to correct defects it knows about. In the latter cases, U.S. law will frequently allow injured parties to sue not only for injuries they have received from the use of the product but for *punitive damages* as well. Punitive damages may amount to many times the amount of actual damages paid to a plaintiff. The purpose of this excess payment is to punish the manufacturer for recklessness or culpable negligence in producing the product, and thus to discourage both that producer and other similar producers from acting negligently or recklessly in the future.

The arguments in defense of strict liability are primarily three. The first claims that strict liability is justified by the doctrine of the "deep pocket." Harm is done, and the entity in the best position to make good the harm done is the producer of the product in question, because it is assumed that the producer is capable of absorbing the cost of making good the harm done. Although this assumption may not be true, nonetheless, the argument goes, any company that produces a product is in the best position to pay damages caused by that product because the company can in effect insure itself against harm its product does. It can either buy insurance from an insurance company to handle strict liability suits, or it can insure itself, adding a small amount to each item sold to cover payments that may arise from strict liability cases.

The second justification claims that through the doctrine of strict liability manufacturers are given a greater incentive to make their products safe than they would have without such liability. Since they know that they can be held strictly liable for harm done by their products, they have an incentive to make their products as safe as they can, given cost and other constraints.

Third, the manufacturers are in the best position to test their products and to foresee possible misuses of the product. The doctrine of strict liability provides an incentive for manufacturers to test more carefully and to pay more attention to harm that misuses of the product might cause. Hence, the doctrine tends to produce safer products, and, since known in advance, it places no undue hardship on manufacturers, who can provide for such payments in their pricing.

Nonetheless, there are several difficulties with strict liability, and some people complain that courts are going too far in assessing strict liability. The critics complain that people should be responsible for their own actions and should take care in using the products they buy. No company can foresee all the misuses of its products. For instance, one person, who was scalded by hot water coming from a shower controlled by a single-handled faucet that mixes hot and cold water, successfully sued the manufacturer of the faucet. Critics in that case claim that any ordinary person knows that one should not turn the faucet to the hottest level and enter the shower without testing the water's temperature. Defenders of the doctrine claim that as a result of that case some faucets are now marked with warnings about the possibility of scalding and others have been devised that automatically shut off water above a certain temperature. The real issue being debated is whether individuals have any responsibility for ordinary care and attention or whether, simply because they suffer damages, someone—preferably some large corporation—must recompense them.

Product liability is not a simple ethical issue that can be settled in the abstract. Producers are morally obliged to produce products that are reasonably safe and up to the standards that the public can rightfully expect given the state of the engineering art. Producers are morally obliged not to knowingly endanger consumers of their products. Producers are morally obliged to warn consumers of possible harm from the use or misuse of their products. Cases of willful negligence, of misrepresentation, and of knowingly producing dangerous products are not cases of moral dilemmas but cases of unethical actions by corporations. But not all cases of harm done by products are of this type. The notion of acceptable risk has its place in the evaluation of product safety and corporate responsibility. Strict liability and punitive damages are legal doctrines that also play a role in helping promote product safety, even if both can be abused.

Since manufacturing in the American system is a competitive enterprise, it is clear that in some instances building safety into a product may put one at a competitive disadvantage. This is the case if consumers are not willing to pay for the added safety and the competition fails to come up to the same level of safety. In such instances, it is not clear that the moral obligation of the manufacturer is to produce the safer product, even though it may be in the best interest of society: If the public will not pay for the increased safety, the producer will not be able to sell the product successfully, given the competition. In such cases, either the society settles for less safety than it could get, or, to keep competition fair, government must mandate attainable levels of safety that all manufacturers must reach. The proper balance between cost and safety, however, is not an issue on which there is a single morally correct answer, or an issue that ethical principles by themselves can settle. Knowingly falling below socially accepted and expected standards is morally culpable, but what that standard is can vary from product to product and society to society.

Production Safety

Just as the level of safety expected or demanded by a society with respect to products may vary, depending on what is possible and what level of safety the society can afford, the same is true of the safety expected and demanded in the production process. At stake here is the safety of workers or employees, rather than customers or consumers. As with product safety, there is a minimum below which hazards in the workplace are not ethically acceptable. These include any dangers that can be easily remedied and any harm that can be easily prevented. For instance, adequate ventilation and reasonable temperatures in which to work are expected, as are safeguards with respect to fire (for example, adequate fire exits), and protection with respect to dangerous machines and toxic substances and wastes.

Some jobs are inherently dangerous, and with these the general rules of determining acceptable risk come into play. Firefighting is a dangerous occupation. Even here, however, firefighters can expect that they will be provided with whatever safety equipment is available and affordable by the community in which they work. They can expect training, and they should take on the job of fighting fires with knowledge of the risks and of how to minimize them. They should be paid adequately to accept that risk. But exactly how much that is may vary widely.

The labor contract with respect to safety is not one that can be ethically negotiated without regard to minimal degrees of safety. Nor is the contract a fair one if the workers have no choice because of high unemployment or great need. They should be informed of dangers and risk where they exist. But dangers and risk should be eliminated to the extent possible. When employers learn of dangers to the health or safety of their employers that neither knew about, the former have the obligation to eliminate them or inform the employees so they can make an informed choice about whether to continue in their jobs.

In the United States the Occupational Safety and Health Act (OSHA) specifies in great detail what safety measures employers have to provide. The law in some cases goes beyond what ethics demands, and not all developed industrial countries have the same health and safety requirements in this regard as does the United States. Some are more and some are less stringent. But whatever the country, there are basic minimal levels of safety that any employer must provide. What are known as sweat shops, in which workers toil in very close quarters in great heat and little ventilation, clearly fall below the moral minimum. The degree of safety and of acceptable risk nonetheless varies with different occupations and different societies. The job of a secretary is typically safer than that of a truck driver, and that of an officer worker is safer than that of a construction worker. Despite safety measures and reasonable precautions accidents happen, due to lack of care, mechanical malfunction, or unknown defects.

Employers are responsible for safe working conditions and are liable for injuries that workers suffer due to faulty equipment or unsafe working conditions. In the United States workmen's compensation is a type of insurance that covers injury to workers on the job. But employers are also liable for harm caused by negligence and by failure to inform the workers of the risks known to management to which they are exposed.

Product safety, production safety, and environmental protection properly involve social as well as individual decisions and choices, risk assessment, and the careful sorting of complex issues. Ethics plays an important role in resolving them. While ethical concerns come into play in setting safety standards for both products and the environment, ethics comes even more clearly into play once the standards have been set. Willfully falling below them is prima facie unethical and a violation of the injunction to do no harm.

Environmental Harm

Who should decide how clean our air and water should be? Since these are common goods, the decisions should be made by all those affected. Since it is a public policy question, the population in general should make it through the political process. Yet voters are often given little information about the trade-offs they as a society are actually making. Americans have typically left it up to government to determine what degree of pollution is dangerous, to decide what degree is acceptable, and to come up with regulations that will punish violations beyond that level. The public has rarely voted on alternatives or been told just what the alternatives are or what it is trading off against what. In some states voters have been asked to vote on specific issues—for instance, whether they want to construct nuclear power plants or establish toxic waste centers. Generally speaking, the public has voted on no comprehensive environmental package. Guidelines determined by various parts of government have been prescribed piecemeal. The claim might be made that the subject is technical and best left to the technicians, but we have seen that any choice of levels involves value judgments and there is little reason to assume that technicians represent or hold the same values as even the majority of the society. Many plausibly claim that, as rational agents, people have a right to decide issues that directly concern and affect them.

The blame for the deterioration of the environment frequently falls squarely on business. Factories pollute; manufacturers pour toxic substances into rivers and streams and bury noxious substances, often without regard to public safety; greedy entrepreneurs denude forests, strip-mine the land, and heedlessly eliminate increasing numbers of species. Business has had a serious and often deleterious effect on the environment. Yet the fact that, with respect to the degradation of their environment, socialist countries have fared no better, and often worse, than free-enterprise countries indicates that the harm may be due more to modern technology and its abuse than to business greed alone.

With the development of modern chemistry and increasing industrialization, a great many possibilities have been created and realized without adequate concern for their side effects and for the sometimes hidden costs of their production. For instance, pesticides and herbicides have been a boon for farmers, increasing crop yield and ridding food products of the pests that have plagued farmers for centuries. But pesticides and herbicides can also have deleterious effects. They can seep into the ground and eventually pollute ground water and wells. They can wend their way into streams and rivers, killing fish, or contaminating them. Eventually, they find their way through the food chain to humans, causing cancer, birth deformities, and other ills. The price of introducing new products often involves a certain amount of risk. In many instances the harm done was, at least at first, not intentional and was unknown. It was only after the incidence of disease and birth defects increased that scientists sought the causes and identified the chemical culprits. Can pesticides and herbicides be developed that do not eventually and indirectly harm people? The answer seems to be yes; and promoting their development is one purpose of governmental controls. Knowing there are safer and equally effective alternatives makes it unreasonable to accept the greater risks and actual harm produced by the outlawed products.

A similar analysis can be given of other activities.[10] Strip-mining and denuding the land of forests are both short-sighted activities. We know that cutting down forests without replanting the trees leads to loss of topsoil and to flooding, both of which cause harm, and both of which can be prevented. Yet in underdeveloped countries the local timber often provides the only source of fuel and of housing material for the local people. They have no resources for reforestation and are concerned with present survival rather than with the long-term impact of their deeds. Large paper mills have less excuse for deforestation, but even they provide some good by their activities—namely, the goods they produce and are able to provide for less cost than they could otherwise.

The issues of pollution raise serious concerns about harm. Other environmental issues are less clear. Treatment of animals is of very great concern to some people and of considerably less to others, and what is proper treatment is debated. Questions such as whether the redwood forests of the U.S. West coast should be opened to lumber companies, and whether and how much land should be preserved as wilderness and kept from commercial development are issues on which there is no consensus. Similarly, how much harm is done by industrial processes and development that lead in one way or another to the elimination of animal species is a debated issue. While some argue in terms of the rights of those species, others claim that only human beings properly speaking have rights. The ground then often switches to

---

[10] Among early works on environmental harm are John Passmore, *Man's Responsibility for Nature*, 2nd ed. (London: Duckworth Publishers, 1980); and William T. Blackstone (Ed.), *Philosophy and Environmental Crisis* (Athens, Ga.: University of Georgia Press, 1974). There is a large and growing literature on environmental ethics. Two useful collections of essays are Tom Regan (Ed.), *Earthbound* (New York: Random House, 1984); and Michael E. Zimmerman (Ed.), *Environmental Philosophy: From Animal Rights to Radical Ecology* (Upper Saddle River, N.J.: Prentice Hall, 1993).

whether harm can be demonstrated to human beings by felling the redwoods; or acting so as to endanger different animal, insect, or plant species; or treating animals with hormones and other drugs, and keeping them in crowded pens in which they can barely move.

In many instances of environmental harm, the harm done is not wanton and produces some good. From a utilitarian point of view we must ask whether more good is done than harm, looking at all those affected, not only immediately but in the long run as well. From a deontological perspective we need to ask whether the activities violate people's rights. From either perspective we must remember that though harming the environment is bad, at least to the extent that it directly or indirectly harms people, the actions that cause the harm frequently have positive effects as well, as in the case of pesticides, which can be of great help in keeping people alive because of higher crop yields than would otherwise be possible.

In dealing with environmental harm, therefore, the task is to minimize the harm done while maximizing the benefits made available by increased scientific knowledge and technological advances, and while respecting the rights of all those affected.

There is no need to belabor the point that direct, intentional, preventable harm is morally wrong. Manufacturers who knowingly dump harmful by-products and chemicals into streams or onto the ground are guilty of willfully harming others. Those involved in the production of radioactive waste know full well the damage such products can cause and the care they must take in disposing of these products. If they fail to take the appropriate measures, they are knowingly causing harm to others. The same is true with respect to farmers who knowingly misuse pesticides and herbicides, to foresters who do not plant trees to replace those they cut, and to strip-miners who do not heal the land they scar.

The problem of environmental harm and pollution is much more complex than this, however. Although the problems of pollution are only one aspect of the ethical problems involved with the environment, pollution raises a number of issues that illustrate an approach to dealing with environmental problems.

Pollution and Its Control

We can distinguish intentional from unintentional pollution, and major from minor polluters. In all cases, what we mean by *pollution* is crucial, and defining it is no easy task. As far as nature is concerned, there is no strict sense of pollution. When the volcano Mount St. Helens, in the State of Washington, erupted in May 1980, it damaged 220,000 acres of timberland; befouled the Touttle, Cowlitz, and Columbia rivers; emitted enormous amounts of sulfur; and spread its emissions in measurable amounts across the United States. In one sense the eruption polluted the air. But the eruption was natural, and the larger amount of sulfur in the air was no more unnatural than the smaller amount in the air prior to the eruption. In a literal sense, nature did not care about the amount of sulfur in the air. Human beings did, because they were adversely affected. What we often mean by *pollution* is the contamination of air, water, and land with substances that harm us or our interests, and in pollution control we are primarily concerned with preventing harm that can be avoided and that results from human activity. That is the only kind of activity that we can classify as moral or immoral.

Pollution, moreover, is sometimes a relative term. Certain gases and chemicals are not dangerous in very small amounts but are dangerous in large amounts. When present in small amounts, they are not usually considered pollutants; they become pollutants only when they reach a certain, dangerous level. Other substances are noxious in even minute amounts and are considered pollutants in whatever amounts they are present. What is considered to be a pollutant in drinking water may not be considered a pollutant in river water.

Since pollution is linked with harm, we wish to prevent the type of pollution that causes harm. For many years people used a variety of materials that either because of their small use did not in fact cause harm or because of ignorance were not known to cause harm. Thus, asbestos for a long while was used both as a fire retardant and as an insulator, with no knowledge that asbestos could cause cancer. When it was determined that asbestos could cause cancer, it became a pollutant to be withdrawn from the human living environment to the extent possible. Those who built with asbestos materials and had no knowledge of its harmful effects had no intention of harming others. (At what point they began to have suspicions, and then knowledge, and what they did thereafter, are questions with moral import.) Similarly, many manufacturers used rivers as dumps for their wastes, and in many instances the ratio of waste to the water into which it was dumped was sufficiently low that no harm was done. The ecosystem was able to dispose of the waste through natural means. In like manner, early motorists were few enough in number that the exhausts that their cars emitted were not dangerous and were carried away by the wind.

Pollution became a major issue when the free use of land, water, and air as means of waste disposal started to cause known harmful effects on others. This happened because of the increasing toxicity of the wastes, the better knowledge of the links between waste and human disease, and the growing number of sources of contamination. The sulfur emitted by one car might be harmless; but the sulfur emitted by millions of cars in a large city can produce harm. There is a threshold above which certain substances become harmful. Determining that level is the job of scientists. The aim of society is to keep such substances below their harmful level. And those who willfully produce those substances in such a way as to create harm are morally guilty of harming others.

One question is how much of given substances is necessary to cause harm. This level is sometimes disputed, and scientists as well as nations may vary in what they consider safe. Once a level is determined, the next step is to try to prevent crossing the harm threshold. The problem here is that very often there is no one person or firm that produces the harmful level. If the harm is caused by the wastes of a single firm, then the solution is relatively simple—namely, to preclude that firm from polluting. Determining how to do that may be a difficult problem both technically and politically, but the situation is exacerbated when multiple sources produce the harmful pollution.

Because pollution can involve harm to others, it has a moral dimension, but because it can be controlled or handled in a number of ways, it has a social dimension that may vary from city to city, state to state, and nation to nation.

Consider the following case. Jason City, a community of 150,000 people, has five factories in an industrially zoned section on the east side of the city. One of the factories is much older than the others and emits three times more sulfur into the atmosphere than the newer plants, each of which emits about the same amount of sulfur as the others. The atmosphere can absorb a certain amount of pollution and carry it away without ill effects to either people or property. Therefore, the city has had no need to do anything about the emissions from the factories, and the factories have not invested in any pollution control equipment. A sixth factory is built. It emits the same amount of sulfur as the other four new factories, but it adds just enough so that now a possibly dangerous level of sulfur is discharged into the air. The pollution may now cause harm. We have said that corporations have a moral obligation not to cause harm to people or property. Who is morally responsible to do what? The oldest factory claims that it was in the town first, and although it produces the most pollution, it caused no harm until the sixth factory arrived. The other four claim that they are minor polluters and would cause no harm if either the sixth factory had not opened or if the first factory lowered its sulfur emissions to the same level as the other factories. The sixth plant claims that it has as much right to emit sulfur into the atmosphere as the other plants, and therefore should not bear any special burden. By itself, it claims, it does no harm.

Clearly, the six plants together cause the harm, even though each one by itself would not cause harm. The moral obligation not to cause harm implies that collectively the plants must reduce and limit the total sulfur they emit. But this does not tell us what each plant should do. Ethics alone will not tell us that, because there are many ethical ways of reducing the pollution to an acceptable level. Let us consider a few.

Jason City might decide that the pollution is small enough, the harm done to residents and property slight, and the benefits to the city from having six plants great enough that nothing need be done about it. The city might decide that if anyone claims damage from the pollution, that individual should sue one or all the plants for compensation. The city could impose a limit on the amount of sulfur any plant can emit. It could prevent the construction of any more plants. It could allow future plants to be built only if they emit no sulfur whatsoever, keeping the emission level at its present rate.

The city might even take it upon itself to supply emission control devices to the plants, thereby controlling pollution at the source, at city expense. It might also tell the six companies that they are causing the pollution, and that they must lower the level or face a series of fines, thus leaving it up to the plants to arrange among themselves how to lower the sulfur to an acceptable level.

There is no one right and best way for Jason City to solve the problem of sulfur pollution, but there are many ways of approaching the problem. It is appropriate, however, that the plants emitting the sulfur control their emissions because the sulfur belongs to them. They have been allowed to use the air to get rid of their wastes when doing so injured no one, but when such a procedure threatens to harm others, then the action can be rightfully curtailed. The claim that because the air belongs to all of us, any of us can discharge what we want into it cannot be successfully defended.

Wastes belong to those who produce them. Just because people do not want their wastes does not release them (or firms) of the responsibility of disposing of their wastes in a way that does not harm others. The principle is recognized with respect to garbage. Individual households in some cities pay to have their garbage disposed of; in other cities this is a service provided through tax funds; and in rural communities people are sometimes allowed to dispose of it by burning it or carrying it themselves to the town dump. Air and water pollutants are industrial wastes, which belong to the plants that produce them as truly as a household's garbage belongs to the household. The method of disposal of such wastes varies with communities. But the principle that the wastes belong to the producer and that producers have no right to harm others by their wastes is a sound moral basis for imposing limits on what pollutants are admissible, in what amounts, and how the rest are to be controlled or disposed of.

Jason City exemplifies some dimensions of the problem of pollution. But the problem has many other facets and dimensions; it is often extremely complicated, and it involves conflicting principles. There is also much uncertainty about facts, the dangers posed, and the probable effects of proposed solutions.

Pollutants produced by many chemical and manufacturing processes are highly noxious. Such chemical byproducts can clearly cause harm. Those who produce these substances have the moral obligation to dispose of them in safe ways; otherwise, they are morally guilty of the harm they produce. Their obligation to dispose of them properly and safely was a moral obligation even prior to government regulation of such waste disposal. After a number of widely publicized reports about improper disposal and the sad effects thereof, the federal government passed a law requiring a "paper trace" that covered the handling of such wastes from the producing plant through the final disposition in a proper facility. Just before the law went into effect, a number of companies—both originators of the waste and haulers—dumped toxic wastes along open roads, to save the cost of hauling the waste to the proper disposal locations. Clearly, such acts threatened the health and safety of people who would be affected by the runoff and seepage into their drinking water supplies. The action was immoral—a blot on the record of the firms involved.

Pollution, we noted, can be ethically handled in many ways. One way is for those who produce harm to reimburse those harmed for the harm done. In this way compensatory justice is brought into play after the fact. When the harm done is both serious and preventable, such pollution is not usually ethically justifiable, even though reimbursing those harmed is preferable to not reimbursing them. In some cases, however, the harm done is not serious and recompense is a satisfactory remedy. The involved parties may even agree, prior to the harm, to a fee that is to be paid those who will be damaged. This is a form of licensing the harm done by compensating those harmed. This might be the procedure, for instance, in dealing with noise pollution produced by airport traffic as it affects those living near the field. The owners of the airport might buy from the neighbors affected the right to produce the noise. (Property values decrease, and the residents suffer from the disturbance of noisy airplanes flying overhead.) One approach to pollution, as these examples show, is to allow it, but to compensate, either before or after the fact, those who are adversely affected.

A second approach allows a firm to pollute but attempts to eliminate the pollution or clean it up before it damages anyone. The cleaning up might be done by the firm that produces it, the firm might hire someone else to handle the cleanup process, or the cleanup might be carried out by some governmental agency or body. In the last-named case, the cleanup might be done at public expense (in which case the taxpayers subsidize the polluting industry) or at the expense of the polluting firms.

A third approach to pollution is to prevent it at the source. This means that the pollution will not be allowed to develop. Government might mandate this, or firms might decide on their own that preventing the damage is preferable to paying for it afterward. If government mandates the prevention of pollution, it may either specify the means to be taken to prevent the pollution or simply require that there be no effluents of a certain type produced and allow the firms involved to take whatever measures they wish to achieve the mandated end. Many firms prefer the latter approach, claiming it offers them greater incentives to find cost-effective means of preventing pollution. Government-mandated procedures are usually not individually tailored to particular needs and so are not cost effective. A variant of this approach is to set certain limits on the pollution to be tolerated, requiring that it be kept at or below a certain threshold level.

The case of pollution caused by motor vehicles raises several interesting aspects of the general problem of pollution. One is the decision about how much pollution and what kind of pollution are to be tolerated from cars. This is a social decision, to be made by society as a whole. It is not appropriately made only by the automobile industry, or only by drivers, because the ill effects of pollution are suffered by all, even though some (e.g., those with emphysema or asthma) suffer more than others. Clearly, the amount of air pollution that produces ill-effects is a technical question. But the amount of pollution that a society wishes to tolerate is a social question that should be decided socially via the political process.

Society can control the harm done from the pollution caused by automobiles in a number of ways. It could prohibit the use of automobiles—a solution that is too drastic to be acceptable, because of the great utility that the automobile provides. It could limit the use of automobiles, either by statute or by taxing cars sufficiently as to prohibit their use by those who could not afford them. It could mandate that cars be made so that they do not pollute or so that they meet certain standards of pollution control. Any such measure will raise the cost of automobiles. It could require that lead and other substances be eliminated from gasoline, thus eliminating at least those pollutants—and so on. Any action society takes, however, will restrict the freedom of drivers, automobile manufacturers, and buyers; raise the cost of driving; or have some other cost in convenience or money attached to it. Hence, society must decide how much it is willing to pay to obtain the level of clean air that it is capable of attaining in various ways. No society can have both clean air and the unrestricted use of large numbers of polluting vehicles.

If we ask who is responsible for the pollution caused by automotive vehicles, the answer is the vehicle manufacturers, the gasoline manufacturers, and the vehicle users. Some may also blame communities that do not provide or no longer provide public transportation, and government policies that subsidized gasoline, for the U.S. dependence on cars. But it is difficult to say that any one person or group was immoral along the way or acted unethically in any given decision. The harm caused by automotive pollutants was not directly intended by anyone or any group but was the unwanted and largely unforeseen result of many different decisions and actions, each of which at the time seemed reasonable and justifiable. The moral issue then becomes, given this state of affairs, who is required to do what?

What makes the issue of vehicular pollution different from the issue of pollution caused by factories is that the actual pollution is caused not by a company or firm, but by individual cars, and hence by individual drivers. Cars driven in a small town might pose no threat to anyone; the same cars driven the same amount in Los Angeles add to the air pollution of Los Angeles, and that pollution, if uncontrolled, would do serious harm to many. Therefore, neither the amount of pollution produced by an individual car nor the number of miles driven can be equated with unacceptable levels of pollution. Why should all car drivers have to pay more to buy cars that reduce pollution when the problem exists only in certain areas? On the other hand, how can one prevent people from driving where they wish? In the United States, California was the first to introduce stricter vehicular pollution-control laws. It chose to impose stricter regulations on car manufacturers than did other states and hence raised the cost of cars made according to those specifications. Should all the cars in the United States be made according to the standards set in California? Clearly, many would think not, and they would not be obviously wrong.

The national standards regarding car-manufacturing are a matter of public policy and should be determined in accordance with the procedures set up for deciding such issues. Some countries have come up with standards different from those in the United States. We cannot say, without thorough investigation, that either of the standards is preferable from an ethical point of view. It may be that each is appropriate for the country involved. In all countries there will be a trade-off of allowed pollution against the expense of pollution control. In this situation it is not unethical for an automobile manufacturer to comply with the standards set by government rather than deciding on its own to make the standards more rigid for its cars, at increased cost to the buyer. Manufacturers may, of course, take the latter course, but this is not an ethical requirement. Unless they have reason to believe the level is too low, the ethical obligation of car manufacturers would be to fulfill the socially mandated standard, and in this instance the manufacturers' ethical and social responsibilities would coincide.

In the United States, some ethical responsibility also falls on the individual car user. All new cars are made with catalytic converters that require the use of lead-free gas. Such gas is more expensive than regular gas. But the converters are effective in controlling pollution to the allowed limit only if lead-free gas is used. For an individual to intentionally pollute by using regular gas, if it is available, is to intentionally contribute to harming people and property. So is tampering with or failing to replace faulty pollution control devices in the car. The harm any individual will do is of course small, but the principle of not harming is violated nonetheless. If many people acted in this way the harm done would be serious, and each guilty person would share in the blame for that harm.

If the onus for reducing automobile pollution falls on vehicle manufacturers, they will pass on the cost of pollution control to their customers. This is only right and proper. Since pollution control is part of the cost of doing business, it is fair that the real costs be reflected in the price of the product produced. If the resulting product becomes too expensive for people to buy, then we shall have to decide whether we as a society want that product more than we want clean air. This is a public policy question, not a free-enterprise question. This approach makes those who benefit from a product bear the cost of its production, rather than having it partially and secretly subsidized by general taxpayers, as when government pays for repairing public buildings damaged by sulfur emissions of private vehicles or factories. This approach, however, requires that the rules be the same for all. For instance, all car manufacturers must be held to the same emission-control levels; otherwise the government would be placing an unfair burden on some and giving others a competitive edge. Requiring that all manufacturers meet certain levels, however, is consistent with allowing each to determine how to achieve those levels.

The problem of pollution is complex and open to a variety of solutions. There is controversy about acceptable levels of pollution, the necessity for producing certain kinds of wastes, the relative benefits involved with producing nuclear wastes for which there are no agreed-upon disposal procedures, and so on. These issues involve corporate, social, and ethical responsibility. But the issues are not always as easy to solve as some who attack corporate policy claim. In dealing with pollution, as in dealing with other issues of social responsibility, it would be helpful to distinguish what is ethically mandatory, what is desirable but not mandatory, what is to be decided by the political process, and how goals are to be achieved. A moral audit—or a social audit, of which a moral audit is a clear part—can be constructed to include an evaluation of corporate actions with respect to pollution. We would all benefit if such instruments helped make clear what the problem is, what the variety of solutions are, and which companies are fulfilling their ethical, legal, and social responsibilities in this area.

Study Questions

1. Are all fast-food chains morally obliged to switch from polystyrene to paper packaging? Are schools? Are individuals?

2. Assume that there is no cost differential between using polystyrene and paper products. Assume that using paper packaging is slightly more harmful overall to the environment than using polystyrene packaging. Assume that McDonald's customers mistakenly believe that using paper packaging is less harmful. What is McDonald's moral responsibility with respect to which packaging it uses? What is its social responsibility? What should it do?

3. Assume the Pro-Environment Packaging Council is sponsored by paper-product manufacturers. Would it be morally justified in instigating children to boycott fast-food chains that use polystyrene instead of paper packaging?

4. What does the rule "Do no harm" require with respect to products, production, and the environment?

5. What are the three steps involved in an ethical safety assessment? Who properly does each? Give an example.

6. What are four conditions for rational risk assessment? Apply the four to an original example in which risk is involved.

7. What are some of the ethical issues involved in building nuclear power plants?

8. Are manufacturers ethically required to make their products as safe as possible? Why or why not?

9. What is the ethical responsibility of automobile manufacturers with respect to pollution? of automobile owners?

10. What are a manufacturer's responsibilities to the public vis-à-vis product safety? How safe do you expect electrical appliances to be? Give an example of what you would consider to be below the state of the art for electric appliances.

11. What is reckless negligence?

12. How safe should cars be? Who properly determines auto safety and how?

13. What do warranties cover?

14. What is strict liability? Is it morally defensible to hold companies strictly liable for the misuse of their products? Why or why not?

15. What are punitive damages? Are they morally justifiable? Why or why not?

16. What is the minimum below which hazards in the workplace are not ethically acceptable?

17. Whether it is unethical to use wilderness areas in the United States for commercial purposes is a debated issue. How would you argue for your views on this issue?

18. Define pollution for purposes of ethical analysis.

19. In what sense is pollution control an ethical issue? a social issue?

20. How may pollution be ethically handled? What do you consider the fairest way to handle the pollution problem of Jason City? Defend your answer.

21. Through its research, XYZ Petroleum discovers a way of refining gasoline for automobiles that will yield fewer pollutants than current methods and will significantly reduce acid rain. But the process will raise the cost of gasoline 6 cents a gallon. The company feels that it cannot competitively sell such gas. It is willing to license its process to other refiners for a fee, but it is unlikely that other refiners will want to adopt the new method unless forced to do so by the government. What is the ethical obligation of XYZ Petroleum vis-à-vis its new process?

22. ABC Cleaning has developed a new process that effectively repels dirt so that garments need never be dry-cleaned. However, the process is toxic and is likely to result in three cases of cancer among employees for every 100,000 hours worked. Should the company be allowed to use the process, and, if so, under what conditions?

23. How safe should children's toys be? Should they be safer than hand tools? How safe should pharmaceutical medicines be? How do you decide?

10

>—:—+>—+—O—+—<>—:—<

WHISTLE BLOWING

The Ford Pinto Case

In the late 1960s American automobiles were losing market share to smaller Japanese imports. Lee Iacocca, then CEO of the Ford Motor Company, wanted a 1971 model to meet the competition. He reportedly ordered that Ford produce a car for 1971 that weighed less than 2,000 pounds and that would be priced at less than $2,000. That meant that the car had to be designed and produced in 25 months rather than the usual 43 months for a new car line. The resulting car was the Pinto.[1] Because of the accelerated production schedule, the Pinto was not tested for rear-end impact until after it was produced. There was no National Highway Traffic Safety Administration rear-end impact standard at the time. Ford engineers knew that testing for rear-end impact is a standard safety procedure. The car was tested after production, and it failed the test, meaning that it fell below the state of the art for cars of that size. The design of the car placed the fuel tank such that if the car was hit from the rear at a speed above 20 miles per hour, it would be punctured by a bolt from the bumper and could possibly burst into flame. Ford did a study and determined that if a baffle (estimated at costing between $6.65 and $11) were placed between the bumper and the gas tank, the Pinto would be comparable to other cars of its class with respect to the danger of fire from rear-end impact. A com-

---

[1] For sources and more details on the Pinto, see Richard T. De George, "Ethical Responsibilities of Engineers in Large Organizations: The Pinto Case," *Business and Professional Ethics Journal*, 1, no. 1 (1981), pp. 1-14; Lee P. Strobel, *Reckless Homicide? Ford's Pinto Trial* (South Bend, Ind.: And Books, 1980); and Mark Dowie, "Pinto Madness," *Mother Jones*, September/October 1977, pp. 24-28.

pany cost-benefit analysis that weighed the cost of adding the baffle against the estimated cost of suits resulting from "excess" accidental deaths and injuries indicated that it would cost the company less not to insert the baffle than to insert it. As a result, the company did not change the design from 1971 to 1978. Nor did the company inform customers that the car was somewhat less safe than comparable cars with respect to rear-end impact or offer them the option of purchasing the baffle.

Between 1976 and 1977 alone, Pintos suffered thirteen fiery rear-end collisions, which was more than double the number for comparable-size cars. As it turned out, suits brought against Ford and the amount it had to pay (estimated at more than $50 million) far exceeded what it saved ($20.9 million) by not correcting the defect—not to mention the cost of bad publicity.

Nonetheless, despite reports of fires in the Pinto, the car sold well through 1978, when it was finally recalled to have the baffle inserted. When the State of Oregon, because of safety concerns, sold its fleet of Pintos at public auction, the cars went for as much as $1,800 each. Obviously, buyers discounted the danger, weighing it against the cost of what was considered adequate transportation at a good price.

Ford's actions with respect to the Pinto have been widely criticized. Harley Copp, a former Ford executive and engineer, was critical of the Pinto from the start. He left the company and voiced his criticism, which was taken up by Ralph Nader and others.

Of course, the Ford engineers were not instructed to make an unsafe car, nor did Ford management set out to do so. That the Pinto was arguably below the state of the art may have been a result of the accelerated production schedule. That the defect was not corrected after the initial production year was the result of a business decision.

Was anyone at Ford at fault? Did anyone at Ford have an obligation to make known to the public the facts that Ford knew but did not make public? If so, who? Why?

Blowing the Whistle

We have seen that corporations have a moral obligation not to harm. This obligation falls on the corporation as such, and internally it falls primarily on those who manage the corporation. Yet other members of the corporation—for instance, engineers and assembly-line workers—are not morally allowed to take part in any immoral activity. Hence, they may not morally take part in any activity that they know will cause harm, including producing products that they know will cause harm. Do they further have a moral obligation to prevent harm, if they are able to do so?

As a general rule, people have a moral obligation to prevent serious harm to others if they are able to do so and can do so with little cost to themselves. As the cost increases, the obligation decreases. If we can save another's life only at the expense of our own life, we are not morally obliged to do so, and giving up our life for another is usually considered an act of heroic virtue. What is the obligation as an employee to prevent his or her company from harming others? The question is a complicated one and leads us to a consideration of what has become known as *whistle blowing.*[2]

Kinds of Whistle Blowing

Whistle blowing is a term used for a wide range of activities that are dissimilar from a moral point of view. Sometimes the term refers to disclosures made by employees to executives in a firm, perhaps concerning improper conduct of fellow employees or superiors who are cheating on expense accounts, or are engaging in petty or grand theft. Students are sometimes said to "blow the whistle" on fellow students whom they see cheating on exams. In these cases, whistle blowing amounts to reporting improper activities to an appropriate person. This can be called *internal whistle blowing,* for the disclosure or allegation of inappropriate conduct is made to someone within the organization or system. Generally, one believes an investigation will follow and a sanction will be imposed. In the classroom situation, if the students are on the honor system, they have agreed to report cheating and are morally obliged to do so. If they are not on the honor system, such reporting may be morally permissible but is not usually required. A similar analysis applies on the job as well.

Someone who reports sexual harassment is also sometimes said to blow the whistle on the offender; this is often because simply speaking to the person has no effect. In this case, the charge is about an offense not against the organization or system, but against oneself; the whistle blowing might be called personal, as opposed to impersonal whistle blowing, in which the potential or actual injury is to others or to the organization rather than to oneself. *Personal whistle blowing* is, in general, morally permitted but not morally required, unless other aspects of the case show that there is immediate danger to others.

Because workers have a right not to be sexually harassed, they should have a means by which to report such harassment if simply speaking to the harasser proves ineffective. Similarly, workers who have other rights violated

---

[2] Some general works dealing with whistle blowing are Gerald Vinten (Ed.), *Whistleblowing: Subversion or Corporate Citizenship? (New York: St. Martin's Press, 1994);* Ralph Nader, Peter J. Petkas, and Kate Blackwell (Eds.), *Whistle Blowing: The Report of the Conference on Professional Responsibility* (New York: Grossman Publishers, 1972); Myron Peretz Glazer and Penina Migdal Glazer, *The Whistle-blowers* (New York: Basic Books, 1989); and Marcia P. Miceli and Janet P. Near, *Blowing the Whistle: The Organizational and Legal Implications for Companies and Employees* (New York: Lexington Books, 1992). For a defense of whistle blowing, see Kenneth D. Walters, "Your Employee's Right to Blow the Whistle," *Harvard Business Review,* July–August 1975. Peter Raven-Hanson's "Do's and Don'ts for Whistleblowers: Planning for Trouble," *Technology Review,* May 1980, pp. 34-44, gives advice on how to blow the whistle. For some detailed accounts of whistle blowing, see Paul Eddy, Elaine Potter, and Bruce Page, *Destination Disaster: From the Tri-Motor to the DC-10: The Risk of Flying* (New York: Quadrangle/New York Times Book Company, 1976); and Alan F. Westin (Ed.), *Whistle Blowing! Loyalty and Dissent in the Corporation* (New York: McGraw-Hill, 1981).

should also have channels through which to get their legitimate complaints heard and acted on. Acts of personal whistle blowing are usually within the organization. But if serious enough, the whistle blower who gets no satisfaction internally might have to report to someone outside. Only a shortsighted firm would force external whistle blowing; a well-managed firm would be so structured as to take care of such cases internally. This is in the best interests not only of the firm but also of the workers and their morale.

Whistle blowing sometimes refers to government employees who divulge to a governmental regulatory or investigative bureau unethical practices in their division or office. It sometimes refers to reporting such things as cost overruns to Congressional committees or to the media. (The former is still considered external whistle blowing, because one goes outside the division or office to alert someone in another part of the government system.) Sometimes whistle blowing refers to leaks by government employees to the media. We can call all these kinds of disclosure *governmental whistle blowing.*

This sort of whistle blowing is different from private-sector whistle blowing, which is by employees on their employers. The obligations one has to one's government are considerably different from obligations to a nongovernmental employer. The reason is that government employees are related to their government both as citizens and as employees and the harm done by governmental employees may have effects not only on the particular division in which they are employed but also on the government and country as a whole. The law recognizes this difference, and Congress has passed special legislation governing and protecting certain kinds of governmental whistle blowers.[3] The laws do not protect those who break the law by revealing classified information, but they protect from dismissal those who reveal waste, overspending, or illegal or corrupt activity within the government bureaucracy. The legislation has been enforced only sporadically, and those who have blown the whistle have usually not fared well in terms of promotion or career advancement, even if they have kept their jobs. No administration has yet signaled that such people, if they have the best interests of the country at heart, are to be rewarded and made examples to be emulated.

We shall restrict our discussion to a specific sort of whistle blowing—namely, *nongovernmental, impersonal, external whistle blowing.* We shall be concerned with (1) employees of profit-making firms, who, for moral reasons, in the hope and expectation that a product will be made safe, or a practice changed, (2) make public information about a product or practice of the firm that owing to faulty design, the use of inferior materials, or the failure to follow safety or other regular procedures or state of the art standards (3) threat-

---

[3] U.S. Merit Systems Protection Board, *Whistle Blowing and the Federal Employee* (Washington, D.C.: U.S. Government Printing Office, 1981). In 1986 Congress revised the False Claims Act. It not only protects those who blow the whistle on government contractor fraud but also gives the whistle blower up to 30 percent of the amount received from a successful suit (Miceli and Near, pp. 247-248).

ens to produce serious harm to the public in general, to employees, or to individual users of a product. We shall restrict our analysis to this type of whistle blowing because, in the first place, the conditions that justify whistle blowing vary according to the type of case at issue. Second, financial harm can be considerably different from bodily harm. An immoral practice that increases the cost of a product by a slight margin may do serious harm to no individual, even if the total amount when summed adds up to a large amount, or profit. (Such cases can be handled differently from cases that threaten bodily harm.) Third, both internal and personal whistle blowing cause problems for a firm, which are for the most part restricted to those within the firm. External, impersonal whistle blowing is of concern to the general public, because it is people or the general public rather than the firm that are threatened with harm.

As a paradigm, we shall take a set of fairly clear-cut cases—namely, those in which serious bodily harm, including possible death, threatens either the users of a product or innocent bystanders because of a firm's practice, the design of its product, or the action of some person or persons within the firm. (Many of the famous whistle-blowing cases are instances of such situations.) We shall assume clear cases where serious, preventable harm will result unless a company makes changes in its product or practice.

Cases that are less clear are probably more numerous and pose problems that are difficult to solve—for example, how serious is *serious*, and how does one tell whether a given situation is serious? We choose not to resolve such issues here, but rather to construct a model embodying a number of distinctions that will enable us to clarify the moral status of whistle blowing, which may, in turn, provide a basis for working out guidelines for more complex cases.

Finally, the only motivation for whistle blowing we shall consider here is moral motivation. Those who blow the whistle for revenge, and so on, are not our concern in this discussion.

Corporations are complex entities. Sometimes those at the top do not want to know in detail the difficulties encountered by those below them. They wish lower management to handle these difficulties as best they can. On the other hand, those in lower management frequently present only good news to those above them, even if those at the top do want to be told about difficulties. Sometimes lower management hopes that things will be straightened out without letting their superiors know that anything has gone wrong. For instance, sometimes a production schedule is drawn up that many employees along the line know cannot be achieved. The manager at each level has cut off a few days of the production time actually needed, to make his or her projection look good to those above. Because this happens at each level, the final projection is weeks, if not months, off the mark. When difficulties develop in actual production, each level is further squeezed and is tempted to cut corners in order not to fall too far behind the overall schedule. The cuts may consist of not correcting defects in a design, or of allowing a defective part to go through, even though a department head and the workers in that department know that this will cause trouble for the consumer. Sometimes a defective part will be annoying; sometimes it will be dangerous. If dangerous, external whistle blowing may be morally mandatory.

Producing goods that are known to be defective or that will break down after a short period time is sometimes justified by producers, who point out that the product is warrantied and that it will be repaired for consumers free of charge. They claim it is better to have the product available for the Christmas market, for the new-model season for cars, or for some other target date, even if it must later be recalled and fixed, rather than have the product delayed beyond the target date.

When the product is so defective as to be dangerous, the situation from a moral point of view is much more serious than when only convenience is at stake. If the danger is such that people are likely to die from the defect, then clearly it should be repaired before being sold. As in the Pinto case, there have been instances when a company, knowing that its product was dangerous, did a cost-benefit analysis. The managers of the company determined how many people were likely to be killed and what the cost to the company would be if a certain percentage of the deceased persons' families successfully sued the company. They then compared this figure with the cost of repairing the defect, or of repairing it immediately rather than at a later date, through a recall. They also estimated the cost to the company if they were not only sued but also fined. If the loss from immediate repair substantially exceeded the probable cost of suits and fines, they continued production.

Such a cost-benefit analysis might seem, at first glance, to resemble a utilitarian calculation. However, a utilitarian calculation would not fail to consider the effect on all parties. The cost-benefit analysis is made exclusively from the standpoint of the company. How much, we have to ask, is a human life worth? If a defective part will probably cause fifty or sixty deaths, can we simply calculate the probability of a certain number of people suing and then weigh that cost against the cost of replacing the part? An adequate moral utilitarian calculation would include the deaths and the injuries, as well as the inconvenience for all the purchasers, and weigh these factors against the dollars saved. The equation is not difficult to solve. We know that we all have a moral obligation not to harm others, when we can prevent it. In such cases, the equation of deaths to dollars is an equation that, from a moral point of view, will always balance out in favor of lives saved. This realization often provides the moral motivation for whistle blowers.

A variety of corporate activities have led people to disclose publicly the internal actions of their companies. In some cases, companies were dumping toxic wastes into a water supply, knowing that it would harm the people who lived near the supply. In other cases, papers were signed by employees certifying that a dangerous defect had been repaired, when in fact no repairs had been made. In the Bay Area Rapid Transit case, three engineers saw a dangerous defect in the system. When their warnings were systematically ignored, and they were told to keep quiet, they felt it was their moral duty to make the danger known to the public.[4]

Whistle blowers usually fare very poorly at the hands of their company, as we mentioned before. Most are fired. In some instances, they have been blackballed in the whole industry. If they are not fired, they are frequently shunted aside at promotion time and treated as pariahs. Those who consider making a firm's wrongdoings public must therefore be aware that they may be fired, ostracized, and condemned by others. They may ruin their chances of future promotion and security, and they also may make themselves a target for revenge. Only rarely have companies praised and promoted such people. This is not surprising, because the whistle blower forces the company to do what it did not want to do, even if, morally, it was the right action. This is scandalous. And it is ironic that those guilty of endangering the lives of others—even of indirectly killing them—frequently get promoted by their companies for increasing profits.

Because the consequences for the whistle blower are often so disastrous, such action is not to be undertaken lightly. Moreover, whistle blowing may, in some cases, be morally justifiable without being morally mandatory. The position we shall develop is a moderate one that falls between the two extremes: That whistle blowing is always morally justifiable and that it is never morally justifiable.

Whistle Blowing as Morally Prohibited

Whistle blowing can be defined in such a way that it is always morally permissible or always morally obligatory. Initially, however, we can plausibly consider as morally neutral the act of an employee making public a firm's internal operations, practices, or policies that affect the safety of a product. In some cases whistle blowing may be morally prohibited, in some cases it may be morally permissible, and in others it may be morally mandatory.

Each of the two extreme positions on whistle blowing, although mistaken, is instructive. The view that whistle blowing is always morally prohibited is the more widely held view. It is held not only by most managers but also by most employees. There is a strong tradition within American mores against "ratting," or telling on others. We find this to be true of children, in and out of school, and in folk wisdom: "Don't wash your dirty linen in public." There is ample evidence that when someone does blow the whistle on his or her company—even for moral reasons, and with positive results for the public—he or she is generally ostracized, not only by the management of the firm but also by fellow employees. The whistle blower is perceived as a trai-

---

[4] Robert M. Anderson, Robert Perrucci, Dan E. Schendel, and Leon E. Trachtman, *Divided Loyalties: Whistle-Blowing at BART* (West Lafayette, Ind.: Purdue University, 1980).

tor, as someone who has damaged the firm—the working family—to which he or she belongs. In so doing, he or she has hurt and offended most of those within the firm.

Rarely are whistle blowers honored as heroes by their fellow workers. A possible explanation might be that, by this action, the whistle blower has implied that fellow workers who did not blow the whistle are guilty of immorality, complicity in the wrongdoings of the company, or cowardice. The whistle blower did what the others were obliged to do but failed to do. His or her presence is therefore a constant reminder of their moral failure. Such a scenario may describe some situations, but whatever the scenario, the evidence is overwhelming that the whistle blower is not considered a hero by most fellow workers.

How can we justify this feeling of most workers and managers that an employee ought not blow the whistle on the firm for which he or she works? Are they not operating under a double standard if they themselves wish to be preserved from injury caused by other firms, even if the means of achieving that protection is the result of someone in another firm blowing the whistle?

The most plausible, and most commonly stated, rationale for not blowing the whistle is given in terms of loyalty. When people join a company, it is claimed, they become part of an organization composed of fellow employees. They are not simply automatons filling positions. They are people with feelings, who are engaged in a joint enterprise. In accepting employment, employees at every level owe something to the employing firm as well as to those with whom they work. Employees owe not only a certain amount of work but also a certain positive attitude toward that work and to their fellow workers. Without such a positive attitude (which we can characterize roughly as loyalty), a worker is either indifferent or disaffected. An indifferent or disaffected worker is clearly not a team player and typically contributes only enough work to keep from being fired. Given the chance, such a worker would gladly leave the firm for a job with another company. Such employees lack loyalty to their employer.

Now, if the indifferent or disaffected worker were to blow the whistle on his or her employer, one might doubt that he or she did so from noble or moral motives. One might be mistaken in assuming ignoble motives, but the natural tendency would be to see the whistle blowing as stemming from the worker's indifference or disaffection. Therefore, it is unlikely that those workers who feel a sense of obligation or loyalty to the firm will look kindly on the whistle blower or the whistle blowing.

This leaves us to consider the loyal worker. What is the basis of this loyalty, and to what extent is it owed the company or employer? In one view, loyalty is based appropriately on gratitude. The firm or employer, after all, gives the worker a job, which is no small consideration in a society in which 4 percent unemployment is considered normal and in which unemployment for some groups in the society has recently reached 18 percent. To be disloyal to your employer is to bite the hand that feeds you—hardly an admirable or praise-worthy action. But even if the worker feels no gratitude, both the worker and the employer profit from their mutual contract, because if workers are to be more than cogs in an impersonal machine, they come to see the company as their company. Workers, in any event, have a stake in the firm for which they work. The stake is appropriately translated into positive concern for the firm, if not full identification with it—a concern that is in part what people mean by *loyalty*.

But even if we concede that an employee appropriately feels loyalty to a firm or to those within it, we cannot agree that such loyalty involves or demands that a worker engage in immoral activities for the firm. Nor need we admit that loyalty is always the overriding consideration in an employee's actions. The flaw in the argument of those who claim that whistle blowing is always immoral is that they make loyalty to a firm the worker's highest obligation and consider it to be always overriding.

On the other hand, those who argue that whistle blowing is always at least morally permissible typically approach such acts from the point of view of the right of free speech. Workers do not give up the right of free speech—a civil right—by taking employment. They usually make no pledge of loyalty; and any claim that employers make regarding an employee's obligation to be loyal to their firm is wishful thinking, or self-serving ideological hogwash that they try to foist on naive employees. There is no obligation of employee loyalty, either as a result of a contract or as an implied condition of employment. But there is the right of free speech.

The right of free speech, of course, is a limited right. One is not free to yell "fire" in a crowded theater when there is no fire. One is legally prohibited from making libelous statements. But one is not prevented from making true statements, whether they be about one's employer or about others. American citizens freely criticize their government and their elected leaders. It would be strange if they did not have a similar right to criticize their employers. Moreover, the argument continues, if the actions of their employers, or of some members of the firm, are morally suspect, or if actions of the firm may in some way damage consumers, workers, or innocent bystanders, or if these actions threaten the interests of shareholders or of other interested parties, then workers clearly have the right to speak out in whatever way, and in whatever forum, they desire. By doing so, they violate no commitment to loyalty because there is no such commitment; they are simply exercising their right to free speech. It may be imprudent at times to speak out, and they may suffer from the often unjust reactions of others, but whistle blowing, or speaking out about a company's practices, is not immoral; it is always a morally defensible act.

This extreme position has much to recommend it. But it is extreme because it makes the right of free speech always overriding, and it fails to consider the harm done to one's firm or fellow workers by the usual kind of whistle blowing. In denying any obligation of loyalty, it implicitly denies any consideration of the harm that one's actions may do to those with whom one is associated, and fails to consider whether there are morally preferable alternatives—or perhaps even morally required alternatives.

Each of the two positions we have described as extreme suffers from the same defect. Each makes absolute one aspect of a complex situation and fails to consider the conflict of obligations, rights, and responsibilities that usually arise in the conditions that lead to whistle blowing. If neither loyalty nor the right to free speech is always overriding, and if neither always determines the morality of a case, it is sometimes possible for loyalty to be overriding, sometimes for the right of free speech to be overriding—and it is possible, therefore, that at times neither be overriding, and that both may give way to some other consideration. This suggests that sometimes whistle blowing may be immoral—as when loyalty is overriding—and that sometimes it is morally justified—as when the right to free speech is overriding.

On whom does the onus of justification rest? Should we assume that whistle blowing is generally morally justifiable, and require that anyone who claims that a given act of whistle blowing is immoral make out that case? Or should we assume that whistle blowing is generally immoral, and require moral justification for those acts that are morally permissible or obligatory? Tradition has placed the onus on those who justify whistle blowing, the common assumption being that it is morally prohibited. We have already noted the general attitude of most workers to whistle blowing, and their negative reaction to the whistle blower. Moreover, unless we are to indict most workers as moral cowards, the relatively rare incidence of whistle blowing indicates that most workers do not feel it is their moral obligation to blow the whistle. Although these considerations do not by themselves show that workers feel it is immoral to blow the whistle, they at least tend to put the onus on those who would claim it is morally obligatory. Finally, the literature on whistle blowing has developed in such a way that those who justify it have assumed the need to do so.

That whistle blowing needs justification makes sense, moreover, if it is seen as an instance of disobedience to the corporation or organization. Frequently, whistle blowers are in fact told by their superiors to mind their own business. To blow the whistle is to go beyond what they are paid to do, and is to fly in the face of orders given by a legitimate superior within the firm or organization. Disobedience typically requires justification if it is to be considered moral—whether it is a case of civil disobedience, disobedience to the corporation, or a child's disobedience to his or her parents. Under the appropriate conditions, obedience is the expected and required moral way to act. Disobedience may be morally justified, but if it is, the onus is on the disobedient person or his or her spokesperson to make out the case.

To admit that whistle blowing is often an instance of disobedience to the corporation and that at least sometimes one (i.e., the corporation) is owed obedience leads us to the conclusion that at least sometimes whistle blowing is morally wrong. That it is sometimes morally wrong seems the general consensus in American society, and there is no reason to challenge the consensus.

But sometimes whistle blowing is morally permissible, and sometimes is even morally obligatory; therefore, it is appropriate to accept the onus of spelling out and justifying the conditions for each.

Whistle Blowing as Morally Permitted

The kind of whistle blowing we are considering involves an employee some-how going public, revealing information or concerns about his or her firm in the hope that the firm will change its product, action, policy, or whatever it is that the whistle blower feels will harm, or has harmed others, and needs to be rectified. We can assume that when one blows the whistle, it is not with the consent of the firm, but against its wishes. It is thus a form of disloyalty and disobedience to the corporation. Whistle blowing of this type, we can further assume, does injury to a firm. It results in either adverse publicity or in an investigation of some sort, or both. If we adopt the principle that one ought not to do harm without sufficient reason, then, if the act of whistle blowing is to be morally permissible, some good must be achieved to outweigh the harm that will be done.

There are five conditions that, if satisfied, change the moral status of whistle blowing. If the first three are satisfied, the act of whistle blowing will be morally justifiable and permissible. If the additional two are satisfied, the act of whistle blowing will be morally obligatory.

Whistle blowing is morally permissible if

1. The firm, through its product or policy, will do serious and considerable harm to employees or to the public, whether in the person of the user of its product, an innocent bystander, or the general public.

Because whistle blowing causes harm to the firm, this harm must be off-set by at least an equal amount of good if the act is to be permissible. We have specified that the potential or actual harm to others must be serious and con-siderable. That requirement may be considered by some to be both too strong and too vague. Why specify "serious and considerable" instead of saying, "involve more harm than the harm that the whistle blowing will produce for the firm"? Moreover, how serious is "serious"? And how considerable is "con-siderable"?

There are several reasons for stating that the potential harm must be serious and considerable. First, if the harm is not serious and considerable, if an action will do only slight damage to the public or to the user of a product, the justification for whistle blowing will be at least problematic. We will not have a clear case. To assess the harm done to the firm is difficult; but though the harm may be rather vague, it is also rather sure. If the harm threatened by a product is slight or not certain, it might not be greater than the harm done to the firm. After all, a great many products involve some risk. Even with a well-constructed hammer, one can smash one's finger. There is some risk in operating any automobile because no automobile is completely safe. There is always a trade-off between safety and cost. It is not immoral not to make the safest automobile possible, for instance, and a great many factors enter into deciding just how safe a car should be. An employee might see that a car can be made slightly safer by modifying a part and might suggest that modification; but not making the modification is not usually grounds for blowing the whistle. If serious harm is not threatened, then the slight harm that is done, say by the use of a product, can be corrected after the product is marketed (e.g., as a result of customer complaint). Our society has a great many ways of handling minor defects, and these are at least arguably better than resorting to whistle blowing.

To this consideration should be added a second. Whistle blowing is frequently, and appropriately, considered an unusual occurrence—a heroic act. If the practice of blowing the whistle for relatively minor harm were to become a common occurrence, its effectiveness would be diminished. When serious harm is threatened, whistle blowers are listened to by the news media, for instance, because the harm is news. But relatively minor harm to the public is not news. If many minor charges or concerns were voiced to the media, the public would soon not react as it is now expected to react to such disclosures. This would also be the case if complaints about all sorts of perceived or anticipated minor harm were reported to government agencies, although most people would expect that government agencies would act first on the serious cases and only later on claims of relatively minor harm.

There is a third consideration. Every time an employee has a concern about possible harm to the public from a product or practice we cannot assume that he or she makes a correct assessment, nor can we assume that every claim of harm is morally motivated. To sift out the claims and concerns of the disaffected worker from the genuine claims and concerns of the morally motivated employee is a practical problem. It may be claimed that this problem has nothing to do with the moral permissibility of the act of whistle blowing; but whistle blowing is a practical matter. If viewed as a technique for changing policy or actions, it will be justified only if effective. It can be trivialized. If it is, then one might plausibly claim that little harm is done to the firm, and hence the act is permitted. But if trivialized, it loses its point. If whistle blowing is to be considered a serious act with serious consequences, it should be reserved for disclosing potentially serious harm and will be morally justifiable in those cases.

Serious is admittedly a vague term. Is an increase in probable automobile deaths from 2 in 100,000 to 15 in 100,000 over a one-year period serious? Although there may be legitimate debate on this issue, it is clear that matters that threaten death are prima facie serious. If the threatened harm is that a product may cost a few pennies more than otherwise, or if the threatened harm is that a part or product may cause minor inconvenience, that harm— even if multiplied by thousands or millions of instances—does not match the seriousness of death to the user or the innocent bystander.

The harm threatened by unsafe tires—for example, sold as premium quality but blowing out at 60 or 70 mph—is serious, for such tires can easily lead to death. The dumping of metal drums of toxic waste into a river, where the drums will rust, leak, and cause cancer or other serious ills to those who drink the river water or otherwise use it, threatens serious harm. The use of substandard concrete in a building, such that the building is likely to collapse and kill people, poses a serious threat to people. Failure to X-ray pipe fittings, as required in building a nuclear plant, is a failure that might lead to nuclear leaks; this may involve serious harm, for it endangers the health and lives of many.

The notion of *serious* harm might be expanded to include serious financial harm, as well as kinds of harm other than death and serious threats to health and body. But as we noted earlier, we shall restrict ourselves here to products and practices that produce or threaten serious harm or danger to life and health. The difference between producing harm and threatening serious danger is not significant for the kinds of cases we are considering.

2. Once employees identify a serious threat to the user of a product or to the general public, they should report it to their immediate superior and make their moral concern known. Unless they do so, the act of whistle blowing is not clearly justifiable.

Why not? Why is not the weighing of harm sufficient? The answer has already been given in part. Whistle blowing is a practice that, to be effective, cannot be routinely used. There are other reasons as well. First, reporting one's concerns is the most direct, and usually the quickest, way of producing the change the whistle blower desires. The normal assumption is that most firms do not want to cause death or injury and do not willingly and knowingly set out to harm the users of their products in this way. If there are life-threatening defects, the normal assumption is, and should be, that the firm will be interested in correcting them, if not for moral reasons, at least for prudential reasons—viz., to avoid suits, bad publicity, and adverse consumer reaction. If serious harm is threatened and an employee can prevent it by reporting it, he or she has the obligation to report it. The argument from loyalty also supports the requirement that the firm be given the chance to rectify its action, procedure, or policy before it is charged in public. In addition, because whistle blowing does harm to the firm, harm in general is minimized if the firm is informed of the problem and allowed to correct it. Less harm is done to the firm in this way, and if the harm to the public or the users is also averted, this procedure produces the least harm, on the whole.

The condition that one report one's concern to one's immediate superior presupposes a hierarchical structure. Although firms are usually so structured, they need not be. In a company of equals, one would report one's concerns internally, as appropriate.

Several objections may be raised to this condition. Suppose one knows that one's immediate superior already knows of the defect and the danger. In this case reporting it to the superior would be redundant, and condition 2 would be satisfied. But one should not presume without good reason that one's superior does know. What may be clear to one individual may not be clear to another. Moreover, the assessment of risk is often a complicated matter. What appears as unacceptable risk to a person on one level may appear as legitimate to a person on a higher level, who may see a larger picture and know of offsetting compensations and the like.

Would not reporting one's concern effectively preclude the possibility of anonymous whistle blowing and so put one in jeopardy? This might be the case, and a person should weigh this consideration before blowing the whistle. We will discuss this matter later in this chapter. If the reporting is done tactfully, moreover, the voicing of one's concerns might, if the problem is apparent to others, indicate a desire to operate within the firm, and so make one less likely to be the person assumed to have blown the whistle anonymously.

By reporting his or her concern to the immediate superior or other appropriate person, the employee preserves and observes the regular practices of firms, which on the whole promote their order and efficiency; this fulfills the employee's obligation of minimizing harm, and it precludes precipitous whistle blowing.

3. If one's immediate superior does nothing effective about the concern or complaint, the employee should exhaust the internal procedures and possibilities within the firm. This usually will involve taking the matter up the managerial ladder and, if necessary—and possible—to the board of directors.

To exhaust the internal procedures and possibilities is the key requirement here. In a hierarchically structured firm, this means going up the chain of command. But the employee may do so either with or without the permission of those at each level of the hierarchy. What constitutes exhausting the internal procedures? This is often a matter of judgment. But because going public with one's concern is more serious both for oneself and for the firm, going up the chain of command is the preferable route to take in most circumstances. This third condition is of course satisfied if, for some reason, it is truly impossible to go beyond any particular level.

Several objections may once again be raised. There may not be time enough to follow the bureaucratic procedures of a given firm; the threatened harm may have been done before the procedures are exhausted. If, moreover, one goes up the chain to the top and nothing is done by anyone, then a great deal of time will have been wasted. Once again, prudence and judgement should be used. The internal possibilities may sometimes be exhausted quickly, by a few phone calls or visits. But it should not simply be assumed that no one at any level within the firm will do anything. If there are truly no possibilities of internal remedy, then the third condition is satisfied.

As we mentioned, the point of the three conditions is essentially that whistle blowing is morally permissible if the harm threatened is serious and if internal remedies have been attempted in good faith without a satisfactory result. In these circumstances, an employee is morally justified in attempting to avert what he or she sees as serious harm by any means that may be effective, including blowing the whistle.

We can pass over as not immediately germane the questions of whether in nonserious matters there is an obligation to report one's moral concerns to one's superiors and whether a person fulfills this obligation once he or she has reported them to the appropriate party.

These three steps can be taken as an analysis of the moral obligation to bring the matter before the attention of those who can prevent it. We noted earlier that everyone has the moral obligation to prevent serious harm to others when they can do so at little cost to themselves. Since one's own good is as important as the good of another, there is no general obligation to sacrifice oneself for another. To do so is generally agreed to go beyond the call of duty. As the cost to oneself grows, the obligation generally diminishes, unless the threatened harm is very great. Once again one must use one's judgment to decide how to weigh the harm to oneself as opposed to the serious harm to others. Yet the general rule applies in the case of serious harm threatened to others by one's own company, and if one can present that harm one has the obligation to do so and to take what steps one can. Hence we can argue that employees have the general obligation to report the threatened harm they perceive to their superiors and to go as high up in the company as they can to prevent it. The obligation to do so sets the stage for the obligation to externally blow the whistle.

If these three steps have been taken, and if the company does not take any action to prevent the harm, then one has exhausted the internal remedies. Having exhausted them is sufficient justification for the employee to turn to external whistle blowing. The employee by using all available internal mechanisms has satisfied any legitimate claim of loyalty to the company and has provided the company an opportunity to prevent the harm without publicity, and so without damage to its reputation. From an ethical point of view, the employee who has taken these three steps without successful remedy is permitted to go outside the company and blow the whistle externally in order to prevent the threatened harm.

Whistle Blowing as Morally Required

To say that external whistle blowing under these conditions is morally permitted does not impose any obligation on an employee to externally blow the whistle. Unless two other conditions are met, the employee does not have a moral obligation to blow the whistle. To blow the whistle when there is no moral requirement to do so, and if done from moral motives (i.e., concern for one's fellow humans) and at risk to oneself, is to commit a supererogatory act. It is an act that deserves moral praise. But failure to so act deserves no moral blame. In such a case, the whistle blower might be considered a moral hero. Sometimes he or she is so considered, and sometimes not. If an employee's claim or concern turns out to be ill-founded, his or her subjective moral state may be as praiseworthy as if the claim were well-founded, but the person will rarely receive much praise for his or her action.

For there to be an obligation to blow the whistle, two conditions must be met, in addition to the foregoing three.

4. The whistle blower must have, or have accessible, documented evidence that would convince a reasonable, impartial observer that one's view of the situation is correct, and that the company's product or practice poses a serious and likely danger to the public or to the user of the product.

Employees do not have an obligation to put themselves at serious risk without some compensating advantage to be gained. Unless they have documented evidence that would convince a reasonable, impartial observer, their charges or claims if made public, would be based essentially on their word. Such grounds may be sufficient for a subjective feeling of certitude about the charges, but they are not usually sufficient for others to act on the claims. For instance, a newspaper is unlikely to print a story based simply on someone's undocumented assertion.

Several difficulties emerge. Should it not be the responsibility of the media or the appropriate regulatory agency or government bureau to carry out an investigation based on someone's complaint? It is reasonable for them to do so, providing they have some evidence in support of the complaint or claim. The damage has not yet been done, and the harm will not, in all likelihood, be done to the complaining party. If the action is criminal, then an investigation by a law-enforcing agency is appropriate. But the charges made by whistle blowers are often not criminal charges. And we do not expect newspapers or government agencies to carry out investigations whenever anyone claims that possible harm will be done by a product or practice. Unless harm is imminent, and very serious (e.g., a bomb threat), it is appropriate to act on evidence that substantiates a claim. The usual procedure, once an investigation is started or a complaint followed up, is to contact the party charged.

One does not have a moral obligation to blow the whistle simply because of a hunch, guess, or personal assessment of possible danger, if supporting evidence and documentation are not available. One may, of course, have the obligation to attempt to get evidence if the harm is serious. But if it is unavailable—or unavailable without using illegal or immoral means—then a person does not have the obligation to blow the whistle.

5. The employee must have good reasons to believe that by going public the necessary changes will be brought about. The chance of being suc-

cessful must be worth the risk one takes and the danger to which one is exposed.

Even with some documentation and evidence, a potential whistle blower may not be taken seriously, or may not be able to get the media or government agency to take any action. How far should one go, and how much must one try? The more serious the situation, the greater the effort required. But unless one has a reasonable expectation of success, one is not obliged to put oneself at great risk. Before going public, the potential whistle blower should know who (e.g., government agency, newspaper, columnist, TV reporter) will make use of the evidence, and how it will be handled. The whistle blower should have good reason to expect that the action taken will result in the kind of change or result that he or she believes is morally appropriate.

The foregoing fourth and fifth conditions may seem too permissive to some and too stringent to others. The conditions are too permissive for those who wish everyone to be ready and willing to blow the whistle whenever there is a chance that the public will be harmed. After all, harm to the public is more serious than harm to the whistle blower, and, in the long run, if everyone saw whistle blowing as obligatory, without satisfying the last two conditions, we would all be better off. If the fourth and fifth conditions must be satisfied, then people will only rarely have the moral obligation to blow the whistle.

If, however, whistle blowing were mandatory whenever the first three conditions were satisfied, and if one had the moral obligation to blow the whistle whenever one had a moral doubt or fear about safety, or whenever one disagreed with one's superiors or colleagues, one would be obliged to go public whenever one did not get one's way on such issues within a firm. But these conditions are much too strong, for the reasons already given. Other conditions, weaker than those proposed, might be suggested. But any condition that makes whistle blowing mandatory in large numbers of cases may reduce the effectiveness of whistle blowing. If this were the result, and the practice were to become widespread, then it is doubtful that we would all be better off.

Finally, the claim that many people very often have the obligation to blow the whistle goes against the common view of the whistle blower as a moral hero, and against the commonly held feeling that whistle blowing is only rarely morally mandatory. This feeling may be misplaced. But a very strong argument is necessary to show that although the general public is morally mistaken in its view, the moral theoretician is correct in his or her assertion.

A consequence of accepting the fourth and fifth conditions stated is that the stringency of the moral obligation of whistle blowing corresponds with the common feeling of most people on this issue. Those in higher positions and those in professional positions in a firm are more likely to have the obligation to change a firm's policy or product—even by whistle blowing, if necessary—than are lower-placed employees. Engineers, for instance, are more likely to have access to data and designs than are assembly-line workers. Managers generally have a broader picture and more access to evidence than do non-managerial employees. Management has the moral responsibility both to see that the expressed moral concerns of those below them have been adequately considered and that the firm does not knowingly inflict harm on others.

The fourth and fifth conditions will appear too stringent to those who believe that whistle blowing is always a supererogatory act, that it is always moral heroism, and that it is never morally obligatory. They might argue that, although we are not permitted to do what is immoral, we have no general moral obligation to prevent all others from acting immorally. This is what the whistle blower attempts to do. The counter to that, however, is to point out that whistle blowing is an act in which one attempts to prevent harm to a third party. It is not implausible to claim both that we are morally obliged to prevent harm to others at relatively little expense to ourselves, and that we are morally obliged to prevent great harm to a great many others, even at considerable expense to ourselves.

The five conditions outlined can be used by an individual to help decide whether he or she is morally permitted or required to blow the whistle. Third parties can also use these conditions when attempting to evaluate acts of whistle blowing by others, even though third parties may have difficulty determining whether the whistle blowing is morally motivated. It might be possible successfully to blow the whistle anonymously. But anonymous tips or stories seldom get much attention. One can confide in a government agent, or in a reporter, on condition that one's name not be disclosed. But this approach, too, is frequently ineffective in achieving the results required. To be effective, the source must usually be willing to be identified, to testify publicly, to produce verifiable evidence, and to put himself or herself at risk. As with civil disobedience, what captures the conscience of others is the willingness of the whistle blower to suffer harm for the benefit of others, and for what he or she thinks is right.

Although we have concentrated on a specific type of nongovernmental, impersonal, external whistle blowing that threatens serious physical harm to the public, the analysis provides a model for dealing with other kinds of whistle blowing as well. What should employees do when the harm threatened is not physical but monetary—to customers, suppliers, or the general public? How serious does such threatened harm have to be? What of unjustified cost overruns on government contracts, or tax evasion, or other illegal activities on the part of a company? When is a worker prohibited from blowing the whistle, and when is a worker permitted or required to blow it?

Internal Whistle Blowing

Impersonal external whistle blowing is the most dramatic and publicized kind of whistle blowing. An equally troubling kind is impersonal, internal, nongovernmental whistle blowing. The analysis of the conditions under which the first kind is prohibited, permitted, or mandatory does not automatically apply to the internal kind. If serious harm is threatened to employees, then the first three conditions come into play and the analysis yields an obligation to internally blow the whistle. But in many instances of internal whistle blowing there is no question of going outside the firm because the harm done is not to employees or to the public but to the firm.

Rather than being an act of corporate disloyalty, internal whistle blowing is more often than not an act of corporate loyalty. However, it usually does involve disloyalty or disobedience to one's immediate superior or disloyalty to one's fellow workers. If done from moral motives, the intent of such whistle blowing is to stop dishonesty or some immoral practice or act in order to protect the interests and reputation of the company or to increase a company's profits.

Those in management positions are usually expected to see that those below them follow proper procedures and obey company policy. But what obligation, if any, does a subordinate have to report that someone above them is padding his or her expense account, or is taking kickbacks on orders placed with a supplier, or is accepting large unreported gifts from suppliers? Most companies would like to know about such activity and stop it. However, unless reporting it is stated as an obligation, such as in corporate guidelines, if those doing the reporting would not in any way be considered accomplices and have nothing to do with the wrongdoing, it is difficult to see how subordinates can have a moral *obligation* to report such activity. In doing so they would help the company, but they might also put their own positions, jobs, or promotions in jeopardy. Workers are not typically hired to spy on their fellow workers or superiors. Nor is it clear that asking employees to act in that capacity would make for a productive corporate atmosphere. There is no general moral obligation for everyone to report every minor instance of wrongdoing of which they become aware. Such a requirement would be impossible to fulfill and would cause more social harm than good. It would turn a normal society into a police state or develop a police-state mentality among its citizens in which everyone watches and reports on everyone else. The cases here do not involve illegal activity or harm to others outside the corporation, and so they are appropriately handled within the corporation. They also involve relatively minor harm to the firm. This does not excuse the activities, but it does affect the obligation of subordinates to report such activity.

Although not obliged to blow the whistle on superiors so acting, are employees morally permitted to do so? Are they ever morally prohibited from doing so?

In the analysis of external whistle blowing, we acknowledged a requirement to try to prevent the threatened harm by reporting it within the firm first. Is there a parallel requirement that before reporting the wrongdoings of a superior one inform that person first? Although this might frequently be the preferable course of action, providing one could do so tactfully and with relative personal impunity, it is not a general requirement. In the cases we are discussing, the action has already been done and the harm inflicted. Because the perpetrators of the prohibited actions in question are acting against the good of the firm, they can claim no right to privacy with respect to those actions and no immunity from being reported. Those above them clearly have the right and often the obligation to stop that activity. Hence, a subordinate who feels strongly about the action may report it. There is no general moral prohibition about reporting wrongdoing, and there is no special prohibition if the wrongdoing occurs within a firm.

A similar kind of analysis applies to reporting the wrongdoings of one's peers or fellow workers.

The analysis changes once the activity is illegal or causes harm to individuals or serious harm to the company. Reporting such activity is morally permitted. Whether it is morally required depends on the severity of the harm, one's position within the firm and vis-à-vis the perpetrator, the firm's general operating procedures, and other pertinent factors. The point is not to look for an automatic rule, but to learn to consider and weigh the pertinent factors in each case.

A company that wishes to foster both collegiality and honesty among its employees will have policies that will help employees work through their responsibilities with respect to issues involving ethical breaches on the part of superiors and fellow employees.

Precluding the Need for Whistle Blowing

The need for moral heroes shows a defective society and defective corporations. It is more important to change the legal and corporate structures that make whistle blowing necessary than to convince people to be moral heroes.

Because it is easier to change the law than to change the practice of all corporations, it should be illegal for any employer to fire an employee, or to take any punitive measures, at the time or later, against an employee who satisfies the first three aforementioned conditions and blows the whistle on the company. Because satisfying those conditions makes the action morally justifiable, the law should protect employees when they are acting in accordance with what their conscience demands. If the whistle is falsely blown, the company will have suffered no great harm. If it is appropriately blown, the company should suffer the consequences of its actions being made public. But to protect a whistle blower by passing such a law is no easy matter. Employers can make life difficult for whistle blowers without firing them. There are many ways of passing over an employee. He or she can be relegated to the back room of the firm or be given unpleasant jobs. Employers can always find reasons not to promote employees or to give them raises. Not all of this can be prevented by law, but some of the more blatant practices can be prohibited.

Second, the law can mandate that the individuals responsible for the decision to proceed with a faulty product or to engage in a harmful practice be penalized. The law has been reluctant to interfere with the operations of companies. As a result, those in the firm who have been guilty of immoral and illegal practices have gone untouched even though the corporation was fined for its activity.

A third possibility is that every company of a certain size be required by law to have an inspector general, an internal operational auditor, an ethics officer, or some comparable person whose job it is to uncover immoral and illegal practices. This person's job would be to listen to the moral concerns of employees, at every level, about the firm's practices. He or she should be independent of management and report to the audit committee of the board, which, ideally, should be a committee made up entirely of outside board members. The inspector or auditor should be charged with making public those complaints that should be made public if not changed from within. Failure on the inspector's part to take proper action with respect to a worker's complaint, such that the worker is forced to go public, should be prima facie evidence of an attempt to cover up a dangerous practice or product, and the inspector should be subject to criminal charges.

In addition, a company that wishes to be moral—that does not wish to engage in harmful practices or to produce harmful products—can take other steps to preclude the necessity of whistle blowing. It can establish channels whereby those employees who have moral concerns can get a fair hearing without danger to their position or standing in the company. Expressing such concerns, moreover, should be considered a demonstration of company loyalty and should be rewarded appropriately. The company might establish the position of ombudsman to hear such complaints or moral concerns, or an independent committee of the board might be established to hear such complaints and concerns. Someone might even be paid by the company to present the position of the would-be whistle blower, who would argue for what the company should do from a moral point of view, rather than what those interested in meeting a schedule or making a profit would like to do. Such a person's success within the company could depend on his or her success in precluding whistle blowing, as well as the conditions that lead to it.

Unions and professional organizations should become concerned with the problem of whistle blowing. They should support their members who feel obligated to blow the whistle on a company; they should defend and support members in their endeavors and prevent them from being fired or abused on the job. They can also establish channels of their own, to which members can report concerns, and then follow up such concerns and force appropriate action.

Although we have concentrated on a specific type of nongovernmental, impersonal, external whistle blowing that threatens serious physical harm to the public, the analysis provides a model for dealing with other kinds of whistle blowing as well.

Because whistle blowing involves disloyalty or disobedience at some level, we start by requiring that it be justified, rather than assuming it needs no justification. To distinguish the various kinds of whistle blowing, listing conditions that make it morally permissible and those that make it morally required is useful as a guide. In personal whistle blowing, there are many instances in which it is permitted but not obligatory. Many people may prefer to change employers rather than blow the whistle, and this may be perfectly justifiable. In all cases, one must weigh the harm done against the good to be achieved and the rights to be protected.

Whistle blowing is a relatively recent phenomenon in the workplace. It is one more indication of the falsity of the Myth of Amoral Business. Whistle blowing should also alert corporations to what can and should be done if they wish to be both moral and excellent. When corporate structures preclude the need for whistle blowing, they protect both workers' rights and the public's good.

Study Questions

1. In your opinion, was the Ford Motor Company or anyone in the company guilty of any ethical breaches? Defend your answer by means of a utilitarian analysis.

2. Did anyone in the Ford Motor Company have an obligation to blow the whistle? Defend your answer.

3. Define *whistle blowing; internal whistle blowing; external whistle blowing; personal whistle blowing; impersonal whistle blowing; governmental whistle blowing; nongovernmental whistle blowing.* Give an illustrative example of each.

4. How might someone argue that whistle blowing is always morally prohibited? What is wrong with that argument?

5. How much loyalty, if any, does a worker owe a firm? Defend your answer.

6. How might someone argue that whistle blowing is always morally permitted? What is wrong with that argument?

7. Under what three conditions is whistle blowing morally permitted? How do you defend the legitimacy of those three conditions?

8. In the kind of whistle blowing developed in the chapter, why must the threatened harm be serious and considerable? Give examples of kinds of harm that you judge to be serious and considerable. What kinds would you not judge to be serious and considerable?

9. In external whistle blowing, why must internal avenues of remedy be tried first?

10. Under what conditions is whistle blowing morally mandatory?

11. Are employees in a subordinate position obliged to internally blow the whistle on their superiors whom they know are padding their expense accounts? Are embezzling funds? In each case say why or why not.

12. Develop guidelines for personal whistle blowing. Defend the guidelines you develop.

13. What can government do to protect whistle blowers? How effective can they be?

14. How can firms preclude the need for whistle blowing?

15. How does whistle blowing indicate the falsity of the Myth of Amoral Business?

16. Using the analysis for external, impersonal, nongovernmental whistle blowing as a model, under what conditions is external, impersonal, governmental whistle blowing morally permissible? Morally mandatory?

17. Jane Fainsell works for an airplane manufacturer and has access to evidence that the company is charging the government for spare parts up to five times what they cost, amounting to about $1 million in overcharges. Is she morally obliged to do anything about this? If so, what?

11

MARKETING, TRUTH, AND ADVERTISING

The May D&F Case

Everyone loves a sale. Americans have become so used to discount houses and the lower prices resulting from competition that many people are reluctant to pay the full price for any item. As a result, sales have become more common. But the notion of a "sale" implies that the item originally sold at a higher price. For how long must it have been sold at that price, and must a store actually have sold any of the item at that price for the item to be legitimately labeled as being "on sale"? What are customer expectations in this regard, and what constitutes deception? These are not easy questions to answer. The Federal Trade Commission 1964 Guides Against Deceptive Pricing states that before a store can claim that an item is on sale at a reduced price it must have been for sale at its regular price "for a reasonably substantial period of time . . . honestly and in good faith and not for the purpose of establishing a fictitious higher price."[1]

May D&F is owned by May Department Stores, Inc., which operates fourteen department store chains. May D&F is not the only store that has been cited for the practices involved in the case, but whereas most stores settle out of court, May D&F defended its case in court. Before being officially charged, it had discussed its policies and its disagreement with the state law depart-

---

[1] Francine Schwadel, "Store's Concept of 'Sale' Pricing Gets Court Test," *Wall Street Journal*, May 15, 1990, p. B7. Other details of this case are also found in "May Unit Cited in Suit for Ad, Sales Practices in Its Colorado Stores," *Wall Street Journal*, June 23, 1989, p. B12; and James P. Miller, "May Stores Ads Ruled Deceptive by State Court," *Wall Street Journal*, June 28, 1990, p. B2.

ment for about a year. The store was officially charged in June 1989. Three counts involved printing inflated prices on its tags, inflating its prices to make its markdowns look larger than they were, and keeping merchandise on continuous sale. As examples, one set of cutlery had been on sale for two years; luggage was continuously sold at a "special introductory price"; and bedding was kept on sale for eight months.

May D&F claimed that its policy was to offer an item for sale for at least ten days at the beginning of each six-month period. That would establish the original price. Few items sold at that price, which was usually not competitive. The store would then place the item on sale for the remaining 170 days, sometimes offering special short-term reductions from that price. At the end of the 180-day cycle, it would raise the price to the original price for ten days and then repeat the cycle. In August 1989, two months after the court case began, it revised its policy so as to charge the original price for 28 out of every 90 days. It further claimed that in a survey 90 percent of its customers did not care whether the item had actually been sold at the original price.

On June 28, 1990, Judge Larry J. Naves of the Colorado State Court decided the case against May D&F, stating that "The clear expectation of May D&F was to sell all or practically all merchandise at its 'sale' price." He fined the company $8,000.

Given current practices and the prevalence of discount houses, do you find May D&F's policy, either before or after August 1989, deceptive and unethical?

The Nestlé Infant Milk Formula Case

Infant milk formula is a common, useful, popular product, widely used in the United States and Europe as a substitute for mother's milk. It comes as a powder that is to be mixed in a specific proportion with sterilized water. It is a useful product to supplement a woman's milk when she does not produce enough for her infant or to substitute for her milk if she cannot or chooses not to breast-feed her infant. In an attempt to increase sales, Nestlé, as well as other producers of infant formula, extended the sale of their product to many countries in Africa. They followed some of the same marketing techniques that they had followed with success and without customer complaint elsewhere.

One standard technique was advertising on billboards and in magazines. A second was the distribution of free samples in hospitals to new mothers as well as to doctors. In themselves, these and other practices were neither illegal nor unethical. Yet their use led to charges of following unethical practices and to a seven-year worldwide boycott of all Nestlé products.

The basis for the complaints was misuse of the products. Many of the women who received samples were poor. When they returned home to their villages, they were unable to buy sufficient quantities of the formula. In the meantime their own breastmilk had dried up. Hence, they stretched formula, diluting it to make it go further. In addition, they often used local, unsterilized water to mix the formula. The overall result was an increase in infant malnutrition and mortality.

Critics blamed the manufacturers of the infant formula, and particularly the aggressive marketing techniques.[2] Specifically, critics charged that the ads for the product frequently showed white women feeding their infants the milk formula from a bottle, thereby sending the message that to be up-to-date, modern mothers should bottle-feed rather than breast-feed their babies. Breast-feeding, however, was preferable from a health standpoint. If the mother had a sufficient supply of breastmilk, the critics maintained, she would not have to worry about buying or stretching the formula, or about contamination from water. At the same time, they said, she could transmit some of her antibodies to help the infant fight disease rather than introduce disease with the contaminated water.

Furthermore, mothers who were given free samples immediately after giving birth were more inclined to bottle-feed than to breast-feed their newborns. The company knew that the mother's milk would dry up and that the mothers would be dependent on the formula when they returned home. In addition, the representatives of the company who went through the wards giving out the samples wore white, and so the mothers easily mistook them for nurses. Therefore, they were more prone to accept and use the formula than if the distributors were easily identified as salespeople.

Because the techniques the distributors used were not illegal, a group that called itself INFACT organized a boycott to apply moral pressure on the infant milk formula companies to change their marketing techniques. The group targeted the Nestlé Corporation, a worldwide corporation based in Switzerland. INFACT asked that consumers refrain from buying any Nestlé products until the company changed its practices. The boycott, which lasted seven years, ended in January 1984. In the meantime, the World Health Organization developed a Code of Marketing of Breast-milk Substitutes, which Nestlé and other companies agreed to follow.[3]

Assuming that the above information is accurate, did Nestlé have a moral obligation to change its practices? Since its practices were legal and accepted in developed countries, why could it not follow them in less developed countries? Did American consumers have any obligation to join the boycott?

---

[2] For details of this case, see John Dobbing (Ed.), *Infant Feeding: Anatomy of a Controversy 1973-1984* (London: Springer-Verlag, 1988), and *The Dilemma of Third World Nutrition: Nestlé and the Role of Infant Formula*, 1985 (a report prepared for and distributed by Nestlé).

[3] Whether they in fact have done so is a continuing matter of controversy. See Nancy Gaschott, "Babies at Risk: Infant Formula Still Takes Its Toll," *Multinational Monitor*, October 1986, pp. 11-13; and *New York Times*, October 5, 1988, IV, p. 2.

Marketing

Once a manufacturer produces a certain product, its aim is to sell it. Marketing is the process by which it does so. Marketing techniques seek to solve a variety of problems in order to sell the product or service that a company produces or provides. Marketing research attempts to determine customer demand and the most efficient and profitable means by which this demand can be met. Often the desired data are not available or not reliable. There are also competitors, who may be interested in the same market, and their actions and potential actions must also be considered. Although many in the business of marketing and marketing research would like marketing to be or become a science, it falls far short of that. Markets can only rarely be predicted with certainty, and the ability to manipulate markets and market demand is much less than many critics claim. Yet the temptation to try to manipulate markets, to lessen one's chances of failure by illegal or immoral means, is often present. We shall examine just a few of the areas where the temptations to act immorally are significant, and where some practices are morally questionable.[4] These areas are competition, pricing, bidding, and consumer marketing.

Competition

We have already seen that competition is part of the free-enterprise system. Competition tends to produce efficiency in the market and benefits the general consumer by resulting in a variety of goods at the best prices. But the competitive market works to the advantage of the buyer only when the competitive process is fair. Although the government plays a role in trying to keep competition fair, government regulation is not enough. Unless those engaged in the competitive process operate fairly and honestly, the system itself is undermined. Moral standards have a role to play and do play it daily, but the temptations to violate the standards of honesty and fair competition for one's personal benefit or that of one's firm are also constantly present.

One major way of undermining competition is through the creation of monopolies. If a firm is able to create and maintain a monopoly in any area, then it has no competitive restraints on its prices. It may consequently charge what it wants, as long as there is a market willing to purchase its product or service at the price it sets. But how does a firm gain a monopoly? Several techniques, some of them questionable, are common. One scenario begins with a large producer of a product coming to dominate the field. Frequently, the producer is the best in the field and wins its market share honestly. It then proceeds to either buy up or undercut the competition. Buying up other firms is not in itself immoral. But if the intent is to eliminate competition, then the

---

[4] Two good collections of articles on ethics and marketing are Gene R. Laczniak and Patrick E. Murphy, *Marketing Ethics* (Lexington, Mass.: Lexington Books, 1985); and N. Craig Smith and John A. Quelch, *Ethics in Marketing* (Homewood, Ill.: Irwin, 1993).

intent is at least questionable, because such action tends to undermine the market system. Undercutting the competition might be done in several ways. One way is simply to price one's product lower than that of the competition. If this is possible because a firm is more efficient, is more productive, and is able to operate at lower cost, or is satisfied with lower profit margins, the process is fair. It is part of the competitive system and leads to the efficiency the system promises. But a large producer may undercut a smaller competitor by selling products for less than they cost to produce, absorbing the loss for a short time, with the intent of capturing the market. It thus forces the competitor also to sell at a loss or lose its market share. If the smaller competitor is unable to operate at a loss or to match prices, it will eventually go under. A large corporation can target its areas of competition; it will keep up its profits in one geographical or product area and use these profits to subsidize its loss in another area, where it wishes to drive out the competition. An alternative to driving out the competition (in the sense of its failing), is to buy up the competing firm just before it fails, at a better price than would have been possible before. Is this morally justifiable? Is it simply part of the competitive market process?

If we admit that monopolies constitute a restraint on the market, which is detrimental to the general public, and are therefore not morally justifiable, then practices executed with the intent of producing monopolies are also not morally justifiable. In the United States, takeovers by large companies must often be approved by government to preclude the formation of monopolies. Forcing out competition by selling products below cost without taking over the competitors is at least morally questionable, though not illegal.

A second way of controlling competition is for a small group of producers of a product to collude for their common good. They may agree, for instance, not to compete against one another in certain areas, dividing up the market among them. Or they may agree on the prices to charge—a practice known as *price fixing*. Such collusion is generally illegal because it undermines the competitive system to the detriment of the buyer. It is also immoral. The collusion may be done so subtly that it cannot be proven to be collusion. This may preclude legal prosecution, but it does not change the immorality of the action.

The growth of giant corporations has tended to make competition in many areas very costly. The growth of supermarkets, which began in the 1940s, has forced most small grocers and vegetable and fruit markets out of business. The prices a supermarket was able to charge were lower than those the small operators could charge for equal-quality goods. The large chains were able to eliminate middlemen, buy in large quantity at better prices, and, through self-service, reduce the cost of labor. They were also able to operate at a lower profit margin because of their large volume. A consequence was the gradual elimination of most small grocers. This was neither illegal nor immoral, because the chains did not force out the small competitor and then raise their prices to the disadvantage of the consumer; they continued to operate as they had before. Consequently, the small grocer gave way before the more efficient supermarket. Furthermore, competition has not been eliminated. The competition is now between large food chains. The small business cannot compete with them on prices, and to survive they must offer service, credit, or something the large chains do not offer. Some people question the morality of a system that allows competition only among the wealthy or among those able to finance large operations. But as long as the general public benefits from the system, there seems no valid moral objection to it.

A company can attempt to stifle competition in numerous ways. Many are part of the system and are morally justifiable, as long as the aim is not to establish a monopoly. Some involve clearly dishonest practices and therefore need not be discussed here. Lying, stealing corporate secrets and plans from a competitor, corporate espionage and sabotage, violation of contracts, dumping products on a market, paying bribes and kickbacks, and so on, are dishonest practices that are part of the competitive system. However, they are not an essential part of it; they tend to undermine it, and are not morally justifiable.

Pricing

Pricing is an important part of the marketing process. A producer wishes to sell its product at a profit and must price its product appropriately in order to do so. The producer must be able to control its costs. But competition, if it is fair, will force the producer to price its product at its true worth. If the price is set too high, the market for it may shrink so that its sales are less than what is required for it to make a profit, or it may not be as attractive to a buyer, who can purchase from a competitor a similar product at a lower price. Unless one is in a monopolistic position, setting prices is in part a result of the market, and one's success depends in part on knowing the market conditions.

We shall deal with only two issues in pricing: overpricing, and markup and markdown.

Overpricing is a special issue in marketing. In general, the competitive system should preclude the possibility of overpricing where this means charging much more than the producer knows the product is worth, thus yielding an excessive profit. There are some who might claim that overpricing is a misnomer because there is no specific limit of justifiable profit. But this claim assumes that prices are competitive, and they are not always competitive. We have already mentioned the possibility that a producer in a monopolistic position can charge more than it would otherwise be able to do. There are other ways, however, that overpricing can take place. In each case they involve either a monopolistic position, force, or ignorance on the part of the buyer. One of the claims made about merchants in poor areas, ghettos, and slums, for instance, is that they overcharge their customers. They are in effect in a monopolistic position; their customers are not mobile enough to go to other parts of the city to buy what they want at competitive prices. They need the goods available at the only source available to them—the local store. The store is thus in a position to charge more than it would otherwise do, to the disadvantage of the consumer. Some store owners in such locations admit that they charge higher prices for goods than stores elsewhere, but they claim that their insurance costs, including rates for fire, robbery, and personal risk, are higher than elsewhere. These factors, they claim, justify their higher prices. Whether this is sufficient justification depends on the relation of these costs to the increase in the price of the goods they sell.

A second area in which excessive rates arise is in the lending of money. For those unable to borrow money in the conventional, competitive way, loan sharks can charge usurious rates. Although they may claim that they are simply providing a service that people need and cannot find elsewhere, they are in fact taking advantage of the need of others, and usually the transactions cannot be described as fair.

In addition to cases of forced need and no other supplier, ignorance on the part of the buyer often provides the occasion for overpricing. This is possible primarily among poorly educated people, but it is possible even among the well educated. Techniques of overpricing vary. They range from simply charging more for goods than they usually sell for, to charging more than an item is worth, on the assumption that the buyer will think that because it costs more it must be better than a lower-priced competing product. In all these cases, the seller counts on the ignorance of the buyer. To do this is to take advantage of the buyer, and that is not morally justifiable. In the long run, the practice undermines the system, sows distrust of all products and prices, and fails to treat people with the respect they deserve.

Markups are a specific form of pricing. Instead of simply determining the price at which to sell to wholesalers, a manufacturer may calculate all the markups for all the middlemen and the retailer, and set or suggest a retail sales price. This price is a guide to the retailer regarding the price at which the item is to be sold. Unless the item is sold at the same price at all outlets, defenders of the practice maintain, the purchaser will be confused as to the real value of the item. For some years, in the United States, the manufacturer's suggested retail price was defended as the fair market price, and attempts were made to declare discounting illegal. But the difference between this practice and price fixing did not withstand the scrutiny of the courts. Competition has led to discount houses and mail-order dealers, who sell products at prices lower than those at traditional retail stores. The suggested price set by a manufacturer takes into account many things: the markups of the wholesaler, the jobber, and the retailer, as well as the various markdowns that the retailer may make in the way of end-of-season or other sales. Setting such a price is allowable. But if by eliminating some of the middle markets a seller can reduce the final price on an item and still make a profit, he or she cannot be prevented from doing so. It remains in the interest of many sellers to sell items at their suggested retail price in order to maintain their profit margins. They may also apply pressure on the producer not to sell the same goods to discount dealers. But if the discount dealer pays the same price to the manufacturer as the regular retailer, the manufacturer frequently has no incentive to yield to the pressure. Although calculating and suggesting a retail sales price are not immoral, trying to enforce such a price stifles competition and is not in the best interest of the consumer. The step from these observations to declaring it immoral is a short one.

We have assumed that the various markups were at least justifiable. A clearly immoral practice, because it is deceptive, is setting a price for a product higher than that at which it is ever sold, so that it can always be sold at a discount. This is deceptive, because to sell at a discount implies a discount from its real price, not a discount from an artificially inflated one.

Although it is illegal to prevent discounts, in 1997 the U.S. Supreme Court ruled that a manufacturer may, under conditions to be worked out over time in response to a Federal court case, place a ceiling on the retail price a seller can charge for a product. A car manufacturer, for instance, can prevent a dealer from selling a car for more than the sticker price, even if the model is in short supply and great demand. Whether manufacturers will impose such limits remains to be seen. But if they do, they can stop price gouging on their products by retailers who might attempt to take advantage of short supplies or long waits for the product. The intent of the ruling was to protect the consumer from overpricing.

Bidding

Bidding is a commonly used practice. It is sometimes used by a seller, as at an auction, to get the highest price. More often, it is used by a buyer, to get the lowest price. It is used in construction projects, by government and large firms in seeking supplies purchased in quantity, and by firms in seeking subcontractors and suppliers. Bidding is a morally justifiable procedure, providing it is fair. Keeping it fair is not always easy.

Not all bidding is secret, as the case of an auction illustrates. But much of it is. How does one justify secret bidding? Why should bidding not be an open process? The answer is that secrecy tends to produce fairer bids and lower prices for the purchaser. This happens in two ways. If the process were open, a firm that could make a profit at a price considerably less than the competition would make a bid only just enough less to win the contract. This bid might well be higher than the lowest bid he would offer if he did not know what the competition was and simply operated on his cost plus what he considered an acceptable, competitive profit.

Second, if the competition were open, a firm might start out at a bid low enough to scare off others from bidding, even though the bid is not the lowest he would offer if forced to make a secret bid. Therefore, secrecy per se is not morally unjustifiable. But if the bidding process is to be secret, then in fairness to all parties it must be kept secret. Any violation of secrecy by any of the parties violates the fairness condition of bidding. Often a government or company will not accept bids above a certain amount. If no bids are lower than that amount, it will not proceed, and will restudy its options. But it may hope to get a bid lower than the highest it is willing to pay. Clearly, the figure it is willing to pay must be kept secret if the bidding is to be fair. Any leaks violate the procedure.

In addition to fraud, using materials inferior to those specified in the bid, and perpetrating other obvious violations of justice, honesty, and fairness, bidding has led to other questionable practices. Two that involve government contracts are common enough to deserve some discussion. One deals with road-building and large construction projects, the other with defense and similar government contracts.

One difficulty many of the states in the United States encounter is that there are only a few construction companies capable of handling a given state's large construction needs, whether for roads or large buildings. Some states, moreover, are committed by state law to using only companies located in their state for state projects. Assume that a state wishes to build a new road and there are only three construction companies in the state capable of building it. How does the state get the best price for the construction job? Usually, a secret bidding procedure is used. But in a state with only three large construction companies, all the managers or owners of the three companies know each other. The temptation is for the executives of the three companies to agree, for instance, on which one of them will get the road job, with the understanding that the second gets some other job they know of, and the third gets the job following that. It would be to their advantage not to compete—to divide up the contracts, agree on what their respective bids will be, and make sure that the lowest bid submitted is sufficiently high to make a handsome profit. Such collusion would in fact be both illegal and immoral. But because such an arrangement would be so easy, so tempting, and so difficult to prove, this might easily take place. How can a state protect itself?

The secret bidding process is one way, but it is open to the defects just described. The state, however, usually gets from its own engineering experts an independent estimate of what the cost of the project should be, and then only accepts bids that are at or below that figure. However, because the costs for large projects are sometimes only guesses (e.g., they have to include unknown inflation rates), there is a great deal of leeway in the process. The need for fairness is obvious, but legal and completely effective ways to control abuses are difficult to formulate.

A second area involves government contracts, for instance, in the defense industry. Two aspects have raised questions of morality. One is cost overruns; another is locking in the government to a single supplier. Let us assume that a government contract for a new airplane is given to the lowest bidder in a fair, secret procedure. The lowest bidder, however, may not in fact be able to deliver the contracted airplane at the quoted price. Once engaged in the process of developing the plane, however, the government cannot change the manufacturer because of these cost increases, simply because it has already invested considerable time and money in the project, nor can it allow the company to go bankrupt and not complete its work. Thus, government has seemed to be forced to live with cost overruns, paying more for projects than it contracted for or making do with delayed production schedules. The limited number of suppliers available to bid is also a factor here. If companies deliberately bid low to get contracts, knowing that cost overruns will be necessary, then their bids are not fair bids, and they get contracts by misrepresentation. This practice is immoral, but again, often difficult to prove, and so is difficult to prosecute legally.

The technique of locking in a buyer can be practiced with individual consumers as well as with governments. It consists in pricing a major item or contract bid lower than the manufacturing cost of the product, with the assurance that the cost of spare and replacement parts, or the cost of the supplies needed to run the product can be priced sufficiently high to guarantee a profit in the long run. Thus, an airplane manufacturer might enter a bid on an airplane contract that is less than its projected development cost, knowing that, on spare or replacement parts, it can overcharge to such an extent that it will make a profit overall. The buyer is locked into purchasing from the company, if that company is the only one that makes the spare parts or the other items needed to use the product. Immorality enters in the form of an overcharge on parts. In government contracts, this has led to some scandals. For example, fifteen dollars were paid for screws worth a few cents, and hundreds of dollars were paid for parts worth just a few dollars. In an attempt to prevent this situation, government may require that the price of parts be included in the original contract or that specifications for spare parts be made available to other possible suppliers.

A third kind of case involves the purchase of goods by a government or large firm. Consider the firm or agency that wishes to buy typewriters. How does it write its specifications for bidding? Several pitfalls are common. There is always the possibility of leaking information to a potential supplier—an unfair practice. This is sometimes done as a result of bribery or offers of a kickback. Both are clearly immoral. There is also the possibility of writing specifications in so detailed and narrow a way that only one supplier can fill the order, thereby undermining the purpose of the bidding procedure. Direct negotiation with that supplier would make more sense and would probably yield better results than bidding because the supplier has no incentive to make his bid low when he knows he is the only bidder.

Bidding is a morally defensible practice in business, but it is open to many abuses, and it must be carefully controlled if it is to be kept fair.

Consumer Marketing

The opportunities for fraud, deception, and unethical practices are endless, but most such practices are clearly immoral and so raise no ethical problems. Advertising poses special problems, which we shall deal with separately. A few of the issues of current concern, however, include truth in lending, unit pricing, and labeling and dating. All of these have become items of consumer concern and the focus of attention by the consumers' movement. The consumers' movement can be seen at least in part as a reaction to marketing practices perceived as unfair or as less fair than they could or should be.

Truth-in-lending concerns the true amount paid by those who purchase items on the installment plan, who get loans to finance purchases, or who buy with credit cards. One sales technique is to state how much an item bought on time or credit will cost in terms of monthly payments. If little or no mention is made of the actual total cost of the purchase, the terms of the loan, or the true annual interest rate, consumers enter into legally binding contracts without full knowledge of what they are agreeing to. Some find out too late that their goods can be repossessed if they miss a payment or that they are actually paying two or three times more than the original price of an item because of interest and other payments.

These practices were not illegal, and a prudent and cautious buyer could have found out the exact nature of the contract into which he or she was entering. But this frequently requires a good deal of investigation and figuring—more than the average consumer is used to. Truth-in-lending therefore became a consumer demand, justified as a means of making transactions fair. The moral demands have been translated into legal obligations as well.

Unit pricing is an attempt to enable buyers to make accurate comparisons based on price. Most consumers would expect, for instance, to pay less per ounce for a soap powder bought in volume than the same brand packaged in a small box. This is not always the case, however. If both the contents of each box and the prices are not stated in round numbers, it is sometimes difficult to know which is the better buy. The same is true regarding competing brands. Yet one of the ways in which competition is supposed to take place in our system is based on price comparison. Pricing techniques that make it difficult to compare prices are not deceptive or immoral, but they do not help the consumer judge on the basis of price. Unit pricing consists in indicating, for example, what 1 ounce of soap costs in each of the packages for each of the brands the store carries. A consumer who wishes to make a choice based on price is helped to do so. The demand for unit pricing is a demand to make transactions fair, and is morally justified. Although marketing techniques may justify packaging in fractions of an ounce, such practices are clearly not adopted to help comparison shopping or competition on the basis of price.

Labeling and dating are other demands consumers have voiced to make the transactions into which they enter fair. When one buys a garment it is often difficult to know exactly what it is made of, whether it is a synthetic fabric, a natural fiber, or a mixture, or what the proportions are of each fiber. In effect, one buys blindly, unless the information is supplied. Availability of adequate information on both sides is a necessary condition if a transaction is to be fair. Hence, demanding such labeling is morally justifiable.

Unless the ingredients of processed foods are listed, in descending order, according to the quantity of each contained in the package, the purchaser does not know exactly what he or she is buying. In the case of perishable goods, unless a date by which an item must be sold is stamped on the product, there is no way for a buyer to know how fresh the product is and how long it can be kept before it spoils. Consumer demands in all these instances are legitimate; these practices not only prevent deception and misleading marketing techniques, but they also help to keep transactions fair, and so help the free-market system to operate as it should.

Advertising

Although moral issues arise in other aspects of marketing, public and governmental concern has tended to focus on the advertising of consumer products to the general public. Corporations are thought capable of handling their own wants and of being qualified to determine on their own what they need. Although they are legally protected against fraud, they are less likely than the ordinary consumer to be taken in by misleading advertising or to be sold what they do not want.[5]

Once a producer makes a commodity, his object is to sell it. To do so he must inform potential buyers that the product is available, what it does, and why it might be a product they want or need. Advertising provides this information to large numbers of people. A product might be advertised through a direct-mail campaign or through use of the media—newspapers, magazines, TV. Advertising, therefore, is part of the process of selling one's products. Because any sale is a transaction between a buyer and a seller, the transaction is fair if both parties have available adequate, appropriate information about the product, and if they enter into the transaction willingly and without coercion. From a moral point of view, because advertising helps achieve the goal of both seller and buyer, it is morally justifiable and permissible, providing it is not deceptive, misleading, or coercive. Advertising can be abused, but it is not inherently immoral.

Before we examine in detail some of the abuses of advertising, we should put aside three morally irrelevant charges brought against advertising. The first charge, that advertising is not necessary in a socialist economic system and that it is an immoral part of capitalism, is vague and for the most part untrue. In every economic system there must be some way of letting potential buyers know of the existence of goods. Any producer must make known that a product is available if people are to know that they can buy it. Displaying an item in a window, so that people can see it, is a form of advertising, as is displaying it on a shelf. In a society of comparative scarcity, where only essentials

---

[5] Among the many books on ethics and advertising, see John T. Lucas and Richard Gurman, *Truth in Advertising* (New York: American Management Association, 1972); and Charles W. Baird, *Advertising by Professionals* (Ottawa, Ill.: International Institute for Economic Research, Green Hills Publishers, 1977). *Business & Professional Ethics Journal*, 3, nos. 3 & 4 (1984), is devoted to issues of ethics in advertising.

are available, people may constantly be on the lookout for products they want, spotting them when they arrive on a shelf. They may then, through word of mouth, transmit the information that the product is available. Before long there are lines of people waiting to purchase the item, and soon it is sold out. Those who did not get the item then wait for it to appear again. Or if an item is a staple, and generally available, people know where it can be purchased and simply go to that store when they need it. In such a society, advertising plays a comparatively small role.

American society is not a society of comparative scarcity; it is one of comparative wealth. Many items are available to the consumer. Competition, moreover, encourages producers to enter a market in which there is consumer demand. If a company had a monopoly on an item, then it would have little need for advertising, once people knew of its availability. Competition, therefore, accounts for the amount of advertising we have in the United States, as opposed to that in the former Soviet Union. The American automobile industry, for instance, produces a great many different kinds of cars—different styles and makes, with different accessories and price ranges. If there were only one kind of car made, clearly there would be less advertising by the automobile industry. Would it be better if there were only one car manufacturer—perhaps the government? The typical American answer is no. Once we allow competition—which has not been shown to be immoral—then advertising is a reasonable concomitant, and as such it is not inherently immoral.

A second charge against advertising that we can dismiss from a moral point of view is its frequent poor taste; it is offensive to one's finer sensibilities. The charge can hardly be denied. But poor taste is not immoral. As members of society, we can make known our displeasure at such advertising, either by vocal or written protest, or by not purchasing the item advertised. However, we should distinguish between poor taste and immorality.

A third charge claims that advertising takes advantage of people, either by forcing them to buy what they do not want or, more plausibly, by psychologically manipulating them to buy what they do not need.[6] According to this view, people are not able to resist the lure of the vast resources available to producers for advertising campaigns. Manipulation and coercion through advertising are immoral, as we shall discuss in detail. But the charge is clearly an overstatement if it asserts that all members of the public are gullible, unsophisticated, and manipulable by media advertising. Advertising would be immoral if it always and necessarily manipulated and coerced people, but it does not. The difficulty is in deciding what is manipulative and what is not; who should be protected from certain kinds of advertising, and who does not need such protection. The notion of protection from advertising is closely linked to government paternalism. To what extent are people to be allowed to make their own decisions, and to what extent should government protect

---

[6] For a critique of advertising and false needs, see John Kenneth Galbraith, *The Affluent Society*, 3rd ed. (New York: Houghton Mifflin Company, 1976).

them against themselves because of its superior knowledge of their real needs and wants? The Federal Trade Commission (FTC) and the Food and Drug Administration (FDA) are the two American agencies with major responsibility for policing advertising. The standards they adopt are frequently more restrictive and paternalistic than morality requires. They have sometimes ruled that advertising is misleading if only 5 percent of the population would be misled by it. Whether morality demands this much protection is among the topics we shall investigate.

We shall consider five areas in which the moral dimension of advertising is of central importance: (1) the immorality of untruthful, misleading, or deceptive advertising; (2) the immorality of manipulation and coercion through advertising, including the question of audience; (3) the morality of paternalism with respect to advertising; (4) the immorality of preventing some kinds of advertising; and (5) the allocation and distribution of moral responsibility with respect to advertising.

Truth and Advertising

A major function of advertising is to sell goods. But this is not its only purpose, nor does it accomplish this only by supplying information. Advertising may educate the public or mold public opinion. Propaganda might be considered a form of advertising for a political party, a religious sect, or some special social group. Let us, however, limit this discussion to advertising in business, with the aim of selling a product. Informing the public of an item's availability is only part of the task of advertising. A manufacturer also wants to influence people to buy the product. Hence, ads are not only informative but also persuasive. Through advertisements, some companies wish to achieve public notice and recognition; they feel that people tend to buy products with a familiar name. The purpose of some advertising is the building of goodwill for the producer, who assumes that public goodwill will eventually help sales.

The approach to advertising that sees the function of advertising only in terms of supplying information takes too narrow a view of its objectives and tends to evaluate it from too narrow a moral perspective.[7] If its proper function were exclusively the giving of information, and if information were always given in declarative sentences, then we could concern ourselves exclusively with the questions of truth in advertising. If what an advertisement says is true, it is morally permissible; if what it says is false, it is immoral. We shall initially approach advertising in this way. In doing so, we shall see the shortcomings of this approach.

Let us start with some distinctions that will be helpful in clarifying the complex question of truth in advertising. With what is truth in advertising

---

[7] For a defense of advertising as information, see Phillip Nelson, "Advertising and Ethics," in R. De George and J. Pichler (Eds.), *Ethics, Free Enterprise, and Public Policy* (New York: Oxford University Press, 1978), pp. 187-198.

contrasted? It can be contrasted with either falsehood or lying. Lying is immoral; stating falsehoods is not necessarily immoral. Suppose, for instance, someone were to tell a story. He could make a number of statements that were not factually true; yet he would not be lying.[8]

The terms *true* and *false* are properly predicated of sentences or propositions. Only a proposition can be true or false. An exclamation, a question, or an interjection cannot be true or false. A statement or a proposition contains a subject and a predicate. The subject has the property or is related to something else stated in the predicate. A statement or proposition is true, roughly speaking, if the stated relation between subject and predicate corresponds to the actual relation in the world between what are designated or referred to by the subject and predicate. Hence, the sentence "This page of this book has words printed on it" is true if this page of this book does in fact have words printed on it. Obviously, this page does have words printed on it. Therefore, the sentence is true. The sentence "This page is colored green" is false if in fact this page is not colored green. This rough characterization of truth and falsehood will suffice for our purposes.

Lying consists, however, not simply in making a false statement. From a moral point of view, lying is an activity. Lying consists in making a statement, which one believes is false, to another person, whom one has reason to think will believe the statement to be true. *Lying consists of my saying what I believe to be false and of my intending that another will believe to be true what is actually false.* I not only say what I do not believe, but I also intend to deceive or mislead the one to whom I make the statement.

Based on this definition, falsehood is not a necessary part of lying. Suppose, for instance, that Tom believes there are four pints in a quart. A friend, who is baking a cake, asks him how many pints are in a quart. Tom replies, "There are four pints in a quart." Actually, there are only two pints in a quart. What Tom said is false. But he has not told a lie; he has made a mistake. Conversely, suppose, as before, that Tom believes there are four pints in a quart and the same person asks him the same question in the same situation. Tom wants the cake to fail, so that his friend will not spend any more time making cakes. So, intending to give false information, Tom says, "There are two pints in a quart." Morally speaking, Tom is guilty of telling a lie, even though, by accident, what he said was a true statement. It is a lie because Tom thought that what he was saying was false; he said it with the intent to deceive, and with the expectation that what he said would be believed.

Whether a statement or proposition is true or false depends on the world; whether a statement is an instance of lying depends on the intent of the speaker.

---

[8] Sissela Bok, *Lying: Moral Choice in Public and Private Life* (New York: Pantheon Books, 1978), is an extended discussion of lying in a variety of contexts. Ivan L. Preston, *The Great American Blow-up: Puffery in Advertising and Selling* (Madison: University of Wisconsin Press, 1975), presents a critique of puffery.

Not all false statements that someone makes, believing that they are false, are lies. Suppose, for instance, a friend says during a chilling wintry day, "I'm as cold as an iceberg." What he says is literally false. His body temperature is about 98.6 degrees, even if he feels cold. But his statement is not a lie. He had no intention of deceiving anyone when he made that statement, nor is it likely that anyone will be deceived by it. We use language in many ways. Part of the normal person's use of language enables one to distinguish by context, phrasing, intonation, and other subtle techniques the difference between a sentence that is literally true and one that is figurative, exaggerated, or not to be taken literally. Metaphor, simile, and hyperbole are all accepted figures of speech. We do not speak only in declarative sentences, and when we do speak in declarative sentences we do not always speak literally. When someone says, "I'm so hungry I could eat a bear," he does not expect people to point out that an average bear weighs much more than he does, that he could not possibly eat a whole bear, or that he probably would not even like bear meat. All that is true, but it is beside the point. He is simply saying, in an expressive way, that he is very hungry. There is no moral reason why we should not use expressive language when we do not intend to deceive and when there is little or no likelihood that we will deceive, even if our statements are not literally true.

We now turn to advertising. Some advertisements contain sentences—express propositions—that are appropriately evaluated in terms of truth and falsity. If an ad makes a false claim, which the advertiser knows to be false, for the purpose of misleading, misinforming, or deceiving potential customers, then the ad is immoral. It is immoral because in the ad the advertiser is lying, and lying is immoral. The problem of truth in advertising, however, does not end here: It is possible to deceive and mislead without making statements that are false, and it is also possible, as we have seen, not to deceive or mislead while making statements that are not literally true.

Consider the following slogan, used by Esso a number of years ago: "Esso puts a tiger in your tank!" The statement, of course, is not literally true. But did anyone think it was literally true? Do we really wonder if, after some customer had put Esso gasoline into his car, he worried about whether it had turned into a tiger? Exactly what Esso meant to convey by its slogan is to some extent a matter of speculation. It clearly did not want its slogan to be taken literally, but rather figuratively. The semantics of advertising properly allows for use of figurative language. To restrict ads to statements that are literally true is to fail to understand the semantics of advertising or of language in general. There is, however, no neat line between allowable figurative language and lying. An obvious exaggeration is not likely to be taken literally. But what is obvious to most people may not be an obvious exaggeration to everyone. Must we protect those who might be deceived by exaggeration by forcing advertising to be literally true in the statements it makes? From a moral point of view, it seems sufficient that the vast majority of those at whom the ad is directed not be misled by it. When discussing responsibility, we used the rule that people are morally responsible for the foreseeable consequences of their actions. The test of what is foreseeable is what the ordinary person of goodwill would foresee in those circumstances. A similar approach can be taken to advertising. An advertiser will know whether he intends his ad to deceive. If he does, then the advertiser acts immorally in placing the ad. But if he does not intend to deceive, and we are to judge the ad on its merits and not on the advertiser's intent, then the ad is morally permissible if the ordinary person to whom the ad is directed would not be deceived. Some ads directed at car owners might be misunderstood by children. This is not a matter of moral concern, however, because the ad is not directed at them but at car owners.

The Better Business Bureaus, the FTC, and the FDA are all concerned with accuracy in advertisements. Advertisers are not allowed to make false statements. Moreover, if challenged, advertisers must be able to document statements making factual claims that are taken literally. These government agencies sometimes go beyond what is morally necessary, according to our analysis. Even if a very small percentage of people might be misled, the ad is not allowed. The action of government agencies in these cases, if morally justifiable, depends not on the question of lying, but on the legitimate extent of governmental paternalism. We shall consider this question later.

Without making any false statements, an ad might be misleading or deceptive. A misleading ad is one in which the ad does not misrepresent or make false claims but makes claims in such a way that the normal person, or at least many ordinary people, reading it quickly and without great attention and thought, will make a false inference or draw a false conclusion. Those who attempt to justify such ads claim that the mistake is made by the reader or viewer of the ad and that the responsibility for drawing the false conclusion rests with the reader or viewer and not with the advertiser. Strictly speaking, this is correct, but clearly, often the intent in such ads is to mislead. They are written or presented in such a way that their effect is predictable. Such ads are immoral because they intend to deceive, even if they do not literally state what is false. The same is true of packaging. If a large box is only half filled, a consumer may erroneously think he will get more in a big box than in a smaller one. If no claim is made that the box is full, no false statement has been made. The mistake is the consumer's. But the maker of the product is morally at fault.

A deceptive ad is one that either makes a false statement and therefore lies, or that misrepresents the product without making any statement.[9] Deception of the eye and mind may take place not only through sentences or propositions but also through pictures, through individual words, or through certain juxtapositions of objects. Such deception trades on a background of ordinary

---

[9] On deceptive advertising, see Frederick Stuart (Ed.), *Consumer Protection from Deceptive Advertising* (Hempstead, N.Y.: Hofstra University, 1974).

expectations. We are accustomed to having the contents of a box pictured on the box. We expect the pictures to be reasonably close to the product within, and when this is not the case, the picture is deceptive. If an item is called "chicken soup," and it contains no chicken and was not made from chicken, the name is deceptive, even if no statement is made that the soup contains chicken or is made from chicken. If an item is advertised as being at half price, and the item was never sold at full price but is always sold at the price indicated, the ad is deceptive.

The semantics of advertising, however, allows a certain leeway in some products. The cosmetics field provides some examples. We expect cosmetics to be packaged in pretty bottles, boxes, or containers. Perfumes would smell as sweet if they were packaged in mustard jars, but they would not sell as well. Face creams without perfume would cleanse and soften as well, but they would not sell as well. Cosmetics are a luxury item, and they are packaged as such. They are sold as much for their promise as for their chemicals. Shampoo, hair rinse, conditioners, and other hair products will not make the ordinary person's hair look like the hair of the models who claim in ads to use these products. Nor will the use of other beauty products make the average person look like the models using them. Is this misleading advertising? Do people actually believe that a product will change their looks, their personalities, their lives? Most people know that the semantics of cosmetics advertising is puffery and do not take the pictures or the implied claims literally. They hope the product will make them more attractive, and the products sometimes *do* make their users more self-confident. This is what the customer is paying for. Repeat sales for such products are an indication that the customer is not being deceived.

Advertisements do not only make statements; their purpose is to try to persuade people to purchase the product advertised. Persuasion may take the form of making statements, but it need not. Many ads simply create associations in the mind of the purchaser. An ad for an expensive scotch whiskey might simply show a couple in evening clothes, sipping a drink, in an elegant room, together with a picture of the bottle of scotch. The association of the scotch with elegance and class is all the ad wishes to convey.

Some ads simply show a picture of the product; the aim of these ads is only recognition of the product—when the consumer sees it on a supermarket shelf, together with eight other brands of the same kind of item. Name recognition has an effect on purchasing. This is not inappropriate. A customer who knows little about the nine items on the shelf knows that at least one of the nine items is advertised. This is at least some information about the product. An item that did not sell would not be advertised for very long. An item that depends on repeat purchases for success must have a fairly large number of users if it is continuously advertised. All this does not mean that the product is the best of its kind, but it is information that makes the choice of products less than random.

The final aspect of truth in advertising that we shall consider is the question of half-truths. A statement made about a product may be true, may not mislead, may not deceive, but may be morally objectionable nevertheless. Sometimes, what the ad does *not* say is as important as what the ad does say. It is immoral to advertise and sell a dangerous product without indicating its dangers. If, for a certain product, the background assumption of the ordinary person is that products of that kind are safe, and the given advertised product is not safe, then the ad and/or the package should include the appropriate caution. We expect lye to be caustic; therefore, if ads for lye emphasize its caustic property, these ads may not have to specify that it burns the skin, although that information should be prominent on the can. But we do not usually expect hair dye to contain lye or to be caustic; therefore, if an ad for such a product does not indicate its unusual potential danger, it would be immoral.

General rules concerning truth in advertising can be summarized in the following way: It is immoral to lie, mislead, and deceive in advertising. It is immoral to fail to indicate dangers that are not normally expected. It is not immoral to use metaphor or other figures of speech if these will be normally understood as the figurative use of language, nor is it immoral to persuade as well as to inform.

Manipulation and Coercion

Advertising not only informs, it frequently also aims to persuade. Persuasion in itself is not immoral. We all attempt to persuade others to do what we wish—to go with us to a movie or go out to dinner. If what we persuade others to do is not immoral, and if we do not use immoral means to persuade them, persuasion is not an immoral activity. Persuasion, however, is different from manipulation and coercion, although all these are ways of getting others to do what we wish. But manipulation and coercion are at least prima facie immoral. They are immoral in business and advertising. The reason is not difficult to state. In Kantian terms, both coercion and manipulation treat another person only as a means to one's own end and deny respect for his or her freedom. Coercion involves force or the threat of force, either physical or psychological. Manipulation does not use force; it involves playing upon a person's will by trickery or by devious, unfair, or insidious means. Both take unfair advantage of a person, and the use of either renders a transaction between the two parties unfair or unjust. Coercion and manipulation in advertising are therefore immoral.

But what constitutes coercion or manipulation in advertising? Can an advertiser truly coerce or manipulate consumers?[10]

A clearly coercive form of manipulative advertising is *subliminal advertising*. An advertiser can insert a message in a music track that is played in a store, in a film shown in a theater, or on TV, in such a way that the viewer is

---

[10] See Tom L. Beauchamp, "Manipulative Advertising," *Business and Professional Ethics Journal*, 3 (Spring/Summer 1984), pp. 1-22.

not consciously aware of the advertisement, even though he or she is subconsciously picking it up. It is possible to do this because a certain threshold of perception must be exceeded before we consciously see a motion picture. The film must be run at a certain number of frames per minute. When a message is inserted between the frames below the threshold of conscious perception, we do not consciously see the message. Despite the fact that we do not consciously see it, tests have shown that we do perceive the message without being conscious of it. Such ads are called subliminal because they are projected below the limit of our conscious perception.

Subliminal advertising is manipulative because it acts on us without our knowledge and, hence, without our consent. If an ad appears on TV, we can tune it out or change stations if we do not want to be subjected to it. If an ad appears in a magazine, we are not forced to look at it. In either case, if we do choose to look and listen, we can consciously evaluate what we see and hear. We can, if we wish, take a critical stance toward the advertisement. All of this is impossible with subliminal advertising because we are unaware that we are being subjected to the message. The advertiser is imposing his message on us without our knowledge or consent. We cannot tune it out because we do not know it is there, nor can we be at all critical of it. A subliminal advertisement may simply flash on the screen the name of a product, or a simple message, such as "Buy X brand of soap." The messages are not complex. Yet they have been shown to have an effect. They are manipulative, and to use them is immoral.

Some department stores and supermarkets have inserted in their music tracks the message "Don't shoplift" or "Don't steal." Studies have shown that stores that use this device have a lower rate of shoplifting than comparable stores that do not use it. Even though the message may advocate moral behavior, the use of the subliminal technique is still immoral. Because we do not know the content of the message or messages we are being subjected to, there is no way of guaranteeing that the message is moral rather than one that is objectionable in some way, or to some people. Because we have no control over the content of a subliminal message, the practice is manipulative; it tends to produce more harm than good, and, from a moral point of view, it is unjustifiable.

Advertisements aimed at preschool children are another fairly clear case of manipulation. At this age, children tend to be very impressionable. They believe most of what they hear and see, are unable to distinguish clearly truth from fancy, and have very little critical skill or experience. They are very susceptible, therefore, to TV advertisements. What is the point of advertisers aiming messages at preschool children? Clearly, they do not make purchases, but they can put pressure on their parents to make the purchases they want. For instance, if a certain children's vitamin is successfully advertised to children on TV, they may be anxious to take that vitamin pill rather than any other. A parent interested in having a child take vitamins may find the job made easier by having the child anxious to take a certain brand and may buy that brand for that reason. Children may also pester their mothers and fathers to buy certain sugar-coated cereals or other products advertised for children. Is this manipulation?

Two replies have been given. One is that the adults in the family make the purchases. If they feel that the product should not be purchased, they should exercise their best judgment. They, and not the children, make the final judgment. If they cannot stand up to their children's demands, that is not the problem of the advertiser; it is the parents' problem. The other reply is that if the parents are the purchasers, the ads for children's products should be aimed at the parents and not at the children.

Ads aimed at children are inappropriate because they create a desire in children for products they do not understand (e.g., vitamins). The intent of the ads is clearly to manipulate the children into applying pressure on their parents to make such purchases. Though the parents make the final decision, the children are still being manipulated for the advertiser's purposes. Such ads take advantage of children, and those who advertise in this way are morally culpable of manipulation and of treating children only as means to their ends.

The situation with respect to adolescents is more difficult. Many ads aimed at this group play on their social insecurity. They are told that unless their breath is sweetened by a certain product they will not be popular, that if they want to attract that certain boy or girl they should use brand X deodorant, or that the key to their making friends is using a certain shampoo or soap. Each of the products does something: reduces bad breath or body odor, or cleans hair and skin. And each of these may to some extent make one more attractive or less offensive. But it is extremely unlikely that any of them, or all of them together, are the basis for making a teenager popular or for winning friends. Adolescents know this; yet they are frequently so insecure socially that the ads play on their fears, worries, hopes, and dreams. Do such ads coerce or manipulate? Only a case-by-case examination can answer this question. The potential for manipulation is present, though not all such ads are manipulative.

The question of audience is relevant. Certain products—alcohol and cigarettes, for instance—are restricted for sale to adults. These and similar items should not be advertised in children's magazines or in magazines aimed at young teenagers. A more difficult problem involves the small minority, such as those people who are gullible or those with a lower than average intelligence, who may be manipulated by ads that are not manipulative to the average adult. From a moral point of view, a general rule would be that it is immoral to gear ads to that group in order to manipulate them, but that for ads aimed at the general public, the usual appropriate moral criterion is whether the ad is manipulative for the average reader or viewer. Society may take a stronger line; the FTC has done so. The arguments for a stronger line, however, have to do with paternalism.

Paternalism and Advertising

The United States Surgeon General has determined that smoking is dangerous to health. We know that drinking intoxicating alcoholic beverages can sometimes lead to alcoholism, to many automobile accidents while driving, and to other ills. Should the United States government and American society allow the spread of the use of these products through advertising? Should we prohibit the advertising of pornography? Should we allow the advertising of marijuana and other illegal drugs? What of "Saturday night specials" and other guns? Are there any limits to what can be morally advertised?

Although there are clearly limits, there is much dispute about where to draw the line. Anything that is illegal to manufacture and sell to the general public cannot legally be advertised to the general public. This poses no real problem because it would be self-defeating for anyone to advertise what is illegal. If someone is selling illegal drugs, for instance, to advertise would be inviting the police to arrest him. We have also seen that it would be immoral to advertise to children what they are prohibited by law from buying. Beyond these clear cases, however, there is little consensus. If an item can be legally sold, why can it not be advertised? What is the proper role of government in protecting people against what will harm them? The question is a political one. In a democracy such as the United States, the answer is that the proper paternalistic role of government should be decided by the people through their representatives and, with a majority rule, limited by the rights of individuals and minority groups.

The Food and Drug Administration (FDA) acts in the people's interests when it requires by law that packaged foods list on the package the ingredients in order of the decreasing quantity. Such information allows the purchaser to know what he or she is buying and makes the transaction a fair one. With respect to drugs, the FDA also acts to protect the consumer. It prohibits the sale of certain drugs, allows other drugs to be sold only with a doctor's prescription, and demands a testing period before approving drugs. It sets high standards—standards that some people and some drug companies claim are too high.

The Federal Trade Commission has prohibited the advertising of tobacco and alcohol on TV. It has not prohibited the advertising of such items in journals and newspapers, though in the case of cigarette ads, one of the Surgeon General's warnings must be included. Some people claim that drinking alcoholic beverages is immoral and that smoking, because it harms the health of the smoker, should be prohibited. They claim that even if such items can legally be sold, the producers of them should not be allowed through advertising to encourage people to smoke and drink.

The philosophy of liberalism, defended eloquently by John Stuart Mill in the nineteenth century in *On Liberty*,[11] espouses the principle that government

---

[11] John Stuart Mill, *On Liberty*, (New York: Appleton-Century-Crofts, 1947).

should not interfere in the actions of individuals if the results of their actions fall mainly on themselves. In both smoking and drinking, the results fall mainly on the agent; hence, the government should not interfere with their use by individuals. The government does more than is required by insisting that packages of cigarettes carry the Surgeon General's warning. The liberal position can be extended to the question of advertising these products: If they are legal and publicly sold, then those who wish to purchase them should be allowed to do so. Those who do not wish to purchase them are not forced to do so simply because they are advertised. Each person can weigh the good and bad effects for himself and make his own decision. If the smoker feels that he gets more enjoyment from smoking a pack of cigarettes a day for twenty-five or thirty years, even if it cuts four or five years off his life, the government cannot legitimately say he is mistaken. Other people will consider that the four or five years of extended life are preferable to the enjoyment of smoking. Neither answer is right or wrong; each is simply a matter of choice or preference. The question allows for a difference of opinion.

The extent to which the FTC has restricted any kind of advertising that might mislead even a very small percentage of the population goes beyond what morality requires of advertisers. The FTC perceives its paternalistic mandate to extend that far. We have no indication yet that the general public feels the FTC has gone too far. Because the amount of paternalism government exercises is a political as well as a moral question, we can distinguish what is morally required from what is politically required without expecting that the two will always coincide.

One further attack on advertising should be discussed before we leave the role of government and paternalism. Some people claim that advertising creates false needs in people. Producers decide not what the people want or need, but what the *producers* want to produce, based on which products will bring the most profit. The producers then manufacture those items, create demand through a high-powered and expensive advertising campaign, and in effect, take advantage of the general population. Because we can correctly call this taking advantage of people, it is immoral.

The attack is not entirely without merit. American producers sometimes do choose to produce what they want instead of what the general public wants. When they do so, it is not always possible to convince people to buy what is produced. Sometimes it is. It is difficult to imagine that people really needed electric toothbrushes. It seems more likely that a manufacturer decided to produce them and then advertised the product. It is also doubtful that Americans really wanted large cars with built-in obsolescence, but for many years they had little choice. Detroit decided what cars would be produced, and Americans picked from what was available. Only when foreign manufacturers entered the market in significant quantity did American car manufacturers switch to producing smaller cars.

What conclusion can we draw from this? The conclusion that advertising can sell anything is much too strong; it cannot. But it can sell some products that people had not thought they needed or wanted before the item was produced. It is difficult to imagine, however, an appropriate solution to this kind of problem—if it *is* a problem. People can purchase what they want. If they do not want to buy electric toothbrushes, advertisements do not force them to do so. If they do not want to buy an Edsel car, an expensive ad campaign will not make them buy one. But if they want small cars and only large cars are available, they may prefer to buy a large car rather than no car. Even here, however, the possibility of free entry into the market by foreign-car makers seems to show that the system of the free market tends to correct itself in the long run. The alternative would be some type of centralized decision-making apparatus, either governmental or private. This body would, presumably, decide that electric toothbrushes should not be made or that small cars rather than large cars should be produced. But how will this group know what should and should not be produced? Will they know better than the individual consumer what the consumer wants? It seems unlikely. In countries where there is such central planning the consumer is generally more poorly served than in the United States.

Our system may be wasteful to some extent. It may produce goods that are not necessary. It may needlessly duplicate effort. All this is true. But a better system, to replace the present one, has not been sufficiently articulated or defended. Furthermore, advertising is not the culprit. We have seen that government can restrict advertising to some extent, in cases where harm to people will result. But the harm must be more clear and present than simply the advertising of what some people think is unnecessary. This sort of governmental decision goes far beyond the kind and extent of paternalism mandated to government by the American people.

Prevention of Advertising

The prevention of advertising, in some cases, comes up against the First Amendment's right of free speech. We have seen that in some instances the government can, with the consent of the people, exercise a certain amount of paternalism. Can it do so by violating the rights of advertisers? Do advertisers have the right, by virtue of the First Amendment, to advertise? The question is a legal, not a strictly moral one. First Amendment rights, as well as other civil rights, can be restricted under certain circumstances. However, government restriction of advertising, in the case of cigarettes and liquor, has not been successfully challenged in the courts.

Another area of advertising presents a different moral issue. Is it moral to prohibit advertising by doctors, lawyers, and other professionals? Obviously, no individual doctor or lawyer is morally obliged to advertise. But is it appropriate for the American Medical Association (AMA) or the American Bar Association (ABA) or other professional organizations to prohibit advertising by their members? Until recently, many professionals were restricted from advertising by their professional associations. Advertising was considered to be in poor taste, vulgar, and unprofessional. Moreover, many professionals claimed, it was not possible to advertise adequately. Reasons given were that the services professionals perform vary from client to client or patient to patient, the relations they develop are personal, and they do not sell a product at a certain price.

The prohibition of advertising by doctors and lawyers, however, has been attacked as being self-serving and harmful to the general public. It has been determined to be a prohibition that tends to hinder competition and free trade. Therefore, these portions of the AMA and ABA codes of professional conduct were declared illegal, and they have been changed.

The arguments in favor of changing them were several. One can be put in utilitarian terms. Essentially, the good gained by the lawyers and doctors and their respective professions was less than the evil suffered by their potential and actual clients and patients. Potential clients and patients were not able to compare doctors or lawyers, as they could compare plumbers and carpenters. The latter could compete through their ads, making known their specialties, rates, and other pertinent information. In picking a doctor or lawyer, one usually had only a list in the Yellow Pages. Store-front lawyers who wished to serve lower-income groups at very low rates, frequently in ghetto areas, were prevented, by the old code, from advertising. This was not in the best interests of people who might be able to use their services but could not afford the services of the typical law firm.

Another argument rests on the right of the individual practitioner to make known his services and to compete, in price and in kinds of services provided, for the business of potential clients. Preventing the individual practitioner from advertising, if he so chose, was a violation of his right to free speech, restricted not by government but by his professional organization. The right of a professional organization to do this has been successfully challenged.

Under the new guidelines, lawyers are still supposed to ensure that their ads are in good taste, so as not to harm the reputation of the profession. "Good taste," however, is broad enough to include a wide range of ads.

The important principle underscored by the ruling on professional advertising is that to prevent advertising is, in many instances, harmful to the public, because it withholds information the public wants and can profitably use; thus, it protects the interests of members of the professions at the expense of the public. Monopolies do not have to advertise because they control the market. A market that allows free entry appropriately allows advertising, so that each of the competitors can make known its product or service, inform the public of its availability, and attempt to persuade the public to purchase the product or service.

We therefore conclude that in some cases it is immoral to prevent advertising, just as in other cases, morality demands that certain advertising be restrained or prohibited.

Allocation of Moral Responsibility in Advertising

In each of the preceding sections we have seen that certain advertising practices are immoral. Who is morally responsible for advertising, and who has moral responsibility with respect to it? We can identify five groups: (1) the producer or manufacturer, (2) the advertising agency, (3) the media in which or through which the advertisement appears, (4) the general public, and (5) government and governmental agencies.

1. Prime responsibility for advertising rests on the one who initiates and directs the advertising. In most cases, this is the producer or manufacturer of a product. The manufacturer decides what and how to advertise. The decisions may be made by the chief executive officer; by the marketing, publicity, advertising, or public relations departments; or by some combination of these and others. In whatever way the decision on advertising is made internally, the company is responsible for the advertising it does or commissions; the company is responsible for its content and accuracy, the medium it chooses, and the like. If it aims ads at preschool children, it is responsible for doing so; if it misrepresents or misleads, it is responsible for doing so. Although primary responsibility is held by the company or manufacturer, it does not hold exclusive moral responsibility.

2. Advertising agencies handle the promotion of a great many goods. They frequently produce ideas for advertising campaigns, which are submitted to and approved by their clients, the manufacturing or producing companies. What is their responsibility?

Because ad agencies do not manufacture the product, they are not responsible for the product as such, but they must be informed of the product's qualities and selling points. Advertising people often work closely with their clients. They frequently know what is true about a product and what is not, what is misleading or deceptive. Sometimes it is the ad writer rather than the manufacturer who comes up with a promotion that is deceptive or misleading in a way that will benefit the manufacturer. The temptation, in such cases, is for the ad writer to feel that responsibility for the ad rests with the manufacturer. The ad writer is simply an agent paid to do what the client asks. The manufacturer feels that the responsibility is that of the ad writer. He, after all, is the specialist. Actually, both are responsible, and neither party can escape moral responsibility.

Frequently, neither the manufacturer nor the ad agency has difficulty with the initial advertising of a product. A good product that serves a need will sell if it is attractively presented. However, as competition increases, the pressure builds. As a competitor's product resembles one's own more and more, the need to find something distinctive as a selling point becomes more difficult. If a company's number one position in the field is threatened, or it slips to number two, the temptation is to keep or regain first place by more noticeable advertising. The temptation to exaggerate, write misleading copy, or consider immoral approaches becomes strong. One is tempted to think in terms of the good of the company, protecting the interests of the shareholders, keeping up profits, and protecting one's job, and thereby to justify practices that one would not ordinarily consider or condone.

Advertising agencies have the moral responsibility not to lie, mislead, or misrepresent products. They also have an obligation to investigate when they suspect that they are being asked to lie, mislead, or misrepresent a product. Ignorance is no excuse, if the typical advertising specialist knows something is amiss in what he or she is told about a product to be advertised. Advertising professionals should not take part in lying or misleading the public; they should try to convince their clients not to push for that approach. Even if they cannot convince their clients, they still have the responsibility not to take part in lying or deception. A good ad agency should not have to resort to unethical practices to sell a product.

3. Once an advertisement or an advertising program has been produced, it can be presented to the public in a variety of forms. The major ones are TV and the print media (newspapers and magazines). Specialized products are usually advertised in specialized journals, trade journals, or through direct mail. General products are usually advertised through TV, magazines, and newspapers.

All TV stations, magazines, and newspapers have the moral responsibility for what appears in their shows or in the pages of their publications. They receive copy or film submitted by the manufacturer or ad agency. Do they have the right to question, censor, or prohibit something they are paid to show or print? Yes, they do. Moreover, they have the moral responsibility not to show or print an advertisement that they know to be false, misleading, or deceptive. They may go even further and choose not to air or print an advertisement they feel is offensive or in extremely bad taste. If they feel that running a particular ad will offend their readers, then they may refuse the ad, though they are not morally required to refuse it. They are morally required to refuse an immoral ad, however.

To show or print an immoral ad would be to take part in an immoral action. We are neither allowed to act immorally nor to take part in immoral conduct by acting as agents for others. But the obligation must be kept within the bounds of reason. We cannot expect every magazine editor to check up on every ad submitted for publication to see whether it is in fact false or misleading. The primary responsibility rests with the manufacturer and the advertising agency that produced the ad. But even if the ordinary professional working on the magazine were to suspect that a given ad is false or misleading, then the ad should be questioned and some evidence sought to show its moral legitimacy. The general principle is that it is immoral for those in control of TV advertising or of advertising in newspapers or magazines to air or print what they know to be immoral. Once again, the temptation will be to claim that the responsibility falls on the manufacturer or ad agency, especially when the account is a big one. But TV stations, newspapers, and magazines cannot cast aside their moral responsibility so lightly.

4. What of the public? Members of the general public do not act immorally when they look at misleading ads. (How would they know they were misleading if they did not look at them?) They also have no moral obligation to take any positive action about them. But if they are concerned about the truthfulness or accuracy of an ad, if they feel an ad is misleading or deceptive, they can perform a public service by making their feelings and perceptions known. They can write to the manufacturing company and complain about the ad, or if they know the responsible ad agency, they can appropriately write to it. They can write to the TV station, newspaper, or magazine that carried the ad. They can write to the local or national Better Business Bureau, the FTC or FDA, or to the National Advertising Review Board (NARB). The NARB was formed in 1971 and is sponsored by the American Association of Advertising Agencies, the American Advertising Federation, the Association of National Advertisers, and the Council of Better Business Bureaus. The NARB's aim is self-regulation by advertisers. It investigates complaints, asks advertisers for substantiation, reports the results to whoever files the complaint, and also prints the results in a monthly press release.

Public pressure can help keep advertising responsible. If advertisers know that members of the public will not only complain about misleading or immoral advertising, but will also cast their vote against a product so advertised by not purchasing it, advertisers would have a strong incentive to keep their advertising moral.

5. Government has taken an active role in regulating and monitoring advertising. The FTC and the FDA enforce only legal standards, however. They do not and should not enforce moral standards if these differ from legal ones. Government is not empowered, in our political system, to be the final arbiter of morality, although through law, it can sometimes legally settle issues about which there is moral controversy. But government does not make actions, policies, or practices moral or immoral by its legislation. Legislators and administrators can certainly listen to moral arguments. Moral arguments, prudential arguments, and legal precedents are all appropriately considered. Government and its agencies should not act immorally, but they are neither capable of nor empowered to legislate morality.

The role of government in the area of advertising is to protect the public interest. It does this in a variety of ways, some of which we have seen. To the extent that advertisers regulate their own behavior, legislation is not needed. When advertisers seek to achieve their own good at the expense of the general public, however, then government plays a legitimate regulatory role.

The role of government as regulator is not without its temptations. Regulatory agencies have sometimes been staffed by people who have worked in the areas being regulated, or who hope to work in the areas regulated. The possible conflict of interest is fairly clear. Who regulates the regulators? Regulators also sometimes take it upon themselves to interpret legislation very broadly, even if this was not the legislative intent. Regulatory agencies can become minor legislators on their own, by writing the regulations that implement the laws. They may, if so inclined, attempt to impose their own moral standards on an industry. They may misinterpret the degree to which the general public wishes or needs paternalistic protection. Regulators, Congress, the president, and the people should be aware of the dangers inherent in governmental regulation.

Advertising is a pervasive activity in the United States. Most people learn the semantics of advertising as they grow up. They learn to discount certain claims as puffery; they learn to read fine print in ads to see if an ad may be interpreted in more than one way. They learn that advertisers make associations but that some associations tell us nothing about a product. Whether or not a movie star or a baseball hero claims to use a beauty product or eat a breakfast cereal tells us more about the star and the hero than it does about the product. Inherent in the semantics of advertising are the notions of lying, misrepresentation, deception, manipulation, and other questionable practices. Those that are immoral should be labeled as such. Public pressure and appropriate government regulation can be effective in curbing the major excesses of advertising.

Study Questions

1. What are some immoral techniques of creating monopolies? Why are they immoral?
2. What is price fixing? What is its purpose? Is it morally allowable? Why or why not?
3. What is overpricing? How can there be such a thing as overpricing if each manufacturer is allowed to set his or her own prices?
4. What is usury? Is it unethical? Why or why not?
5. What are some moral issues in pricing? Give examples of some of them.
6. Is secret bidding morally justifiable? Why or why not?
7. How might cost overruns and "locking in a buyer" be immoral?
8. What is truth-in-lending? unit pricing? labeling and dating? Are these morally required or simply socially or legally required?
9. Is advertising itself immoral? Why or why not?
10. Is all advertising manipulative? Why or why not?
11. Define lying. Is lying the same as telling a falsehood? Why or why not? Illustrate your answer by examples.
12. Are figures of speech literally true? Do they constitute lying? Give examples of figures of speech used in advertising.
13. What is a misleading ad? Give an example of one.
14. What is a deceptive ad? Give an example of one.
15. Can an ad be immoral and not make any verbal statement? If so, how?
16. Is persuasion immoral in itself? is manipulation? coercion?

17. Is subliminal advertising morally permissible? Why or why not?

18. What is paternalism? How does it enter into discussions of advertising? How much paternalism is morally justifiable?

19. Is it morally permissible for professional associations to prevent their members from advertising? Why or why not?

20. Who holds primary moral responsibility for advertising?

21. What is the moral obligation of ad agencies with respect to advertising? of the media? of government regulatory agencies?

22. A company that manufactures vitamins has made vitamins for preschool children that look and taste like candy. The company advertises heavily on children's TV programs. Although the ads mention health benefits from the vitamins, that message is clearly secondary to the message of the good taste and colorful packaging to which the preschool children react positively. Is such advertising morally justifiable? Why or why not?

23. Consider the statement "Whatever it is ethical to produce or whatever service it is ethical to provide, it is ethical to advertise." Do you agree? Why or why not?

24. A hospital advertises that its "success rate" in treating breast cancer is higher than that of the local community hospital. The statement is factually correct. Is the hospital morally justified in running such an ad? Why or why not?

12

>–:–‹›–•–O–•–‹›–:–‹

PROTECTING INTELLECTUAL PROPERTY, CORPORATE DISCLOSURE, AND INSIDER TRADING

Boesky, Milken, and an Insider Trading Case

In the second half of the 1980s the United States was in the midst of a period of corporate restructuring. Takeovers of one corporation by another and corporate mergers were the rage. Rumors of corporate takeover were frequent and spread quickly. The stock of a company that was targeted for a takeover frequently rose in price, simply on the basis of being targeted, because those taking over a company usually had to pay more than the present stock price in order to acquire enough shares for the takeover. Anyone with knowledge of an actual takeover and of the amount the targeted stock would bring had privileged information that was closely guarded.

In January 1985 Ivan Boesky, an arbitrager for Ivan Boesky Corporation in New York, was reported to have received a call from Michael Milken, who was the head of high-yield securities of the financial firm of Drexel, Burnham, Lambert, Inc. in Beverly Hills.[1] The two had worked together before and would continue to work together, earning over a billion dollars. Five years later both ended up serving prison terms. But on this particular January day Milken told Boesky that he had learned of a merger between Occidental Petroleum Corporation, which Milken's firm was representing, and Diamond Shamrock. According to the terms of the merger, which had not been made public, Diamond Shamrock's stock would go up in price and Occidental's

---

[1] This account is based on James B. Stewart's report, "Scenes from a Scandal: The Secret World of Michael Milken and Ivan Boesky," *Wall Street Journal*, October 2, 1991, p. B1. Milken denies that he made the call in question.

would fall. Both the law and Drexel, Burnham, Lambert's policy prohibited Milken from trading the stock—hence, his call to Boesky. Their prior agreement on such deals was to split their profits evenly. On the basis of that phone call, Boesky immediately set about buying as much of Diamond Shamrock stock as he could. He sold short as much Occidental stock as he could, in anticipation of replacing the Occidental stock with shares that he would buy after its price fell. Thus, they would make money on both stocks.

Although the information came from the inside and was accurate, things did not turn out as anticipated. The Diamond Shamrock board of directors unexpectedly turned down the merger. Milken had no prior knowledge that this would happen and learned of it only when the news was publicly announced. Then there were no buyers for Diamond Shamrock's shares, which fell dramatically, and the price of Occidental's shares rose. By the time Boesky was able to sell his Diamond Shamrock stock and cover his position in Occidental, he and Milken had lost $10 million.

Consider this one case, and ignore the many other deals for which Milken and Boesky eventually went to jail. In this case, did they do anything unethical (ignoring the issue of whether what they did was illegal)? Does it make any difference that they lost money rather than made money? Does it make any difference that their inside information, though accurate, was not definitive, since the decision to merge was not ratified? In this case, is there any significant difference between the information they had and rumors that might emerge as a result of heavy buying of Diamond Shamrock's stock and heavy short positions in Occidental?

In Japan there are few laws governing the sale of stock, and rules are made and enforced by Japan's Ministry of Finance. In 1990 the Ministry decided to sell 5 million shares in the government-owned Nippon Telegraph and Telephone Corporation.[2] They set the initial offering price very high and then pushed the stock and encouraged brokerage houses to do likewise. Eventually, the stock fell to one-third of the initial price, and noninsiders lost $80 million.[3] The government and the brokers came out ahead. No laws were broken, and nothing illegal was done. Yet one can still ask: Did the Ministry act ethically? Until recent years, the argument Japan gave for its absence of laws against insider trading was that the stock market was in effect a market for insiders. Because of the interlocking common to Japanese firms, almost the

---

[2] "Japan Plans to Sell 5 Million NTT Shares over 7-Year Period," *Wall Street Journal*, November 21, 1990, p. C9.

[3] Kenichi Ohmae, "The Scandal Behind Japan's Financial Scandals, *Wall Street Journal*, August 6, 1991, p. A16. See also James Sterngold, "Japan's Scandal: No Laws to Break," *New York Times*, July 15, 1991, p. D3; and Clay Chandler, "Japanese Stock Scandal Sends Strong Message: Small Investors Beware," *Wall Street Journal*, June 25, 1992, p. 1.

only players in the market were large corporations, all of whom acted on inside information. Those not on the inside were marginal. In recent years, however, more small shareholders, as well as foreign buyers, have entered the market. The players have changed, but the rules have not.

Information is a crucial key in the stock market, as in other areas of business, and information in business is the topic of this chapter.

If one company were to hijack a truckload of TV sets from another company, or if an employee were to embezzle funds from his employer, we would have no hesitation in calling the acts immoral. We know what it means for a company to own TV sets or money, and what it means for someone to take these wrongfully. However, our concept of proprietorship is less clear when it comes to knowledge and information. If I take information or knowledge from you, I do not physically deprive you of it. We may both have it and have it equally. My taking it from you does not leave you without it because knowledge and information are different from physical objects. If, furthermore, we lived in a society in which all goods were shared, knowledge and information would be among those items that would be shared most freely, because each person could enjoy the benefit of the knowledge and information without depriving anyone else of their use.

Information and knowledge are vital aspects of many businesses, and special information may give one business an advantage over another. Hence, in a competitive situation, one business may not wish to share its knowledge and information, although doing so would not lessen its own knowledge and information. Information and knowledge, moreover, often represent a financial investment by a firm. Some knowledge is costly to obtain or develop. A marketing study, for instance, may represent a great deal of time and money, and a company's desire to keep such information secret is understandable.

Who owns knowledge and information that have been developed by people in a corporation? Who owns knowledge and information about a corporation? From a moral point of view, what may be kept secret and what must be disclosed? In a broad sense, the term *trade secrets* refers to all knowledge developed by a firm, which it guards as proprietary; in a narrow sense, trade secrets designate an alternative to patents and copyrights as a means to protecting inventions, formulas, and the like. Protecting intellectual property, insider information, and disclosure are three aspects of questions pertaining to knowledge and information in business. They have generated much discussion.[4] Many people are demanding and receiving more and more disclosure of information from corporations. At the same time, computer theft is rising, and corporations are trying to devise ways of keeping corporate information both secret and secure.

---

[4] See Stanley Lieberstein, *Who Owns What Is in Your Head?: A Guide for Entrepreneurs, Inventors and Creative Employees* (Pensacola, FL: Wildcat Publishers, 1996); and Russell B. Stevenson, Jr., *Corporations and Information: Secrecy, Access, and Disclosure* (Baltimore: Johns Hopkins University Press, 1980).

Intellectual Property

The notion of property is best analyzed as a bundle of rights.[5] The exact nature of the bundle varies from society to society and from one kind of property to another.

When people think of property, they often think first of what is called *tangible* property. As the name implies this is physical items that we can touch. To own or to claim such items as one's property is to claim that one has certain rights with respect to those items. One has, for instance, the right to the exclusive use of the items for whatever legitimate purposes one wishes; the right to sell, trade, discard, destroy, or otherwise dispose of them; the right to keep, preserve, store, and do any number of any other things one wishes with them. That is what we mean when we say that they are ours.

Clearly, however, the bundle or set of rights that attach to what is called *real* property is somewhat different. Real property refers to land and to the buildings and additions on the land. Although we can claim the right to exclusive use of real property, and the right to use it more or less as we wish, there are restrictions on the use we can make of it. We cannot use our land as a toxic dump site, simply because it is ours. Dumping toxic waste on our land may harm others, which we are morally prohibited from doing. Nor does it make much sense to claim that we have the right to destroy the land. It remains, despite what we do to it. The right-to-use that one has of a house one rents to others is different from the right that one has to a house that one uses oneself. Although in both cases one owns the house, one's rights to the use of it differ in the two cases. The bundle of rights that constitutes real property, thus, overlaps somewhat with the bundle of rights that constitutes tangible property but is in someways a different bundle.

The same is true of what is called *intangible* property—money, stocks, bonds, and other financial securities. A U.S. $1 bill is a piece of paper that is worth a certain amount for purposes of trade. It is in effect a promise to pay upon demand the value represented by the face amount on the bill. When I deposit money in the bank and then a month later withdraw that amount, I do not expect the same bills with the same serial numbers. I would expect that if the bills were tangible property. I would expect back exactly what I had deposited. But with money, what I expect back is an equivalent amount, not the same physical bills. Similarly a stock certificate represents a certain portion of ownership of a corporation. The value of that certificate will fluctuate. But the certificate does not give me any claim to any particular piece of equipment or furniture of the corporation. As the name implies, what I own is not anything tangible that I can touch. It follows that my bundle of rights is different with respect to intangible property than it is with the two previous kinds.

---

[5] See Lawrence C. Becker, *Property Rights: Philosophic Foundations* (Boston: Routledge & Kegan Paul, 1977), and James O. Grunebaum, *Private Ownership* (New York: Routledge & Kegan Paul, 1987).

A fourth type of property is *intellectual* property. Intellectual property is constituted by a bundle of rights governing products of the mind or intellect. The rights that one has with respect to these products are different from the bundles of rights that constitute tangible, real, or intangible property. Intellectual property is significantly different from the other types of property because it can be shared with others without losing any part of it oneself. If someone steals my car, I no longer have it. If someone steals my idea, I continue to have full use of it, although I no longer have exclusive use of it. On the other hand if others come up with the same idea that I do, their idea is as much theirs as mine is mine. None of us has exclusive use.

When it comes to intellectual products, be they ideas, the expression of ideas, inventions, discoveries, and so on, the initial question is: To what sort of intellectual products can anyone make any valid ownership claims? Can one properly own ideas, or mathematical equations, or scientific formulas, or facts about the world? If there are intellectual products of which one can legitimately claim ownership, what is the bundle of rights that constitutes intellectual property? It is easier to answer the second question than the first, and legally the bundle of rights approach has been used to implicitly answer the first question as well. There are three recognized ways by which legally, and ethically as well, one can protect intellectual property, and to a large extent that protection determines the bundle of rights that one has with respect to intellectual property. The three ways are copyright, patent, and trade secrecy.

Copyrights and Patents

While trade secrecy is the legal right to keep one's information, ideas, plans, projects, and so on secret, copyrights and patents give their holders certain rights with respect to their products on condition of their making them public in certain prescribed ways.

Generally speaking we can not own ideas. One reason is that others may have similar ideas, and there is no way of preventing them from having them and no reason to deny the legitimacy of their having them independently. But we can lay ownership claims to the expression we give ideas, for instance, in the printed word. Copyrights were instituted in order to protect the written expression of ideas. Thus one could express one's ideas in a book or play or poem, and publish that. If in doing so one copyrights the material, then one has the exclusive right to sell that material and to profit from it. Others are prevented from copying it for sale and from claiming that the words are their own. To do either is to infringe on the rights of the one who owns the copyright. Although originally instituted to protect the written word, copyright protection has been extended to a large variety of expressions of ideas, including recordings, works of art, films, video tapes, and computer programs. The U. S. copyright law formerly protected copyrighted material for an initial period of twenty-eight years, renewable for an additional twenty-eight years. This did not coincide with copyright practices in many countries of Europe and elsewhere, and U.S. law has been brought into conformity with international copyright agreements that protect copyrighted material for the life of the author plus seventy years, and with respect to corporate authors for a period of ninety-five years. When someone buys a copyrighted book they buy the physical object, which is their tangible property. But the contents of the book are protected by copyright. One can resell the book, but not the story or information or the expression of the ideas contained therein. A doctrine called *fair use* permits one to copy some or all of the work, under certain conditions, and usually for one's personal, not for commercial, use.

Patents cover not the expression of ideas but inventions. The rationale for offering such protection is that unless there were some way of guaranteeing a certain period of time after producing a new invention so that the inventor could recover his expenses and make a profit, society would kill the incentive to come up with new inventions or products or pharmaceutical drugs. Developing one's ideas in tangible form takes time and often a considerable investment of money. If as soon as a new product appeared a competitor could freely copy it and produce it without having invested any time or money in its research and development, the competitor could price the product below the price at which the original inventor and producer, who had to recoup his costs, could sell it. Every company would see that it was to its advantage to wait until someone else had come up with a new or an improved device and then copy it. Patents give inventors protection for their innovation. Patents filed before 1995 afford protection for a period of seventeen years from date of issuance or twenty years from the date of application, whichever is longer. Since January 1, 1995, the period is twenty years from the date of application. After that period the products fall into the public domain and may be freely copied. Prior to that period a patent gives the patent holder the right to the exclusive use of that item. Patent holders, if they wish, may also sell their rights to exclusive use or they may license the use of the product to others, making it available to them for a fee.

Patents do not prohibit *reverse engineering*. This is a process in which a product that has appeared on the market can be taken apart and inspected to learn what is new and how it is made. A patent prevents direct copying. But it does not prevent learning from the new product or developing a competing product that will perform the same function somewhat differently. Often it is not worth the investment of time and money to develop such a product if the original is available by a license from the patent holder.

Both copyrights and patents require that the intellectual products be made available and are thus socially useful. Because they are socially useful, it is appropriate for society to encourage their development. Yet it is also appropriate for that protection not to last indefinitely, for everyone's ideas build on the ideas of others. Everyone's expression of ideas is due in part to the work of others from whom one learns and on whom one builds. Whatever new knowledge a person or company produces is always an increment to past knowledge that has been developed by society in years past and passed from one generation to the next. Any new invention is made by people who learned a great deal from the general store of knowledge, before they could bring what they knew to bear on a particular problem. Though we can attribute inventions and discoveries to particular efforts of individuals or teams, they are also the result of those people who developed underlying knowledge and passed it on to others. In this way, every advance in knowledge is social and belongs ultimately to society, even though for practical purposes we can assign it temporarily to a given individual or firm. It is therefore appropriate that one's property rights be limited and that the contribution be added to the free store of the human inheritance of knowledge.

Trade Secrets

Unlike copyrights and patents, trade secrets are not revealed, and once revealed are no longer secrets and no longer legally protected. Within certain limits, one can keep secret whatever one wishes, providing that he has no obligation to reveal it. Trade secrecy clearly does not prevent others from coming up with the same ideas, since they have no way of knowing what anyone else is keeping secret. Inventions and products under development are often kept as trade secrets until they are sufficiently advanced to seek patent protection for them. Several companies may be working on a very similar product and know that they are in a race to see who can develop it first and secure a patent for it. Nonetheless, to the extent that they are kept secret, trade secrets are legally and ethically protected.

Three indicators are useful in determining what information is appropriately secret, what information belongs to a given firm, and hence what information an employee has a moral obligation not to reveal.

- First is the amount of security the company employs to maintain the secrecy of the information. A company may treat the information—techniques or inventions, or consumer and/or supplier lists—as highly confidential; that is, it takes measures to ensure that the information is not available routinely by restricting access, and so on. If such measures are taken, then the employees with access to that information know that it is considered secret by the firm. Usually, the employees are not only cautioned about the secrecy of the data or information to which they are given access, but also are required to sign an agreement not to divulge the information.
- Second is the amount of money that a firm has spent in developing the information. Strict security regulations for information that is in the public domain, or that can be easily developed, make no sense. Elaborate safeguards make sense only where the information is costly to produce and important to the financial future of the firm.
- Third is the value of the information to a competitor. Again, it is unlikely that a firm will initiate great security to protect information valuable

only to the firm itself. If, however, the information could be used by a competitor to gain a competitive edge, then it is reasonable that the originating firm be permitted to protect its investment.

To get a clearer picture of trade secrets and ownership of intellectual property we can look at three typical, though hypothetical, cases.

Case 1: John Knosit was head of a research team of CDE Electric. His team was working on developing a cheaper and more effective filament for light bulbs. Six months ago, a rumor circulated in the industry that the team had made a breakthrough, and all that was required was final testing. This would put CDE Electric far ahead of its competitors. Five months ago, X Electric hired John away from CDE, offering him $25,000 a year more than he had been getting. No mention was made of his work on the new filament. After he had been in his new position for three months, his superior approached him and said that X Electric had hired him because of his work on the filament, and that he would have to develop the filament quickly for X Electric or be fired. John knows how to develop the filament. Is he morally justified in developing it for X Electric?

Case 2: Jane Berry works as sales manager for Pretty-Good Refrigeration. She is hired by Even-Better Refrigeration to fill a similar position in their firm, at a sizable raise in salary. Before she leaves Pretty-Good Refrigeration, Jane makes a copy of the customer book, which contains the list of Pretty-Good Refrigeration's customers, the contact person in each firm, the kind of equipment each purchased, when it is due for replacement, and other similar information. She brings the list with her and then systematically contacts the people on the list at the appropriate time, promoting the products of Even-Better Refrigeration. She believes that Even-Better Refrigeration products are superior to Pretty-Good Refrigeration, and because she knows both products she is able to mount a convincing sales pitch. Does she act morally in doing so?

Case 3: Henry Mangel is assistant human resources manager of Dirt-Brown Construction Company. He has worked for the company for five years. During that time he has learned a good deal about the company's personnel management techniques, which were implemented and proved to be successful. Partly as a result of his innovations, the workers have been content and their productivity has increased. He is hired by Grass-Green Construction Company as their personnel manager. At his new job, he immediately introduces a series of changes based on his experience at Dirt-Brown Construction and uses some of the techniques he learned as well as those he introduced there. Is he morally justified in doing this?

The three cases share a common feature. In all three cases, a person goes from one company to another, bringing certain knowledge from the first company. The person uses that knowledge in the second company. Is it appropriate to do so? Does the knowledge belong to the worker or to the firm at which he or she worked? What kind of knowledge belongs to a company, and how can it be protected?

Consider the first case. John Knosit was the head of a research team. He was appointed to that position, presumably because of his leadership ability and because of his knowledge and skill. These belong to him. He takes with him his own knowledge, skill, experience, and personal qualities wherever he goes. But while employed by CDE Electric, he works on a specific project. The company pays his salary while he works on the project. It also pays the salaries of his fellow teamworkers. The company provides the laboratory in which they conduct their experiments; it supplies all the materials they need. When they develop the new filament, the company will take out a patent on it. Clearly, the filament belongs to the company. But John knows how to develop the filament. Is that knowledge his?

To get some perspective on the question, suppose that while working for CDE Electric John went to X Electric and offered to sell them, for $50,000, the process he had developed. Most people would readily admit that to do so would be immoral. The reason it is immoral is that the process belongs to CDE Electric. Even though John knows the process, it does not belong to him. He is morally restricted in what he can do with that information, and giving it or selling it to others is not morally allowable. His being hired by X Electric does not change the status of his knowledge of the filament. That still belongs to CDE Electric. Hence, he cannot, morally, develop the filament for X Electric as he is commanded to do. John's superior at X Electric acts immorally in commanding it, and if John does as he commands, John also acts immorally.

A short utilitarian analysis will help us see why it is immoral to develop the filament for X Electric. Consider the consequences for all those involved. John benefits because he gets to keep his job and his handsome increase in salary. X Electric benefits because they get the filament quickly and cheaply. They will therefore be able to compete easily with CDE Electric. In order to get around patent laws, they may have to make minor modifications so that the filament is not identical. But the cost of doing that will not be anything like the cost of developing the original filament. Because they do not have to recoup research and development costs, they will even be able to market the new bulbs more cheaply than CDE Electric. CDE Electric is the loser. It still has the filament, but it has lost its competitive edge; it will lose to X Electric part of the market it would otherwise have had to itself. And because of the research costs, it will make less profit.

The harm that CDE suffers, however, is offset by the benefit that X Electric reaps. If we then add in the benefit John receives, John's action seems morally justifiable. This, however, is not the case. For we have not yet considered the result or effect of the practice on the rest of society. Suppose that hiring team leaders in order to gain trade secrets from them becomes a practice. Any firm that spent money—perhaps millions of dollars—to develop a new product or idea would expect to lose that investment to a competitor, who would obtain the information by hiring away its developer. In each case, the second company would benefit at the expense of the first. Clearly, every company would see that it is not in its best interest to develop any product or idea. They would all be better off waiting for someone else to develop a product or idea. In the end, no one would develop products or ideas. The result of the practice in the long run, therefore, would be very serious, not only for society as a whole but for the companies—all companies—that now benefit from research and development. Taking the broad consequences into account, we see that the practice is an immoral one.

What conclusions can we draw from this consideration? If the analysis is correct, we can legitimately claim that a company is allowed to protect the products and ideas it develops in its research and development programs, for at least a certain amount of time.

The analysis, though plausible, is not universally accepted, however. There are some who argue that John Knosit is the real inventor of the product because it is the result of his genius or ingenuity, and it rightfully belongs to him. He developed it while working for the company, so the company has the "shop right" to it—that is, the company has the right to use the invention for its own ends. But it has no right, this view maintains, to prevent John from taking that knowledge with him and using it for the benefit of his new employer, if he so chooses.

Because of controversies of this type, certain practices have become more or less standard in industry, and laws have been developed to help regulate the use of information and inventions. Patent laws are one obvious device that help companies achieve some protection in the use of products developed by those in their employ. A company can protect its interests in other ways as well. It can, for instance, fragment its projects so that very few people know the total project. It is also typical for a firm to require that people who work for it in development areas keep sensitive information they acquire as employees of the firm (including information on products the employees themselves develop) confidential for a certain length of time, even if they leave the company. This is specified in a contract, which details what an employee may and may not reveal. Employees must often sign such agreements before they are given access to the company's research and development. Should an employee break this contract, he can be sued for the damages incurred. The contract itself, in such cases, sets not only the legal but also the moral framework within which to decide the morality of a given act of disclosure. In general, the practice is morally defensible, even though some companies abuse the practice. Abuse occurs when the contract violates an employee's rights by imposing unreasonable limitations on what the employer assigns to an employee in terms of his or her knowledge. Firms will sometimes subtly coerce the employee to sign unreasonable agreements. For instance, the employee will be asked to sign a condition of employment *only after* leaving his or her other position and becoming ready to work for the new firm.

The right of the company to be the first to use and profit from its research is nonetheless in general morally defensible. As we have seen, however, this does not mean that it has the exclusive right to what it develops forever. Nor does this mean that if it develops a product that would benefit society, it can for its own reasons indefinitely prevent it from ever becoming known. Knowledge is not something that one can keep locked up for as long as one likes. Patents, appropriately, do expire. Long before they expire, any new idea that can be reverse-engineered may be so engineered and copied with just sufficient changes so as not to infringe on the patent laws. Competition thus enters the field. However, the delay that such copying requires after the original item appears is sufficient for the originator to recoup his or her research expenses. Interestingly, the formula for Coca-Cola has never been patented precisely in order to keep it secret. Chemical analysis has not yielded the formula. The formula for Coca-Cola is one of the best-kept trade secrets in history. From a moral point of view, there is no objection to that secret remaining a secret of the company indefinitely; no demonstrable harm would befall society even if the secret eventually died with its keepers.

If a cheap substitute for gasoline was found, however, oil companies might consider it to be in their own interests to keep such a product from being developed. If the product was discovered in their laboratories, they might prefer to lock up the process in their company safe until it was necessary to use it, rather than compete with their own oil interests. Could they morally do so, and could they morally keep those employees who developed it from divulging the formula *forever?* No. The good that society would reap from the oil substitute would far exceed the damage done to the oil company by the substitute's appearing on the market. The developer has the right to be the first to market the product and to protect its investment in development so as to recover its cost. But this right is a limited one.

Case 2 raises a somewhat different issue. Jane Berry makes a copy of the customer book, a list of Pretty-Good Refrigeration's customers. She does not take the original; therefore, the information is still available to Pretty-Good Refrigeration. To whom does the list belong? The list is in the company's book. It does not contain simply a list of purchasers, such as might be obtained from an industry trade list. It was generated by employees of the company, and they were paid for their services while it was generated. The list therefore belongs to Pretty-Good Refrigeration. By taking the list with her, Jane is stealing information that does not belong to her. She uses it, moreover, for her own ends and at the expense of her former employer. As in the previous case, the information rightfully belongs to the company, and in taking it, Jane acts immorally.

What if instead of taking a copy of the customer book Jane goes to her new employer with the list memorized? Does this make a difference? The answer is clearly no. What is immoral is not the fact that she took a certain amount of paper from Pretty-Good Refrigeration but that she took its annotated customer list. That list belongs to the company. Whether she takes it in her head or on photocopied paper does not matter. The information is not hers, and she uses it immorally when she uses it to take away the customers from her former employer.

Case 3, however, is different from the other two. In Case 3, Henry does not take what does not belong to him. He steals no secrets from the company. What managerial skill he learns while working for the company belongs to him. It is not patentable information, and it is not guaranteed by copyright or any other law. A person who works for a firm earns his pay by discharging the duties of whatever position he holds in the firm. As a human resources manager, Henry performed his duties. In doing so, he gained experience. He had ideas for improvement, and these were implemented in the firm, to the firm's advantage. But managerial techniques and organizational structures that one develops do not belong to the firm for which one works.

Let us test this claim. Suppose that while working for Dirty-Brown Construction Henry went to Grass-Green Construction and offered to sell them his managerial ideas for $50,000. What would we say of the morality of that action? A proper first reply is that it is unlikely that Grass-Green Construction would be interested. Managerial ideas are not the kinds of things one can simply take and implement; each firm has a particular structure and dynamism. A consultant might come in and do a study of how to increase the efficiency of a firm, but no consultant would simply offer an idea regarding management and expect to receive much, if any, money for it.

If Henry's ideas are good, could he legitimately consult on the side? The answer, of course, depends on the firm he is working for and the nature of his agreement with the firm. His employer could make it a condition of his employment that he not consult, and of course he should not consult for the company's competitors. His consulting, however, is different from his selling information that belongs to the firm. The skill that one develops and the experience that one attains on a job belong to the employee, not the firm. If he can sell his experience and skill for more to another employer, the employee is entitled to do so. Each company, unless it hires only unskilled labor and does all its training and hiring from its own ranks, hires people who have acquired knowledge, skill, and experience working for other employers.

The distinction between the information and knowledge that belong appropriately to the employer, and the information and knowledge that belong appropriately to the employee, is not always an easy one to draw. Several guidelines may help. Information that is available in the public domain is not secret. Even if a firm independently develops information in its own laboratory, if the identical information is available in technical or popular journals, the firm cannot claim proprietary rights to it. If such material is publicly available, an employee violates no trust or obligation of loyalty if he or she uses that knowledge in a new position. Similarly, if the information can be easily generated by those competent to do so, then the restriction on an employee's using such information in a new position is minimal, if it exists at all.

From the foregoing analysis we can conclude that firms have the right to protect certain kinds of information if it belongs to them, and that they can legitimately impose restrictions on their employees not to divulge such information. The analysis provides some rough guidelines. But the conclusion should not be taken to be stronger than it actually is. In particular, we should note two points. First, the employee's obligation not to sell or give to another what properly belongs to the firm is a moral obligation. Attempts to reinforce the moral obligation through law have been only minimally effective. Some employers have attempted to restrain their employees from working for competing firms for a period of two years after they leave their own company.[6] Such agreements, even if signed, have generally not held up in court because they violate the right of the employee to change jobs. The attempts of the firms to issue injunctions against competitors who are pursuing research with the help of a former employee have usually been unsuccessful. Some companies have emphasized the ethical obligations of employees both before they begin work on certain projects and just prior to their leaving the service of the company. They have also attempted to keep them loyal by offering consulting fees for a period of one or two years, and by giving them retirement benefits, or other benefits that they would not normally receive, in return for not revealing trade secrets.

The second point again concerns the information that a company can appropriately keep secret. Some, it seems, would prefer to keep all aspects of their operation secret. They have been reluctant to disclose any information at all, unless forced to do so by law. The foregoing guidelines concern only certain kinds of information—namely, what is closely guarded, is expensive, and, if divulged to a competitor, would cause serious harm. However, a great deal of company information is not of this type. There are some interesting borderline cases. Many firms have claimed, for instance, that the salaries of their top executives were trade secrets. If the competition knew what these salaries were, they could more easily lure top executives to their own company. But clearly, what a top executive makes is not something he is required to keep secret from others who might want to employ him. His total compensation is also of interest to stockholders. Such information is now a matter of public record. Companies' claims to secrecy have to be balanced against claims of the employees to freedom of speech and movement, and against claims of the government, stockholders, and the public to information that concerns them and that they have a right to know. Last, claims to secrecy must be balanced against the right of society in general to benefit from socially useful information and knowledge.

---

[6] For one comment, see Meredith K. Wadman, "More Firms Restrict Departing Workers," *Wall Street Journal,* June 26, 1992, p. B1.

Industrial Espionage

Because business has become global, the guarding of information and the stealing of information have become issues not only of one firm's competing against another but also of espionage sponsored by national governments. Ironically, with the end of the Cold War, the spying that was characteristic of one government on another has been transformed at least in part into spying on the world's industrial companies in the forefront of technological development. American companies have become the major targets, especially those in the electronics, laser research, biotechnology, aerospace, and other industries of the future—their technology, marketing plans, contract bids, and software are of particular interest.

In the past few years the issue has become public, both as a discussion of the proper use of the U.S. Central Intelligence Agency in spying on companies in other countries has surfaced and as the United States government has raised charges of spying by intelligence services of other countries. Russia, France, Japan, Israel, Egypt, and the People's Republic of China are among the nearly one hundred countries that have purportedly sought the trade secrets of U.S. companies.[7]

As is true of most military espionage, industrial espionage depends to a large extent on public sources for its information. It consists of carefully gathering, organizing, and analyzing data available in published articles, reports, interviews, sales promotions, and the like. Up to 90 percent of intelligence is gathered in this way, and it is both legal and moral to so acquire information.[8]

The second most effective way to obtain intelligence on a company's trade secrets is through the company's employees. We have already discussed what information belongs to employers and what belongs to employees. But foreign nations use many techniques other than hiring away employees or buying secrets from them. China has been accused of giving Chinese employees in key American firms free trips to China in order to build their loyalty and make them willing to discuss their work. It also sends students to study in American university departments where they will have access to knowledge and information in which the government is interested. Some nations require that U.S. firms abroad hire local nationals, some of whom turn over information they acquire to the local government intelligence bureaus.

Clearly unethical are the invasive and surreptitious methods of tapping phones, compromising computer systems, and outright stealing of secrets. Less clear are such borderline activities of electronic eavesdropping as picking up traffic from portable telephones. Since such phones are not secure and operate by using radio waves that may be picked up inadvertently as well as

---

[7] Norm Alster, "The Valley of the Spies," *Forbes,* October 26, 1992, pp. 200–204. See also Roderick P. Deighen, "Welcome to Cold War II," *Chief Executive,* 82 (January–February 1993), pp. 42–46; and John J. Fialka, "U.S. to Toughen Stand on Spying Against Firms," *Wall Street Journal,* April 30, 1993, p. A4.

[8] Ronald E. Yates, "Spies Shift to Corporate Snooping as Global Competition Intensifies," *Chicago Tribune,* March 1, 1993, p. 1.

by design, companies often take precautions against such listening. But such eavesdropping is not illegal, and what goes over the air waves is arguably public, since public access to such calls is possible and is known to be such. Is it up to those using such phones to make sure that they say nothing compromising while using them, or is the burden of not listening on others? However one answers that question, it is unethical to invade others' privacy, to harass them, or to use listening devices to hear conversations in closed rooms. What about collecting and sifting through a company's garbage? Most companies shred sensitive material. Is what a company discards fair game for competitors? Or what is the morality of following a company's employees or executives to see where they go and whom they meet? Such meetings together with other information may provide clues as to mergers, marketing plans, or new developments. If there are no invasion of privacy and no harassment, on what grounds could following a person be prohibited?

The United States and other nations differ in their approach to intelligence gathering and helping companies from their countries. France and Japan, for example, use their national intelligence agencies to help specific firms, whereas the United States does not. But in August 1992 Robert Gates, then director of the CIA, indicated that the CIA would perform three tasks: report to government policy makers intelligence on world economic trends and techniques used by other nations in trade negotiations with the United States; monitor developments in technology; and report intelligence gathering by foreign countries on U.S. firms.[9] Some legislators believe that U.S. intelligence services should help American firms as much as other nations help their firms. But even if they did, they could not justifiably use unethical methods. Nor do the rules governing wartime intelligence activities automatically transfer to corporate intelligence.

Individual companies, such as Motorola and Intel, have established their own intelligence units, both to study the competition and to prevent espionage by their competitors. Individual intelligence companies have also sprung up, some of which were started by former intelligence operatives from both the CIA and the KGB. Whoever runs the intelligence gathering, whether it be specialized companies, corporations, or government, the rules are the same. No group is allowed to do what is unethical in pursuit of its goal. But exactly what is unethical is not always clear in this new and rapidly developing area.[10]

Corporate Disclosure

Trade secrets include those items of information and knowledge to which a firm has proprietary right, which it can legally and morally protect and refuse

---

[9] Gerald F. Seib, "Business Secrets: Some Urge CIA to Go Further in Gathering Economic Intelligence," *Wall Street Journal,* August 4, 1992, p. A1.

[10] For a discussion of intelligence gathering among U.S. corporations, see Lynn Sharp Paine, "Corporate Policy and the Ethics of Competitor Intelligence Gathering," *Journal of Business Ethics,* 10 (June 1991), pp. 423-436.

to reveal. At the other end of the information spectrum is a large amount of information that a public corporation must, by law, reveal.[11] The information that a corporation is morally obliged to disclose coincides with much that is legally required, though pressures for increased disclosure are based for the most part on moral arguments.

The moral basis for disclosure of corporate information rests primarily on two second-order, substantive moral principles: (1) Each person has the right to access the information he needs to enter into a transaction fairly, and (2) Each person has the right to know those actions of others that will seriously and adversely affect him. Each of these requires some defense.

We have discussed the first of these principles several times. A transaction is fair if those who are a party to it have access to the appropriate information and freely enter into it. They cannot fairly participate in a transaction if they are denied pertinent information. On the other hand, it is not necessary for each party to make sure that the other party is properly informed. What is necessary is that each party have access to the appropriate information. A transaction is fair even if one of the parties does not take advantage of information that is available to him and that he could use profitably. This principle probably requires no more explanation here, even though it can be defended by using a utilitarian, a Kantian, or a Rawlsian approach.

The second principle can be derived from our earlier analysis of moral responsibility. We saw that each person is morally responsible for his actions and their effects. He is responsible to those whom his actions affect, and he is morally bound not to harm others unless there is some overriding reason for doing so. Respect for persons, a contract formed behind a veil of ignorance, and a utilitarian calculation all lead to the conclusion that, if we are going to engage in some action that endangers others, then we are morally bound either to warn them or not to perform the action. Though we are not morally permitted to harm others, we are permitted to do some things that might cause others harm, providing we take the precautions necessary to prevent harm to them, including warning them. For instance, if a road crew is authorized to dynamite a pass, it is morally allowed to do so only if the crew takes proper precautions to assure that no one gets hurt. The obligation not to hurt others involves the potential victim's right not to be hurt and his right to be warned of actions that could hurt him, even if they are legitimate. If a company intends to build a nuclear power plant in a certain location, those in the vicinity of the site have a right to know this. If such a plant potentially endangers them, they have the right to this information. They may have further rights as well. But a basic right, and the one by virtue of which they can rationally take other action and exercise other rights, is the right to be informed.

---

[11] Concerning the U.S. rules on disclosure, see Paul Munster and Thomas A. Ratcliffe, *A Guide to Financial Statement Disclosure* (New York: Quorum Books, 1986); and James T. O'Reilly, *Union's Rights to Company Information*, rev. ed. (Philadelphia: Wharton School, 1987).

In our discussion of disclosure, we shall deal with three questions: To whom must disclosure be made available; morally, what must be disclosed; and what form should disclosure take?

1. Based on the two principles stated previously, a corporation has the moral obligation to disclose appropriate information to those with whom it enters into transactions and to those whom its actions affect seriously and adversely. In broad terms, those affected are (a) the shareholders and potential shareholders of the corporation, (b) the board of directors,(c) the workers, (d) government, (e) the corporation's suppliers and agents, (f) the consumer of the corporation's product, and (g) the general public, whether or not they are consumers of the product. A different kind of disclosure is appropriate for each of these groups.

The actions of a corporation may seriously and adversely affect its competitors. Yet if the harm results from legal and moral activities, such as producing a better product, making a technological breakthrough, pursuing an aggressive marketing strategy, or increasing efficiency, then the corporation owes the competitor no special information. If a competitor's plant is adjacent to that of the corporation, however, and an explosion that may cause harm to the competitor's plant is possible, then the competitor has the right to be informed of the danger, just as every other neighbor does.

2. What morally must be disclosed? Because each group relates differently to the corporation, what is to be disclosed will vary from group to group. In each case the two principles apply.

a. Disclosure of information to stockholders and to potential stockholders has caused a great deal of debate. Corporations have argued that in disclosing information to these groups they were making information available to their competitors—information that by right the corporation should be allowed to keep secret. The argument in favor of secrecy, however, conflicts with the right of these groups to information. A partial solution has been effected by the Securities and Exchange Commission. It requires the disclosure of certain information by all corporations to shareholders and to potential shareholders. Disclosure to potential shareholders in effect means disclosure to the general public. Because the same information is required from all competing corporations, the conditions of competition are kept fair.

Those who own stock in a corporation are its legal owners. It would seem that they have the right to know everything about a corporation that they choose to know. Yet because disclosure of trade secrets, for instance, would compromise those secrets to the detriment of the owners, shareholders do not have the right to be informed of everything, nor are they routinely informed of everything. What they have a right to know includes information on the management of the corporation, its financial position, and its general plans for the future. They are routinely informed in some detail of these matters through the annual shareholders' meeting and the corporation's annual report, which is sent to all shareholders. They are informed of the net sales of the company, net earnings, return on shareholder's equity, earnings per share, dividends, working capital, and the assets and the liabilities of the corporation. The annual report usually includes an overview of the corporation's activities, possibly something about its research and development, a list of the members of the board of directors and the corporate officers, a financial balance sheet, information on the corporation's debts and taxes, and possibly some information on its retirement plan and similar pertinent information. This information is necessary if a shareholder is to evaluate how his investment is being managed. Because he has a right to vote for members of the corporation's board of directors, he is also informed about them: Who they are; what position they hold, either in the corporation or in other companies; and how many shares of the corporation's stock each one owns. If new members of the board are to be elected, shareholders are informed who they are. For many years, the salaries of a corporation's top officers were considered a trade secret. This information is now, by law, reported to the shareholders; this is appropriate because the shareholders are owners of the corporation.

Once information of this sort is disclosed to the shareholders, it also becomes a matter of public record with the Securities and Exchange Commission (SEC). The information is therefore available to a corporation's competitors. More important, it is available to potential purchasers of the corporation's stock. Before investing money in a corporation—if the transaction is to be a fair one—one has the right to know something about the company one is investing in: its assets, the dividends it pays, its growth or lack of growth, the price/earnings ratio of the company's stock, its assets and liabilities, and its management.

The information disclosed to shareholders and to potential shareholders has for the most part been financial. Those who defend this policy argue that the financial details of a corporation are the pieces of information that are necessary to judge its management, and also to judge whether one is making a sound investment. But there are some who feel that other kinds of information are of interest to shareholders and potential shareholders. The proposed Corporate Democracy Act, for instance, desires "to increase the flow of information to consumers, shareholders and workers about employment patterns, environmental matters, job health and safety, foreign production, directional performance, shareholder ownership, tax rates and legal and auditing fees."[12] The act spells out in detail a great deal of information about distribution of the work force by sex and race, about records submitted to the Environmental Protection Agency, and about overseas operations. In some cases it would require such information be included in the annual report; in others, it would require only that a corporation make such information available on demand to its shareholders.

---

[12] Mark Green and Robert Massie, Jr., (Eds.) *The Big Business Reader: Essays on Corporate America* (New York: Pilgrim Press, 1980), p. 592.

The right of shareholders to information about the company is a right that no one denies. But exactly what they have the right to, in addition to what is already required by law, is a matter of debate. Corporations have argued that investors are interested only in financial information, and they claim that they already supply much more than the vast majority of investors are interested in having. They also argue that, beyond a certain point, the increase of information results in a decrease in understanding on the part of all except the expert in accounting. An investor who is interested in whether the corporation is acting morally, however, may well be interested in how the corporation operates from the point of view of hiring women and minorities, how often its employees have blown the whistle, and whether the corporation is operating, for example, in China. These and other issues are not irrelevant if one wishes to evaluate the corporation from a moral point of view. If shareholders and potential shareholders demand such information, they have a right to it. Uniform disclosure by all large corporations, however, can be achieved only by making such disclosures legally mandatory. A moral audit would, of course, provide this information.

Shareholders are legally represented by members of the board of directors of a corporation. Shareholders, therefore, should be informed about the operation of the board and the actions of its members. Shareholders have a right to know not only for whom they are voting but also how the nomination procedure for board members works, how the board functions, who sets agendas, how often the board meets, what the committees of the board are and who serves on them, the number of meetings each board member has attended in the previous year, and the reasons for the resignation of any board members. If a board member resigns in protest of board or corporation action, such information is of direct and pertinent interest to shareholders. At the present time, this information is generally not disclosed.

b. The members of the board of directors are the legal representatives of the shareholders, so they owe the shareholders appropriate information, as well as honest service in their interests. Yet board members need not make public everything they learn. Because they are legally and morally bound to look after the interests of the corporation, and to evaluate the corporation's activities and the performance of management, they have the right to independent access to the information they desire. The owners' right of access is exercised through the members of the board, and this access cannot be appropriately restricted by a decision of management.

c. What must be disclosed to the workers? They have a right to know the conditions of work, including their rights, benefits, and obligations. This follows simply from the fact that this information is necessary if the contract between employer and employee is to be fair. The worker must know in advance what he is contracting into. He must also be informed of any danger to his health the work he performs might produce. If a corporation learns that a certain substance with which employees have been working is dangerous to them, it has the moral obligation to inform the workers of this. Such information not only directly affects them but also changes the background conditions of their employment. Workers may choose to work in a dangerous or somewhat unhealthy environment for extra pay, but they must be informed of such conditions.

Workers also have a right to know the general policy of the corporation in the areas in which they have moral concerns. If they do not wish to work for a company that practices discrimination, they should be able to find out whether their company does engage in such practices. The other items of moral concern we have previously discussed may all be of moral concern to workers. If so, they have a right to such information.

Workers also have the right to know, in ample time, about decisions made by management that will directly and adversely affect them. The decision to close a plant and to dismiss all the employees working there, we have seen, is a decision that they have the right to know about in sufficient time to make alternative plans, especially if the corporation does not intend to help them relocate or find other jobs.

d. Government has the right to know that corporations are complying with the law. Despite the fact that government receives a great deal of information from corporations concerning their activities, it is still very difficult for the federal government to obtain adequate information on the activities of mammoth conglomerates. The information required of small and middle-sized corporations raises few problems from the point of view of adequate disclosure. The information reported by the large conglomerates and multinational corporations tends to be aggregative rather than broken down into the activities of each of the subsidiary units. The difficulty of mandating adequate reporting from these giants makes control difficult. In some cases, the government needs more information before it can even get an idea about what specific additional information it must have. Ralph Nader, among others, has proposed federal chartering of corporations, rather than the present system of state chartering, as a means of gaining greater governmental control over large corporations and their operations. Information about their operations is a necessary prerequisite to adequate control, and adequate information is not now available to the government.

e. The corporation, from a moral point of view, should disclose to its suppliers whatever is necessary to make the contracts between them fair. The same general principle applies to a corporation's disclosure to its agents. They should know enough to fulfill, in turn, their responsibilities of disclosure to their customers.

f. Consumers should be informed of any dangers posed by the use of the product they purchase. They properly expect that the item they buy will be reasonably safe if properly used. If a product is caustic, they should be so informed. If it is poisonous, they should be warned. If it is defective, they should be notified in some way before it is purchased. They should know what a food product or a drug contains, what an article of clothing or upholstery material is made of, and so on. Government regulations have been passed, frequently as a result of consumer pressures, mandating the disclosure of information about consumer products—for example, the estimated gas mileage of a new car or the efficiency of air conditioners.

A customer cannot usually obtain information about such things as the morality of the corporation's employment practices or its overseas operations. Such information, of course, should not be carried on every box of cereal a company sells. But if customers, by their purchases, wish to vote for a company that behaves morally, and, by withholding purchases wish to vote against a company that engages in immoral practices, they should have some way of determining a company's policy. Obviously, we cannot expect any company to assert that it is engaging in an immoral practice. But we can expect that customers will have access to information about a company's employment policies, overseas operations, suits successfully brought against it, government fines it has paid, and similar details, from which customers can draw their own conclusions about its morality.

g. The term *general public* includes more than simply a corporation's customers or potential customers. The potential customers of an airplane manufacturer, for instance, would be airlines, governments, and possibly individual firms. Yet the location of an airplane manufacturing plant, the closing of such a plant, and its operation have a large impact on the area in which it is located. Those directly affected by such a plant include not only those employed by it but also those who live near it.

The closing of a plant may seriously and adversely affect the workers in the plant as well as the shops and stores that have opened to serve those workers. Communities frequently have zoning regulations and negotiate the terms under which a plant can locate in a community. They rarely negotiate any conditions for the plant's closing. Certain conditions, such as a specified amount of advance warning of a closing, as well as specifications about closing procedures, similar to opening procedures, would be appropriate.

Information concerning environmental impact, pollution, and the possible dangers of the operation to the surrounding population would also be of interest to the general public. The building of nuclear-powered electric plants poses particular problems. The dangers of radiation are greatest to those nearest the plant. Morally, such plants cannot be built without informing those in the vicinity of the danger. But if the dangers are considered low enough by the licensing authorities, this information is all that is required. Currently, the consent on the part of those who will be directly affected, in case of an accident, is not required, nor is there agreement on whether it is possible to state meaningfully what the chances of an accident occurring are. The moral issues here go beyond the question of appropriate disclosure. But it is agreed that public disclosure is appropriate where the actions of a corporation seriously and adversely affect the general public.

3. What form should disclosure take? We have already touched indirectly on some of the appropriate forms of disclosure. Shareholders are informed of a corporation's activities through the annual report and the annual shareholders' meeting; government is informed of a company's activities through legally mandated reports, and, where appropriate, through on-site investigations and inspections; and workers are informed of the conditions of employment prior to their employment. In some of these cases the information required is disclosed routinely, though reports. In other cases it is supplied only on direct request from a party authorized to receive it. Information that is a matter of public record is available to the general population. If some action will directly endanger certain people, then that information must be conveyed directly to them.

The appropriate channels for reporting information concerning the moral dimensions of some of a corporation's actions have yet to be decided upon, much less standardized. The moral audit to which we referred in Chapter 9 fits into the question of disclosure at this point and will, if developed, be an appropriate vehicle for such information.

Problems arise when a corporation engages in an activity that is immoral, illegal, or dangerous to the public. We cannot expect the people engaged in such activities to disclose the fact that they are acting in that way. We have already seen the conditions under which an employee is morally allowed and morally required to inform the public of conditions that will seriously injure people. But some questions still remain concerning disclosure of such activities.

Problems arise with respect to members of the professions who work in one way or another for a corporation. Lawyers, engineers, accountants, and sometimes doctors and nurses, fall into this category. They owe a certain loyalty to the corporation that employs them or pays them. However, they are also professionals, and as such, they are expected to maintain certain standards of conduct in the exercise of their profession. Suppose an accounting firm conducting an independent audit turns up a discrepancy in the company's books. It reports it to the president and perhaps to the chairman of the board. Suppose the discrepancy involves bribery or embezzlement, and the company decides simply to take the loss. Should this be reported to the shareholders? If the company does nothing about it, does the accounting firm or the individual accountant have any obligation to make known the facts of the case?

Suppose the corporation's lawyers are asked how to cover up some illegal procedure or act. Do they have any responsibility to make that fact known, as well as the procedure or act? Should they go to the board? And if the board does not take action, should they go to the shareholders or the government? If health measures are enforced only when there is danger of governmental inspection, or if the company doctor finds that more and more workers show signs of a work-related disease, does he fulfill his responsibilities by simply reporting this to management? If management takes no remedial action and does not inform the workers, does the doctor have any obligation to inform them?

These questions are related to disclosure, within the firm, to shareholders, management, the board, and the workers. Some of these questions are covered by codes of professional conduct of the individual professions, and some are covered in individual firms by the firm's policy statement of its ethical code of conduct. Where neither is the case, then the rules that apply to whistle blowing can be modified to handle these questions.

Confidentiality raises another set of problems. Some of what a professional learns about his client or patient is confidential and is not a proper matter for disclosure. The rule with respect to lawyers was once so severe that even if a lawyer learned, in his professional relation with a client, that the client was going to commit a felony, it was considered improper for the lawyer to disclose that information. That rule has recently—and appropriately—been changed. Journalists claim the right not to have to disclose their sources, but this does not mean that they are not required to document their stories. Investigative reporters often seek information about the wrongdoings of a firm, a group, or an individual and make this information public. They have no right to lie, but they do have the right to make known wrongdoing where they discover it, especially if it involves a cover-up by those who should appropriately disclose it.

Not all wrongdoings by members of a firm need to be publicly disclosed. But if members of a corporation have engaged in bribery, taken kickbacks, or covered up defects in a product, such information should be reported to the board of directors and possibly to the shareholders, together with a report of any action taken against such persons. A moral firm does not reward immorality with raises and promotions. One way shareholders can judge the morality of a firm is by knowing how it deals with those who are guilty of wrongdoing, even if done in the name of, and for the sake of, the company.

Corporations have typically been reluctant to disclose information about their activities. If left to themselves, some of them would consider all their internal operations trade secrets. However, if they wish to remain within the law, they must disclose what is legally required. Should they disclose more, and if so, how much more? The analysis we have given indicates the basis for deciding what should be disclosed. Corporations frequently see the issue of disclosure in an adversarial context—a struggle between their desire not to disclose and the unreasonable demands of environmentalists, consumer activists, and the enemies of capitalism. The relation need not be an adversarial one. A corporation that wishes to act morally and to fulfill its moral obligations will be amenable to discussing the demands made upon it. It will, moreover, establish channels to hear those who have claims to press and demands to make. This does not mean that every claim for information is justifiable. Either the board, the officers of a corporation, or both must in the final analysis decide what disclosure, beyond what is legally required, is appropriate. But they should base this decision on what the corporation's customers, shareholders, or the general public wish, and on the arguments they give in defense of their demands. Shareholders' meetings are only one forum for raising and discussing these questions. Such meetings are more and more frequently used, often because this is the only channel available to those who have concerns about corporations, their policies, and their activities. It is possible to find other channels, and they are needed; they are certainly not beyond the organizational capacities of most large corporations.

Insider Trading

Insider information is information that someone within a company has but that is not available to those outside the company. This includes not only trade secrets, which we have already discussed, but also company strategy and plans. The moral problems connected with insider information concern the use individuals may make of such information while they are still members of a firm. Two aspects of the question raise special problems. One is that of someone within the firm using information for his or her own private gain, at the expense of the firm. This is called conflict of interest. The other is the use of insider information by someone within a firm to secure personal advantage over those not in the firm. The most serious instance of this concerns inappropriate insider trading.

We have seen that some information belongs to a company and that some information belongs to the employee, who may use it in another firm. In our discussion of the corporation and of the responsibility of employees within it, we distinguished between employees as persons and the roles they play or the function they perform within a corporation. We can also distinguish between information belonging to individuals which they can use as they wish, and that which does not belong to them and which they cannot use as they wish.

An employee of a firm fills a certain position within the firm. We saw that employees cannot morally do what is immoral, even if they are expected or commanded to do so as part of their job. While filling any position in a firm, individuals remain moral beings and persons. They cannot compartmentalize themselves into persons and employees. Hence, any information they receive or absorb in their capacity as employees they retain in their capacity as human beings. As human beings they have certain interests and a private life. They are interested in advancing their own good as well as the good of the firm for which they work. Of all the information and knowledge they receive in their capacity as employees, what can they morally use for their own benefit?

Consider the following fairly obvious case. A vice-president of a railroad company is involved in planning the expansion of the railroad. He and others work on the most desirable route for the railroad to take. He has access to the plans of the company and knows well in advance where the railroad expects to put its new line. The company does not disclose its plans to the public. It tries to keep the route secret until it can purchase or negotiate the right-of-way. If it were to divulge its intent, the price of the land would rise significantly. The vice-president, knowing the route, purchases as much of the land along the projected route as he can. He intends to buy the land as cheaply as possible from its present owners, who of course do not know the railroad's plans, and then sell the land to the railroad at as high a price as he can get. He knows in advance the amount of money the railroad has projected for purchase of the land, and therefore he knows how much he can hold out for. Does he act morally in doing this?

The company will certainly not look kindly on his action. He is increasing the cost of the land to the company and profiting at the company's expense. Such action will probably result in his being fired. But is he not free to exercise his private right to buy and sell land, to look after his personal finances, and to invest as he wishes? What, if anything, is wrong with his action? The crux of the situation is that he used information that he received in his corporate capacity—in his position as the company's vice-president—for personal gain in his private capacity. The information was not available to him in his capacity as a private individual. It was not public knowledge, and it was knowledge available to only a few persons within the company. The basis for calling his action unethical is that he used information that was not his. He used it for his private gain at the expense of the company. The company might call that a breach of loyalty. More serious is his use of information to which, as a private individual, he had no right. This is sometimes called *misappropriation*.

The distinction between the information one has as occupant of a certain position in a firm and that which one has as a private individual has wide application. In casual conversation, employees frequently emphasize their importance by dropping information they have gained because of their position in a firm. They do this to impress the people to whom they are speaking—a form of one-upmanship. Frequently, no harm is done, but sometimes great harm is done. Those who have access to personnel files, for instance, have no right to divulge what they know about an employee if the information is learned only through their work and is not otherwise available. Morality demands confidentiality of records, whether or not one signs a contract not to divulge such information. Similarly, many plans, discussions, or memos that pertain to a company's business, and to which employees have official access, do not belong to them in their private capacity. From a moral point of view, one is not free to divulge such information casually, for personal profit, for monetary gain, or even to feel important.

The second case of the illegitimate use of insider information also concerns personal gain, not at the company's expense but at the expense of those not connected with the company. This typically occurs in trading the stock of the company for which one works. What is morally allowable in this respect and what is not?

Those who work for a company are in a position to know it better than those who do not. They can judge the efficiency of management on a daily basis. They can estimate worker satisfaction and productivity. They can sense whether the company is developing, and whether management is dynamic and anxious for expansion and growth. On the basis of this information, they may be in a better position than others to decide whether to invest in the company by buying its stock. Such information is not privileged. It lacks the specificity of the sort of insider information that would make its use immoral when deciding whether to buy the company's stock.

Consider the following two cases, however. The management of Company A, in its private planning sessions, decides that buying Company B as a subsidiary would be a profitable move. Such takeovers frequently result in the stock of Company B rising to the price that Company A will offer for the stock in its purchase offer. Adam Agile of Company A buys stock in Company B before any news or rumor of the takeover gets out. He makes a handsome profit. In the second case, Nancy Nimble, an officer in Company B, buys a large block of stock in her own company, as soon as she sees that the takeover is likely to occur. She too acts prior to any news or leak of the takeover and reaps the reward of a sizable profit. Are their actions morally justifiable?

In both cases the two people act on inside information. They are guilty of misappropriation. Neither one harms either company. If their action is inappropriate, whom do they hurt? As a result of their inside information, they are able to act on knowledge not available to the general public or to other traders in the stock market. A charge of immorality can be based on the fact that to buy and sell stock, both parties to the transaction should have access to the appropriate information. Their interpretation of that information, or their diligence in analyzing the information available, as well as their personal situations, make some people buyers at the time others are sellers. But the use of inside information makes the transaction an unequal one, and hence an unfair one.

In these cases, Adam purchased stock in a company other than his own. Officers, board members, and large shareholders of publicly owned corporations are legally required to disclose the purchase of stock in their own company. They do not have to disclose their purchase of stock in other companies. Construed strictly, Adam's action was not insider information, when this is taken to mean knowledge of the actions of one's own company and the purchase of that company's stock. In a broad sense, however, it was insider information. Nancy used the same information to purchase stock in Company B. From a moral point of view, the two cases are similar. If one acted immorally, so did the other. Both took advantage of special knowledge to make a profit, which they would not have been able to do without inside information.

In the foregoing cases, however, there was no manipulation of the stock and no other unfair practice took place. Corporations are required to disclose or release information promptly, to avoid special privilege to an insider. But clearly those on the inside frequently have access to the information before it is disclosed. Because they have that information in their capacity as corporate agents and not as private individuals, they inappropriately use it to achieve personal gain at the expense of the general public. This, of course, does not mean that they cannot buy and sell stock in their own companies. It simply means that, morally, they cannot take unfair advantage of their special insider information.

The Securities and Exchange Commission (SEC) has in recent years attempted to crack down on insider trading. In 1988 Congress passed a law raising the maximum penalty for illegal insider trading to ten years in prison and criminal fines up to $1 million for an individual and $2.5 million for a company, plus civil fines of treble damages. It also holds firms liable for actions of their employees if the firms knowingly and recklessly fail to detect and prevent insider trading. The SEC has started prosecuting about twenty cases a year—far more than in the past. In 1987–1988 the media dramatized the SEC's prosecution of those guilty of illegal insider trading by publicizing pictures of highly placed members of the financial community being led from their offices in handcuffs.

The Securities and Exchange Commission considers an "insider" anyone who has pertinent information that is not publicly available and that gives the trader an advantage over the public.[13] Thus, secretaries, lawyers, consultants, financial printers, and others who have access to inside information and who might ordinarily be considered outsiders become insiders because of their knowledge—as do all others who are given the pertinent information. Many companies go to extreme lengths to keep takeover and similar plans secret. They use code words for the companies involved, shred memos, and guard against tapped phones and electronic surveillance. Such measures are evidence both that the firms involved believe it is in their best interests to keep their plans secret and that those who act on such information, act on information to which only a privileged few have access.

The SEC argues that insider trading will dampen the public's interest in investing in what people feel is an unfair market, one in which insiders have all the advantages. But the SEC has its critics. They claim that the practice of insider trading is so widespread that the SEC investigations barely scratch the surface and are not worth the money or effort poured into attempts to stop such trading. Furthermore, they claim, insider trading has not discouraged investor interest in the stock market, and hence the SEC's fears are unfounded. Finally, some, pointing out that insider trading is allowed in a number of countries, such as New Zealand, argue that it is not unethical in itself and should not be illegal in the United States.[14] The 1987–1988 insider trading scandals were based on the mistake of making certain kinds of insider trading illegal. There would have been no scandals if the actions of those con-

---

[13] Gary L. Tidwell and Abdul Aziz, "Insider Trading: How Well Do You Understand the Current Status of the Law?" *California Management Review*, 30 (1988), pp. 115-123, illustrates the law through mini-cases; see also C. Edward Fletcher, *The Law of Insider Trading* (Durham, N.C.: Carolina Academy Press, 1991); and Robert C. Rosen, "An Accountant's Guide to the SEC's New Insider Trading Regulations," *CPA Journal*, 63 (February 1993), pp. 67 ff.

[14] Daniel Seligman, "An Economic Defense of Insider Trading," *Fortune*, September 5, 1983, pp. 47-48, argues that insider trading should not be illegal, as do Jonathan R. Macey, *Insider Trading: Economics, Politics, and Policy* (Washington, D.C.: AEI Press, 1991), and Hayne E. Leland, "Insider Trading: Should It Be Prohibited?" *Journal of Political Economy*, 100 (August 1992), pp. 859-887. Arthur M. Louis, "The Unwinnable War on Insider Trading," *Fortune*, July 13, 1981, pp. 72-82, details the difficulties of enforcing the law.

victed, such as Dennis Levine and Ivan Boesky, had not been illegal. These actions should not be illegal because they make the market more efficient.

The arguments mustered in defense of currently illegal insider trading hinge primarily on efficiency, where this means that insider trading moves the price of stocks closer to where they would be if all available information were utilized. The claim is that with all information available—that is, when it becomes available—a stock that is a takeover target will go up a certain amount. That is the actual value of the stock. Hence, the purchase of the stock by people with knowledge of all the facts helps move the stock to that value, and indirectly gives the market information that is actual but not yet publicly available. To this argument are added two others.

The first draws a scenario of three traders in a stock. Trader Agnes for reasons of her own is interested in selling stock Z. Trader Baker, again for reasons of his own, is interested in buying stock Z and buys 1,000 shares at 50. Trader Charlie, who has inside information that the stock is about to be taken over, buys 500,000 shares of stock Z at the same time as Baker, and they both get the same price. According to the view that insider trading is unethical, Charlie is unethical while Baker is not, even though they buy the same stock at the same time for the same price from some anonymous source. We cannot, the argument concludes, consistently hold that the one trade is allowable and the other not.

The second argument claims that by buying stock Z Charlie does no one any harm. If an action is ethically wrong only when and because it does harm, then Charlie does not act unethically. Charlie does not force Agnes to sell any stock, and, by placing a bid for a significant number of shares, will probably raise the price of the stock, thus making the price more advantageous for Agnes than it would otherwise be. Charlie's action thus increases the amount Agnes receives for the stock. In this way the price is more reflective of the real situation than it would otherwise be. Hence, no injury is done to Agnes. As a result of Charlie's bid, the price that Baker pays for the stock might be higher than it would otherwise have been. But we know that the stock is going to go up considerably. Thus, no real harm is done Baker, who is going to make a profit when the stock goes up. Because neither other buyers nor other sellers of the stock, nor those who continue to hold stock, suffer any harm, the action is not unethical and so should not be made illegal.

The arguments are deficient in a number of ways. First, efficiency is not the only important factor in the market or in ethical thinking. Fairness is central to both. Unless traders in the market believe that the market is fair and that all participating in it trade on equal terms, they will not have confidence in it. If you know a game is rigged against you, your incentive to play is certainly diminished. If the system is rigged in favor of certain players, then even if you continue to play, you can certainly prefer to play in a fair game than in the only one available. Hence, the alternative to an unequal, and to that extent unfair, system is a fair system. If the insider makes the market more efficient by trading on privileged information, and if the gain is an increase in information, then all would benefit more and the market would be more efficient if the information, as soon as it is available to the insider, were made public for all to act on. Allowing information to affect the market indirectly instead of directly is accepting second best.

Second, consider the issue of fairness in another way. The market presupposes equality in the transaction between the two contracting parties. Each acts for his or her own reasons. In other markets the rule of *caveat emptor* has given way to either informed consent or other forms of full disclosure of information. Use of insider information in the stock market is in effect a return to the doctrine of *caveat emptor* and hence is unfair, as fairness is judged in other market transactions.

Third, the claim that no one gets hurt ignores the counterclaims of Traders Agnes and Baker that they are in fact harmed by Trader Charlie. Suppose the information held by the insider that a takeover is imminent and that the price of the stock will jump by 10 points in two days were known by the person about to sell. Unless Agnes were forced by extreme circumstances to sell, there is no doubt she would wait two days and reap her assured profit. The fact that Charlie knows of the takeover and Agnes does not is why Agnes would claim that Charlie took unfair advantage of her, even if Agnes received somewhat more than she would have if Charlie had not bought stock in company Z. Charlie is not a lucky speculator; he acts on sure information. Agnes would not feel that Baker had taken advantage of her, assuming that Baker had no knowledge of company Z that was not in principle available to Agnes. Fairness is a component of the total situation, not simply of the price one receives for shares. The situations of Baker and Charlie are different, and hence their actions are different from an ethical point of view, even if the result to Agnes is the same.

Furthermore, Baker would not accept the assertion that he was not hurt because he still made money when the stock went up after the takeover. Surely Baker would be correct in claiming that, although he made money on the stock, he could have bought the stock at a lower price, and so could have made more than he did, if Charlie had not bought Z on inside information. He would thus correctly claim that he, as well as Agnes, had been done an injustice by Charlie.

The mistake of those who attempt to justify insider trading in terms of market efficiency is that, believing in the Myth of Amoral Business, they see the market as an impersonal mechanism, which does not care who gains or loses in its transactions. Winners and losers are beside the point, because the market is simply an efficient means of matching buyers and sellers. Yet even though the stock market acts impersonally, it mediates transactions between people, and transactions between people are properly subject to moral rules. Clearly, those who buy and sell do care who gains and loses. Both parties desire and deserve a fair market.

Finally, those who act on inside information violate their fiduciary obligations to the companies they or their firms represent and may do harm to them thereby. Dennis Levine, who worked for the investment banking firm of Drexel Burnham Lambert, bought stock in firms that he learned were takeover targets. He drove up the stock of target firms that Drexel's clients were interested in acquiring. If we assume that Drexel was guiltless and that its clients were interested in making their initial accumulations at the lowest prices possible, Drexel's reputation for handling sensitive deals was certainly seriously damaged.

Those who engage in illegal insider trading misappropriate—and thus steal—information that they properly have only in their corporate role and that they inappropriately use in their private capacity for personal gain. Even if the actions of insiders moved the stock in which they traded in the direction that those who paid them or their companies wanted the stock to move, that would be beside the point. If an action is unfair to others, the fact that it produces the result one's client wants is no justification. One is not ethically allowed to act unfairly, even if it benefits one's client or firm.

Insider trading is difficult to control. To prove successfully the case against accused insiders is often not easy. Moreover, those who have access to foreign currencies (e.g., a Swiss bank account) can buy stock from abroad with less fear of their activities being detected. Nonetheless, because insiders use for their personal gain knowledge they have only as corporate agents, because the transaction is based on unequal knowledge, and because harm is done to those without the inside knowledge (and sometimes to the insider's firm), the arguments against the justifiability of insider trading are stronger than the justifications thus far given for it.

A closely related issue concerns not insiders but investment advisories. One such advisory service, for instance, run by Joseph Granville, is so influential that it is able to influence the market—at least in the short run. In January 1981, a recommendation by Granville to "sell everything" led to a dramatic drop in the stock market.[15] Granville knew that this would happen, as did those who work for him, who had this information before others. Those who buy Granville's investment service got the information and were able to act on it before the general public. Knowing that once generally known Granville's recommendation would lead to a precipitous drop in the market, they could have sold short, making a profit when the market declined. Is acting on such information comparable to acting on insider information?

In both insider trading cases and the Granville case, one party has information that is not public information. But the cases are different. Insiders trade on knowledge that will be appropriately public and that they know only by virtue of their corporate position. The advice of an investment advisory is based on generally available information. The advice is paid for by subscribers to the advisory, and that advice is therefore proprietary. No one else has a

---

[15] Alexander R. Hammer, "Stocks Decline Sharply as Trading Soars to Record," *New York Times*, January 8, 1981, p. 1; see also Thomas Petzinger, Jr., "A Debate on Ethics: Who Should Benefit by Kaufman's Ideas?," *Wall Street Journal*, August 20, 1982, p. A19.

right to such knowledge, even if having such knowledge can at times help one make a better investment than otherwise. If any advisory were found guilty of trying to manipulate the market, the situation would be different; and any such activity is immoral. There may be cases in which the SEC is uncertain whether manipulation is actually intended. But investment advisories do not have shareholders to protect, as members of a board are required to protect the interests of their shareholders. The supposed knowledge of advisories can be more appropriately characterized as guesses, even if their guesses are sometimes shrewd, and following them leads to financial gains.

In another incident, R. Foster Winans, who wrote the column "Heard on the Street" for *The Wall Street Journal*, used information prior to publication for his own gain. Although he was not guilty of insider trading, he was prosecuted for misappropriating information that belonged to his employer.[16] Although the issues raised by the Granville and Winans cases are in part similar to insider trading, they are not the same should be kept distinct.

Information plays a central role in modern business. Information is vital for the adequate evaluation of business activities. The tension between a corporation's urge for secrecy and the right to know of those affected or involved can strain a corporation's relations with the public. But if a corporation responds to this tension creatively and openly, it can lead to the exercise of more responsibility on the part of a corporation and to greater acceptance of corporations on the part of the general public.

Study Questions

1. In the Boesky–Milken case, did they act unethically? Defend your claim in some detail.
2. What knowledge belongs to a company and how can it be protected? Illustrate your answer by examples.
3. What is property?
4. Distinguish tangible, real, intangible, and intellectual property from one another.
5. Can intellectual property ethically be owned? Explain why or why not.
6. What do copyrights cover and what protection do they offer?
7. What do patents cover and what protection do they offer?
8. What is *reverse engineering*? Is it morally justifiable? Why or why not?
9. What are the purpose and justification of copyrights and patents?

---

[16] Stuart Taylor, Jr., "Justices, 8–0, Back U.S. on Conviction of Wall Street Writer," *New York Times*, November 17, 1987, p. A1; see also Nathaniel C. Nash, "'Insider' Definition in New Law Urged," *New York Times*, November 17, 1987, p. A40; and Pu Liu, Stanley D. Smith, and Azmat A. Syed, "The Impact of the Insider Trading Scandal on the Information Content of the Wall Street Journal's 'Heard on the Street' Column," *Journal of Financial Research*, 15 (Summer 1992), pp. 181–188.

10. Why is the right of a company to knowledge rightly limited to a certain period of time rather than being unlimited?

11. What are *trade secrets?* Give an example of one.

12. What are three factors an employee might consider to determine what company information is appropriately secret?

13. If a product is developed by an employee of a company in its labs, to whom does the knowledge belong? May it be sold by the employee? May a former employee make it available to his new employer?

14. What is industrial espionage?

15. Does it make any difference from an ethical point of view whether intelligence is gathered by one company spying on another or by a government spying on companies from another country?

16. What are some ethically permissible ways of gathering intelligence on a company? What are some ethically impermissible ways? Why are they not permissible?

17. What disclosure is morally required of a corporation to stockholders? about the board of directors? to workers? to government? to the general public? Why is such disclosure appropriate?

18. What is insider information? Can such information morally be used for one's personal benefit? Why or why not?

19. What is *insider trading?* When, if ever, is it unethical? If it is unethical, why is it? If it is not, why is it allowable?

20. What is *misappropriation?* Give an example of misappropriation.

21. Why is the use of insider information in stock market transactions unfair or immoral?

22. ABC Cleaning has produced a safe new product that when sprayed on clothes effectively repels dirt so garments need never be washed or dry cleaned. If it sold the product and the product were widely used, no one would need ABC Cleaning's services. Consequently, ABC Cleaning's management decides not to market the product and sets out to destroy any information about it. Is management ethically justified in doing so?

23. Sally Smith, the president and chief executive officer of X Company is involved in planning the takeover of Company Y. She has a neighbor who is facing financial difficulties. She suggests to the neighbor that the neighbor buy as much Company Y stock as he can afford because its value will go up soon. She does not tell him why it will go up. The neighbor buys the stock. Is the neighbor guilty of unethical insider trading? Why or why not?

13

>─┤◆〉─○─〈◆├─◄

INFORMATION
TECHNOLOGY, ETHICS,
AND BUSINESS

The Apple versus Microsoft Case

Most people would readily agree that stealing is wrong and that the misappropriation of another person's property is stealing. In the area of computer software, however, what constitutes stealing or misappropriation is not always clear. Copyright law seeks to help define the legal parameters of intellectual property and the rights of a person in the intellectual property he or she creates. But copyright law was originally intended to cover the written expression of ideas, and the transfer of some of the concepts to computer software has far from been an exact fit. In 1964 the Copyright Office started treating software as "literary works." Although the 1976 U.S. copyright law did not explicitly mention computer software, the 1980 Amendments did. Nonetheless, the interpretation of the law has proceeded via judicial decisions, and judges in different U.S. districts have handed down judgments that have not always been consistent. The U.S. Supreme Court has not handed down any decisions, and so to some extent there is no binding national interpretation.

One of the unclear areas concerns the so-called look and feel disputes, the most prominent of which is the *Apple versus Microsoft* case.[1]

Apple had produced the Macintosh computer and had developed a distinctive graphical user interface to go with it, including pulldown screens or

---

[1] For details of this case, see *Apple Computer, Inc. v. Microsoft Corporation*, No. C-88-20149-VRW, United States District Court, N. D. California, *Federal Supplement*, 799 (1993), pp. 1006-1047. For a summary and commentary, see "The Ups and Downs of Look and Feel," *Communications of the ACM*, 36, no. 4 (April 1993), pp. 29-35.

windows, windows within windows, and a variety of icons for a variety of different tasks (e.g., a file folder represented a file, a trash can represented discarded files). When Microsoft introduced the now very popular software program Windows, which was written not for Apple computers but for IBM compatible computers that use MS-DOS as the operating system, it included many of the features that were previously available only on Apple computers.

Apple Computer, Inc., sued Microsoft for 189 infringements of its software copyrights. Although U.S. District Judge Vaughn R. Walker of the Ninth Circuit, who heard the case, threw out many of the claimed infringements on a variety of technical grounds, the heart of the controversy lay in Apple's claim to the "look and feel" of its software. Apple maintained that although individual instances of copying might be allowed for various reasons under copyright law, Apple had a right to claim protection for the artistic interpretation it had designed in the look of the computer screen produced by its software. Although, for instance, the general idea of using icons could not be protected by copyright, its distinctive display—its special look—could be protected. The "feel" at issue referred to the use of a string of keystroke sequences that people would employ in using the program, which gave the program a distinctive "feel."

Apple Computer, Inc., clearly wanted to protect its originality and the market appeal that this originality provided. For its part Microsoft wished to make its DOS system more attractive, to offer DOS users some of the advantages previously available only to Apple users, and so gain greater market share. The motives of each are clear. But what belonged to Apple, and did Microsoft inappropriately use what did not belong to it? The crucial question is this: If we consider all of the individual items that Apple claimed Microsoft copied, whether or not protected by copyright, can the *combination* of those in an artistic or creative manner be protected?

Our concern here is not with the technical legal aspects of the case, for those were argued by the respective lawyers and decided by Judge Walker. Our concern, rather, is with what morally belongs to whom in such a controversy. Is there any way to argue that one or the other side was morally right in its claim, even though the copyright laws did or did not grant the disputed property right? Is what is morally correct here decided by law—meaning that without a legal decision there is no right or wrong or that there is no claim to a right unless it is protected by law? On utilitarian grounds, is more good than harm done for software-producing firms, users, and society in general if the look and feel of computer software is protected by copyright? Are there ownership rights to an artistic and creative screen design that should be respected?

The Electronic Privacy at ABC Control Case

The notice of termination would arrive seemingly out of the blue. Suddenly and unexpectedly Barbara Hanley and Jim Sampson, who worked for ABC Control [a fictitious company], would be told that they had been terminated from the firm—Barbara for sending personal e-mail from her company computer and Jim for spending too much time surfing the Web at recreational sites and downloading pornography. Both would be stunned. They had received no warning. They did not know they were in violation of company policy—since none had been promulgated. They did not know they were being monitored. And their productivity and work output had not diminished since they were favorably rated at their last annual evaluation.

"I hate to do this," Sarah Hanson, vice president of Human Resources (HR), argued to Alan Stephens, executive vice president of ABC Control. "Somehow it doesn't seem fair. We've not warned them, and they have been good productive employees up until now."

"I know,"replied Alan. "But when Arthur [Arthur Pesinsky, director of information systems] brought me the reports, I saw no alternative. Clearly, they have abused company resources, and we have to draw the line somewhere. We were monitoring Barbara prior to possible promotion, and Jim happened to be the first one caught by our new Sequel Technology Net Manager software that lets us track our employees' use of the World Wide Web."

"We're not the first ones to do this, you know," he continued. "Employees at Los Alamos National Laboratory have been fired for surfing adult Web sites, Southern California fired an aerospace engineer for spending time on an Internet forum of home repairs, and Electronic Data Systems, among other companies, has fired employees for similar reasons. We have to protect ourselves. The courts have ruled that whatever goes out on e-mail from a company belongs to the company. We have not only the legal right to review whatever is sent, but if there is any criminal activity we also have the obligation to turn over our backup tapes of any e-mail message to the authorities. We don't have a written policy on all of this, but anyone who reads the newspaper knows that e-mail is not private, and all employees with any common sense should know that they shouldn't spend their work time on either private correspondence or nonjob-related Web surfing. Downloading pornography can even open us up to possible suits for sexual harassment for allowing a sexually hostile environment for our other employees."

"Nonetheless," Sarah retorted, "not all companies monitor their employees' e-mail and their use of the Web. They trust them and respect their privacy. If there is an abuse or a complaint or someone is not performing up to expectations, then appropriate action can be taken. But in the absence of any negative complaints, why should we snoop on our employees, even if we're legally allowed to do so? We don't listen in on their phone calls. Why should we monitor their e-mail or Web use?"

"You can't have it both ways, Sarah," Jim replied. "We don't want to block any Web sites. But if we treat our employees as adults and honor their privacy, then they have to take responsibility for their actions and act as they know they should. If they abuse the respect we show them and they are found out, then they should suffer the consequences."

"I'm still not comfortable with summary dismissal. Somehow it doesn't seem fair. And what message will it send to our other employees?"

"It should send a strong and clear message, I would hope. Anyone with any sense will understand that e-mail messages are not private, that surfing the Web for nonwork-related sites is unacceptable, that their illusions—if they had any—of electronic privacy were mistaken, and that they should do the work they are hired to do while on the job. What they do at home is their own business, unless, of course, they access their work computers from home with their modems, instead of getting their own private accounts on AOL or some other service."

"Why couldn't we first give them a warning or a reprimand?" continued Sarah.

"We could," said Alan. "But that would be a very weak message to our other employees. Break the rules you know you should obey and the company will give you a warning. No. We need something with teeth and drama to bring home to everyone how serious the issue is. It's a shame for Barbara and Jim. But they brought this on themselves."

"HR has a responsibility for our employees," Sarah finally said. "Give me a chance to work through a policy on this before sending them their termination letters. There has to be a better way to handle this, to protect the legitimate interests of the company and to respect the privacy of our employees. Give me forty-eight hours to come up with a policy."

"OK," said Alan. "Forty-eight hours."

>-!-+>-●-<+-!-<

What policy do you recommend Sarah go with?

Business and Computers

Businesses have adopted computers in their daily activities, and computers are quickly transforming the way office work is organized, communication takes place, and business is done. The computer revolution has accordingly raised a number of moral issues in business.

Some moral issues deal with computer hardware—for example, with the morality of its production, sale, and abuse. Many of these problems, such as the question of whether it is moral to sell computers to the secret police of an oppressive regime in a foreign country, raise issues that are not peculiar to computers. Computers may help oppressive regimes control a country's people, but so do radios, cars, and guns. Everyone is morally bound not to aid and abet criminals or those engaged in immoral activity. Producers and distributors of computers fall under this general rule, just as all other producers and distributors do. Computer manufacturers make products that are, or might be, sensitive and are covered by special governmental restrictions on selling them to certain foreign countries. But aside from such restrictions, no special moral issues are raised by the sale of computers, nor are any special moral issues raised by the theft of terminals, or willful damage to computer centers. It is immoral to steal computer terminals, just as it is immoral to steal anything else.

The social impact and use of computers raise other moral issues. Issues related to the displacement of workers by computers are partially questions of business ethics, partially questions of social practice. Whenever employers consider the introduction of new equipment or new technology, they should consider the impact of the equipment or technology on their employees. Will the new equipment replace employees, require that they be retrained, or necessitate additional employees? If it will mean laying off employees, then this factor should be carefully considered before the equipment is purchased. In addition, adequate attention should be paid to the terms and conditions under which the employees are to be terminated, giving full consideration to their rights. Once again, however, computers raise no special moral problems in this respect.

There are, however, some areas in which the introduction of the computer into business either raises familiar problems in a somewhat different way or raises new problems. We shall consider four such areas: (1) computer crime; (2) responsibility for computer failure; (3) protection of computer property, records, and software; and (4) privacy of the company, workers, and customers. Three basic concepts emerge in many of the cases in these areas and will require special attention: information, privacy, and property.[2]

Computer Crime

The notion of computer crime has become fairly common. It is simple enough to understand in its gross aspects. We know that it is immoral to steal from others, and whether we do so physically, by stealing cash from a drawer, or electronically, by transferring money into our account from the account of others, makes little difference. We know that harming others is immoral, and whether we produce that harm with a computer or by other means makes little difference, from a moral point of view.

Stealing via computer is immoral, just as is stealing by any other means. But stealing by computer has raised a number of problems for businesses. The computer theft plaguing business is of three types. One is the actual stealing of funds or assets. A second is the stealing of information. A third is the stealing of computer time.[3]

---

[2] A useful collection of articles on ethics and computers dealing with responsibility, privacy, and software as property is Deborah G. Johnson and John W. Snapper (Eds.), *Ethical Issues in the Use of Computers* (Belmont, Calif.: Wadsworth, 1985). See also Deborah G. Johnson, *Computer Ethics*, 2nd ed.(Englewood Cliffs, N.J.: Prentice Hall, 1994); and W. Michael Hoffman and Jennifer Mills Moore (Eds.), *Ethics and the Management of Computer Technology* (Cambridge: Oelgeschlager, Gunn & Hain, Publishers, 1982).

[3] For information on computer crime, see August Bequai, *Technocrimes* (Lexington, Mass.: Lexington Books, 1987); John A. Buckland (Ed.), *Combating Computer Crime: Prevention, Detection, Investigation* (New York: McGraw-Hill, 1992); and Donn B. Parker, *Computer Crime: Criminal Justice Resource Manual*, 2nd ed. (Washington, D.C.: U.S. Department of Justice, National Institute of Justice, Office of Justice Programs, 1989).

Computer Theft of Funds

The stealing of funds or assets by computer has resulted in the loss to business of what is conservatively estimated to be $3 billion annually. The thefts carried out by computer are of many kinds. If the theft is by an outsider, it requires breaking into the firm's computer system. If it is by an insider, it requires the surreptitious introduction of appropriate commands into the firm's computer system.

The incidence of such crimes is rising. Yet many firms, banks included, are reluctant to report computer crimes and, if they find the culprit, are loath to prosecute. They do not wish to publicize the fact that their computer system has been compromised and is not entirely secure; this would create doubts about the firm, which might result in losing customers or depositors. So the firms have either written off the losses or tried to collect the amount of the loss from insurance companies. It is not uncommon for an employee who is found guilty of computer theft to be made to restore whatever money he or she still has, to be dismissed, and then to be let go, unprosecuted. The thief would be fired, but soon hired by another firm anxious to use his or her computer skills. Many are not caught. Insurance companies have begun refusing to pay unless the guilty party, if found, is prosecuted. And some states have passed, or are considering, laws that make it illegal not to report computer crimes. But reporting them and pressing charges are two different matters. Furthermore, the media do not report such crimes, even though they report bank robberies.

Those reluctant to prosecute, in addition to the reasons just stated, sometimes argue that there *is* a difference between computer crimes and other crimes—a difference that makes them no less crimes, but that, insofar as punishment is concerned, changes the punishment that is appropriate. Consider the difference between the James gang robbing a bank and a computer operator stealing the same amount of money from a bank by setting up a special account into which he or she siphons off any fractional part of a cent in the daily interest due to each account. That fractional part of a cent is not usually credited to the depositors; it remains with the bank. The thief thus steals from the bank what may only dubiously belong to the bank. But there is no face-to-face confrontation. There is no overt violence. There are no threats made, no guns fired, no physical harm either threatened or done to people. In crime by computer, there is a physical distance—the yards or miles of space between the computer operator and whatever is being manipulated; a psychic distance, because the operator sees no human being face to face, perhaps trembling in fear. The operator may imagine that he or she is faced with impersonal electronic and bookkeeping challenges—a game—rather than with human beings who may be harmed. Crimes by computer are intellectual crimes rather than crimes of force. They require work and imagination of an intellectual sort, which has traditionally inspired respect. They are crimes committed by white-collar workers—and white-collar crime has always been treated as less serious, as deserving of less severe punishment (if any punishment at all) than physical, violent crime.

Although this states the view both of many culprits and of many employers, it carries little moral weight. White-collar crime is still crime, even if it is not violent. The fact that banks and other firms do not wish to prosecute despite losses is an indication that perhaps they are not entirely blameless. They have adopted a technology that they cannot completely control and security measures that fall short of what they wish the public to believe or know. They can be morally faulted on both counts. Reluctance to prosecute simply compounds the offense, making more likely further losses because of computer theft. If the worst that can happen to the apprehended thief is that he or she must return the stolen money, the deterrent to computer crime is almost nonexistent.

The incidence of computer crime, therefore, raises special problems for management.

Unauthorized Computer Entry

In addition to money, one can steal, by computer, a company's trade secrets, its corporate data, and anything else the firm stores or files in its computer. Corporate espionage is easier by computer theft than before the widespread introduction of computers; it is more likely to occur and is on the rise. Such theft once again raises no special problems. It is clearly immoral. But the vulnerability of computers to outside intrusion requires at least some brief discussion.

In the present stage of computer development, we have not even developed rules of computer etiquette, much less of computer ethics. Over the years locksmiths have guarded their art with great care. Only a select few are taught how to pick locks and gain entry to areas protected by locks. The same is not true of computers and computer locks. It is illegal to break into another's home or office; there is no question about the immorality of the practice. Is it immoral—or illegal—to break into another's computer file? The law is not always clear, nor are the moral intuitions of many people, including those in the business world.

Some university computer instructors encourage their students in computer courses to try to break into the university's secured computer operations. Some seem to condone attempts to break into other computer networks and systems as well, to compromise them. This is done for fun, or as a means of testing the students' skill, developing their proficiency, or uncovering weaknesses that can be remedied to make the systems or networks secure. Other universities frown on any such attempt to enter files or systems to which one is not given direct access. Is surreptitious entry, even when not illegal, immoral? Is such entry a violation of privacy or a violation of property? Is it legitimate to "look around," providing there is no change made in data or commands, and no copying? What are the proper limits to protection of knowledge, data, or information? Our intuitions are clear about entry into homes and offices. Is entry into someone's computer system or file comparable? If not, why not?

It is not surprising that our intuitions differ on a number of questions relating to computers in business. Because the questions are new, we have not had the time to develop our moral intuitions in this area. Intuitions concerning the morality of murder, theft, and perjury are the result of a great deal of social thought, practice, and experience that have been distilled into maxims or principles that are accepted by society and passed onto children as the accepted moral norms to follow. We have not yet reached consensus on the morality of many aspects of computer use.

In August 1983, one or more young men using a home computer broke into the computerized radiation-therapy records of cancer patients at Memorial Sloan Kettering Cancer Center in Manhattan. This was not the first such entry, and the hospital had left messages in the computer asking the culprits to stop. There have been reports of similar entries at the nuclear weapons laboratory at Los Alamos.

The boys who broke into Sloan Kettering changed the master program so that anyone entering the system would reveal his or her password. Hospital officials asked the intruders via the computer to call them so they could determine whether the intruders had changed any records that would endanger the patients. A boy phoned and apologized but refused to say how he had broken into the system. The hospital offered him free access to its computer if he would stop his break-ins. But he did not need it. Twenty other illegal entries were recorded, some of which gave false leads to the culprit's identity.

Was the intrusion morally wrong? After all, what harm was done? If the intruder simply exercised his skill in entering, and did not change any records, what is wrong with that? The reply is that there are at least three things wrong with it. First, it involves entry into another person's file, which is an invasion of property. One of the senses of property involves the right to exclusive use. Entering another's file is a violation of that right. The intruder might claim that no harm was done by entry—that is, that no changes were made in any records. But how is one to be sure of that? The fact that someone who is unauthorized enters a file or system means that the owner of that system cannot be sure that no changes were made. Changes made in computer records can be made so as to leave no trace. Even if there were backup records, one could only be sure that no change had been made in a record by checking the record with the backup—a costly and time-consuming procedure. Moreover, which records should be checked, and how often? What of the programs themselves? Have they been altered? Has a virus or a logic bomb—a command programmed to be activated at a certain date and time, or when certain entries are made—been planted? Unauthorized entry causes all these concerns, costs, and damage. This is the first basis for claiming that unauthorized access is immoral. The second is the potential violation of privacy. Patient-doctor confidentiality is a clearly recognized principle. Hospital records are privileged information, access to which is allowed by morality and law only to certain people. The same is true of the records of a business. To intrude into these records is at least a violation of privacy. Once again, damage is done, whether one actually looks or not, for once it is known that someone has gained illegitimate entry, no one knows what has been seen and what has not. This undermines the confidentiality of the records and of the process, and so of the doctor-patient or employee-employer relation. Third, the system is itself compromised. The Sloan Kettering computer system was part of Telenet, a large computer network. If the boys were able to break into part of that system, then there is worry that they can break into other parts. Hence, harm is done not only to Sloan Kettering but also to the other sixty subscribers to the system and to its owners and operators.

There is a counter argument to this line of reasoning. It claims that if nothing is changed by a hacker, and the system is not secure, by violating it the operators of the system are given an inducement to build in more safeguards against those intruders who might do damage. In the Sloan Kettering instance, this was not a motivation for the break-in, because the perpetrator did not reveal how he managed to violate the system. But even if he had, the argument in defense of hackers is defective. Computer hacking is like using a plastic credit card to open an office door so that the owner will put a better lock on it. The usual assumption is not that we can enter wherever we are able to penetrate, but that we are not allowed to penetrate except where authorized. The latter principle is the one that we follow in the other areas of our lives. The principle that more good will be done by penetrating, wherever we can do so electronically, does not hold up under scrutiny. If teachers wish to teach their students how to safeguard systems, and if they wish them to have practice breaking codes, they should set up the codes to be broken. We do not teach students of locksmithing how to pick locks by telling them to see how many locks they can pick, or how many banks they can successfully enter simply to "look around."

The possibility of surreptitious computer entry and the safeguarding of computer systems and the data they contain raise special problems for corporate managers.

Theft of Computer Time

What of stealing computer time? This can be done either internally or externally. Surreptitious entry into a system does not mean that automatically one has access to private files. One might simply break into a system in order to use the computer for one's own purposes. The fact that the entry is surreptitious is enough to make the act morally suspect. Use of a computer by an unauthorized user either steals time, which is usually sold, or involves unauthorized use. There is no general rule that allows someone, for instance, to use another person's typewriter when the typewriter is not in use by the owner. Simply because one can gain access without physical trespass does not change the morality of the act. But the morality of use of computer time by a firm's employees who have authorized access is less clear. May they use the computer for their personal use on their own time if the computer is not in use?

The firm pays the same amount for the computer whether or not it is in use. The employee has authorized access and does no harm to any company records or files. Why is using a computer not like using a blackboard, which one erases when one is finished? Do we really believe it is immoral to use a blackboard in an office after hours, providing one is allowed to be in the office after hours? Is use of a computer any different?

There is no consensus on the use of computer time by employees when a computer is idle. IBM does not allow any personal use of its computers. General Electric allows employees to use the computer for personal purposes during their own time, when the computer is not in use; Equitable Life encourages employees to use its mainframe from their home terminals and allows family use as well. In such a situation it is impossible to say that one should not use a company's computer for one's personal use. One must say that one can use a computer to the extent that the owner allows. Because company policies differ, it is in the best interest of companies and employees for each company to determine its policy on the private use of the company's computer, and to notify its employees of the policy. Without a policy, numerous conflicts can arise and have arisen.

Who, for instance, owns the job-related results that an employee develops on his own time, though with the allowed use of the company's terminal? If the terminal was used without permission, then the employee's claim of individual proprietorship could be challenged. But with company permission the case becomes more difficult. This situation is the one that obtains at many universities as well as in businesses. Stanford, Cal Tech, MIT, and Yale are all involved in trying to set policies on intellectual property. Stephen Wolfram, when at Cal Tech, developed a program to manipulate complicated algebraic expressions, and it turned out to have commercial applications. Cal Tech felt it had a right to some of the royalties Wolfram receives, because the program was developed while he was on the staff, using Cal Tech's materials. Yet Cal Tech does not claim the royalties of those who write books while on the staff, even if they do so on the computer. If Wolfram had quit his job and taken none of his data with him, then reproduced the program on his own computer, would the program have been his, or would it still have been partly owned by the university?

The solution found by many universities and companies is to enter into signed agreements, stating what the rules of computer use are, who gets rights to what, and how royalties are divided, if there are any.

Although the fact that computer systems are so vulnerable raises special problems for business, most companies have not yet adequately considered them.

Computers and Corporate Responsibility

We have already seen that corporations can be held morally responsible for their actions that affect others. Because ultimately the corporation acts only through human individuals who act for it, the individuals are morally responsible for what the corporation does. They must assume the responsibility for actions attributable to the corporation, if it is assumed at all. The same is true with respect to computers. Computers, no matter how sophisticated, are simply machines. They are incapable of assuming responsibility, and responsibility cannot be correctly ascribed to them. Anything they do can be traced back to human beings, who are ultimately responsible.

Because human beings are the ones who must accept moral responsibility, no one can legitimately blame a computer, in a moral sense, for anything. The computer does what it is programmed to do. If it is poorly constructed, it may not do what one expects it will do; if a program is defective, it will not give the anticipated results; and if the data fed into it are faulty it cannot be expected to correct them. Hence, whatever mistakes the computer makes are the fault of human beings, and whatever harm is done to human beings by computers is the fault of human beings. Computers have become a means for human beings to attempt to avoid responsibility. We commonly hear the excuse given that the computer malfunctioned or that the mistake is a computer error. Mistakes, however, are human mistakes, not computer mistakes, and responsibility for mistakes rests with human beings, not with computers.

The development of computers, which have many different aspects, raises the question of human moral responsibility—and in law, of liability—in some new ways. How much responsibility does a programmer have for checking a program before it is sold or marketed? Programmers usually work for software companies and the programs they write are "work for hire." Legally their employers both own the programs and are liable for them. If the program is defective, or if it does not do, under some unusual conditions, what the company purchasing or ordering it thought it would do, who is responsible for harm caused employees or customers? How much responsibility and liability appropriately fall on the programmer, how much on the software company, how much on the using company? If a system is unable to handle a payroll properly, is it the fault of the programmer, of the engineers who overload the computer, or of those who are in charge of the overall operation? Assigning responsibility may sometimes be difficult, but the fault can always be placed at the feet or on the shoulders of human beings. And if they perform their actions in their official capacity, the results of their actions are attributable to the company for which they work. If a company wishes to operate morally, it will accept the responsibility for attempting to foresee and prevent any harm through the use of its computers, and it will also make good any harm it does through computer use or failure.

Just as human beings are morally responsible for the harm done other human beings by computers or through their use, so human beings are responsible for any use to which computers are put. Computers, like other areas of modern technology, are not good or bad in themselves. They can be used to benefit or to harm human beings and whether they are used to benefit or harm is up to human beings.

The Year 2000 Problem (Y2K) is a classic case for raising the question of responsibility in programming. Early programmers in the 1960s and 1970s devised a variety of means to save computer memory space, which was extremely limited and so precious. By representing a year by its last two digits and omitting the "19" as understood, programmers were able to save memory space and so save money. They assumed that their programs would be superseded by the year 2000 and so did not anticipate any difficulties. But the practice continued into the 1980s and 1990s when memory space was readily available in order to ensure compatibility with older parts of a program that were still in use. Unless changes were made in computers, chips, and other devices containing dates, computers and computer-operated machines (such as elevators) could stop or malfunction when the year 2000 arrived because they would misinterpret "00" as being the year 1900.

We can raise the question of the point at which it was the responsibility of programmers to foresee the coming change of century and to program accordingly. Mainframe computers have very complicated code running millions of lines. The cost of checking all that code was very expensive. When should information system managers have informed their companies of the need to spend the millions of dollars it would take to fix the problem, and when should managers have spent those millions? Many companies waited until the last few years to take any action. In cases of resulting computer failure is the original programmer responsible, the firm for which he or she worked, or the end user? Companies adversely affected have sought remedy from the firm that supplied them with the program. Customers seek remedy from the company that caused them harm or inconvenience. The chain of responsibility is a long one and the courts are left to sort out the myriad claims.

Companies that sell commercial programs, such as word processing or spread sheet programs, to individual customers typically include an agreement. The agreement specifies the conditions under which the product is sold, and if one breaks the shrink wrap or seal, one implicitly accepts the agreement. The purchaser buys a license to use the program, usually on one or at most on two machines, and the purchaser implicitly agrees to this restriction. The agreement usually contains a stipulation that the provider is not responsible for any consequent damages the user may suffer by using the program, and that the provider is liable only for replacing a defective disk. The agreement is, of course, a one-sided one and is not the result of negotiation. Is such an agreement a fair one, or is it in fact a forced agreement, since all programs carry similar terms? If one wishes to use a word processing program, the terms are set out on a take it or leave it basis. The alternative is use a typewriter or write by hand or create one's own word processing program.

Some software providers were selling newly written programs as late as 1998 that were not year 2000 compliant. They claimed that this was justifiable because by the year 2000 they would have an upgraded version that the user could purchase. Since they did not have to mention whether or not the programs were year 2000 compliant, they broke no law. They claim that the agreement purchasers accepted by opening their product protects them from any claims made by the purchaser. Purchasers who assumed that any product purchased in 1998 would be useable in 2000 and beyond were mistaken. Clearly, however, such software providers took advantage of their customers and ethically had the obligation to make their software year 2000 compliant before selling it. The issue of responsibility for software, however, is a slowly evolving one. Ethical intuitions vary because the medium is still relatively new and changes so rapidly. Nonetheless, ordinary notions of responsibility and liability for harm are applicable.

Firms that utilize computers are responsible for safeguarding them from misuse. Banks, for instance, take great precautions with the physical security of their vaults. But billions of dollars are sent electronically across the country every day, with much less security. Many firms do not know for certain whether their computerized networks and systems are secure, not only from those seeking illegal entry but also from those wishing to sabotage the systems physically. The firms nevertheless have responsibility for safeguarding their funds.

As we move from communicating with mainframes by telephones and terminals to communicating by radio waves, problems will increase. It will be more difficult to safeguard transmitted data from interception because the legal status of data so transmitted is not protected by law, as are data transmitted by telephone lines or computer linkages. There are laws against wiretapping, but there are no laws against picking up radio waves. Are data in the air, in the form of radio waves, something that one can claim one owns? Or is air use free to all? When someone has a conversation with someone else and they are overheard, no one steals their property. If someone purposely listens when others speak in a low voice he or she may be invading the speakers' privacy, but simply overhearing does not.

Listening to radio messages or CB chatter violates no one's rights, and senders assume others may be listening. Why is sending business information between computers by radio waves different? Many such messages are scrambled or coded; but is intercepting them wrong? Is it either a violation of privacy or of property? To some extent, what constitutes property is a social matter, and a social decision is required to determine what is legitimate and what is not. As a society we have not yet decided how to treat the contents of radio messages and the data they may carry. Until we do, the morality of various practices cannot be definitively determined.

Technology makes possible great speed in transmitting messages. But unless those businesses that use computer networks consider the possibility of theft and interception and take adequate measures against them, they fail in part of their responsibility. How can managers guarantee shareholders that funds sent electronically are secure if managers do not know that they are in fact secure? Consideration of this aspect of computer use puts a burden on management, which managers often are not technically competent to handle.

But ignorance is not an excusing condition here because the responsibility for such security includes the obligation to determine possible breaches. The obligation to protect a firm's funds falls on managers, and they cannot shift this responsibility to computer departments. Managers will undoubtedly have to work with and rely on computer specialists, but the managers retain ultimate responsibility. How to adequately fulfill this responsibility remains an unsolved problem for many managers.

As we search for legal means of protection, and applicable moral norms, we, as a society, must look at the implications of computers for our ordinary definitions of property and privacy—both of which are being stretched beyond their ordinary meaning.

Property: Information and Software

With respect to computers, we can raise questions of property rights regarding programs, data, and, as we have already seen, computer time. Does a program developed by an employee belong to the employee or to the employer? Does the algorithm used to solve a problem constitute general knowledge or proprietary knowledge? Does reproducing a program in a different computer language constitute new knowledge, or should it be compared to translating an article from one natural language to another? Are computer languages properly proprietary? What constitutes intellectual property must be determined before we can make valid judgments about who, if anyone, properly owns such property, under what conditions, and for how long. Property interests and claims of privacy often overlap in this area, and both can clash with claims of the "right to know." Some of these clashes are being raised in the courts. Yet the issues are not only legal but also moral. We shall first look at data and information as property; next, at the protection of computer software; and then at some cases involving the ownership of programs by employers and employees.

Data and Information

One difficulty with many discussions of computer cases is that the term *information* is used all-inclusively. People speak generally of "information systems" and of "processing information." But to get clarity in many cases, we should distinguish facts, data, knowledge, and understanding. Another difficulty is that we use the word *program* to cover a great variety of different things, all of which have in common the fact that they are in some sense the product of the incorporation of a sequence of commands, and these commands will result in the electronic machine, which we call a computer, performing certain operations. Similarly, we use the word *computer* to refer to a wide variety of machines and parts of machines, ranging from silicon chips to parts of automobiles, to personal computers, to mainframes. Just as Eskimos have many different words to describe kinds of snow, so we can use a variety of different words to characterize the different kinds of information, computers, and programs.

Let us, then, start by defining some terms. By *fact* we shall mean a statement of the way the world is. The way of the world is independent of our knowledge of it. Furthermore, the individual appropriation of facts does not deprive anyone else of them. Facts, knowledge, and information are all infinitely shareable. We can all know the date of the discovery of America, or that five times five equals twenty-five. This knowledge on the part of one person does not prevent its being known by others, and no harm is done the first person if someone learns from him—at least no harm is done *qua* knowledge. But the discovery of some facts, as well as the collecting and storing of facts, often involves time and expense, and this provides a basis for claims to some facts as proprietary, at least for a short period of time.

Knowledge can be of facts, and in part knowledge consists of facts as known. *Understanding* consists of knowledge that is integrated in some unified way and evaluated. The word *information* is sometimes used to include data, facts, and knowledge, as when we speak of information systems. But though information systems might include knowledge in the sense of interpreted facts informed by theories, systems strictly speaking do not know. They simply contain symbols that can be interpreted by those who can know, just as books might contain written words that when read by others transfer knowledge to the readers.

What computer systems can be properly said to contain and manipulate are *data*. What is entered into a computer are *data*. The entered data can represent either words, letters, or numbers, and so the data can represent facts in coded fashion. So far as computers have developed, they do not know anything in the sense that humans do, nor do they understand anything. But computers can handle data and manipulate them with great speed. Data may represent falsehood as well as facts, and the two should not be confused.

Although facts available to all cannot be owned, data representing facts can be owned. Data entered into a computer can be owned, at least in some of the senses of ownership. Suppose we enter into a computer the distance between one hundred major American cities and a table of one hundred square roots. The distance between cities is a fact of the world, given certain conventions. The distance between cities has been measured and is available; it is knowledge that no one owns. The fact that New York and Boston are 190 air miles apart does not and cannot belong to anyone. The square root of a number also cannot belong to anyone. This is not a fact about the world but a mathematical fact—which, given most theories of knowledge, is a fact about numbers and mathematical operations. The square root of four is two. No one can own that. If no one can own the individual facts, can anyone own the collection of one hundred distances and one hundred square roots? The answer is again no. The combination can no more be owned than the individual facts. But the facts can be entered as data into a computer. The facts cannot be owned, but the data can be owned, for the data entered into the computer belong to whoever owns the computer and entered the data into it. In saying that the owner of the computer owns the data, all we mean is that he owns the computer and whatever is put into it. They are his in some of the important senses of ownership. Data cannot be possessed as objects can, and hence data cannot be owned in this way, even though printouts of data can be owned in this way, as can tapes and floppy disks. But data can be owned in the sense that the owner has the right to exclusive use of the data as put into the computer. The same facts can be stored as data in other computers. The data in each of the computers may be similar, as tokens of the same type. But each owner has the exclusive right to the use of the data in his computer. If he uses the data to produce something else, that product in turn also belongs to him. Because the data are his property, he has the exclusive right to manage the data, the right to the income from the use of the data, the right to replace or erase them, the right to keep them indefinitely, and the right to transfer them to other computers. No one other than the owner, therefore, has the right to erase or tamper with these data, nor to copy them without permission, because copying them, although that does not violate the original owner's use (because the data will still be in his file), does violate his *exclusive* use.

If the data in a person's computer are his and he has exclusive right to their use, then it makes no difference what the data are or represent. The data are his. But part of the notion of property also involves liability for its use. One cannot use one's property in any way one wishes. If, for instance, one owns a gun, one cannot legitimately use it to harm or threaten harm to others. The same is true of data. Someone's owning data does not give him the right to use them any way he wants. But providing he harms no one and threatens no harm, then the data are his to use as he wishes.

We shall use these definitions and distinctions to help solve a number of cases and answer a number of questions later in this chapter.

The Protection of Computer Software

If we have a problem we wish to solve by a computer, we can start by thinking through the steps necessary to solve it. This logical process might be first diagramed in a flowchart. In some cases an algorithm—a logical statement (or formula) of how to solve a problem—is involved. This is then translated into a high-level computer language, such as BASIC or Java. The result is a program that will direct a machine either to perform certain actions or to manipulate special data entered into it in certain ways. Such a program is called a *source code*. This in turn is translated by a compiler or assembler into an object code, in machine language of ones and zeros, which controls the passage of electrical impulses.

Japan has decided to protect both computer software and hardware through the use of patents. The United States initially decided to cover software with copyrights and hardware with patents, but in recent years some software has been patented. Neither patents nor copyrights were originally developed with computers in mind, and numerous difficulties have arisen. The line between software (programs used to run computers) and computer hardware (the physical computer) is becoming less and less clear, as is the line between physical and intellectual property. Some programs are of the "read-only" variety, and these may simply control a certain activity—for instance, the working of part of an automobile engine. Such a program is not read, in the usual sense, by a human being. It may be on a silicon chip. It is simply instructions to a machine.

Copyrights were originally intended to protect the written word. They were extended to cover works of art, films, and records. And, as we have seen, they have been further extended to cover some computer programs. To be eligible for copyright in the United States, an item must be intelligible to human beings. The courts originally decided that because a source code is understandable by human beings, it can be covered by copyright, but they were reluctant to grant copyrights to object codes—which are written in machine language consisting of ones and zeros, and which are probably not intelligible to human beings.[4] Yet the object code is simply a translation of the source code, and courts have granted protection to object codes as well. Exactly what can and cannot be copyrighted is being decided by the courts on a case-by-case basis. But the issues involving the protection of software raise moral as well as legal questions.

Even when a program that was not readable in any ordinary sense by human beings could not be copyrighted, we could still ask to whom it belonged. If we buy a car with a silicon chip that governs the injection of fuel, we own the chip as well as the other parts of the car. We have the right to the exclusive use of the chip as part of the car, in the sense that no one has the right to take it. But do we thereby have the right to the program embedded in the chip? Is it ours to duplicate as we wish—whether we are private individuals or competing car manufacturers?

If the data and the programs—insofar as they are considered data—are the property of the owner of the computer, then clearly a program that one generates for one's own use belongs to oneself and cannot morally be copied, any more than it can be erased by another person without permission. This does not answer the question of whether a program that is sold can be copied. But to answer that, we need to know the background conditions governing sales and the rights to reproduce what one has. Here law is pertinent, because it sets the public rules of commerce, which are necessary in order to determine the morality of transactions made possible by them. This is true both within and outside of firms, as we shall see.

Attempting to solve moral issues related to computers is often complicated by the lack of any established and agreed-upon practices. Many com-

---

[4] For details of the evolution of protection for the object code through court decisions, see Tobey B. Marzouk, *Protecting Your Proprietary Rights in the Computer and High Technology Industries* (Washington, D.C.: Computer Society Press, 1988), pp. 21-23.

puter programmers for example, feel no proprietary claim to the programs they write; they trade them with others or allow others to copy them freely. Others claim proprietary rights even if they do not copyright their programs. Therefore, the question of how to handle programs is often not clear. Should one treat all programs as if they are the property of others, or should one treat them all as common property, unless they are copyrighted?

Another difficulty is knowing exactly when enough changes are made in a program to make it a new program. If Company *A* commissions a computer service to write a program to handle its payroll, can the computer service, after completing the job, simply modify the program and sell it to Company *B*, to handle its payroll? Or does the original program belong entirely to the original purchaser? Must the computer service start from scratch with each program? If Company *A* paid for all the time involved in producing the first program, is it fair for Company *B* to pay considerably less because the program had been basically developed, and paid for, by Company *A*? Is it fair for the computer service to charge both companies the same amount, even though it spent a great deal of time—for which it was paid—in the first case, and considerably less time in the second case?

The logical process or algorithm constitutes the heart of a program. Because mathematical equations and logical processes cannot be copyrighted, courts originally ruled that computer algorithms could not be copyrighted. But then the protection one gets for one's program is protection for the particular string of commands one writes to implement the algorithm. In a very complicated program involving thousands of steps, this may be enough. But frequently the difficult task is not writing the steps but solving the logical problem. Why is it fair for someone to take that algorithm and write a program based on it, when simply translating a program from one high-level computer language to another is considered a violation of copyright? There is fertile ground for many disputes over whether a program is a slightly changed copy of a copyrighted program or an original program based on the same algorithm as another program. Similarly, when is a computer algorithm sufficiently changed to become a different algorithm? There is usually more than one way to solve a programming problem and to write a program that has a certain outcome. These issues are perplexing to computer and software manufacturers, as well as to businesses and individual users.

Program Property Rights between Employer and Employee

Let us now consider the following set of cases.

Case A: Joan Cullen works for a large firm, Company Z, in the marketing department and does most of her work on computers. During several weekends and evenings, working on her home personal computer, she writes a program that will facilitate her work and make her more efficient. She transfers the program to the office computer and uses it daily. After several months she gets an offer from another firm. When she leaves Company Z, she takes her program with her and erases it from Company Z's computer.

Case B: This is the same as Case A, except that Joan develops the program, on her own time, using Company Z's computer during weekends and evenings. Her company allows her access to the computer during these times.

Case C: This is the same as Case B, except that Joan leaves the program in Company Z's computer and takes only a copy of the program with her when she leaves.

Case D: This is the same as Case B, except that Joan takes neither the program nor a copy with her when she leaves. She rewrites the program when she goes to her new job.

Case E: This is the same as Case D, except that Joan develops the program on company time.

Case F: This is the same as Case B, except that Joan does not write her own program. Instead, she modifies a copyrighted program that Company Z has purchased from a commercial supplier of software. When she leaves, she takes her modified program with her, leaving behind the original.

Case A poses no serious moral problem. Joan takes a program that she developed on her own time, using her own computer. The fact that she used it on the job was of benefit to her employer. But she is the only one who used it. Although it makes her more efficient, and its use by her replacement might make that person more efficient, she does not owe the program to the firm. It is hers, and she can rightly take it with her.

In Case B, Joan writes the program on her own time, but with the computer facilities of her employer. Who owns the program?

To answer this question, consider Cases D and C first. In Case D, Joan rewrites the program at her new job. She does not take the program from Company Z. Does she take anything from Company Z that belongs to it? No; she leaves the program with the company. The program in her head does not belong to the company, even though she developed it while working for the company, for it was not a program she was paid to develop or told to develop, or one that she produced on company time. Nor was it a trade secret of the company's. If it had been a trade secret, then she could not legitimately reproduce it for a competitor. But her experience is her own, including in this case the knowledge of the program she developed. She can legitimately rewrite the program to help her in her work for her new employer.

In Case C, Joan takes a copy but leaves the original program. As a result, the employer does not have exclusive use of the program. But because Joan developed the program on her own time, what could be the basis for a claim to exclusive use by the company? Because Company Z allowed employees to use its computer, it has no claim to exclusive use of the products they develop. Yet because the program was written and stored in the company's computer, and since it was job-related, is there not some weight to the claim that because the company's facilities were used, the company has some right to the product? Because there may be a dispute here, we can see how helpful it would be if agreements were reached about ownership of programs before disputes arose.

How much of the company's resources were actually involved in producing the program? If the proportion of assets of the company and of the employee's time are reasonably matched, then the claim of the company is potentially greater. If, in monetary terms, the amount of computer time is very small, the claim of the programmer is much greater. Because the employer did not prohibit Joan's use of the computer, and because she wrote the program on her own time, Company Z cannot support the claim that the program belongs exclusively to the company. Joan may therefore take a copy of it. Nor would it be wise for the company to establish a contrary policy. Consider adopting the principle that no programmer should ever make any program to improve his or her own work unless he or she is willing to sign it over to the company. What would the results be? The programmer's incentive to produce such a program on his or her own time would be killed. The effect on the company would be to get poorer work performance from its workers. Hence, the overall effects of adopting that principle are neither in the interest of companies nor in the interest of employees. The only possible reason for adopting the principle is to keep one's competition from getting the use of programs. But what one loses by losing an employee to the competition, one gains in getting new employees from other companies. Thus, that principle, if adopted, would clearly produce less good for all concerned than would its opposite.

Providing, therefore, that the cost of getting the copy is minimal, taking a copy is morally permissible. To assume that the cost is minimal and that Joan gets the program while still an employee of the company are small enough assumptions to raise no serious moral problems. If while an employee of Company Z Joan uses a few sheets of company paper to write notes of ideas she does not wish to forget when she gets to her new job, she does not act immorally. In such an instance, paper is considered by most companies to be an expendable item, and such use should not be confused with an employee's routinely taking paper and other items home in any quantity, for his or her strictly personal use. For someone who works with computer programs, a printout or a floppy disk is comparable to other items of an expendable kind. The main issue in the case is not the use of expendable supplies but the copying of the program. And on that point, because exclusive use by the company cannot be justified without a prior policy to that effect, Joan's copying her program is legitimate.

A related issue is whether Joan owes Company Z anything in addition to leaving the program in the computer. No one will know it is there unless Joan tells them. If the program appears by name on a list of programs in the computer, no one will know what it is or does. Unless Joan lets Company Z know that the program is in the computer, indicates what it is for, and provides documentation about its use, the company gains nothing. But if Joan is required to provide documentation—which can be an onerous job—this might well be a disincentive to producing the program in the first place. Once again, clear guidelines would help. In their absence, Joan has no obligation to provide the documentation.

In Case C, she may take the program; may she also take it in Case B? The difference in the two cases is that in Case C she leaves a copy of the program, but in Case B she does not. Is she required to leave a copy of the program? If it is correct that Joan does not have to leave documentation, even if she leaves the program, there is little reason to stop her from taking the program out of the computer entirely. Not only does it do no good without documentation, but also its presence might actually cause confusion, or at least take up storage space.

Joan might have asked her superior whether the company wanted her to leave the program, or she might have asked permission to take a copy of the program. If taking the program represented any significant amount of expense, permission would be required. But if her superior did not even know she had developed and used the program, asking permission is more than is required. Once Joan asks, moreover, she implies that her superior has the right to refuse permission. If she does ask, then she is required to abide by her superior's decision.

We might ask whether a company should adopt one of these policies: Whatever employees produce on the company's computer, on their own time, (1) belongs to the employee, (2) belongs entirely to the company, or (3) belongs in part to the company. A company can morally choose any of the three alternatives. But it should choose one and so inform its employees. In the absence of any stated policy, it is not implausible to assume that what one produces on one's own time is one's own. Some companies, as we noted earlier, even allow families to use the company's mainframe for personal computing.

Case E is more difficult. In this case Joan wrote the program on company time. It is not only job-related but can legitimately be considered as part of her job. The program therefore belongs to Company Z. When she goes to her new job and re-creates the program, does this amount to copying a program (and so is morally prohibited) or is it using an algorithm (and so morally permitted)? For her to rewrite the program, she would most likely remember the algorithm rather than recall all the specific commands that constitute the program. Mathematical algorithms cannot be copyrighted or patented, but computer algorithms can now be copyrighted. It not likely that either the algorithm or the program Joan wrote was copyrighted. Still, it belongs to her employer. Can the same be said of the algorithm? The moral basis for such a claim is weak. One may not take a program directly, nor may one directly reproduce for a competitor the identical program. The distinction between data and the ideas represented by the data here becomes crucial. The exception would be if the algorithm could be defended as a trade secret. But we have discussed the rules for trade secrets in Chapter 11, and this case does not fall under them.

Case F raises another set of issues. In this case, the program belongs neither to Joan nor to her employer. What one buys when purchasing a program is the program's use. Company Z cannot copy the program to sell or give it to another user—assuming the program is covered by a copyright. When Joan changes the program, she adds something to it. Does she thereby make it her program? How much change must be made before a program is no longer the original program is a difficult issue, as we have noted. But if we assume that the basic program is one of considerable complexity, and Joan modifies it only somewhat, then the basic program is not hers, even though the final program she works with is not identical to the original. Hence, she does not have the right to take either the program or a copy with her. But she may remember how to alter the program and use that knowledge to alter the same, or a similar, program at her new place of employment.

These examples demonstrate a few of the complexities involved in program use. The wise firm will establish guidelines and ground rules governing computer use and programs before problems arise.

Computers and Privacy

Privacy is a relative term. Notions of privacy vary greatly from society to society. Moreover the term is used to cover a great variety of actions and cases. Two kinds of privacy have special relevance with respect to computers, however, which we can call information privacy and electronic privacy.

Information Privacy

Information privacy refers to a claimed right on the part of individuals to keep information about themselves private. Exactly what this claim covers is, however, both vague and controversial. Clearly I have the right to keep my thoughts to myself and I have no obligation to reveal them. They are my thoughts, I own them and I can keep them to myself or keep them private. There is some information about myself known only to me which is similarly covered. There is some information about me known to me and only to one or a small number of other people. Is this covered by a claim to privacy? I may wish my medical records to be private in the sense that they are available only to my doctors and other similarly authorized people. Some people claim that they have ownership rights over all information about them. But that cannot be the case, since some information about them is a matter of public record, some is shared by people who have observed them at certain places and times and have no obligation not to reveal this, and so on. What information about me do I have a right to keep private, and what is at stake?

The fears of many people concerning computers and privacy can be described as the Big Brother syndrome.[5] We know that computers are capable of assembling large amounts of data, making the assembled data easily and readily available. We know that large amounts of data are assembled on each of us. Our bank keeps a record of our financial transactions—our checks and deposits—on computer tapes; our credit rating is filed in computers; hospitals keep our medical records in computers; MasterCard and Visa keep our records on computer; and the IRS keeps all kinds of information on us in computers. It is, moreover, possible to assemble and collate all of this information. Someone—Big Brother, the government, or someone else—can at least in theory assemble all the information about us and use it for a variety of purposes. There may be errors that we do not know about, that we have no way to correct, and that yet are used to make decisions about us. Some people fear that their privacy is invaded in the process. The capacity for collecting, storing, and retrieving information far exceeds anything generations prior to ours had to face. The capacity to assemble such information raises questions about whether our privacy is in fact invaded by the collection of such information, whether our rights are in any way violated, and whether we are threatened with potential damage. There are moral issues in the collection and use of information that require some reflection and that may yield moral problems for which we have no ready answers.

Let us extend the distinction between data and facts or information in several ways. If we cannot own facts, then we cannot own facts about ourselves, any more than we can own other kinds of facts. Consider the implications in the following ways.

First, suppose that the statement "John had an operation ten years ago" is a fact. John cannot own that fact. It is a fact known by those who knew John was in the hospital, by the doctor and nurses in attendance, and by those to whom John told that fact. That fact is entered as data in the computers of the hospital, in the computers of the insurance company that paid for the operation, and perhaps elsewhere as well. The fact belongs to no one, although the data belong to the owners of the various computer systems. Do they have the right to sell those data? Does John have any rights because the data represent facts about him? There are also other facts about John that others know. If they can use their data as they wish because the data are theirs, and if no one owns facts, might not all sorts of threats to John result from the improper use of the facts or data?

---

[5] See David Burnham, *The Rise of the Computer State* (New York: Vintage Books, 1984); and David F. Linowes, *Privacy in America: Is Your Private Life in the Public Eye?* (Urbana: University of Illinois Press, 1989). Concerning the computer and privacy, see Andrew E. Wessel, *The Social Use of Information: Ownership and Access* (New York: John Wiley & Sons, 1976); Alan F. Westin and Michael A. Baker, *Databanks in a Free Society: Computers, Record-Keeping, and Privacy* (New York: Quadrangle Books, 1972); and Martin O. Holoien, *Computers and Their Social Impact* (New York: John Wiley & Sons, 1977).

We should be careful of our distinction. Facts are statements about the way the world is, and hence, by definition, true; *data*—as we have been using the term—are neither true nor false. When interpreted, data may yield false-hoods. This may be because falsehoods rather than facts were entered into the computer as data, because mistakes were made in entry, because the pro-gram was defective, or for a variety of other reasons. Hence, although one owns one's data, there is no guarantee that the data represent facts. One is responsible for the interpretation and use one makes of one's data—for mis-takes, harm done, and so on. The issue of responsibility is not solved but is perhaps more clearly defined by distinguishing facts from data. The term *information*, when used to cover both facts and data, tends to obscure the issue and location of truth. In its broad sense, information, unlike facts, can be false; but in a common, narrow usage, information is considered equivalent to facts and by definition true. Keeping data and facts distinct helps us state, and so resolve, a number of issues.

The definitions we gave of *fact* and *data*, moreover, are compatible with several restrictions on use of data and on the method of learning facts. Although the fact that John had an operation is owned by no one, it does not follow that it is properly common knowledge, for ownership is not the only way of preventing use or dissemination of facts. Nor does the statement that no one owns facts mean that everyone has a right to know all facts. Society can—and our society does—for good reason, recognize certain areas of privi-leged communications, of secrecy, and of privacy.

Patient-doctor confidentiality, priest-penitent confidentiality, and lawyer-client confidentiality are all instances of privileged communication. Society recognizes that statements that patients, penitents, or clients make are appro-priately kept confidential. The facts revealed in such disclosures may not be freely repeated, and any records kept of them are confidential as well. That the records are kept on computers changes nothing in this respect. The data belong to the lawyer or doctor, but the facts they represent may not be dis-closed except under certain conditions, and anyone who has legitimate access to the data is also bound by the same strictures of confidentiality. If this were not the case, the practice of law and medicine would be seriously impaired. There are restrictions, therefore, on the use that one can make of one's data, even though the data are owned. Confidential data may not be sold or other-wise transferred, copied, or divulged to outside parties without authoriza-tion.

Does the circumstance that the facts are about us give us any special right to them? The answer seems to be clearly no, because we have no right to facts. But we have no obligation to make known personal facts about our-selves, and if we make them in confidence, we have the right to insist, and expect, that they will be kept confidential.

Are the facts that John subscribes to a certain magazine, that he pays bills on time, and that he buys certain products facts to which John has a right? The answer again is no. These are, at least in part, facts about John that are not confidential. The fact that he subscribes to a certain magazine is known by him, by the magazine and some of its employees, the postman, and others along the way who might see the magazine in his mailbox, or the secretary who distributes the mail in his office. His name is on a list of all the subscribers to that magazine. He knows that it is. Does the owner of the list have the right to sell a list with John's name on it? Unless the relation is confidential, the owner of the list does have the right, because John's subscription is a fact, and because the data are the owner's—unless by selling them he does John some harm, for he has no right to use his data to harm John or anyone else. The owner's selling his list to another magazine, to be used for promotional purposes, or to some other advertiser, in general does not harm John, even if it increases the amount of mail he gets. But if the list were to be used in ways that did harm John, he would have the right not to have his name given to others. The reason is not that John owns facts about himself, but that he has a right not to be harmed. The same is true of his credit rating. If information about the way he pays his bills is to be given to others and used for some purpose that may harm him, then he should at the very least know that this is being done and should have access to that information so that he can correct it if it is in error. This again is in virtue not of his owning the facts but of his right not to be harmed.

What of one's right to privacy?[6] This is ground for keeping confidential facts about people. Our society recognizes areas of privacy for the individual, into which others have no right to penetrate, unless serious harm is threatened to others. Our thoughts are our own, as are our beliefs. We have no obligation to reveal them, even though it is a fact that we are thinking certain things and have certain beliefs. There are other private areas in our lives that we have no obligation to divulge any information about. We have the right to keep these secret; and if others try to find out about them, they may violate our privacy. Hence, surreptitious surveillance, wire-tapping, bugging, and so on are violations of privacy, which are allowable under law only in very special circumstances.

Many believe that, although having records about us in various places is allowable, the gathering of all of this data, through the use of computers, somehow violates our privacy. Yet why and how it does so is not clear. Facts about us do not belong to us; therefore, if those who have facts about us, stored as data, own that data and have the right to sell it or give it away (providing it does not harm or threaten to harm us), then collecting these data in one place does not violate our right to privacy. Nonetheless, there may be good grounds for objecting to the process if such a collection may be used to

---

[6] On privacy, see Ferdinand David Shoeman, *Privacy and Social Freedom* (New York: Cambridge University Press, 1992); Ferdinand David Shoeman (Ed.), *Philosophical Dimensions of Privacy* (New York: Cambridge University Press, 1984); J. Roland Pennock and John W. Chapman (Eds.), *Privacy* (New York: Atherton Press, 1971); and Warren Freedman, *The Right of Privacy in the Computer Age* (New York: Quorum Books, 1987).

harm us, and if we have no opportunity to verify what it contains, to correct errors, or to rebut false statements. This is the root of the concern, and although often presented in terms of privacy it is more appropriately a case of possible harm. The right of workers to inspect their files is an instance of a general right that applies to all people—against credit agencies, governments, and any others who maintain and use such files in ways that directly affect, and harm, us. Clearly, we should be notified of any such files kept on us, and rules governing their use should be established and enforced. Such mandatory notification and enforcement obviously require appropriate legislation.

In addition to the Big Brother syndrome, the computer makes violation of information privacy possible in other new ways.

Employees, we noted, have a right to privacy. When employee records are kept in computer files rather than filing cabinets, employers are bound to secure that information at least as well as they secure filing cabinets. Yet many managers have no idea how safe such files really are or how open they are to compromise. They know the usual means of protecting physical files by lock and key, but they often simply trust their information systems or computer department to do what is necessary to safeguard computer files. Obvious passwords are sometimes used, and compromise is easy, especially for workers in the firm with access to other files. Floppy disks containing sensitive personal information are frequently much less closely guarded than are paper files containing similar information.

As more and more personal data are kept on computers and disks, more and more people will have authorized, as well as easy unauthorized, access. The rules for handling these data are often left unspecified, and different companies differ in their rules. But every company has an obligation to determine that any system containing confidential records is secure and that employees with access to such files are informed of, and trained in, security procedures. They should also understand the importance of confidentiality. Computer access is much easier to compromise and more difficult to control than physical access. Keys to doors can be made such that duplication is difficult, if not impossible. Employees are not likely to give a key to others because when they do so they no longer have the key. But they can give an access code to others and still have it themselves. Access codes, moreover, can often be easily used to gain entrance into other parts of a system. Unless due care is taken, this is much easier than getting from one room to another when one has the key to the first. Computers have been adopted by many companies so quickly and in such numbers that insufficient care has been taken about security. But privacy is an obligation that managers owe to their employees, just as they owe security of funds to shareholders. Employees have the obligation to respect the privacy of files, to control their curiosity when it is possible for them to gain unauthorized access to files, and to protect the confidentiality of records and files to which they have authorized access. The problems of providing privacy and security in the age of the computer are related and demand a corporation's serious thought and effort.

Electronic Privacy

The second area of current privacy concern in business is electronic privacy. This refers primarily to the use by employees of e-mail and the Internet. How much privacy do and should employees have and how much may they legitimately expect in these areas?

Many employees think of e-mail as comparable to regular mail. The laws governing U.S. mail are very strict and Americans are used to the protection of privacy that such laws provide. Others think of e-mail on the model of the telephone, which also is private and cannot be tapped without a court order. Most states in the United States mandate that if calls are monitored by a company both parties to a conversation must be advised of that fact. Employees often figure that there is no or very little cost involved in sending an e-mail, and that it is comparable to the cost of making a local telephone call at work, or perhaps of using a piece of paper and an envelope, the cost of which is negligible and so generally allowed.

The status of e-mail, however, is legally comparable to neither regular mail nor to telephone use. U.S. courts have declared that computers belong to the company that purchases and owns them, and that everything on the computer is hence company property, including e-mail sent or received by employees. Moreover, most companies routinely make and keep archives of all e-mail sent and received. These may be accessed by law enforcement officers, as well as by corporate management. A consequence is that many employees operate under the mistaken belief that their e-mails are private, when in fact legally they are not. This gap between current belief and legal fact is the source of a good deal of difficulty. Because there is so much misinformation, and because policies vary widely from corporation to corporation, every corporation, in fairness to its employees, owes it to them to make clear what its policy on e-mail privacy is.

There is no one ethically manadatory policy. A company may decide that it trusts its employees sufficiently that it adopts a policy that says that it will consider employee e-mail confidential, and that it will not read archived e-mail, even though if required by law enforcement agencies it will allow them access. Such a policy lets employees know exactly how much privacy they have, and they can act accordingly. Another company may feel that company e-mail should be used exclusively for strictly business purposes, and it may so inform it employees, telling them that their e-mail may be read at any time by their supervisors or managers, by others in senior positions, or by security personnel. Such a policy will be perceived by employees as an indication that the corporation does not trust them. But the policy is not unethical, as long as it is promulgated clearly, and preferably often. Some companies have their computers set to post a warning message to the effect that e-mail is not private each time an employee accesses the company e-mail program. There are positions between these two. Whatever policy a company adopts the essential ingredient is that it be made known to all employees and that, if the policy is restrictive, it be reiterated sufficiently often so that it is in fact known by them.

The situation with respect to use of the Internet is in some ways comparable and in some ways different. It is comparable in that the computer belongs to the employer and any use of it to access the Internet is recorded and is legally available to the company. It is different in that the problems that Internet access poses are somewhat different from those posed by e-mail. Two of them are misuse of time and access to nonjob-related, and even to illegal sites.

The issue of misuse of time comes from the temptation to browse the Internet often and to follow link after link or to spend a great deal of time in chat-rooms. Both can consume a great deal of time and can take away from the work an employee should be doing. Taking a ten-minute break by surfing the Internet is perhaps no different from taking a ten-minute break to get coffee, and both may be allowed. Whether or not they are is a matter of company policy. Yet because of the temptation to spend a good deal of time on the Internet, some companies restrict access, some set limits on the time one may spend, and some monitor use to determine abuse. Some companies allow employees to use their computer for personal use after working hours; some do not. As with e-mail, the company may set its policy. What it owes its employees is a clear statement of that policy.

The use of the Internet to access pornography poses another problem. Such access, from the point of view of being job related, may be no less job related than accessing sites about fishing, or home decorating, or any other topic. One difference is that if the screen is visible to others besides the user, it can produce a sexually hostile environment, and so be a violation of sexual harassment laws. Since use of the Web can also be tracked by the sites one accesses, some companies also fear the harm to the company's reputation that may result from having their company linked to pornographic sites, or by having the company subject to pornographic ads as a result of some employee's contact. Accessing illegal sites, such those dedicated to child pornography, is clearly not something that can be defended under the guise of employee privacy, since no one has the right to break the law in private or to break the law on the job.

The upshot is that despite the beliefs of many employees, e-mail and Internet use are not covered by the right to privacy, either legally or ethically. The correlate is that companies have the ethical obligation to inform their employees of the company's policy with respect to what employees are allowed and not allowed to do in these regards, how much or how little privacy they have, and what will and will not be monitored, under what conditions and by whom. Too few companies have given adequate attention to the need to develop a clear policy and even fewer have adequately made the policy clearly known to employees.

The computer, in all these and other ways, raises new problems for business and places new responsibilities on corporate managers. The major difficulty is that change in this area is taking place so fast that inadequate thought has been given to the moral implications involved in the changes. Not only is there no consensus on many issues, and on the legitimacy of many practices; many managers do not even know there are issues about which they should be concerned, or that they should be establishing policies to prevent future difficulties. Because there often is no consensus on issues, and because the intuitions of different people differ on the propriety of practices involving computers and their use, the need for clear moral thinking and moral argument is especially important in this area.

Study Questions

1. What is the "look and feel" issue in computer software disputes?
2. If in the ABC Control case the institution were a university and the policy were to govern state employees (faculty and staff), should the policy be any different? Should a policy for students be the same, more restrictive, or less restrictive than the one for employees?
3. In what four areas does the use of computers raise new problems or familiar problems in a new way? Specify the new problems.
4. Stealing by computer is immoral. What moral obligations do firms have when subject to computer theft? Why are firms often reluctant to prosecute violators?
5. What is the difference between robbing a bank with a gun or with a computer? Do the differences make any moral difference? Explain.
6. Is surreptitious entry of a computer system immoral? Why or why not?
7. What defense is sometimes made for hacking? Is the defense sound?
8. What general rule can we apply in deciding the morality of use of computer time? Present a moral defense of the rule.
9. Who is responsible for harm done by computer use? What does this imply?
10. What are the differences among data, information, and facts?
11. Can data be owned? Can facts? Explain why or why not.
12. Distinguish a source code from an object code. Is there any moral difference between copying one or the other? Why or why not?
13. If an employee develops a program on his or her own time and uses it at work, to whom does the program belong? Why?
14. If an employee develops a program on company time, to whom does the program belong? Why?
15. May employees take copies of a program with them from one job to another? algorithms? Why or why not?
16. What is information privacy?

17. Do individuals own facts about themselves? Must they divulge facts about themselves? What are the implications for databases?

18. Does selling mailing lists violate a person's right to privacy? Why or why not?

19. What is electronic privacy?

20. Write a policy for a company covering employee use of e-mail and the Internet that you think is fair to all concerned, and give an ethical defense of the policy.

21. Does compiling information about a person violate that person's right to privacy? Why or why not?

22. How does the computer used in business affect the employee's right to privacy? Explain.

23. A marketing firm, Nosey A, buys data from a variety of sources and uses them to compile information banks on individuals. It then uses that information to draw profiles of those individuals, including their spending habits, the kinds of products they buy, and the like. It in turn sells those profiles to other firms or parties. Is the firm's activity morally defensible? Why or why not?

24. Would it be ethical for credit card companies to sell Nosey A the details of all the purchases made by its card users?

14

WORKERS' RIGHTS: EMPLOYMENT, WAGES, AND UNIONS

The Air Traffic Controllers Case

At 7:00 A.M. on August 3, 1981, the members of the Professional Air Traffic Controllers Organization (PATCO) went on strike.[1] The strike was called after over 95 percent of the members had earlier rejected a contract negotiated between the union and the Federal Aviation Administration (FAA).

The union sought a $10,000 increase across the board in base pay, a reduction in the work week of its members to thirty-two hours, and retirement after twenty years of service at 75 percent of the member's highest gross salary. The FAA negotiators offered an average wage increase of $2,300 in addition to the $1,700 that all federal employees were scheduled to receive, and retirement after twenty-five years or at age 50 after twenty years, at 50 percent of average base salary for the three years of highest pay. The controllers were federal government employees; hence, their salaries and the agreement had to be approved by Congress.

In the past airline pilots had gone out on strike. Their strike was legal and ethically justifiable, despite the harm done to the traveling public. The

---

[1] For details of the strike and two comments on it, see Herbert R. Northrup, "The Rise and Demise of PATCO," *Industrial and Labor Relations Review,* 37, no. 2 (January 1984), pp. 167-184; and Richard W. Hurd and Jill K. Kriesky, with "Reply" by Herbert R. Northrup, "Communications: `The Rise and Demise of PATCO' Reconstructed," *Industrial and Labor Relations Review,* 40, no. 1 (October 1986), pp. 115-127. See also *New York Times,* August 3-7, 1981, and Arthur B. Shostak and David Skocik, *The Air Controllers' Controversy: Lessons from the PATCO Strike* (New York: Human Sciences Press, 1986).

pilots, however, were employees not of the government but of the airlines. In contrast, the air traffic controllers were federal employees, governed by the Civil Service Reform Act of 1978, which prohibits strikes by those subject to it. In 1981 William Clay (Missouri Democrat) had introduced a bill in the U.S. House of Representatives that would have permitted the air traffic controllers to strike. Thus, although illegal, their right to strike was not beyond consideration.

Nonetheless, on August 3, the PATCO strike was illegal. On August 4, President Ronald Reagan issued a statement warning the controllers that if they did not report for work within forty-eight hours, they would be terminated. He added, "I respect the right of workers in the private sector to strike. . . . But we cannot compare labor management relations in the private sector with Government." Moreover, he noted that each had taken an oath: "I am not participating in any strike against the Government of the United States or any agency thereof, and I will not participate while an employee of the Government of the United States or any agency thereof."[2] Lane Kirkland, president of the AFL-CIO, responded that air traffic controllers, just as other workers, had "a basic human right, the right to withdraw their services, not to work under conditions they no longer find tolerable."[3] Ultimately, 875 air traffic controllers returned to work before the deadline; the 11,301 who did not return were terminated. In addition, the Federal Labor Relations Authority decertified PATCO.

The strike inconvenienced many travelers, but it did not cause a shutdown of all flights. In fact, with the controllers who did not walk out or who returned, as well as with supervisors and military controllers, about 50 percent of scheduled flights took off, and they gradually moved back to normal. The strike was a failure. The government had refused further mediation and showed its resolve. The move to permit federal government employees to strike has yet to gain the momentum it had prior to the strike. Moreover, some saw the Reagan administration's decertifying of PATCO as setting an example of what has been termed "union busting" in the private as well as the public sector.

The PATCO strike was not the first strike by government employees. U.S. postal workers, who were government employees at the time, had gone on strike under the Nixon administration and had not been fired, just as employees of various states had gone on strike even though they were legally prohibited from doing so. Reagan's action was legal, but it was not mandatory. Was it fair, all things considered? Should air traffic controllers and other (even though perhaps not all) government employees have the same right to strike that workers have in the private sector? Is it fair for the government to prohibit strikes by government employees and not be required to bargain or submit to some independent mediation process?

---

[2] *New York Times*, August 4, 1981, p. B8.
[3] Stuart Taylor, Jr., "Strikes and the Law," *New York Times*, August 4, 1981, p. A14.

Employment-at-Will

Any consideration of the right to strike comes, of course, only after a worker is employed, and it is only one of the rights to which workers have a claim. Free enterprise allows capital, resources, and labor to flow freely, and, ideally, where they flow is determined by the market. But labor is significantly different from capital and resources. Labor is not simply a commodity to be bought and sold. For by labor we always mean the labor of human beings, and human beings have rights, which they do not give up by becoming employees.

What of the transactions between worker and employer? Can we subsume these into a contract or agreement and treat them as we would any other contract? Are there aspects of an employer-employee relationship that cannot be negotiated? Are there certain assumptions about workers' rights and obligations, and about employers' rights and obligations that form the background for worker-employer contracts, and are these assumptions justifiable?

We have seen that the implicit contract between society and corporations is that the latter are allowed limited liability and the opportunity to reap profits from their activity on condition that they benefit society by providing goods and services at reasonable prices and that they provide employment for the members of society. Of course, no individual corporation provides employment for all the members of the society, and corporations are free to hire the people it needs and wants. Similarly, since slave labor is immoral and illegal, no one can be forced to work for another or for any particular corporation.

The contract between employers and employees is generally viewed as a kind of transaction, and we have seen that transactions are fair or just if both parties have access to appropriate information, both benefit by the transaction, and both enter into the transaction freely. This general approach in the United States led to the development of a legal position known as the doctrine of *employment-at-will*.[4] According to this doctrine, employers are free to hire whomever they choose and to fire them whenever they choose, for any reason or even for no particular reason. Similarly, individuals are free to work for whomever they choose who offers them a job or position, and they may quit whenever they wish, for any reason or even for no particular reason. Because the agreement is a mutual one, and both are free to enter an agreement, the employment agreement can be initiated and terminated "at will." Hence the name of the doctrine.

Although the doctrine sounds fair and symmetrical, it has come under greater and greater attack and has been more and more circumscribed by law,

---

[4] Lawrence E. Blades, "Employment at Will vs. Individual Freedom: On Limiting the Abusive Exercise of Employer Power," *Columbia Law Review*, 67 (1967), pp. 1405-1435, reviews pertinent legal cases. David R. Hiley, "Employee Rights and the Doctrine of At Will Employment," *Business & Professional Ethics Journal*, 4, no. 1, pp. 1-10, argues that employees have a defensible right to their jobs. Patricia H. Werhane, *Persons, Rights, and Corporations* (Englewood Cliffs, N.J.: Prentice Hall, 1985), discusses employment at will and its relation to workers' rights.

for ethically justifiable reasons. It does not take much imagination to realize that although the doctrine sounds symmetrical, the relation of an individual worker to a large corporation is not an equal one. Because the ordinary worker must work to get the wherewithal to live, he is both forced to work (and often must accept work not of his preference) and lives in fear of losing his job if he has no contract guaranteeing him a secure position. He is not free to set the conditions of his employment the way the employer is free to set the conditions for the potential employee. The employee cannot work for whatever company he or she chooses but is obviously limited by the openings available and by the choice or choices offered. Frequently those seeking employment are grateful to find even one position offered to them, since the alternative is no work and so no income. The employer, on the other hand, sets the conditions of employment, and if one person refuses them usually there are others waiting for a chance to accept an offer. If the conditions are such that no one applies, the company can make the position more attractive. If any particular employee quits, the company rarely suffers more than some inconvenience and if the firm wishes to keep someone who is leaving to take a better position, the firm can make its own position more attractive than the competition's. Employment-at-will, therefore, is not a symmetrical relation.

Moreover, there are other ethical considerations that militate against unrestricted use of the doctrine. Since transactions are fair only if there is no force or coercion and both parties enter the agreement freely, care must be taken to make sure that workers are not forced by circumstances not of their making, such as high unemployment, to accept whatever is offered them. To ensure the requisite freedom, society must find ways to keep socially produced desperation out of the labor market. In addition, ethics precludes employers from setting terms that are unethical as conditions of employment. We have already seen that employers must do what they can to make working conditions reasonably safe. Selling oneself into slavery is not morally permitted. Although the doctrine of employment-at-will says that employers may hire whomever they choose, this has come to be seen as much too broad a doctrine. It is unfair to exclude some people from the possibility of being hired because of their gender, race, religion, and other nonjob-related criteria. If all or a majority of companies each individually chose such criteria, the possibility of employment for members of the designated group would no longer exist. American society has thus come to restrict the doctrine of employment-at-will by outlawing racial and other kinds of discrimination in both the hiring and the firing process.

The doctrine of employment-at-will is compatible with the claim that no particular applicant has a right to the job or position for which he or she applies. The final decision is up to the employer. No applicants can rightly claim that they have the best credentials or that they are better qualified than the other applicants and therefore have a right to the job. Who is best qualified for the job is a decision properly made not by the applicants but by the person or firm doing the hiring. Candidates can claim the right to be treated fairly and the right not to be discriminated against on the basis of nonjob-related criteria. But if they are turned down, for instance, because their potential employer thought they were "overqualified" for the job, that is a decision for the employer to make. To claim otherwise is to force employees on firms, which would be as unfair as it is to force firms on employees.

Just like employment in any society, the doctrine of employment-at-will takes place within social and legal contexts, which constitute the background conditions for its implementation. An ethical analysis of employment must examine those conditions, as well as the specific activities of individual employers. Individual corporate employers do not create those conditions but may benefit from them. Workers may have rights that they exercise against the system as such, as well as rights they exercise against specific employers. And for a society to respect the rights of its members, a society may have to require certain actions of those who provide the employment. What rights, if any, do workers have?

The Right to Employment

Prior to employment in a particular job, workers have rights against the system because of their place within it. As opposed to specific rights concerning conditions of employment, these rights are general rights against the society or system as such and therefore have a special status. To the extent that they are human rights, they are held by all human beings, no matter what the politico-economic system in which they live. The appropriate implementation of these rights varies with the resources, level of development, and politico-economic structures of different societies. The right to employment is one of these.

The right to employment is not a right that is recognized in the United States, where unemployment is both expected and accepted. The right can be derived from the right to work, another right that is not recognized in the United States, but one that is listed in Article 23 of the Universal Declaration of Human Rights[5] and is recognized in many countries. Whether there is truly a right to employment, which should be recognized in the United States, depends on whether it is a justifiable claim. We shall therefore look at the argument that supports it and look as well at alternatives to the recognition of that right, which do exist in the United States.

In those countries in which the only employer is the government, each able-bodied person can exercise the right to employment directly against the government. In such countries the right is frequently joined with a correlative obligation to work—an obligation that government enforces against the able-bodied. In the free-enterprise system, the right to employment is not a right that can be exercised against any particular employer. In the United States, no

---

[5] See Ian Brownlie (Ed.), *Basic Documents on Human Rights*, 3rd ed. (Oxford: Oxford University Press, 1993), p. 363.

one has a right to any particular job or position. Even the fact that one is the most capable person for a position does not give one the right to it.

Because the right to employment is derived from the right to work, we should start with this. As a human right, the right to work applies to all human beings, merely by virtue of their being human. But the right is appropriately implemented differently, both in different societies and for people of different ages and circumstances. Infants as well as all other human beings have the right to work; but because they are physically and mentally incapable of working, it is not a right they actively exercise. Adults in primitive societies exercise the right differently from those in advanced industrial societies.

We can roughly divide the population of the United States into four groups. One group is composed of children too young to work, or at least considered too young to work full time in our society. Either they are incapable of working because they are infants or very young children, or they are required to go to school and so are legally precluded from working full time. After a certain age they may be allowed to work part time. A second group consists of retired workers. They have worked for a certain period of time and have now left the work force. A third group consists of those unable to work—whether because of sickness, injury, or other infirmity. The fourth and largest group consists of adults who are able to work.

The group of able-bodied adults can be further subdivided. The largest subgroup consists of those actually in the work force—those who are self-employed, employed by government, by someone else, or by a firm. The second largest subgroup consists of those who work at home but who are not employed. These include housewives, mothers of small children, and others with no outside employment, who do not seek employment. There is clearly a difference between *work* and *employment*. A person who raises a family and "keeps house" works but is not employed. A person who sculpts, writes, or makes his or her living in a similar way also works but is not employed. Children who work at home or for the family are not employed, but they work. Consider a small family on a farm: The husband and wife work in the fields, care for the animals, and work in the house; the children do chores in the morning and evening and go to school between times. All the members of the family work. None are employed, but none are unemployed either.

The third largest group are the unemployed. This group can be further subdivided. It includes young adults who want to work but are unable to find their first full-time job, as well as those who work at home but want outside employment. It includes seasonal workers, young or older—for instance, fruit pickers, who work in certain seasons and are unable to find work in other seasons. It includes the *hard-core unemployed*, who do not have work and who have given up looking for a job. It includes the *structurally unemployed*—that is, those who had work in a certain industry but who are unable to find that sort of employment, are unable to relocate, and have no other skills to sell. It includes as well the *cyclically unemployed*—that is, those who are unemployed because of a cutback in the number of workers employed by firms, owing to recessions or depressions; and the *frictionally unemployed*—that is, those who are temporarily out of work for a short period while changing jobs.

Employment usually implies both an employer and a wage; work implies neither of these. Defining work is notoriously difficult. We can, however, determine what the right to work involves without deciding precisely what is and is not work, or how we distinguish work from play or from other kinds of human activity.

The right to work as a universal, human right, is itself a derived right. Defenders of the right have attempted to derive it from the right to life, the right to development, and/or the right to respect. In each case the derivation hinges on certain assumptions and background conditions. Thus, the right to work can be derived from the right to life to the extent that access to work is necessary to obtain the wherewithal to preserve life. The right to life carries with it the right to engage in those activities, compatible with the exercise of the rights of others, necessary to sustain life. To the extent that work is the typical means by which adults produce the goods they need and want to sustain themselves and those dependent on them, the right to work is a derivative of the right to life. The right so derived is a negative, not a positive, right. The derivation hinges on the assumption that if we are deprived of work, we are deprived of the means of sustaining our life and the lives of our dependents. In a society in which preventing people from working threatens their lives, the right to work is easily derived from the right to life.

Although the assumption that people in general produce the means of their subsistence is correct, it is not necessarily the case that each adult person able to engage in productive labor must be allowed to do so to prevent him from dying, for society can so arrange what it produces to sustain not only those who work and those dependent on them, but others as well. In the United States, for instance, a variety of welfare programs are justified on the basis of a recognized right to life, which can be sustained without recognizing a right to work.

The derivation of the right to work from the right to development, despite a certain plausibility and appropriateness in some societies, is also tenuous. If work or productive activity is a means by which human beings develop themselves physically and mentally, then to the extent that we have a right to such development, and to the extent that work is necessary for such development, we have the right to work. But at both critical junctures the link is weak. For even granting the right to development, such a right could be implemented by education, leisure activity, and other nonwork-related means. Furthermore, many kinds of work do not develop a person either physically or mentally. Thus, a frequent charge brought against much industrial work is that it is stultifying and prevents rather than fosters development.

The derivation of the right to work that hinges on the right of all human beings to respect provides its most solid basis. Human beings belong to human society. An able-bodied, competent member of society has and plays a role in it. Each has a right to do so. No adult is "excess" or "expendable," and the recognition of this fact is part of what it means for people to have the right to respect. Work is the typical way by which human adults assert their independence and are able to assume their full share of responsibility in a community. Work involves the taking of our place in the community, whether it is work in the home, in the fields, or in the factory or office. Our self-respect as well as the respect of others is closely linked with what we do, how we express ourselves through our actions, and the extent to which we assume the full burden and responsibility for our lives and our part in the social fabric. If we are not allowed to work, we are not allowed to take our rightful place in society as contributing, mature, responsible adults. The right to work is in this way closely related to the right to respect and is derived from it, for every society.

For this reason, to deprive a person of a productive role in many societies is a form of ostracism, tantamount to punishment, and justifiable only for a serious social offense or crime.

The right to work can be interpreted as both a negative and a positive right. As a negative right, no one, including the government, may legitimately prohibit someone who wishes to work from doing so—that is, within the normal restrictions for negative rights, such as not infringing the similar, equal, or more important rights of others. As a positive right, it requires at least that our society accept us and give us the opportunity for full membership, including the opportunity for participation in the productive activity of society.

The relation of respect and the right to work is implied in Article 23 of the Declaration of Human Rights, which insists on the "free choice of employment" (thus precluding forced labor, slavery, or gross exploitation) and on "just and favorable remuneration ensuring for himself and his family an existence worthy of human dignity."

As with most other rights, the right to work rises to consciousness only at a certain historical time. In the idyllic society of an imaginary tropical island where needs are few, food is plentiful, and the population is small in comparison with the land and resources available, the right to work would not arise. It is not explicitly raised, although it is implicitly implemented in a traditional society, for in such a society everyone has a place in the social order—whether that society is one of hunting, herding, or agriculture, and whether it is organized on tribal, feudal, or other similar lines. Each adult is accepted into the community and participates in the activity of the adults of that community. Nor would one tend to invoke the right in a country where land is plentiful and where there are many alternative ways to keep oneself and one's family flourishing with dignity. The right to work was not an issue when there was always an alternative to the jobs available. Finally, the right to work would tend not to arise in a society that had a chronic shortage of labor. If the demand for labor always exceeded the supply, the notion of the right to work would have little, if any, importance, except in its negative sense.

The right to work typically arises when the supply of labor exceeds the demand, when large numbers of people have no available alternative to earning their living by working for others, and when the social fabric characteristic of tribes and extended families, in which all share in whatever is available, breaks down. Historically, the right to work became an issue with the advent of industrialization, in which the means of production were owned by only a few and the typical worker earned his living by working for a wage.

In an industrialized society, the line between the negative and the positive interpretation of the right to work often blurs. Preventing one from working in a traditional society involves depriving one of access to work or to a place in the society. In an industrial society, those who depend on employment for wages can be kept from working by being kept from employment. One might actively be kept from employment, by some action or intervention—blackballing, or the like—or passively, when no employer needs workers. Unemployment might, in this latter sense, result from the system. It is not the active result of employers discriminating or refusing, out of malice, to employ people. No individual employer has the obligation to employ others, and employers, acting individually in their own interests, cannot be blamed if collectively they cannot provide work for all who want it. The system is to blame, not individual employers within it.

In such a situation, the right to work is equivalent to the right to employment for those able, willing, and desiring work and unable to engage in productive work if not employed. Properly speaking, the right to employment is not itself a human right but becomes a specification of the human right to work appropriate in industrialized society. The right to employment is properly exercised by the unemployed against the society with such a system, because it is the system that is responsible for preventing them from working. Americans have come to accept the system because of the goods and wealth it produces and have provided welfare as an alternative to employment. But welfare, critics claim, has masked the right to work and has kept its violation from general consciousness. For although welfare does indeed preserve life, it does not allow the able-to-work who receive it to take an active, productive part in their society, with the concomitant respect and self-respect that go with having work or employment.

To say that the right to employment is exercised against the system or society does not mean that it is exercised only against government. For just as business benefits from the system adopted by society, business appropriately shares in meeting the obligations of society to those members who suffer as a result of the system. Government, however, would have to enforce the right. It might use tax incentives to motivate firms to retain employees they might otherwise fire. Government might require and help firms to retain or relocate workers when plants are shut down. It could give businesses tax benefits or subsidies to provide training for the unemployed. It might mandate cuts in the time worked by all workers in a firm—with a corresponding cut in salary—rather than allowing layoffs when these are economically necessary. Government can also directly serve as a clearinghouse for openings and applicants, aid in relocating the unemployed, supplement insufficient wages through a negative income tax, or, finally, serve as a temporary employer of last resort.

These and other similar requirements placed on business may seem like interferences with their freedom, and of course they are. But the freedom of business is, and always has been, legitimately circumscribed by the rights of the individuals in society. Such interferences perhaps seem severe only because as a society we have not seriously considered the right to employment.

To the extent that the right to work has received any attention in labor law in the United States it has been in the sense of a negative right. Thus, for instance, some have claimed that *union shops* (in which union membership is required for employment either on or after the thirtieth day of beginning employment) prevent those who do not want to join the union from working, or at least from working where they choose. Legislation on the union shop has varied from state to state in the United States, ever since Section 14(b) of the Taft-Hartley law allowed states to outlaw such shops.[6] *Right-to-work laws* in this context mean laws that outlaw union shops and thus preserve the right of all workers to work without the obligation to join or belong to a union. But although the legislation and debates surrounding union shops have been couched in terms of right-to-work laws, such laws touch only a small portion of what the human right to work covers. Whether such laws are truly for the benefit of the worker is a hotly debated issue. The existing right-to-work laws, therefore, do not implement the human right to work we have been considering; and having preempted the terminology, they make discussion of right-to-work laws (in the sense of positively implementing the right) confusing and difficult.

Yet the right to employment is compatible with the best in the United States' tradition of free enterprise and peaceful and productive labor relations, and implementation of that right does not necessarily lead to socialism or to disruption of the free-enterprise worker-management relation.

In the United States, the failure to recognize and address the right to employment has to some extent been mitigated by a variety of public programs, from unemployment insurance to welfare programs. Unemployment insurance, as the name implies, is a type of insurance program. It is available only to those who have such insurance, and the minimal requirement is that one must have been previously employed. It is thus not available to those leaving school who have not been previously employed on a full-time basis, nor is it available to women, for example, who have been working in the home raising a family and who wish at a certain time to join the work force. It is also not available to those who have been out of work for a longer period than that covered by the insurance. As a stopgap measure for those temporarily unem-

---

[6] Labor Management Relations Act (Taft-Hartley) of 1947, 8(a)(3), 29 U.S.C. 158(a)(3) (1982).

ployed or for those between jobs, it is on the whole adequate and serves an obvious need. For the others, however, it does nothing.

Welfare programs come to the rescue for some of those not eligible for unemployment insurance and in need of help. Such programs serve another obvious need. But there is a difference between providing support for those who cannot work outside the home because of disability, or the need to care for children, or some other similar reason, and providing support for those who both can work and wish to do so. For the latter, the absence of work can be and very often is demoralizing and, as we have noted, leads to loss of both self-respect and respect from others. The reason for their unemployment is not theirs, but in some sense the society's or the system's. That failure is only partially made good by charity or by welfare payments. And what is not made good marks the difference between welfare and recognition of the right to employment.

In the United States, the notion of full employment is often equated, for practical purposes, with the right to employment. The right to employment, however, is not identical with full employment. Full employment is an aim or goal that, if reached, would go a long way toward implementing the right to employment for all those seeking it. But *full employment* is usually defined, in the United States, as being compatible with a certain level of unemployment. (Some have even suggested that 10 percent unemployment in the United States might constitute full employment.[7]) Moreover, unemployment figures ignore the discouraged or hard-core unemployed, who have given up looking for work. Full employment, moreover, is a societal goal, not a right. It is a goal properly adopted by a society in which unemployment is a result of the socioeconomic system. But there is an important difference between full employment as a *goal* and the *right* to employment. As a societal goal, full employment is appropriately balanced against other societal goals, such as control of inflation. The right of individuals, however, is different from societal goals and should not be weighed simply as one good against another. A right is an entitlement that should be respected even at the cost of some other good. (For instance, there is no right to single-digit inflation, even though that is desirable.) Government might attempt both to implement rights and to control inflation; but the difference between considering full employment simply as one goal among many and considering the right to employment as a valid individual claim against society is fundamental.

---

[7] See Bill Neikirk, "Unfortunately, we may now be close to `full employment'," *Chicago Tribune,* May 1, 1983, sec. 5, p. 3. The 1983 *Economic Report of the President,* p. 41, says, "It would be imprudent to use macroeconomic policies to reduce the unemployment rate below its inflation threshold level of six to seven percent."

If the *right* to employment were taken seriously, American society, American business, American government would all have to take a different approach to problems of unemployment and welfare than they have. A new approach would require imagination and experimentation. As a nation the United States lacks neither the means nor resources to implement the right, but as a society it has not yet been either forced or willing to recognize it.

The Right to a Just Wage

The right to a just wage, sometimes called a living wage, is a right derived from the right to life, the right to employment, and the right to respect. For some people the problem of what constitutes a just wage is a pseudoproblem: A just wage is whatever the market determines. For them, there is no sense in taking any other approach. The market matches buyer and seller with respect to labor, as with anything else. But clearly that approach, if it claims to be not simply a statement of how wages are set but of how they should be set, demands justification. If setting wages by the market is indeed just, then it should be possible to spell out why it is just. And once spelled out the reasons can be carefully analyzed to see if they are sound.

Fairness can be taken to mean several equally plausible things, and what is fair according to one justifiable principle may be unfair according to another.

We have already seen that according to Marx's labor theory of value, a just wage is a contradiction in terms. Wages cannot be just because all wage labor involves exploitation. The way to achieve justice is to do away with wage labor and replace it with some other form of distribution. But we have also seen that this analysis has not convinced many Americans or West Europeans or Japanese. Except for a small number of Marxist critics, we do not hear workers complaining about being exploited because they receive wages.

We can, however, do without the notion of exploitation and substitute for it less controversial concepts that will enable us to state clearly the problems of wage differential and its justification. The need for a theory of a just wage is not eliminated by doing away with theories of exploitation, but its focus is shifted. A system that allows "anything the market will bear" is not acceptable from a moral point of view. A pure market approach to labor—and to wages as the price of labor—will not do. An unrestricted free-market approach leads historically and potentially to a variety of injustices, yet a theory of a just wage can include the market as one of the determinants of wages. A theory that does so must place limits on the market through social institutions acceptable to the rational participants in the system, each armed with appropriate knowledge.

The solution provided by the Marxist approach suggests, in some ways, the need for proper institutions. It misplaces its criticism, however, by focusing on private property. The marginal-productivity approach to wages ignores background institutions and often sees such institutions as restrictions on free contracts and markets rather than as necessary prerequisites if they are to be morally defensible.

We can talk meaningfully about a just wage only in relation to a system. A just legal and political system must at least provide an income floor and must keep desperation out of the market by providing alternatives to forced acceptance of any wage offered, regardless of conditions. Only within a set of what can be called fair background institutions can the market be allowed to determine wage differentials. This approach makes no attempt to set wages according to some scale of worth, social usefulness, or need, and allows all of these to enter in, if those engaged in the process so choose. Hence, adopting this approach, we can say that what is just is whatever the market produces within the confines of a just system, in the way of wage differentials. If we claim that the results are not just, then we must argue that the background conditions are defective, that additional background institutional limitations are necessary, or that the market is defective. This approach also allows us to judge the morality of excessively low wages in less developed countries, where charges of injustice can often be sustained because of the lack of appropriate background institutions, with the result that the labor transactions are not free but forced.

Exploitation and discussion of what constitutes a just wage are not issues of vital concern among American workers because our system of background institutions has been developed and modified so as to be generally acceptable to them. The market system in the United States is severely restricted; the labor market operates only within certain parameters. Minimum wage laws put a floor on the lower limit, and unemployment insurance and a variety of welfare programs provide an alternative to employment at starvation wages. Such legislation helps keep desperation out of the market. Unions helped to equalize the wage negotiation process by equalizing the power of both parties in the transaction. An effective full-employment bill or legal recognition of the right to employment at an adequate wage would do even more to equalize the bargaining process for all. But at the lower limits, where the charge of exploitation is most likely to occur, there are floors; thereafter the market allows for wage differential. At the upper limits of management, if morality enters, it is not because of claimed exploitation, according to some theories, but because the multiple of minimum to maximum wages is too great.

Although in general the approach to wages in the United States is both morally justifiable and acceptable to most Americans, and although exploitation is not a burning issue in American labor relations, it does not follow that the notion of a fair or just wage is absent from the American scene. But the locus of the discussion of fairness has come to center on equality and discrimination rather than on exploitation or minimum wage. Thus, the argument is that the market needs further restraints. And some people have argued for correction of the market by other norms, as we shall see.

Before looking at the contemporary scene, however, we can usefully cast a glance at the historical development of fair-wage theory. Some of the present charges of unfairness stem from the prior implementation of a criterion of fairness we no longer use. If we are not fighting against habitual unfairness, but are moving toward a changed version of fairness, the means by which we move might well appear in a somewhat different light than otherwise.

If we go back to the nineteenth century, we find a doctrine of a just wage spelled out, for instance, in some of the papal encyclicals. In general, a fair wage was one sufficient to keep a family at a reasonable level of life beyond bare subsistence. This notion contained several assumptions and allowed a great deal of variation from society to society. It assumed that there was one primary wage earner, who was typically male and typically the head of the family. A fair wage, therefore, was by definition a wage sufficient for a male head of a family to raise his family and support its members at a level comparable to that at which the other members of his society—or more particularly, his social class—lived. It was expected that as one's family grew one's expenses increased. Therefore, seniority was to count toward an increase in wages, even if one's work and productivity were comparable to those of entry-level workers performing a similar job. Women had a full-time job at home keeping house, cooking and cleaning, raising children, and managing the household. They were sometimes forced by economic need to work; but they would not have to work outside the home, and certainly not full time, if the male head of the household were paid a fair or living wage. Thus, Pope Pius XI, in his encyclical *Quadragesimo Anno* (1931), called the necessity of a woman's working to help support a family "an intolerable abuse," which was "to be abolished at all cost."[8] When they did work outside the home, women were marginal contributors to a household income, and because their wages were typically supplementary, it was considered fair to pay them less than men. It was also considered fair if single men were paid less than married men because they needed less. And children, if they worked part time, could be paid very little, because whatever they received was gravy for themselves and the family.

Fairness was thus to a large extent connected to need, and a judgment was made not on the basis of individual need but on the need of classes of people—male heads of households, single males, females, and children, in that order. Part of Marx's fierce attack on the capitalist system was its tendency to pay less than a fair wage to the male head of a household, forcing women, and finally even children, to work. This state of affairs was in part rectified by laws that limited child labor and then limited female labor.

To our contemporary ears such a view of a just wage seems strange. But the principle is a defensible one: Namely, that wages should be proportional to classes of need. We have now substituted several other principles for that one, the main one of which is that equal work deserves equal pay. Thus, it makes no difference whether the work is done by a male head of a household, by a single male, or by a female—single or married. Need is beside the point, except at the bottom, where it is handled by minimum-wage laws and welfare programs. What one deserves is equal recompense for equal work.

[8] Claudia Carlen, (Ed.), *The Papal Encyclicals* (Wilmington, N.C.: McGrath Publishing Company, 1981), vol. 3, p. 426. See also Pope John Paul II, *On Human Work* (Washington, D.C.: Office of Publishing and Promotion Services, United States Catholic Conference, 1981). For other approaches to wages, see C. Kerr, *Labor Markets and Wage Determination* (Berkeley: University of California Press, 1977); and Adrian Wood, *A Theory of Pay* (Cambridge: Cambridge University Press, 1978). For a Marxist critique of wages, see John Roemer, *A General Theory of Exploitation and Class* (Cambridge, Mass.: Harvard University Press, 1982).

According to this principle, many of the old, customary practices are prejudicial and discriminatory. The change in the criterion of fairness that was to be used in wage distribution took place during and after World War II. During that war, American women entered the work force in large numbers, and many remained there. And with the increase of divorce, one can no longer assume that males rather than females are the heads of households. One's family situation is no longer a pertinent consideration, and now fairness demands that each person be considered on the basis of the work he or she does rather than on need, family status, or other considerations. Women have fought for equality in the labor market and have attempted to have the old customs replaced by new ones. The fight has been a long one, and women still make less than men. But the general principle of equal pay for equal work has been adopted in legislation, and it is a principle to which there is no vocal opposition.

Equal pay for equal work, however, is not a simple principle, nor an unambiguous one. It admits of at least five levels of initial interpretation: (1) on an international level, across an occupation or position; (2) on a national or regional level, across an occupation or position; (3) on an industry level; (4) on a company level; and (5) on an individual or interpersonal level. Thus, some claim that U.S. multinationals should pay all their personnel in similar positions at the same rate, regardless of whether they are in the United States, in Europe, or in less developed countries. This position is not required by justice. Wages should always be considered in the context of background institutions as well as of the local cost of living. Nor has the case been made that equal pay for equal work demands that people holding similar positions anywhere in the United States receive similar pay, or even that a given company pay all its people at the same rate, wherever they are in the United States. The cost of living varies, and the labor markets are different in different part of the country. There is no reason why a company must pay everyone in its employ what it must pay in the sector where the cost of living is highest or where the supply of people it needs to employ is not plentiful.

The principle of equal pay for equal work has been used successfully in uncovering and uprooting discrimination (on the basis of race and sex) within a particular firm in a given location. In such cases it has been used either in class-action suits or on the basis of interpersonal comparisons. If a man and a woman are performing similar tasks, and have equal training, seniority, and competence but are paid different wages in the same firm at the same location, there is certainly a prima facie case for claiming discrimination.

Equal pay for equal work, however, does not quite mean what it might be interpreted to mean if taken literally, even within a given firm. Consider a college or university.

Professors of computer science, engineering, business, or medicine receive a considerably higher salary on entry and thereafter than do professors of English, history, or philosophy, at the same college or university. Why is that not a violation of the principle of equal pay for equal work? And if an assistant professor teaches the same number of students and courses as does a senior professor, publishes the same number of articles or books in a given year, and serves on the same number of committees, why should the assistant professor not receive as high a salary as the senior professor? The answer in the latter case is seniority, a system superimposed on the principle of equal pay for equal work. It is not without justification, because although the assistant professor (the junior person) receives less upon entry, he or she can expect to receive comparable increases over time, as did the senior member. And in the long run, they will have received comparable, if not necessarily equal, pay for equal work. The practice in universities, moreover, parallels the seniority system in the private business sector and is justifiable if the system is justifiable.

In the former case, the only justification for the difference in salaries between the pay of the professor of computer science and the professor of English is that of the marketplace. The market, if fair, is blind concerning sex or race. But discrimination on the basis of skill is permissible. The skill of the computer scientist is not greater in his domain than the skill of the English professor. But the computer scientist's skill is in shorter supply than the skill of the English teacher; the computer scientist therefore commands higher pay. The justification is that in the long run the market, by differential reward, will signal the need for more computer scientists and for fewer English professors. Students interested in income will pay attention to these signals and act accordingly. Those who refuse to do so and take their chances on receiving appointments as English professors should realize that they will receive less than computer scientists with comparable training. Such wage differentials help allocate human resources to where they are most needed, and are justifiable because of the efficiency they thus promote.

This justification takes into account the system, as any justification should. Those who knowingly choose poorer-paying positions cannot legitimately complain that their positions are poorly paid. No one is forced to take a particular position, and those willing and able to develop the skills for which there is most demand will receive the best returns. Professors of some subjects may receive less pay than people with similar training in industry, but presumably there are attractions in the teaching profession that compensate for less pay. If this were not so, there would be a shortage of qualified people in academia, and the pay for professors would have to be increased as it has increased for professors of computer science. Because professors of the humanities are in less demand outside of academia, the pay sufficient to attract and hold professors of the humanities is less than what is necessary to attract and hold professors of computer science. Therefore, they are paid different wages, even though a professor of English and a professor of computer science may teach the same number of students, serve on similar committees, and teach a subject that is just as important to society.

Comparable Worth

An argument similar to the one justifying pay differentials for professors teaching at the same university in different departments is sometimes used to justify paying teachers less than those with similar education who perform tasks of equal social importance. The market determines whether teachers receive more or less than those with equal training and responsibility in non-teaching positions. Yet in certain areas this justification has been challenged under the new claim of *equal pay for comparable work.* That principle is presented as a principle of justice, in terms of which we can judge that some wages are unfair and demand rectification. Implicit is the claim that the market fails in certain areas, and therefore changes in background institutions need to be made. The impetus, as in the case of equal pay for equal work, is claimed discrimination.

Some traditionally female jobs—nursing, elementary-school teaching, and secretarial work, among others—have remained low-paying positions. Women continue to be the major group of people attracted to these positions, for reasons that are not altogether clear. The question that has arisen is whether the pay for these positions is low because of the nature of the work or whether the pay for these positions is low because women are attracted to them. If secretaries were primarily men, would secretarial pay be as low as it is? The contention of some people is that the positions would not be low-paying if they were filled primarily by men. Hence, they consider the low pay for such positions to be discriminatory. The case was difficult to make under the principle of equal pay for equal work, as written into law and as generally interpreted, because the small percentage of men in such jobs received the same pay as women. This, then, is the reason for the more recent claim that the principle of equal pay for equal work implies the principle of equal pay for comparable work; and if the law does not include this latter principle, new legislation is needed that does embody it.

The issue was raised explicitly in a case in the State of Washington. In the Washington case, Judge Jack E. Tanner ruled that women employees of the state (members of the state's public colleges and universities excluded) had been underpaid and deserved compensation.[9] He based his ruling on Title VII of the Civil Rights Act of 1964, which bars paying women less than men performing "comparable" jobs. Judge Tanner based his decision on a "comparable skills" study adopted by the State of Washington. According to the study, points were attached to various factors, such as responsibility, knowledge, skill, working conditions, and accountability. The results showed that occupations in which women dominated received about 20 percent less than occupations that ranked in the same place on the scale but in which men domi-

---

[9] *American Federation of State, County, and Municipal Employees (AFSCME)* v. *the State of Washington* (1983). In 1985 the U.S. Ninth Circuit Court of Appeals reversed the decision. The U.S. Supreme Court has not decided any comparable worth case and is not scheduled to do so.

nated. Thus, a ranking of 97 points was given to both laundry workers and truck drivers. But truck drivers, who are mostly male, received a maximum of $1,574 a month, and laundry workers, who are mostly women, received only $1,114. A secretary II received $1,324 for a 197-point job, but an electrician received $1,918. In making his ruling, Judge Tanner claimed he was simply applying standards that the state had determined. Implications of the ruling for other states without a commitment to such a study, or for the private sector, therefore, may be nil.

The State of Kansas, for instance, has a law dating back over 100 years that requires the state to pay the "prevailing wage," as determined community by community, for various services. It thus determines its wages by the market as it operates in the private sector. The determination of wages in the public sector is notoriously difficult because there is often no measurable product, and the determination of productivity in the various sections is fairly arbitrary. One solution is the adoption of a step system, according to which those who supervise others are to receive more pay—a principle that operates in a great many firms and that leads to very high salaries in the more complex and very large firms.

If we prescind from the Washington study, however, and the determination of state salaries on the basis of that study, we can ask whether the principle of equal pay for comparable work is a morally justifiable one. There are three arguments against it, which are serious enough to make it a questionable principle.

First, the argument of equal pay for comparable work assumes that some fair determination of comparable work is not only possible but morally justifiable. There are many measures of work and of comparability. One of the arguments for the market is that different people weigh the various factors differently. The market gives priority to no one set but considers them all, the end result being a mix of all the factors with their various weights. Secretaries may have as much responsibility, and need as much skill and knowledge as electricians or truck drivers. The conclusion that therefore they should be paid at the same rate does not follow, for a great many other factors enter into these jobs. If women, as some do, prefer the pay of a truck driver to the pay of a secretary, they should be able to enter that market. If entry is denied them, then that is where the injustice lies and where remedy is needed, rather than in adjusting salaries elsewhere. The comparable work argument cannot be used fairly if it is used selectively—that is, only in the instances where women are paid less and dominate the occupation. Such selective use of a principle is not an application of a morally justified principle, and such use of the principle seems only a rationalization for what is perceived for other reasons as unjust. If there is discrimination—and we cannot deny that there is—then discrimination should be addressed. The attack in this instance misses its proper target.

Second, the approach of comparable worth, if accepted, will not help to reduce discrimination; it will help to reinforce it. If it is true, as some claim, that women are discriminated against by being forced into secretarial jobs, nursing jobs, and so on, raising their pay in those jobs may well increase, not decrease, the likelihood that those jobs will remain filled predominantly by women. The incentive for women to go into other fields will be diminished and the incentive for them to enter those fields will be increased. If there is discrimination in those areas, the best solution will be to remove barriers to the entry of women into other areas and to change the incentives that push them into those areas. If there are truly alternative opportunities, and if women still choose those occupations, despite lower pay, then their choice may call for social analysis; it does not call for compensatory justice.

Third, the claim of equal pay for comparable work undercuts the market mechanism and raises more problems than it solves. We have argued that if we have proper background institutions, the market is the best determinant of wage differential, above the minimum. This leads to the most efficient use of talent and results in talent being drawn to where it is most needed—in the long run. To introduce a scale of comparable work into government would imply that the scale is morally justifiable (and if in government, then also in the nongovernmental sector). This in turn would ultimately lead to the imposition of pay scales and wage determination by government.

In the private sector, a rating service would generate competing and conflicting rating services, with different scales; then government would be required to set norms and determine the salary scale to be used. The result would be grossly inefficient and ultimately arbitrary. We need not only speculate that it would be so. Numerous countries have tried to do away with the market, and wages or remuneration have been set by government—the USSR was a case in point. The results were not perspicuously just or rational. An assumption that things would be different in the United States seems unwarranted.

If equal pay for comparable work is a justifiable principle, it has not yet been shown to be such.[10] Consideration of the principle does illustrate, however, how discussion of the justice or fairness of wages can and does take place within the system of American free enterprise.

Executive Compensation

Although we have discussed the necessity for a bottom for wages, we have not addressed the question of the justifiability of upper limits. What is the proper maximum ratio of highest to lowest wages? Within a company, is a ratio of seven to one high enough, as some socialist countries maintained and enforced? Is a thousand to one too high? If the lowest-paid worker gets $4.35

---

[10] For a fuller discussion of the issue, see Steven E. Rhoads, *Incomparable Worth* (Cambridge: Cambridge University Press, 1993); Paula England, *Comparable Worth: Theories and Evidence* (New York: Aldine de Gruyter, 1992); and Linda M. Blum, *Between Feminism and Labor: The Significance of the Comparable Worth Movement* (Berkeley: University of California Press, 1991).

an hour, should management at its highest levels make no more than $435.00 an hour? Or no more than $4,350 an hour? Is there a proper multiple? There seems to be no way to decide that a multiple of five or seven or ten or one hundred is the proper upper multiple. If this is true, we should not attempt to set one. Rather, we should ask what background institutions are appropriate to keep income differentials from skewing our society in undesirable ways, robbing those less well off of their dignity and personal or social esteem. One solution available, which we already use, even if we do not use it as well as we might, is taxation. In Japan, for instance, multiples are kept low because large incomes are taxed at such high rates (e.g., up to 83 percent) that there is little to gain by increasing the multiple. It would not make a great deal of difference if the multiple of one person's earnings was considerably more than another's if there were a fair method of progressive taxation. One solution to high incomes, therefore, is to judge not the fairness of the wage or income but the proper and fair rate of taxation on that income.

Complaints about executive compensation, however, do not focus only or mainly on the multiple of the salary of executives to ordinary workers, even though that multiple is much higher in the United States than anywhere else in the world. Two other frequent complaints are that executive salaries go up even when the company's profits decline or when it loses money, and that executives often receive handsome increases at the same time that the company is laying off workers in order to save money. The criticims are often, although not always, right in this complaint. A CEO might well have performed admirably and deserved a raise for having prevented the company from losing more than it might have under different management or than other comparable firms did in the same market. Yet a sense of fairness argues that in cases in which the company performs poorly, the CEO should not benefit.

What seems appropriate is that an executive's compensation should be tied to the company's performance and that it should be set by some portion of the board of directors that is truly independent of the person whose salary is being set. A board that is chaired by the executive in question and the members of which were chosen by that executive can hardly be considered impartial and objective. The most commonly suggested way of tying the executive's compensation to the company's performance is through stock ownership or stock options, especially if the options are set reasonably higher than the price of a share when the CEO is hired and if they cannot be exercised for some length of time, for example, five years. This both provides the executive with a challenge and encourages a long-term perspective. If the company performs well and its stock rises, the CEO reaps the benefits through the exercise of the options. If the company does poorly and the stock falls or remains the same, the CEO does not benefit, and suffers with the sahreholders and workers. Of course, a company's stock may rise and fall based not on performance but on the general movement of the stock market up or down. But even in these cases the financial fate of the CEO is tied directly to that of the shareholders.

The more difficult and controversial issue is giving the CEO a substantial raise for improving the stock price by firing large numbers of employees. Although such downsizing might improve the efficieny of the company, if the financial health of the company required cutting wages, it does not seem proper that those who are fired suffer all the burden. If the point was to save money in wages, then the CEO should not be given a raise, which money could have been used to keep on more employees. The argument is plausible on the face of it, and some CEOs have refused raises when they have downsized, in part to help the morale of the remaining employees. Other companies feel that unless they reward the CEO for taking such action, he or she will not take it. The distinction between not receiving a raise and still benefiting from the rise in the price of the stock because of stock options mollifies only some of the critics.

In 1992 the Securities and Exchange Commission, partially in response to public demand, issued new executive compensation rules, under which appropriate data must be publicly stated in a standard form, all compensation is to be disclosed, and the firm's compensation committee is to disclose the factors on which the compensation decision was made.[11] This does not prevent excess executive compensation, however one defines that, but it does make it easier for shareholders and the general public to know how much executives are paid. In this way, it helps clarify the public debate about what constitutes just or fair executive compensation.[12]

The Right to Organize: Unions

In a just society, among the institutions necessary to achieve a system of fair wages, unions have played an important role.

The gross annual income of such corporate giants as General Motors, Standard Oil, and Ford is larger than the gross national product of Austria, Norway, Finland, or Greece, not to mention that of many less developed countries. An individual facing the corporate colossus is no David standing before Goliath. The individual who takes on a large corporation is more like David facing a whole army.

We have already seen that an agreement between two contracting parties is fair if each of the parties has access to adequate, appropriate information, and if each enters into the transaction freely, without coercion. But what of

---

[11] Michael A. Schwartz, "Executive Compensation: A Brief on the SEC's New Rules," *Directors and Boards*, 17, no. 2 (Winter 1993), pp. 59, 61.

[12] For more on executive compensation, see Derek Bok, *The Cost of Talent: How Executives and Professionals Are Paid and How It Affects America* (New York: Free Press, 1993); Graef S. Crystal, *In Search of Excess: The Overcompensation of American Executives* (New York: W. W. Norton & Company, 1991); Ira T. Kay, *Value at the Top: Solutions to the Executive Compensation Crisis* (New York: Harper Business, 1992); and Fred K. Foulkes (Ed.), *Executive Compensation: A Strategic Guide for the 1990's* (Boston: Harvard Business School Press, 1991).

contracts between an individual worker and a giant corporation? Can such a contract be fair, and can the worker deal as an equal in negotiations with the corporation?

Individual workers, of course, are no match for large corporations and are in a very weak position with respect to negotiation. Individual workers are most often given the choice simply of accepting employment on the terms offered by a firm or of not accepting such terms and conditions. If the number of firms is fairly small and the number of employees in search of work comparatively large, then the firms are clearly in a position of superiority in any negotiation and they can offer employment on terms that favor themselves. Even if they do not offer the lowest wages possible, it is in their interest to offer lower rather than higher wages whenever possible. The system of competition, in theory, should offset this advantage. But when the labor supply exceeds the demand for labor, this does not happen. Hence, workers have found it to their advantage to organize into workers' associations, or unions, in order to deal with managers on more equal terms. By forcing management to deal with workers as a group rather than individually, the workers are in a better position to make the terms of any labor contract fair, at least in the sense that it is freely accepted by both sides.

How is the claimed right to form unions justified? The justification in the free-enterprise system stems from the prior right of individuals to the greatest amount of freedom compatible with a like freedom for all. This includes the right of individuals to pursue their own ends and the right to associate with others to achieve common ends. The free association of workers to achieve common ends leads to the organization of labor unions. Because labor unions are the product of united workers, the unions have the same rights as the workers. The derivation and justification of unions parallel the derivation and justification of corporations. Unions are thus as morally legitimate as corporations. Unions, moreover, have no special rights beyond those of the individual workers, except those that are due organizations under their legal status. Union activity may be justly limited by government—for instance, if the workers in a field create a monopoly of labor in that field. Monopoly power goes beyond the rights of individuals and therefore of unions. Just as a government can legitimately regulate or preclude monopolies in industry, it can also do so with unions. But this does not mean that government can legitimately outlaw unions, for workers have the right to free association. Workers in unions can also do what they are allowed to do as individuals—jointly provide insurance for members, build up savings in case of need, establish funds to carry on strikes or civil suits in defense of workers, and so on.

Unions and their activities can be morally evaluated, just as corporations and their activities can be morally evaluated.[13] Charges of corruption

---

[13] For a discussion of unions, see Richard B. Freeman and James L. Medoff, *What Do Unions Do?* (New York: Basic Books, 1984). An interesting article about Canadian policy is William L. Batt, Jr., "Canada's Good Example with Displaced Workers," *Harvard Business Review*, 83, no. 4 (July-August 1983), pp. 6-22.

within unions need little discussion here. If union leaders use union money illegally, or for their own private purposes, such actions are clearly immoral.

Is it fair for unions to restrict membership in certain trades so that the number of members will be kept lower than the demand for them? Such a device obviously makes each member more valuable and therefore able to command a higher wage. But he or she is able to do so at the expense of those who would like to enter the marketplace and are prevented from doing so. If it is unfair for businesses to restrict trade and gain monopolies, it is unfair for some workers to restrict other workers from pursuing their interests and engaging in the type of work they prefer. Both are attempts to curtail competition for the benefit of the one restricting entry.

Although workers have the right to form and join unions, workers have no *obligation* to do so. What then is the moral status of union shops? In a union shop the union typically does not restrict union membership; often, the point of a union shop is to encourage membership. But a union shop allows only union members, or those who join the union within thirty days of employment, to work in the plant or industry. The argument given in defense of a union shop is twofold. If a plant is allowed to hire nonunion labor, then it can hire such labor at nonunion rates. Once a plant is able to hire people at less than union rates, it will find it to its advantage to do so. As a result, it will tend to replace union labor with nonunion labor, and the success that unions have achieved will thus be undercut. The second argument claims that if a plant hires both union and nonunion labor and treats them equally, workers will have little incentive to join the union. Why should they, if they receive the same benefits without having to pay union dues? The result in this case is once again to undercut and weaken the union, deplete its coffers, and make it financially impossible to fund its activities.

Although both arguments carry a good deal of weight, they are not conclusive. For there is no obligation that everyone who benefits by the actions of others must somehow support those actions or contribute to the activities of the group from whose actions they benefit. If a particular enterprise agrees to hire only union labor, however, it does not thereby violate the rights of potential nonunion workers because the latter have no right to work for that enterprise. The right of union members must be balanced against the right of an individual worker to seek a job and to have the option of not joining a union. He should not be forced to do so if he does not wish to do so. He should not be prevented from working or have his options narrowly restricted because he prefers not to join a union. Therefore, we have a conflict of rights. The controversy has been resolved in various ways in the United States. Because the Taft-Hartley Act has left the decision of whether there should be union shops to the individual states, the decision becomes one of law and public policy. Such a policy may be written into a contract between a union and a given enterprise. The issue in some states has been decided at the polls. Right-to-work laws that guarantee the right of a worker to seek employment without joining a union have been passed in some states. If this means breaking up the union shop, it robs unions of one of their key implements. The last word on the controversy has not yet been spoken.

Unions have a specific constituency—their members. They do not claim to serve directly the larger society or to have the good of society as their primary aim. Their goal is to protect and promote the interests of their members. They typically take management as their adversary. Unions have championed the right to strike and have used it as an effective weapon. They engage in collective bargaining and press the demands of the workers as forcefully and fully as possible. They have achieved a good deal of success.

Can unions properly be faulted for ignoring the public good and for sacrificing it in order to achieve their own ends? The union practice of featherbedding, for example, preserves the jobs of those employees who would otherwise be laid off because of technological improvements. A frequently cited case—during the transition from steam to electric trains—was the requirement that each train have a fireman, even though the train was run by electricity and did not need a fireman. The fireman was carried on each run, although he had no work to do. He continued to be paid, and this pay eventually came out of the pockets of those who used the train. Unions have also been accused of fueling inflation by seeking higher wages in an unending spiral—each demand fueling other demands that in turn raise the demands of the first group. Each raise increases the cost of the products produced, and in the long run may lead to unemployment and recession.

Unions, like businesses, sometimes act in terms of vested interests, to the detriment of the general good. Union leaders claim, however, that in the long run (even in the particular instances cited), their actions lead to more good than harm, not only for their own workers but for all workers and for society in general. Such claims are a shorthand version of a utilitarian argument and can be properly evaluated only by considering particular cases and by attempting to evaluate the good and bad done to all those affected by the actions in question.

Individual workers are legally bound by the contracts entered into on their behalf by their union representatives. Yet we can legitimately ask whether workers are morally so bound, and whether they are bound even if they have voted against a contract supported by a majority. There is room for moral disagreement, for instance, about the justifiability of strikes by workers that are not called or sanctioned by union leaders. Whether these "wildcat strikes" are morally justifiable depends on the facts and circumstances of the case, the nature of the organizations involved, the agreement made by members with their unions, the degree of trust the workers have in their leaders, and similar considerations.

To have said this much, however, seems to have assumed the right to strike on the part of unions, and we should ask whether this is in fact a right, and if so, how it is justified.

The Right to Strike

In relations between labor and management there are four major groups involved, not merely two. The four are labor, management, government, and the general public. From a moral point of view, it is essential to remember that all persons who make up these groups are human beings, and they do not stop being human beings by becoming workers, managers, a part of government, or a part of the general public. Workers and managers are persons, beings deserving of respect, who have the moral obligation to do what is right and to avoid doing what is wrong. They thus have both moral rights and responsibilities that take precedence over their role-related rights, duties, or positions as workers or managers. Hence, despite the adversarial relation of workers and managers in the American free-enterprise system, both deserve respect from the other and deserve to be treated as human beings, regardless of their differences. This general background truth, though simple, obvious, and powerful, is often ignored.

Government, the third party, has the task of giving all the members of society—and so, both workers and managers—a reasonable degree of security from both internal and external violence. It has the obligation to provide for the adjudication of disputes, and it also has the duty to safeguard the common good and protect the rights of all its citizens. The fourth participant in labor relations is the general public. By *general public* we usually mean all the people considered, without regard to their particular roles. The general public as such has no rights, but each of the persons making up the general public has rights. They have the right, for instance, not to have violence done to them by another. Each person has the right not be killed arbitrarily and without just cause, even if such killing would somehow produce good for the rest of society. To speak of the rights of individuals means, we have seen, that there are certain claims that each individual has against society that cannot be overridden by some calculation of the good to be achieved. If their rights are to be respected they can only be overridden by the stronger rights of others, not simply by a claimed maximization of good.

Given this background of worker-management relations, do workers have a right to strike? If a strike is seen as an extension of an individual worker's freedom to refuse employment, or to refuse to accept employment on certain conditions, then it seems clear that workers—workers in associations or unions—have a right to strike. One obvious exception is in a nonvolunteer army, in which soldiers are drafted and required to serve for the common good. But if employment is freely engaged in, then, whether the employer is private industry or government, the right of the worker to choose not to work carries with it the right of workers, collectively, not to work. Nonetheless, the right is morally restricted by at least two considerations. One consideration is respect for a valid contract. Inherent in valid contracts is the moral obligation to live up to them unless there are seriously overriding moral reasons not to do so. These reasons must involve conflicts of serious moral obligations, not simply the desire to achieve greater good or welfare. Hence, if a contract includes a no-strike clause, it should be respected for the term of the contract. The second restriction is consideration of the rights of the general public to protection, medical care, and other necessities of life. Strikes by public-sector employees—police, firefighters, and hospital workers—thus pose serious problems.

The right to strike has been widely accepted. The discrepancy between the power and resources of big business and the resources of the individual worker historically put the worker at the mercy of management. Workers have had to unite to gain a position of equality from which to bargain with management about higher wages, shorter hours, vacations with pay, safer working conditions, retirement plans, and other similar benefits. Management has frequently passed on some of the cost of these benefits to their customers, in the form of higher prices. But increased productivity has often made it possible for companies to retain the same rate of profit despite paying higher wages to workers. The unions have also helped ease the plight of nonunion workers by bargaining for standards that have become the norm for all.

Once we have granted the right to strike, however, a question arises about management's right to hire other workers in the place of striking workers. The right of management to hire whomever it wishes at whatever conditions they mutually agree on undercuts the effectiveness of unions and strikes. Management in some industries is not able to do this. In the United States, for instance, in 1981 and again in 1994, the major league baseball players went out on strike for higher wages. Because there are a limited number of baseball players of the quality of the professional players, and because one cannot form a team simply by hiring people willing to play, the strikers did not worry about others being brought in to replace them. In other industries, however, unskilled laborers have sometimes been brought in by management to replace strikers. This has often led to violence against those who chose to work under those conditions, who are called strikebreakers. Violence against strikebreakers, however, violates the rights of those people. Moral considerations here demand solutions other than violence. Striking employees are usually considered employees of a firm unless fired, even though they have no contract governing them if the strike occurs after a contract has terminated. Strikebreakers are either temporary replacements or employees hired to replace those who have been fired and those on strike. Unions, however, have learned to deal with management's right to hire strikebreakers and have often become strong enough to preclude this practice. One effective technique involves the solidarity of workers, both the skilled and the unskilled, within a firm. If all the workers in a firm refuse to work when any strikers are fired, and until they are rehired and a contract signed, the possibility of a strike being broken by imported workers is lessened or precluded. Other techniques have also been used. The point is that there *are* methods of achieving the aim of a strike while respecting the rights of all involved. Consciousness of the rights of all persons will help keep strikes, as well as other forms of dispute settlement, within moral bounds.

But what of the harm done to the public by strikes?

Here it is necessary to distinguish between rights and good. If the workers of a particular industry, the auto industry, for instance, go on strike, then a certain amount of harm is done to the general population. Those who ordered cars or who wish to buy cars may not have them available for purchase. Steel mills may suffer from lack of orders from the automotive industry and may have to lay off workers. Such harm may produce public pressure on automobile manufacturers to settle the strike. It may also prepare the public for the higher prices they will have to pay for cars as a result of the settlement of the strike. But the harm done to the public in this instance does not violate any of its rights. People do not have a right to be able to buy a car whenever they have the money to do so. It may be their desire to be able to do this, and we might say that their ability to do so helps the general welfare. But no one's rights are violated when this is not the case. Hence, the harm done to the public in this case does not override the right of workers to refuse to work, or to refuse to accept certain terms in a negotiated contract. Nor does the public have a right to buy cars at a certain price, so that consideration cannot be used to offset the workers' right to strike.

There may be times, however, when the public's rights *are* violated by a strike. In such cases the *right* of the public must be weighed against the *right* of the workers to strike. A frequent example is public-sector strikes. The general public has the right to protection by police and firefighters. Does its right to such protection override the right of police and firefighters to strike? Clearly, the considerations here are different from those in the auto industry, for in these cases we are weighing competing rights and not rights versus good.

The right of workers in the public sector to strike is controversial. In the United States, *public-sector strikes* are strikes by federal, state, and municipal employees. Should teachers, firemen, policemen, municipal hospital employees, and members of the armed forces be allowed to strike? Enough strikes by public school teachers have taken place that a precedent for their right to strike has been established. The claimed harm to children has not been as great as was feared. Firemen, policemen, and municipal hospital employees have also gone on strike in various parts of the country. When they do, they not only harm the city, state, or federal bureaucracies or departments that hire them, but they also endanger the lives and safety of ordinary citizens who have no say in the settlement and no responsibility for the negotiations. Is this fair? A strike by employees against an employer aims at forcing him to suffer greater damage by failure of the workers to work than he would suffer by giving in to their demands. Is the same true of public-service strikes? Firefighters, police, and municipal hospital workers work for the city or state, and they are paid from money raised by public taxes. If their demands are not totally unreasonable, if the wages or other benefits they seek are in line with what others in the private sector are making, then by striking they apply pressure on the members of society to bear an increase in taxes or take cuts in the services they receive. The pressure is appropriately placed on the public because these people work for the public.

But what of the lives threatened by such strikes? The problem is a difficult one, and one that has been handled in a variety of ways. Sometimes the supervisory personnel in the organization take over the basic jobs; sometimes police are called upon to man the firehouses; sometimes the state militia or the army are called in to handle the jobs of those on strike. Sometimes, too, if a true emergency arises, those on strike—or at least some of them—pitch in to help.

Members of the armed forces have raised the question of their right to strike, but they have won little support. The qualities that are important in battle are immediate response to authority and trust in one's commanders. Soldiers are no more permitted to do what is immoral than anyone else. Yet within those bounds obedience is essential to their survival and to their effectiveness. Is such obedience undermined by the development of a strike mentality? Some people argue that it is. When, after all, would a strike by the military be most effective? When the military is most needed, is the reply. Yet that is precisely the time when a strike is most inappropriate, from the point of view of those who wish to be defended by the military. What about strikes in peacetime by a peacetime army? The case justifying the military's use of the strike technique has yet to be forcefully and convincingly made, but that does not mean it cannot or will not some day be made.

The justification for public-sector strikes is that strikes are the only effective way such workers can make their plight known and can apply pressure to achieve some of the benefits enjoyed by the workers in the private sector. Whether strikes are the only way or whether mandatory arbitration is not an acceptable alternative is at the heart of the issue.

The adversarial relation of workers and management in the American system is not in itself unethical or immoral. Yet simply because workers have the *right* to strike does not mean that workers *ought* to strike. The exercise of a right to strike is often shortsighted, and from an economic point of view may in the long run as well as the short run not be in the interest of the workers, management, or the general public, whose lives are disrupted in one way or another.

Are there, however, no other moral restrictions on the right of workers to strike? Are there no moral considerations that should be fulfilled before a strike is undertaken? Is there no moral obligation to seek negotiation rather than confrontation? Is it not better from a moral point of view to give up the right to strike and to enforce impartial negotiations to which both unions and firms must submit?

It is not a violation of a right to require that it not be exercised capriciously. It can be legitimately circumscribed. Although labor and management at the time of negotiations have adversarial roles, they need not act out those roles to their detriment. In a given firm, workers and management can function together. If workers benefit when the enterprise is successful, then the fate of both management and workers is bound up with the success of the firm. If management alone benefits, then workers have less incentive to contribute to the success of the firm. But their welfare is associated with the firm's continuing to operate, and so continuing to provide them employment. Neither side benefits when workers do not work; therefore, neither side benefits more from a strike than they would from a negotiated settlement. A negotiated settlement, moreover, would tend to disrupt the public served by the firm less than would a strike. A negotiated settlement, therefore, is in the best interest of all concerned, providing that the negotiations yield fair results.

The consideration of the general good is not sufficient to override the right of the workers to strike, but it is sufficient to provide the basis for legislation requiring attempts at negotiation prior to a strike. There are difficulties with any such law. Such negotiations are fruitful only if both parties negotiate in good faith and make reasonable demands and concessions. A party that enters into negotiations by setting demands that must be met without change is not really entering into a negotiation. Good faith and goodwill are difficult, if not impossible, to mandate by law. But even when good faith is lacking, a forced period of negotiation prior to a strike does provide what is sometimes called a cooling-off period. If such a period is legally mandated and a good faith effort at negotiation is required, there is at least a chance for a settlement. Such legislation is morally legitimate. Though such legislation cannot morally take away the right of workers to strike, it can legitimately delay the exercise of that right.

What of legally mandatory arbitration by a third party acceptable to both labor and management? If the industry is one that protects the public (e.g., police) or serves it in such a way as to fulfill its rights, then we weigh the right of the public to protection, for instance, against the right of the police to strike. In given circumstances and conditions, it is possible that the public's right will override the right of the police to strike. In such a case, binding legally mandatory arbitration is permissible. The condition for its being morally justifiable is that the arbitration be truly impartial. In industries that provide goods or services to which people have no right, then we once again are forced to weigh good against rights. If our previous analysis is correct, we cannot outlaw strikes on the basis of an argument in favor of the public good, even though the government may mandate attempts at arbitration before a strike. The threat of a strike, in this instance, is an inducement to management to negotiate in good faith. If, to preclude wage increases, a government temporarily suspends the right of workers to strike for higher wages, it must, in justice, also preclude the right of industry to increase prices that place workers at a disadvantage.

Despite all of this, many settlements in labor relations that come about from voluntary negotiations (which is the ideal, and therefore the preferable approach to labor relations) are shortsighted. And many settlements from mandated negotiations or from strikes are also shortsighted. This is because the negotiators frequently look only at the interests of labor and management.

They do not consider the long-range impact on society or on the industry itself, or, in the long run, on the workers and management. Society would profit if labor and management were to take a long-range view, considering the good of society, of which they are a part, as well as of their own short-range good. If labor and management would cooperate with each other and with other industries, they would probably help to serve the common good by arriving at socially helpful solutions to disputes, and also help to control inflation. The problem is that no one has the answer to the question of what is the proper way for all industries to act. In those countries where the government makes all the decisions, the results are not demonstrably better than in those in which the various sectors and individuals are allowed to negotiate for their own good.

In the United States, labor and management have traditionally seen themselves as adversaries, and most American labor law has developed from this premise. There are, however, two indications of possible future change. The first is the placement of union representatives on corporate boards. The first time this happened was in 1980, when Douglas Fraser, president of the United Auto Workers, took a seat on the board of directors of the Chrysler Corporation. There was some worry at the time about possible conflict of interest because the board of directors negotiates the labor contract with union representatives. Not all directors need to be present at all meetings, however, and, where conflict of interest is a danger or an issue (as in the board's negotiation with labor over contracts), a member can be excused. Labor has not been anxious to join boards, and management has not been anxious to have designated representatives from any area, unions included. But at least a dozen companies added union representatives to their boards in the three years following the Chrysler precedent, and others may do so. If they do, this will signal a significant change in the adversarial relation of management and labor.

The second indicator of change is the significant decline in the number of union members in the United States, which in part reflects the changing composition of the American labor force. By 1989, only 17 percent of American workers belonged to a union. The traditionally unionized occupations—factory workers—have declined significantly, and the number of white-collar workers has increased. Whether unions have served their function and will be replaced eventually with government guarantees of workers' rights and negotiated contracts remains to be seen.

Morality cannot supply the concrete solutions to labor disputes or to the specific agreements to which negotiations must lead, but it can provide a general framework within which labor disputes can be negotiated. It can specify the conditions of justice under which such negotiations should proceed. And it can clarify the right of the parties, which any solution must respect. In the long run, only by observing moral norms and constraints can we expect that solutions to labor problems will be truly accepted and so lead to general long-term social peace and stability. The attempt to make all our actions—including our actions as workers or industrialists—conform to moral norms is simply an attempt to act as true human beings in all our relations with others.

Study Questions

1. Was the PATCO strike in 1981 ethically justifiable? Why or why not? Was President Reagan's action in firing the air traffic controllers ethically justifiable? Why or why not?
2. What is the doctrine of employment-at-will? What ethical and/or legal limitations apply to it?
3. What is the right to employment? the right to work?
4. What does it mean to say a right is a *human right?*
5. Can the right to work be justified? If so, show how. If not, show why not.
6. What is the negative right to work? the positive right to work? Illustrate each.
7. Why does the right typically arise in an industrial society? Explain.
8. Against whom is the right to employment exercised? Explain.
9. What is a *union shop?* Is it ethically justifiable?
10. What is a *right-to-work law?* Is it ethically justifiable?
11. Why is the right to employment not identical with full employment? Explain.
12. What is the right to a just wage? How can it be justified?
13. Why isn't the market alone morally sufficient to set a just wage?
14. What background institutions are needed to speak of a just wage?
15. What does equal pay for equal work mean? How can it be defended as ethically justifiable?
16. How can paying senior people more for equal work be justified? Explain.
17. What does equal pay for comparable work mean? Give some examples.
18. What are some arguments against equal pay for comparable work? Evaluate the arguments.
19. What is an ethically justifiable way to determine the pay of a CEO of a large corporation. Explain.
20. Is it fair to raise the pay of a CEO who raises the value of the company's stock by firing large numbers of employees in order to save money? Explain.
21. Are unions morally justifiable? Explain.
22. What four major groups are relevant to any strike consideration? Explain how they are relevant.
23. How can strikes be ethically justified? Explain.

24. What are *public-sector strikes?* Are they justifiable? Does it make any difference what field the workers are in? Does it make any difference whether the workers are municipal, state, or federal employees? Explain.

25. Why is fair negotiation preferable to strikes?

26. Can morality alone settle labor disputes? If so, how? If not, what can morality do with respect to such disputes?

27. Oil Company X is doing drilling offshore on the coast of Florida. It has brought in employees to work on the rig from eight of its various divisions around the country. The workers receive different wages, depending on their location and other factors. They will work on the rig about eight months before returning to their regular jobs. Should Company X pay all the employees doing similar work the same amount, should it pay each according to the regular salary that employee earns, or should it use some other way of figuring wages? What is fair in this situation?

28. American communities depend heavily on electricity. Would it be ethically justifiable for all the workers of electric power plants (which are privately owned) in a state or region to go out on strike? Why or why not?

15

WORKERS' RIGHTS AND DUTIES WITHIN A FIRM

Case Studies: Drug Testing and the Right to Privacy

Case 1: Drug and Polygraph Testing at Company X

"I'm tired of pandering to the supposed privacy rights of employees," Arnold Moss thundered as he slammed his fist down on the table. "I'm the CEO of this company and I have rights too. Anyone who is drug free and honest will have no objection to taking a periodic drug test or to taking a lie detector test when necessary. I have the right to hire whom I want and to fire whom I want. I also have the right to make sure that this company provides a drug-free environment for all of us who work here. And I have the right to make sure that all the employees of our company are honest. I would have no objection to doing so. Why should any honest person object? Only acid heads and crooks would hide behind some cock and bull story about privacy rights."

Sam Hempin, the union representative sitting opposite him at the table shifted uneasily in his chair. "You may not like it, Mr. Moss. But whether you like it or not and whether you agree with it or not, every worker has a right to privacy—even on the job. Requiring urinalysis, with someone watching as an employee provides the specimen, is clearly an invasion of that person's privacy. And their dismissal if they prove positive, even if their job performance has been up to par, is a further invasion of their privacy. What an employee does on his or her own time is properly of no concern to this firm unless it harms the firm in some way or impairs the employee's functioning. Nor is it any business of the company if an employee stole something as an adolescent or even while in the employ of another company and was neither charged nor punished for it. Yet that is what your polygraph people want to know when they give their tests. You know very well that the 1988 Employee Polygraph Protection Act prohibits pre-employment and random post-hiring polygraph testing."

"I know what the law says. It was passed by those liberals. That doesn't make it right. And if now and then someone failed the test who was honest, at least I'd have a better chance of hiring honest employees than I do now. And don't forget the law allows federal, state, and government employees and firms that do sensitive work under contracts with the Defense Department, the FBI, or the CIA to use pre-employment polygraph tests. If it's good enough for the government why shouldn't it be good enough for the private sector? The law is inconsistent and doesn't make sense."

"While we're on the law," he continued, "at least the Supreme Court had the good sense in *National Treasury Employees v. Von Rabb* to turn down the union's complaint of invasion of privacy by drug testing."

"Come on, now," retorted Sam. "You know that decision was based on narrow grounds of freedom from unreasonable search, and the case dealt with employees involved in drug interdiction, carrying firearms, and handling classified material. Our company makes paper products—hardly a sensitive area. Why do we need drug testing and polygraph tests? The employees find them demeaning and an invasion of their privacy. Even when legal they are unnecessary and there are better and more effective ways to deal with any problems that arise. You know very well that someone who used a hard drug two weeks prior to the test might test negative while someone who smoked a little marijuana a month earlier might test positive. What the company's concern should be is how each person performs, not what they do at home. And any real thief would probably know how to fool the polygraph, while the nervous honest secretary might fail it."

"I know all that. But I want people here who are drug free and if I can avoid the problems that drug users usually bring with them, I think I have the right to hire the people I want. And as far as the unreliability of polygraph tests, we of course would never use that evidence as decisive. Yet if someone refused to take such a test, I'd have strong suspicions about that person. I'm willing to state our policy up front and I want only those people as employees who agree with it, want to work in the environment we create, and are willing to take the tests we think necessary or appropriate."

"Mr. Moss," replied Sam, "you simply don't get it. This is not about what people are willing to submit to. This is about privacy rights. The union cannot agree to the terms of employment you want to set. It is not a matter of protecting the guilty. It is a matter of principle and of protecting the innocent."

Are Moss's or Hempin's arguments stronger? Are drug and polygraph tests an invasion of privacy? Should companies in the private sector use such tests routinely in either pre-employment screening or after hiring people?

Case 2: National Treasury Employees Union v. Von Rabb.[1]

In this U.S. Supreme Court case the union challenged the United States Customs Service's drug-testing program, which required a urine analysis of all employees who applied for promotion or transfer to positions that involved drug interdiction, required them to carry firearms, or involved the handling of classified material. Applicants were told that their selection was contingent on successfully passing the test; provision was made for the greatest privacy compatible with ensuring the specimen belonged to the person tested; and the test results could not be used for other purposes or turned over to any other agency. The program was started not because of any drug problem among the employees of the Customs Service, but rather as a preventive measure. The government's rationale for the program was that its agents involved with drug interdiction should be physically fit and have unimpeachable character; that to ensure the safety of others, those who carry firearms must be drug free; and that those who handle classified material must be free of the possibility of bribery or blackmail to which drug use would open them.

The union argued that searches should be based on probable cause and that the program was not so based; that the required urinalysis was an invasion of privacy; and that the tests were not required for the Service to achieve its aims. Those who tested positive and could offer no satisfactory explanation were subject to dismissal, regardless of their on-the-job performance, which constituted a further invasion of their privacy.

Case 3: Skinner v. Railway Labor Executives Association[2]

This U.S. Supreme Court case concerned regulations of the Federal Railroad Administration that required private railroads to perform blood and urine tests for drugs on all employees involved in major train accidents; that authorized breath and urine tests of employees who violated certain safety rules; and that enabled a supervisor with "reasonable suspicion" to determine whether an employee was under the influence of alcohol or drugs. The government argued that the safety of both the traveling public and the employees justified the regulations. The employees countered that the regulations requiring urine testing violated their right to privacy and that the ends hoped for by the regulations could be attained without such a violation.

While in the National Treasury Employees Union case the Court recognized the right of applicants to privacy and to freedom from unreasonable search, it ruled that the government's interests outweighed their privacy interests. In the Skinner case, although the majority of the Court recognized the right of the employees to privacy, it ruled that the regulations were permissi-

---

[1] 109 S. Ct. 1384 (1989).
[2] 109 S. Ct. 1402 (1989).

ble because the safety of the public outweighed the employee's right to privacy. Are these legal judgments morally justified?

The U.S. Supreme Court's rulings on drug testing in these two cases were narrow rulings and related to the legitimacy of government regulations in this regard. The issue was raised under a possible violation of the Fourth Amendment to the Constitution, which guarantees freedom from unreasonable government searches. The Court extended the scope of the amendment to include privacy.

From a moral point of view, we could argue that in the two cases decided by the Supreme Court the right of the general public to safety overrides the right of the employees to privacy, which is violated by mandated urine tests in which specimens are collected under supervision. Both cases, however, were judged with respect to the Fourth Amendment to the Constitution, which provides a guarantee against unreasonable search or seizure by the government. It does not govern drug testing in the private sector. Many employers claim the right to maintain a drug-free workplace, a right that comes up against the employee's right to privacy. From a moral point of view, under what conditions, if any, may employers in the private sector require drug testing by urinalysis? What moral rights do employees have against employers in such circumstances? How do you construe the right to privacy, and how important is it vis-à-vis other rights?

Although workers have a moral right to privacy, exactly what this right involves with respect to drug testing is far from clear. The reason is twofold. First, the notion of privacy is at least in part culturally determined. Hence, to speak of a human right to privacy, as if it were a right that could be substantively described as inherent to all human beings, is to misunderstand it. The right is part of the respect due to persons and can be derived from that respect. But how that respect is demonstrated with regard to privacy varies, at least to some extent, from culture to culture. Second, the right to privacy, like all other rights, is a prima facie right. But how high it stands on a scale of rights is not clear, and it often tends to be overridden by a number of other rights that take precedence when the two conflict.

No one can plausibly claim a right to take illegal drugs. Therefore, that cannot be used as a defense for those who refuse to submit to drugs tests at work. Some employers claim the right to maintain a drug-free environment on the job. The question is what means they may take to achieve such an environment since employees can legitimately claim a right to privacy. The employee's right to privacy enters the picture in two ways. Since employees have no right to take illegal drugs, they have no right to do so on the job. But they do have the right to a private life once they leave the job. They therefore can plausibly claim that what they do off the job is of no legitimate concern to their employers as long as what they do does not adversely affect their job performance. Moreover, drug testing is done through urinalysis, which is the most common and least expensive means, and blood tests. The surest way to determine that the urine sample comes from a particular person is to observe the production of the specimen—which many people claim is an invasion of their privacy. Hence, two issues are involved here: Whether drug testing violates the employees' right to privacy to do what they choose on their own time off the job; and whether the means used for testing violates their privacy with respect to very personal bodily functions.

The Rights of Employees Within a Firm

A simple approach to the rights and duties of employees states that employees as employees have all those, and only those, rights and duties that they negotiate with their employers as conditions of employment. This approach, however, is too simple and is seriously misleading. Employees and employers are not mere abstractions. Potential employees are first of all human beings and rational agents, ends in themselves and worthy of respect. As moral beings they carry with them in all their endeavors and undertakings the moral obligation to do what is right and to avoid doing what is wrong. Neither on the job nor in any other aspect of their lives are they free to do whatever they choose. They remain bound by the moral law in all their activities. An employer—whether we mean by employer the corporation as a legal entity or the actual persons who act for the corporation—is also bound by the moral law. Hence, neither side in the hiring process has the moral right to set whatever terms it wishes. Both sides are bound not only by law but also by morality. For instance, if someone wishes to sell himself into slavery to raise money to give to his family, he is legally and morally prohibited from doing so, and everyone else is legally and morally prohibited from making him a slave.

The background conditions for any contract between employer and employee are the conditions set by morality, law, local custom, and by the existing social circumstances in which the contract is made. Most people who start out in the employment market would like to earn as much as possible. Usually they have no work experience. If they also have no work skills, what they can offer is their time, their labor power, their ability to learn, and their intelligence, developed by however much schooling and training they have had. They offer these to the employer, who in turn has work of some kind available, for which he promises a certain compensation. A wage laborer works for wages—a certain amount of money per hour, week, month, or per piece.

The development of industry in the nineteenth century taught us many lessons. Workers fought for and secured legislation that protects them and their interests in many areas. Many workers in the past had to face the problem of how to live if they were laid off, fired, injured, or retired. Unemployment insurance, workman's compensation, and social security have helped alleviate the worst of those problems for large numbers of employees in the United States.

Employees have bargained collectively as well as individually for certain rights and privileges and have committed themselves to fulfilling certain obligations. Some employees have more to offer employers than others. Some people have special skills, much accumulated experience, and character or other traits that are in short supply and therefore in great demand. Such people can bargain better than those with no special skills, experience, or traits. Hollywood movie stars; stellar baseball, basketball, or football players; and top executives of large corporations all command handsome salaries or compensation for their work. Teenagers often work at jobs that pay the minimum allowable by law, and they are happy to find even those jobs. The range of pay is enormous, as is the range of other types of compensation. The tasks required—from menial to professional to entrepreneurial—are also extremely diverse. Yet we can make some general statements about the rights of all workers.[3]

Rights in Hiring, Promotion, and Firing

Although we cannot specify here all the restrictions that should be placed on the employment-at-will doctrine, in addition to the limitations already mentioned, if job offers are to be truly fair, employees have the right to know the real conditions under which they are hired. If the position is only a temporary one, they should be so informed. If there is a probationary period, they should know the length of it, and what is expected of them if they are to be kept on. If they are expected to fulfill conditions beyond those stated in a job description, these should be stated. If employees might be terminated simply because the employer feels someone else might do the job better, that too should be made clear from the start. Some people would not accept a position under these conditions; others would. If the employer does not volunteer all of this information, the potential employee has the right to ask and to have his or her questions answered honestly. The clearer the conditions of employment—including promotion, salary increases, and possible termination—before a person is hired, the more likely it is that the employment agreement is truly fair. In general applicants have the right to be judged only on the basis of job-related criteria, and they have the right to equal consideration with other candidates. They should not be discriminated against on the basis of nonjob-related criteria.

The rights to rest periods, vacations, holidays, and work days of reasonable length are all generally acknowledged in American society. Because Social

---

[3] Some useful works on workers' rights include David W. Ewing, *Freedom Inside the Organization* (New York: McGraw-Hill, 1977); Gertrude Ezorsky (Ed.), *Moral Rights in the Workplace* (Albany: State University of New York Press, 1987); David W. Ewing, *"Do It My Way or You're Fired!"* (New York: Wiley, 1983); Mary Gibson, *Workers' Rights* (Totowa, N.J.: Rowman & Allanheld, 1983); Alan F. Westin and Stephan Salisbury (Eds.), *Individual Rights in the Corporation* (New York: Pantheon Books, 1980); and Robert O'Neill, *The Rights of Government Employees* (New York: Avon Books, 1978).

Security payments are usually an insufficient replacement for salary, workers also have a right to some sort of retirement or pension plan after completing a certain number of years with a firm. Such plans are usually part of a contract and have become a legitimate expectation of workers. To fire employees shortly before they retire, so the firm will not have to pay them a pension, is clearly unjust and violates the employees' right to the pension they have earned.

Once hired, employees have the right to cost-of-living increases periodically and to fair consideration for merit salary raises and should be given the reason for lack of such increases if they might usually be expected. Employees have no right to promotion unless promotions are automatic, or are generally expected or promised. But employees do have a right to fair and regular evaluation and consideration for promotion, and they have a right to be informed of the reasons for lack of promotion when it might usually be expected. As in hiring, employees should be promoted on the basis of job-related criteria, especially their performance, and should not be discriminated against because of their gender, race, religion, and other inappropriate criteria. Women have frequently encountered what have become known as "glass ceilings," which are levels of upper management beyond which they are not promoted. Although in some companies women are breaking through such barriers, where they exist they are clearly unethical.

Promotion within a firm is not a right and not guaranteed, and there are usually more people technically eligible for positions than there are openings. Some people are passed over time after time and promotions given to those junior to them in both years with the firm and in years of experience. Unless there is some kind of nonjob-related discrimination involved, such practices are not unethical. Some people rise to the level of their competence or of their perceived competence; some rise to the level of their incompetence. Some are simply unlucky, being in the wrong position at the wrong time, while others luckily are in the right place at the right time. What is unethical is treating people unfairly, failing to give them appropriate consideration, or discriminating against them by the use of inappropriate criteria.

Those firms with a policy of not firing employees who have been with the firm beyond a certain probationary period, even when the firm is in financial difficulty, tend to enjoy greater employee loyalty than other firms. It is not hard to understand why. According to such policies, both lower-level and management-level employees are kept on. If an individual has risen to the level of his incompetence, he may be shifted laterally or moved to another position, or helped to improve. Concern for one's employees is a function of good management and also implements the moral injunction to treat people as ends in themselves. Nonetheless, firing or letting employees go is not unethical in itself.

To offset the disparity between the power of the employer and that of the employee, unions usually have contracts with employers, guaranteeing employment at a certain level for a certain period of years and requiring that a firm terminate an employee only for "cause." This precludes arbitrary firing, or firing at will or at whim. Civil service also provides job security for government employees who also can only be fired for "cause." The same is true for educators who have been granted tenure at their institutions. But there remain a large number of people who are subject to the doctrine of employment-at-will. This includes both high-level executives and nonunionized beginners in many occupations, as well as those workers not covered by union contracts, civil service regulations, or tenure systems. Do they have any rights with respect to their jobs? Although the employment-at-will doctrine says no, there are good arguments in defense of the right to job security, at least of a certain type.

People are fired for many reasons. A common one is an economic recession, which forces a firm to cut back on production and so to decrease the number of people it needs to work for it. But there are other reasons as well. Inefficiency, immorality on the job, chronic lateness or absenteeism, and lack of ability to perform at the level expected are all common reasons and are all examples of reasonable cause. Other reasons are less clearly justifiable, such as incompatibility with management or with other workers, lack of respect or deference to superiors, poor attitude toward work, voicing of dissent, or an employer's belief that he or she can find someone who can do the job better. In some instances, an employer fires an employee simply because the employer dislikes the employee for personal reasons, or because the employee refuses the sexual advances of the employer, or because the employee knows of an irregularity in the firm and cannot be trusted not to expose it. Has the employee no right in these instances?

Employees, from the lowest-paid employee in the corporation to the president, do not have the right to continuance in their jobs if they do not perform adequately or if the firm is not able to continue employing them. But fairness requires that workers not be fired arbitrarily. Arbitrary firing violates the ordinary expectations assumed by workers when accepting employment. They properly expect to be treated as persons deserving of respect; they are not objects to be discarded or replaced at whim. But exactly what rules should govern the termination of employment is a controversial issue. Two general principles are often applied, however.

One principle states that the longer one has been employed by a firm, the greater the obligation of the firm not to fire, except for cause. Those who give many years of acceptable service deserve more consideration than those who are new on the job, and should be helped, encouraged, and given a chance to improve; they should be transferred to less demanding jobs where possible. This is minimal recompense for employee loyalty. On the other hand, a beginner is seen as being on probation. Although even a beginner should not be fired on a whim, the reason for termination can be less substantive if the term of employment is short. The reason given in favor of that principle rests on what a probationary period means. Another consideration is that unless a firm is allowed to fire beginning people whom, for one reason or another, it does not want, it becomes chained to employees simply by virtue of having initially hired them. Even civil service regulations allow for probationary periods; and academic tenure is not usually mandated except after six years of full-time teaching.

The second principle states that the employer should inform the employee of the reason for the termination of employment. This principle is derived from the obligation to treat persons with respect.

Some people argue that respect for persons requires more than simply being informed of the reason for one's dismissal, because the reasons given may be false, inadequate, or unjustifiable. One may be told that one is fired for refusing the sexual advances of one's superior, for instance, but being told this is not sufficient to make the firing morally justifiable. The reason for the firing is itself morally unjustifiable. Hence, some argue, respect for persons requires that one should be fired only for legitimate cause and that employees who dispute the legitimacy of the stated cause should have recourse to due process, such as that available in law (and under a system such as the civil service). The reasons stated for the firing, if challenged by the employee, must be considered adequate by an impartial judge, arbitrator, or other third party. Evidence must be produced in case an employer's charge against an employee is denied by the employee, and a chance for the presentation of a defense must be allowed the employee. Such procedures are in fact followed by some large firms. They are not as likely to be implemented by small employers, who work closely with their employees. Small employers do not have the facilities or personnel to carry out such formal procedures; moreover, the closeness of daily contact makes it unlikely that an employee who is kept on—under what the employer considers duress—will find any satisfaction on the job.

The extent to which an employee has a right to due process in the case of firing is still being debated. But there is ample precedent in the areas of civil service, union contracts, and tenure systems to show that due process is practicable in cases of firing. There are laws that prohibit the firing of whistle blowers in government positions, and many have suggested that such laws be extended to cover the private sector as well.

When firing is done for cause, and the reason is financial exigency, union rules require that layoffs be made under rules of seniority, according to which those last hired for any kind of position are those first fired. This rule has been affirmed by the courts even when those fired have been hired for affirmative-action reasons.

The doctrine of employment-at-will does not require that either employer or employee give advance notice of termination of employment, although this has become a common custom in many fields. It constitutes acknowledgment that the termination of employment on the part of either party causes some inconvenience to the other party, and the advance warning gives them both a chance to make alternative arrangements. When an employer fires an employee for reasons of efficiency, some firms either by contract or unilaterally give the employee a certain amount of severance pay to provide a financial cushion until he or she finds another job. When executives are fired, some firms allow them to continue to use the firm's address, or to look for a job from an office in the firm, where telephone and secretarial services are available. Even when firing is morally justifiable there are ways of softening what is always a blow, and a firm that truly treats its employees as persons will do what it can to soften that blow—especially when the firing is for the firm's financial reasons, rather than because of what the employee did or failed to do.

Employees who are being laid off, or those whose appointments will not be renewed, deserve as much advance warning as possible. Whether this is, strictly speaking, a moral right is debatable. But it is clearly the morally preferable way of acting when an employer has an option, and advance notice, of periods ranging from several months to as much as a year or longer, is a contractual agreement in some fields.

Plant closings raise these issues in a dramatic way. In 1988 a U.S. federal plant-closing bill was passed[4] that mandates that any business with over 100 employees must give at least 60 days' notice of any plant closing or major layoff. Several states have passed more stringent bills. Such bills typically require more advance notice of a factory's closing, continuation of health insurance (e.g., for three months after being laid off), unemployment compensation, counseling, and retraining. In states that do not have such laws, laid-off workers have turned to litigation in an attempt to get legal recognition of what they consider their rights. They have met with mixed success, because many employers still firmly defend employment-at-will as their right. Erosion of the doctrine has clearly taken place, however, and more restrictions to it, based on workers' rights, seem likely.

Employee Civil Rights and Equal Treatment

There are many kinds of rights. Civil rights are legal rights that entitle each person covered by them to certain treatment or that guarantee noninterference in their acting in certain ways. The right to equal employment regardless of race or sex makes it illegal for employers to discriminate in their hiring practices with respect to these. The right to freedom of speech allows each citizen to express his or her views publicly, and prevents others, especially government officials, from interfering in such expression. A moral right does not depend on positive law, but a moral right might also be a civil right. Not every moral right is written into law, nor is the state the source of moral rights. People have such rights simply by virtue of being moral agents and worthy of respect. The rights to life, liberty, and the pursuit of happiness are among these moral rights.

---

[4] The Worker Adjustment Retraining and Notification Act (WARN). The act allows the payment of 60 days' wages and benefits instead of notice.

By contract and position, one can secure other special rights. A business executive of a certain level may earn the right to eat in the executive restaurant; other employees have the right to eat in the company lunchroom. Those not employed by a firm have no general right to eat in the firm's lunchroom or restaurant, or to use facilities of the firm. Special rights are not moral rights. However, if such special rights are extended under certain regular conditions and are then denied to a particular individual for no defensible reason, failure to extend them may be a violation of a moral right to equality of treatment.

Civil Rights on the Job

Many disputes have arisen about whether employees are allowed to exercise their civil rights, either on or off the job, if the exercise of such rights is in some way perceived by their employer as being detrimental to the good of the firm. Do workers have the right to criticize their company, its management, or some of its decisions, either on or off the job? Many managers complain that workers who criticize the company on the job sow disaffection, unrest, and discontent among other workers. This clearly hurts the company and affects its productivity. Hence, they argue, it is right to fire such people. Some companies go so far as to claim that speaking or writing against the company and its policies during off-hours is disloyal and harmful to the company, and that people who so act are rightly open to censure and dismissal.

The right of employees to freedom of expression on their own time is a civil right that their employer cannot morally deny them. Employers have the right to demand work of a specific kind from their employees, and while they are working they can be expected to do certain tasks assigned to them. But no employer has the right to deprive his employees of their civil rights off the job. Because freedom of expression is one of their rights, they are free on their own time to say what they choose. This includes criticizing their employer, but not, of course spreading lies about him. Also not defensible as a right are verbal abuse, divulging secret or confidential information learned in one's capacity as an employee, or revealing the legitimate plans or activities of the firm.

Employees, as members of society, have the moral right, moreover, to the most extensive liberty compatible with a like liberty for all. They have the right to belong to the church of their choosing, to live their private lives as they wish, and to engage in political or social activities as they desire. An employer violates these rights if he penalizes his employees for what they do on their own time. Employees are properly evaluated for their work on the job, but this evaluation should not extend to their nonjob-related activities as long as these do not adversely affect their job performance. There are borderline cases, of course. An employee who is an alcoholic should not be fired for drinking off the job, but his drinking may affect his performance on the job, which is the only proper criterion for job evaluation.

Whether employees have a complete right to freedom of expression on the job is not a clear-cut issue. They do not have the right to sow disaffection and foment employee unrest during their working hours. But they do have the right to organize, form unions, raise grievances, and so on, on their own time at work—whether on coffee breaks, lunch breaks, or before or after hours. Fairness requires procedures whereby workers can register their complaints against those above them and receive a fair hearing. Their right to complain about grievances to those above them, and to go higher up the managerial ladder than their immediate superior, is, moreover, not properly considered to be sowing disaffection. Their right to free speech at work cannot be legitimately taken from them, but the right cannot be so exercised as to interfere with one's regularly assigned tasks, or in such a way as to be disruptive of the orderly functioning of the firm.

On the job, workers have the right to equality of treatment. They should receive equal pay for equal work, regardless of sex, race, or religion. They should all have equal opportunity for advancement. They should be evaluated fairly and only on job-related criteria. They have a right not to be fired for non-job-related matters or for registering legitimate complaints. Established procedures for hiring, promotion, layoffs, and firing should guarantee that the worker's right to fair treatment is respected.

The Right to Treatment with Respect

The right of an employee to be treated like a human being is a moral right. It is an extremely broad and, in many ways, a vague right. Nevertheless it is a central right. Its foundation is straightforward: Each person is a human being, a moral agent deserving of respect. We saw in our study of the Categorical Imperative that to treat a human being only as a means is immoral. Thus, an employer who treats his workers *only* as a means to his profit, or *only* as a way of getting done what he wants done, treats them immorally. They are not machines or objects. What does this imply about their treatment? Can we translate the notion of respect for human beings into specific conditions of labor?

Because workers are human beings worthy of respect, they should not be treated like slaves, nor can they morally contract into such treatment. Their work should not be demeaning, nor should the conditions of work be unsafe, unhealthy, or in general not suitable for human beings. These vague statements are translated into different work conditions, depending on the country, the standard of living, the kind of work, and the availability of safety and other equipment. In the United States the Occupational Safety and Health Administration (OSHA) sets and regulates standards for health and safety on the job. Its function is morally justified, even though its specific regulations may be challenged. The conditions it prescribes are not morally mandatory for all societies. Nonetheless, in all societies employees deserve health and safety protection, they are entitled to know the dangers to which they are subject, and workers who willingly undertake dangerous work should be recompensed appropriately.

The right to be treated with respect also means that workers should not be made to work in stultifying jobs or be considered replaceable parts in the productive process. This falls short of the claimed right to meaningful work.[5] This right is a doubtful right at the present time, even though it is a worthy ideal, because a good deal of work is dull, requires little skill or imagination, and is not intrinsically fulfilling. Yet such work need not and should not be stultifying or oppressive. The right to treatment with respect requires interpretation, and specific rights derived from it must be argued for and defended. Yet it is a legitimate basis for demanding specific conditions worthy of human beings. Among these is the right to freedom from sexual harassment.

Sexual Harassment

The right to freedom from sexual harassment in the workplace has come to the fore in recent years. Sexual harassment is demeaning and fails to show people the respect they deserve.

Office romances are not uncommon, and drawing the line as to what constitutes sexual harassment is sometimes difficult. Yet in general it consists of *unwelcome* sexual advances or requests for sexual favors, sexual jokes, or verbal abuse, and physical or verbal conduct imposed on an employee, submission to which is either explicitly or implicitly a condition of continued employment or advancement. The courts in the United States have recognized two types of sexual harassment: quid pro quo harassment and hostile environment harassment.[6] The first type involves submission to sexual requests or advances as a condition of continued employment or of some job benefit, such as promotion. The second requires the employer to keep the workplace free from actions or words by other employees or managers that create a hostile, intimidating, or offensive environment such that it interferes with the employee's work or performance. Words or actions of a sexual nature or with sexual overtones that interfere with one's work or make an employee uncomfortable constitute sexual harassment. Complaints made to the individual responsible for such conduct are sufficient to show that the words or acts are unwelcome. If they persist, this becomes a clear violation of the employee's right to freedom from sexual harassment. The right of the employee to be free from sexual harassment imposes an obligation not only on other employees, supervisors, and management, but also on the employing firm to provide an harassment-free environment. Wise companies will have antisexual-harassment policies and procedures for handling complaints.

---

[5] The right to meaningful work is open to a great many interpretations. For some discussions of this right, see Ezorsky (Ed.), *Moral Rights in the Workplace,* section 1.

[6] Robert K. Robinson, Billie M. Allen, Geralyn McClure Franklin, and David L. Duhon, "Sexual Harassment in the Workplace: A Review of the Legal Rights and Responsibilities of All Parties," *Public Personnel Management,* 22, no. 1 (Spring 1993), pp. 123-135.

Privacy, Polygraphs, and Drugs

Employees have a moral right to privacy. They work for their employers for a certain period of time each day, and the rest of their time does not belong to the company but to themselves. They should be allowed to do what they want during that time, free from company interference. When they are employed, they do not surrender the right to privacy in their personal lives, nor does this privacy end when they enter the corporation's walls. Some aspects of their lives do not affect their capacity to do the work expected of them. Consequently, corporations have no right to inquire about such things, nor to keep such information on record in personnel files. Workers have a right not to answer personal, nonjob-related questions and have a right to know that no such material is kept in their files. They have a right to know their evaluations and other information in their personnel files, as well as to enter rebuttals about such information if they believe it to be erroneous. They have a right, if they have personal lockers or desks, not to have them searched without good cause, and then only by those authorized to do so for job-related reasons. The conditions of privacy of lockers and desks should be clear and should be made known to employees.

Although the right to privacy in these respects is frequently violated, the validity of the claims is not seriously disputed. However, three other issues involving privacy have raised a great deal of discussion: polygraph testing, drug testing, and testing for AIDS.

Polygraph Testing

A polygraph or "lie detector" is a machine that tests and records simultaneously a number of physiological reactions—such as perspiration and heart rate—of a subject as questions are posed by an investigator. The subject's reactions are traced onto a paper tape and then analyzed. The theory behind polygraphs is that when the subject lies his or her physiological response is different from when the subject tells the truth. Until 1988 the test was widely used by business and government for two purposes. One was to prevent the hiring of those who might steal from the employer or might be security risks in a sensitive position. Retailers suffer considerable losses from employees. Hence, retail employers claimed that they wished to weed out prospective employees who had stolen in the past. They claimed the only sure way to do this was to have all prospective candidates for a job submit to a polygraph test and ask them, for instance, whether they had stolen on previous jobs. Similarly, the government used polygraph tests on candidates for positions requiring security clearance or other sensitive work. The other use was to help find the culprit in instances of theft or of other crimes within a company. If goods or a sum of money had been stolen, some companies required that all those suspected submit to polygraph tests in order to determine the culprit.

If the polygraph tests worked with perfect accuracy, they might be ethically unobjectionable even though they might be abused by some employers to find out information they had no right to know. But they are not reliable. They both indicate in some cases that people who are telling the truth are lying and that people who are lying are telling the truth. Since the machine measures physiological reactions, it is possible to learn how to control those reactions and so "fool" the machine. Those most likely to learn to do this are those people the operators of the machine are most interested in detecting. Innocent but very nervous people often react in a way that can be interpreted as lying. Moreover, given the recorded readings, different polygraph specialists would sometimes come up with different interpretations about whether the subject was lying in response to a particular question.

Those who used the tests for pre-employment purposes claimed that they had the right to hire or not hire anyone they wished among the applicants. If all applicants were required to take a polygraph test, no candidate was being discriminated against. If some applicants who were innocent of stealing in the past failed the test, that was unfortunate. But since no candidate has a right to an opening in a particular business, their right to that opening could not have been infringed. As long as there was a sufficient number of applicants that the business could choose from among those who passed the test, the using firm had no problems. The firm admittedly might now and then hire someone who beat the machine. But the firm might hire that person anyway if it did not use the polygraph test, and, firms claimed, using the polygraph test reduced the number of potential thieves they hired.

Did the taking of a polygraph test violate the applicants' right to privacy? It might in three ways. First, it might if the questions asked were of a type that the firm had no right to ask. In order to arrive at a base of physiological reactions, the polygraph examiner asks a number of supposedly innocuous questions, such as one's name, date of birth, where one went to school, and so on. Against such a base one can then test reactions to such questions as whether one ever stole from a previous employer, whether one ever shoplifted as an adolescent, and whether one thought it was permissible to take small objects such as pencils home from work. Do employers have the right to know whether a person shoplifted as an adolescent or ever took anything from a former employer? Although we can understand that they might like to know such information, even if it does not necessarily serve as an indication of the future action of the subject, potential employees have no obligation to reveal such information. If applicants are unwilling to answer the questions posed, they can refuse to do so or to take the polygraph test—but if they do, they will not be considered for the job. Hence, they are forced to answer the questions if they want to be considered for the job.

Second, the range of questions employers sometimes asked went well into other areas that some employer might wish to know about but into which employers have no right to go, such as one's sexual preferences, religious beliefs, political affiliations, home life, and drinking habits. Firms have the right to ask questions that are job-related; they do not have the right to probe into one's personal life about nonjob-related activities. The temptation to do so with polygraphs was considerable.

A third objection is that those taking the test had no guarantee that the results of the test would be kept private. They had no way of knowing how the results would be used, whether they would be stored or destroyed or put into a computer for use by other potential employers, to whom they would be available, or anything else. If they were not hired, they usually did not know whether it was because they failed the polygraph test.

A possible reply is that although the polygraph test might be used in such a way as to violate a subject's right to privacy, safeguards can be placed on its use to preclude that. The questions asked might be appropriate and given in advance to the subject, who would agree to answer them. The results might be available only to the person directly involved in hiring and destroyed immediately after being used for initial employment purposes. However, this reply would not handle the objections of those who feel degraded by being required to submit to such a test, or those who claim that it is a violation of one's privacy to be forced to submit to a machine that records and reveals their physiological (and indirectly their emotional) responses, which are private in the sense that they are not available to others without machines.

Any argument in defense of the machines eventually falters on the fact that they are unreliable. From the subject's point of view, the unreliability is especially serious when the subject is interpreted as lying when actually telling the truth. If someone is turned down for a job on this basis, that is a violation of one's right to fair treatment. Moreover, if a person does not wish to submit to the test for any number of reasons, that person is automatically excluded from jobs for which taking the polygraph test is mandatory.

The opposition to the use of polygraphs mounted until a U.S. federal law, the Employee Polygraph Protection Act, was passed in December 1988, prohibiting pre-employment polygraph testing, and random post-employment polygraph testing. The law allows polygraph use in the case of theft, embezzlement, or sabotage. An employee has the right to refuse to take the test and cannot be fired for such refusal. No employee who fails the test can be fired because of that; other evidence must be found that is sufficient to warrant dismissal. No questions on sex, politics, or union activities may be asked, and all questions must be furnished in advance. Individual states may pass more restrictive measures with respect to polygraph use.

The U.S. federal law applies to private-sector employees, but not to federal, state, and local government employees or to firms doing sensitive work under contracts with the Defense Department, the FBI, or the CIA. It is not clear why it is inappropriate to use polygraph tests in the private sector but not in the government sector, since the tests are equally unreliable in both. The argument might be that, with respect to positions that involve handling material on which the security of the nation rests, the tests might be helpful as a preliminary screen, which would be followed up by a detailed investigation of any accepted candidate. The polygraph test would then supply only one piece of information that would be part of a temporary file, with no one given access to secret information until all information was verified. But this is not what the law says. Without some such rationale, if the test violates the right to privacy and to fair treatment in the private sector, it seems to do so as well in the public sector. An argument strong enough to justify such violations would have to be in terms of the rights of the citizenry not to be endangered by the employment of those who might undermine the nation's security.

The reaction to the law on the part of some private-sector employers has been to adopt paper and pencil "honesty tests" as part of their pre-employment screening. These are supposed to measure the subject's honesty and propensity to steal. They have not been shown to be reliable, they can easily be beaten by those who wish to learn how they are constructed and evaluated, and they can easily be faulted on grounds similar to those used to fault pre-employment use of the polygraph.

Drug Testing

The use of drugs in the United States has increased to alarming proportions. The effect of drugs on users can be serious, ranging from temporary physical or psychological impairment to death. The direct and indirect cost to businesses in terms of increased accidents, liability payments, health insurance, absenteeism, and theft to purchase drugs is escalating to staggering heights.

The use, possession, sale, or possession of illegal drugs at work is often grounds for discipline, up to and including discharge. Since the actions are illegal, such action by an employer raises no ethical problem. Employers have no obligation to protect those who break the law.

Drug users may be adversely affected for some time after having actually taken a drug. Hence, what they do on their own time, into which an employer has no right to pry, might affect their performance on the job. Because of this, many employers would prefer to hire people who do not use drugs and screen job applicants by having them submit to pre-employment drug tests. Furthermore, in order to preclude harm that drug users might do, some companies have instituted post-employment drug testing to determine which employees do use drugs. Is such use an invasion of the privacy of job applicants and employees? If it is, is it justifiable? If so, under what conditions?

Although drug testing is not foolproof, it can be made highly reliable. Nonetheless, there are various problems. About 10 percent of initial testing produces false positives—that is, the test indicates the presence of drugs when the person has not taken drugs. The usual urine tests used to detect drugs do not indicate what drug has been used. Someone who smoked marijuana might test positive for up to a month afterwards. Someone who used a hard drug, such as cocaine, might test negative only a week or less after using the drug. The test does not indicate whether the person who used the drug is in any way impaired. The test does not show whether the subject is a habitual, infrequent, or one-time user. The test will show positive as a result not only of illegal drugs but also of prescription drugs, including such things as cough medicine containing codeine. Hence, it would be unfair to extrapolate from any given instance of a positive result to any conclusion with respect to the subject who tests positive. To be absolutely sure that the urine sample is not tampered with and that it is from the person being tested, the producing of the sample must be observed. Such observance violates at least some people's sense of privacy, and they find it demeaning.

What is morally permitted in this area? Since the right of privacy is one that individuals can forgo, one's privacy is not invaded if one willingly reveals otherwise private information or willingly submits to testing of various kinds, including drug testing. Hence, any strictly voluntary program of drug testing is acceptable. The difficulty arises when the testing is mandatory.

Since the tests are known to produce false positives, it would be unethical to make any decisions seriously affecting someone on the basis of such possibly erroneous information. If tests are to be used in a justifiable way, any positive reading should be followed both by a second test and by an interview with the person to determine whether he or she is taking any medication or anything else that might account for the positive result. All information about the test results should be kept confidential, made available only to those who have the need to know them, and destroyed when no longer necessary. If as a result of a true positive reading an applicant is turned down for a position, that person in fairness should know the reason and such a rejection should not preclude the applicant from reapplying for a position at some reasonable time (e.g., six months) in the future.

But why screen for drugs in a pre-employment situation in the first place? There seems to be little justification for it unless the position for which people are applying is in some way dangerous to themselves or others or in some way particularly sensitive. Most people would not want to ride in an airplane or bus operated by someone on drugs. Pre-employment testing is one way to screen out drug users from the start, although the conditions above are appropriate. For most jobs pre-employment drug screening is not clearly appropriate, for it attempts to determine facts about a person off the job that are not directly pertinent to the job. To that extent, such tests constitute a violation of a person's right to privacy, and to overcome that right some other right that overrides it is necessary.

On the job the situation is similar. The conditions for the proper use of testing apply. Involuntary random testing suffers from the same difficulties as preemployment testing. If it is morally justified, the reasons must be important enough to override the employees's right to privacy.[7] Random drug testing

---

[7] The California Supreme Court has ruled that random drug testing by private employers violates employees' right to privacy as protected by the California constitution. A Minnesota statute, on the other hand, permits such testing. There is no national policy, and the U.S. Supreme Court has not issued any ruling on the practice.

also tends to cause uncertainty and uneasiness among workers, since they never know when they will be called. Defenders of the practice claim that this is the point: Since workers do not know when they will be tested, they have an incentive not to use drugs. That random drug testing actually decreases drug use has not been demonstrated. Nor has it been shown that companies that use random testing suffer fewer injuries or other difficulties than do companies that do not use random drug testing. If drugs affect a worker's performance, then that performance is the basis for action. What action is appropriate? Many companies follow procedures they have established with respect to employees adversely affected by intoxicating beverages. These are sometimes called employee assistance programs.[8] Employees are tested if there is cause, based on job performance, to believe that they are adversely affected by drugs (including alcoholic beverages). If they truly test positive, they are offered treatment, help, and counseling. Frequently, they are warned that if they refuse treatment, or if they accept treatment but are later again adversely affected by drugs, they will be terminated. Nonetheless, refusal to submit to testing should not mean that one is automatically subject to dismissal. The cause should be failure to perform adequately. By itself, suspicion of drug use is not adequate cause for dismissal.

In sensitive occupations, if testing is the only way to ensure that people are able to do their jobs adequately (e.g., are not under the influence of drugs when flying a commercial jet), then regular testing of all those in that position is preferable to random testing. Random testing does not achieve the results for which the testing is done. Testing of all those in a similar sensitive position from the highest to the lowest is one way of removing any stigma from testing and of making it less demeaning. The test then does not indicate suspicion or imply that people at one rank or level are more trustworthy that those at another level, causing invidious comparisons. If the president of a company dealing with sensitive issues is unwilling to submit to regular drug testing, workers below the president may well question why they are required to submit to such testing.

Testing for AIDS

The emergence of AIDS (Acquired Immune Deficiency Syndrome) has raised issues about workers' rights. One issue concerns the right of the person with AIDS to privacy. The second is the right of the person with AIDS to nondiscriminatory treatment. The third is the claimed right of other workers not to be exposed to a fatal and communicable disease. This last right of others is a real right. But all the evidence so far indicates that AIDS is not transmitted by casual contact such as that occurring between fellow workers. Hence, the right of workers not to be exposed to fatal diseases is not violated by hiring or

---

[8] James T. Wrich, "Beyond Testing: Coping with Drugs at Work," *Harvard Business Review,* January–February 1988, pp. 120–129, is a good treatment of handling the problem of drugs in the workplace.

keeping on employees infected with the AIDS virus. Workers who have such unfounded fears may well pose a problem for an employer. A proper response, however, is not to violate the rights of someone with AIDS, but a program of employee education with respect to the facts about the transmission of AIDS.

What of the rights of those with AIDS? Is their right to privacy violated if their condition is made public without their consent? The answer is clearly yes, for if that information is made known to those who have no need to know it, then the person with AIDS is likely to be treated very differently from other people—shunned, avoided, or in other ways mistreated. The same is true of anyone who tests positive for the AIDS virus, even though as yet a great many people who test positive show no signs of the disease.

Because those with AIDS have the right not to be discriminated against, they should be treated on the job as people with any other type of physical disorder, handicap, or disease. There is no special reason for a general pre-employment test of employees for AIDS unless they are applying for special kinds of jobs. Applicants to the armed forces are given medical examinations and are turned down if they have any of a great many different medical problems, including AIDS. The rationale is that in time of war they will undergo great physical stress and the safety of the nation depends on their being able to perform adequately. That argument does not apply to most nonmilitary jobs.

Doctors, nurses, police, and others who might have occasion to deal with the injured or give CPR should be given the proper equipment to protect themselves from being infected and should use such protection routinely. They have no special need to know who has AIDS for purposes of emergency treatment.

The situation becomes more difficult as the condition of infected employees deteriorates and possibly affects job performance. The right to privacy remains, but if the same accommodation is to be made for these employees as for those with other disabilities, then clearly supervisors and others in charge of job allocation and performance evaluation must be informed.

As yet there is no special legislation governing the treatment of those with AIDS on the job, and the existing legal and moral rules of privacy and fair treatment seem to suffice. The high cost of AIDS testing has precluded the routine use of such testing in pre-employment situations. If an inexpensive test is found and such testing becomes commonplace, then the above arguments with respect to the right to privacy in polygraph and drug testing can come into play with appropriate modifications.

Quality of Work Life

In addition to concern with workers' rights, concern is growing for the quality of work life—a relatively new arrival on the American social scene. Quality of work life is a reflection of the affluence and level of technological development present in American society, which has become concerned with the general quality of life. American society has found that the blessings of advanced technology have brought with them certain dysfunctional aspects, of which pollution and the deterioration of the quality of air and water are the clearest examples. The general concern with the qualify of life has been carried over into the workplace as concern for the quality of work life. The concern also reflects the changing conditions of American work and the changing attitudes toward work. American labor is no longer dominated by nineteenth-century concerns, and work itself has changed since then. In the United States, by 1980, only 16 percent of the workers were employed in manufacturing—the traditional kind of work that dominated trade-union concerns and formed the focus of analyses of the condition of the working class. Forty-six percent of the American work force is now employed in the service sector of the economy. The concerns of these workers are not necessarily the same as those of factory workers.

Although there are still disputes over wages, vacation, retirement, and safety, workers have begun to turn their attention to qualitative rather than quantitative aspects of their work life. These are not yet stated in terms of rights, and the demands are still to some extent unfocused. But they are growing concerns to which management will eventually have to respond.

The following are four aspects of the qualify of work life that will throw some light on what is meant by the phrase. The components can be scaled, though not always quantitatively, for analytic purposes. The first concerns the conditions of labor; the second, the organization of the work performed; the third, the relations of workers among themselves, with those above them, and with the tools or machines with which they work; and the fourth, the attitude of the worker to work.

Conditions of Labor

Workers have traditionally focused on the number of hours worked, the amount of pay received, the number of days of vacation and sick leave provided, and the level of seniority accruing to length of service. They have also been somewhat concerned with safety on the job—for example, with screens around dangerous machines, adequate ventilation, sufficient light, noise levels below certain decibel ratings, protection from radiation or noxious chemicals and gases, ladders of a certain strength, and so on. Some of these concerns have been translated into industry codes or OSHA regulations that specify levels that must be met. Each of the foregoing items is quantifiable and specifiable, and one can plausibly argue that the quality of work life is significantly improved when these are met at a high, as opposed to a low, level. However, all of these considerations, although necessary for a high quality of work life, are not sufficient to ensure it.

Conditions of labor also refer to the atmosphere in which work is done. Pleasant surroundings are preferable to grim, dirty, or unpleasant ones, even if, strictly speaking, one has no particular right to pleasant surroundings. Adequate space rather than cramped quarters, and air-conditioning where appropriate, are two other examples of improved working conditions. A change in dress codes, so as to minimize the distinction between labor and management, is another subtle aspect of changing work conditions. At IBM, technicians wear jackets and ties, as does management. At one GM plant, managers go tieless, as do assembly-line workers. The improvement in working conditions at other companies involves the breaking down of what are perceived as invidious distinctions, and no longer are there separate restrooms, restaurants, and recreational centers for workers and managers.

Improving the conditions of labor requires that one start from the existing conditions. The better the existing physical condition, the more concentration on other conditions—aesthetic, psychological, and personal. But improving these conditions, even more than improving physical conditions, requires consultation with, and input from, workers. The improvement of working conditions cannot be done only from above and then imposed on workers; workers should not only be considered but also consulted as to which improvements they desire and which they value more than others.

Improvement of working conditions thus includes a variety of concerns.

In 1993 the U.S. Congress passed the Family and Medical Leave Act, the aim of which was to help balance the requirements of work with legitimate family demands. The act requires that employers of fifty or more employees provide their employees with up to twelve weeks of unpaid leave for the birth or adoption of a child or for the serious illness or injury of a family member. After the leave, the employer must return the employee to the same or an equivalent position as he or she held before. Many European countries have more liberal maternity leave policies; some have better paternal leave policies; and others fall short of the U.S. policy with respect to leave for caring for elderly parents. What is morally required is not some specific amount of leave but recognition that employees have family lives and responsibilities. The conditions of labor should recognize this fact and include provisions for it.

The Organization of Work

The division of labor leads to greater and greater repetition of tasks. At its worst it consists of doing one mechanical task (e.g., tightening a certain bolt, on an assembly line). Such work is inherently dull and stultifying. Many such tasks could be done as well, and probably better, by robots. Increasing the quality of work life involves lessening the division of labor, allowing workers to carry on more complex or more diversified tasks. This is true as well with respect to office and secretarial work, which can be either mechanical, routine, and dull or more varied and diversified. If the goal is a higher quality of work life, then work should be as interesting and fulfilling as possible to those engaged in it. Some people may well be comfortable with jobs that are not very demanding and are fairly routine, but it is difficult to imagine anyone being satisfied with deadening, stultifying work.

Although worker self-management has not received much support from most American workers, what has received support is greater worker participation. Workers can frequently contribute to improvement in the work they do if allowed to have input. Grouping workers into teams that handle a variety of different tasks, holding weekly worker meetings to discuss improvements in the productive process, and allowing workers to take part in some of the planning and policy sessions of a firm are all techniques that have been tried, and they have helped to improve the quality of work life for the workers affected.

Lessening the division of labor by the use of teams of workers and worker participation in general are not yet recognized rights, but workers are expressing these wishes more and more frequently.

Worker Relations

The relation of workers to others, and to their tools, is an area difficult to quantify. We can speak of cordial and less cordial relations, competitive and cooperative, supportive and destructive ones. We can also speak of arrangements that produce certain types of relations—hierarchical as opposed to collegial, arbitrary as opposed to rule-governed. We can speak of treating people with respect or treating them like things, and this can be specified in greater detail. The tone of voice in which directions or orders are given may reflect the relations between the person in a superior position and the one in a subordinate position. Some may argue that there should be no distinction between superior and subordinate, and that everyone should be on the same level. The initial implausibility of this claim in any large-scale operation leads one either to press for only small-scale operations or to try to rethink organizational structures.

Any suggested changes can be measured against productivity. Changes may lead to greater or lesser productivity. If they lead to less, then this is a cost that must be considered. Whether the cost is too great depends on how much difference the changes make to those involved. A number of innovations have been adopted, at least on a small scale—for example, flexible time, when employees set their preferred schedules rather than being bound by the traditional nine-to-five day. This can be very convenient. Some people have children who come home after school and they wish to be home by three to greet them. Others might wish to drive home after six to avoid the traffic jams they would otherwise encounter. Some people are early risers; others are night people, who prefer to sleep late in the morning. All these considerations can be taken into account in a flexible approach to work schedules, in many operations. In some, they are not possible. The point is that thought can and should be given to workers and their needs and preferences, when at all possible—and it is possible more often than many managers believe. Day-care centers for the small children of workers are another innovation some firms have adopted to improve the quality of work life. Workers can spend their lunchtime or breaks with their children. The increase in productivity may be worth the cost of providing the centers. Whether or not it is, such centers certainly help the morale of the parents involved.

The relation of workers to tools and machines is a subtle but important area. Craft workers consider tools an extension of themselves and, in a sense, become one with their tools, but this is not the typical relation of industrial workers to the machines they work on. Machines should be kept subordinate to workers, and the structures of a plant or firm should build machines around people rather than people around machines. Technology has made possible the reduction of drudgery in many jobs, but new technology is sometimes introduced without consideration of the people who will use it. Computer terminal screens that are difficult to read and cause eyestrain are one example; and computer operators who are virtually chained to their screens can easily replace the nineteenth-century picture of workers chained to their machines. Work networks must not only be efficient, from a technological point of view, but should also enhance rather than diminish concern for the people who use them. It is unlikely that many people will feel toward their computer terminals what craft workers felt toward their tools, but it is possible to keep the terminals from becoming tyrants.

Worker Attitude

What attitude should workers and society take toward work? Is work punishment for the human condition, or is it a means of self-expression and development? Technology opens up possibilities not previously available. Will we use technology for the benefit of people, or will we use it to repress them and their energies? The change in work from manufacturing to service, and from machine-operating to machine-tending, is bringing about a search for a new conception of work and an attitude that fits the new reality. How can alienation be diminished and worker dissatisfaction lessened? The answer is not always clear, although various experiments are being tried. But concern for the quality of work life seeks answers to these questions as it seeks to make work meaningful and fulfilling.

Worker attitude is often related to worker involvement—the more involvement the better the attitude. Yet workers have reacted negatively to attempts at worker involvement that they see as being aimed merely at increased productivity. They perceive such programs as being ultimately manipulative. Worker involvement can include more worker autonomy, more worker responsibility, and more worker interaction with management than is ordinarily the case, but this may require breaking down strict hierarchical lines. However, as quality of work life improves, workers' attitudes toward work will change; they may see it not as something one must do to live but as an activity that is part of one's life, growth, and self-expression. That is the ideal.

The changing conditions and forms of work are forcing a rethinking of work and its place in workers' lives. Discussions of quality of work life are a sign of the change and will play a role in the change. We can expect concern for the quality of work life to be translated into more and more specific demands that are in better accord with the realities of changing work conditions. Such changes will eventually come to be expected and will be considered entitlements and rights, just as the concept of worker rights and the specification of those rights have developed up until now.

Employee Duties

The list of a worker's obligations depends in part on his or her job or position, but we can specify in general some obligations that hold true for all employment.

Workers are morally obliged to obey the moral law, and they are legally obliged to obey the civil law at work, just as during all other times. Hence, they should not steal from their companies, even in little ways—taking stamps, pencils, paper, or other materials. If they feel they are underpaid, they should let this be known, bargain for more pay, or find other employment. They have no right to adjust their pay by taking things they want from the company.

They are obliged not to lie, not to spread false information, not to sexually or otherwise abuse or harass others. They are morally obliged to treat their fellow employees, whether above or below them, with respect.

They are also obliged to fulfill the terms of their contracts. If they are hired to work an eight-hour day, they should work that amount of time. They should work conscientiously at their jobs and live up to the terms of their contracts. This is an obligation of justice.

The obligations of workers are sometimes spelled out in contracts and job descriptions. The latter are often extremely vague, and exactly what a person in a particular position is obliged to do may be unclear. A person in such a position has no obligation to do the maximum, although if he or she wants a promotion, he or she may choose to do more than is expected or required. Workers have the obligation to perform adequately; they do not have the obligation to break records, work overtime, or do jobs other than those that come with the position. Conversely, however, there is no moral objection—at least in most cases—to their doing more than can be legitimately expected of them.

Employees are obliged, in addition, to consider the interests of the firm for which they work. For instance, they should not work parttime or consult for a competitor, nor is it appropriate either to undercut their firm or to help a competitor do so by solicited public statements. Unsolicited public statements concerning their private, but negative, opinion of their employer are also inappropriate.

Managers are in most cases employees of the firm for which they work. Their obligation is to manage efficiently and fairly. This includes respecting the rights of their employees and creating an ambiance in which all can work together for the benefit of the firm.

Management usually emphasizes the obligations of workers much more frequently than it mentions the rights of workers. Therefore, it is often easier to learn what is expected of one than to know when one's rights are being unjustly ignored or violated.

Worker Loyalty and Obedience

Do workers owe loyalty to their firm, as well as an honest day's work? The question is an ambiguous one. While they work for a particular firm, workers should not subvert it or sabotage its activities. But loyalty to a firm does not require that employees should be unwilling to change employers, or that they should not criticize their employer. What can a firm legitimately expect from an employee, in addition to what it can command or demand?

Consider the following three hypothetical cases.

Case A: Susan Monroe works for ABC Construction Corporation. Her immediate superior has drawn up an estimate for a project, and on the basis of the resulting bid, the company has received the contract. Though the contract has already been signed, Susan's boss asks her to verify her calculations, which is part of Susan's job. In doing so, Susan discovers an error. The result is that there will be a slight loss for the company rather than the anticipated profit. Susan points this out to her superior, who tells Susan to forget the error and mention it to no one; otherwise she will be fired. Her superior does not report the error to her own superior.

Case B: Sam Jones works for XYZ Printing Company. He is in charge of ordering high-quality paper for the firm. A salesman from O. Good Paper wishes to land a large contract from XYZ Printing and offers Sam a new Ford, as a gift, if he gives him the contract. Sam refuses the car. The next day he learns that Tom Brand, who is in charge of ordering lower-quality paper for XYZ, placed an order with O. Good Paper; he also knows that Tom is driving a new Ford.

Case C: Lewis Cage is director of personnel at a large firm. He is in charge of hiring new personnel, keeping records, and issuing notices of dismissal. His firm has just hired a new president, from a competitor. On his first visit to Cage's office, he tells Cage that he (the president) is not prejudiced. He believes in hiring the best people for a job. But, he goes on, he does not like to work with Jews. He tells Cage that if there are any Jews working for the firm, he should keep his eyes open for any excuse to have them fired. He also tells Cage that he should also not consider Jewish people for any future opening in the firm. Cage, unbeknownst to the new president, is Jewish.

The three cases raise a variety of issues dealing with worker obedience and worker loyalty. Before analyzing the cases, we shall state a few general principles. Many firms expect obedience, and in fact many employers regard it as a prime virtue. Employees are to do what they are told, how they are told, and when they are told. They are frequently not asked to think creatively or to inquire too deeply into the workings of the company. They need only follow orders. Some people are paid to be leaders; others are paid to be followers. When workers accept positions, they agree to do what the positions require, including what those above them tell them to do. This view makes of obedience a blank check, to be filled in by the employer.

Though obedience can be morally justified, there are clear moral limits to obedience. No one can be morally obliged to do what is immoral. This statement needs little defense; it is essentially a statement of self-consistency. If we were morally obliged to do what is immoral, we would be morally obliged to both do, and not do, the action in question. Every command by an employer to employees has two parts. One is the fact that the employer tells the employees to do something, or gives them an order, which he expects will be obeyed. The second part constitutes the action the employees are told to do. If the action falls within the area of work of the employees, and if it is not an immoral act, then the employees are rightly expected by the employer to obey the command. For instance, if the vice-president for finance tells her secretary to type a letter to the auditors before typing a letter to the accounting department, she can rightly expect him to follow her instructions. If she hands her secretary her personal Christmas shopping list, with instructions to spend the weekend buying the items on the list for her, the secretary may well protest that doing her shopping is not part of his job. If the vice-president tells the secretary to come to her apartment that evening to spend the night with her, the secretary clearly has no moral obligation to do so, and if the secretary reads her intent correctly, the secretary may have a moral obligation *not* to do as the vice-president commands.

Loyalty is also a quality expected and demanded by many firms. A worker for such a company does not merely give it minimal time and effort. The employee is part of the enterprise, is a member of the team, and is expected to show loyalty to the company in a variety of ways. If the company has a vacancy in a branch office, company loyalty may demand one's being willing to move to the branch office. An offer by another company, at somewhat higher pay, is to be refused because of loyalty, even if the other offer is not matched. If the company is sued or maligned, the loyal worker defends the company. In these and in many other ways, an employee can show loyalty. Being loyal in these ways is morally permissible, but it is not morally obligatory. One has no general moral obligation of loyalty to one's employer, even though employers would like to have loyal employees.

We can now turn to Case A. What, if anything, should Susan Monroe do in the situation described? She is told by her immediate superior not to say anything about the error to anyone. If she does as she is told, she will be obeying her immediate superior. Does she owe anything more to the company? Suppose that by going over her superior's head, to the vice-president, she can bring the error to the company's attention and some adjustments can be made so that the company does not lose money on the project. Does she have an obligation to the company to do so? If she does go to the vice-president, perhaps nothing can be done, and she will simply get herself fired for disobeying her superior. Sooner or later the company will find out that it will lose money on the project. Will Susan be made the scapegoat, because she was supposed to verify the calculations? These and similar considerations are likely to come to Susan's mind. The approach she is implicitly taking is a utilitarian one. What are the consequences for all concerned if she does go over her superior's head? What are the results for all concerned if she does not?

Another approach is to try to weigh the obligation to obey her superior against her obligation to inform the company of facts that may adversely affect it. The latter is an obligation of loyalty. The former is one of obedience. Each is prima facie defensible. Which carries more weight in this situation?

The first thing Susan should do before going above her superior's head is attempt to reason with her superior, thusly: If there is a mistake, it will be found out sooner or later. Will it be better for all concerned to find out sooner rather than later? How will the superior try to remedy the situation, if at all? Will she take the blame when the error is found, or will she put the blame on Susan?

The case is not clear-cut; but because it is internal to the company it reflects a difficulty not only for Susan but also for the company. Susan can argue that she owes obedience to her superior and that in doing as she is told she also shows loyalty to the firm. She does not know what will happen, and is not responsible for what does happen. If the firm suffers a small loss, the firm will not be ruined. Susan is not being asked to do anything immoral. If she had been asked to falsify a record, or to sign a statement that the figures were correct, she could not morally do so. But she is simply being told not to report a mistake, and unless it is her duty to report it (i.e., unless it is a part of her job to do so) she is not doing anything immoral.

Companies might learn from such cases. A company should have a mechanism by which to protect those who have something to report to higher echelons of a firm, but who are threatened with dismissal by those immediately above them if they do so. A firm should also not tolerate attempts by anyone to cover up mistakes or immoral conduct by threatening to fire those subordinates who report the mistake or conduct.

Case B raises somewhat different problems. Sam Jones acted properly in refusing the car offered by the O. Good salesman. Does he have a further obligation to find out whether Tom Brand received his new Ford from the O. Good salesman? If he finds out that Tom did receive it from the salesman, should he report it to the appropriate person in his own firm? Should he, or should XYZ Printing also report the incident to O. Good Paper?

In the absence of any written guidelines, does one have an obligation to investigate and report wrongdoings in one's firm? To what extent are we our brother's keeper in a firm, and does loyalty require that we report wrongdoings in the firm by others? Does a company or its employees have an oblig-ation to report the wrongdoings of other firms' employees to their employers?

Once again the situation could be clarified if XYZ Printing Company had a policy on these issues. If it were policy not to accept any gift, or any gift worth more than $25, for example, Sam would certainly know that he should not accept the car. But he did not accept it. Does he have an obligation to report that the salesman offered him a car? If there were a company policy that such offers be reported, then he should do so. Those to whom he reported could then watch other areas of the company dealing with that salesman; or they could stop dealing with that salesman altogether and let O. Good Paper know what they were doing, and why.

In the absence of such guidelines, however, Sam is not morally obliged to investigate Tom's conduct. He is not Tom's supervisor and has no responsi-bility for his actions. If he does investigate, and if he finds out that Tom took the car, he is not morally obliged to report it to their superior. He might talk to Tom about it, or he might report that he was approached by the salesman and let those above determine whether Tom was similarly approached. If they choose not to investigate, that is their decision. Loyalty to one's firm does not imply that one should be on constant watch to make sure that those over whom one has no authority are acting morally.

Case C involves discrimination and injustice. One can never morally do what is immoral. Hence, the order to find a pretext to fire people because of their religious beliefs, and the order to practice discrimination based on reli-gion in hiring, are both orders that Lewis is morally prohibited from carrying out. The irony is that if Lewis obeyed the order, he would have to find a rea-son for having himself fired. That reason would be found easily: Lewis should not follow the order of the president, and because he disobeys the order to have Jews fired, Lewis gives the president grounds to fire him.

Does a company not have the right to hire whom it pleases? Can anyone rightly force a company to hire people it does not want working for it? Does the president not have the right to issue the order he gave Lewis? The answer is that although no one can force a company to hire certain people, companies are obliged, both by morality and by law in the United States (Title VII of the Civil Rights Act of 1964), to hire on the basis of job-related characteristics and should not discriminate on the basis of sex, race, color, religion, or national ori-gin. To refuse to hire qualified people because of religion is discriminatory, and firing people because of their religion is also discriminatory. Neither prac-tice is morally justifiable.

Lewis could report the order to the board of directors of the company. If they agree that the president's policy should be followed, Lewis could then report the situation to the appropriate government agency.

Lewis could take another approach—to ignore the order, and wait until he is called to task, or fired for not obeying orders. This, however, puts an excessive burden on him—a burden that loyalty to the company cannot legit-imately demand. There are times when injustice within a company can be rectified only by forces outside a company, and recourse to them is morally justifiable.

Obedience can be demanded of employees, as long as what is commanded is job-related, and neither illegal nor immoral. Firms may wish their employees to be loyal, but loyalty cannot be demanded. It must be developed, encouraged, and, ultimately, earned.

The moral concerns of workers, as well as their moral rights, have received too little attention from corporations. A firm that takes morality seriously will set a moral tone from above, and will pay close attention to the moral concerns of its employees. It will make sure that its structure facilitates the expression of employees' concerns regarding their moral and civil rights.

Study Questions

1. Does the fact that one works for the government affect the justifiability of drug testing? Why or why not?
2. Why is it not correct to say that workers have only those rights that they negotiate as conditions of employment? What other rights do they have? Explain.
3. What constitutes just cause for firing? Give specific examples.
4. What are two moral principles that apply in any case of firing? Explain what they are and how they should be applied.
5. Do employees have a right to promotions? vacations? pension plans in their jobs? If so, under what conditions? If not, why not?
6. What rights do employees have in plant-closing cases? Do they have moral rights in addition to those guaranteed by law? Do employees in small firms have the same moral rights in the case of a plant closing as do employees of large firms?
7. Distinguish *civil* from *moral* rights. Give examples of workers' rights of each kind.
8. To what extent do employees retain the right of freedom of speech on the job? off the job? Explain and give examples.
9. How does the right to treatment with respect affect conditions of employment? Explain.
10. Do pre-employment polygraph tests violate a job applicant's right to privacy? Why or why not?
11. To what extent, if any, is post-employment drug testing morally justifiable?
12. What rights do those who test positive for AIDS have on the job?
13. How might the quality of work life be improved with respect to conditions of labor? the organization of work? worker relations? worker attitudes?
14. Name some of the obligations of employees to their firms.

15. Do workers owe their firms loyalty? If so, to what extent, and how is the obligation defended? If not, why not?

16. What obedience do employees owe the firms for which they work? Explain.

17. Are employees obliged to report the wrongdoings of others in the firm? Why or why not?

18. Can loyalty be demanded of employees? Why or why not?

19. Karolyn Kline is the manager of a plant that makes computers. She suspects that Tim Hoskins is on drugs. His eyes are glassy, he seems to drift off every now and them, and the number of rejects from his work lately is higher than usual for him, although still within the normal number made by people in his job. The plant has a drug employee assistance program. What should she do? What are the ethical limitations on her options?

16

>–I–‹›–O–‹›–I–‹

DISCRIMINATION, AFFIRMATIVE ACTION, AND REVERSE DISCRIMINATION

The *Weber* Case

In the case of *United Steelworkers of America v. Brian F. Weber et al.*[1] Brian Weber, a member of the United Steelworkers Union and an employee of Kaiser Aluminum & Chemical Corporation, complained that he was being treated unfairly as a result of an affirmative-action plan that Kaiser and the union had agreed upon. The Kaiser plant was in Gramercy, Louisiana. Until 1974, Kaiser hired as craft workers for the plant only persons who had prior craft experience. This almost precluded blacks from such positions, because they had been excluded from the craft union. Prior to 1974, only 5 out of 273 (1.83 percent) of the skilled craft workers at Gramercy were black. Because 39 percent of the work force at Gramercy was black, there was basis for at least a prima facie claim of past discrimination, either in the union or in the plant, or both. As a result of a collective-bargaining agreement between the union and Kaiser, an affirmative-action plan was adopted at fifteen plants—including the Gramercy plant—and black hiring goals for craft positions were set. In the Gramercy plant, the goal was eventually to have 39 percent of the skilled craft positions filled by blacks. In order to reach this goal, an on-the-job training program was set up to teach craft skills to nonskilled workers. The program was open to both whites and blacks. At least 50 percent of the openings were to be reserved for black workers. In the choice of both whites and blacks, selection was based on seniority.

---

[1] *United Steelworkers of America, AFL-CIO-CLC v. Weber*, 99 S. Ct. 2721 (1979).

In the first year of the program at Gramercy, thirteen workers were chosen for the program—six whites and seven blacks. The most senior black selected had less seniority than several of the white applicants who were rejected. On behalf of himself and the other rejected whites with more seniority than the blacks, Weber claimed that he and the others had been unjustly discriminated against. The District Court decided in favor of Weber, the Fifth Court of Appeals for the Fifth Circuit upheld the decision, but the Supreme Court overturned it. The Court acted on the legal aspects of the case. We shall consider the moral aspects.

Was the setting up of the program by Kaiser and the United Steelworkers Union morally justifiable? The program was part of a collective-bargaining agreement, and so both management and labor were represented. The program was not one that was established unilaterally by Kaiser. Moreover, both Kaiser and the United Steelworkers Union were, at least in the Gramercy situation, prima facie guilty of past discrimination, as reflected in the small number of blacks among their skilled workers. Clearly, the policies of both organizations had to change. But simply changing the policies would not be enough, because the pool of black skilled craft workers was extremely small, and there was no clear way for that number to increase. The policy adopted was one of affirmative action. It had as its aim the training of workers already employed at Kaiser; it did not bring workers in from the outside. The benefit of such a program was that it not only helped increase the percentage of blacks in the skilled positions, but it also gave those black workers—who had possibly been discriminated against by the system—a chance to improve their position. The intent of the program was morally justified. Were the details? Weber did not claim that the union and Kaiser did not have the right to establish a program. He argued that the program established was unfair to him and others. Was it?

If there had not been the need for affirmative action with respect to blacks at the plant, the new training program would not have been established. When there was no such program, no one, including Weber, could claim that he had a right to one. Moreover, as a result of the affirmative-action program, whites, who as a class did not need any special program to gain entrance into the union and the craft positions, were also to be given the opportunity for special training. Hence, white workers could not argue that as a class they were being discriminated against. Furthermore, this training program was just that—a training program. No whites were displaced from their jobs; no blacks were given jobs automatically because of the training program. Presumably, when a position had to be filled, it would be filled with a qualified applicant. The training program added blacks as well as whites to the pool from which craft positions could be filled. So far, there seems to be no injustice for anyone to complain about.

The complaint of Weber was not that whites as a class had been discriminated against, but that a small class of whites—namely, those with more seniority than the blacks accepted into the program—had been discriminated against. The basis for the complaint was that in choosing the trainees, seniority alone did not count. But it is not clear why it alone should have counted. Weber and the others seem to have claimed that the seniority rule was to take precedence over the 50 percent rule and that it was unfair that the rule should read, "at least 50 percent blacks." Yet if the 50 percent rule had not been adopted by Kaiser and the Union, then it would have been possible for all the trainees to be white. And if that were the case, the training program, instead of helping to alleviate the imbalance of whites and blacks, would have exacerbated it. Under those conditions the training program would have been not only unnecessary, but one could argue it would have been preferable not to have it. If the alternative was either no program or a program that mandated that at least 50 percent of the trainees be black, a white such as Weber would arguably have been better off with the latter than with no program.

Justice William J. Brennan, Jr., wrote the majority decision for the Supreme Court and concluded that, from a legal point of view, Title VII of the 1964 Civil Rights Act prohibits requiring preferential treatment because of race, but it does not preclude permitting voluntary affirmative-action programs to correct racial imbalance.

Nonetheless, some critics continue to maintain that the case is an instance of invidious reverse discrimination and that as such the training program as established was not ethically justifiable. Was the program unfair to Weber? Was it unfair in general to white male workers at Kaiser? If it was, could an alternative program have been established? If so, describe that program. If not, was no program ethically preferable to the one that was instituted? Why?

Discrimination

The term *discrimination* is usually used in a pejorative sense with respect to employment, but there is also a morally neutral sense of the term. We discriminate between those things we want and those we do not want. We can discriminate between good apples and bad ones in a fruit market, and we are allowed to choose those we wish. We can also discriminate between people on the basis of qualifications. If a position requires the ability to type, that requirement will serve to discriminate between those who have the ability and those who do not. What we are not morally allowed to do when discriminating between people with respect to work is to use improper criteria. Improper criteria in the job market are nonjob-related criteria. Discrimination in the job market has come to mean discrimination in the pejorative sense.

Because workers have the right to equal treatment, discrimination on the basis of nonjob-related characteristics when hiring, firing, or promoting people is immoral. Few dispute this statement, which is fairly easy to demonstrate using a utilitarian, a Kantian, or a Rawlsian approach.

Consider the practice of discrimination from a utilitarian point of view. We see, immediately, that harm is done to those who are discriminated against. If the practice is widespread and repeated in successive job situations, the harm done is serious and long-lasting. It affects not only the individuals but also their families. Those who do get the positions and promotions they would not get under conditions of fair competition do benefit. The good done to them, however, is probably not as great as the harm done to those discriminated against. But let us assume that the good is equal to the harm. In this case, the morality of the practice hinges on the results to others and to society in general. We can first consider the companies in which discrimination is practiced. If they did not discriminate, but hired and promoted only on the basis of merit, they would undoubtedly hire and promote some of those they discriminate against. Hence, they are not getting the best people possible. To that extent they suffer some harm and experience no benefit. What about society as a whole? It also suffers. Systematic discrimination produces a class of people who are treated unjustly. They cannot help but feel anger against society, an anger that will show itself in many ways—from violence to seething ill will. Other groups in the society will also have cause to worry about whether they will be the next group to be discriminated against. On the whole, more harm than good is done by following the practice of discrimination than by not following it. Discrimination is therefore an immoral practice.

We can reach the same result by a Kantian-type analysis. Can discrimination be made universal consistently? In fact, it can. People might not like the kind of society in which they were to live if discrimination were made universal, but the action is not self-contradictory. It passes the first of the three Kantian tests, but it fails the next two. Discrimination does not treat people as ends in themselves. They are not considered as persons; they are treated as members of a class with a certain characteristic. As a result of that characteristic, they are not given equal treatment, and they are not treated with respect. They are made means to the ends of the dominant class's desire to maintain its superiority and its class prerogatives. And if we were to ask whether rational human beings would be willing to live in a society that discriminates rather than in one that does not, could we expect anything other than a negative answer?

Using a Rawlsian-like approach, we should consider the decision that rational people would make if they were behind the veil of ignorance. If they did not know where they would end up, would they prefer to live in a discriminatory society or in a nondiscriminatory one? Clearly, the least advantaged would be better off in a nondiscriminatory society than in one that discriminates. Therefore, the rational person, not knowing where he or she would end up, would see that the morally preferable, the morally just society is the one that does not practice discrimination. Discrimination, moreover, directly violates Rawls's principles of justice because it does not allow either equal freedom to all or equality of opportunity.

Because it seems so clear that discrimination is immoral, we should pause to consider why discrimination has been so widely practiced in our society. Part of the reply comes from historical circumstances. To understand why people discriminate is not to justify their doing so; and although condemning the practice, we can at least understand the human motivation for it.

Blacks have been one chief group against whom discrimination has been practiced for a long period of time, and in a systematic way.[2] The reason for the discrimination stems from the fact that, with but a few exceptions, blacks in the United States were slaves until freed as a result of the Civil War. Many whites did not even consider them human beings. This attitude towards blacks enabled the whites to live with the immoral institution of slavery. The Emancipation Proclamation could not instantly change the attitude of those who considered blacks slaves, inferior to whites, and nonhuman. Neither amendments to the Constitution nor legislation granting the blacks the rights of citizens could change the views and attitudes of such whites—Southern or Northern. Attitudes are not easily or quickly changed. Moreover, the blacks were uneducated and were used to living in extremely poor conditions. When they were freed, they could leave the plantation and seek employment elsewhere, but they were not trained to work in factories or to run their own affairs. They were easy prey for entrepreneurs, who hired them for a pittance. After they were freed, the standard of living of many blacks was little, if at all, improved over the slave days. Some were even worse off. The whites in both the North and the South, who had felt superior to the slaves, continued to feel so. The well-to-do felt superior because they lived better, had more money, and could hire the blacks cheaply; and the poor whites felt superior simply because they were white. The color of their own skin was all they had to feel superior about, but they found it enough. The blacks were forced to live in segregated areas, and were discriminated against in schooling, opportunities to gain advancement, employment, and almost every aspect of social life.

Women are another group against whom discrimination in employment has been practiced.[3] The historical situation with respect to women is more complicated and more controversial than that of blacks. During the nineteenth century and the early part of the twentieth century, other than the movement for women's suffrage, little was said or written concerning discrimination against women. The majority of women did not seek employment outside of the home. The man in a household was considered the head of the family and the breadwinner. We have already seen, in Chapter 14, that men were paid more than women for the same work because it was assumed that men had to support their families whereas women either had to support only themselves

---

[2] For a fuller discussion of this topic, see Bernard R. Boxill, *Blacks and Social Justice,* rev. ed. (Boston: Rowman & Littlefield, 1992).

[3] For a fuller discussion of this topic, see Marilyn French, *The War Against Women* (New York: Summit Books, 1992); Janice Wood Wetzel, *The World of Women: In Pursuit of Human Rights* (New York: New York University Press, 1993); and Susan Gluck Mezey, *In Pursuit of Equality: Women, Public Policy, and the Federal Courts* (New York: St. Martin's Press, 1992). Barbara S. Gamble (Ed.), *Sex Discrimination Handbook* (Washington, D.C.: BNA Books, 1992), is a guide to federal and state legislation dealing with sexual discrimination.

or had to contribute to the support of a family in which the man already worked. The allocation of pay was based on a combination of both work and need, a criterion that many people in former times considered appropriate. Women who did not work, or who worked to supplement their husband's income, benefited from the fact that their husbands were paid more than women. With hindsight, we can now see that the women who were underpaid for their work were actually being discriminated against. As women joined the work force in greater numbers, as divorce increased, as more women became heads of households, and as it became clear that single men were also paid more than single women, a movement gradually formed. Women demanded equal pay for equal work, equal opportunity for women, and an end to discrimination against women. Old habits die hard, however, and much discrimination, often in subtle forms, continues to the present day. Its historical roots are nonetheless important to remember.

Ethnic groups have also been the object of discrimination: the American Indian, Asians, Hispanics, Italians, Irish, Poles, Czechs, and so on. At one time or another, members of religious sects, including Jews, Catholics, and Mormons, have been discriminated against. In each case, the people in question were different from the majority of Americans, in that they lived on reservations or in ghettos, or were immigrants or migrant workers. Eventually, most of them were assimilated, but sometimes only after two or three generations. And before assimilation, they suffered discrimination in the job market as well as in other areas of life.

Discrimination is unjust and causes harm to those against whom it is practiced. Compensatory justice demands that restitution be made to those harmed. The compensation should be equivalent to the harm suffered, and it should be paid to the one harmed by the one who caused the harm.

If a black or a woman working for a company has been receiving less pay for the same work done by white males, then compensatory justice requires that the company pay the black or the woman the amount he or she did not receive during his or her tenure with the company. Few cases, however, are that simple. Those who were discriminated against and have since died cannot be compensated by payment. Should their children or their heirs be compensated? Those who were never hired by any of the firms to which they applied cannot easily say which ones turned them down because of discrimination. Even if they could say which firms were guilty of discrimination, for what amount should they be compensated? Should they be paid a certain sum by all the companies that turned them down, or by all the firms that would have turned them down had they applied to them? None of these questions is easy to answer.

Some people have urged that certain groups or classes of people who have been discriminated against should be identified. The members of that group deserve compensation of some form from the group of people and companies that have discriminated, or who have been the beneficiaries of discrimination. In concrete terms, the class of all blacks, women, Chicanos, American Indians, and Asians are considered to be the major bearers of the burden of discrimination. If an individual in any of those groups has not been personally discriminated against, it is very likely that his or her parents have been, or that some other ancestor or relative has been. If by chance a few who bear no scars of discrimination receive compensation, that is better than large numbers never receiving any compensation.

Who is to pay the compensation? Those who have benefited from discrimination are said to be American corporations and American white males. Even if some individual white males did not benefit directly, they benefited indirectly as a result of the systematic discrimination that has favored them throughout their lives. Similarly, even if a particular company did not discriminate, it took advantage of the climate of corporate life that discrimination fostered.

Of what should compensation consist? It could not, in justice, consist of monetary payments, for there would be no way to determine these in an equitable way. The only sort of compensation possible, the argument goes, is that the class of people who were previously discriminated against be given special privileges and opportunities to make up for the absence of such privileges and opportunities in the past. A variety of target goals have been proposed. Some urge that every firm have the same proportion of women, blacks, Chicanos, and Asians as is found in the general population. Others favor the idea that proportions in each type of position should be equal to the proportion of each group in training for that position. But this is considered unsatisfactory by those who feel that fewer women and blacks, for instance, are in engineering schools than should be because discrimination has steered them away from such professions.

At what rate should those previously discriminated against be taken into companies and given promotions? Some would set targets and quotas for each year until the proper proportion is reached. Some simply advocate an affirmative approach—that is, making sure that places are open to those qualified. Others seek preferential hiring—a term that can be interpreted in several different ways—of women and minorities.

Before we look into the specifics of some of these proposals, we should examine carefully the approach to compensation in terms of classes. Is such an approach fair, just, and proper? In arguing that discrimination was immoral, we saw that harm was done to the one discriminated against, that benefit was provided to the one chosen, and that harm was done to society and to the companies that engaged in the practice. Suppose we follow the class or group approach. If people from the previously discriminated-against groups were chosen in favor of more qualified white males, we would have an instance of discrimination, even though the discrimination was against white males and in favor of blacks and females. Less qualified people would still be chosen over more qualified people. Harm would be done to the group and to the individuals discriminated against, as well as to the companies and to society. If discrimination was wrong because of these results in the first instance, it cannot be right when the results are similar in the second instance. After years of this practice, we would have a group of white males who had suffered discrimination, and we would have to start the cycle all over again. The argument that white males are the group that had previously benefited will not be convincing to the individual white males now being discriminated against. They will rightly claim that they are not guilty of past discrimination and that it is unjust to punish sons for the sins of their fathers. The children of immigrants from Italy or Poland or Ireland will cry out even louder for justice. Their parents were discriminated against, just as blacks and women were. Do they not deserve compensation too? But under the proposed system, they are the ones threatened with direct discrimination, after having suffered indirectly from the discrimination against their parents.

Other objections have been raised against the class approach to compensation. How much black blood is necessary for one to be considered black and therefore eligible to belong to the class of those to get recompense? How much American Indian blood, or Mexican blood, and so on, is necessary? This is not an insuperable obstacle, because the number of borderline cases may be small in proportion to the number of clear cases. Yet it does raise some problems. Should those who have succeeded despite discrimination receive compensation? There are, of course, successful and prosperous blacks and women. Some are in the professions; some are in business. Some were born in middle-class communities; some were born well-to-do. Some were born in the slums and worked their way up the ladder to success, however *success* is defined. Their children may not have suffered discrimination. Should they be recompensed? Many women now in college have lived their lives so far during the period of the rise of the women's movement. They have not been discriminated against in school. They frequently come from families supported by their fathers. If their fathers are white, they probably benefited from the discrimination against blacks and women, which aided their fathers' success. Should these young women be compensated for discrimination?

The class approach to discrimination and recompense suffers from many forms of inequity. One assumption is that without discrimination no white male would have been successful in the competition of the marketplace. This seems unlikely. Furthermore, it assumes that all white males somehow make up a class that can and should be penalized. Discrimination, however, was practiced by those now at the senior levels, not by those who will suffer the cost of reparation. In our earlier discussion of responsibility, we saw that, for someone to be responsible, and to be properly censurable and punished, a causal connection is necessary. But those being punished in the class approach to discrimination are not those who are causally responsible for discrimination, and those who benefited most are not those who will suffer the major effects of this new discrimination.

The conclusion to which we are reluctantly brought is that the class approach to discrimination and compensation itself involves discrimination, produces harm to those who did not cause it, does not solve the social problems of discrimination, and is immoral. Yet we saw that the individual approach is not sufficiently extensive and that it ignores many who still suffer indirectly from the discrimination practiced against their parents. Is there any way to satisfy the demands of compensatory justice without continuing discrimination in another form—frequently called *reverse discrimination?*

We suggest four answers. First, the problem is not simply one of individuals, classes, or groups; the problem involves all members of society. Past discrimination was a result of social structures; therefore, these have to be changed, and some beneficial structures must be built that give at least some compensation for those still suffering from the effects of discrimination. Second, in an attempt to change existing conditions, the government has mandated equal employment opportunity for all. Although this is morally proper, some claim it is not enough. Third, affirmative action can be taken to ensure that members of those groups previously discriminated against are not further ignored by the system. Fourth, preferential hiring can be implemented to achieve affirmative-action goals. Each of these deserves further discussion.

Changing Social Structures

Discrimination against women, blacks, and other minority groups was not necessarily done consciously or with personally malicious intentions. It was an effect of certain ways of doing business, certain patterns of thinking and acting, and certain social structures. These must be changed. A necessary first step has been raising the consciousness of the ordinary citizen and of those people holding responsible positions in business. Discrimination has been illegal since the Civil Rights Act of 1964, but legislation cannot change people's attitudes and their old habits. These have been changing slowly, under constant pressure from both minority associations and women's groups, as well as from individuals who push for their rights, sue when appropriate, and jostle those who tend to revert to old habits.

People who, as individuals, have been discriminated against can bargain or sue for compensation, but those who suffer the effects of discrimination in a less specific manner cannot. In many ways, society as a whole is to blame for past discrimination. So society should bear the burden of compensation when direct individual reparation by a business or individual is not available. Though the claim is plausible, its implementation raises questions. For instance, what is to count as evidence of suffering from past discrimination, either directly or indirectly? Similarly, what is to count as evidence of having profited, directly or indirectly, from past discrimination? Who should bear the cost of compensation? What form should the compensation take? There are no easy answers to these questions, but we suggest some approaches.

No specific condition is evidence of past discrimination: neither poverty, nor a poor education, nor failure to get and keep a good job, however *good job* is defined. All of these are often the result of discrimination. But other causes also contribute to poverty, poor education, and failure to get a job of one's choosing. From a social point of view, need we distinguish between the help given to the poor or to the poorly educated, who were discriminated against, which is called compensation, and the help we give to the poor and the poorly educated simply because they are poor and poorly educated? There is little to gain in attempting to make such fine distinctions. If one of the results of racial discrimination is poverty and poor schooling, then justice requires that attempts be made to get rid of poverty and to improve schooling. But it is also appropriate for society to do these things for all the poor and the poorly educated. Society should make available the opportunities for people to rise above the poverty level, to take part in the mainstream of social activity if they wish, and to have available the schooling and more advanced educational opportunities that allow them to better themselves and to compete on an equal footing with others.

The attempts to make black schools equal to white schools have not been successful. Obviously, more must be done in this regard. The problem of how to achieve the desired end of equal educational opportunities for all has not been satisfactorily solved. It is a problem that requires more work, thought, experimentation, and money. Society should supply all of these in greater quantity than it has thus far.

Improving education for blacks by improving their schools is a slow approach. It will take several generations of people to produce any real effect. We first have to provide good, basic schooling at the elementary level, then improve the junior high and high school levels, so that blacks can compete on the college level and then go on to professional schools. The process is obviously long and drawn-out. What of the blacks and other minority members who have had poor elementary school training and are now in high school, or those who have had poor high school training and are having difficulty in college? Thus far, the best that can be done is to provide remedial help wherever possible. Those who earn engineering degrees or medical degrees must have mastered the requisite knowledge. They are not passed through because they are the victims of past discrimination, nor do many advocate that they should be. No one would want to consult a doctor who was not properly trained or entrust his or her life to a building designed or built by an incompetent engineer.

Industry, however, can provide special training, financed by business as well as by public funds. Business can appropriately be asked to take the lead in such programs, and to make some contribution to them, for two reasons: Because businesses in the past have practiced discrimination, and because businesses, once they hire minorities, will benefit by the training they give such people. Government can appropriately be asked to contribute because such programs represent society's effort to make restitution for past social injustice.

The situation with respect to women is in some ways easier and in some ways more difficult, because it is more subtle. It is easier because at least white women have in recent years gained access to as good schools as men and have had the opportunity to receive adequate education for a variety of jobs and professions. They have been discriminated against, however, in both the hiring and the promotion processes. But these are both remediable, and important first steps have been taken. Obviously, however, not many women have made it to the top of their professions and firms, considering the number of women in them. Proportional representation at the top takes time; women have to compete with men and have had the opportunity to do so for too short a time. Those impatient with this approach want more women at the top, now. Those with more patience claim that promoting women to the "level of their incompetence" too soon will not help but hinder the cause of women in general. There are admittedly still too many barriers to and at the top, which must come down, and which will come down with time and with steady pressure.

On the other hand, the situation of women is more difficult than for blacks and minorities because women are a majority. Some of them feel they are oppressed by language, which gives dominance to men, and by culture, which stereotypes them and forces them into certain roles. There is less agreement about whether there is such discrimination and oppression of women by men, nor is it a matter of males against females on these issues; a significant number of women are unsympathetic to the radical position of the women's movement, and there are men who sympathize with it. The social problem of stereotyping women and men in textbooks, in the media, and in business has been persuasively raised. Some change has been made—less than many think is appropriate—but change does continue, and society is surely, if slowly, moving in the direction of greater equality of treatment for women.

Racial, sexual, religious, and other kinds of discrimination have always been immoral. Discrimination is now illegal in many areas and is under attack in areas that are beyond the reach of the law. We must still provide equal access to all, making up for past discrimination by improved schooling for those who have suffered from poor schooling, improved training for those who have not had access to training, and improved chances for advancement through affirmative action and preferential hiring. Changes in our social structures are essential.

What we have not suggested is that either businesses or individual white males be directly penalized unless they can be identified as perpetrators or direct beneficiaries of specific discrimination in the past. There are some who claim this permits the guilty, or at least those who have benefited from discrimination, to remain without censure or penalty. However, just because a white male has been successful in business, we cannot know whether his success is owing to discrimination. Presumably, if there had been no discrimination, some white males would be successful. Unless we have evidence to determine which are which, we do some an injustice by condemning or seeking retribution from all. One solution may be for society to appropriately tax all people who do well financially, in order to help those who need financial assistance. Society taxes businesses for the social good. Such taxation can be defended as justifiable, even though we cannot say exactly which company benefited from discrimination and to what precise extent it benefited, or which company practiced it, to what extent, and whether wittingly or unwittingly.

Equal Employment Opportunity

Since 1963, the United States Congress has passed a series of laws that attempt to implement the right of each person to equal treatment with respect to employment. The Equal Pay Act of 1963 guarantees the right to equal pay for equal work and is aimed especially at wage discrimination against women. The Civil Rights Act was passed in 1964 and was amended in 1972 by the Equal Employment Opportunity Act. It prohibits all forms of discrimination based on race, color, sex, religion, or national origin. The most important section of the act, known as Title VII, prohibits discrimination in employment. It applies to all employers, both public and private, with fifteen or more employees. The purpose of the act is to target the major employers. Nonjob-related discrimination is, of course, morally prohibited no matter how few workers one employs. But the act's reporting and other requirements are onerous enough to impose unreasonable cost on small businesses that employ only a few people. In 1967 the Age Discrimination in Employment Act was passed (amended in 1978). In particular, it protects those between the ages of 40 and 70 from discrimination because of age. All of these acts are enforced through the Equal Employment Opportunity Commission (EEOC). In addition, there have been several acts and executive orders that regulate government contractors and subcontractors, and that require equal opportunities for the handicapped, disabled veterans, and veterans of the Vietnam War.

Taken together, these form a solid basis for implementing equal opportunity. But laws alone cannot in fact extend equal opportunity to all. The laws provide an incentive not to discriminate, and they specifically provide legal recourse for those who suffer discrimination in employment. But as with any legal procedure, filing charges requires time and energy, and the victims of discrimination are frequently loath to pursue the matter, especially if another job is available.

Equal Employment Opportunity (EEO) places certain responsibilities on employers of fifteen or more people, and these begin with the specification of a job requirement. In making employment decisions, employers are to consider only job-related criteria. Sex and race are not job-related criteria for the vast majority of jobs. One result of EEO has been to prohibit the stereotyping of jobs. Before the EEO laws, it was common practice to list jobs in the newspaper under either "male" or "female." It was expected and accepted, for instance, that a secretarial job would be listed in the "female" column and a truck driver's job would be listed in the "male" column. This is no longer allowed or done. Although most truck drivers are still males and most secretaries are females, a company can no longer advertise its positions in this way, nor should it consider applicants on the basis of sex. Males can be secretaries as well as females, and females can be truck drivers as well as males. There is nothing in the nature of either job that requires one to be of a certain sex. Hence, sex is a nonjob-related characteristic for both jobs—as well as for most others.

The EEO laws require an employer to give greater care to writing the job description for a position than many employers did prior to the laws. The descriptions should state the actual qualifications needed for the job. Only if the job description is clearly and accurately written can prospective employees know if they are qualified, and only if the description is clear and accurate can employers both make and defend unbiased judgments concerning who the best applicant is.

Once a clear and accurate job description has been drawn up, EEO laws discourage the asking of nonjob-related questions on application forms and during interviews, since if such information is solicited and provided it cannot legally be used as a basis for refusing to hire. If it is, that is the basis for a claim of illegal discrimination. The list is not exhaustive. But the types of questions that should not be asked concern age, marital status, race, religion, sex, plans to have children, and arrest (as opposed to relevant conviction) record. Of course, some nonjob-related characteristics, such as sex and race, may become immediately apparent in an interview, but they should not be the basis for the final decisions of whom to hire.

Laws can, however, only go so far. If someone refuses, without saying so, to hire women and blacks, the laws do not force them to do so. More is required than simply equal opportunity laws, and this is part of the purpose of affirmative action and some executive orders.

From a moral point of view, equal opportunity is a moral right of all people. It is built into the two principles of justice developed by John Rawls. But equal opportunity has several dimensions, and equal employment opportunity is only one of them. Although people now have the legally guaranteed right to equal consideration for a job regardless of race, sex, and national origin, applicants must be qualified for the jobs in order to compete for them. Is there equal opportunity to get the education, training, and experience that jobs require? We certainly cannot assume that each person has the equal opportunity to develop his or her talents to an equal extent. Children raised in a ghetto have many fewer opportunities for development than do children in affluent communities. Sex stereotyping still persists in many schools, where girls are subtly led into some courses and boys into others. Because the schools of our country are not equal, there are differences in the quality of education that children receive. There are also native differences in human beings; some are more intelligent than others, some are stronger than others, some are more energetic. Family also makes a difference. Some families are nurturing and help children develop, providing them with values and support that sustain them throughout life. Others provide little support, encouragement, or positive values. The law does not take upon itself the remedying of all these differences—nor can it. Does morality demand that equal opportunity take all these differences into account, and that those who have greater advantage in the natural lottery of talents be somehow handicapped so as to make everyone equal? Some people believe so. But that is not demanded by law, nor is it clearly a moral demand.

The demands for equal opportunity have as their aim overcoming discriminatory practices. However, they do not do anything to overcome the disadvantages of people who have been discriminated against in the past. The network of information concerning job availability, for instance, was developed in such a way that minorities and women were ignored. In order to make up for such subtle and indirect discrimination, many believed that positive, affirmative action had to be taken. The result has been a program of affirmative action, of which some aspects are mandated and implemented by executive orders and government regulations.

Affirmative Action

The promise on the part of businesses not to engage in discrimination is not enough to offset the effects of past discrimination, nor is it enough for them simply to refrain from discrimination. An active rather than a passive approach is required. An approach mandated by government and advocated by many groups has become known as *affirmative action.*[4] Unfortunately, affirmative action has come to be equated by many either with quotas or with reverse discrimination. But it need not and should not be confused or identified with either of them.

As originally intended, affirmative action operates on four levels: (1) active recruiting of women and members of minority groups in a job search, (2) equalization of criteria so as not to give preference to any group, (3) adequate training for senior positions, and (4) promotion of women and members of minority groups to senior positions.

Who should practice affirmative action? Those firms and institutions that have a small number of minorities and women in proportion to the general population (or in proportion to the number of persons qualified for the positions in the firm or organization) are prime candidates for affirmative action. Though the small percentage of women and minority members does not prove active discrimination in the past, it presents prima facie evidence of either active discrimination or of cooperation in discriminatory conditions in other parts of society. The head of a scientific laboratory that has no women

---

[4] Some of the more recent works on affirmative action include Steven M. Cahn (Ed.), *Affirmative Action and the University* (Philadelphia: Temple University Press, 1993); Susan D. Clayton, *Justice, Gender, and Affirmative Action* (Ann Arbor: University of Michigan Press, 1992); Gertrude Ezorsky, *Racism and Justice: The Case for Affirmative Action* (Ithaca, N.Y.: Cornell University Press, 1991); Michael Rosenfeld, *Affirmative Action and Justice: A Philosophical and Constitutional Inquiry* (New Haven: Yale University Press, 1991); and Raymond Bron Taylor, *Affirmative Action at Work: Law, Politics, and Ethics* (Pittsburgh: University of Pittsburgh Press, 1991).

may plead that he has never had good women candidates. The question then becomes, why have so few women gone into science? Is there any reason other than that sexual stereotyping took place from infancy on? But if indeed there is a shortage of women in a certain field of science, it would be ridiculous to demand that, within the next two or three years, all laboratories add women scientists. The patterns that lead to women choosing scientific fields must be established if women are to be represented in adequate numbers in all laboratories.

Business has less excuse for not hiring women. Many women are eligible for executive traineeships, just as they are eligible for other kinds of work in business. The training is neither so long nor so specialized in many cases that it may justify long delays in hiring women in appreciable numbers. Though the same case cannot be made for all minority groups, because of the fact that a smaller percentage of minorities go on to college, growing numbers of minority members are available for managerial jobs. The problem here is why more minority members do not go on to college. What forces of discrimination have to be overcome to change that pattern? It seems justifiable to assume that more members of minority groups would choose college and the kinds of jobs it can lead to if they had the chance.

Active Recruitment

The first level of affirmative action involves the active recruiting of women and members of minority groups. This represents a change from the way many positions were filled in the past. Probably no woman or minority member was ever turned down in competition with a white male for certain positions because no woman or minority member *knew* of the opening. Openings were filled by the "old boy" network. If one employer had an opening for a good job, he would call up his friends and ask whom they recommended, or write to a few select universities and hire one of their best graduates. Affirmative action requires that jobs be advertised publicly, and not simply by word of mouth to one's friends. It also requires adequate advertising in the outlets commonly used by those interested in certain kinds of positions. If in addition there are special publications that are more likely to be read by women and minority members, then the opening should be listed in these. Affirmative action goes even further, if a reasonable number of women and minority applicants do not apply. In such cases, active soliciting of applications from members of these groups may be in order. Affirmative action, as the name suggests, consists of actively seeking applicants from the previously discriminated-against groups rather than waiting for them to take the initiative. This is not too much to demand. Typically, those who have been discriminated against by a certain firm or kind of business tend not to apply there, on the assumption that the future will be like the past. Those who have discriminated, or who give prima facie evidence of having participated in a discriminatory social syndrome, should take the initiative to contact groups whom they have previously ignored. This may be more costly in time and money than the old way of hiring. The extra burden is part of the cost of compensation and an appropriate form of reparation.

Equalization of Criteria

Discrimination is often subtle. If for a position one chooses criteria in terms of what skills white males are typically good at, one can write a job description that can be filled only by white males. If standard tests are skewed in such a way that white males excel at them, and if these tests are used to screen candidates, then white males will appear as the most qualified. Hence, we must ask, are the criteria themselves free of bias and prejudice? Are they fair? Are they relevant to the position advertised?

The fairness of criteria and tests has taken many strange turns. Some claim that blacks should not be discriminated against for using "black English" and for not writing standard English fluently. The argument may hold if the command of standard English is not necessary for the job, but it does not hold true for a job in which a person must write memos, letters, and reports for a range of American readers. This does not constitute prejudice, any more than not hiring a Mexican who cannot write English would constitute prejudice, if the job called for such a skill. More plausible are the claims that many of the objective tests designed to test intelligence or work skills are culturally slanted in favor of middle-class white males. The problem is a difficult one. Research has so far proved to be inconclusive, and even where the result seems to bear out the claim, it is not clear how to devise a test that will be fair to all, or how to weigh the built-in bias in favor of a certain group.

Other sorts of bias are built into job criteria. Frequently, a position calls for a college degree. The reason for demanding a college degree is not because one needs to know a particular subject that was taught in college. Any degree in any major will do. The assumption is that anyone who had the discipline to work for four years for a degree is a better candidate than someone who does not have that sort of background. But in many cases a person who has worked at a job for four years shows as much discipline as the person who attended college, and perhaps even more.

Discrimination that is built into job criteria is difficult to root out by law. Employers are free to draw up their own job descriptions, and no government bureaucrat can presume to know better than an employer what qualifications an employer needs in an employee. But pressure can be brought to bear, by those within a firm as well as by unions and professional associations, to rid job descriptions of built-in discrimination.

Adequate Training

We have already noted that many women and minority members have only in the past decade or two entered a large number of firms and institutions. They are still poorly represented in top positions. To remedy this situation, affirmative action has been taken by a number of firms. Such firms have established training internships for women and members of minority groups, in which they become apprenticed to a senior executive, for six months or a year. They learn what executives do and how they do it. The firsthand apprenticeship has served as an effective means of advancing those who have taken part in them. This is affirmative action. Instead of letting the natural process work, this technique has advanced people faster. The internships are usually available only to women or minority members in the firm, those who have been there a certain length of time and who compete for the positions. Does this mean the internships are discriminatory against white males? The answer seems to be clearly no. When vacancies occur for regular positions, white males are eligible for them and compete with women and minority members. The best person for the job should be chosen. Women and minority members need such internships to compete adequately with many white males, who for years had access to special privileges.

Promotion to Senior Positions

Affirmative action in hiring is not significant unless those hired have a chance to compete fairly for advancement and raises. In these areas, just as in hiring, many firms have had built-in prejudices and biases in favor of white males. Their background assumptions have frequently favored the white male. Managers have usually assumed that married women would not accept a promotion that involved transfer to another city, whereas they have offered such positions to men and later found out whether they would accept the transfer. Managers have assumed that single women would soon get married, or leave to have and raise children. Minority members were stereotyped as blue-collar workers, and racial prejudices about intelligence and ability were prevalent, even when proved false by performance. These and other assumptions were not spelled out in promotion criteria.

Affirmative action in promotion means that higher-level positions are truly open to competent women and minority members. It means searching through personnel records and inviting women and minority members to apply for positions that they may otherwise feel would not be open to them. It involves counseling them (if in fact they are passed over) as to how they can improve their chances for the next opening. Once again, what may seem like favoritism is justifiable, in order to equalize the predispositions in favor of the white male that still linger consciously or unconsciously in the system.

Affirmative action does not mandate quotas. If quotas mean hiring unqualified people, it is difficult to see how they can be morally mandatory. The unqualified will be let go after a short while or will remain at their entry level indefinitely, will be passed over by those qualified and eventually will lose their self-respect. Quotas will not supply role models for women and minority members, nor will they improve their image among managers in general. Quotas, however, can be distinguished from the expectation that firms will make reasonable progress toward hiring members of those groups grossly underrepresented, if the pool of applicants is sufficiently large. Making such progress is a reasonable moral expectation.

Hiring token women and members of minority groups is not affirmative action. Tokenism is not an adequate way to fulfill the moral responsibility to break the pattern and system of discrimination. The moral obligation to take affirmative action goes beyond satisfying the letter of the law.

Reverse Discrimination

If discrimination using nonjob-related criteria of race, color, sex, religion, or national origin is unjust when used against women or members of minority groups, it would also be unjust when used against white males. Refusing to hire a white male because he is white or because he is male is no less discriminatory than refusing to hire a black because he or she is black, or a woman because she is female. Discrimination against white males is often referred to as *reverse discrimination.* Reverse discrimination is unjust because it is a form of invidious discrimination, and we have already argued that discrimination on the basis of race, sex, and other nonjob-related criteria is unjust. Past discrimination does not justify present discrimination. The argument that white males have practiced discrimination in the past and that white males continue to be the beneficiaries of such discrimination considers all white males as forming a class. But it is usually not those white males who practiced discrimination or who were the greatest beneficiaries who are hurt by reverse discrimination. Most often the white males who suffer from reverse discrimination are young white male job seekers who have not practiced racial or sexual discrimination in the past.[5] Placing the blame for past discrimination on a class of people does not justify either holding every member of the class guilty or penalizing only certain members without regard to their individual culpability.

A standard way of filling a job is to announce the opening with a description indicating the qualifications necessary for the job. The implied agreement between those who advertise job openings and those who apply for them is that the person most suited for the position will be chosen. The criteria to be used in making the selection are understood to be job-related. It is unfair to use nonjob-related criteria because the use of such criteria breaks the implicit conditions of seeking and granting jobs. It is unfair to raise expectations when hidden criteria are being used, which, if known, will tell some

---

[5] Frederick R. Lynch, *Invisible Victims: White Males and the Crisis of Affirmative Action* (Westport, Conn.: Greenwood Press, 1989). For other discussions of reverse discrimination, see Kent Greenawalt, *Discrimination and Reverse Discrimination* (New York: Alfred A. Knopf, 1983); Alan H. Goldman, *Justice and Reverse Discrimination* (Princeton, N.J.: Princeton University Press, 1979); and Barry R. Gross (Ed.), *Reverse Discrimination* (Buffalo, N.Y.: Prometheus Books, 1977).

people that they will not be seriously considered for the job. To use criteria other than those stated or those obviously job-related is to mislead, deceive, raise false hopes, and violate an implied practice governing hiring. If a person is denied a job solely because of sex, race, or religion, that person is a victim of discrimination.

This implied agreement should not be misconstrued. No job applicant can plausibly claim a *right* to any particular job. The right to choose someone to fill an advertised position rests with the employer. There is no implied agreement that the "most qualified person" has a right to the job. This follows from the fact that no applicant has a right to any particular job. What constitutes the most suitable person to fill the job is determined by the employer, and that choice may or may not tally with the one whom any individual applicant considers the "best qualified person." What is included in the implied agreement is that anyone hired must satisfy the advertised criteria, providing there are applicants who do satisfy the criteria. To hire someone who does not satisfy the stated criteria over someone who does satisfy the criteria is prima facie unfair to the latter person. From this it follows that hiring women or minority members who are unqualified over qualified male applicants is unfair. If such a practice is followed in order to fill a quota, filling quotas in such a way is unfair. But this leaves open the question of whether it is fair or just to hire qualified women or minority members over equally or more qualified white males. Crucial to answering this question is the answer to another question: Can hiring women or minority members in order to rectify past discrimination or to balance one's work force be a legitimate aim for a firm? If so, then fulfilling that aim is a consideration that a firm may appropriately take into account in advertising and filling positions.

Balanced or Preferential Hiring

Preferential hiring is the hiring of women or minority applicants over equally or more qualified white males. Is preferential hiring a form of reverse discrimination, and is it therefore immoral?

A great deal of controversy has surrounded this question,[6] and some people simply equate preferential hiring with reverse discrimination. By assimilating the one to the other, they draw the conclusion that the practice is not morally justifiable. But the issue is not clear-cut and should not be summarily dismissed. If preferential hiring were simply and always reverse discrimination, it would, given our argument above, be unjust.

In order to give a better perspective, we might discuss *balanced hiring*, that is, the hiring of qualified women or minority members in order to balance

---

[6] For some discussion of preferential hiring, see William T. Blackstone and Robert Heslep, *Social Justice and Preferential Treatment* (Athens, Ga.: University of Georgia Press, 1977); and Marshall Cohen, Thomas Nagel, and Thomas Scanlon (Eds.), *Equality and Preferential Treatment* (Princeton, N.J.: Princeton University Press, 1977).

the composition of one's work force for any one of several organization-related reasons: To help make up for past discrimination; to provide role models in certain positions, such as in schools; to achieve a desired diversity that makes the employee composition more attractive for all applicants regardless of sex or race; and so on. If and when justified, preferential hiring equals balanced hiring.

Is preferential hiring ever justifiable? We can reject two interpretations immediately. One might claim that preferential hiring is not a form of discrimination because it *chooses* someone on the basis of sex, race, or religion rather than *denying* someone a position for these reasons. The distinction, however, will not stand up to scrutiny. If a white male is hired because he is white and a black male is not hired, and we are told that the black male was not discriminated against and that the white male was simply preferred *because* of the color of his skin, we would certainly call the choice one of racial discrimination.

In the second interpretation, one might claim that it is permissible to use preferential hiring if the announcement indicates that preference will be given to women or minority members. This, the claim goes, would indicate the rules of the game, would not deceive, and hence would be morally permitted. Consider, however, an ad for a job that included these words: "Women and minority members need not apply." Or an ad that indicated preference would be given to white males, even though one need not be a white male to do the job described. Surely we would say that such ads were discriminatory, as would be the practice. The same can be said of the reverse situation—when preference is given to women or minorities. If employers use a nonjob-related criterion, such as sex, race, or religion to hire people, they discriminate, whether they announce openly that they are or whether they do so without making it public.

To clarify the moral status of preferential hiring as balanced hiring, however, consider the following job announcement with respect to each of the situations listed:

> **Wanted**   Computer programmer. Must have knowledge of *Unix* and Java, plus at least two years of programming experience. Salary: open, depending on experience. An equal opportunity employer. Call 555-7625.

Situation 1: Sally Hanson and Tom Byers both apply for the job. Sally knows *Unix* but does not know Java. She has had only one year of experience as a programmer. She applies, figuring she has nothing to lose. Tom knows *Unix* and Java and has three years of experience as a programmer.

(a) Tom gets the job. He is the more qualified of the two.
(b) Sally gets the job. The employer needs more women in his work force to meet affirmative-action goals.

Situation 2: Sue Jones and John Green apply for the job. Sue fulfills all the listed requirements. John knows *Unix* and Java but has only one year of programming experience.

(a) Sue gets the job. She is the more qualified of the two.
(b) John gets the job. The employer prefers to hire males.

Situation 3: Sandra Hopkins and Henry Thompson apply for the job. Both Sandra and Henry know *Unix* and Java, and both have had two years of programming experience.

(a) Sandra gets the job. The employer wants more women in his work force to meet affirmative-action goals.
(b) Henry gets the job. Henry is a veteran, and the employer gives extra credit to veterans.
(b) Henry gets the job. The employer prefers to hire males.

Situation 4: Sarah Hall and Peter Brock apply for the job. Sarah knows *Unix* and Java and has had two years of programming experience. Her former employers stated that she was only adequate on the job. Peter is a computer whiz. He knows *Unix*, Java, and three other computer languages. He has had four years of programming experience and is rated as outstanding by his past employers.

(a) Sarah gets the job. The employer wants more women in his work force to meet affirmative-action goals.
(a) Peter gets the job. Regarding job experience, he is the better of the two applicants.

In Situation 1, it is appropriate that Tom rather than Sally get the job because he has the specified qualifications, which she does not have. If Sally gets the job because she is a woman and the firm wishes to meet its affirmative-action goals, then the firm has achieved its purpose in a way that does an injustice to Tom. If the qualifications listed are not the qualifications required for the job, and if the firm is going to consider someone with lesser qualifications if that someone is female, then the job description should be written differently.

Clearly, if the situation with respect to qualifications were reversed, as they are in Situation 2, we feel that it is inappropriate for John to be hired rather than Sue. Sue has all the stated qualifications. John has only one year of experience. The reason the firm gives, in Situation 2(b), is that it prefers to hire males. Hiring John, who does not have the stipulated qualifications, rather than Sue, who does, is a classic case of discrimination. The employer's only criterion for choosing John over Sue is that John is male. Is there a difference between Situation 2(b) and 1(b)? In both cases, a person who does *not* meet the stated qualifications for the job is chosen over a person of the other sex who *does* meet the qualifications. In both cases, the person is chosen on the basis of sex, a nonjob-related characteristic. The difference in the two cases is that in 2(b) the reason is personal preference, and in 1(b) it is a desire to fulfill an affirmative-action goal, with or without personal preference for hiring women. Does achievement of the goal outweigh the injustice done to Tom?

In order to answer this question, we might try a utilitarian approach. Consider the following rule: Managers should hire women who do not meet stated job requirements, rather than men who do, when the choice is between two such people and when the firm should make progress toward fulfilling affirmative-action goals. If we calculate the good and bad effects of the rule on all concerned, we can decide whether the practice is morally justifiable.

The good effect for Sally, at least initially, is that she gets the job. The bad effect for Tom is that he does not get the job. Would the results be equal if Tom got the job rather than Sally? The answer is no. If Tom got the job rather than Sally, Sally would not feel that an injustice had been done because she knew she did not have the stated qualifications. Tom, however, would feel that an injustice had been done to him because, despite his qualifications, he did not get the job and someone unqualified did. Therefore, just by considering the two people directly affected in the first instance, more good overall would be done by hiring Tom than by hiring Sally.

Next, consider what happens after the person hired is on the job. If the job actually requires knowledge of Java, Sally will not be able to perform that portion of her job. She could, of course, learn it. But this takes so much time that, if it were really necessary for the job, she might be fired for lacking this knowledge, before she would have had the time to learn it. This would not happen if Tom were hired.

How does the practice affect the company? Hiring Sally helps the company achieve its affirmative-action goal, but if she cannot perform adequately in the job, her performance hurts the firm. Hiring Tom helps the firm do its work but does not help it achieve its affirmative-action goal. What is the effect on the other workers? If they feel that Sally was hired because of affirmative action, she will probably not be well treated or thought of by her fellow workers. This will have an adverse effect on Sally. And because she cannot do what the job calls for, the other workers are likely to resent her being hired. They would have no such feelings toward Tom.

The practice of hiring women who do not meet the stated requirements rather than hiring men who do results in more harm than good. Hence, it is immoral and should not be adopted as a practice.

In the analysis, certain assumptions were made, one of them being that Sally could not learn Java quickly enough to be able to carry out her job well. If she could learn Java quickly enough, then the job description was not an accurate statement of the qualifications needed for the position. The real qualifications would then be knowledge of *Unix* and one year experience as a programmer, together with the ability to learn Java quickly. But if those were the real qualifications needed, we would have an entirely different situation, the kind described in Situations 3 and 4.

In Situation 3, both Sandra and Henry have all the required qualifications. Assuming that those are the only qualifications needed for the job, both candidates are equally qualified. Hence, there is no job-related criterion on the basis of which the employer can choose one of them rather than another. The firm could with justice make its decision in a random way—for instance, by tossing a coin. Situation 3(c) is puzzling. Is this an instance of discrimination? The employer chooses Henry only because Henry is a male. Is it proper for the firm to do so when it could choose either of them, indiscriminately, by tossing a coin? Is it wrong to choose one of them because of sex when it is right to choose either of them? The answer is yes. To choose a male applicant rather than an equally qualified female applicant, simply on the basis of sex, is discriminatory. It would be better to choose between them by the toss of a coin rather than on the basis of sex, because the toss of the coin gives them each an equal chance at the job.

What of Situations 3(a) and 3(b)? In each case the employer uses a criterion other than job-related qualifications. Is this fair? The answer is yes. But this answer requires some defense. Situation 3(a) is a classic case of justifiable preferential hiring. It is justifiable because in hiring Sandra rather than Henry, the employer is able to meet another need of the firm—namely, making progress toward its affirmative-action goal. The need of the firm is not identical with a job-related qualification. But, in a broad way, it is an employment-related criterion; it does not spring from a prejudice. It does no injustice to Henry because he is not being turned down in favor of someone unqualified. The job could properly go to either of them. If an employer can serve affirmative-action goals by hiring a qualified woman over an equally qualified man, this is a step, even if a small one, in the direction of making up for past discrimination by the firm.

Government jobs allow a certain amount of credit to an applicant who has served in the armed forces and has been honorably discharged. This is considered both a reward for past service to the government and to the country, and perhaps an incentive to others to join the armed forces. Such service credit is not inappropriate in private employment, though it is not required by law. By giving military-service credit, the employer helps the country achieve certain goals. But the fact that the company gives such credit should be made known in advance. It should not be used as a criterion after the fact. If the policy is to give government-service credit, then it should be given consistently. If, in Situation 3(b), giving Henry credit for military service is part of the firm's policy, it is justifiable. If giving Henry credit for military service is just a device used to decide this case, then it is an inappropriate device. If the firm has the policy of giving military-service credit, the problem then becomes how one is to balance military-service credit against affirmative-action goals. Both policies are governmentally and socially approved. Which takes precedence is not clear, and to decide it requires more information. For instance, how close to meeting its affirmative-action goal is the firm? How much weight does it give for military service? However the firm finally makes that decision, it should be able to defend the choice, giving reasons for its weighting of the various factors. If they are equally weighted, then we are back to tossing a coin.

Situation 4 demonstrates another aspect of preferential hiring. In Situation 4(a), Sarah gets the job. In Situation 4(b), Peter gets the job. Both outcomes are morally justifiable. Preferential hiring is morally justifiable to achieve affirmative-action goals and to make up for past discrimination. But as long as a firm makes reasonable progress toward affirmative-action goals, it is not required in any specific case to hire a woman or a minority member rather than a white male. As in Situation 4(a), the company may properly decide to hire Sarah. She satisfies the job qualifications. The qualifications, we shall assume, are appropriate to the job she will fill. She will be able to handle the job and will in no way harm the company. Someone else has stronger credentials in the field, but this does not make Sarah any less qualified for the job. By hiring her, the company gets a qualified person and helps achieve its affirmative-action goal, which is an employment-related criterion.

In Situation 4(b), the company hires an excellently qualified worker. He has more skills than the job requires. Even discounting his additional knowledge, his past ratings are higher than Sarah's. As far as job qualifications go, he can be shown to be the stronger candidate on the basis of job-related qualities. The firm cannot be blamed for choosing him, and no injustice is done to Sarah if he is chosen. No injustice is done to him, however, if Sarah is chosen.

We can generalize from our discussion of these varied situations.

1. Affirmative action does not justify hiring unqualified women or minority members in preference to qualified white males.
2. Qualified women and minority members can morally be given preference, on the basis of sex or race, over equally qualified white males, in order to achieve affirmative-action goals.
3. Qualified women and minority members can morally be given preference over better-qualified white males in order to achieve affirmative-action goals.
4. Preferential hiring is not mandatory in any given case, though overall, a firm must make adequate progress toward achieving affirmative-action goals.

These generalizations can be applied to promotion as well as to initial hiring. Firing raises a special problem. Many companies use the rule: "last on, first off." Unions generally support this rule and often agree to it in contracts. The rule protects seniority rights. Senior people, under this rule, have more job security than junior people. Older people usually have a harder time finding a new job than do younger people. Older people have put down roots, which are more difficult to pull up than newly planted roots. Older people usually earn more than beginners and therefore may be prime candidates for a firm that wants to save as much as possible by laying people off during a recession. This is why unions favor the rule. Supporters of the rule argue, moreover, that it does no injustice to the young because in the natural course of events the young grow older. What they lose in their youth they gain in their older age.

The rule is compatible with the foregoing four principles, when properly modified to apply to firing instead of hiring. Where two workers—for instance, a woman and a man—have comparable jobs, have worked the same amount of time, and have performed equally well in their jobs, then the woman can be given preference, in order to help the firm achieve affirmative-action goals. But because affirmative action and preferential hiring are of recent vintage, many of the people most vulnerable to layoff under the seniority system are those hired under affirmative-action guidelines. Hence, a period of recession and the resulting layoffs tend to undo most of the good done by affirmative-action programs. Is the seniority rule sacrosanct? Or would more good be done by violating it and giving preference to achieving affirmative-action goals? (This would mean keeping on junior women and minority members and laying off white males senior to them.) An argument has not yet been mounted to support a breach of seniority rules in favor of affirmative action—at least, none that is adequate to convince the Supreme Court, union leaders, or many members of the general public.

The Supreme Court has moved very slowly and carefully in deciding cases that involve reverse discrimination. It has chosen to rule narrowly rather than broadly in such cases as *Bakke, De Funis,* and *Weber.* The issue, however, is amenable to moral analysis and argument.

Two Cases: *Bakke* and *Stotts*

Two cases stand out as landmark decisions by the Supreme Court with respect to issues of affirmative action and reverse discrimination. The cases were decided on legal grounds, but the decisions have been argued in moral terms as well. Each of the cases, moreover, has reflected public sentiment and each has influenced public sentiment with respect to these issues. The *Bakke* case set limits on reverse discrimination, and the *Stotts* case gave preference to seniority over affirmative action. No one argues that special preference should be given to any group, whether minority or majority, indefinitely. The ideal is for all people, regardless of race, sex, or national origin, to have truly equal opportunity and freedom, and to be allowed to develop as fully as possible. Those who believe that the *Stotts* decision marks the beginning of the end of affirmative action are probably overreacting to the decision. At some time in the future, the need for affirmative action and preferential hiring will no longer exist, and at that time these programs will no longer be necessary. But the process will require time, and the dismantling of the programs will undoubtedly occur slowly.

The Bakke Case

In the case of *Bakke* v. *Regents of the University of California,*[7] Allan Bakke applied for admission to the Medical School at the University of California at Davis. The university had set aside sixteen places for minority students out of a class of one hundred. Minority students could request to be considered by a separate admissions committee, which applied less stringent admission criteria than the regular admissions committee. Bakke, a white male, applied for admission to the medical school twice and was twice rejected. Yet his grade-point average, his Medical College Admission Test (MCAT) scores, and his overall "benchmark" rating by the university were considerably higher than those of some of the minority students who were admitted.

Bakke sued for admission and won. The court decision was upheld by the Supreme Court of the State of California. The United States Supreme Court, on June 28, 1978, ruled that Bakke had been unlawfully denied admission and that race could be considered in admissions criteria. Exactly how that was to be done was not clear, but we can look at the moral issues involved nonetheless.

The Supreme Court of California indicated that either increasing the number of people admitted in order to allow minorities, or the admission of all disadvantaged persons, regardless of race, on some special criteria, would be legally acceptable. From a moral point of view, either of these alternatives would be morally acceptable. For what was unfair in the Bakke situation was depriving Bakke, simply on the basis of his race, a chance to gain admission to medical school on an equal footing with all other applicants. If we agree that each person has a right to an equal opportunity for such admission, then having a standard based on race is unfair.

The counterarguments are that the standard admission procedure is skewed in favor of whites because of the nature of the MCAT, that whites have access to better colleges, and that blacks have restricted opportunity in many areas of society. But the proper response to this argument is to change the criteria so that they are fair for all, rather than change them only for certain applicants from minority races. What was unfair at the Davis Medical School was not the changing of the rules to encourage more minority candidates to apply, but the way the rules were changed.

The question of quotas was also at issue in the Bakke case. There was not simply affirmative action to encourage more minorities to apply, or a change in the requirements so they would be fair to all. There was a quota—a certain number of places that were set aside for minority students. If that number had been added to the one hundred places originally available, then there would be less basis for charging injustice, although there might still be some. But because the sixteen places were subtracted from the original one hun-

---

[7] *Regents of University of California* v. *Bakke,* 98 S. Ct. 2733 (1978).

dred, Bakke legitimately claimed an injustice had been done to him; his chances were lessened because of his race.

Quotas, as we have already seen, cannot be morally defended as a means of achieving racial balance; they cannot remedy the injustice of past discrimination. What the *Bakke* case helped to underline was the need for policies that are fair to all, yet geared, in some affirmative fashion, to help right the wrongs of past discrimination. The same is true in the area of employment. Finding such policies requires imagination and ingenuity. It requires, especially, a readiness to rethink one's procedures objectively and honestly, and a willingness to change them as necessary so they are truly fair.

The Stotts Case

The *Firefighters v. Stotts*[8] case involved black firefighters in Memphis, Tennessee, who were laid off prior to whites with more seniority. Carl Stotts was a black district fire chief in Memphis. In 1977, the black firefighters filed a class-action suit charging the Memphis Fire Department with hiring and promotion discrimination. In 1980 the city and the black firefighters agreed on an affirmative-action plan, which was approved by a federal judge. Under the plan, the percentage of blacks rose from 4 percent to 11.5 percent. When financial difficulties forced the city of Memphis, in May 1981, to lay off firefighters, it followed the seniority rules negotiated with the union: The last on were the first off. The blacks protested, and the federal district court mandated that the same percentage of blacks be kept in the department. As a result, seventy-two whites with seniority were laid off or demoted, but only eight blacks.

The city of Memphis and the union appealed the ruling. A federal appeals court upheld the ruling. The U.S. Supreme Court overturned the lower court, indicating that bona fide seniority systems were protected by Title VII of the 1964 Civil Rights Act, that class-action suits could not be filed for such cases, and that only individuals who can prove they are victims of discrimination can sue for protection under affirmative action. Once again, the legal grounds need not concern us. Is the last-on-first-off rule morally justifiable?

The argument against the rule is that the blacks were hired under affirmative-action programs. If the last hired were the first fired, then the good accomplished by the affirmative-action plans would be defeated. If it was appropriate for blacks to be hired in preference to whites, providing both were qualified for the job, then it should be right to keep blacks on in preference to whites, providing both are qualified. *Seniority* refers to length of time on the job. But people with different amounts of seniority may do essentially the same jobs and be equally qualified. If one must terminate people, to be in accord with affirmative action plans (which are allowed, encouraged, and

---

[8] *Firefighters Local Union No. 1784 v. Stotts,* 104 S. Ct. 2576 (1984).

sometimes mandated by government), one should not terminate only on the basis of seniority if goals of racial balance will be adversely affected. The attainment of such goals has at least as much social and moral merit as seniority. To use only seniority rules as a basis for determining who will be laid off is to institute a revolving-door policy for women and minorities: They will be hired only to be fired. In the interim, firms will claim to be exercising affirmative action, but in fact, little will change in the composition of the permanent work force in these firms. The argument seems reasonable. But it did not persuade the Supreme Court.

The Court held that seniority takes precedence over affirmative action and that only individuals who have been the victims of direct discrimination have the right to claim preferential treatment. A moral argument in support of this decision is that both minorities and white males earn seniority. The seniority principle is blind when it comes to race, sex, or any other characteristic. Using this principle is therefore fair because it allows all to compete equally. It may, in some cases, interfere with the progress made toward affirmative-action goals. It does not necessarily do so and will do so even less as more and more women and minorities find positions in companies in which they were previously underrepresented. Moreover, the seniority system establishes certain *rights* of employees. These cannot be violated even to achieve good ends.

The decision in this case has been called ambiguous, and to some extent it is. In none of the three cases we have considered have there been clear defenses of principle. The Supreme Court has preferred to make narrow rulings rather than clearly endorse or clearly curtail affirmative-action programs. In this way the Court reflects the ambiguity with which affirmative action is greeted by the general population.

By 1998 a reaction against affirmative action as practiced was evident in some areas. Just as the *Bakke* case had arisen in a California university, so the reaction first appeared in California universities. In 1995 the University of California's Board of Regents voted to abolish preferential admission based on race, gender, religion or national origin. In November 1996, California voters approved Proposition 209, which outlawed racial preferences in education, contracting, and public employment. Nor was California unique. Federal courts ruled that racially reserved fellowships at the University of Maryland were illegal, as was the University of Texas Law School's policy of dual-track admissions. The reaction was not against affirmative action as originally conceived, but against set-asides and preferential treatment. At the same time, however, businesses had widely embraced the notion of diversity in their work force. The emphasis on diversity paralleled the aims of affirmative action and may or may not involve preferential treatment.

Although it is clear that past injustice must be rectified, it is also clear that no individual's rights should be violated to achieve racial balance in all areas of society or of the workplace. The attempt to balance the rights of both women and minorities and of white males has led to excesses on both sides. There is no easy way to achieve the necessary and just balance. Therefore, society must keep trying to achieve the balance until the problem eventually recedes because a reasonable approximation to a just situation has been achieved. Until that time arrives, both law and moral reasoning must be constantly invoked to find the best solutions to an extremely difficult problem.

Study Questions

1. Explain the issue in the *Weber* case. Was the Supreme Court decision morally justifiable? Why or why not?
2. What kind of discrimination is immoral?
3. Show why racial and sexual discrimination are immoral by means of a Kantian-type analysis; by using a Rawlsian approach; by using a utilitarian approach.
4. Explain what compensation in terms of classes means. Is it fair or just? Why or why not?
5. Is there a way to satisfy the demands of compensatory justice with respect to discrimination and not be unjust to any group? What three ways suggest themselves?
6. Define affirmative action.
7. On what four levels can affirmative action operate?
8. What does affirmative recruitment consist of? Give an example.
9. What does "equalization of employment criteria" mean? Illustrate your answer by an example.
10. What part does training have in affirmative action? Explain.
11. What does affirmative action in promotions mean?
12. Does affirmative action mandate quotas? Why or why not?
13. Define reverse discrimination.
14. What is preferential hiring? Is it the same as reverse discrimination? Explain your answer.
15. Is preferential hiring ever morally justifiable? If so, under what conditions?
16. What is balanced hiring?
17. Is balanced hiring justifiable? Explain why or why not.
18. Can affirmative action be reconciled with seniority rules? If so, how?
19. Explain the issue in the *Bakke* case. Was the Supreme Court decision morally justifiable? Why or why not? Could it be defended on utilitarian grounds? If the university had added more places to the entering class and reserved those for minority students, would that have been morally justified? Why or why not? In this latter case, since Bakke's chances of entering were the same as they would have been, could he rightfully claim that adding more places in this way was unfair to him? Why or why not?

20. Explain the issue in the *Stotts* case. Was the Supreme Court decision morally justifiable?

21. Jack Fasttrack has risen quickly in the company. He is bright and aggressive, and he has eleven years of sales experience with the company. He and many others in the firm think he is the best qualified to be the next vice-president for sales. He is passed over, and the position is given to Julie Star, an MBA who is good at sales but who has been with the company only four years. She is the first woman vice-president in the company's history. Have any of Jack's rights been violated?

17

>—┤—◄►—•—Ο—•—◄►—├—◄

ACCOUNTING, FINANCE, CORPORATE RESTRUCTURING, AND ETHICAL INVESTING

The ethics of the financial community has come under increased scrutiny as a result of deregulation and the restructuring that took on a great deal of prominence starting in the 1980s. The issues are many. We shall deal with accounting, finance and banking, restructuring of various kinds, and the responsibility of individual investors.

Savings and Loans: A Case Study

Banking-type financial institutions typically make money by investing or loaning money they receive as deposits at higher rates of return than the interest they pay on deposits. Savings and loan associations, or "thrifts," were established to provide mortgages for individual home owners. The original concept was that the thrifts would operate locally. They would receive deposits from local patrons who would get a basic rate of interest, and the thrift in turn would lend that money to local people interested in buying or building a home. The federal government, through the Federal Savings and Loan Insurance Corporation (FSLIC), guaranteed the deposits made in such institutions (as of 1980) up to $100,000. Until the mid-1960s, the thrifts were closely regulated by the government, which limited the amount of interest they could pay, the amount of equity they had to maintain, and the kinds of investments they could make. In return for tight control, the thrifts had the federal government's guarantee that the deposits of their customers were safeguarded.

Beginning in the late 1970s, regulations governing savings and loan associations were progressively eased. In the early 1980s deregulation took place in that industry as well as in many others. The result was that the thrifts could pay higher interest rates, could operate with lower equity, and could invest in a wider variety of instruments than previously. Interest rates increased, and in order to keep customers, thrifts raised the rates they were paying and offered a variety of securities of deposit at even higher rates. They did this in order to keep depositors from withdrawing their money and putting it where they could receive even higher returns. In addition, many thrifts held mortgages that were fixed at a rate much lower than the rate the thrifts were paying to their depositors.

In this situation the temptation was to lower equity and to invest in instruments that paid high returns. Since the rate of return is directly proportional to risk, some thrifts invested in risky instruments. An almost predictable result was that some of the investments went sour, and some thrifts no longer had enough to cover deposits. By the time some of them started actually going bankrupt and closing, many of them were in poor financial shape. In 1989, of the 3,000 U.S. savings and loan associations, or "thrifts," 515 were insolvent. Since all deposits up to the insured limit were covered by the federal government, no depositor would lose any money. But where would the money to cover all deposits come from? Unlike a business that fails, the losses would not be suffered by the company and its creditors. The losses would be covered in large part by the American taxpayer, for an estimated total of up to $200 billion. Is this fair?

In instances in which thrift managers engaged in fraud, embezzlement, or other illegal activities—and there were many of these—they can be ethically faulted.[1] What of those cases in which thrift managers were guilty only of faulty judgment, over optimistic assessments of investment opportunities, or imprudent investments? Although these are not necessarily moral faults, those who deal with other people's money have greater obligations—fiduciary obligations—to their clients than those who deal with their own money. Do imprudent and risky investments in such instances constitute reckless behavior and violate fiduciary obligations? Whether or not particular managers of the failing and failed thrifts are morally faulted, is it fair that the taxpayers bear the costs? It would be unfair for the government to renege on its guarantee of deposits. Yet

---

[1] For a detailed description of particular instances of such activity, see Stephen Pizzo, Mary Fricker, and Paul Muolo, *Inside Job: The Looting of America's Savings and Loans* (New York: McGraw-Hill Publishing Company, 1989). See also James R. Barth, *The Great Savings and Loan Debacle* (Washington, D.C.: AEI Press, 1991); Lawrence J. White, *The S & L Debacle: Public Policy Lessons for Bank and Thrift Regulation* (New York: Oxford University Press, 1991); and Kathleen Day, *S & L Hell: The People and the Politics Behind the $1 Trillion Savings and Loan Scandal* (New York: W. W. Norton & Company, 1993).

was it financially responsible of the government to continue to guarantee deposits in thrifts without regulating their operation? Who bears moral responsibility in this case? The S & L scandal is often traced back to the deregulation of the industry. Is the fault deregulation or the way deregulation was or was not implemented? Finally, the S & L crisis caught the American public and the American government unawares. How is it possible that so many S & L's were close to insolvency without their status becoming public long before it was too late to do anything about it? Does moral responsibility for this scandal lie with the bank regulators and auditors, with the accountants, or with the accepted standards and practices by which they operated?

Accounting

In one sense, accounting is simply the process by which any business keeps track of its financial activities by recording its credits and debits and balancing its accounts. Firms hire those with accounting training to help the firms maintain their books in accordance with generally accepted accounting standards and principles. Those who work in a firm's accounting department are employees of the firm and work for it. Such employees have no special obligations beyond those of other employees. They may not, of course, take part in fraud or other unethical activity. They should not falsify documents or sign as correct any document they feel is not correct. But in these regards they are no different from any other employee of the firm.

The situation is considerably different, however, when we consider not members of a corporation's accounting department, but independent Certified Public Accountants (CPAs) or those who work for the large accounting firms, because these accountants both do and do not work for the corporations that hire them to certify or audit their books. The point of an audit or of outside certification of a corporation's financial statements (of its income, balance sheets, earnings, financial position, equity, and changes in its financial position over time) by a certified public accountant is not so much to benefit the corporation as it is to benefit the public and maintain the public's confidence. The ideal intent of certification is to satisfy the shareholders, the government, potential shareholders, and the general public that the corporation's accounts are in order and that the certified report accurately represents the financial situation of the corporation. However, there is a difficulty built into the process from the start. The CPA or accounting firm is paid by the corporation but serves society's interests. There is clearly the potential for a conflict between satisfying the interests of the corporation that pays one's fees and satisfying the interests of the general public that wishes an objective, impartial financial review.

In our discussion we shall focus on two aspects of accounting. The first is the least controversial and deals with the actual difficulties encountered by individual accountants in their daily work. These are issues that arise within the context of accepted practices. The second deals with larger questions of the accounting procedures and practices themselves and the accounting profession's enforcement of its rules.

Ethical Issues for Accountants

Accountants face a great many pressures from clients who want them to do what is illegal: underreporting income, falsifying accounts, taking questionable deductions, illegally evading income tax, and engaging in outright fraud.[2] None of these pose difficult conceptual issues from a moral point of view. They are illegal and unethical. This fact does not lessen the pressure to act unethically that many CPAs feel and to which they are subject. But the ethically correct thing to do in these issues is not in question.

Other difficulties involve requests to alter financial statements in order to achieve certain purposes (e.g., so the company will be able to get loans the client could not otherwise get) and requests that accounts deviate from standard accounting practices for any number of reasons. Corporations prefer to have their earnings rise in a gently sloping line. They prefer to avoid spikes in earning charts and to balance out windfall earnings over several quarters or years. Some would prefer to keep some assets in reserve in case of a poor quarter or year. They would prefer, therefore, that sometimes their reports not accurately reflect their actual situation. Sometimes this is legal, as when a company defers receipts or defers shipments so that they fall in another quarter or year. Sometimes it is not, and companies seek creative bookkeeping techniques to achieve their goals. The pressure to supply such techniques or to approve them often falls on the CPAs.

Fee setting, billing clients whom one knows are on the verge of bankruptcy, working for clients who can no longer afford their services, and resisting offers to work on a contingency fee basis form another set of issues with an ethical dimension. Still another set of issues involves deciding how to handle mistakes, especially when some accountants feel they are unable to keep up with the constant changes in regulations, law, and accounting practices and rules. A CPA should undertake only those tasks that he or she is competent to perform; but the knowledge that one is over one's head sometimes emerges only as one is sinking. Similarly, the temptation to overcommit oneself and to allow too little time for carrying out one's tasks with the proper care all possibly lead to unethical behavior and practices.[3]

---

[2] Don W. Finn, Lawrence B. Chonko, and Shelby D. Hunt, "Ethical Problems in Public Accounting: The View from the Top," *Journal of Business Ethics,* 7 (1988), pp. 605-615, analyzes a survey of CPAs.

[3] For discussions of ethics and accounting, see Abraham J. Briloff, *The Truth About Corporate Accounting* (New York: Harper & Row, 1981); Ford S. Worthy, "Manipulating Profits: How It's Done," *Fortune,* June 25, 1984, pp. 50-54; and Norman E. Bowie, "Accountants, Full Disclosure, and Conflicts of Interest," *Business & Professional Ethics Journal,* 5 (1986), nos. 3 & 4, pp. 59-73.

The American Institute of Certified Public Accountants (AICPA) publishes professional rules to guide and govern certified public accountants.[4] Accountants are governed by three codes: Generally Accepted Accounting Principles (GAAP), Generally Accepted Auditing Standards (GAAS), and a Code of Professional Ethics (COPE). The AICPA Rules require independence of the firm or accountant from the client. This means they cannot hold any financial interest in the company. The intent is clearly to avoid conflict of interest. If the accounting firm is to certify a company's financial statements, it should have no incentive, owing to financial holdings in the company, to make the firm's financial situation look better than it is. The Code demands integrity, objectivity, competence, and compliance with standards set forth in GAAS and GAAP. The Rules guard client confidentiality, prohibit contingency fees (e.g., according to which no fee is charged unless a certain specified finding is attained), and preclude encroachment on the client of another accountant or accounting firm and the payment of commissions to obtain a client.

The client is responsible for the financial statements. The CPA does not guarantee the accuracy of the statements. The accountant is neither required nor expected to investigate in depth the accuracy of the data presented in the reports. A CPA might become suspicious of some entries and question them, and must refuse to certify a statement that is misleading. But the client, not the CPA, is responsible for maintaining accurate records, and it is not the CPA's job routinely to check those records against all other documents or inventories. The CPA certifies that the financial statements conform with generally accepted accounting principles.

For many practicing accountants, obeying the Rules is the guide to ethical behavior. However, for some critics, it is not the honesty of individual accountants as they try to live up to the Rules that is the problem. They attack the rules and the system itself as ethically deficient.

The Accounting Rules

The major issue is the (at least) apparent conflict of interest, to which we already referred, that is built into the American accounting system. Critics claim that, although the purpose of certifying the accounts of a corporation is to assure the general public that the corporation's accounts are correct as reported, the system is not set up to guarantee this result. The major stumbling block is that the accounting firm certifying a company's accounts works for the company whose accounts it is auditing. Although the accounting firm is independent, in the sense that it has no financial holdings in the company it is examining, its client—the one who pays its bills—is the company it is examining. It may be fired by that company and replaced by another accounting firm as the client wishes. There is at least on the surface an unavoidable con-

---

[4] The CPA "Code of Professional Conduct" is in *AICPA Professional Standards* (Chicago: Commerce Clearing House, 1992), vol. 2, pp. 4269–4909, with later updates.

flict of interest in the operation of any accounting firm. It has the temptation to do nothing to cause disfavor with the company that hires it. Hence, although it is supposed to strive for objectivity, objectivity is not easy to achieve under the circumstances.[5]

A second complaint stems from the fact that the accounting firm simply certifies that the company's accounts are correctly presented and are in accord with the generally accepted accounting and auditing standards. The accounting firm has no responsibility to verify the information it is given by the company whose accounts it is certifying. Furthermore, it has no responsibility to make public any internal discrepancies, fraud, or other irregularities it may discover, even though it may not, of course, itself engage in any cover-up or falsification of the records it does certify. The CPAs are caught between the requirement of confidentiality with respect to the client and the public's interest. Because this is the case, the system does not really assure those interested in the financial health of the company—shareholders, potential shareholders, and to some extent the general public who do business with the company— that the company's records are accurate and reflect its actual financial situation. Furthermore, there are various acceptable methods of handling debits and credits, and those reading financial reports are not always appraised of which alternative methods might have been used and why the one that is used was chosen over the others. Loans and debt are cases in point. If a loan is not likely to be recoverable in full, it is misleading to carry it at its full value. How and when to reduce it for accounting purposes, however, is open to a good deal of discretion, nor can a CPA always know which loans or investments may turn sour and lead to a company's failing.

The public often wonders when businesses go bankrupt how it is that the financial reports did not indicate the seriousness of their plight. The reply that this is not the obligation of the auditor is formally correct, but it is an indication of the problem, rather than an answer to the problem. If it is not the auditor's job to do this, then whose job is it? Can the public interest be protected if it is no one's job to reveal when a corporation is in financial difficulty? If accountants performing audits were paid by the government and required to report an instance of fraud or financial irregularity to the government rather than to the client, would the public be better served than it currently is? The answer is at least arguably yes.

In 1988, the Financial Accounting Standards Board (FASB), which sets standards that the Securities and Exchange Commission requires corporations to follow, proposed requiring that corporations carry as a liability their expo-

---

[5] James C. Gaa and Charles H. Smith, "Auditors and Deceptive Financial Statements: Assigning Responsibility and Blame," *Contemporary Accounting Research*, 1, no. 2, pp. 219-241, argue for changes in the accounting codes. I. C. Stewart, "Ethics and Financial Accounting in the United States," *Journal of Business Ethics*, 5 (1986), pp. 401-408, calls for fairness in financial reporting. John L. Casey, *Ethics in the Financial Marketplace* (New York: Scudder, Stevens & Clark, 1988), uses fictional vignettes to raise ethical issues.

sure in terms of retirees' health care benefits. The proposal was adopted as FAS Standard 106 and took effect for large companies in 1993 and for smaller companies in 1995.[6] This method more accurately reflects the company's financial exposure than does the former practice of simply listing the amount paid for this purpose in the past year. Yet, because the new reporting method would at least initially diminish annual corporate earnings considerably, the proposal generated great opposition. Opponents also claimed that future projections were no better than a guess. What do fairness and accuracy in reporting require in this case? What do they amount to when actual liabilities such as this need not be reported? Should corporate opposition be sufficient to preclude and determine reporting regulations? Are the regulations for the benefit of the firms or of the public? These are legitimate questions, raising ethical concerns that deserve at least discussion. Critics claim that accounting firms would take the lead in changing reporting requirements to better serve the public if the firms were not paid by their clients, whose interests are not always served by such reporting regulations.

Another area of controversy is the reporting of stock options.[7] Stock options, it is claimed, have been the engine driving many of the companies in Silicon Valley and are credited with the success of so many start-up companies there. Microsoft and Intel, among others, are very generous in their stock options, giving them not only to their executives but to most, if not all, of their employees. Having options gives employees a stake in the firm and in its success. It is through stock options that 2,200 of Microsoft's 11,000 employees became millionaires by 1997.

The controversy comes not so much from the awarding of options as from the method of accounting for them. Under U.S. tax laws options are not counted as a cost or liability when they are issued, if they are valued as of the market price on the day of issue. So if many employees are paid in options and receive a lower salary because of this, although the cash paid as salary is counted as a cost to the company, the options are not. Furthermore, when the options are exercised, the difference between the price of the stock when the option is exercised and the issue price of the option is considered a cost for tax purposes, even though the company doesn't actually spend any money. Yet options are a true liability, and when exercised they dilute the value of the other stock of a company, and reduce dividends, because there are a greater number of shares among which to divide profits.

In 1993 FASB tried to alter the reporting method and met such opposition that it backed down, requiring only a footnote in the annual report which indicated the company's estimated options expense. In 1997 the *New York*

---

[6] Stephenie Overman, "Time to Rethink Retiree Benefits," *HR Magazine*, March 1993, pp. 52-53; and William H. Steinbrink and Charles D. Weller, "Volatile Accrual: What You Need to Know About FAS 106," *Management Review*, May 1993, pp. 59-60.

[7] For a good account of employee options see Justin Fox, "The Next Best Thing to Free Money," *Fortune*, July 7, 1997, pp. 52-62.

Times hailed Microsoft for presenting an alternative quarterly income statement that accurately presented the cost of its options.[8] Opponents of such reporting claim that the real cost of options is unknown because they might become worthless if the stock falls below the issue price. Nonetheless, shareholders and those interested in purchasing stock in a company have the right to know the actual estimated cost that options pose for a company.

If there is a conflict between public interest and the interest of their clients, which interest is an accounting firm to put first? If the point of audits and certification were truly to protect the public interest, then accountants and accounting firms would be ethically obliged to place that interest above the interests of their clients. But they are not clearly required to do that, and hence they are in an ethically ambiguous position.

To the extent that accounting firms have taken on the additional task of consulting firms, they have increased the potential for conflict of interest. If the same company both suggests a policy and then audits the results, it is likely to be tempted to make the results look as favorable as possible. Faced with this temptation, some firms have attempted to construct "Chinese walls" between their auditing departments and their consulting departments, such that neither knows what the other is doing.

Critics would prefer changing the system so as to preclude the present built-in conflicts of interest. As yet, no widely acceptable alternative has emerged.

The accounting profession itself has responded to public concern by scrutinizing and revising its own rules, yet the AICPA has not been conspicuous in its ability or desire to police itself, enforce its codes, and take punitive actions against those who violate them. In this respect, it fares no better than other professional associations.

Finance and Banking

Of the many financial institutions, banking is perhaps the most visible to the general public. There are many kinds of banks—investment banks, commercial banks, and savings banks, among others. There are also a variety of other financial institutions, such as savings and loan associations, that are not strictly banks but that perform functions similar to those of banks in that they take in deposits and use them to make loans. Other institutions, such as insurance companies, pension funds, and brokerage houses, are all involved in financing and investing. A large number of ethical issues arise in considering the myriad activities of financial institutions. We shall briefly examine only three. One is the BCCI scandal, a second is the international debt of less developed countries, and a third is secrecy and disclosure.

---

[8] Floyd Norris, "Microsoft, A Pioneer in Quality Accounting," *New York Times*, November 16, 1997, Section 3, p. 1.

The Bank of Credit and Commerce International

The scandals associated with the Bank of Credit and Commerce International (BCCI) are of particular interest because they were international in scope, affecting people in many countries. The bank's activity on a worldwide scale dramatically raises the issues of how national governments can control multinational institutions, who has responsibility, and what is needed as commerce and finance operate more and more on a global level.

The BCCI story is a convoluted one, the details of which are still unfolding, but the main thread of the narrative is clear enough.[9] Agha Hasan Abedi, a Pakistani banker, convinced Sheik Zayed of Abu Dhabi to use some of his vast oil-generated income to fund a Karachi-based bank that would compete with Western banks and serve to help less developed countries. Started in 1972, the bank grew to control more than $20 billion in 400 branches and subsidiaries located in over 70 countries. Chartered in Luxembourg and carrying on many of its operations in the Cayman Islands, both of which are noted for lax banking regulations, BCCI effectively escaped any effective government control for almost twenty years. When threatened with possible governmental action, it often succeeded in paying off high-level officials who dismissed or impeded further investigations.

One result was that it became the bank of choice for laundering drug money, facilitating illegal arms deals, providing a haven for the wealth siphoned off by corrupt rulers of a number of countries, and serving as a conduit for illegal operations of both individuals and nations. Its customers included the CIA, the PLO, Manuel Noriega, Saddam Hussein, and a variety of drug lords, among others. It allegedly engaged in blackmail, extortion, kidnapping, and murder.

Since there was no accountability, those who ran the bank could and did funnel money from the bank into their own pockets, keeping just enough of a cash flow to pay those who wished to withdraw money. By 1991, when authorities finally closed the bank first in the United States and Great Britain and then worldwide, scarcely $10 billion of its $20 billion commitments could be found. In the United States, where its operation was very limited, no individuals lost money. Even if they had, because their accounts were federally insured, the American taxpayer would have covered the losses. The vast majority of small customers in poor countries were not so lucky; nor were many poor countries themselves (such as Nigeria and Botswana, among many others), which had used the bank extensively and had deposited large sums of money in it.

The existence of such a rogue bank is scandal enough, but equally scandalous and more disturbing to many was the fact that it was able to operate so

---

[9] For details of the scandal and how it was uncovered, see Jonathan Beaty and S. C. Gwynne, *The Outlaw Bank: A Wild Ride into the Secret Heart of BCCI* (New York: Random House, 1993); and Peter Truell and Larry Gurwin, *False Profits: The Inside Story of BCCI, The World's Most Corrupt Financial Empire* (Boston: Houghton Mifflin, 1993).

long with impunity. How lax is national and international control of banks that BCCI was not stopped earlier? How effective are audits and bank regulations when the BCCI can secret away billions of dollars without any trace? How safe are banks when billions of dollars in assets can disappear, leaving a bank insolvent, and no one notices? How moral are governments that use outlets such as the BCCI for their own covert activities, and how moral are governmental officials and regulators who impede investigations into such banks? These are among the more troubling questions that demand answers. Unfortunately, the answer to the question "Can this happen again?" seems to be yes.

As finance becomes more and more international, effective international standards need to be developed and enforced, and cooperation among regulators in different nations needs to be increased.

The events in the late 1990s in Asia reinforce this need. The banking systems of Thailand and Korea, which were considered among the Asian tigers, had engaged in practices very similar to the U.S. savings and loans. They were restricted by few regulations and because of the influx of money from their booming economies and foreign investors, they made large, unsecured loans. The economic bubble burst in 1997 and in 1998 in country after country, affecting even the richest of them all, Japan, whose stock market lost more than 50 percent of its value from its all-time high. Lack of effective regulation, as well as some cronyism, are among the cited causes for the Asian financial meltdown. Such financial disasters inevitably affect the people of a country, even though they have no part in the causes of the banking difficulties. Greater governmental regulation is clearly needed. Since banking is international, international regulation is necessary, even though there is no international body capable of passing and enforcing such regulation.

Banks and World Debt

The situation with respect to banks and the debt of underdeveloped nations follows a somewhat similar pattern of what might be called reckless investment. When the price of oil rose dramatically in the 1970s, oil-rich countries had an abundance of money, much of which was deposited in American banks. The banks in turn sought investment and loan opportunities. Huge unsecured loans were made to underdeveloped countries, often for unrealistic projects. Once the oil boom receded, many of the countries were left not only with their debts, but also with the need to pay interest on them. In many cases the loans were made at initially low interest rates, which escalated as the cost of money increased. As a result, the borrowing countries were faced with the prospect of having to pay off their loans in hard currencies, which they did not have. Sometimes a large portion (up to 70 percent) of the hard currencies they made from exporting goods to the United States and Europe went to pay the interest on their foreign debt. Consequently, those countries had little or no hard currency to buy what they needed abroad to enable them to develop. As inflation increased at home, the people of those countries (who had no hand in the loans) faced a bleak future in which unemployment would rise and their standard of living fall. The countries could not develop their productive capacities and would have to use their wealth indefinitely into the future to pay the interest on their loans. If they refused to pay, they would lose all chance of any future loans, which would be necessary for them to finance their development.

The situation was not only abysmal for the debtor countries, but bad as well for the banks that had made the loans, since it was extremely unlikely that in the foreseeable future any of the large debtor nations could repay their loans, and many could not pay the whole of the annual interest due.[10] Although the loans would never be paid in full, the accounting system enabled the banks to carry them at their face value.

As a result of the situation that developed, a number of issues arose. Is it fair to the people of developing countries to hinder their progress and condemn them to a future without hope, in which they simply work to pay off the interest on their debt? Is it fair for the American people, through the government, to take over the bad debts made by banks and bail them out for their poor management? On the other hand, is it fair to allow the banks with these bad debts to fail and hurt large numbers of individuals and corporations tied to their assets? We once again have a scenario in which if any of those involved in the lending and borrowing acted unethically, they should be made to bear the consequences of their action. To the extent that they acted using bad judgment or were reckless or imprudent, there is little argument for immunizing them from paying whatever penalty is appropriate, if they could do so without endangering a great many innocent people both in the United States and abroad. The difficulty is trying to find how to defuse the international debt situation in such a way that the innocent do not have to pay for the sins of the guilty.

One step in the right direction has been for banks to start writing off some of the debt as unpayable and putting aside other assets to cover their obligations.[11] Selling off part of their debt at a discount to others is another strategy some have taken.[12] A large number of other solutions have been suggested, as governments and peoples around the world realize that something must be done.

The ethical dimensions of the situation are complex. It is difficult to pinpoint unethical actions or place ethical blame. Some blame falls on the banks that acted recklessly. Some falls on the borrowing countries that recklessly accepted loans or used them at best injudiciously when one evaluates the consequences for the people of the country. Some falls on the leaders and entrepreneurs in those countries who misused or misappropriated funds and who

---

[10] See Georges Enderle, "The Indebtedness of Low-Income Countries as an Ethical Challenge for Industrialized Market Economics," *International Journal of Applied Philosophy,* 4 (1989), no. 3, pp. 31-38.

[11] "The Crushing Monster," *Time,* July 27, 1987, pp. 36-38.

[12] Jaclyn Fierman, "Fast Bucks in Latin Loan Swaps," *Fortune,* August 3, 1987, pp. 91-99.

not infrequently deposited their own funds safely abroad. Those on whom blame falls deserve to bear the brunt of the difficulties of a solution.

Ethically justifiable solutions are those that do justice to all those affected without allowing anyone to profit unduly at the expense of others and without imposing all the burdens on any single group of those affected. The banks should bear a good deal of the burden. To some extent the rich countries benefited and can be expected to bear some of the costs of rectifying the situation. This means government and the taxpayer paying some price. But that burden is in justice secondary to that borne by the banks and the debtors. The people of the underdeveloped countries are already bearing a good deal of the hardship, and a just solution should not impose more costs on them. Rather, it should relieve them to the extent possible of their debt burden, while enabling them to develop their resources so as to become productive members of the international community.

Secrecy and Disclosure

Banks have moral obligations of confidentiality on the one hand and disclosure on the other. The obligation to maintain confidentiality stems from the right of depositors to privacy. One aspect of that right is that their accounts and transactions should be kept confidential. How much money we have and what we do with our money is in most cases no one else's business. Yet the right to privacy does not preclude our having to report our holdings for tax or legitimate other purposes. Furthermore, our right to privacy does not enable us to conceal illegal payments we might receive or make. The government has the right to learn the details of our accounts if there is valid reason—for example, that the information is pertinent to the investigation of a felony.

What then of secret bank accounts?

Such accounts were long the rule, for instance, in Switzerland. What is wrong with secret accounts? The problem lies not in the fact that they are secret but in the illegitimate uses that unrestricted secrecy allows. The problem is clear if one thinks of illegally acquired money—for instance, from drug trafficking. Secret accounts allow drug dealers to deposit their ill-gotten funds and then to place that money in legal investments. Such "laundering" of money is impossible to trace if bank accounts are totally secret, even from governments with cause to suspect felonious actions. Other ethically dubious uses of such accounts are as storage places for individuals or corporations in underdeveloped countries who use such accounts as repositories for money that they remove from their country, often money that is earmarked for capital or other improvements in the country. The alleged secret bank accounts of former President Marcos of the Philippines are a case in point. Secret accounts can thus become part of a plan for criminal and unethical activity. It is their part in such activity that renders secret accounts, at least in these circumstances, unethical. There may be legitimate reasons for secrecy, and governments have no right without sufficient cause to infringe on privacy by gaining access to information on private bank accounts. But when they have sufficient cause, the inability to trace money is a hindrance to justice. And it is a sufficient hindrance that it overcomes any right to privacy.

The rules of bank secrecy were an impediment in the investigation of U.S. insider trading cases. The U.S. government sought, initially unsuccessfully, to trace money through Swiss accounts. The Swiss ultimately changed their laws, allowing the United States to pursue its investigation.[13] But some strict limits on secrecy still stand. Balancing the right of individuals and firms to confidentiality with the right of governments to pursue evidence of felonious action through bank deposits and exchanges is a delicate task. Not all government investigations may be appropriate, and indiscriminate release of information on individual accounts to government would be a prima facie violation of an individual's right to privacy. Yet banks are no more allowed to take part in or abet criminal activity than anyone else or any other institution.

On the other end of the spectrum, banks are morally obliged to disclose to customers and potential customers complete and accurate information concerning, for instance, the loans they make to their customers. Banks are morally precluded from charging exorbitant interest rates—known as usury. The maximum permissible rate is often set by law. We have argued that for any transaction to be fair both parties must enter in it freely and both should have access to appropriate information. In cases in which the bank is the lender, it is clearly in the position of strength and power with respect to the borrower. There is therefore all the more need for banks to make completely clear to borrowers the conditions of any loan, the real interest (rather than simply monthly payments), and the conditions and penalties for defaulting. Clarity requires that customers be informed in language they can understand.

How banks are to treat their loans in statements of their financial positions is a topic on which we have already touched. Customers who place their savings with banks have the right to know the actual financial situation of the bank, and disclosure to them is as appropriate as to shareholders.

Banks have been among the institutions that have helped finance a great deal of the restructuring of American business. Banks and their employees thus come to have access to inside information about planned and impending corporate takeovers. As insiders they have the obligation to keep such information confidential, as well as not to trade on it for their own accounts. On the other hand, they have the obligation to make pertinent information public and available to all at the same time. Disclosure in this case means that in principle no one is given the information and the opportunity to act on it before it is made known publicly.

A significant factor in the Asian banking crisis resulted from the fact that the banks in most of the affected countries did not have to disclose their real

---

[13] Stephen Labaton, "Group of 7 Asks Money-Laundering Curbs," *New York Times,* April 20, 1990, p. C1; Alan Riding, "New Rule Reduces Swiss Banking Secrecy," *New York Times,* May 6, 1991, p. C1; and "The End of Banking Secrecy in Liechtenstein," *International Living* 9 (February 1990), p. 19.

assets. Japan's real estate was the most expensive in the world, and by most standards unrealistically priced. Real estate in turn was accepted as collateral for loans. When reality finally caught up with the price of land and it fell by half or more, banks continued to carry mortgages at their face value. Banks in Thailand and Korea did the same. The result was the general economic collapse we already noted. Arguably, that could have been avoided had accurate information been required, and the veil of secrecy lifted.

Corporate Takeovers and Restructuring

The trend toward corporate mergers and takeovers that developed especially in the 1980s has been called the restructuring of American business. The trend continued into the 1990s, when it was joined with the downsizing of many firms. The number of takeovers of one company by another often brought about significant changes in the companies taken over, and the threat of takeover frequently promoted, if it did not force, changes in many other companies.[14]

In the 1960s and early 1970s companies began to merge in unprecedented numbers. Efficiency and diversification were two common rationales for mergers, acquisitions, and the building of corporate conglomerates. Efficiency was achieved if, for instance, two producers of the same product were combined so as to take advantage of their larger size to be able to buy in larger quantities and so more cheaply. Some companies took over companies from which they had purchased supplies or parts, in order to save the cost of middlemen. Diversification, it was claimed, helped a company during an economic downturn. A company with elastic demand might suffer more than a company with inelastic demand as money became tight. In such times the profits from the one part of the conglomerate would help ease the fall-off from the other part. The rationales seemed to make sense. Except for the danger of forming monopolies, there is no apparent ethical reason to fault such mergers and takeovers.

The 1980s saw a change in corporate restructuring that both raised ethical concerns and spawned a host of takeover strategies and defenses that were ethically questioned. In a friendly takeover, one company buys another with the acquired company's consent. A hostile takeover is one that takes place against the wishes of the acquired company's managers.

The rationale given for the takeovers in the 1980s was that the companies were undervalued by the market when one compared the price of their stock against the assets of the firm. Those holding the new perspective argued that companies were undervalued because they were inefficiently run. If taken over and run under new management, they could be made efficient. Efficiency

---

[14] For more detailed discussions of takeovers, see Abbass F. Alkhafaji, *Restructuring American Corporations: Causes, Effects, and Implications* (New York: Quorum Books, 1990); and W. Michael Hoffman, Robert Frederick, and Edward S. Petry, Jr. (Eds.), *The Ethics of Organizational Transformation: Mergers, Takeovers, and Corporate Restructuring* (New York: Quorum Books, 1987).

frequently meant selling off the less productive parts of a firm or conglomerate. In some instances the rationale of diversification, which meant that one portion of a company might be more profitable at one period and another portion at another period, was ignored and the less productive part of the firm was now seen as inefficient.

Because a more efficient firm will produce greater profits, an acquiring firm will offer a premium above the current price for the stock of the target company. The higher price is offered to the shareholders, who sell their stock for the profit. The newly acquired company is then restructured by the new management. Often portions of the old company are sold off to raise money to pay the acquisition costs of that company. The portions sold off might be the most profitable (referred to as the "crown jewels") or the least profitable. Sometimes, unprofitable or less profitable plants are closed down, or the work force is reduced. Frequently, the management of the company that is taken over is replaced by new management.

Since the management of every company wishes to continue in its position, the threat of a takeover spurred some companies to restructure before being taken over—to sell off parts of the company, to close plants, to lay off workers. In some cases pension funds were raided by increasing the annual projected rate of return from, say, 3 percent to 15 percent. This would free up money that had been put aside to cover pension payments. Some managers decreased the amount of stock outstanding by buying it back. In order to do so, the companies frequently borrowed against their assets, replacing stock with loans. The rationale and justification for all this activity was increased efficiency.

The major issue of ethical concern was not takeovers or mergers, as such, but hostile takeovers.

Ethics and Hostile Takeovers

One set of ethical debates for and against hostile takeovers is between those both pro and con who implicitly accept a utilitarian approach to ethics, even though they do not necessarily identify themselves by that label. Another set, both pro and con, argues in terms of justice and freedom. Debate on both sides has not always been clear or unbiased. Any ethical evaluation should give each side its due, consider all affected, and remain cognizant of the common good.[15]

The implicit utilitarians ask whether more benefit is achieved—both to the participants and to society as a whole—by allowing hostile takeovers than

---

[15] M. C. Jensen defends takeovers as efficient in "Takeovers: Folklore and Science," *Harvard Business Review*, November–December, 1984, pp. 109–121. See also David J. Ravenscraft and F. M. Scherer, *Mergers, Sell-Offs, and Economic Efficiency* (Washington, D.C.: Brookings Institution, 1987); David L. McKee (Ed.), *Hostile Takeovers: Issues in Public and Corporate Policy* (New York: Praeger, 1989); and John C. Coffee, Jr., Louis Lowenstein, and S. Rose-Ackerman (Eds.), *Knights, Raiders, and Targets: The Impact of Hostile Takeovers* (New York: Oxford University Press, 1988).

by outlawing them. Defenders of takeovers argue primarily that they promote efficiency and that the threat of takeovers is an incentive for managers to work harder and more productively, as well as to raise profits for their shareholders, rather than leaving that task to a more efficient takeover manager. Takeovers thus help the economy as a whole, foster restructuring that would not take place without them, and make America more competitive with foreign firms.

Those on the other side deny that the good consequences of efficiency will outweigh the bad consequences of hostile takeovers in the long run, pointing not only to the predictable plant closings, sell-offs, and displacements, but also to the growing internal debt that companies take upon themselves to finance the takeovers—debt that they may not be able to service during any kind of a downturn in the economy and that, in case of failure, will represent enormous losses that will threaten the whole system.

Moreover, the critics argue, the primary benefit achieved by the takeover frenzy has been the multiplying of paper profits. As a result of all the takeover activity we have raised the level of the stock market and the price of individual shares, but we have not increased productivity, created new jobs, or strengthened our economy. Since we have been building on sand, the illusion of efficiency has blinded us to the real situation, which is a weakening rather than a strengthening of our economy. Hence, the activities have overall been deleterious, and because they harm society, they should be seen as unethical.

Deciding between the two positions is no easy matter because the situation is extremely complex, because we have too little experience with the practices in question to be able accurately to predict what their long-range consequences will be, and because many of the supposed facts stated by one side are contested by the other. Nonetheless, whichever side is correct, it is clear that if we could preserve the good effects of takeovers while eliminating the negative effects, from a utilitarian perspective the situation would be better than it currently is. This means distinguishing among takeovers. Those that truly increase long-range efficiency, taken broadly, would on the whole be justifiable. Those that do not, and that are carried out only to amass quick gains for speculators, would not be justifiable. Thus, one strategy would be to eliminate quick gains without preventing companies interested in long-range benefits from taking over a target company.

The second set of debates focuses not on efficiency or good over bad consequences, but on freedom versus fairness or justice. The benefit of this approach is that it allows us to make well-founded ethical decisions now, rather than waiting for anticipated or predicted consequences—such as the failure of junk bonds or the onset of a recession.

The issue of freedom from government regulation is a familiar one for staunch defenders of the free market. In the case of finance they argue that corporate raiders should be free to raid, that managers and corporations should be free to protect themselves, and that shareholders should be free to accept or reject takeover bids. To this extent their argument amounts to a defense of the current practices, which have developed without government restraint and interference, and which they claim should continue like that. The market will weed out the bad from the good and the advantageous from the disadvantageous much more effectively than will government legislation.

The argument is valid up to a point, and that point is where freedom violates rights or justice. We are not free to do whatever we want if what we do harms others and violates their rights or is unjust. The claimed injustice in hostile takeovers varies. Sometimes it is the injustice done to workers and communities when plants are closed. Sometimes it is to the shareholders of the acquiring corporation, whose stock frequently falls as a result of a takeover attempt. Although the shareholders of the company taken over usually receive a premium on their stock, it is not the fiduciary obligation of the raider to care for their interest, but for the interests of its own shareholders, which it fails to serve if its own stock values fall.

This line of debate, like the utilitarian one, has its merits. It raises issues that should be seriously considered in attempting to morally evaluate any particular takeover. But neither line shows that hostile takeovers are necessarily unethical.

The wave of takeovers also led to the development of takeover and defense strategies, each of which might be submitted to ethical appraisal. These include greenmail, golden parachutes, and leveraged buyouts, among others. Many of the practices have been criticized as being unethical and misguided, raising more problems than they solve, and protecting inefficient managers.[16]

Greenmail

To the extent that we treasure individual freedom of action, we should not, without compelling reason, make actions illegal that are not unethical. If there is in fact nothing *inherently* wrong with a hostile takeover, then it should not be legally prohibited. Yet there are unethical ways of pursuing such takeovers, and such activities are legitimate legislative targets.

One type of takeover threat on which legislators have focused is the practice known as *greenmail*. Although some potential raiders buy up 5 percent of a company's stock and announce their intention to take over the company (as they are legally required to do), they are willing to allow the attacked company to repurchase from them the stock they have acquired if the target company pays a higher than market price for their shares. This is not illegal. Should it be? Is it unethical?

The argument against it is, first, that the declaration of the company's intent is dubious. If the intent is really to take over the company, why bargain to sell back the acquired shares? Second, the practice involves two different

---

[16] Allen Michael and Israel Shaked, *Takeover Madness: Corporate America Fights Back* (New York: John Wiley & Sons, 1986), describes many of the practices as used by particular corporations.

prices for the same kind of company stock: one the market price to ordinary shareholders, and the other a premium price to the raider. The dual price system that it creates for common stock is not consistent with the usual concept of stock ownership and stock value. Third, while this is not legally extortion, those who wield greenmail get their higher price through threat. Whether they are more at fault than those who pay greenmail is a debatable question. This tactic of threat by a raider in order to be paid off to remove its threat either forces or induces the attacked company to buy back stock it would not otherwise have bought, and to buy it back at a premium, for which the other shareholders receive no perceptible benefit, except the continued management of the company by its present managers.

One defense of the practice counters by arguing that there are good and bad greenmailers. Good greenmailers propose a restructuring plan to management and induce management either to follow their plan or to restructure in some other way in self-defense. The profit a greenmailer receives should be considered payment of a consultant's fee for the restructuring they proposed and the restructuring they induce management to make. Thus, the greenmail payment does not harm the other shareholders but benefits them.

This defense is defective, however, because the practice, if considered as a consultation, is certainly a forced one, on terms set by the greenmailer. To that extent even "good" greenmail is importantly different from a consultant's services, and arguably unethical. In addition, the threatened company neither must do any restructuring nor must learn of the predator's restructuring plans in order to fend off the greenmailer; it need merely buy the greenmailer's stock at a higher price.

Legislation aimed at preventing greenmail attempts to specify conditions for a bona fide takeover offer or attempt. One suggestion is that any raiding company should be required to have available 100 percent funding to carry through any announced takeover. This would preclude coercion that has no effect but to line the pockets of the greenmailer. A question is whether government intervention is either the necessary or the best response to that practice. The name "greenmail" is obviously modeled on "blackmail." But a blackmailer either threatens harm, which it is the proper province of government to prevent, or threatens disclosure, which it may not be the proper province of government to prevent, even though it may well be unethical to make such a threat. The analogy with greenmail fails on both counts.

Another piece of proposed legislation requires a longer delay than is required at present between announced intentions and vote by the shareholders on the proposal. Yet another requires all shares of a company's regular stock to be sold at the same price, effectively precluding greenmail. Although there is no ethical objection to any of these practices, ethics does not prescribe any one rather than another of them, and a question can legitimately be raised about the need for any such legislation.

If a company is threatened by greenmail, it always has the option to refuse to pay it. If it refuses, it may be subjected to a takeover bid. If so, then either it can attempt to restructure itself and make its case to its shareholders, it can seek a "white knight" or some company interested in a friendly takeover, or it can yield and be taken over if the greenmailers are really serious in their takeover bid. Any of these options, as well as other strategies, preclude the need for paying greenmail. In paying greenmail, the managers of a company must ask whether they are in fact serving the best interests of their shareholders as they are supposed to. The money they use to pay the greenmail in the long run comes from the pockets of the shareholders. From the point of view of the shareholders' interest, paying greenmail is justified only if such a move serves their long-term interests.

Golden Parachutes

Another phenomenon that hostile takeovers has spawned is known as the "golden parachute." This practice consists of guaranteeing that the chief officers of a company are given a certain set of benefits—sometimes a multimillion dollar payment—if the company is taken over and the executives are fired or their positions are eliminated.

The justification given for such a practice is twofold. First, it increases the cost to the predator company. But given the scale of large takeovers, the cost of golden parachutes is unlikely to prevent a takeover. Second, it gives the chief executives an incentive to work toward the interests of the shareholders in case of a takeover threat.

Should there be a threat, the executive's job is in danger. The natural reaction would be to fend off the threat by whatever means are available to protect one's position. But protecting one's position may not be in the best interests of the shareholders, whose interests the executive should really have at heart. The golden parachute is supposed to remove from the executive the fear of dismissal, by making dismissal financially acceptable; hence, the golden parachute enables the executive to act in the best interest of the shareholders.

Critics object that this is an inappropriate use of a company's money. Most executives are already very well compensated in their jobs, and they are paid precisely to manage the company as best they can for the benefit of— among others—the shareholders, even at some possible detriment to themselves. They are also well paid in part for taking the risk of working without job security. They should not need job insurance to do what is best for the company. If they do not act for the benefit of the shareholders in a takeover threat, they violate their fiduciary duty. In that case they deserve to be fired, not compensated for being the type of person who would sacrifice shareholder interests for their own. Moreover, high-level managers often own considerable stock in their companies and often have stock options—all of which will go up if the company stock is bought at a premium. As a consequence, there is already an incentive for them to act in the interest of shareholders. If, as some claim, companies cannot get senior officers to serve for companies that may be takeover targets without golden parachutes, the preferable alternative would be stock options that link the executive's interests with those of the shareholders.

If shareholders vote to offer the company's executives golden parachutes, that is their right. It might be considered foolish by some, but it would not be unethical. However, if, as is usually the case, the offer of a golden parachute is made to the president by the company's board of directors—many of whom might have been appointed by the president of the company—then the justification for it is less clear. Such action should be in the interest of the shareholders, and it is not clear that it is.

Several bills have been proposed making golden parachutes illegal, even though they are not clearly unethical. Those who propose that they should be illegal argue that they do not serve the shareholders and act only to protect possibly inefficient managers who are in danger of losing their jobs if the firm is taken over. Whether golden parachutes are proper and whether they should be made illegal are two different issues. In addition, a prior question to be answered is whether legislation that forbids the practice is preferable to action taken by the stockholders themselves, who are the claimed victims.

Leveraged Buyouts by Management

A reaction to takeovers on the part of some managers has been the Leveraged Buyout (LBO) by management, usually in association with outside financiers.[17] The strategy here is to "take private" a publicly owned company by buying up its stock. The money for the buyout comes from what have become known as "junk bonds." These are bonds issued against the assets of the company. They are called junk bonds because they are below investment grade. They pay a high yield because they are risky, in the sense that the company that issues them may not be able to pay the interest due on them. In an LBO the company replaces its stock, which it buys back and which represents equity in the company, with bonds, which represent debt. In an economic downturn, if a company is not able to operate profitably and it is funded by stock, it does not pay dividends. In the same situation, a company funded by junk bonds is required to pay the interest on the bonds, and if it does not or defaults, it goes into bankruptcy.

The high yield of the junk bonds has made them attractive to a wide variety of investors—including groups that in the past have been conservative, such as pension funds, savings and loan associations, and banks. This situation has led to criticism of junk bonds as a means of corporate restructuring both because of the possibility of widespread corporate failure in a recession and because of the damage done to a wide range of investors if the junk bonds fail.

---

[17] Robert F. Bruner and Lynn Sharp Paine, "Management Buyouts and Managerial Ethics," *California Management Review,* Winter 1988, pp. 89-106, suggests how to deal with conflicts of interest in such buyouts.

From an ethical point of view, LBOs raise a serious issue of possible conflict of interest. The managers of any firm have a fiduciary responsibility to the shareholders of the company. Can they fulfill that duty at the same time that they are the purchasers of the stock from the shareholders? The reason the managers engage in an LBO is to benefit themselves. Do they do so at the expense of the shareholders they are supposed to serve? Clearly, it would be in the interest of the managers to purchase the stock at the smallest possible premium above its current price. But as the representatives of the shareholders it is their duty to get for the shareholders the highest price possible. Whereas the conflict is obvious, the ways to avoid the conflict are less clear. But unless the managers can arrive at a price that would have been arrived at if the transaction were an "arm's length one"—that is, unless they can offer the shareholders a price that both management and the shareholders would consider fair from an outsider—they violate their fiduciary obligations.

Management knows the operation of the company from within and is in the best position to know its real and potential value. It operates with information that is not available to the shareholders, or with insider information. Under ordinary circumstances, managers are not supposed to operate on that knowledge for their own profit, as we saw in the discussion of insider trading—yet here, they are both insiders and the ones offering to buy back the stock in the company. Once more, although it is possible to be fair in such an operation, the possibility of unfairness is sufficient to motivate some people to argue that LBOs should be illegal.

An LBO often has the same effect on a company that a hostile takeover has. The restructuring is similar. Because management has replaced stock with debt, it is anxious to pay off that debt as quickly as possible so that it can reduce the interest it pays. One way to do that is to sell off portions of the firm, close down plants, and fire employees. To the extent that these are negative results, they are the same as in a hostile takeover, and the arguments against the LBO are similar. Defenders counter that, as a result of an LBO, management is no longer forced to work toward short-term or quarterly results to please or attract shareholders. Consequently, it can be truly efficient, while at the same time working toward long-range goals. These may include research and development, even though critics charge that takeovers usually result in less research and development because of the burden of debt.

The American tax laws favor LBOs because the interest paid on corporate loans is deductible as a business expense. On the other hand, corporate profits are taxed twice, once as corporate taxes on a corporation's profits and a second time when they are paid out as dividends and so as income to the shareholders.

Do leveraged buyouts with junk bonds threaten the financial stability of society sufficiently to justify governmental interference? Similarly, if a firm buys back its own stock and takes on a huge debt that it must then service in order to make itself unattractive as a takeover candidate, is it up to the government to interfere?

If the role of the government is to protect the innocent and to help keep the economy running more or less equitably and smoothly, does it properly enter into how companies run themselves, who takes over whom (unless the action violates antitrust laws), how a company defends itself, or how shareholders react to it all? Shareholders, especially large institutional investors, have forced over sixty companies to submit to them "poison pill" proposals— a variety of options or other guarantees that become operative only in case of a takeover and serve to increase the cost of the takeover to the acquiring firm. The aim is to make the takeover too costly; but it often fails to achieve that end. Such action by *shareholders* is not prima facie unethical, because it represents the shareholders' free use of their own funds. It is arguably preferable to government regulation.

The role of the government in this area is not clear and is now being debated. The difficulty is that the debates tend to be about specific proposed pieces of legislation, and there is little discussion of the whole picture, of which these various practices are interrelated parts.

From an ethical point of view, those actions that are unethical and threaten serious harm to the community can properly be made illegal, but they need not be. Not all harmful acts must be made illegal. Some may be tolerated if they produce more good than harm overall, or if enforcing them threatens the freedom or other values of those whose actions are controlled.

There has been too little debate about the ethics of the different practices, all of which have become equal targets for legislation. The proposed legislation has been reactive, piecemeal, and basically conservative, and in the long run it would produce little significant change in the financial community.

Restructuring and Change

Although the contemporary restructuring of American corporations has been defended in terms of efficiency, it is not yet clear whether the wave of takeovers has been efficient. Critics claim that no new products have resulted, along with no increased productivity and no new jobs. On the other hand, plants have been closed, large numbers of people fired, and firms reorganized to the detriment of their corporate cultures. The process has also tended to undermine corporate loyalty and to increase the level of fear about job security. Actions have been taken that would not have taken place without the threat of takeovers and that earlier were justified in terms of responsibility to workers and communities, and the need to have some flexibility in times of recession. Moreover, even from a utilitarian point of view, efficiency as currently defined is not the only value to be considered.

A second complaint is that takeovers have been fed by large institutional holders of stock, such as pension funds. The managers of such funds have the fiduciary obligation to try to maximize the results of investments. In any takeover bid they would therefore, critics claim, be obliged to vote in favor of a takeover that pays a premium for their stock, even if it were not in the best long-term interests of the company. They could take their funds and invest them elsewhere. Since that and the tax structure favor takeovers and LBOs, it is not surprising that these have flourished. Are they in the best interest of the nation and economy as a whole? If not, then a piecemeal approach to takeovers and related practices may not be the best approach. Corporate restructuring has raised the issue of the need for legal restructuring to accommodate the new situation.

We can join both the utilitarian and the deontological approaches in an effort to evaluate restructuring financial practices by considering the implicit contract of finance with society. As a basis for this line of ethical analysis, we can go back to the justification for the free-enterprise system and the implicit contract between society and business. Society allows business to operate because it receives certain benefits—including jobs, products, services, and taxes—from it. Business in turn stays within the rules because it can achieve its ends only in a stable, safe, well-organized society. When society no longer receives its expected benefits, or when it is hurt more than helped by the activity of business, then society is allowed and should be expected to change the rules, since the conditions justifying the original contract have changed. This is in some ways similar to the utilitarian analysis above, but joins to it the notion of implied contract and so of fairness.

The point is to look at the newly developing system as a whole, rather than simply looking at the improper motivation of the few or at changes in particular businesses without looking at and possibly changing the system. The system has a great many vested interests built in that are of questionable value to the system and could well be changed.

If the old system was ethically sound and defensible, it does not follow that the new system is. If the new system is ethically sound and its practices are demonstrably justifiable, no harm will have been done by subjecting it to ethical scrutiny. In fact, such scrutiny will quiet doubts some may have about it and hence bolster it at a time when it can use such bolstering. If the new system is in general ethically defensible but some of the current practices are ethically unsound, then we can change those practices and in the process strengthen the system. And if unremediable injustices are inherent in the system, that is a good reason to look for an alternative system of capital financing.

Central to the market is competition, and central to acceptable competition is fairness. In addition to fairness, the market should operate to the benefit of society in general. Under the U.S. system, society is able to place restraints on business and is justified in doing so when it believes it will be better off with than without such restraints and when it believes it is being harmed by their absence. No individual, group, or firm has an unrestricted right to make large amounts of money or to make money at the expense of the general social welfare. A society rightly allows people to make large amounts of money if this provides incentives for increased production, efficiency, inventiveness, risk taking, and other activities or results that help the general well-being of society.

The insider trading scandals of the late 1980s were directly related to impending takeovers. Since insider trading is unethical, we might take as a working hypothesis the claim that the insider trader scandals are a symptom of something wrong not with a few individuals but with the investment industry more broadly. If there is a cancer in the investment industry, we should not worry so much about the symptom—after all, the actions were illegal and some people have gone to jail—as about the cause. To treat insider trading as a symptom raises the question of whether there is more wrong than simply a few greedy people breaking the law. It asks what their actions are a symptom of; and if we are to cure the cause of which this is a symptom, we must open up the whole system to scrutiny, subject all its parts to ethical evaluation, and scan all the central components. In such a scrutiny, a principle of caution advises that we change as little as possible to produce the needed cure, while a radical principle calls for the overthrow of the system as a whole. A middle ground is possible.

Instead of simply seeking better enforcement in such cases as the Levine-Boesky scandals, can we preclude the cause? For instance, why allow the possibility of someone—anyone—making millions in a few days as Ivan Boesky did? Defenders of free enterprise want people to have an inducement to take risks, to increase productivity, and to be handsomely recompensed for their efforts when appropriate to benefit the whole. Free enterprise does not need the possibility of an individual's making $4 million in four days to achieve these ends, unless doing so is a byproduct of benefiting society, and not just themselves.

We can ask whether there should be positions such as arbitragers, who make a market in a firm's stock, in which the temptations and gains are possibly enormous. The aim of the inquiry is to get at the source of the corrupt practices, which are certainly linked to the vast sums at stake. A challenge to those in finance is to consider other structures that better prevent abuse. If in fact arbitragers perform a valuable service to the business community, we can still restructure the system so that the rewards are commensurate with the service performed, while eliminating the great abuses to which they have been shown to be open. If the root of the abuses is personal greed, the system would be better off if arbitragers were well paid for their work by their firms but were prohibited from trading for themselves as one of the conditions of their employment—a condition that can be set by the firms without federal legislation. Although any such new rules would also be open to violation and circumvention, the possibility of enormous personal gain would be greatly diminished. The system would also be better off if the financial firms avoided even the appearance of conflict of interest, acted on a set fee for services basis, and did not trade for their own profit in any merger or takeover.

Is the major ethical problem at its roots hostile takeovers, some of the ways that such takeovers are conducted, some of the financing developed to support them, or some of the defensive mechanisms developed to offset them? As we have seen, we can evaluate from a moral point of view hostile takeovers, junk bonds, greenmail, and the host of defensive tactics potential takeover targets have developed. Yet there is a sense in which doing so is like tackling a brush fire piecemeal. As we handle one practice, another dubious practice develops elsewhere.

The root of the problems in the finance industry has been identified by some as greed. And the greed of a few, critics argue, has become infectious. While executives were previously content with large salaries, stock options, and annual incomes of $1–$2 million a year, the news of others making many times that in a few days, weeks, or months escalated the game. It seems it was not only the money but also the prestige of "keeping up" that was the driving factor.[18]

If the root of the problems in the finance industry has been correctly identified as greed, the solution is not to attempt to change people so they are not greedy or to motivate them to control their greed, but to establish structures that eliminate the temptations to which many succumb. Pernicious greed is nonproductive and has as its only aim the quick acquisition by almost any means of personal gain. The remedy is to preclude such gain while continuing to reward those who contribute to society's welfare through the production of goods and services. A plausible target is short-term capital gains.

In this regard, Warren Buffett, a billionaire involved in many takeovers, suggested that all short-term gains be taxed at 100 percent. If that proposal sounds too draconian, it can easily be softened to tax at 100 percent only those short-term capital gains from hostile takeovers that exceed, for instance, $1 million in any year. The target is not orphans, widows, and small investors. Short-term gains on commodities might also be excluded, since the aim is to prevent not productive practices but counterproductive ones.

The point is that with some change, such as a modified 100 percent tax on short-term gains above a certain high amount, the trades that Ivan Boesky engaged in would yield him nothing, and hence the incentive to engage in them would be eliminated. Inside trading could still be regulated by the present rules; no new legislation would be required. Eliminating short-term capital gains from hostile takeover attempts would preclude the benefit of greenmail and hence remove the motive for the practice. With only long-term capital gains as a source of profit, the incentive for many of the takeovers would be diminished. Hostile takeovers would still be possible, but those that took place would tend to be productive in a way that many in the 1980s were not. Only those that were planned for long-term gains would take place. Taxing short-term gains at 100 percent would preclude trading and working for the quarterly report, a practice that is frequently bemoaned but never attacked in practice.

If speculative profit—that is, profit for profit's sake with little if any return to society—is the aim of corporate takeovers, then society acts within its

---

[18] Karen W. Arenson, "How Wall Street Bred Ivan Boesky," *New York Times*, November 23, 1986, p. F8.

rights to preclude such profit. One way to preclude it is to try to legislate against its being made. A second way is to take away the incentive to engage in those practices by making them unprofitable. The first approach legislates only after a practice develops; the second prevents the development of new practices with the same aim.

At the least, society can appropriately demand an argument justifying the benefits of short-term capital gains—or of such gains above some reasonable amount—from hostile takeovers. Are such takeovers necessary for restructuring, for efficiency, and for the common good of the society? The present situation arguably calls for both a new, hard look at the ethical justification for the existing structures and practices, and a willingness to make radical changes, if necessary.

Downsizing

As the 1990s emerged, restructuring via downsizing joined the restructuring via mergers and takeovers that was rampant in the 1980s. Although the argument was still efficiency, the threat now was not only predators but competition, especially international competition. Downsizing involved making do with fewer workers, both at the managerial and at lower levels. Firms that had long traditions of not laying off workers, such as IBM and Levi-Strauss,[19] when faced with decreasing profits or with actual losses, joined the multitude of other firms that sought to be "leaner" and more efficient, doing as much and as well with fewer employees. The ethical issue is not whether a firm can let employees go, if layoffs are financially necessary in order for the firm to survive. It can. The questions are, first, whether in fact layoffs are the best method to achieve efficiency or whether they in fact reduce the morale and loyalty of the workers and undermine efficiency; and, second, whether in laying off employees firms do as much as they can and should to ease the blow, to treat them with the respect and consideration they deserve, to help them move or retrain, or otherwise to ease the negative results of being discharged through no fault of their own.

Whether in fact downsizing is the best way to achieve efficiency, of course, depends on the particular company and its actual situation. Few companies purposefully expanded their labor force beyond what they needed. Expansion often took place in the middle management range, where it is difficult to match costs and returns. On the other hand, if demand for a product falls, then, unless the employees engaged in production can be retrained or shifted to some other growing part of the company, the work force is typically reduced to match production. Layoffs, or downsizings, are not in themselves unethical. Levi Strauss took its action reluctantly as demand for its jeans declined due to competition. Such downsizing, and downsizing of managers,

---

[19] Ralph T. King, Jr., "Its Share Shrinking, Levi Strauss Lays Off 6,395," *Wall Street Journal*, November 4, 1997, p. B1.

to make a firm more competitive is difficult to fault from a moral point of view, although some critics say that even in these circumstances companies that have had a tradition of permanent employment for their workers break faith with the implicit contract they had with their employees. The ethically questionable instances of downsizing are those carried out solely for its effect on the market price of the company's stock. Since downsizing results in lower costs, market analysts often react positively to downsizing by a company as an indication that it is doing what needs to be done to increase its profits. Downsizing does not always result in cost cutting in the long run, as when a company that lays off a worker who earns $15.00 an hour plus benefits has to pay $65 an hour from an outside contractor to get the same work done.[20] Seldom does management figure in costs that are not easily quantifiable, such as the morale of the remaining work force. Nothing erases loyalty like downsizing, which sends all employees the message that they are expendable. Diminished loyalty hardly energizes the remaining workers who now have to do the same work that many more people previously did.

When downsizing is necessary and truly improves efficiency, the ethical issue still remains of how it is done. Levi Strauss, in announcing that it was closing eleven of its U.S. factories and letting 6,395 of its employees go, simultaneously told the workers it would pay them all, shop floor workers and executives alike, for eight months, give them three weeks additional pay for every year with the company, and continue their paid health insurance for eighteen months, among other benefits.[21] Giving fired employees a reasonable severance package, including continuation of their health insurance, and providing help in finding other employment are parts of the ways to treat employees as worthy of respect even if they are being fired. Explaining the reasons for the downsizing and the rationale for letting go those who are fired also shows respect for the employees. The opposite message is sent by summary dismissal with few, if any benefits, and such dismissal is hardly ethically justifiable. Also questionable is the tactic of firing employees to save money and simultaneously giving fat raises and bonuses to top management, and continuation bonuses to those lucky enough to still have their jobs. Apple Computer rightly came in for criticism when it fired workers and eliminated its dividends but gave its CEO a salary of $2.5 million plus a bonus.[22] If the aim is to save money, then giving large salary increases and bonuses is not the way to do so and raises doubt about the stated motive. Workers do not have any right to lifelong employment with a firm, but they do have the right to be treated with respect, and companies have the obligation to do as little harm as possible in firing workers who have done good work and would normally be kept on.

---

[20] "Alex Markels and Matt Murray, "Axing for Trouble: Call It Dumbsizing: Why Some Companies Regret Cost-Cutting," *Wall Street Journal*, May 14, 1996, p. A1.

[21] David Cay Johnston, "At Levi Strauss, A Big Cutback, With Largess," *New York Times*, November 4, 1997, p. C1.

[22] "The Hit Men," *Newsweek*, February 26, 1996, p. 47.

Ethical Investing

Given the restructuring of corporate America, what is the moral responsibility of the shareholders of a corporation, and how should moral considerations enter into investing?

Institutional investors are now major players in the stock market. They often claim that they are forced to opt for short-term gains. Thus, they often turn out to be more speculators than investors. If the tax structure discouraged large short-term gains more than it does, institutional investors would be encouraged to take greater interest in the companies in which they invest and to have more concern that those companies do well in the longer term. The pressure on management to manage ethically as well as effectively would come from the shareholders rather than from outside predators. Management in turn would not need to sell poison pills, buy back the company's stock to increase its debt, or offer management golden parachutes.

Although institutional investors exert the greatest force in the market, the stock of most public firms is now owned primarily by small investors,[23] usually through the intermediary of institutional investors who manage their pension funds, 401(k) retirement funds, insurance funds, mutual funds, and the like. But the general public has not sought to exercise the control that ownership has traditionally brought with it. Fund managers seek to maximize returns for their clients, who in turn take little interest in using the leverage they have to affect corporate policy. Nonetheless, the instruments for significant change are available.

What then are the ethical responsibilities of investors?

Moral responsibility involves a causal connection to an action or result that is morally evaluated, and moral responsibility is properly ascribed and assumed only if the action in question was done knowingly and freely, and if there were no excusing conditions. We have seen that the corporation can correctly be said to act, even if it acts only when those within it act. In a family-owned or closely held corporation, the owners of the corporation and the principal managers are typically the same people. Hence, the owners, as managers, have responsibility for what the corporation does. The shareholder of a large, publicly held corporation is a part owner of the corporation. Shareholders may own a very, very small part indeed. Moreover, their ownership is usually separated from management; the majority of shareholders are in no sense managers, and have no direct voice in the management of the corporation. They have a vote proportional to the number of shares they own—a vote that they can exercise at the annual shareholders' meeting on the issues presented for a vote by management. But the small shareholders have no say in what is put on the agenda, nor do their votes carry much weight. Even large shareholders may own only a very small percentage of the stock of a giant corporation.

---

[23] Ronald B. Lieber, "Who Owns the 500?" *Fortune*, April 29, 1996, p. 264, says that according to the consulting firm CDA Equity Intelligence small individual investors own "roughly 80 percent of the outstanding shares of Fortune 500 companies."

Managers, strictly speaking, work for the shareholders, who are the owners of the corporation. The managers act as agents for the shareholders. Yet any individual shareholder has in fact little, if any, control over the managers.

Frequently, individuals invest in a company simply as a result of a broker's or a market analyst's suggestion. The concept of being responsible for what the company does because one owns a share of a company is not part of the consciousness of many shareholders. The situation is magnified when people own stock through a pension or retirement plan, through a life insurance policy, or through a mutual fund. Though their money is invested in certain stocks and they own a certain portion of these stocks, they frequently have no idea what stocks their money is invested in, or how much of each stock they own. Hence, it seems farfetched to hold individual shareholders responsible for what the managers do on the basis of the claim that the owners are ultimately responsible for what the corporation does. Limited liability shields the personal property of the stockholders from creditors and from those who file suit for damages of a negligent or criminal type; but the shareholders are penalized for what the managers do and for which the corporation is sued. When the corporation pays a fine, the shareholders in effect pay it, even though they had nothing to do with the action in question. On the other hand, they also gain by actions management takes that, even if immoral, add to the profit of the firm.

Shareholders cannot be held morally responsible for what the firm does since the shareholder is in fact very distant from the causal relation between an action of the corporation and its effects—but this does not relieve shareholders of all moral responsibility.

First, no one is ethically allowed to invest in an unethical operation. If we know an operation is unethical, we have the ethical obligation not to invest in it or, if we are already invested in it, to withdraw from it. Clearly, because the basic transaction of selling cocaine is unethical, it would be unethical to invest in a cocaine ring, even if one were guaranteed extremely high returns on one's funds. If Murder, Inc., were quietly seeking investors, investing in that enterprise would be unethical. The general principle is that if a corporation is established for an immoral end, then no one can morally support its activities through the purchase of its stock. The ordinary public corporation does not have an immoral end. Yet by analogy we can argue that even if a company is established for a legitimate end, if it in fact has a policy of engaging in unethical practices, then no one can morally support its activities through the purchase of its stock.

Thus, if it is unethical for a company to engage in racial discrimination, or in child labor, then it is unethical to invest in a company that follows such practices. If it is unethical to produce and sell "Saturday night specials," then it is unethical to invest in a company that produces such handguns. If it is unethical to produce and sell intoxicating beverages, it is unethical to invest in a company that makes and sells them. We have not argued that holding stock of companies that produce cigarettes or tobacco is necessarily unethical. We have argued, rather, that *if* these and other practices are unethical, then it is unethical to purchase stock in companies that adopt those practices as part of their policies. The present point is that one cannot ethically hold stock in companies that have unethical policies, and that in cases where the ethics of a practice is disputed, one must follow one's own beliefs in the matter. Consistency requires that if one believes that making and selling cigarettes is unethical, then one is ethically required not to own stock in such a company.

Note that the question is not whether the company is legal. Drug-pushing and Murder, Inc., are, of course, illegal. But simply because a company operates legally does not mean that it necessarily operates ethically. The law may tolerate unethical behavior. The law is the only guide that interests those who believe in the Myth of Amoral Business. But if one understands that not everything that is legal is ethical, then one can ask whether the firm, company, or enterprise in which one is interested in investing is ethical. In some instances this will be a matter of dispute. There is a difference of opinion whether companies that produce and sell tobacco products, intoxicating beverages, "Saturday night specials," and nuclear weapons act unethically. In these cases we are ethically obliged to follow our conscience. If we believe that producing certain goods is unethical, then to be consistent we must admit that investing in such a company is also unethical.

The situation is more complicated in most cases. What makes a company unethical? The easy cases are those in which companies engage primarily in unethical activity. Just as we would be willing to condemn the drug-pusher and the murderer, so we would condemn those who carry on unethical activities in business. But do we ethically condemn the person who is generally law-abiding and ethical, but who slips every now and then—who now and then misrepresents, or now and then takes pencils or small items at work? We should condemn the action, but we do not necessarily shun the person. What about companies? How clean do we want them to be in order to be considered ethical, and for how small an offense should they be shunned?

There are at least three considerations in answering such questions. One is the company's policies. If a firm makes a fraction of 1 percent of its earnings or profits from some questionable activity, is that sufficient to condemn it? If Company X makes less than 1 percent of its profit from its operation with companies that use child labor in a country in which this is tolerated, is that sufficient to call the company unethical and so to refuse to invest in it? The answer is arguably yes because the practice is one that is consciously adopted as company policy. To be consistent, we should hold that how much or how little a company makes from an unethical practice is beside the point. Any amount made from such activity is sufficient to taint the company. Unethical policies are unethical even if they represent a very small portion of a company's policies.

The second way of evaluating a company is in terms of its record. How does it treat its employees? How does it fare with respect to the number of women and minorities it hires compared to the pool of available employees?

Does it promote women and minorities to the level of upper management? How safe are the products the firm produces? How safe are the conditions it provides for its employees? Does it pollute or ravage the land? Does it consider the impact of its activities on the community and ensure that it does no harm? Does it close down plants without advance warning, or lay off workers in any downturn? How many suits have been filed against it by workers, and what do the suits claim? All these questions can and should be answered, even though it is often difficult to get the answers, since disclosure of much of this information is not required by law. Nevertheless, answers to such questions are important if we are to evaluate firms from a moral point of view.

In considering these questions, we have to ask not only what the company's record is but also what its present policies are. If the company discriminated in the past with respect to hiring women but is now engaged in affirmative action, is that acceptable, or does the fact that it once practiced discrimination suffice to taint it and render it unethical? Present policies arguably dominate, unless the company's history shows that it tends to continue unethical practices even though it claims to have policies that prevent them. Once we get answers to all these and similar questions, we must then attempt to determine whether the firm is sufficiently unethical for us to refuse to own its stock. Since some of the questions and answers may be controversial, borderline, unclear, or ethically ambiguous, there is sometimes room for some honest differences in moral judgment.

The third issue is whether a company is to be held responsible for anything that any of its employees do, or whether it is to be held unethical only if the action done by a corporate official is part of company policy. If a firm—such as some defense firms—is found guilty of paying bribes or violating bidding procedures, and the corporate CEO claims that this was the unauthorized action of a lower manager, is that sufficient to exonerate the firm? It is not legally sufficient; is it morally sufficient? Should we hold a company responsible for anything done in its name by its members? A two-pronged test is reasonable here. First, are the structures of the company such that they either permit or encourage such activity, even though it is not part of company policy? If so, the company as well as the offending official is morally at fault. Second, after the fact, has the company taken appropriate action to prevent similar occurrences in the future? Did the company fire the guilty official and issue and enforce strict rules that actively discourage similar action on the part of others? Unless the answer is yes, the sincerity of the company is questionable. Disclaimers by companies are easy to issue. The tests of action are what count if we wish to take ethical investing seriously.

From an ethical point of view, before we can be excused from responsibility because of ignorance, we must be sure that our ignorance is not culpable. In general, this means considering whether ordinary persons would have known or could have known if they paid sufficient attention and exercised proper care. This rule applies in investing. How much investigation do we expect the average shareholder to carry out before investing? How much is reasonable, given the limitations on any individual's time? The short answer is that one must pay some attention to the activities of the companies one invests in, including their ethical track record. But less is reasonably expected of the small shareholder than of the large shareholder or of the institutional investor.

The difficulty of obtaining adequate and appropriate information lessens the small shareholder's responsibility. But if we know that a company is engaged in unethical activity, then clearly we should not invest in that company. And if we learn that the company we hold stock in is engaged in unethical activity, then we should separate ourselves from the company by selling our stock in that company. If there is no easy way to determine the ethical quotient of a company, then the cost of determining it is beyond what the ordinary person can be expected to expend in either time or money, given the small amount of the investment.

The analysis is not quite the same with respect to large investors and institutional investors. Because of their greater assets, they can afford to determine with greater care than the individual investor the ethical quotient of the companies in which they invest. Hence, more care can be expected of them prior to purchase. Moreover, once they own large shares of a company, they can influence the actions of companies in a way small investors cannot, by voting their shares in an ethically responsible manner and by bringing up for vote issues that the corporation does not. To get an item on the agenda of a stockholders' meeting usually requires controlling at least 3 percent of the voting stock of the company. Institutional investors, either alone or in concert with other similar investors, may get issues on the agenda for a vote—whether they concern takeovers, affirmative action, plant-closing policies, product or plant safety, or any other issue. Large shareholders may also be in a position to influence corporate policy from within a firm in a way that small shareholders cannot. Hence, large shareholders might legitimately not sell stock in a company if they in good faith intend to produce a change in corporate policy and have some hope of doing so.

Ethical investing guidelines place ethical demands of a minimal sort. They say that one cannot ethically invest in companies that as a policy or as a regular practice violate the moral minimum required of all companies. They do not demand that one invest only in exemplary companies or only in companies that do more than abide by the moral minimum.

As we have seen, social responsibility is different from ethical responsibility. Similarly, socially responsible investors may wish to do more or to do something different from ethical investors. Any ethical investing plan is socially responsible, but a socially responsible investment plan may use a variety of criteria in deciding on companies in which to invest, some of which may demand meeting more than minimal morality standards and others of which may have no relation to ethical concerns.

A number of criticisms have been leveled against ethical investing, and it is useful to see what these are and see how they can be answered.

One argument claims that the demands of ethical investing are too stringent and so are impossible to follow. If the claim is right, then, since *ought* implies *can,* we are responsible only for doing what we can in this area—but we are responsible for doing that much. The argument, however, implies more than this: It implicitly claims that ethical investing is impossible either because all companies act unethically; or because there is no way to avoid investing in unethical companies since any alternative form of investing one's money—in certificates of deposit, in a bank, in a savings and loan corporation—simply provides others with money that they reinvest in the stock market on the basis of the best returns they can get.

The reply in each case is straightforward. The claim that all companies are unethical is much too strong and implausible and goes against most people's perception of the business world; hence, that argument fails. But if it were correct, then there is even more reason than otherwise for the general public to demand that companies obey the moral minimum and enforce this demand by withholding support to the extent possible. To the second claim, that we cannot avoid investing indirectly, the answer is that banks, savings and loans, pension funds, insurance companies, and other institutional investors are bound by ethical constraints just as individuals are. The general tenor of this kind of argument against ethical investing is one of adherence to the Myth of Amoral Business and should be seen as such.

Another attack on ethical investing claims that if some individuals and institutional investors do not invest in companies that act unethically, other less scrupulous individuals and institutions will; hence, one cannot bring moral pressure to bear on companies in this way. If only unprincipled investors hold stock in some companies, then there will be no ethically sensitive shareholders to help change the practices of those firms from within by voting their shares.

The answer to this argument is multiple. First, simply because someone else will act unethically in no way justifies our acting in the same manner. Second, small shareholders cannot change company policy, so the argument that they can act from within does not hold. Third, the ethical investing criteria developed above allow large and institutional investors to continue holding stock in a company that adopts some unethical policy, if there is reasonable hope that the shareholders can force the company to give up that policy. But if there is no practical hope of doing so, then divestment of such stock is ethically required.

Another frequently used argument claims that ethical investing demands too much because it looks only at specific policies and fails to consider the broader picture. We cannot expect perfection in or from business, and we must also consider the good done by the profits earned by investing in profitable companies. Fund managers have the responsibility to get the best possible returns for their clients. University endowments have the responsibility to get the best returns for endowment funds so that they can give more to students in the way of financial support. The fiduciary responsibility of those who invest money that is not their own, the argument continues, precludes imposing their own ethical criteria on how they invest. The law represents the general social consensus, and so they should invest in any legal way they can that maximizes the investment funds they manage.

The argument is not simply a utilitarian one arguing that possibly more good is achieved by investing without regard to ethical criteria than otherwise, but also a deontological argument that those in charge of large funds have a fiduciary duty to maximize returns. Neither version of the argument works.

No one can have an ethical obligation to act unethically. Hence, no fiduciary obligation can demand that one maximize returns by unethical investing. The obligation can only be to attempt to maximize returns within the constraints imposed by law and morality. The point about not imposing one's own ethical values is confused. One is obliged not to act unethically, where this means one is obliged not to do what is objectively wrong. It is not the case that each person has his or her own ethics. What the argument might plausibly hold is that in disputed cases the manager of an institutional fund should not apply his or her own moral decision on the case in deciding not to purchase the firm's stock. The argument claims that if such investment managers believe that tobacco and liquor companies should be avoided, they should put aside their own beliefs as being not very widely shared. However, even this version of the argument is too strong, for it assumes that the fund manager cannot achieve the same returns for the fund's clients by excluding such stock in the fund's portfolio—an assumption that has not been demonstrated. Nonetheless, it would be appropriate both for fund managers to make known to the general managers of the fund that they are using such criteria, and for the fund to make such information known to those who may purchase shares in it.

A number of mutual funds have become available that screen investments using a variety of different ethical and social criteria. Some screen out tobacco and alchoholic beverage companies, and others screen out arms makers. The mixes are not infinite, but the variety is fairly large and growing larger. What is significant about these funds is that, although some have done poorly, others have done extremely well financially. The latter show that ethical investing need not yield lower returns than investing that pays no attention to ethical criteria. Yet we should be cautious of any claim that by being ethical in business one is guaranteed bigger financial returns than otherwise; sometimes being ethical means being satisfied with lesser returns.

The final argument we shall look at claims that there is no evidence that ethical investing actually applies pressure on companies to change their policies. The reply here is threefold. First, that is not the only reason for ethical investing. Even if companies do not change, that is no reason for others to indirectly engage in unethical practices by providing them with funding. Second, there is some evidence that the strong protests against American companies operating in South Africa had some effect, since so many of them withdrew from South Africa in one way or another. Third, ethical investing should be seen as only one part of an overall strategy to apply moral pressure on companies to operate ethically.

At its best, ethical investing should be coupled with ethical consumer purchasing. Consumers vote with their dollars, just as investors vote with theirs. If the companies that act unethically or have unethical policies were shunned not only by investors but by consumers as well, then the pressure would be strong enough to have a significant influence on firms. The difficulty of obtaining and disseminating appropriate information is a large, but not insurmountable, hurdle. It is often extremely difficult to know which company produces which product. But we do know that cars, computers, and large appliances all bear the names of their companies. The Nestlé boycott is an example of ethical consumer pressure. If the students who protested in favor of divestment of the stock of companies that did business in South Africa had also refrained from purchasing the products produced by those companies and had convinced others to do so as well, their effectiveness would have been much greater than it was.

Although ethical quotients on companies are still difficult to obtain, there are some efforts to generate such information for consumers.[24] If there is sufficient interest and demand, such information will become more readily available.

We can expect companies to be no more ethical on the whole than the general population. The more consumers and investors demand that companies act ethically and back up their demands with ethical investing and purchasing, the more companies will be forced to respond to the demand for ethical behavior, just as they respond to other demands that affect their ability to succeed in business.

Neither investors nor those in finance can afford to ignore ethical norms or to avoid considering and abiding by them in their practices and dealings. The challenge of thinking and acting ethically means going beyond vested interests, short-term profits, and conventional morality to consider the investment community's role and actions from the perspective of the common good. Only if financial practices are justifiable from that perspective do they benefit the public, and only if the public benefits should it accept or allow such practices.

Study Questions

1. How did the system's structure of "thrifts" help lead to unethical behavior?
2. Do accountants who work for a corporation in its accounting department have any special ethical obligations because they are accountants? Why or why not?

---

[24] See, for instance, Steven D. Lydenberg, Alice Tepper Marlin, Sean O'Brien Strub, and the Council on Economic Priorities, *Rating America's Corporate Conscience.* (Reading, Mass.: Addison-Wesley Publishing Company, 1987); and Amy L. Domini and Peter D. Kinder, *Ethical Investing,* (Reading, Mass.: Addison-Wesley Publishing Company, 1986).

3. To whom do CPAs owe their loyalty?

4. Why are CPAs necessarily faced with a conflict-of-interest situation? Can anything be done about this?

5. What do the letters GAAP, GAAS, and COPE stand for?

6. May CPAs ethically work on a contingency fee basis? Why or why not?

7. What are some complaints about the system under which CPAs work?

8. Should corporations be required to list as a liability their financial exposure in terms of health care benefits to their retirees? Why or why not?

9. Are employee stock options a liability to the assets of the company? If so, how should they be reported? If not, why not?

10. What ethical lessons can be learned from the BCCI scandal?

11. What are the ethical issues in the international debt of underdeveloped countries?

12. Under what conditions is complete bank secrecy ethically unjustifiable?

13. What are a bank's ethical obligations of disclosure?

14. What is a friendly takeover? A hostile takeover?

15. Are hostile takeovers morally justifiable? Why or why not?

16. Develop the utilitarian arguments for and against hostile takeovers.

17. Develop the deontological argument against hostile takeovers.

18. What is *greenmail*? Is it morally justifiable? Why or why not?

19. What are *golden parachutes?* Are they morally justifiable? Why or why not?

20. What are *LBOs?* Are they morally justifiable? Why or why not?

21. How might long-term versus short-term gains be used to separate ethically justifiable from ethically unjustifiable hostile takeovers?

22. In some instances, the workers of a firm have bought out the firm when it was threatened with a hostile takeover. Does the fact that the LBO was a worker action rather than a management action change the ethical evaluation one might make of the buyout? Why or why not?

23. When, if ever, is downsizing ethically justifiable? Explain.

24. Is there an ethical way to downsize? Explain.

25. Can the typical small shareholder be held responsible for what the firm does? Why or why not? What of the institutional shareholder, such as pension plans or mutual funds?

26. What are the ethical responsibilities of small shareholders?

27. How do the ethical responsibilities of large shareholders and institutional investors differ from those of small shareholders?

18

>─┼─◄►─•─O─•─◄►─┼─◄

PROFESSIONS IN BUSINESS
AND
PROFESSIONS AS BUSINESS

The Manville Case

In its heyday, asbestos was used in over 2,500 products. It does not burn and is an excellent fire retardant as well as an excellent insulator. It is resistant to heat and to chemical reaction. Its virtues led to its wide use, including brake linings for cars, roofing for houses, insulation in schools, and heat protection in hair dryers. One manufacturer even wove asbestos into children's pajamas and advertised them as a safety feature in case of fire. During World War II the U.S. government mandated that shipbuilders use asbestos in navy vessels to help prevent the spread of fires aboard them. No substitute was known for many of its uses.

But the news about asbestos was not all good. As early as 1932, reports began to appear in the medical literature that asbestos carries with it possible health risks. The U.S. Navy Department and the U.S. Maritime Commission recognized the risk from asbestos insulation in 1943. Those involved in the manufacture of asbestos products were exposed to direct health hazards. Their claims were covered under workers' compensation laws. The threat to those who used the products was more tenuous. But Dr. Kenneth Wallace Smith, Johns-Manville's corporate medical director from 1952 to 1966, testified that in 1952 he told corporate executives that he believed insulation workers "were exposed to the same potential hazards" as manufacturing workers.[1]

---

[1] Stephen Solomon, "The Asbestos Fallout at Johns-Manville," *Fortune*, 99, no. 9 (May 7, 1979), p. 204. For other details on Manville and asbestos, see Jordan H. Leibman, "The Manufacturer's Responsibility to Warn Product Users of Unknowable Dangers," *American Business Law Journal*, 21

Despite such reports, Johns-Manville and other asbestos manufacturers did not warn those who handled or used its products of any potential danger until 1964, when a study by Dr. Irving J. Selikoff of the New York Mount Sinai School of Medicine reported the results of a study demonstrating the link between exposure to asbestos and a variety of health problems. Asbestos is now known to cause asbestosis (scarring of the lungs) and mesothelioma (cancer of the chest lining), as well as other respiratory illnesses and cancers. After that study, Johns-Manville issued warnings that its asbestos products posed potential health hazards. Whether the warnings indicated the true seriousness of the danger is still debated.

The second act of the Manville case opened after 1964 when those who were adversely affected by Manville's asbestos products started filing claims for damages, both actual and punitive. The company responded to the suits with the defense that it could not be held responsible for harm done by its product when it did not and could not know that it was harmful. Furthermore, since the government had mandated its use in navy shipyards, Johns-Manville maintained that the government should bear part of the costs of any payments that the company might be forced to make.

The Supreme Court of New Jersey ruled that Johns-Manville had to pay damages under strict liability laws. It rejected the claim of lack of culpability as irrelevant; it also rejected the state of the art defense that Manville's lawyers used to justify the company's failure to warn users of the dangers associated with the company's asbestos products. The court did not find Johns-Manville guilty of negligence. Rather, it ruled that because the products were dangerous, even if the company did not know about the danger, the cost of the damage should fall on the manufacturer rather than on the individual user. The danger may well have been unseen by both manufacturer and user, but the manufacturer should bear the cost of harm rather than the user. Interestingly, the court also commented that even if it was true that the company was not aware of potential harm, the claim that it could not be known given the state of the art of science at the time begged the question of how much earlier the harm could have been known if the company had spent more on relevant research.

Critics cite the knowledge of harm that existed as early as the 1930s. Given the knowledge in the medical journals, what should the doctors working for Johns-Manville have been doing? When did they have suspicions of a health hazard to users as well as producers of asbestos products? How diligently did they pursue the possibility of harm? What responsibility did they have to potential users, even though those users were not employees of Johns-Manville? Where does a corporate doctor's responsibility as a doctor end, and to what extent are such doctors simply employees of the company that pays

---

(1984), pp. 403-438; *Beshada v. Johns-Manville Products Corp.*, 90 N.J. 191, 447 A.2nd 539 (1982); and *New York Times*, September 2, 1982, p. D2.

their salaries and obliged to obey orders rather than to worry about harm to workers or users of a firm's products? We have already discussed the conditions under which whistle blowing is prohibited, permitted, and mandatory. How do those criteria apply in this case? What should the doctors have done? Is their responsibility different from that of those workers who were not members of the medical profession? Does being a member of the medical profession—or of any other profession—carry with it special obligations?

>─┼─◆>─O─<◆─┼─<

The curtain rises on the third act of the Johns-Manville saga in 1982, by which time 16,500 claims totaling at least $2 billion had been filed, with the number increasing monthly. The net worth of the company was $1.1 billion. Although it was still making a profit, the company took the unprecedented step of declaring bankruptcy under Chapter 11. This reorganization would prevent new suits from being filed against the company. In addition, some of the insurance companies that covered some of Johns-Manville's claims argued that they had been defrauded because Johns-Manville had not revealed to them data it had linking asbestos to health hazards. They also argued about whether their liability (which totaled $364 million) began when the workers were exposed to asbestos or some twenty to forty years later when the asbestos-related disease manifested itself. In 1988, faced with potential claims of $87 billion, the Johns-Manville Corporation established a Personal Injury Settlement Trust to pay out more than $2.5 billion to asbestos claimants. The company emerged from bankruptcy reorganized as the Manville Corporation. Suits continued to mount, and the Trust temporarily stopped payment in 1990 to restructure payments, which were based on arbitration, so that it could cover the more than 150,000 claims still pending. In July 23, 1993, Federal Judge Jack B. Weinstein authorized the Trust to pay out $154 million to 4,000 claimants whose cases had been settled by 1990.[2] In 1995 Judge Weinstein approved a class action settlement that equalized payments to present and future claimants. It provided for payments of 10 percent of the settlement amount for seven categories of disease. Thus, for cancer of one lung, scheduled for $60,000, a claimant would receive $6,000. By December 1997 the Trust had paid more than $720 million to over 140,000 claimants, with 135,000 cases still pending.[3] Payments continue to be made.

Some analysts saw the legal ploy of filing for bankruptcy as an attempt to avoid further suits and punitive damages. The suits and countersuits by the insurance firms were also criticized by some as a delaying tactic and an attempt to avoid payment of legitimate claims. Many claims lapsed because the statute of limitations in some states ran out. On the other hand, some peo-

---

[2] *Wall Street Journal,* August 5, 1986, p. 14; *New York Times,* July 24, 1993, p. A39.

[3] Summary details of the Trust are available on the Internet at the Manville Personal Injury Settlement Trust web site (http://www.mantrust.org).

ple filed claims who had already received compensation from their companies under workman's compensation laws.

Deeply involved in all of the suits, of course, were lawyers. What responsibility do corporate lawyers have to justice or to the welfare of those who may have been harmed by the company for which the lawyers work? Is the job of corporate lawyers simply to do the best they can for their employers, if necessary trying to stretch the law, ignoring its spirit and working only by its letter? Is justice not something they appropriately worry about but leave up to the courts to decide in the U.S. adversarial system? If this is so, are the ethical obligations of a corporate lawyer, as a member of a profession, different from those of a corporate doctor who works for the same firm? Are both bound to work exclusively for the benefit of their corporate employer, as the corporation dictates, as long as they stay within the limits of the law?

The Professions and Business

The professions are inextricably intertwined with business. Corporations, for example, in 1991 spent $84 billion on legal services. Lawyers sometimes are employed directly by corporations, others form partnerships and sell their services, and still others have independent practices. The health professions form an important part of social life. Drug companies are among the corporate giants; hospital, doctor, and medical insurance bills take a significant part of the average worker's salary. Engineers build our roads, skyscrapers, bridges, and plants. They are hired in great numbers by corporations to design cars, airplanes, washing machines, electric toothbrushes, and the many other mechanical and electronic objects that form part of our daily life.

As modern society becomes more complex, it requires greater specialization and specialized knowledge. In the United States, automation has taken over many of the routine jobs formerly performed by unskilled labor. The need for advanced training and the growth of the service professions have encouraged more people to go to college and to professional schools. Schooling has in turn provided business and industry with a pool of trained workers to take on the jobs that require communication skills, computer programming knowledge, engineering expertise, accounting procedures, legal practices, and a variety of specialized information.

The trend toward specialization has led groups to identify themselves as professions, and to seek the prestige and wealth that have become identified with professions. Professionalism and the professions raise special problems from the point of view of ethics. Their rapid growth makes the problems more pressing.

In dealing with the professions and professionalism, the first problem is to identify what we mean by a profession or by professionals. What is a profession? Typically, professions have been self-governing, and society has allowed them a large amount of autonomy. Is such autonomy justifiable? And does it carry with it special moral or ethical responsibilities? A second topic for investigation follows from these questions: professional ethical codes. Professional codes make demands on members of the professions, demands that are not always compatible with the loyalty and obedience expected by many employers. The role of the professions in business therefore requires examination, as do the activities of professional organizations. Because the members of many professions are self-employed, we should also look at the professions as independent businesses.

Whatever fields are characterized as professions, and whatever roles are played by professions, it is always people who fill professional roles and are members of professions. Members of a profession are people first and members of a profession second. Hence, there is no special ethics that allows people in a profession to do as professionals what it is immoral for others to do. Lawyers, for instance, have no right to lie or cheat or mislead in order to help or to defend a client. Doctors in their role as doctors may not for the good of medicine experiment on their patients without the patients' informed consent, nor may they lie to patients for the patients' good. Those in professions do have a special relation to ethics because of the roles they fill as members of a profession. But *more* is appropriately expected of them because of their roles, not less. In order to determine the proper moral obligations of members of a profession, we must understand the role of professions in society.

Professionalism and the Professions

The history of the professions is still being written. How it is written depends on whether we identify the professions first and then write their history, or whether we specify certain criteria that must be met for a group or field to qualify as a profession, and then investigate which groups or fields have met those criteria.[4] The trend toward specialization has led more and more groups to identify themselves as professions and to seek the prestige and wealth that have become identified with professions.[5]

The confusion about what constitutes a profession is reflected in the linguistic confusion between the terms *profession* and *professional*. We have no single, unambiguous term to refer to a member of a profession; *professional* is the term we use. But many people who are, in one sense, professionals do not belong to professions. Professionals in this sense do full time, for pay, and with considerable expertise, what others do occasionally, without pay, and as amateurs. Thus, a professional is someone who earns his or her living by practicing some skill or engaging in some activity that requires expertise, but which others do as a hobby, for pleasure, or in their spare time. Members of the various trades are professionals. There are professional carpenters,

---

[4] Magali Sarafatti Larson, *The Rise of Professionalism: A Sociological Analysis* (Berkeley: University of California Press, 1977), is a good introduction to the rise of the professions.

[5] As early as 1974, Jane Clapp assembled in *Professional Ethics and Insignia* (Metuchen, N.J.: Scarecrow Press, 1974), over 100 codes of groups that identify themselves as professions.

plumbers, auto mechanics, bricklayers, barbers, and so on. Professionals know their craft, devote their full working time to it, usually are paid for what they do, and take a certain pride in doing their job well. We speak of professional actors and actresses, writers, painters, gardeners, and athletes—many people who do professionally what many other people do at an amateur level. Many activities are professional activities in this sense, but not all these activities constitute professions.

With some justification, the witch doctor has been proposed as the paradigm of a member of a profession. A witch doctor has arcane knowledge; he controls access to that knowledge and initiates his successor to his role; he performs an important service to his society; he commands respect and prestige. These are characteristics that tend to designate professions. In the West, two occupations have served as early exemplars of the professions. The doctor, from ancient times to the present, has performed a needed service for society, has controlled and had access to specialized knowledge, and has been given status and prestige, though not necessarily wealth. In the Middle Ages, priests made up an acknowledged profession. They had special powers and knowledge, controlled entry into their ranks, exercised a large degree of autonomy, and served an important social function. They were the educated members of society and professed the faith from the pulpit. By extension, other scholars came to be considered members of the scholarly professions. They, too, had access to and controlled knowledge, performed a service to society, and had something to profess. They were called *professors* and formed a *profession.* Two other groups that had some early claim to being members of a profession were professional soldiers, especially officers, and engineers— those who designed and built aqueducts, cathedrals, palaces, and roads.

In the contemporary world, the paradigms of the professions are the medical and legal professions. Other occupations often considered professions are engineering, pharmacy, architecture, and nursing. Some people consider journalism a profession, as well as accounting. University teaching is probably a profession, though high school and grade school teaching are probably not. Many other groups claim professional status: actuaries, insurance underwriters, school administrators, public administrators, social workers, and paramedics, among others. The professions traditionally carry with them prestige, respect, social status, and autonomy. In recent times they have also been regarded as well-paid occupations. Hence, the desire of more and more groups to have their activity recognized as a profession is understandable.

Does it make any difference whether or not society considers a group to be a profession? Would plumbers do better work if they were a profession instead of a trade? Would doctors perform less well if they were a trade rather than a profession? The answer depends on what society allows members of a profession that it does not allow others, and what it expects from members of a profession that it does not expect from others. Traditionally, society has allowed professions greater autonomy than it allows the trades, arts, or business. Members of a profession set their own standards, regulate entry into the profession, discipline their own members, and function with fewer restraints than others. They frequently set their own tasks, are not closely supervised, and do not punch time clocks. In return for such increased autonomy, however, they properly are expected to serve the public good, to set higher standards of conduct for their members than those required of others, and to enforce a higher discipline on themselves than others do. The trade-off granted by society is that it imposes less social control, on the condition that the profession be self-regulating and self-disciplinary. The standards to which members of a profession are to hold themselves are usually expressed in a professional code (most often called an ethical code) of conduct, promulgated and enforced by a professional organization. Those groups wishing to gain the status of a profession frequently organize into a professional association and promulgate a code of professional ethical conduct.

Professional Ethical Codes

The argument in favor of allowing a profession to govern itself is based on two claims. The first is that the knowledge that members of the profession have mastered is specialized, useful to society, and not easily mastered by the layperson. The second is that members of the profession set higher standards for themselves than society requires of its citizens, of unskilled workers, and of those in the business world. The profession is appropriately in a position to know how its members should behave, to be alert to violations of the standards its sets, and to censure or dismiss from its ranks those who do not live up to the profession's standards.

Doctors and lawyers are two groups that plausibly make both claims. Doctors have a large body of specialized knowledge. They study for four years beyond college, do an internship, and then sometimes go on to further specialized study. The knowledge they have is clearly useful to society, and though some knowledge of health care is accessible to the layperson, much is not. The medical profession has developed a specialized vocabulary and an impressive technical jargon. Mastering the vocabulary and jargon is part of a doctor's knowledge and expertise. Doctors perform a service that laypersons need and want. Moreover, people wish to be able to trust their doctors. They want to be assured that those to whom they entrust their health and lives are competent. Hence, it is reasonable for society to demand that only those competent should be allowed to practice medicine. Society reasonably requires proof of training, knowledge, and competence, and identifies those qualified to perform medical services by requiring a licensing procedure.

Who does the licensing? The state does. But the state is not competent to decide what a doctor must know or to grade the tests of those who wish certification. Because the knowledge is technical, only those already trained— that is, doctors, or representative doctors—make up the medical examinations, set requirements for entry into the profession, and certify those who pass. The profession, therefore, decides what knowledge a person must have to practice medicine legally; it sets the curriculum of medical schools. Because doctors decide how many students the medical school can handle, they control entry into the market. They decide not only how many people will be trained, but also who will be admitted to medical school, what these people must learn, and who will be allowed to practice medicine. They set the standards for the practice of medicine. Lawyers similarly control legal education, bar examinations, and the standards of the legal profession. Because both groups control entry into the field and set policy for remaining in the field, both groups act, in many ways, like monopolies. Why should society allow these groups to have so much power when it denies such power to business?

The reply is based on the second claim—namely that the professions set higher standards for themselves than society sets for other groups. What exactly does this mean? Though originally the claim was best understood in moral terms, its present meaning is no longer clearly that of morality. What would it mean for members of a profession to hold themselves to higher moral norms than those applied to other members of society? Obviously, it would not mean that members of the profession were merely to refrain from cheating their clients or to refrain from lying to their patients. Honesty is a moral requirement of everyone, as is telling the truth. The higher moral norms to which members of a profession were to adhere, in the past, were norms that went beyond the requirements of minimal morality. Doctors, for instance, were expected not to work only for money, but to serve patients even if they could not pay for medical services. Lawyers, too, were expected to put their thirst for justice above their desire for fees. They were expected, therefore, to be willing to defend some people who could not afford to pay for their services. Tradespeople, shopkeepers, and businesspeople are not expected to work without pay. To expect members of a profession to do so is to expect more of them than society demands of others.

Members of a profession were also expected to take a different approach to their time and commitments than ordinary workers. Doctors and lawyers were not expected to punch a time clock. They were expected to work as many hours as their professional duties required, which frequently amounted to more than the standard work week of others. Doctors, especially, were expected to be ready to provide their services at inconvenient times of the day or night, when necessary.

Another way in which members of a profession were expected to follow a higher standard was in their personal as well as their professional conduct. They were expected to set an example of proper conduct and to be above suspicion. They were expected not only to refrain from improper conduct but also to be *known* to refrain. This is more than is expected of others.

In these and other ways the professions, at least in earlier times, were expected to adhere to higher moral standards than other people. They were in turn given more respect.

The benefits that accrue to members of a profession are legitimate to the extent that they live up to a higher moral code than others.

An individual can only be a member of a profession if he or she is part of a constituted, self-regulated, properly defined group. The group as such, moreover, has moral obligations that each of its members shares by belonging actively to the profession. The moral status and responsibilities of professions in many ways parallel those of corporations and corporate responsibility. We can correctly speak of the responsibilities of the medical profession. But the profession acts only through the actions of its members, who are the ones who must assume the responsibility of the profession. Thus, if the medical profession is entrusted by society with the regulation of the profession, then each of its members has the obligation not only to live up to proper standards but also to make sure that other members of the profession do so. If society allows the medical profession to control access to the profession, the profession has the moral obligation to make sure that medical care is available to all, and not just to the well-to-do or to those who live in urban areas. That is the responsibility of both the profession and, necessarily, of those within it.

This leads to professional ethical codes.[6] If the argument given so far is valid, members of a profession, both individually and collectively, have special moral obligations. How adequately are they reflected in professional ethical codes?

Typically, professions no longer set higher *moral* standards for themselves, but they do set professional standards, sometimes called *ethical standards*. These, to a large extent, though not immoral, frequently have little to do with moral standards. Doctors and lawyers claim to know the proper role members of their professions should play in society. They claim to set high professional standards to protect society against incompetent practitioners, frauds, and quacks. They know the subterfuges to which members of their profession are prone, the means by which doctors or lawyers can be immoral or unethical without public awareness of their activities. Because they have virtually exclusive access to their specialized knowledge, some may be tempted to use it to achieve their own ends at the expense of the public. Such practitioners can best be restrained by those within the field who have comparable knowledge. Accordingly, doctors and lawyers argue that they should be given autonomy and should be allowed to be self-regulating, not because they adhere to higher norms but because they are best equipped to know how their peers should act, and are therefore best able to judge when they act improperly.

This argument in favor of self-regulation by the professions is plausible. If accepted by society, then society can allow these and similar professions more autonomy than other occupations. The standards to which members of the profession hold themselves are stated in their professional ethical codes.

---

[6] Peter Y. Windt et al. (Eds.), *Ethical Issues in the Professions* (Englewood Cliffs, N.J.: Prentice Hall, 1989), reprints eighteen professional codes, including those of the American Bar Association, the American Medical Association, the National Society of Professional Engineers, and the American Institute of Certified Public Accountants.

Before we look at professional codes of conduct, however, we should note that the argument in defense of autonomy presents some difficulties. Although the ordinary person does not spend four years learning medicine, he or she can learn something about medicine. The ordinary person can also tell to some extent when a doctor seems unsure of himself or herself; when the patient is not being given all the facts; and when a diagnosis turns out to be wrong or a treatment inappropriate. It is not true that only doctors can judge other doctors. The ordinary people who make up society can judge certain aspects of medical practice and the results of some medical activities. The doctors' expertise is not as exclusive as some doctors would like others to believe. The same observation is true of lawyers.

Nor is it always the case that doctors are better judges of doctors and lawyers of lawyers than are the laypersons untrained in these professions. Ordinary citizens serve on juries to judge evidence of crimes; the evidence, when technical, is made intelligible to the jury members. Similarly, laypersons could serve on trial boards to judge the charges of unethical or immoral conduct on the part of doctors and lawyers. Laypersons could either master the knowledge necessary for a particular case or have the case explained in a non-technical manner so that they could make an intelligent judgment on the issue.

Members of a profession know the pitfalls of the profession from the inside. But self-regulation by a profession is justifiable only if the general public is satisfied that a given profession is effectively policing itself, that its code requires higher standards than nonprofessional occupations, that its members are living up to the code, and that the profession is promoting the general good.

Does restricting entry to the medical profession, for instance, promote the general good? The extent to which doctors restrict entry to the profession may be justified by the absence of facilities for training more doctors. By restricting entry, however, doctors can protect their own positions. A potential conflict of interest clearly exists. The more that doctors restrict entry, the fewer doctors there are, and consequently they can demand more money for their services. Doctors were not always well paid. The old-time country doctor and the general practitioner received modest pay, worked long hours, were frequently called out at night, and did not complain loudly when someone could not pay. They were a service profession (somewhat like priests and ministers), and it was considered improper for them to charge or to receive high fees. As professions change, so should society's view of the professions and of their autonomy.

Although professional codes of conduct were once expected to state high standards, they now serve a variety of purposes. Some codes are simply used to indicate that the group is a profession. The code is brought out and referred to on ceremonial occasions, and is sometimes read by new members upon initiation to the profession. Some codes state a set of ideals that members of the profession should try to attain and by which they should guide their practice. But failure to attain the ideals is expected, and few members of the profession actually achieve the goals stated. Other codes or parts thereof are disciplinary. They state the minimum conditions that a member of the profession must satisfy. If he or she falls below that minimum, he or she is subject to sanction by the profession, the most serious of which is expulsion. Still other codes spell out the etiquette of the profession. A single code may include a statement of ideals, a set of disciplinary rules, and standards of professional etiquette.

If a professional code is to serve as a basis on which a profession claims autonomy from the nonprofessional social control to which other groups are subject, the code should have the following characteristics:

1. The code should be regulative. The inclusion of ideals is not necessarily inappropriate. But the code should make clear which of its statements are ideals and which are punitively regulative. Unless a code actually regulates the conduct of the members of a profession, the profession has no public statement to which society can hold the profession. Society allows a profession autonomy on condition that it holds its members to higher norms than those to which others are held; therefore, these norms must be publicly available and must be perceived as being higher than other norms.

2. The code should protect the public interest and the interests of those served by the profession. Unless the public benefits by granting the profession autonomy, it should withdraw this privilege.

3. The code should not be self-serving. Codes can be used to serve the interests of the profession at the expense of the public. Certain regulations (for instance, those concerning the setting of fees or the restricting of advertising) protect the profession and are not in the public interest. Code provisions that prevent competition within the profession are generally not in the public's interest; they tend to emphasize the negative, monopolistic aspects of the profession.

4. The code should be specific and honest. A code that simply says that its members should not lie, steal, or cheat requires nothing of them that is not required of all others. If a code is honest, it deals with those aspects of the profession that pose particular and specialized temptations to its members. The profession is allowed autonomy because it knows the special pitfalls of the profession—its shady areas and its unethical, though not quite illegal, practices. Unless these are addressed, the profession is not truly regulating itself.

5. The code must be both policeable and policed. Unless the code has provisions in it for bringing charges and applying penalties, it is no more than a set of ideals. Unless a profession can demonstrate by its record that it does police its own ranks, society has little reason to believe that it is doing so. In such cases, it has no justification for allowing special privileges to the profession. Society should then, appropriately, legislate concerning the members of the profession and control their activities, as it controls those engaged in other occupations.

Not long ago, the codes of both the medical and the legal professions came under attack. The provision that prevented advertising by doctors and lawyers was successfully challenged as restricting trade and preventing competition. The setting of fees for professional work by the respective organizations was also successfully attacked as artificially setting rates, serving the profession at the expense of the public, and preventing competition. Neither the American Bar Association nor the American Medical Association has been especially anxious to discipline its members. Frequently, they act only after a lawyer or a doctor has been found guilty of a felony. It is not clear that such limited action justifies special privileges.

Although professions can enforce their codes, they are not courts of law and cannot act as such. Violations of a code are subject to limited discipline. Expulsion from the professional association is typically the severest penalty that can be enforced, together with public exposure of the act. Censure is a more frequent penalty.

Professional codes are supposed to govern the professional activity of all members of the profession, whether they are working for themselves or for an employer. The codes may set higher standards than the employer wishes his or her employees to adopt, or that the company code allows.

Professional codes usually ignore such problems, which at least some members of a profession face. Professional codes often specify obligations to the client or patient, to the employer (if there happens to be one), the public, and the profession. What are professionals to do when they find that these obligations conflict? For instance, what if a company's doctor is told not to release information about mounting evidence that the workers in the plant are suffering from an employment-related health hazard? Does his obligation to public health and to his patients (the workers) take precedence over his obligation to his employer?

The 1983 National Association of Accountants Code of Ethics for accountants working within a firm suggests (does not require) that accountants report improper activity (bribery, fraud, false accounting) to top management and the board of directors. But rather than require whistle blowing if no remedial action is taken, the accountant is advised to resign. The guide for these accountants is what is required by law. If law requires public disclosure, the code requires it. If the law does not require public disclosure, the code counsels silence. Because the code requires no more than the law does, the code does not satisfy the conditions for a profession's autonomy, and this is partial grounds for not considering accountancy a profession.

The professional codes give no indication of what action to take when the profession itself acts inappropriately. Professional codes do not consider this possibility. Furthermore, the professions have not adequately considered their collective responsibility to society, or how it is to be met. Our discussions of corporate responsibility and accountability can be fruitfully applied to the professions. Work along these lines is still in its early stages. But unless professions both acknowledge and live up to their collective responsibilities, society has no moral warrant for not tightly controlling them through legislation.

Professional Ethics

Ethical codes do not exhaust the issues of ethics in the professions.[7] They do not usually deal with a great many of the more pressing issues with which the professions are grappling. That is not their purpose. Codes are general guidelines for professional action, and they specify particular prohibitions and ideals, each of which can be evaluated from a moral point of view. As we have noted with regard to the prohibition on advertising, particular items of professional codes can be and are sometimes challenged and revised.

Many of the ethical issues that arise within each profession are not covered by the profession's code. Some of these are intertwined with public policy issues; others are intertwined with issues of business ethics; still others are intertwined with both. For instance, ethical issues in medicine often gain media attention as a result of advances in medical technology; these issues raise ethical questions not only for those in medicine but also for those in business and for those involved in formulating public policy. The ethics of organ transplants, of the use of fetal tissue, of various forms of surrogate motherhood, and of genetic engineering are pressing and prominent issues in medical ethics. Each of them has implications for public policy as well as for business ethics. Suppose that kidney transplants are ethically justifiable under certain conditions and that there is a shortage of available kidneys for transplant in the United States. In India it is legal for people to sell a kidney, for which they may receive up to $10,000. Is it ethically permissible for a company to buy and sell human kidneys internationally? The question is an issue in medical ethics, in the ethics of public policy, and in business ethics. Simply because it is legal in some countries for people to sell their organs does not make it ethically right. Nor does the fact that such kidneys are available make it ethically permissible to buy them since doing so promotes, supports, and encourages the practice.

For-profit hospitals, pharmaceutical companies, medical technology companies, and the like are all businesses. Their business practices are intertwined with the medical-related work they do. The professionals they have working for them will face complex ethical issues—some of which are more

---

[7] There is a large literature on professional ethics in general as well as on ethical issues within particular professions. Among the many available, see Michael D. Bayles, *Professional Ethics*, 2nd ed. (Belmont, Calif.: Wadsworth Publishing Company, 1989); Alan H. Goldman, *The Moral Foundations of Professional Ethics* (Totowa, N.J.: Rowman & Littlefield, 1980); Mike W. Martin and Roland Schinzinger, *Ethics in Engineering* (New York: McGraw-Hill, 1983); David S. Schrader, *Ethics and the Practice of Law* (Englewood Cliffs, N.J.: Prentice Hall, 1988); Tom L. Beauchamp and LeRoy Walters, *Contemporary Issues in Bioethics*, 3rd ed. (Belmont, Calif.: Wadsworth Publishing Company, 1989); and Andrew Jameton, *Nursing Practice: The Ethical Issues* (Englewood Cliffs, N.J.: Prentice Hall, 1984).

clearly issues in medical ethics or in business ethics, and others of which are a mixture of the two. A comparable state of affairs holds for engineering firms, where issues of engineering ethics and business ethics frequently overlap, converge, and are intermingled; for newspapers, television, and the media in general, where issues in media ethics are mixed with issues of business ethics; and for legal firms in which issues as mundane as advertising have both a legal and a business side for ethical analysis.

Ethical issues seldom fall neatly into the kinds of divisions people have devised to study and discuss them: business ethics, medical ethics, legal ethics, engineering ethics, media ethics, and so on. Insofar as any of the activities enter into the business realm, they have aspects of business ethics. As a result, there is a fair amount of carryover. Arguments that hold for the legitimacy of advertising in general, for instance, are likely to be applicable to legal, medical, engineering, and other kinds of advertising as well. Privacy with respect to medical records and the right of people to give informed consent before being subject to medical experiments carry over into the right of workers with respect to their medical records and to their being subject to experimentation in the workplace.

Members of the various professions face special problems related to their work, which sometimes raise ethical issues specific to the profession. The specialized study that constitutes the various fields of professional ethics has proven to be useful. But the professions are all part of the broader society, and their codes should cohere with the broader ethical norms of the society, whose good the professions should serve.

Professional Organizations

Members of a profession tend to gather and organize into professional organizations and associations, just as workers tend to gather into unions. The role of the professional association is to promote the profession's interests, to provide a forum for discussion, and to disseminate information concerning the profession. Professional associations also tend to be both the promulgators and the enforcers of professional codes. Although this is appropriate, some professional associations need policing.

A professional association has the de facto (if not always the legal) power to control entry into the field, dismiss certain practitioners from the field, set policy for its members, and restrict access to publication for those whose work it does not approve. Such organizations are sometimes asked for advice by government; publishers ask them for definitive texts; and others ask them to recommend consultants and experts. The power of the officers of professional organizations is often uncontrolled and sometimes excessive. Such power can be damaging to those members of the profession who disagree with the organization's leadership or policies. Professional organizations are often able to silence opposition to the organization's policies and prevent minority views from being heard on public as well as professional issues. Such cases have led to the suggestion that professional organizations should be subject to independent review by those outside the profession; that there should be lay participation in hearing disciplinary cases under the code; and that an independent group should serve as the recipient of complaints made by the public against members of the profession, and follow the handling of the complaint by the profession.

Professional associations have tended both to monopolize power in the area of the profession's prestige and to safeguard the vested interests of their members. The failure of those in the professions and professional associations to police their ranks erodes the basis for society's trust of the profession and for its autonomy. In professional codes, provisions for reprimand, censure, and expulsion are usually phrased so as to preserve secrecy rather than to publicize immoral activities by members of the profession. If a profession has higher moral standards than those required by law, the professional organization should not only make these standards generally known but should also reveal infractions of these standards by members of the profession.

Because the professions have access to and control over specialized knowledge, the public is dependent on them for the effective use of this knowledge. The members of the profession are in the best position to know how their fellow professionals can abuse this knowledge and how they can take advantage of the public. Yet professional organizations rarely inform ordinary persons of ways to protect themselves against malpractice or unethical or immoral behavior by a member of the profession. Nor do professional societies ask for increased competition within professional ranks, greater disclosure regarding the activities of their members, lower fees, and so on. Changes that the professions could make that would be in the public interest would be a higher code of ethics, greater disclosure of their activities, and active encouragement of demystification of their jargon and simplification of their language.

Professional associations should also provide a forum within the profession or industry, at which members can raise ethical issues that the association can face and provide solutions for—or work toward solutions—that can be morally justified to the general public. To ask the professionals in an industry to help the public achieve more disclosure about a profession or industry might seem like asking them to go against their own best interests. But it is in the general interest of the professions, and of industry, to foster and develop public trust. There is no better way to do so than by full, understandable, and proper disclosure.

Professional societies have often failed to fulfill their obligations in the defense of members of the profession who lose their jobs or are otherwise penalized for following and living up to the code of the profession. Those who work for an employer (e.g., a corporation) are sometimes asked, or are required, to perform some action that violates their professional code. For instance, the typical engineering code states that the safety, health, and welfare of the public shall be held paramount in the performance of professional duties. Suppose an engineer for a tire company sees that the tires being produced are unsafe, reports this to his superiors, including the board, and gets no reaction except to be told to keep quiet and mind his own business. But he knows that the code of his profession requires that he hold the safety of the public paramount, and accordingly he informs the newspapers that the tires are unsafe. This leads to an investigation, to a recall of the tires, and to a penalty for the tire manufacturer. Typically, this engineer would be fired; perhaps he would be blackballed in the industry. And typically, no professional engineering organization would come to his defense for upholding its code. Yet such a defense seems professionally and morally mandatory if professional organizations expect their members to take their codes seriously and to live by them.

The Professions in Businesses

The case of the whistle blower in the tire factory manufacturing defective tires is a classic instance of a professional conflict between the demands of a professional code and the demands of an employer. Although any employee may have blown the whistle (e.g., on a tire manufacturer), the engineering code places a special, more stringent obligation on engineers than on others to be concerned with public safety.

A professional code of conduct appropriately demands more of professionals than of ordinary workers. If professionals are self-employed, they may be able to live according to a higher standard of conduct. But what if they are employed by a corporation that demands they conform only to the letter of the law? Do they have special obligations because of their role as members of a profession, and does a company act immorally if it does not respect these higher obligations?

The situation is especially difficult for doctors, engineers, nurses, and others who work for large corporations, hospitals, or firms. Doctors not only in corporations but also in HMOs are finding an increased tension between their professional responsibilities to their patients and the orders they receive. Some HMOs do not authorize certain tests, referrals, or procedures that a doctor feels are necessary for the best care of his or her patient. In such cases should the doctor inform the patient of his or her recommendation, even though the HMO won't pay for it? What if the HMO specifically instructs the doctor not to mention alternatives that are not covered? Does that take precedence over the care for the patient the doctor would under different circumstances recommend? Engineers and nurses are often treated as if their only duty is to obey orders—do what they are told. What does a nurse do when hospital rules require doctors to scrub before an operation but one doctor refuses to do so and tells the nurse to mind his or her own business? What do engineers do when they believe that the safety of some design is questionable, advise against using it, and are told that for cost reasons the company refuses to change the design? What if an actuary sees that what he has produced is used in a way that he did not intend, or that it may be misleading, even though in his report he took pains to make sure his methods and assumptions were clear? Perhaps in none of these cases will the danger to the public be serious enough to mandate whistle blowing. But in each case, a professional would rightly feel that his or her professional code demands taking some action. Does loyalty to one's professional code take precedence over loyalty to one's employer?

There is no agreement on the appropriate answer. The typical professional code is not written to handle this problem, nor do the professional societies insist that employers respect the right of professionals in their employ to follow the letter and the spirit of the professional codes.

Members of the professions, just as everyone else who works for a firm, have the obligation *not* to do what is *immoral*. They have the obligation to employ their knowledge as they deem appropriate and to warn of unsafe products, illegal activities, and dangerous work conditions. But they do not have the responsibility to make final judgments that appropriately belong to management. Typically, an engineering judgment, a legal judgment, and a medical judgment are only part of the relevant information that goes into to a managerial judgment. Professionals should make their professional views and concerns known. They should insist that public safety be protected when it is clearly threatened. But they have no obligation to insist that their way of doing things be observed, or that their fears carry the day in a disputed area. The special obligations of those in professions require them to do more than others, be more sensitive to how their work is used, and be more alert to violations of ethical standards in their firms. Yet even here we can distinguish between what they are morally required to do as individuals from what they are professionally required to do. The limits on what they are professionally required to do are set not only by the code but also by the extent to which the profession as a whole is willing to support them.

Journalists have long fought for the right to preserve the secrecy of their sources. In their fight against the courts, they have generally been supported by their fellow journalists, their newspapers or TV stations, and the news media in general. Such support is an indication of a profession's commitment to a principle. The right to preserve the confidentiality of one's sources is a right that journalists have insisted on and convincingly defended. A right to confidentiality is claimed and generally given to priests in the confessional, to lawyers and their clients, and to doctors and their patients.

Members of the various professions may have special rights and duties that outweigh their obligations to corporate loyalty and obedience. But until the profession as a whole—its members and its professional organizations—stand up and defend those professionals who strive to live up to the professional code by which they are supposed to live, neither the public nor most employers will take such rights and duties very seriously.

We can draw several conclusions concerning professional rules and moral obligations.

1. Professions and members of professions deserve more autonomy in their actions than do others, providing they impose upon themselves, and live up to, higher demands than those required of others. The specific nature of these higher demands will vary from profession to profession. But in general they will concern serving and protecting the welfare of society—the general public, and their clients or patients in the realm of their professional expertise.
2. When one becomes a member of a profession, one not only incurs individual moral obligations insofar as he or she fills an individual professional role but also shares in the collective moral obligations of the profession.
3. The moral obligation of the members of a profession thus extends beyond each one's individual activities. A member of a profession has the obligation to police his or her professional peers, to help change professional structures if they need changing, and to be concerned with the impact of the profession on society. (This aspect of professional moral obligation, we have noted, is ignored by professional ethical codes.)
4. Members of a profession sometimes encounter special moral problems in business, because of conflicts of interest and conflicts between one's professional obligations and the demands of one's employer. Professions should help defend those members who live up to the professions' higher standards in those cases.

Because members of professions are moral beings first and only secondarily professionals, professional ethics cannot appropriately relieve a person of the general moral obligations that apply to all people. To choose to be a member of a profession is to choose greater, not lesser, moral obligations, and it is only to the extent that its members fulfill these moral obligations that the professions deserve respect.

The Professions as Business

To contrast the professions and business is to give only a partial picture, for many members of the professions are also businesspersons. Lawyers and engineers frequently move up the corporate ladder to management positions. Lawyers, doctors, accountants, consulting engineers, and members of many other professions are in business for themselves. As more and more groups claim the status of a profession, the line between the professions and business blurs even more.

In considering the professions as businesses, we shall focus only on a few aspects that tend to distinguish them from other businesses: restriction of entry to the field, restrictions on competition, and service to the public.

We have already seen that the medical profession has practical control of most aspects of the health industry. For many years there has been a shortage of doctors—at least in certain portions of the country. Rural areas and ghettos, for instance, are poorly served. Doctors as a profession set the standards that must be attained to practice medicine. They control the degree requirements for the M.D.; they also decide how many students should be trained in their medical schools and how large the medical schools should be. They set up the testing and other procedures required before one is allowed to practice medicine. All of these practices can be justified. Yet when doctors trained abroad have difficulty being licensed, and when the shortage of doctors remains chronic despite a large pool of applicants for medical school, the profession is open to the charge of restricting entry. The charge is reinforced by the fact that doctors now are typically among the more affluent members of society, whereas in previous eras they were among the less affluent. The responsibility for supplying doctors for all sectors of society is held collectively by the profession. It is, moreover, a responsibility that individual members of the medical profession cannot simply ignore as being not their concern or their moral obligation.

Entry into the legal profession has also become more difficult than it once was, even though the supply has kept up with, and at times even exceeded, the demand.

Would society be better off if it were deprofessionalized? Have the professions become too strong? Have they won protective legislation that makes their services necessary, without reason? Could midwives and paraprofessionals perform some of the services that are now the exclusive right of doctors? Are lawyers really needed to draw up wills, file for divorce, and defend those charged with minor offenses? Can the law be simplified so that the intelligent layperson could adequately handle these and similar tasks? The answer to these questions is still hotly debated. Yet a comparative study in the United States and other countries provides evidence that we are overlegalized and overdoctored.

What of the other professions? The techniques of licensing and claims to specialized knowledge have made entry into certain areas difficult, as we have noted. When used to keep fees up and to keep competition out, such techniques are clearly not in the public's interest.

Restrictions on competition among those already in a profession affect two areas in particular: professional limitations on advertising and the setting of fees.

The prohibition on advertising by doctors, lawyers, architects, and members of other professions has a long history (see Chapter 11) and is not restricted to the United States. The prohibition, moreover, has frequently been included in codes of professional conduct and backed up by law. Many reasons are given for the prohibition. Some point to the outrageous claims made by quacks and peddlers of patent remedies for diseases ranging from the plague to cancer. Others claim that if doctors, lawyers, and similar professionals could advertise, the public would be poorly served. The best advertisers rather than the best practitioners would probably get the most patients and clients. Furthermore, the personal relation of doctor to patient and lawyer to client is developed and not just promoted. Such relations are neither fostered nor established by advertising. A third claim is that advertising undermines the dignity of the profession. Clearly, though the arguments carry some weight with respect to some advertising, they do not make a very strong case for the total prohibition of it.

The prohibition against advertising by the professions has been found to be unconstitutional—an abridgment of First Amendment rights of freedom of speech and the press. The professional codes have been changed to reflect this ruling. Yet we have not seen a rash of advertising by doctors, lawyers, architects, and others. Why not? There are two possible answers. One is that the members of these professions have been raised on the prohibition against advertising, are unaccustomed to advertising, and are therefore not advertising from past habit. The other is that the absence of advertising has always benefited the professions and not the public. Lack of advertising reflects a lack of competition. By restricting entry, doctors have all the patients they can handle. Why seek more through advertising? Thus, removing the law against advertising and removing the statement in the codes against advertising have had little effect on actual practice.

The second area of concern is the setting of fees by the professions. Is this unfair restraint of trade? Members of the professions, it is claimed, should not haggle over fees. To do so would be demeaning, undignified, and, in a word, unprofessional. A second argument claims that a sliding-fee schedule would give the professional an upper hand when faced with a desperate individual who needs his or her help, but put a professional in a poor bargaining position vis-à-vis a large firm. The same service would cost the individual who could least afford it more than it would the rich corporation. The claim is that the setting of fees assures equal access and guarantees equal fees for equal work. However, this does not justify the reluctance to reveal fees or the lack of competition in setting professional fees. The ordinary person rarely shops around to inquire how much the various doctors in a town charge, nor is this part of general knowledge. The ordinary person's approach to medical and legal service is strangely removed from consideration of the fees that members of the profession charge. There is no obvious competition on the basis of fees. Some professions have even recommended minimum fees to be charged for certain services, a practice clearly in the interest of the profession and not in the interest of the public.

The practice of "payment by results" further protects the self-interest of the professional at the expense of the public. It is rarely practiced by doctors. They do not charge only if the patient gets better or only if the patient survives the operation; they charge for the use of their skill and their time. The practice of charging by results is more common in civil suits in which lawyers take a certain percentage of the amount awarded their clients if they win the suit and nothing if they do not. However, the temptation is to sue for a larger amount than otherwise is justifiable, so as to collect higher fees.

The dual role of businessperson and professional involves many potential conflicts of interest in which making money is opposed to serving the client or patient as best one can. Such conflicts make disclosure all the more necessary. Those professions that prefer to work under a veil of tacit secrecy must be more open to the public scrutiny of their business practices.

The professions are an important aspect of the American business scene. Actions of the professions and their members can and should be evaluated from a moral point of view as objectively and critically as the actions of business.

Study Questions

1. In the Johns-Manville case, did Dr. Smith have an obligation to inform workers of potential risk when management did not do so?
2. Was it ethically permissible for the company to file for bankruptcy if its aim was to avoid future suits for asbestos-related claims? Why or why not?
3. What is a *profession?* Distinguish a *profession* from a *professional.* Give examples of each.
4. Does it make any difference whether or not society recognizes a group as a profession? If so, why? If not, why not?
5. In what ways has society allowed professions more autonomy than other groups?
6. State the argument in favor of allowing a profession to govern itself. State an argument against it. Which argument is stronger?
7. In what ways have members of professions set higher standards for themselves than society sets for other groups? Illustrate with examples from two professions.
8. What is a professional ethical code? Is it morally binding? Why or why not?
9. Under what conditions is self-regulation by a profession justifiable?
10. If a professional code is to justify a profession's autonomy, what characteristics should the code have? Why?
11. Can codes serve some useful function? Which ones?
12. What is the role of a professional association?
13. How might professional associations foster moral practices by its members?
14. Do members of professions have any special moral obligations, different from those of other employees or workers? Why or why not?
15. Do members of a profession (e.g., doctors) have any collective obligations as members of that profession?

16. Is the prohibition against advertising by members of a profession morally justifiable? Why or why not?

17. A company doctor, Helen Mack, starts to notice an increasing number of cases of emphysema among the long-term workers in the company's plant. She reports this to management and is told to keep monitoring the number of cases but not to say anything to anyone else. The next year, as the number of cases increases, she believes she has found a correlation between the age of the ventilating system in different parts of the plant and the incidence of the disease. She reports this finding to management and is told to keep monitoring but not to make any tests or say anything lest she upset the workers. Does she have an ethical obligation to do as she is told? Does she have an ethical obligation to do something other than what she is told?

MORAL ISSUES IN INTERNATIONAL BUSINESS

19

>─┼─◆>─•─O─•─<◆>─┼─<

THE INTERNATIONAL BUSINESS SYSTEM, MULTINATIONALS, AND MORALITY

The Bhopal Case

On December 3, 1984, a poisonous cloud rose silently above the Union Carbide plant in Bhopal, India. Before it dissipated it had killed over 3,000 people and had injured over 200,000 others. It was the worst industrial disaster on record. It took place in a less developed country and was caused by modern technology used by a foreign subsidiary of an American-based multinational chemical corporation. Yet it raised the question of the obligations of multinational corporations operating in less developed countries.

The Bhopal case is complicated, and there are differing accounts of what actually led to the disaster.[1]

The Bhopal plant, which produced Sevin, a widely used agricultural pesticide, had been expanded by Union Carbide at the request of the Indian government to provide more jobs. As an incentive, the government allowed Union Carbide an exception to India's 1973 Foreign Exchange Regulation Act, which allowed at most 40 percent foreign ownership of companies located in India. The Indian government allowed Union Carbide, Inc., the American parent company, to own 50.9 percent of Union Carbide, India, with the Indian government and Indian interests holding the remaining 49.1 percent of the company's shares. The Sevin the plant produced was sold in India and increased

---

[1] For details of this case, see *New York Times,* January 28, 30, 31 and February 3, 1985, front pages; June 23, 1987, p. 6; June 22, 1992, p. C5; Larry Everest, *Behind the Poison Cloud: Union Carbide's Bhopal Massacre* (Chicago: Banner Press, 1985); and Paul Shrivastava, *Bhopal: Anatomy of a Crisis* (Cambridge, Mass.: Ballinger Publishing, 1987).

crop yields by about 10 percent, providing food for an additional 70 million Indians. Prior to the expansion of the plant, Union Carbide had shipped to India Sevin made in the United States.

The Bhopal plant had indeed provided employment for a number of Indians, and it had attracted a large population of other Indians, who formed a large shanty town outside of the plant grounds. Sevin is made from Methyl Isocyanate (MIC), which is kept in large vats in liquid form, prior to turning it into the pesticide. For a variety of reasons, on that December evening the liquid in one of the tanks turned to its gaseous form and escaped through the plant's vents. The fatal cloud passed over the shanty town, wreaking its havoc.

In 1984 the Bhopal plant was operating at a loss and was producing only about one-third of its capacity. It was run entirely by Indian managers and workers. Union Carbide, Inc., had made a safety inspection in May 1982 and had found a large number of safety deficiencies. Union Carbide, India, had reported that all the deficiencies had been or were being corrected. However, on the night of December 3, five safety devices that had been originally installed were inoperative or failed. Among these a scrubber, which was to detoxify leaks, was under repair; the refrigerator unit, which was to keep the MIC cool, had been shut off for six months, while the refrigerant was being used in another part of the plant; and a metal barrier that was to keep water from leaking into the MIC liquid had been removed and not replaced. In addition, the concentration of chloroform, which was to have been monitored daily, had not been checked for six weeks and was thirty-two times that needed. Water, either by sabotage (as Union Carbide claims) or by accident, entered the tank, causing the temperature to rise and the MIC to turn to gas. Two lower level employees failed to take proper measures when this happened, and it was only after a supervisor hosed the tank for forty-five minutes with cold water that the leaked stopped.

Union Carbide claims sabotage. Others place responsibility for the accident on Union Carbide's failure to use the same automatic safety mechanisms in India as it did in its plants in the United States and its failure to supervise the running of the plant closely enough. Others attribute the accident to poor management on the part of the Indian executives who ran the plant, to the Indian workers who were not adequately trained, and to the Indian government, which was lax in enforcing its safety standards.

Who should have been held responsible for the disaster, and what sort of compensation should have been paid to those injured and to the families of those killed?

The issue of compensation was not finally settled until 1992, almost eight years after the tragedy. Immediately after the accident, American lawyers swarmed over Bhopal seeking to file suits on behalf of those killed or injured. Suits were initially filed in the United States because Union Carbide, Inc., was an American company, because settlements are much higher in the United States than in India, and because American law allows for punitive damages, whereas Indian law does not. The Indian claims totaled over $15 billion. The total assets of Union Carbide, Inc., were about $10 billion. The company was insured for damages of up to $200 million.

Union Carbide initially offered $50 million in compensation. Although the Indian government paid $794 to the relatives of those killed in cases for which the government was responsible, Prime Minister Rajiv Gandhi rejected Union Carbide's offer, stating that Indian lives were as valuable as American lives and that the government would seek compensation equivalent to that typically paid in such incidents in the United States or $500,000 per fatality. All the Indian cases were consolidated by the Indian government and presented in New York before U.S. District Judge John F. Keenan. The U.S. court refused to hear the case and transferred it to the Indian courts, as the proper venue. Judge Keenan also recommended negotiations to achieve an out-of-court settlement. If the case went to court and if Union Carbide could prove that the tragedy was the result of sabotage, it could be relieved of paying any compensation. While the company and the Indian government bickered, those injured and the families of those killed received from both corporate and government sources only token amounts: $550 to families of those killed and $83 to those injured. The final out-of-court settlement in 1992 amounted to $470 million.

The Bhopal plant was closed immediately after the accident and has not been reopened.

Who was morally responsible for the harm done? If, in fact, the tragedy was a result of sabotage, should Union Carbide be held responsible? If Union Carbide, Inc., had held less than 50 percent interest in the Bhopal plant, would its responsibility have been different? What was the moral responsibility, if any, of the Indian government in the incident?

Morality and the International Economic System

Thus far, we have considered the morality of the free-enterprise system in the United States and the morality of a variety of business practices within that system. But the American system is not an isolated one. The United States is a world power; just as its political interests extend far beyond its borders, so do its economic interests. Lenin called the last stage of fully developed capitalism "imperialism." He claimed that the developed countries were able to reduce the level of exploitation of their own workers by shifting the worst aspects of exploitation to their colonies. However, this colonial theory had to be modified once the European industrial powers lost their colonies. The United States, moreover, was never a colonial power in the sense that England and France were. The present-day version of the Leninist charge is that the capitalistic, advanced industrial nations of the world are able to prosper because they exploit the people and resources of the Less Developed Countries (LDCs) of the world. The brunt of the attack on the developed industrial countries often falls on the activities of their Multinational Corporations (MNCs).

The international economic system is not simply an extension of the American system. Involved in the system are a great many other countries, each with its own economic system, together with its own political system and its own social and historical background and institutions. The total international economic system is a result of the extension and interaction of all of these.[2]

When we examined the capitalist system in the United States (see Chapter 7), we noted that government fulfills many necessary functions, such as keeping competition fair, providing a safety net for those who through no fault of their own cannot compete, and protecting the interests of workers and consumers. It was only in the context of a developed social and political system that we found the American system to be ethically justifiable. What of the international system?

We can, of course, analyze each national system, just as we did the American system, to see whether each one is ethically justifiable. But that is not our present concern. Rather, if we look at the total international stage on which business operates, can the system as a whole be ethically justifiable?

We can sort out three issues in sketching an answer to this large question. The first concerns the unequal distribution of wealth. Unlike individual nations, there is no international redistribution system according to which the wealthy are taxed to help support the poor. This is the basis for the claim of some nations that a new international economic order is ethically required, which would redress the imbalance.[3] Short of that, we can ask, what obligations, if any, do rich countries have to poor countries? We shall postpone a discussion of this question until Chapter 21.

The second issue arises from the fact that, although the American system of free enterprise is situated within the framework of the American legal, political, and social system, there is no comparable international framework for international business. Business in the United States is constrained by various laws, by a set of accepted ways of conducting business, by a variety of understood practices and shared values, and by unions, consumer groups, environmental groups, and a host of other informal organizations and mechanisms. It is within this framework of what we can call "background institutions" that business operates. Although background institutions vary from society to society, there are many similarities among those in most of the developed countries. The number of such restraints are fewer in the less devel-

---

[2] Some general discussions of the international system are Richard Falk, Samuel S. Kim, and Saul H. Mendlovitz (Eds.), *Toward a Just World Order*, vol. 1 (Boulder, Colo.: Westview Press, 1982); Peter G. Brown and Henry Shue (Eds.), *Boundaries: National Autonomy and Its Limits* (Totowa, N.J.: Rowman & Littlefield, 1981); Charles Beitz, *Political Theory and International Relations* (Princeton, N.J.: Princeton University Press, 1979); and Robert F. Meagher, *An International Redistribution of Wealth and Power* (New York: Pergamon Press, 1979).

[3] "Declaration on the Establishment of a New International Economic Order," in United Nations General Assembly, A/9556 (Part II), May 1, 1974, *Study of the Problems of Raw Materials and Development: Report of the Ad Hoc Committee of the Sixth Special Session.*

oped countries, both because they have had a shorter time to develop them in response to business activities and because those countries are often too poor to be able to afford the kinds of governmental agencies, such as the Occupational Safety and Health Administration and the Federal Drug Administration, that are expensive to run.

The absence of effective background institutions on the international level is even more striking. Although international law covers some areas, it is not always enforceable (especially against large and powerful countries). The United Nations and its commissions have no power to enforce its guidelines governing trade and commerce. And there is no international police force that is capable of enforcing even agreed-upon rules. Although the nations of the world are not totally in a state of nature, the rules that govern the interactions of nations, trade between nations, and the actions of large corporations that operate in many countries are dependent on agreement, moral persuasion, indirect pressure, and goodwill. The need for ethics is greater in this kind of situation than in a society with a fully developed, enforced set of background institutions.[4]

This brings us to the third issue. If we grant that ethics is important in international business, whose ethics should business follow? In discussing ethical relativism, we saw that this is a specious question: There is no American ethics as opposed to a German or a Japanese or a Russian or a Turkish ethics. At both a basic level and at a high level of generality, ethics is the same for everyone. In all countries murder, stealing, lying, and breaking contracts are wrong. No society could function if these basic norms were not observed for the most part. Nor could business operate. Business operates on trust that contracts will be honored, that goods promised will be delivered, that those who receive goods will pay for them, and so on. Similarly, the high-level norms of utilitarianism and Kantianism can be applied universally, and almost all nations of the world have recognized the Universal Declaration of Human Rights.

Nonetheless, we have noted that American business practices have developed and are ethically justifiable within the framework of American background institutions. These include customs and laws, neither of which are determined in detail by ethics. There is no reason to think that only American customs and laws are ethically justifiable and that therefore American companies must act in all countries just as they do in the United States. On the contrary, it is appropriate for foreign individuals as well as foreign companies to observe the laws and customs of the countries in which they find themselves, providing that these customs and laws are not themselves unethical. On the world stage there are many ethically justifiable mixes of values, many different ethically permissible ways of living, many different ethically accept-

---

[4] For a fuller discussion of business ethics in the international realm, see Richard T. De George, *Competing with Integrity in International Business* (New York: Oxford University Press, 1993); and Thomas Donaldson, *The Ethics of International Business* (New York: Oxford University Press, 1989).

able systems of law. As a result, although American companies that operate in different countries are required to act ethically in all of them, they are not ethically required to act the same in all of them. Yet a company of integrity cannot change its ethics as it moves from country to country. To attempt to do so is to give up any semblance of acting ethically or with integrity.

Multinational Corporations and Ethics

Multinationals are corporations that operate extensively in more than one country, usually through branches or subsidiaries engaged in production, marketing, or both. Multinational corporations have their headquarters not only in the United States, but increasingly in Japan, Germany, and other industrialized countries as well. Even some less developed countries, such as Brazil, have developed multinational corporations that operate in many countries. For purposes of simplicity, however, we shall focus on American multinationals, in part because they were among the first and because in the 1960s and 1970s they bore the brunt of criticism.[5] Critics of multinationals loudly proclaimed that multinational corporations operate to benefit themselves and their interests, with no moral or legal constraints on their activities.

Multinational corporations are not immoral in themselves. The fact that Japanese firms operate in the United States, either independently, as Sony does, or in cooperation with an American corporation, as Toyota does (with General Motors), is no reason to call them immoral. Nor is the fact that Ford has factories in Germany a reason to feel that it operates immorally. But when large multinationals operate in less developed countries, critics claim that, although they do not *necessarily* operate immorally, often they do *in fact* operate immorally. Developed countries are able to control foreign firms. Less developed or developing countries are not able, or are less able, to do so, especially when the firm has greater total sales than that country's gross national product.

On the international level there is no effective way to prevent firms from forming cartels and controlling prices and production. We see this clearly in the case of OPEC (Organization of Petroleum Exporting Countries). Critics charge that the large international oil corporations (the seven largest have been called the Seven Sisters) have conspired to limit the production of oil, creating false shortages, and driving up the price without any regard to whom they hurt by such action. Because these companies operate internationally, it is not possible for any government to check their books, worldwide, or to prevent such collusion. Other multinationals are charged with supporting repres-

---

[5] Of the many attacks on America multinational corporations, see, for example, Richard Barnet and Ronald Mueller, *Global Reach: The Power of Multinational Corporations* (New York: Simon & Schuster, 1974). A set of conference papers discussing the ethical issues of multinationals is W. Michael Hoffman, Ann E. Lange, and David A. Fedo (Eds.), *Ethics and the Multinational Enterprise* (New York: University Press of America, 1986).

sive governments that serve the interests of the MNCs, exploiting workers in less developed countries, marketing dangerous drugs and unsafe equipment, and disrupting the culture and traditions of other nations. We shall start by looking at some of the general attacks on American multinational corporations. We shall then examine some particular charges and cases.

The following are three general, major charges: (1) MNCs operate immorally in the less developed countries by exploiting workers, by exploiting natural resources, and by reaping exorbitant profits; (2) MNCs compete unfairly in the LDCs, to the detriment of the host countries; and (3) MNCs are a major cause of the impoverishment of the LDCs and of the unrest found there. Each of the charges has some basis in fact and history.

Multinationals and Exploitation

Multinational corporations operate in less developed countries for a variety of reasons. They seek cheap labor, available resources, tax shelters and relief, and markets. If they did not think they could make a profit in a less developed country, they would not establish subsidiaries there. In seeking cheap labor, they operate just as they do in the United States. Many textile factories, for instance, moved from New England to the South to take advantage of cheaper labor there. Were the Southern workers exploited because they were paid less than Northern workers? We cannot conclude that they were simply because the workers were paid less; the charge of exploitation requires more than the existence of a comparatively low wage scale. In discussing a fair wage, we saw that this requires background institutions that are just, which include minimum-wage laws and welfare programs as alternatives to workers having to accept *any* wage offered in order to live. In many LDCs fair background institutions of this sort are woefully lacking. Under such conditions, it is difficult to speak meaningfully of a fair wage set by the market. Without the restraints imposed by background institutions, the market does not guarantee fair wages; the market inclines firms to go in the direction of paying the lowest wages possible. Sometimes this is lower than what is required for subsistence. To the extent that this is the case, the wage is not a living wage; it does not allow the worker to live in dignity as a human being, and it can be ethically faulted. Some MNCs are guilty of paying such wages, and that practice can be ethically condemned. But the situation is more complicated than a blanket condemnation would warrant.

In many situations, multinationals pay the same rate as the local employers. If the other employers fail to pay a living wage, they are as guilty as the MNCs. But in other cases, local businesses criticize the MNCs for paying more than the going wage. The businesses complain that the multinationals thus attract the best workers, leaving the less skilled or less productive workers to work in the locally owned firms. Furthermore, they say that the multinationals force up the wages that workers in general expect, in some instances to more than local firms can afford. The MNCs are thus caught between contradictory demands. Some critics demand that they pay more, and others demand that they pay less than they do.

The solution is to pay a living wage, even when this is not paid by local firms, and otherwise to pay only as much as necessary to get competent workers, given the competitive situation of a particular region or country. Although most people would not expect the MNCs to help develop labor unions or to lobby for the passage of minimal wage or other laws, the MNCs should not work against any such developments. And to the extent possible, they should foster an atmosphere in which the development of fair background institutions is facilitated.

The exploitation of resources raises a different problem. Mineral resources represent one of the assets of a country. The resources, however, do little good unless they are removed from the earth and sold or used. There is no moral demand that resources extracted from one country be used only in that country. If that were the case, oil-poor countries would be precluded from buying the oil they need. The complaint against multinational corporations, therefore, cannot be simply that they extract minerals and ship them out of the country. The complaint is that the MNCs buy the mineral rights for a very low price and sell the minerals abroad for a much higher price. The natural-resource wealth of the LDCs is thus being extracted and diminished. Those who are profiting by the extraction are not the less developed countries but the MNCs. The complaint is well taken. It was just such a situation that led to the OPEC nations' raising the price of oil, ensuring a large return on their diminishing assets. Oil-depletion taxes in the United States are a means by which states seek to be repaid by those who extract oil, thereby making the state that much poorer in resources. Once a state's nonrenewable resources are used up, it has lost that portion of its wealth. Taxes reaped from the depletion, however, help offset the loss.

LDCs can take measures to offset exploitation of their resources by MNCs, and more and more are beginning to do so. Multinational corporations are morally bound not to take advantage of the LDCs, and governments are morally permitted to impose regulations or taxes on the extraction of minerals. The United Nations has drafted a "Charter of the Economic Rights and Duties of States," which includes a chapter on multinationals and the rights of states with respect to them. The UN has also established a Commission on Transnational Corporations and an Information and Research Center to monitor multinationals and to draw up a code of conduct for MNCs. These are all steps in the direction of helping the less developed countries to control the blatant abuses of multinationals. The LDCs can tame the MNCs and ensure that their presence helps the host country, by providing employment, transferring organizational knowledge and productive techniques, and paying their fair share of taxes.

If American MNCs pay workers very low wages, pay little for natural resources, and sell in the United States at the regular prices the products they produce in LDCs, they clearly have the opportunity to make significant profits. They can also price their products somewhat lower than the going price for similar products produced in the United States. They thereby gain a greater share of the market, without reducing their profit margin by more than is necessary to undersell the competition.

Those Americans who felt the LDCs were being treated unfairly complained; those in the United States who felt they were losing jobs to cheap labor abroad complained; and those who felt they were faced with unfair competition complained. The complaints were often justified, and various remedies have been suggested or tried. Import taxes on some of these goods have forced up the price and reduced the profit; export taxes imposed by the LDCs have helped the LDCs share in some of the profits of the multinationals. Competition has developed among the MNCs themselves, so that the profit margin has been driven down—to the benefit of the consumer. But international background institutions are still not adequately developed, and codes cannot be effectively enforced.

MNCs try to play one less developed country against another in an attempt to get the most favorable conditions possible. Only slowly are LDCs learning that they can play one company against another as well. They can establish laws governing the allowable growth of MNCs; they can require companies to hire a certain proportion of a firm's managerial staff from the local population; they can demand that profits be reinvested in the host country instead of being sent to the parent country; and they can renegotiate initial conditions of operation to their own benefit, after a firm has developed an expensive plant in the host country and is unable to move elsewhere.

The Unfair Competition of Multinationals

The charge that MNCs compete unfairly in the LDCs has two major components. One is that the MNCs are able to operate on especially favorable and uncompetitive terms. The MNCs can borrow money from local lenders at favorable rates because they are sound and competitive. The result is that little local capital is left for local firms, and the rates for the capital that is left are often higher than for the MNCs.

The second charge is that MNCs do not carry their fair share of the cost of social development, which imposes greater burdens on local industries. MNCs frequently utilize advanced technologies, which local companies do not have or cannot afford. The MNCs are thus able to be more productive. The result is that they not only pay higher wages but they also hire fewer people than the local firms who produce the same product. They are thus able to underprice the competition and often force local firms out of business. The MNCs also negotiate low tax rates, and by manipulating transfer payments among their affiliates worldwide, they pay little tax anywhere. The overall result is unfair competition. Hence, the MNC does the host country little good.

These charges are often well founded. But at least some of the LDCs have found ways of countering the dominant position of the MNCs, as many policies adopted by Latin American countries show.[6]

Capital formation is a crucial issue for developing countries. Capital is often in short supply. Under such conditions, LDC national policy can restrict the amount that a multinational corporation can borrow; and it can require that MNC profits be reinvested or loaned within the host country. The difficult situation many Latin American countries find themselves in, however, results more from external borrowing by the country or local firms than from MNCs tying up all the local capital—even though that is sometimes a contributing factor. The national debt of some Latin American countries is so large that the country must use a major portion of the money it receives from exports merely to pay the interest on its loans. The moral blame, if blame is to be assessed, falls on MNCs, on the lending banks, on the borrowing countries and their elites, on oil-exporting countries, and on the policies of the developed countries. Except for purposes of determining instances of compensatory justice, however, determining blame is less important than finding solutions to the debt and to the capital-development problems of LDCs. Latin America faces a worse debt problem than many African countries, which were too poor even to qualify for loans or to attract MNCs.

The charges that MNCs use advanced technology, are more productive, and undercut local firms are in part true. Some people urge MNCs to utilize more labor-intensive productive processes and thus equalize competition with local firms and increase employment opportunities for the local population. However, competition in itself is not unjust. Some less developed countries have taken a more positive approach to the problem. They have allowed foreign companies to establish only firms that do not compete with local firms. A country gains little or nothing by allowing a foreign company to operate to the detriment of a local producer of the same product. But a country can gain if a foreign enterprise establishes a plant that produces and sells locally a desired product not produced locally.

The less developed countries give multinationals tax advantages in order to attract them. But this makes sense only if the multinational in other ways contributes to the wealth, development, and good of the country. Transfer payments are related to taxes. Transfer payments are payments made by a multinational to its various divisions or affiliates. Where profits are highly taxed, it is to the benefit of the MNCs to put low prices on products sold to other parts of the firm, thus claiming low profits. Where profit taxes are low, they put high prices and claim higher profits on products sold abroad to other affiliates. This in turn lowers the profit and taxes paid by the affiliate in the

---

    [6] See Fernando Henrique Cardoso and Enzo Faletto, *Dependencia and Development in Latin America* (Berkeley: University of California Press, 1979); and Michael Novak and Michael P. Jackson (Eds.), *Latin America: Dependency or Interdependence?* (Washington, D.C.: American Enterprise Institute for Public Policy Research, 1985).

receiving country. A multinational is able to change prices from country to country to suit its needs, transferring prices at intervening countries where necessary, prior to selling a product in the United States. The United Nations' Code of Conduct on Transnational Corporations proposes that MNCs engage in "arm's length" pricing—that is, it proposes that prices among an MNC's affiliates be figured as if each affiliate or division were truly independent. Less developed countries can demand this.

The attacks on MNCs have not been misplaced. But the age of the multinational robber baron is slowly drawing to a close. The financial crisis in many countries makes them unattractive places in which to invest, and in other countries governments are learning from one another how to use MNCs to their own advantage. Abuses still take place, but as government controls increase, firms have more reason to adopt policies that do not grossly exploit a host country. The more responsibly MNCs behave, the less likely a host country will impose restrictive legislation on them.

Multinationals and Impoverishment of Less Developed Countries

The charge that MNCs are the cause of the impoverishment of less developed countries and of the unrest found there is partly correct. Colonialization was a mixed blessing for most nations. To some extent the substructure of the countries was developed. Roads were built where none existed before, water was made safe to drink, schools and hospitals were built, as were airports and railroads. Industry was imported and work and capital provided. But in the colonies and in general, the people of all LDCs were poor before colonization. Hence, the sense in which they were impoverished is not in the ordinary sense of the word. They were impoverished culturally. Their cultures were disrupted; Western ways were imposed on the people, and if not imposed then imported and made attractive, so as to seduce many of the local population. Division, unrest, and raised expectations that could not be fulfilled were the results. Some responsibility falls on the more developed countries for enticing people with goods and products they could not afford and did not previously want or need. Moreover, people of the less developed countries were also impoverished in a comparative sense. Poverty is not only an absolute condition; it is also relative. When all are poor, people do not feel as poor as when they are poor and others have much more. By increasing their wealth, the rich make the poor relatively poorer. In these two senses, the industrial countries are in part responsible for the poverty and unrest of the less developed countries.

There is a third sense in which the developed countries are partly responsible for the impoverishment of the LDCs; paradoxically, this is related to the gains made by the LDCs. The more developed countries have helped eradicate some of the diseases—such as smallpox—that ravaged some countries; through medical technology they have decreased the infant mortality rate and increased the average life expectancy of the people of many countries. At the same time, this has contributed to the population growth in many LDCs, which poses enormous problems and leads to increasing poverty and starvation.

Fourth, several MNCs have directly helped produce starvation in some countries. The typical scenario is this: An MNC goes into a country and buys up large portions of the productive land. It then grows cash crops for export, whereas, before, local farmers grew food for local consumption. The best land is thus taken out of production for local consumption, people are no longer able to grow their own food, and the result is frequently increased malnutrition or starvation. Multinational corporations have played this role and continue to play it. Multinational corporations, just as do other corporations, have an obligation not to harm and must consider the consequences of their actions. They cannot act with moral impunity. Some LDC governments, moreover, are learning to control the actions of multinationals in the agricultural sector. They are requiring cooperation with local farmers, limiting the amount of land that can go into cash crops, and taxing profits for the benefit of the people. All of this requires governments that are not corrupt, that do not benefit by colluding with MNCs at the expense of the people, and that are strong enough and stable enough to control and restrict MNCs. The number of countries in which these conditions prevail is growing, but unfair practices have by no means been eliminated.

The abuses of multinational corporations in less developed countries need not, and should not, be denied, ignored, or excused. But even taken at their worst, and as a whole, they do not establish the case that the American free-enterprise system rests on the exploitation of LDCs. That less developed countries offer potential markets cannot be denied. That continued expansion by American companies is made easier by such markets is obvious. But the claim that the developed countries depend on exploiting less developed countries does not follow from the claims we have examined. The arguments do show that there is a tendency on the part of MNCs toward injustice, which must be controlled. Some practices are immoral and should be changed. The advantages that the system brings to less developed countries at least offset the costs imposed by it on them. As in our analysis of the free-enterprise system in the United States, the arguments that critics mount do not show that the extension of the system through American-controlled multinationals is inherently immoral.

The role of the multinationals is not, however, the same as the role of the United States in international economic affairs, even though they are related. The United States, because of its size, wealth, and global importance, intervenes in the economy of many nations even if it does nothing to them directly. Its internal monetary and fiscal policies, for instance, affect the interest rates other countries must pay for loans, and influence inflation rates. Its import and export policies also influence what happens in many MNCs. Does the

United States have obligations toward other countries? It has at least the obligation not directly to harm them through its practices. Where it has knowingly and willingly done harm, it owes reparations. Furthermore, the United States has sometimes acted benevolently, but despite its good intentions has caused harm. This happened, for instance, when it sent sugar to Bolivia for humanitarian reasons. The distribution of the sugar required all the distributive resources of the country. As a result, the local wheat growers were unable to transport their wheat to market and were forced out of business. Although the United States intended no harm, it was causally responsible for it. In this case the United States is more guilty of paternalism than of exploitation. The United States can help avoid unintended harm by working more closely with local governments and by replacing paternalism with cooperation. If the United States wishes to help a country, it can support programs developed by the country itself, especially when these help the poor, provide employment, and lead to self-improvement. Whether the United States has obligations to other countries, based not on charity, reparations, or self-interest but on the rights of other countries, we shall investigate in Chapter 21. Its obligation not to harm other countries, however, is not necessarily violated by its adherence to a free-enterprise economy and the extension of that system into the international domain.

Ethical Guidelines for Multinational Operations

The striking structural difference between the American system and the system of international business is the paucity on the international level of background institutions—which include laws and accepted practices, moral norms, and social demands—to control or guide international business. The situation is doubly bad with respect to less developed countries, which tend to have inadequate background institutions internally as well. This situation makes possible many great abuses. It underlines the need for developing adequate background institutions and provides grounds for arguing that there is a moral imperative to help establish just international background institutions. Their absence, instead of being a license to act immorally, is a demand that they be established. Until they are, morality has a greater rather than a lesser role to play in the conduct of multinationals.

Although MNCs are not inherently immoral, we can fruitfully evaluate, from a moral point of view, the activities of individual multinationals in specific countries. Neither the less developed countries nor all multinationals are the same. Yet, based on our discussion thus far, we can list a number of moral norms that apply to U.S. multinationals (and those of other developed countries as well) operating in less developed countries.

The first norm, "the moral minimum," is the norm to *do no intentional direct harm*. This moral minimum applies to all actions of all people, corporations, and countries. To do intentional direct harm is to willfully harm another, and unless done in self-defense or with some similar overriding reason, it is generally immoral and widely recognized as such. When applied to the relations of U.S. companies and LDCs, it has a number of obvious implications. Dumping toxic products—such as the children's pajamas containing fire-retardant asbestos fibers, which were prohibited for sale in the United States and Europe—would be one example of doing harm knowingly and willingly and taking advantage of the lack of legal restraints to the detriment of the consumer. Similarly, selling pesticides and drugs that the seller knows will be misused or even, if properly used, will cause harm—an action of which some American multinationals are guilty—is prohibited by this rule. Obviously, gross pollution of air, land, and water is precluded. Less obviously precluded is the acquisition of the prime farmland previously used for growing local foodstuffs, and its conversion to cash export crops, if this leads to starvation or serious malnutrition for the local population.

The second norm builds on the first. Not only should the multinational do no direct intentional harm, but if its activity is to be morally justified, its activity must benefit the host country. This means that good to the multinational cannot be traded off against harm—even unintentional, indirect harm—to the host country. A typical utilitarian analysis might seem to justify a transaction that produced great good to the multinational and serious harm to the host country as long as the good was greater than the harm. But if one takes a broader point of view, given the already poor condition of the host country, to make its lot worse in order to better the position of the United States or of a U.S. MNC is to deepen that country's problems and to make the gap between developed and less developed countries greater rather than less—hence the justification for this second norm.

A corollary to this norm is that the good of the country is not the same as the good of corrupt leaders or the good of an oppressive elite of the country. The good of the country must include the good of the ordinary people of the country. This distinction is crucial.

The third norm is to respect the human rights of the workers, consumers, and all others in the host country. Like the first norm, this applies to all companies operating in all countries. But it is primarily in the LDCs that multinationals tend to violate the norm, primarily because of the great poverty and high unemployment rates found there and because of the frequent absence of protective local legislation. This norm prevents not only engaging in slavery and apartheid, but also paying less than subsistence wages and failing to provide adequate and safe working conditions. If local companies are guilty of violating this norm, that cannot be taken as justification for acting in like manner. The argument leads not to the conclusion that if others violate rights we are allowed to do so also, but to the conclusion that if others violate rights and we cannot compete effectively without also violating rights, either we do not compete or we attempt to get background institutions that protect the human rights of all.

This leads to the next two norms. The fourth norm is to promote the development of just background institutions internally within the country as well as on the international level.

The fifth norm requires a multinational to respect the laws of a host country and to respect as well its culture and local values, providing these do not violate human rights or impose immoral laws. If apartheid is immoral, then even if it is legal, a multinational has no more right to engage in the practice than do the local firms. Yet, given that caveat, multinationals should respect the local laws and cultures and seek neither to undermine them nor to replace them. To do either would be a violation of the first norm of doing no harm, and this fifth norm is simply an application of that first one. Moreover, as a guest in a foreign land, an outside multinational generally has no right to interfere with the local government and should not stand in the way of or lobby against reforms or laws that protect the workers or consumers, even if such laws make operating in these countries less profitable.

There is a narrow line between, on the one hand, working toward just background institutions in LDCs and on an international level and, on the other hand, observing one's proper place by not interfering with the internal affairs of a country and respecting its culture and values. Nonetheless, it should be clear that supporting a government's efforts in establishing just background institutions constitutes neither inappropriate interference nor the promotion of self-interest at the expense of the host country.

These five rules are examples of the kind of rules that can be generated and defended with respect to the actions of multinationals in less developed countries. Following these rules will preclude many of the unjust practices with which multinationals are so often charged.

Multinationals and Human Rights

We have seen that multinationals are obliged to respect human rights wherever they operate. Exactly what this means, however, is not a simple or non-controversial task. The UN Universal Declaration on Human Rights is a widely accepted beginning point. Starting from there we can talk about the obligations of multinationals with respect to human rights on three levels, and the issues raised in each are somewhat different. On the first level, the multinational has the obligation to respect the human rights of all those with whom it has contact—its employees, its suppliers, its customers, the people in communities who are impacted by its actions, and so on. Most of the rights listed in the Universal Declaration, however, are rights that people have against governments: the right to liberty, the right to be free from slavery and torture, the right to equality before the law, the right to freedom of thought and religion, and the right to an education, for instance. The right to freedom from slavery clearly also applies to corporations and prohibits them from using slave labor. The Declaration includes the right to employment under favorable conditions and the right to a just wage. There is also the right to an adequate standard of living. These economic rights restrict multinationals in various ways and prohibit gross exploitation. Although there is much debate about exactly what constitutes a just wage in particular locations and what adequate standards of living are, multinationals for the most part acknowledge these rights, even though sometimes they, as well as local firms, violate them. When multinationals are at fault, a good investigative press tries to pick up on it and various interest groups have their eyes open for violations by multinationals.

The second level has to do with multinationals using contractors or suppliers or engaging in joint partnerships or joint ventures. Just as multinationals may not directly violate human rights, so they may not indirectly violate them by using contractors or suppliers or joining partners who violate human rights. Just as they may not employ slave or child labor themselves, they may not purchase items from those who employ such labor. Local firms that employ child labor violate the human rights of the children just as the multinationals who employ them do. Although international consumers and organizations can put pressure on multinationals that they cannot put on local firms, the violations are no less violations if done by indigenous firms than if done by multinationals. This fact puts on the multinationals the obligation to ensure that the contractors, suppliers, or partners with whom they work do not violate human rights. Many U.S. multinationals inspect the premises of the contractors or suppliers they use to make sure that the working conditions are safe, that children are not employed, and that workers are decently paid. This is not something above and beyond what is required of them. It is what they are obliged to do. They must take whatever reasonable measures they can to make sure that they do not indirectly violate human rights by working with local companies that do violate them. The larger the multinational and the more business it does with local suppliers where violations of human rights are suspected, the greater the effort the multinational is required to make to ensure that it is not indirectly violating human rights.

The third level in which human rights come into play is the level of operating in countries whose governments engage in egregious violations of human rights. We noted that many of the rights listed in the Universal Declaration are rights that people have against their government—such as freedom from torture, freedom of thought and religion, and equality before the law. Governmental violations of human rights may be a result of governmental policy that directly affects multinationals, such as the apartheid laws in pre-1991 South Africa, or it might be the result of government actions of a political nature that do not directly involve multinationals. The first case, in which the government policy involves multinationals, is in fact a subset of our discussion concerning the first level. Multinationals may not directly violate human rights, even if the law of the land directs them to. Multinationals could not ethically follow the South African apartheid laws that required them to discriminate against blacks. The issue then became whether they could ethically do business in such a country if they did not obey the laws.

The question of whether multinationals may operate in countries in which the government seriously violates human rights but does not require that multinationals do so is hotly debated. In some cases, such as Burma (Myanmar) in the 1990s, conditions became so bad that in order to apply pressure on the government to end its political oppression, to recognize the results of fair elections, and to respect basic human rights; the U.S. government prohibited new investments there by any U.S. person or firm. But carrying on business in other countries that are known violators of human rights is more controversial. The Chinese government, for instance, is accused of imprisoning political dissidents simply because they protest the government's actions; of having engaged in a brutal action against its citizens in Tiananmen Square in Beijing in 1989, killing many protestors; of severely controlling the practice of religion; of using forced labor in some of its factories; and so on. Under these conditions, are multinationals ethically permitted to do business in China and other countries with similar records? Clearly, they may not do so if they either directly or indirectly engage in violations of human rights on the first two levels, that is, by violating human rights themselves or by using suppliers that do. Nor may they do so if they directly help the government of the country to violate human rights by providing the means or the finances for them to do so. Beyond that there is less agreement, although if they do operate in such countries, they should do what they can to help prevent abuses of human rights. Individual companies may not be able to do much, and usually cannot, and should not enter into local politics. Yet multinationals together or large multinationals that have contact with high government officials sometimes can have an impact and make a difference. Some multinationals have decided against doing business in countries that grossly violate human rights; others have decided to enter such markets cautiously. At the very least, whether or not they are able to bring about changes in governmental policy, while operating in such countries they must take all measures possible to ensure that they do not violate human rights either directly or indirectly.

International Codes

The absence of effectively enforced international background institutions does not mean that there are no accepted international standards governing business and that therefore any company of integrity must develop them from scratch. We have already noted the basic moral norms common to all societies and necessary for the conduct of business. But we should not ignore standards that have been hammered out since the late 1970s and that have been incorporated into a variety of codes. The United Nations' proposed Code of Conduct on Transnational Corporations is but one example. Although not all of its standards are ethical standards, many of them are, such as "respect for human rights and fundamental freedom" (item 14), "abstention from corrupt practices" (item 20), standards on transfer pricing (item 33), consumer protection (items 37–40), environmental protection (items 41–43), and the disclosure of information (item 44). Agreement has been reached on these and most of the other items of the code, with only a few remaining in dispute.[7]

Nations that accept the final set of standards may either accept them as goals or adopt them into national legislation. However, all the work that has gone into that document clearly should be a starting point for both national codes and a variety of more specific industry or business codes.

Industrywide codes have also been established. Two types are most significant. One type is exemplified by the UN code governing the sale of infant formula.[8] This is an international set of standards that has been agreed to by the infant formula companies worldwide. In those cases in which the companies are not in full compliance, the public and certain groups have acted as watchdogs, monitoring compliance. Failure to live up to the code led, for instance, to a call for the renewal of the Nestlé boycott in 1988.[9] The second type of code is exemplified by the industrywide Guiding Principles of the "Responsible Care" program adopted in 1988 by over 170 members of the Chemical Manufacturers Association (CMA) of the United States.[10] These principles are a self-imposed set of standards of safety and responsibility with respect to the production, sale, and disposal of chemicals worldwide. Since 1990 the chemical manufacturers of various countries have adopted codes of practice based on the CMA's Guiding Principles, have adopted specific targets to improve their safety performance, and have set up norms against which they can be judged and they can judge themselves. There are no official sanctions for failure to comply, but companies committed to the principles indicate that they will apply peer pressure to help ensure compliance.

The adoption of the principles followed Bhopal and other disasters. This industry self-regulation perhaps was undertaken in order to avoid governmental regulation. Nonetheless, it is self-regulation worldwide, and pressure for compliance is coming from members of the industry itself. It can serve as a model for other industries as well. Companies of integrity in each industry can take the lead in articulating appropriate industry norms and in committing themselves to living up to them.

The difference between self-regulation of business and governmental regulation is not necessarily an adversarial one. A company that wishes to act ethically in international business may well find itself in competition with other companies from the same or from different nations that for reasons of

---

[7] United Nations, Economic and Social Council, E/1990/94, June 12, 1990, contains the "Proposed Text of the Draft Code of Conduct on Transnational Corporations." For an overview and discussion of other codes, see John M. Kline, *International Codes and Multinational Business: Setting Guidelines for International Business Operations* (Westport, Conn.: Quorum Books, 1985).

[8] See *International Code of Breast-milk Substitutes* (Geneva: World Health Organization, 1981).

[9] See Chapter 11 for details of the case. The Action for Corporate Accountability sounded the call. Nestlé denied the charges and promised to abide by the code.

[10] The Guiding Principles of the program were published in full-page ads in the *New York Times* and the *Wall Street Journal* on April 11, 1990.

profit behave unethically. If big enough and strong enough, the ethical company may nonetheless compete successfully, although it would prefer the rules to be the same for all. Since no company can control the actions of all other companies, a company of integrity may desire and lobby for national and international standards that make the rules of competition equal for all companies. In this case, government may legislate what those companies that wish to compete ethically desire. Thus, the relations of government and business often coincide, and the picture of government as the watchdog and regulator of business, and of business and government on opposing sides, offers only limited and partial views that hide other important relations.

Automotive safety provides an example in which competition on safety has played a more effective role than government regulation. Rather than wait for government to mandate airbags, some auto manufacturers introduced this safety feature prior to regulation as a selling point. Given the internationalization of markets and competition, once one company takes the lead in this regard, others not only in that country but throughout the world are pressured by the market to do likewise.

This illustration shows the importance of leadership on the part of some companies and industries. The principle of noblesse oblige obtains here. Setting higher standards than the existing norms takes imagination and courage. To serve as an example, the company must somehow be visible, and that often means the company must be large and already be an industry leader in productivity or quality of goods or market share. Leaders can set standards by their actions against which other companies are judged.

The best starting point in the further development of standards for international business is self-regulation by business within the guidelines and standards that already exist. A general rule is that government should do only what business is unable or unwilling to do on its own. Business is best suited to know where the potential for abuse lies. It is gratuitous to assume that all firms wish to exploit such potential, for if they did, the general public would sooner or later call for remedies. In some instances, industries can and do set standards and police themselves. U.S. antitrust laws recognize the danger that self-regulation is open to some abuses and collusion. Internationally, since we have no worldwide government, the dangers exist. Hence, both nationally and internationally, we cannot depend solely on self-regulation by business. But government is not the only necessary body that sets standards; also important are a variety of private bodies, media, enlightened consumers, and vocal workers' groups. When the conditions of competition are structurally unfair, then self-regulation does not work. It is here that the role of government comes in. But just as there are unethical companies, so too there are unethical governments. In these cases the subjugated, exploited, and abused people, other countries and governments, and other groups can provide some counterweight.

Although government is presently only national, controlling abuses by transnationals can in part be achieved by governments acting in concert. The

BCCI case demonstrates what is needed. The BCCI scandal was an international phenomenon in which no government had adequate control over the banking facilities worldwide that allowed the abuses to take place. Secrecy in banking is part of the problem, and that is an issue that must be resolved in part by the banking industry and in part by the countries of the world agreeing on conditions under which secrecy is not overriding. Any countries that refuse to regulate the banking industry within their borders can be forbidden access to banks in other countries that agree to such standards.

Standards can be reached in a variety of ways: by a commission of the United Nations to which all concerned parties have access; by agreements among nations directly; and by agreements and standards drawn up by the banking industry, with or without outside representation, such as the standards drawn up by the chemical industry. Other models—such as one involving model codes drawn up by groups or commissions composed of practitioners, governmental representatives, academic experts, and the general population—are possible. In any case, all such groups should start from what already exists in the way of standards, both in the industry in question and in other areas.

If negotiations are not carried on government to government, then individual countries must adopt any model code or any code reached or presented. Only if all or most countries adopt them will they be effective worldwide. Those who refuse to adopt them, unless they can defend such refusal on reasonable ethical grounds—which will indicate a defect in the negotiation process or the end result—can appropriately be pressured to accept by public opinion, by refusal to do business in that area with that country, or by other means.

In addition to government, standards can be enforced through the media, which often serve as a watchdog when not dominated and constrained by government or big business; through the general public, both as workers and as consumers; and through the large number of intermediary groups in society, from unions and environmental and consumer groups to churches and Amnesty International, scholarly associations, and grass-roots movements, clubs, and groups. Given the lack of international enforcement by an executive body, these intermediary groups become essential in the more informal enforcement of standards. Publicity, for instance, takes on a crucial role and is an effective tool in the enforcement of standards, providing the people so informed of infractions are moved by the stories, news, and results of the investigative reporting they receive. The media, after all, made known the *Valdez* spill and publicized the Bhopal disaster. The media probed and brought to public attention the BCCI scandal. The positive role of the media is to encourage firms to abide by generally acknowledged standards or face public exposure. The negative task is to uncover violations to expose. But without a public interested and responsive to reports of violations, the media are ineffective.

Ethical standards adopted by firms are a reflection of ethical standards held by people. Hence, the importance of public opinion and public pressure cannot be overstated. In the end it is public input that makes the difference between standards that are respected and followed and those that are benignly ignored or allowed to atrophy.

The solution to acceptable international standards for business depends not only on business and government but also on the many people whom business and government serve. In the last resort, people get both the business and government they demand and so in a sense deserve. The same is true worldwide.

We can now turn from a consideration of general codes to a moral evaluation of some particular practices and cases. We shall continue to concentrate on American-based firms. Many moral issues are involved in the charges made against American multinationals. We can illustrate and sort out some of these by discussing two controversial situations: the marketing abroad of pharmaceutical drugs that are prohibited in the United States and the transfer of dangerous industries to underdeveloped countries.

Multinational Drug Companies

The control of pharmaceutical drugs is probably more restrictive in the United States than in any other country in the world. The Food and Drug Administration (FDA) has adopted stringent requirements for testing drugs, and any drug allowed on the market in the United States must pass long and comprehensive testing. The FDA also determines which drugs require a doctor's prescription.

The argument in defense of the FDA's actions is that lives and health are at risk in the taking of any drug. Unless a drug is found to be safe, it should not be sold. If a drug is known to have certain dangerous side effects, it should be sold only under certain conditions, for people under a doctor's care. If the drug is known to cause cancer or some other serious illness, it should not be sold at all, or only under rigidly controlled conditions. The drug thalidomide was not authorized for sale in the United States but was prescribed by doctors in Europe. Its use by pregnant women resulted in large numbers of seriously deformed babies in the 1950s. Such disasters explain the FDA's insistence on high standards.

American drug companies, however, often feel that the FDA standards are too rigid; that the testing required is too expensive, cumbersome, and long; and that it is inappropriate to impose U.S. standards on the operation of U.S. companies in other countries. They claim that as long as they do not act illegally in those countries, there is no reason why they should not market whatever is allowed.

The morality of the action of these companies is not settled by determining whether what they do in other countries is legal. On the other hand, the morality of their actions abroad is also not settled by simply determining whether they live up to American standards abroad.[11] The standards may be appropriate for Americans but inappropriate for people of some other countries because of special circumstances in those countries. We can distinguish several typical cases and investigate them from a moral point of view. Consider the following three hypothetical cases.

Case 1: Drug Company XYZ produces a drug that relieves the symptoms of migraine headaches. It is marketed in the United States and is initially thought to be safe enough for sale over the counter. After it is widely used, however, it is determined that one of the side effects in a significant number of patients is severe depression, sometimes leading to suicide. The drug is therefore considered too dangerous for sale over the counter in the United States and is allowed only for use by those under a doctor's care. Doctors are warned of the dangerous side effects and are cautioned to be alert to signs of depression in their patients. The drug is sold in many countries besides the United States. After the U.S. action, some other countries take similar action. Others do not. Drug Company XYZ continues to market the product in these other countries. It is sold over the counter, and no information is provided about its possible dangerous side effects.

Case 2: Drug Company MNO develops and tests a drug that is slightly more effective than insulin for diabetics. After some use, the drug is found to produce cancer. It is forbidden in the United States. Drug Company MNO continues to market it where it is not forbidden to do so.

Case 3: Drug Company ABC develops a drug that helps cure glaucoma. There is no other effective drug for this ailment on the market. After some extended use, the drug is found to produce cancer in a significant number of cases. The drug is taken off the market in United States. The drug company continues to market it in those countries in which it is legal to do so.

The three cases raise a number of different issues.

Is the action of Company XYZ morally justifiable, and if not, why not? In trying to decide, consider two substantive second-order principles that might apply. Principle 1: A drug company should not sell any drug that it knows to be harmful in any way. Principle 2: A drug company should not sell any drug that it knows to be harmful without informing the purchaser of the harmful effects.

The first of the principles is too strong. In Case 1, Drug Company XYZ was allowed to sell the drug in the United States to those who had a doctor's

---

[11] Some specific attacks on the drug industry are contained in Milton Silverman, *The Drugging of the Americas* (Berkeley: University of California Press, 1976); and Milton Silverman, Philip R. Lee and Mia Lydecker, *Prescriptions for Death: The Drugging of the Third World* (Berkeley: University of California Press, 1982).

prescription for it. It is morally justifiable for the FDA to allow some drugs, which have possibly harmful side effects, to be sold. The reason is that the side effects are usually less serious than the illness that is being treated; the risks involved are worth taking, providing the patient and the doctor know about them and decide to take the risks, exercising due caution. The second principle is morally sound. We can justify it in a number of ways. If we consider the purchase of the drug as a free transaction, such transactions are justifiable if both parties have the relevant knowledge concerning the transaction, and freely enter into it. If the drug company knows of the drug's ill effects but does not disclose these to the purchaser, the purchaser does not have the information necessary to make a competent decision concerning the transaction. To keep this information from the buyer is morally inappropriate because the buyer will assume that the product is safe. The transaction is thus not morally justifiable. We can reach the same conclusion by asking whether the drug company is treating the purchaser as an end rather than simply as a means of earning profit. Because it does not warn him of dangers of the drug, the company treats him only as a means, and hence treats him immorally.

Adopting the second principle, Drug Company XYZ therefore can be morally faulted, not for selling the drug but for selling it without informing the potential purchaser of the dangers of its use. Note that if this analysis is correct, it is morally permissible for Drug Company XYZ to market the drug as an over-the-counter product in the countries where this is allowed—even though it is not allowed to do so in the United States and other countries—providing its side effects are clearly indicated and users are properly warned. The argument does not claim that the U.S. standards are the only appropriate ones, that all countries must adopt them, or that drug companies must adhere to them wherever they operate. This is not morally required. Standards other than those adopted by the FDA may be appropriate in other countries. But some standards are necessary. It would clearly be wrong to sell drugs that did little good and were known to be harmful, even if the selling of such drugs were legally permitted in some countries. It would also clearly be wrong to sell drugs without adequate warning of possibly harmful side effects. Drug companies are morally bound not to inflict harm on others knowingly. To the extent that they do, drug companies act immorally even if they act legally.

In Case 3, there is no other drug for the disease, whereas in Case 2, an alternative drug is available. The argument for marketing the drug (in Case 2), which is only slightly more effective but more dangerous than insulin, is difficult to make. We might argue that if the company makes the risks known to the public, then it may sell the drug to those who wish to buy it. But why anyone would wish to buy it is not clear because the harm significantly outweighs the benefit of using it instead of insulin. Thus, if we assume that only those who really do not know what they are doing would use this drug instead of insulin, we can conclude that, despite its issuing a warning, the drug company is trading on the ignorance of the consumer. To so trade at the consumer's expense is to take unfair advantage and hence to act immorally. The case, however, is not as clearly immoral as it would be if the drug were marketed without any warning of its dangers.

The drug in Case 3 helps cure glaucoma but tends to produce cancer in some people. There is no other drug on the market for this ailment. Once again, the drug can be morally sold only if those who buy and use it are informed of its dangers. But even when informed of the risks, people may choose to use it, preferring to chance getting cancer rather than suffer blindness. That the drug is not allowed in the United States indicates that the FDA does not think the risk is worth the cure. But others may feel differently and weigh the odds differently. If a person is relatively old, and if the drug takes many years to produce cancer, the person may feel the risk is worth taking. His or her doctor may agree.

A principle implicit in this analysis is the principle of informed consent. In order for the transaction to be morally permissible, the purchaser of the drug must be truly informed. A warning sentence, in small print, on page three of a technical information sheet inside the box is hardly adequate notice of the danger. The purchaser should be informed of any danger before purchasing the drug, and the information (e.g., on the box) should be readily visible and understandable.

If adequate information about the ill effects of the drug is not supplied to the potential purchaser, the practice is immoral. If adequate information is supplied, if there is no alternative drug, and if the risk is reasonable, the sale of the drug is still justifiable, whether or not its use is allowed by the FDA in the United States. However, if there is a similar or better product available, one that does not have the ill effects of this particular drug, the latter should not be marketed at all. The principles apply to drug companies wherever they operate.

Some countries are unable to fund the kind of extensive testing operations that are conducted by the United States government or required by it. These countries have passed laws, however, that prohibit a drug company from marketing a drug that has been prohibited for sale in the country of origin. Some drug companies, wishing to market their drugs but also wishing to abide by the law, have adopted a number of practices for which they have been morally condemned. Some have added an inert substance to a drug so that, technically, it is not the same item, even though it has all the same effects. Then the drug has been marketed in the foreign country under a different name. Others have produced the drug that has been outlawed in the United States in some third country, where it is not outlawed, and then they have shipped it elsewhere. Both of these practices are within the letter of the law in the countries where the drugs are finally sold, even if they are clearly outside the spirit of those laws. The morality of *these* practices depends not on whether the law has been circumvented but on whether the companies that act in this way are doing harm to the people who take the drug, and whether they are supplying adequate and appropriate information. Their critics claim the drug companies frequently fail to supply such information. If this is so, then the companies act immorally.

These cases illustrate some of the difficulties of dealing with multinationals. How laws can be rewritten to prohibit the sale of drugs outlawed in the country of origin is an unsolved problem. Some solutions might be that all nations adopt similar rules and standards or that an agency, such as WHO or UNESCO, set minimal standards. Some nations might then adopt more stringent regulations. Until international standards are adopted, the temptation of drug companies to abide only by the legal minimum in each country will remain. Succumbing to the temptation will benefit the drug companies, mainly at the expense of the poorer and less developed countries—those who in the long run will be least able to cope with the negative effects of such drugs on their people.

The Transfer of Dangerous Industries to Underdeveloped Countries

Consider the following case: Asbestos USA (a fictitious name) produces asbestos products for the U.S. market. It competes with asbestos products made in Mexico. It is able to compete, despite the fact that Mexican labor is so much cheaper than labor in the United States, because it operates more efficiently and with more advanced equipment than do the Mexican companies. We now know that asbestos causes cancer. Those exposed to it for long periods had a significantly higher rate of cancer than others. The rate was especially high for people who worked in asbestos plants. The United States therefore passed legislation requiring the introduction of a series of safeguards for people working in asbestos plants. Asbestos USA calculated the cost of implementing the safeguards and decided it could not implement them and still stay in business. Rather than close down completely, however, it moved its plant to Mexico, which has not passed comparable safety legislation. Asbestos USA continues to market its products in the United States, even though it manufactures its products in Mexico. There, it operates its equipment in the same way (i.e., without safeguards) as it did in the United States; however, it has to pay its workers only the going wage for the industry in Mexico.

By moving its plant to Mexico, is Asbestos USA acting immorally?

Exposure to asbestos tends to produce cancer in a significant number of people. This is the overriding consideration to which the American government reacted when it passed legislation requiring safeguards. No company, it has ruled, has the right to expose its workers to cancer if this can be prevented. The ruling is a defensible one. It applies to all industries and to all asbestos manufacturers. But obviously the U.S. rule applies only in the United States; it does not apply to asbestos factories in other countries. If Asbestos USA's imports were subject to an import duty, it would have little incentive to move to Mexico. But because this is not the case, it moved its plant. This move is better for its shareholders than if the company had gone out of business. The asbestos products would be bought from Mexican firms anyway, so why not have an American company selling asbestos products to the United States, as well as Mexican companies? These considerations, however, fail to respond to the major issue: Is it moral to expose employees to the danger of cancer when this can be prevented? If the answer is no, then it is not moral to so expose Mexican workers.

Which second-order principle is applicable to this case? Here is one possible principle: It is immoral to hire anyone to do work that is in some way dangerous to his or her life or health. But the principle, as stated, is too strong. Any job might be dangerous in some way; therefore, if it were immoral to hire someone to do work that was in any way dangerous, no one could be hired to do many jobs that seem perfectly acceptable. But we must also acknowledge that some jobs are more dangerous than others. Firefighters are paid to put out fires, but they know they risk their lives in doing so. Police are also paid to risk their lives. Yet most people would be reluctant to say that hiring people to do these jobs is immoral. The immorality, therefore, does not come from hiring people to do work that involves risk to life or health. But we can defend the principle that it is immoral to hire someone to do work that is known to the employer to involve significant risk without informing the prospective employee of that risk. This application of the principle of informed consent is defensible, as guaranteeing a fair exchange between consenting adults.

If we adopt this principle, then Asbestos USA could be morally right in hiring workers in Mexico, with working conditions that would not be allowed in the United States, if the potential workers were warned of the dangers. We can assume that once warned of the dangers, the workers would agree to work in the plant only if they received more pay than they would for comparable work in a factory in which they were not exposed to the danger of cancer. If this were not the case, it would be an indication that the people who were hired were in some way being forced into the jobs—were not free agents, contracting freely and knowingly to do dangerous work at pay they considered appropriate to make up for the increased risk. A contract between employer and employee is fair if both parties enter into the contract with adequate appropriate knowledge and if both freely agree to the terms of the contract.

The critics of Asbestos USA contend that the Mexican workers, even if they are informed of the dangers and are paid somewhat higher wages than other workers are paid (Brazil requires triple pay for dangerous work), are forced because of the lack of work in Mexico to accept employment in asbestos plants, at less than adequate pay. Hence, the critics contend, despite protestations regarding informed consent, the workers are forced to take such jobs and are exploited in them.

Informed consent is *necessary* if the action is to be moral, but it is not *sufficient*. There are some things (e.g., selling oneself into slavery) to which no one can morally consent. There are also some conditions that are immoral for an employer to impose on his or her workers, even if the latter agree to work under those conditions. Consent is not enough because people who desperately need money may agree to work under almost any conditions. Built into capitalism is the tendency of employers to pay workers as little as possible and to spend as little as possible on a safe work environment. In the United States, this tendency has been offset by unionization and government legislation. In countries where it is not offset, employers can take unfair advantage of workers and engage in immoral practices. If Asbestos USA wishes to operate its plant in Mexico, it can morally do so only if it informs the workers of the risk, in terms they can understand; if it pays them more for undertaking the risk; and if it lowers the risk to some acceptable level. It need not be at the same level demanded by the Occupational Safety and Health Act (OSHA) in the United States, but morally, it cannot be at a level so high that risk is maximized rather than minimized. It would also be immoral not to eliminate risks that could be removed without extravagant cost. If, in Mexican plants, asbestos particles float freely through the air, collecting like cobwebs, and if workers are not even given paper masks, it is clear that minimum safety standards are not being observed.

Why does the Mexican government not pass laws similar to those in the United States concerning safeguards for workers? Why do not all nations pass such laws, so as to preclude such moves as that made by Asbestos USA because it would be unprofitable? The answer is that not all countries are as affluent as the United States. A wealthy country can afford to spend more to protect the health of its people than can a much poorer country. The standards of cleanliness and safety that the United States can enforce by law are much higher than those that businesses in many countries could afford. Traditions also vary from country to country. There is no reason to think that the traditions of the United States are the only right ones and that all the world must become like us. This attitude is itself condemned by many because it is considered a form of U.S. imperialism. The United States is a democratic country, and its people enjoy a large measure of freedom. Some other countries are not democratic or are much less so. The literacy rate and the level of education of the average person are much higher in the United States than in many other countries. Americans must be careful not to set their standards as the model of what every nation should do if it wishes to be moral. U.S. standards do not constitute the moral norm. Although morality is universal and does not differ from country to country, conditions do differ from country to country, and therefore, what morality demands in different countries may well vary. What may be required by the principle of utility in one country may not be required by the same principle in another country, because the consequences of adopting the practice in each of the two countries may differ significantly. What may be prima facie right in both countries may be the proper thing to do in one country but not in the other because of conflicts with other duties or rights, owing to differing circumstances.

We return to our example of Asbestos USA. The Mexican government sometimes passes laws concerning health and safety which are different from those passed in the United States. We cannot conclude that the Mexican government cares less for the welfare of its people than does the American government for its citizens. U.S. industry is more technologically developed than Mexican industry. Mexican industry is more labor-intensive, on the whole, than U.S. industry. Mexico seeks to attract foreign industry to help develop its potential, to train its people in work skills, and to bring in tax and other revenue. Imported industry also provides work for Mexicans who would otherwise be unemployed. Suppose that for these and similar reasons the Mexican government decides that it gains more by allowing somewhat unsafe factory conditions than by setting standards that would preclude the development of industry in the country. Suppose that the workers prefer working in Asbestos USA to not working at all. We can complain that it is unfair for people not to have work or that the contract of employment with such people is not free and hence morally marred. But granting all of this, it might still be true that Mexico and the Mexican people benefit more by Asbestos USA locating its plant in Mexico than by its not being there. If this were the case, then the move of Asbestos USA would not be immoral, providing it fulfilled the foregoing conditions.

Does this mean that it is moral to export cancer-producing industries to Mexico and other countries, where the regulations are more lenient than in the United States? The argument so far has considered Asbestos USA an isolated case. What will be the effect on Mexico and its people twenty years hence if such industries move there in significant numbers? Are the country and the people better off without such industries? How will the cancer cases be treated? What will happen to families of workers who get cancer? Are health provisions and pension plans provided for the workers?

Companies that wish to act morally must consider and attempt to answer these questions.

Ideally, there should be international agreements on minimally acceptable standards of safety in industry. In the absence of such standards moral sense and pressure must function until law can equalize the position of the worker vis-à-vis the employer. But moral sense and pressure seem to play little role in the policies of many international corporations. Paradoxically, some underdeveloped countries see the conditions for moral action, which have been discussed here, as impediments to the development of their countries, as requirements that keep them underdeveloped, and as the moralizing of Americans who are basically well off and do not understand other situations, including the aspirations of other people. The difficulty of knowing what will benefit the people in such countries most and of knowing what the people truly want—as opposed to what some governmental leaders say—is enormous. The difficulty forces us to be careful not to confuse what is morally right with what is proper for Americans. But American companies that are operating abroad and wish to be moral should not ignore the moral dimension of their actions; they should not simply follow the letter of the law in the countries in which they operate.

Is Asbestos USA immoral if it does not pay its Mexican employees the same wages that it paid its U.S. employees? The claim that it is immoral if it does not is a difficult one to sustain. Justice requires that people who do the same work should receive the same pay. A Mexican could rightly complain of injustice if he were paid less than an American for doing similar work in the same factory. But the principle applies only within the same factory, plant, or office.

The desirability of international minimal wage standards is obvious. But there is no visible movement in this direction, and multinational corporations on the whole have not attempted to promote such standards.

Finally, is it immoral for Asbestos USA to produce products in Mexico for sale in the United States? Suppose a German company made cars in the United States exclusively for export to Germany. Would we claim that the German company was exploiting the United States? It is difficult to develop a principle under which we would make such a determination. Earlier, we suggested the principle that unless a foreign company benefits the country in which it operates, it exploits that country for its own advantage and so acts immorally. This rules out as immoral exploitation of one country, *A*, by another, *B*, that dominates *A* in such a way that *B* can force *A* to act contrary to *A*'s own best interests. But if we consider the building of plants in sovereign states by firms from other countries, the host countries are able to prevent and prohibit such exploitation. If Asbestos USA were to force the demise of Mexican asbestos companies, it is difficult to see why it should be tolerated. But if it does not, there are many ways Asbestos USA might help the economy other than by producing its products for the Mexican market. It supplies work for its Mexican employees, teaches skills to the people it employs, pays taxes to the government, provides work for those who must build the plant in the first place, and purchases materials it needs locally to the advantage of the local economy. The workers in turn use their wages to buy goods, food, and shelter and so help support others in the economy. The Mexican government might well consider the trade-off to be to its advantage.

This analysis does not exonerate Asbestos USA on all counts. It has argued that Asbestos USA is not automatically guilty of the immoral practices attributed to it by typical critics.

We have not touched on the question of what the moral obligations of a multinational are in a country in which the government is repressive and in which the leaders care more for their own good and benefit than for the good of their people. If a government itself exploits its people and encourages foreign exploitation of its people by foreign firms that pay taxes to the government, or pay government officials directly, the government acts immorally. If a firm knowingly and willingly exploits its workers, even if it is legal to do so, it also acts immorally. But whether a particular firm is exploiting its workers often requires detailed investigation.

The critics of multinationals will have little patience with the analysis we have given of Asbestos USA. Even if multinationals *can* operate morally, they would assert that multinationals typically do not act morally. By outlining the conditions under which multinationals might act morally, the critics would maintain, we have given the impression that multinationals do act morally and that attacks on them are unwarranted. Such was not the intent. The temptations to act immorally are great in the international arena, and it would be surprising if many companies did not succumb. If moral restraints are ineffective, then the restraints on such activity must be international restraints. The abuses of multinationals underscore the need for effective international controls—controls, however, that the present international climate has not strongly fostered.

The Interconnection of American and International Business

The American business system and the international business system are inextricably intertwined. This means that ethics in international business involves ethics in American business and vice-versa.

In this regard, consider only the export of industry and protectionism. The export of American manufacturing has been faulted from many points of view. Whether the United States can continue in its preeminent world role without a strong and vital industrial base is a hotly debated topic. There is no consensus on the answer to the question of whether the United States is in a postindustrial, service, or information stage of development and, if it is, whether that is a positive or negative condition. Some people complain when a company moves its factory from the Northern part of the United States to the Sun Belt, where it can find cheaper labor. Yet many argue this is morally and economically acceptable. But when the same company for the same reasons—namely, to lower labor costs—moves from the United States abroad, then many of these same people condemn the action as immoral. The reason for the difference, they claim, is that although the Northern states may be adversely affected by the first move, the Sun Belt states benefit, and the overall benefit to the country balances out the harm done. When industry is exported, however, then Americans lose jobs and harm is done to the country as a whole from the loss of industry as well as jobs. This adds to unemployment, reduces the national tax base, and benefits the company at the expense of the country.

The argument is a one-sided view, however, for it considers only the company and the United States. It fails to consider the fact that exporting industry in this way helps provide jobs for people in the host country, where typically the unemployment rate is staggering. Are jobs more important for Americans than for the unemployed of other countries? To argue only in terms of the benefits for the United States and its citizens is not to take a broad enough perspective. The perspective for the evaluation of good and bad in the moral context is the broadest possible perspective—that is, all those affected by an action should be considered. From this perspective, the moral problem and the proper evaluation are more difficult to determine. This does not mean either that the export of industry is necessarily moral or immoral; it means that from a moral point of view not only are the interests of Americans to count, but the interests of others are to count as well. If the United States can prosper while others also prosper, so much the better. If, in order for the disadvantaged to prosper at all, the standard of living of Americans must be somewhat reduced, then that is a cost that morality may impose and that Americans as well as others similarly affected should be willing to pay.

A like analysis can be made with respect to protectionism. The argument in favor of protectionist policies is that they protect home industries from foreign competition. They help preserve jobs for workers at home. Typically, they also raise the cost of items protected for consumers at home. Especially when used against less developed countries, protectionism denies others access to our market, doing them greater harm than the benefit done to our own industry. As a response to protectionism practiced by other developed countries, the tactic may be justifiable if its aim, and actual end result, is the elimination of protectionism by all sides. But to the extent that it deprives LDCs of markets, it simply exacerbates the plight in which they now find themselves. The moral justification for such action is at best not clear and is apparently lacking.

Ethics in international business is complex. The problems are pressing and require careful analysis and discussion. Ethics for international business constitutes one more layer of analysis that business must consider in any business activity. Ethics by itself will not tell a business how to act, but it can tell a business how not to act. In this sense it is a sieve through which business decisions must pass. Only those that pass through it are morally acceptable. But which of those that pass through it are the best from a business point of view must of course be decided by those in business. The moral level achieved in international business will be a reflection of the morality of those engaged in such business. Yet ultimately, fairness and global justice will require not only honest businesspersons, but also just background institutions that enable all to compete on the same terms and that provide for those whom the international business system fails to benefit.

Study Questions

1. Are chemical companies ethically required to install the same safety devices they use in their U.S. plants in plants they build in less developed countries? Why or why not?

2. If an American company builds a potentially dangerous plant in a less developed country and if the American company does not have majority control of the plant it builds, does it have any ethical obligation to ensure how the plant is run after it completes construction? If so, what obligation does it have? If not, why not?

3. Of what is the international system of capitalism composed?

4. What are the basic differences between the economic system of free enterprise as it exists in the United States and the economic system as it exists worldwide?

5. What are *background institutions?* What function do they serve with respect to business?

6. What is a *multinational?*

7. Are multinationals immoral? Why or why not?

8. Can individual nations control multinationals? Why or why not?

9. Present and evaluate the charge that MNCs operate immorally in LDCs by exploiting workers, exploiting natural resources, and reaping exorbitant profits.

10. Present and evaluate the charge that MNCs compete unfairly in LDCs to the detriment of the host country.

11. Present and evaluate the charge that MNCs are the major cause of impoverishment of LDCs.

12. What general norms can be applied in morally evaluating the activities of MNCs operating in LDCs? How are those norms justified?

13. On what three levels do considerations of human rights face multinationals?

14. May multinationals ethically operate in a country that engages in gross abuses of human rights? Why or why not?

15. What standards of ethical conduct for international business already exist?

16. What is the "Responsible Care" program?

17. What is the role of self-regulation in international business?

18. What groups other than government play a role in setting norms for international business?

19. Should drug companies not sell any drug they know to be harmful in any way? Why or why not?

20. May a drug company morally sell harmful drugs without informing the purchaser of the harmful effects? Why or why not?

21. Are FDA standards the only morally permissible ones for all countries?

22. Is it moral for drug companies to add an inert substance to a drug and market it under another name in order to circumvent the law of a country that outlaws U.S. drugs outlawed in the United States?

23. Is it immoral to hire anyone to do work that is dangerous to his or her health or life? Is it immoral to do so if one warns the prospective employee of the dangers?

24. Are U.S. traditions and laws the only morally justifiable ones?

25. Why might Mexico adopt less stringent safety requirements for workers than the United States?

26. Is it morally sufficient for a U.S. company to comply with the laws of the foreign country in which it operates? Why or why not?

27. What does the principle of equal pay for equal work require?

28. Is it unfair for a U.S. firm to pay Mexican workers in Mexico less than it pays U.S. workers in the United States for the same kind of work? Why or why not?

29. Is it immoral for a U.S. firm in Mexico to make products exclusively for export to the United States? Why or why not? How might multinationals be controlled?

30. Is it morally defensible for a U.S. firm to close down its U.S. factories and move its production facilities to underdeveloped countries to take advantage of cheaper labor costs? Why or why not?

20

>─┤─◆>─◦─<◆─┤─<

CORRUPT CONTEXTS, CULTURAL DIVERSITY, AND INTERNATIONAL BUSINESS

The Case of General Motors and Apartheid

In 1926 General Motors opened its first factory in South Africa. It preceded by many years the introduction of what were to become known as apartheid laws, which began to be passed in 1948. In 1950 the South African Group Areas Act designated areas by race. In 1953 the Reservation of Separate Amenities Act mandated racial segregation. The 1956 Labor Relations Act reserved certain jobs for whites. These and a host of other laws enforced racial segregation and guaranteed white domination.

Under apartheid, the blacks in South Africa suffered extreme oppression. Although they constituted the overwhelming majority of the population, they were allowed to live on only 13 percent of the land. The other 87 percent was reserved for the whites, who constituted only 17 percent of the population. The whites controlled the gold and diamond mines, the harbors, and the industrial areas. Blacks who wished to work in these areas were required to live in townships outside of the major cities. Because only males were allowed in the townships, the workers were separated from their families for the major part of the year. The blacks could not vote, own property, organize politically, or join unions. They were systematically paid less than whites for the same work. They were not allowed to hold managerial positions of even the lowest kind. They were forced to use segregated eating, dressing, and toilet facilities.

General Motors, like many other foreign-owned corporations in South Africa, did not have any part in passing the apartheid legislation. Yet they were all bound by the laws, just as were the local firms. The laws were passed gradually, and the society changed accordingly. As each of the apartheid laws was passed, it could be ethically faulted. Should General Motors or any of the other foreign companies have obeyed the laws? Could they have done otherwise?

The answer to the second question came in 1977 from Leon Sullivan, a black Philadelphia pastor and a member of the GM board of directors. Convinced that apartheid was immoral and that GM could not morally follow the apartheid laws, he proposed a set of principles, known as the Sullivan Principles. Among other provisions, these principles prohibited GM from following the apartheid laws and required nonsegregation in the company's operations, equal pay for equal work regardless of race, and the promotion of qualified black workers over white workers. Sullivan's proposal was not only that GM follow the principles but also that other American companies band together to follow them. In this way it was both less likely that the South African government would prosecute any company for breaking the law and possibly that the apartheid laws could be undermined from within.[1]

Both deontological and utilitarian arguments were employed to justify companies that followed the Sullivan Principles operating in South Africa. From a deontological point of view, the companies could correctly state that they were not engaging in either racial segregation or discrimination. From a utilitarian point of view, they could argue that they were producing more good than harm for all concerned and especially for the blacks and for South Africa.

Sullivan initially proposed the principles to twelve major American companies. By 1986, of the 280 American companies operating in South Africa, 172 had become signatories of the principles. In addition, in 1985 Roger Smith, chairman of the board and CEO of General Motors, helped found the U.S. Corporate Council on South Africa to apply pressure on the South African government to end apartheid. Most of the black nations of South Africa had already imposed economic sanctions on South Africa, as had most countries of Western Europe. In 1985 the United States froze new credits to South Africa, and in 1986 the U.S. Congress passed legislation restricting trade, investment, and lending.

Nonetheless, in 1987 Sullivan declared the ten-year experiment in following the principles a failure because it had not succeeded in undermining apartheid from within. He held that following the principles no longer constituted a justification for companies operating in South Africa, and he called for their withdrawal. In doing so, he joined a large number of other observers who claimed that any American company in South Africa by its presence and its taxes lent unjustifiable support to the South African government and in fact did more harm than good.

---

[1] For details of apartheid and a list of the Sullivan Principles, see Oliver F. Williams, *The Apartheid Crisis: How We Can Do Justice in a Land of Violence* (San Francisco: Harper & Row, 1986).

In 1987 General Motors sold its holdings in South Africa.

Whether or not the sanctions and the Sullivan Principles were effective, in 1991 the South African government began to repeal the apartheid laws. In 1993 the white rulers agreed to end apartheid completely and to allow universal elections under a new constitution. Thereupon most countries rescinded their sanctions, and some American companies that had left South Africa began returning. In 1994 apartheid officially ended.

Was General Motors justified in staying in South Africa as long as it did? Would it have been justified in staying on longer?

U.S. Multinationals in South Africa

U.S. companies began moving into South Africa as early as the 1880s. At that time, these firms employed only whites and sold their products almost exclusively to the white community. The white community was the economically advanced and productive sector of the country and supplied the market for goods. The blacks lived in their own sections of the country, according to their traditional tribal ways. The whites set up and controlled the government. The blacks did not take part in any governmental activities, were not educated, and were not considered able to run the government or to have any impact on it. The whites exercised a colonial type of paternalism over the blacks.

Whatever we might think about the morality of such colonial paternalism, it is understandable how and why companies from the United States initially saw both their market and their employees as coming from the white community. These companies wanted to expand their markets and make a profit, and South Africa was a ripe market to develop. With time and the changes of over half a century, colonialism fell out of favor in other parts of Africa; the native inhabitants took over the reins of power in country after country and ran their own affairs. Even in South Africa, some changes did take place. As factories expanded, they found that there were not enough whites to fill the jobs available, and blacks were found able and willing to work in these factories. Fear of their achieving control was, in part, what had motivated the government to draw up and enforce the apartheid laws in the first place. But as blacks entered the labor force, they also had money to buy goods and so represented a potential market.

American-controlled multinationals moved into South Africa in greater numbers to take advantage of the low wages they could pay blacks and the large market that South Africa represented. The profits earned by American South African subsidiaries were often twice as high as those earned by the home-based mother company. Many black-dominated countries in Africa placed embargoes on goods manufactured by U.S. companies operating in South Africa. But the local market was sufficient to make the operation of subsidiaries in South Africa profitable for IBM, Ford, General Motors, Goodyear, Firestone, Exxon, Mobil, Kellogg's, Eli Lilly, Kodak, Control Data, and over three hundred other U.S. companies.

U.S. multinationals would not have opened subsidiaries in South Africa unless it was profitable to do so. South Africa had four conditions that made it attractive to U.S. companies. First, it had a stable government. U.S. companies are reluctant to open plants in countries with an unstable government, for fear of losing their investments because of nationalization or constant domestic turmoil. U.S. companies, therefore, have an interest in helping to preserve stable governments. They have tended not to care whether the government is repressive or dictatorial. That, they often claim, is a local, political matter. In addition, from a business point of view, a strong, stable government is a guarantee of the safety of their investment. Second, South Africa had a large potential market of 28 million people. Even though only 17 percent of the population is white, they represented a market of close to 5 million people, and the other 23 million formed a pool that could be increasingly tapped. The U.S. companies were the chief suppliers of consumer goods and of advanced technology. Third, South Africa has a large and cheap supply of labor. The standard of living of the blacks was extremely low, and the scale paid them by South African firms was about one-fourth the wages paid to white workers. As more blacks were brought into the work force, the market for manufactured goods grew. Fourth, South Africa is rich in minerals. It can provide from within its own borders the materials necessary for manufacturing, as well as ship to the parent U.S. companies raw materials needed for production in the United States.

All four conditions supply both the reasons why multinationals wanted to locate subsidiaries in South Africa and the reasons why critics of such firms charged them with immoral exploitation and with supporting repressive regimes.

U.S. firms were not unaware of the charges of immorality, but for a long time few of them responded to the charges by withdrawal. They felt the moral pressure from stockholders and from other vocal groups in the United States, however, and initially responded in a number of cases by adopting the Sullivan Principles.

Divestment and Disinvestment

Although multinationals operating abroad are outside the control of the U.S. government, American-controlled multinationals are not beyond the control of the American parent company. These companies are controlled by their respective boards of directors, which are in turn subject to the interests of the shareholders. American shareholders could, at least in theory, determine the practices of the U.S. multinationals.

We have already discussed ethical investing. We know that because every person has a moral obligation not to engage in immoral practices, no one may ethically invest in a firm that engages in unethical practices. The issue for stockholders in the United States was whether firms that followed the Sullivan Principles in South Africa were nonetheless engaged in unethical practices. As more and more people became interested in this issue, it became easier and easier to learn which companies operated in South Africa and, of these, which ones followed the Sullivan Principles, and to what extent. Those who felt that any business activity in South Africa was morally unjustifiable were able to sell their stock in those companies.

Just as individuals should not support firms that engage in immoral practices, so institutions also should not invest in such firms. Because corporate bodies usually make larger investments than individuals, they have a correspondingly greater responsibility concerning the investments they make. Critics claimed that churches and universities should take the lead in ethical investment practices because they are appropriate models for moral behavior. They argued further that the churches and universities could force the U.S. companies out of South Africa by *divesting,* or selling their stock, in protest.

Those who argued against divestment rejected the idea that the universities and churches could effect the withdrawal of these companies from South Africa by selling their stock in protest. If they were to sell their stock and drive the price of the stock down, they said, it would simply be purchased by traders who would be delighted to get it at a lower price, confident that it would soon rise in line with its actual worth. Some of the institutional shareholders claimed that they were more effective voting from within the company than they would be voicing disapproval as outsiders.

During the 1970s and the early 1980s, groups on campuses throughout the United States sought to get their local endowment associations to divest themselves of companies operating in South Africa. In some cases these groups were successful and in other cases they were not. Nonetheless, they showed how pressure might be brought to bear on institutional investors and in turn on multinational corporations.

In May 1987, when Sullivan called for *disinvestment,* or the selling off of their holdings in South Africa by U.S. firms, a number of people and firms disagreed with his assessment and continued to affirm that the best way to break down apartheid was by U.S. firms operating according to the Sullivan Principles within South Africa. Others agreed with his assessment. By the middle of 1987 U.S. firms in increasing numbers began to leave South Africa.

By the end of 1987 not only General Motors but also many of the largest U.S. firms—IBM, Eastman Kodak, Coca-Cola, Exxon, Procter & Gamble, and others—had left or had started leaving. The issue then became how they were leaving and whether some were leaving in name only but continuing to operate in South Africa in fact. Some firms, including IBM, sold their holdings to newly created offshore employee trusts. They financed the sale to the workers, who agreed to pay back the loan over a set number of years. Other firms sold to white South Africans. Kodak not only sold off its holdings in South Africa but also refused to sell any of its products to South Africa. Still other firms sold their holdings but continued to sell their products to the new owners. Although most of the departing companies mentioned the moral issue and the pressure they felt because of it, they also cited the deteriorating economic conditions in South Africa as part of the reason for their disinvestment there.

The Lessons of Business in South Africa

The experience of U.S. multinationals in South Africa allows us to derive a number of lessons about how to operate in the context of a structurally immoral society. The lessons can be generalized beyond opposition to apartheid to apply in other situations in which the official structures or government policies violate human rights.

Leon Sullivan highlighted the fact that a company of integrity cannot obey unethical laws. If a foreign company cannot operate in a host country that has such laws without obeying them, then it cannot ethically operate in such a country. If it wishes to be ethical, it will be forced to withdraw. A number of U.S. banks came to the correct conclusion that they could not operate ethically in South Africa because their loans and other activities directly supported the government and its interests. They reluctantly left South Africa.

Moreover, as Sullivan also pointed out, simply refusing to follow the apartheid laws was not sufficient justification for remaining in South Africa; for the American companies helped the South African government indirectly in a number of ways, only one of which was through taxes. To offset the indirect support the companies gave the government, they had to take active steps to undermine the government's unethical practices and laws. Passive resistance was not enough; they had to be proactive in their approach, including promoting actions opposed to apartheid, pressuring the government to change its practices, publicizing their opposition to it, and supporting sanctions and other external attempts to influence the government to change.

The signatories to the Sullivan Principles openly disobeyed the apartheid laws. The South African government tolerated their disobedience only because the companies had joined forces. Whether the government would have ignored any individual company's breaking the law is a moot point. But a large number of major U.S. firms that join forces wield an enormous amount of power and influence because of their great economic contribution to the country in which they are located. The South African experience is not unique, even though it is one of the clearest examples of the importance and possibility of joint corporate action.

Whether the U.S. companies that followed the Sullivan Principles helped break down apartheid from within is still debated. But that action, as well as the economic sanctions imposed by a large number of countries, surely had a role in the South African government's final repeal of the apartheid laws and the entry of the majority of the population into political life and political power. The influence of multinationals and of outside governments should not be underestimated. Although a fine line can be drawn between a country's internal affairs—into which foreign companies and other countries have no right to interfere—and a country's unethical practices, the host country cannot ignore these practices if it wishes multinationals to operate therein and if it wants to trade or carry on similar interactions with other nations. Hence, companies that operate in countries that institutionalize violations of human rights can and should refuse to follow such practices and can do so most effectively if they do it jointly and openly.

The South African experience shows that shareholders can hold multinationals accountable if they truly wish to do so. Shareholders can demand to know what practices the companies follow in their subsidiaries abroad. If immoral practices are discovered in an operation abroad and if enough people in the United States refuse to purchase the product or stock of the manufacturer in question until the immoral practice is stopped, then a plausible assumption is that the practice will be changed when the economics of the situation demand it. In the case of South Africa, however, the student protests that impelled many university endowments to divest their portfolios of stock in companies that operated in South Africa would have been more effective if the students had also refused to purchase the goods of such companies rather than simply demanding that their university sell its stock. As we will recall from Chapter 11, the INFACT coalition boycott of Nestlé products sent a clearer and stronger message to Nestlé about its action than the universities' divestiture of their Nestlé stock would have.

The nations that had imposed sanctions lifted them largely at the request of the African National Congress, the major representative of the blacks in South Africa. The purpose of the sanctions was to pressure the government to end apartheid and to end the violation of the black population's human rights. Hence, it was appropriate to listen to representatives of those who were oppressed. That is a lesson well taken. Nonetheless, the sanctions and the disinvestment by American companies had a serious negative impact on the South African economy. The end of sanctions has not been enough to restore the economy's previous vigor. Nor are all the U.S. companies that left South Africa anxious or willing to return, at least until the political and economic situations stabilize. Although the companies may have left South Africa primarily for a moral reason, often an economic motive was also involved; there is no moral requirement that any company return, and most are unlikely to do so without economic reasons for that action.

Bribery and the Foreign Corrupt Practices Act

Among the many corrupt practices that multinationals face, endemic bribery is cited more often than any other. The claim is frequently made that in some parts of the world it is simply not possible to do business without paying bribes. That claim must be treated with some skepticism. While bribery is certainly widespread in some countries, whether bribes are *necessary* for multinationals to do business is the real issue. We can distinguish between what may be necessary, respectively, for local businesses and for multinational corporations to function. Moreover, we should note that in no country is bribery publicly justified as being ethically proper. It could not be, for bribery is a means by which some people get special treatment in preference to others for no other reason than that they pay sums of monies. Bribery undercuts efficiency in the market, skews the allocation of resources and goods, often imposes unjust costs on third parties, and leads to further corruption, since such payments are not legal and cannot be reported in generally accepted accounting procedures. Hence, calling bribery unethical and a form of corruption is not an example of the United States imposing its norms on other countries.

In 1977 the United States passed the Foreign Corrupt Practices Act (FCPA), which made it illegal for any American company to pay bribes to higher governmental officials in foreign countries. The law was an attempt to level the playing field for American companies operating abroad. The law also intended to establish a model that other countries might follow, and the UN Commission on Transnational Corporations has proposed a norm for all transnational corporations comparable to that imposed on American companies by the FCPA.

The FCPA targets payments to higher level government officials because such payments not only undermine an efficient market but also corrupt the officials, who are supposed to govern for the benefit of the people of the country. Excluded from the bill are small payments to lower level officials which may be necessary to get them to perform their official functions—called facilitating or "grease" payments. Thus, a small payment to a customs official to inspect a company's shipment at a border is permitted and reportable, providing that the payment is not an attempt to get the official to do anything illegal, such as passing contraband goods or not charging appropriate tariffs. These small payments are considered comparable to tips left for waiters. Nonetheless, some companies find such payments morally objectionable. Some U.S. firms have jointly protested such payments and in some countries have succeeded in operating without paying them. Moreover, there is no hard evidence that, overall, U.S. firms have suffered competitively because of the Foreign Corrupt Practices Act.[2] The law has also given U.S. companies an understandable excuse—if one was needed—that they can make when approached for bribes.

What of bribes to nongovernmental personnel? Although these are not prohibited by the FCPA, they can still be evaluated from an ethical point of view. The major questions that must be answered are: Do they involve unfairness to anyone or violate anyone's rights? Must they be kept secret, such that they cannot be reported as a business expense? Are they truly necessary in order to carry on business? Unless the answer to the first two questions is negative and to the third positive, the payment is prima facie unethical. In some cases what is considered a bribe is actually extortion—namely, payment made to prevent some unjustifiable harm by the party demanding payment. Although the extracting of extortion is to be morally condemned, the paying

---

[2] Paul J. Beck, Michael W. Maher, and Adrian E. Tschoegl, "The Impact of the Foreign Corrupt Practices Act on U.S. Exports," *Managerial and Decision Economics,* 12, (no. 4) (August 1991), pp. 295-303.

of extortion, while generally wrong since it promotes an immoral practice, may in some cases be justified on the basis of results or as the choice of the lesser of two evils. However, such an excuse will likely be more appropriate for a small local business that truly has no alternative than for a multinational corporation that always has the alternative of not doing business in such a context and that has enough power and influence to refuse such payments.

Although in 1977 when the FCPA was passed the United States hoped that other countries would follow its example by passing similar legislation, for almost twenty years none of them did. Nonetheless, over that period of time the public reaction to bribery in country after country changed. Governmental corruption involving bribery led to the jailing of two former South Korean presidents, to the resignation of the presidents of Brazil and Venezuela, to the fall of Italy's Christian Democrat and Socialist parties, to crises in Japan, and to indictments of government officials in many countries in which bribery had supposedly been acceptable.

Finally, in 1996 the Organization for Economic Cooperation and Development (OECD)countries agreed that they would all no longer allow their corporations to deduct foreign bribes as a legitimate tax deduction. In 1997 the twenty-nine OECD countries agreed to outlaw bribes to foreign government officials. Although each individual country's legislature had to approve the agreement for it to take effect in that country, even some corporations in Europe and Japan that had fought the control of bribery supported the agreement. Although some details have still to be worked out, the agreement was an important step in leveling the international business playing field and in officially condemning bribery.

International Business in Unsettled Contexts

Although business prefers settled internal conditions, at present a number of potentially attractive markets are in unsettled contexts. Chief among these are the countries of the former Soviet Union and of Eastern Europe.

Following the peaceful revolutions in Eastern Europe in 1989 and in the Soviet Union in 1991, these countries entered unchartered waters as they moved from socialism to some sort of market economy. No country has done what these countries are doing. Although the transition has varied to some extent from country to country, in all of them the move to a market economy has involved hardship and a certain amount of corruption, bribery, extortion, and the gamut of unethical business practices.

Government control in the USSR and in the socialist countries of Eastern Europe was ubiquitous. The state or government owned all the means of production. Housing, too, was state owned, as was industry. The government was the sole employer, and it in turn provided highly subsidized housing, free education, free medical care, and old age pensions. Productivity was not very high, and the standard of living was correlatively low. There were laws, but there was no real rule of law. Nonetheless, the state provided security. Government control was total, and hence other sources of control were minimal.

In the USSR the overthrow of the communist regime was a protest against the domination by the Communist party and its control; it was *not* a fight for capitalism or free enterprise. How much of socialism the Russian people want to give up remains an open question. The problems in Russia are many, for having overthrown communism and repudiated the former system, the Russians have been left with little in the way of a system under which to operate. Socialist laws have still not been effectively replaced by other laws, and debate continues on which laws to adopt. With the legal system under revision, the police and courts were less and less effective and not free of corruption. As the traditional background institutions that lend stability to a society disintegrated, there was increasing need for morality to function as a source of social order. However, there was little public morality left to play that essential role.

The ordinary Russian workers have little. The 1996 wage of the average worker was 27 percent below what it had been in 1992. With rampant inflation since 1991 their savings have disappeared. As late as 1998 the government was unable to pay many of its workers on time and owed them several months' back pay. Many Russian workers regard anyone who has been able to succeed in these circumstances as crooked: They believe the successful must have been former communist officials or bureaucrats who took advantage of their past position, or members of the Russian "mafia" criminally amassing wealth, or entrepreneurs exploiting others.

Absent during the transition period from socialism were the laws, customs, nongovernmental organizations, effective and fair means of taxation, enforcement of contracts, and other aspects of what we have called background institutions. Their absence has encouraged the worst aspects of the capitalism that Marx described and excoriated.

Officially, the development of small entrepreneurs was both encouraged and hampered. It was encouraged because it was clear that one of the failures of the old system, which relied exclusively on centralized control, was simply not effective. Hence, some of those in charge at least in theory realized the need for entrepreneurs to develop small businesses and for decentralization to replace the former command economy. At the same time, the tax structure and state bureaucracy made operating a small business difficult.

Moreover, the former state structures of distribution are to a notable extent still in place. In Russia large factories and enterprises remain an important economic reality, and sources of supplies are still often geared toward those enterprises. As a result, small businesses have a very difficult time getting the wherewithal to conduct their business. If goods are earmarked for the large factories and are not available to the small entrepreneur, the small businesspersons effectively cannot function. The only way they can operate, given the skewed—and they claim unfair—allocation system, is by getting what they can where, when, and how they can. In practice, this most often means paying bribes to those who have access to the needed materials—whether those are managers in factories willing to sell what has been allocated to them, or shippers and middlemen who divert shipments to the small business for a fee, or black marketeers and other people who steal what they can sell.

The climate for the entrepreneur in Russia is very volatile. The laws are constantly changing and the tax rates and rules, too, are in a state of flux. The status of ownership of much property is still uncertain. With the end of socialism and the breakdown of social order, crime increased, extortion became common, and a powerful Russian mafia developed.[3]

For a long time the status of privatization was equally unsettled. Under socialism, the people were said to be the owners of the means of production, but simply owning the factories, shops, and stores does no good if they are not productive; and most of them needed an influx of money to retool and modernize.[4]

The result was a condition of great confusion and uncertainty. The state was ineffective in its new role. Market forces were not yet in place. The transition period led to high unemployment and the closing of many factories that simply could not compete. Whereas they had been able to sell shoddy goods in the former command economy, they could not in an economy where goods were available from the West. The social services formerly provided by the state were no longer readily available. The status of apartments and housing was often in dispute, and ownership was not clear.

The transition to a market economy demonstrated the need for effective background institutions, and especially for enforceable contracts, social understandings, standard business practices, and acceptance by the general population, if the system was to be ethically justifiable. In a chaotic and unstable context, business ethics has a larger role to play than otherwise. Yet, paradoxically, in such a context it is often difficult to decide what is just: for justice depends in part on a context.

The claim that in order to operate in Russia as a small entrepreneur one had to pay bribes and buy supplies where and when one found them without questioning their source was probably correct. Let us suppose that it was. Is one ethically allowed to operate one's business this way? The obvious answer is no if there is any other alternative. But if the allocation system is itself unfair and corrupt, if government bureaucrats get their share of payments and ignore (if not condone) the diverting of goods based on bribes, can the small entrepreneur be held to a standard of ethical behavior that is proper in a less corrupt environment? To hold businesspersons to that standard is in effect to prevent them from becoming private entrepreneurs and to leave all enterprise to the criminal element.

---

[3] See Stephen Handelman, "Inside Russia's Gangster Economy," *New York Times Magazine,* January 24, 1993, pp. 12 ff.

[4] For details of privatization in Russia see Joseph R. Blasi, Maya Kroumova, and Donald Kruse, *Kremlin Capitalism: Privatizing the Russian Economy* (Ithaca: Cornell University Press, 1997).

Under such circumstances, basic fundamental ethical norms still apply. Extortion, physical harm and threats, robbery, lying, producing defective goods, dumping toxic wastes—all remain unethical, whether or not they are effectively policed. The outright stealing of goods by some of the managers, who received materials and immediately shipped and sold them abroad at a price below their market value is unethical by any standard.

Arguably, however, practices that would be clearly wrong, for instance, in the United States, might be ethically justified for people in those circumstances. When, for instance, might the paying of bribes to receive legitimate supplies necessary for one's business be allowed? One justifiable answer is when they are not bribes but are part of the cost of doing business. Bribes are payments made to receive special advantage at the expense of others under some orderly system of entitlements. In the absence of an orderly system of entitlements and the special advantage, and hence harm, done to others, we are no longer describing what is generally thought of as bribery. We have a disorderly system in which goods are not rationally allocated either by the market or by the government and in which there is no fair market price. The price of goods is determined by supply and demand in a rough sense. But if all private entrepreneurs are in the same system and if goods are available only through the payment of fees beyond those listed on an invoice (if there is one), then that is the way and the cost of doing business. The payments do not undermine a free market, but in this case can be said to be part of a developing market.

A kind of utilitarian argument might also be mounted according to which both society as a whole and consumers benefit from private entrepreneurs taking the risks of private business and providing goods and services under an inefficient and chaotic system. In this way, these private entrepreneurs benefit society much more than would be possible if they decided not to carry on such businesses and left people without goods and services or if they left all enterprise to criminal initiatives.

This justification is clearly conditional and temporary. As the system becomes organized and regularized, then the status of such payments changes and becomes disruptive rather than productive and unethical rather than marginally justifiable. Moreover, this line of reasoning justifies at best those who are forced to pay what we shall continue to call bribes. It does not justify the actions of government officials who demand bribes or of police who require bribes in order not to enforce what law there is. These actions are part of the problem and can in no way be considered a way station toward the solution.

Similarly, it is difficult for the small entrepreneur to know what taxes are owed when the government for all intents and purposes does not know and is unable to provide adequate information or to police any rules it does establish. In such a situation is failure to pay one's taxes unethical? Although it is unethical to avoid paying our fair taxes in an ordinary system, we could hardly call the developing Russian situation a system in any functional sense. Hence, small entrepreneurs could plausibly follow whatever rules there are that are most favorable to them—for example, delaying payment where this is not clearly illegal.

The appropriate generalization in these conditions is that more cannot be asked of those in business than the situation warrants. General ethical demands must be placed in context, and in the Russian context the conclusions we come to from an ethical point of view diverge from the conclusions we would come to in a normal situation, primarily because the country has no stable, just background institutions.

In such circumstances, it is difficult to know what "just" or "fair" means in a great many instances having to do with property because property is a bundle of rights relative to a system of rights. What constitutes property in the United States is a function of our laws that grant property rights and provide a system under which property can be legitimately transferred. Under the Soviet system, private property was not allowed, and the system of rights that developed was significantly different from the system of property in the United States. What was fair or just as well as what was possible under the two systems differed. But under which system were, and in some cases are, Russia and the countries of Eastern Europe during their transition, and which notions of property and justice apply? The problem was the absence of a clear system in these countries. In some ways, then, business ethics requires a background system within which to operate. Nonetheless, as we have already seen, both the ordinary citizen and outside observers appropriately condemn violence, outright robbery, the misuse of political or police power for private gain, and the like.

Given such an environment, how should foreign, for instance, American, firms, act? Although American companies are not required to do business in Eastern Europe and Russia in exactly the same way as they do in the United States, they are also not allowed to ignore moral norms, even if these are not either enacted into law or are not effectively enforced in the host country. Whereas the multinational can choose whether to operate in such countries and determine the conditions under which it will operate, the native entrepreneur's choices when setting up in business are much more restricted.

Does this not imply a double standard, since we gave a limited defense of local entrepreneurs working within the system? The answer is no. The reason is that the situations of the local entrepreneur and of the American multinational are very different. First, we can plausibly argue that the local entrepreneur has no choice but to operate within a corrupt system or not to operate at all. The American multinational, on the other hand, has a very real option of not operating there at all, while continuing to operate everywhere else that it already does. Second, the multinational does not need to engage in bribery. It has available hard currency, which is in such great demand that, if anything, it needs to give some attention to the fact that it can skew the allocation of resources to the serious disadvantage of local firms. If bribes are demanded, a U.S. company can and should point to the U.S. Foreign Corrupt Practices Act as an added reason for not paying bribes to public officials. If bribes are actually necessary to conduct business, the U.S. company can protest through official governmental and intergovernmental channels, it can use the media to expose the demands, and it can band together with other American companies similarly situated to jointly refuse to pay such demands. In short, unlike the local entrepreneur, the U.S. company has a large variety of options, such that the multinationals have no justification for engaging in such practices.

Because of its strong position, the multinational in such a context has a positive obligation to set an example of ethics in business and to encourage the development of background institutions conducive to stability and to business practices that benefit the society as a whole. As an outside interest entering the country for the company's benefit, it should not be exploitative and seek its good at the disadvantage of the local population. To do otherwise is to adopt the carpetbagger syndrome; it is exploitative and hence is unethical, even if legal.

International Industrial Espionage, Discrimination, and Questionable Products

There are no special rules governing the operation of multinationals from one developed nation in another developed nation. The general rules of morality, of course, apply, and multinationals must abide by the just laws of the various countries in which they operate. We have already seen that the developed countries on the whole have an adequate set of background institutions that constrain the excesses to which business might be prone. We have also observed that such countries are able to defend their own interests. MNCs must, of course, consider cultural differences and practices if they are to succeed in different countries. Nonetheless, a number of issues arise, three of which we shall briefly discuss here: industrial espionage, racial and gender discrimination, and questionable products.

International Industrial Intelligence and Espionage

With the end of the Cold War, international intelligence agencies no longer had clearly defined enemy targets. Yet intelligence operations did not suddenly disappear, nor did the sophisticated and not-so-sophisticated means of collecting intelligence vanish. In a number of instances, the targets switched from foe to friend and from military secrets to industrial and commercial secrets.[5]

---

[5] See, for instance, Peter Schweizer, "Our Thieving Allies," *New York Times,* June 23, 1992, p. A15; and Douglas Waller, "The Open Door: U.S. Firms Face a Wave of Foreign Espionage," *Newsweek,* May 4, 1992, pp. 58-60.

We can distinguish overt from covert intelligence gathering and governmental from private intelligence gathering. Most intelligence consists of gathering information from a variety of sources, piecing it together, and analyzing it carefully. This is as true in peacetime as in less peaceful periods. There is nothing unethical about such intelligence production if it is based on public sources—corporate reports, public announcements, public relations documents, published interviews, and so on. Nor is there anything inherently unethical about a government carrying on such research to benefit corporations within its borders. Most governments do something along these lines and make the results available—some more generally and some more specifically—to certain industries or corporations that they see as tied to their national interests. The closeness of relations between business and government varies from country to country. It is unlikely any American company would receive sensitive information about foreign competitors from any U.S. government agency because this would give it a competitive advantage over its American competitors. This is not true in all countries. Is it fair for the governments of some countries to help their corporations while the governments of other countries do not? The answer seems to be yes, it is fair, for there is no moral rule that mandates the relation of government and business. What is not fair is when the means used to gather information is itself unethical.

Stealing trade secrets, surreptitiously entering into a company's computer system to find confidential information, paying (or blackmailing) a company's employees to divulge privileged information, tapping a company's phones or bugging its offices, photocopying papers or copying computer disks from a visiting executive's hotel room are all clearly unethical. Other techniques, however, are less clearly wrong. Some of these include monitoring the air waves for messages that go over portable phones, following corporate executives to see whom they meet, buying drinks for key employees in the hope of getting them to reveal in otherwise casual conversation what a competitor might want to know, and sifting a company's refuse after disposal for useful information.

The justification for military intelligence gathering by governments has typically been national security. The extent to which that justification legitimizes stealing state secrets, monitoring offices with listening devices, and placing moles within another country's government or industry is open to debate. But an argument based on national security cannot justify the use of such means for industrial espionage. All the same, some governments engage in such practices, as do some firms. The response to such practices, insofar as they are unethical, is for companies to take protective countermeasures and for governments to enter into enforceable agreements concerning such activities. No country openly admits, much less justifies, such surreptitious activities. Agreements to mutually refrain from them, however, are often easier to obtain than to enforce, and both companies and governments must realistically take measures to protect their secrets from unethical encroachment.

Racial and Gender Discrimination

We have already discussed racial and gender discrimination in the United States. We can extrapolate from that discussion to a U.S. multinational's operation in other countries. Since such discrimination is unethical, a U.S. multinational may no more engage in such discrimination abroad than it may in the United States. But the situation may be considerably different in the two cases.

Consider countries in which women are not equitably represented in the work force or in management positions, and there is either prima facie evidence of or blatant discrimination against women. What obligation does a U.S. company have in such a culture? Clearly, it may not discriminate, whether or not the local companies do. Does it have a further obligation to help break down gender-based discrimination by doing more than observing fair employment practices in hiring and promoting its employees? The argument for requiring affirmative action on the part of companies in the United States was the fact that they had discriminated in the past as a group. Suppose the American firm in question is opening a new plant or office and hence had no opportunity to discriminate in the past. Does the argument for affirmative action hold for a company coming from outside? Does the example of U.S. companies in South Africa that followed the Sullivan Principles apply here, even though gender discrimination is not usually mandated by law?

While the U.S.-based company with integrity cannot discriminate, it is not clear that it must take the lead in breaking down such discrimination by means other than its example and its practices. If the women that it promotes to executive positions have difficulty working effectively with other companies that have a tradition of male domination, it must do the best it can to balance fair treatment of the women and the financial interests of the company. This will be easier in some cultures and countries than in others, but in no country should a company simply assume that women cannot be effective in high positions. Even countries such as Pakistan and India, where women have been notoriously poorly treated, have had women as heads of government.

The same analysis seems to hold with racial discrimination as well. Several countries in Europe are facing discrimination problems comparable in some ways to those in the United States. Are these problems that U.S. companies have a special obligation to address? The answer seems to be no, even though the U.S. companies may not practice racial discrimination, even if mandated by law. Beyond this, however, although U.S. companies may have such an obligation in the United States, there seems to be no special obligation that these companies have to practice affirmative action, to seek out those nonnationals whom the local companies discriminate against, or to employ them in numbers corresponding to their representation in the employment pool. Practicing nondiscrimination, and in this way setting an example, is required. Such an example is especially needed when unemployment is increasing in some European countries, such as Germany, where guest-workers are no longer welcome and German firms prefer to hire German nationals.

But there are limits both on what U.S. firms can do in such contexts and on what they are required to do beyond refusing to practice racial discrimination.

Questionable Products

The U.S. companies' export of tobacco and of weapons has raised a number of ethical charges by critics.

Although tobacco products are legally produced and sold in the United States to those over 18 years of age, cigarette packages, for instance, carry a warning from the surgeon general about the danger of smoking to one's health. The campaigns against smoking and the health hazards posed by secondary smoke have led to a decrease in cigarette sales in the United States. To make up for this shrinking market, U.S. cigarette companies have aggressively sought foreign markets. In the absence of legal restraints, they target teenagers in the hope of capturing lifelong users. If no notice of potential harm is required, none is carried. Cigarette smoking is as injurious to the health of non-Americans as it is to Americans. Is it ethical for tobacco companies to aggressively advertise smoking to teenagers abroad when it may not do so in the United States, and to seek to develop large markets without any warning of the dangers of smoking?

Tobacco companies defend their actions in the United States on the basis that cigarettes are sold to adults who are informed of the possible dangerous consequences of smoking. Cigarette advertising is banned from American television to prevent child and teenage addiction. If, despite warnings, adults are willing to take the health risk for whatever reasons, then because they are members of a free society, government will not prevent them from doing so. That defense does not work if advertising and promotions target teenagers, and if no warnings of the dangers of smoking are given together with the product.

The former Soviet republics, countries of Asia, and many less developed countries are all potentially lucrative markets that U.S. tobacco companies are cultivating. By 1994 Philip Morris had a controlling interest in the formerly state-owned Czech tobacco company, had captured a large share of the cigarette industry in Russia, and had agreed to produce Marlboros in China.

Are such practices by tobacco firms ethically justifiable?

Weapons sales are another area of questionable international trade. Trade takes place both by private manufacturers and by governments.

Corruption is often imposed by violence, and violence frequently comes on the end of a bayonet, rifle, submachine gun, or tank. Ideally, each legitimate government has the monopoly of force in its society. This means that it controls the weapons and has the largest arsenal in the society—an arsenal sufficient to defend itself and its people and to enforce the law.

In addition to weapons used for law enforcement, weapons are generally legitimate only for peaceful means, such as hunting for food, possibly for sport, and for self-defense needs.

The sale of arms by anyone who knows or even has reason to believe they will be used for any illegitimate purpose is unethical, just as is their use. Drug lords use armaments of all kinds when threatened, as well as to threaten. Not only is this use of arms unethical, but providing the weapons for this use is also unethical.

It is more difficult to fight corruption if the corrupt are armed. This link between arms and corruption makes it difficult, sometimes even impossible, to effectively fight corruption without also controlling access to arms. The ultimate nightmare is that a crime syndicate gets nuclear devices and holds a city, country, or multinational hostage for extortion payments. Yet the difference between nuclear devices and submachine guns or automatic weapons is one of degree, not of principle.

It is idealistic to think that weapons manufacturers will limit the arms they sell and will voluntarily restrict their sales, even though they may not ethically sell to corrupt parties—be they private or governmental. Realistically, the restrictions must come from each nation, from the general public, and possibly in some instances from international agreements.

A society that is serious about fighting corruption will be serious about controlling firearms. To want the one and not act on the other is to desire an end without having the resolve to achieve that end.

The major arms suppliers are the United States, Russia, France, China, and the United Kingdom. Russia's need for hard currency has led it to seek new markets for its arms, often at what are considered bargain basement prices. How many arms does a nation need for self-defense? Is it either ethical or wise for any country to supply other countries with the arms a country desires for aggression? Are those who supply such arms partially responsible for the aggressive wars that are fought with the arms they provided? Foreign aid to less developed countries has often been given primarily in arms. In 1992 the European Community considered a novel approach: making economic aid dependent on a country's cutting its arms spending.[6] With the end of the Cold War and the consequent cutbacks in U.S. defense spending, American defense contractors became more dependent on foreign contracts. Arms sales to the Middle East, especially Saudi Arabia, increased significantly after the Gulf War. Who decides what arms sales are ethically justifiable? If the U.S. government authorizes the sale of arms to a given country, does that equal ethical justifiability?[7] If U.S. arms manufacturers depend on foreign sales, does their need justify the sale of arms to whatever extent a designated friendly government desires? Who decides and who is responsible for the tragedy of wars that erupt using such arms?

---

[6] Wolfgang H. Reinicke, "Arms Sales Abroad: European Community Export Controls Beyond 1992," *Brookings Review*, 10, no. 3 (Summer 1992), pp. 22-25.

[7] Jeff Cole and Sarah Lubman, "Bombs Away: Weapons Merchants Are Going Great Guns in Post-Cold War Era," *Wall Street Journal*, January 28, 1994, pp. A1, 4-5.

Illegal drugs are a third category of questionable products. The issue is not whether illegal drugs should be sold as long as they are illegal. Rather, the issue is whether multinationals can legitimately engage in trade and manufacturing with and in countries in which drug lords in effect wield great power. May multinationals deal or trade with such people or operate in such countries? If not, what are they allowed to do to protect themselves? These questions raise the broader issue of operating in destabilizing environments.

Operating in Destabilized Environments

How should multinationals function in destabilized environments in which corruption is rampant and the country's government, though not corrupt, is ineffective in controlling corruption? Some of the countries in South America form a case in point. For instance, operating in a country such as Colombia, where drug lords exercise great power and the government is less than effective in controlling them, is extremely difficult. Nonetheless, two points are clear.

First, there is no ethical justification for any company, American or other, supplying anyone involved in cocaine production with ether or methyl ethyl ketone, which are used in reducing coca leaves to cocaine. Moreover, since these chemicals are known to be used in producing cocaine, any company supplying these chemicals to any firm or person in Colombia, or in any other locale in which the transfer of the materials to cocaine producers in Colombia is likely, has the obligation to make sure that the purchasers are engaged in legitimate activities and to the extent possible that the chemicals will be used for legitimate purposes. Greatly increased purchases by any party without corresponding legitimate output constitutes grounds for refusing to supply the chemicals in the amounts requested. This is an obligation that other companies do not typically have.

Second, other companies, whether they be manufacturing, service, banking, or other, have the ethical obligation not to supply known narco producers and traffickers with goods or services. No American company is obliged to operate in Colombia. If it does, it has special ethical obligations that it does not have when it operates in many other countries. The special obligations come both because the company is foreign and because of the locale in which it is operating. No company is ethically allowed to aid or abet in any way narco producers or traffickers; and given the prevalence of the drug trade in Colombia, each firm must make sure as best it can that it does not supply goods or services to those in the drug trade. Ignorance in this context is no excuse. Companies are obliged to take affirmative action in checking on the legitimacy of those with whom they deal. Companies that do not live up to this obligation directly or indirectly aid or abet the drug trade and are to that extent ethically culpable. If American companies cannot guarantee that their hands are reasonably clean in this regard, they are ethically required either to change their policies so that they can guarantee reasonably clean hands or to leave the country.

The obligation of noncomplicity falls not only to the firm as such (that is, to the managers and high-level executives) but to all the other employees as well. Lower level workers cannot excuse their engaging in activities that they know aid and abet drug traffickers on the grounds that they are just obeying orders. One can no more use that as an excuse than one can excuse killing innocent people because one's boss or superior commands it. Although their culpability may be reduced, it is nonetheless real. Those in positions of setting policy have greater responsibility.

In each case, we can distinguish the responsibility of individuals from the responsibility of the firm as such and from the responsibility of firms in an industry or region that follow similar practices. In the case of dealing with drug traffickers, an industrywide policy or a policy of all U.S. companies against such dealings is more effective than individual company policies that may incur greater expenses for the company and force it to operate at a competitive disadvantage. Moreover, corporate, industry, and group policies, should be consistent with national and international policies aimed at fighting the drug trade.

A multinational that operates in such conditions has directly involved itself in Colombian society. It employs Colombians, and it benefits by its operations in Colombia. If it had no operation in the country, it could consistently claim that it has no responsibility to do anything about the drug situation there. But it cannot both operate there and claim no involvement; by its presence it is involved. It is not easy for a foreign firm to operate with integrity in Colombia, but claiming a neutral stance on the drug problem is not an ethically credible alternative.

Any company, just as any individual, has the right to defend itself and to establish its own contingency plans for crises. It should, however, cooperate with legitimate local security, military, and police forces in order not to hinder ordinary police and security measures and operations. For this reason, strictly independent measures are ethically suspect. An analogy can be drawn between civilians carrying weapons to defend themselves rather than relying on the police. If the practice becomes widespread, it quickly leads to an outlaw-type society where anarchy reigns and the strongest determine policy. Even if it does not become widespread, it still is unacceptable behavior, for it threatens legitimate expectations and undermines civil authority.

What is the ethically appropriate position for U.S. firms in Colombia? They should acknowledge by their actions that they are in a foreign country and act as guests should act; they should help local civic efforts, just as many companies do in the United States; and they should work with Colombian officials and security forces, again just as American companies do in the United States. The point here is not that U.S. companies should behave in all respects in Colombia as they do in the United States. Rather, there are some appropriate ways of acting that cross borders, and cooperating with legitimate authority is one of them.

Such cooperation involves several levels. Crisis management is based on local initiatives and does not require corporate approval. Such behavior should be made known to all employees, and individuals should be expected to act accordingly. At the level of the firm, those in charge are responsible for directing the firm in accordance with the approved procedures. The firm cannot fight or solve the problems of drug trafficking or guerrilla warfare by itself, nor should it. It appropriately cooperates with both other American firms and with the Colombian government.

At first it might appear that those firms that try go it alone show the greatest courage. After all, they defend themselves and stand alone as did the gunslingers in the days of the old American West. But their courage is misplaced, just as a gunslinger's courage in any civilized society is inappropriate. True courage is exemplified by those who, despite threats, cooperate with the lawful authorities and work with them against the illegal elements in the society. The courage to stand with others against the enemy is preferable to standing alone and possibly cooperating with the enemy of the host country.

The Colombian government has for a long time spoken of waging war on the drug lords. The term *war* carries with it a variety of connotations, but primarily that of a type of civil war, with the drug lords holding parts of the country. They have mercenary troops and arms; they fight by terror and attack innocent civilians; and they deal in drugs, which have become the bane of country after country. Their aim is money and what money can buy. Just as during World War II it would have been unethical for Americans to trade or cooperate with the enemy, so it is unethical for those companies that operate in countries such as Colombia to trade or to cooperate with or to fail to oppose the enemy, in this case the drug traffickers.

A state of war authorizes certain actions that are not authorized in peace. But these are not to be determined by individual firms acting unilaterally, even though self-defense is a legitimate activity within the limits set by society.

Operating in a war-torn country is dangerous and difficult. Although no foreign firm is obliged to operate in such conditions, if it chooses to do so, then it ought to act appropriately. "Appropriately" means cooperating fully with legitimate authority and joining with others in refusing to deal with or to help those engaged in drug production or trafficking.

We can generalize this discussion to other contexts as well, and in all of them the following key guidelines apply: It is wrong to do anything unethical, even when fighting unethical forces; it is legitimate to protect one's property and personnel by private means if public means are insufficient, but restraint is always required; it is appropriate to join with others in opposing violence and corruption; it is mandatory to cooperate with legitimate local and national government authorities; and it is the obligation of large and powerful corporations to take the initiative in organizing ethically justifiable responses, which usually include exercising moral imagination and using the public media to spotlight immorality and to mobilize opposition to it.

Outsourcing, Slavery, and Child Labor

International outsourcing is the practice of a company manufacturing or contracting all or parts of its product abroad. Through such outsourcing a company can purchase what it needs more cheaply abroad than making it itself, or if it manufactures the product itself, it does so using cheaper labor than is available at home. International outsourcing takes advantage of differentials in labor costs. Although such outsourcing by American companies is condemned by some because it transfers jobs from the United States, in itself it is not unethical. Nonetheless, some practices involved in international outsourcing are unethical.

Slavery, is, of course, immoral. Hence, it is unethical knowingly to buy goods made with slave labor, because doing so fosters the continuation of slavery as well as profiting from it. Child labor is illegal in the United States and in many other parts of the world, but it is not illegal everywhere. Is it ethically permissible for American multinationals to employ child labor where it is the local custom? Is it permissible to purchase goods made by child labor? There is large agreement in the United States that neither practice is allowable from an ethical point of view. But what exactly is permitted and prohibited is not always clear.

The International Labor Office claims that 25 percent of children between the ages of 10 and 14 are working not only in Asia but even in parts of Western Europe.[8] Child labor is not simply a matter of children working. Often they are paid nothing or are charged more for their room and board than they earn, making them bonded servants working long hours in extremely poor conditions. They are in effect slaves. Anti-Slavery International claims that worldwide more than 100 million people are in effect slaves and 16 million of them are in China alone.[9]

Because child labor is of many kinds, ranging from slave labor to children brought to work by their mothers to help them, some distinctions are appropriate, but still some generalizations may be made. All full-time child laborers are deprived of even rudimentary education and are condemned to impoverished lives. Multinationals do not help the situation of such children by dealing with suppliers who use such labor, even if the working conditions are tolerable. On the other hand, some might question whether U.S. multinationals do more harm than good by adopting a general policy against child labor. Theoretically, this is possible, but as a general rule multinationals are prima facie ethically bound not to deal with sources that use either slave or child labor. Any exception requires specific and detailed justification. Nor can multinationals claim ignorance about the workers who produce the goods they buy or the conditions in which they work. Large companies have the

---

[8] "Danger: Children at Work," *Futurist*, 27, no. 1 (January–February 1993), pp. 42-43. See also Martha Nichols, "Third-world Families at Work: Child Labor or Child Care?," *Harvard Business Review*, 71, no. 1 (January-February 1993), pp. 12-23. "Slavery," *Newsweek*, May 4, 1992, pp. 30-39.

[9] Hongda Harry Wu, *Laogai: The Chinese Gulag* (Boulder, Colo.: Westview Press, 1992), presents a detailed analysis of forced labor in China.

resources to investigate those with whom they do business. They can inspect the factories or plants. Levi-Strauss has set standards that its contractors have to meet in order to continue their contracts. Specifically, child labor is prohibited, at least the prevailing local wage must be paid, and reasonably safe and healthy working conditions must be provided. In addition to standards, companies can also take other imaginative approaches. Some companies have set up schools for the children of women workers who traditionally take their young children to work with them; others pay the parents the equivalent of what the children would be paid in addition to their own wages, if the children are sent to school; and still others have established training programs for the children. Yet other alternatives are possible, while still keeping costs at a competitive level.

In 1997 the U. S. government placed a ban on the importation of goods made by child labor in bondage. As a result more manufacturers started placing labels on their goods, especially their rugs, indicating that they have not been made by child labor. Whether such labeling can be trusted is debated, but nevertheless importers are making special efforts to verify how the goods they sell were made. The International Labor Organization (ILO) monitors child labor throughout the world and has campaigned for countries to adopt measures that would reduce and eventually eliminate such labor. Part of the solution to child labor is the elimination of the poverty that drives it in less developed countries. But paradoxically one of the best ways to eliminate poverty is through the education of the children who will be trained to do the kind of work required in a developed country. The child labor problem is one that will not disappear overnight. But refusing to buy products made with child labor places the emphasis in the right place and applies pressure for change.

International Business in Different Cultures: Japan

In recent years more controversy has arisen with respect to trade and business between the United States and Japan than between the United States and most other developed countries. The issues have ranged from Japan's purchase of American landmarks such as Rockefeller Center in New York City and Columbia Motion Pictures to charges of Japanese dumping of semiconductors on the American market to Japan's lack of reciprocity in opening its markets to American firms.

The differences stem in part from the two nations' different social conditions and different views of ethics.[10] The relation of business and government differs quite sharply in the two countries, even though both are capitalist democracies. In addition, their differing background institutions have caused their respective judgments of the justice of particular practices to diverge.

---

[10] For a description of the Japanese approach to ethics, see Iwao Taka, "Business Ethics: A Japanese View," *Business Ethics Quarterly*, 4, no. 1 (January 1994), pp. 53-78.

Although since 1998 there are signs of change, large Japanese firms traditionally received strong support from the government and were intertwined with other Japanese firms in a system known as *keiretsu*. These interlocking firms traditionally deal with one another, and over time they develop a feeling of obligation to each other. Thus, if one firm within the system falls on hard times, it is not unusual for the other firms to do what they can to help it. If one firm has bought supplies from another within the system for many years and the supplier has helped the main firm in the past, the main firm will feel obliged to continue to purchase from the supplier, even if its prices may be somewhat higher than those offered for the same products by a U.S. company. The American company may feel that this is unfair competition and that it is being prevented from entering the Japanese market. The Japanese firm may feel it is obliged to consider factors other than price. Who is correct?

For a long while the U.S. discount toy company, Toys 'R' Us, had a very hard time breaking into the Japanese market. It encountered roadblocks at every turn. But this reception was not very different from the reception accorded even a Japanese firm that wishes to sell at discount. Until very recently Japan's laws and local regulations in effect prohibited discount stores in order to protect neighborhood retail stores. One result was that Japanese tourists abroad could purchase Japanese-made electronic goods, for example, more cheaply abroad than they could in their native land. Was this unfair to U.S. firms? Another difficulty U.S. companies have encountered is the excessively high cost of land in Japan. To the Japanese, American property—including Rockefeller Center—seems very cheap by comparison. The fact is, however, that U.S. firms were charged no more to purchase land in Japan than the Japanese firms were. And as for American resentment of Japanese land purchases in the United States, it is true that if Americans wished to prevent foreign ownership of American land or buildings, they could do so.

Although the Japanese have a higher savings rate than Americans, the U.S. standard of living is higher than Japan's. Each side has complaints about the other, and each has suggestions for change; yet each can plausibly defend its practices from its own point of view. In such a situation, what is judged fair or ethically acceptable is dependent on one's general perspective and view of justice. This is because justice is in part determined by the system in which a particular practice is evaluated: its constitution, laws, commonly accepted customs, values, beliefs, social structures, and so on. Each of these components may be evaluated from the point of view of whether they are just but without them many social arrangements cannot take place. And only within a system is justice in many instances possible.

When differences arise as a result of different cultures, unilateral charges of unfairness or injustice are rarely effective in producing change. Rather than either side declaring what is just or fair in some absolute sense and attempting to impose its view on the other, each side, armed with its conception of what is just, can negotiate terms of trade that each would prefer to no trade at all. The parties need not agree on a conception of justice. Rather, they need agree only that the final arrangements that both accept are just from each of their perspectives. This does not mean that either side is accepting what it considers an injustice or a violation of its principles. It means that each is willing to give up some of what (on its view of justice) it thinks it deserves in order to obtain the trade that it desires.

If U.S. businesses feel they are being unfairly kept out of Japanese markets, either individually or through the U.S. government they can negotiate changes in the entry rules, providing they have something to offer the Japanese in return. And what the United States has to offer, of course, is continued entry to American markets. Sometimes the appropriate negotiations are between firms, sometimes between governments. In the case of South Africa, American companies could not ethically compromise on apartheid. In the case of Japan, however, there is no valid basis for claiming structural immorality, and so negotiation and compromise are ethically defensible ways of resolving differences.

Cross-Cultural Judgments, Negotiation, and International Justice

The pluralism worldwide means, of course, that standards are different and sometimes conflict. Within an individual country, unless there are gross violations of human rights, each country can set its own rules. If these rules are unfavorable to external competition, other affected nations can retaliate if they are in an equally strong economic position. Such retaliation often prompts the other party to reconsider its policies in the light of its broader interests and desirable international interactions.

A cross-cultural judgment concerns practices, institutions, general systems, or theories other than those of one's culture, society, or system. These judgments are the product of a country's own point of view or concept of justice inasmuch as it is impossible to adopt all points of view at once or to make judgments from no point of view. One society's perception may lead it to condemn other societies or their practices as unjust, to speak and write against them, to refuse to deal with them, or to take other actions against them. All these responses may be appropriate, and they are comparable to the kinds of actions individuals may take within their own society toward practices or companies or persons they consider to be acting unjustly or unethically. Yet most nations do not subscribe to the principle that if nation *A* believes that nation *B* is acting unethically, then nation *A* may directly interfere in the internal practices of nation *B*, despite the use of boycotts and sanctions.

Different systems can be just, and justice does not require that all countries adopt the U.S. view of justice, changing their political, social, and economic systems to match or suit those of the United States. Liberal theory tends toward the position that there is no single best combination of values, beliefs, and practices or only one just society. Some nations, however, hold their view to be the uniquely true one.

Sovereignty is part of the international system, and international business takes this as part of the background on which justice is built. Of course, some people attack sovereignty as unjust. However, that attack itself, when raised from considerations of justice, presupposes certain background institutions, assumptions, and beliefs, and, if the attack is to succeed, more is required than simply attacking sovereignty. In the present international context, sovereignty is apparently here to stay for the indefinite future, although some recent international agreements and arrangements have involved concessions with regard to sovereignty. For example, the members of the European Community have given up the right to impose tariffs on each other.

The need to resolve disputes arises once interaction takes place. Cross-cultural dialogue may lead to a better understanding of systems of justice other than one's own, to a realization of changes needed in one's own society, and to joint consideration of common problems. Moreover, despite important differences, many values and beliefs of different systems of justice do overlap and converge. There is cross-cultural consensus on some issues and near consensus on others. There is consensus, for example, that slavery is unjust both as an institution and as a social system. As an instance of near consensus, most theories, including the socialist, the liberal, the Confucian, and the egalitarian, agree that racism is unjust. The near-universal consensus on apartheid is instructive for studying specific cross-cultural responses to a system that has been almost universally condemned as unjust.

Existing conditions must serve as the starting point for change. In the absence of any universally agreed upon concept or theory of justice, justice within transactions—or what can be called international transactional justice—is properly characterized not in substantive terms but in terms of reciprocity. A transaction or practice is just if all those importantly affected by it freely and reciprocally agree to it as just. Although we can expect vested interests to dictate in part what justice claims are made, the key to just progress in the international arena is reciprocity, which in turn involves negotiation and compromise and the absence of coercion.

If the agreement in question is to be between states, reciprocity requires acknowledgment of the formal equality of states vis-à-vis one another in the context of international relations and international law. National sovereignty limits the extent to which any nation must abide by a tribunal higher than itself. International law does not at present play the mediating and adjudicating role that law does, for instance, in the United States, and it operates either by consent or by the power of strong versus weak nations. Nonetheless, there is a significant basis of common interests in survival, trade, and exchange among almost all states. Moreover, a sufficient background has already been developed by tradition, custom, and law for speaking of international justice and for determining some of what is just and unjust with respect to states. To the extent that nations accept these background conditions, they form a basis from which they can develop additional just international structures. In attempting to arrive at such structures, we can build on those practices on which nations already agree.

Exchange and trade are dominant forms of interaction on the international level, and transactional justice governs such activities. It requires that equals be exchanged for equals and that those who enter into a transaction enter freely, with each seeking to secure its own good. To the extent that transactions are forced or take place at forced prices, they are unjust according to most theories of justice. Forced transactions are one form of exploitation, and if one state exploits another, compensatory justice comes into play. The component of reciprocity is essential in just commutative transactions. If two agents with different conceptions of justice wish to trade and if their differing conceptions lead to different evaluations of the terms of the exchange, they must reach some accommodation, some agreement on terms, or some third position between the opposing positions that both are willing to accept. If these conditions are not met, then the transaction will either not take place or will be forced and therefore unjust.

On the international level, states that are relatively equal in power, such as the United States and Japan, cannot force their terms on the other. Their equality of status provides the conditions for arriving at transactions that both parties agree to be just, even though they base their judgments on different conceptions and theories of justice.

Since reciprocity involves acknowledgment that the other party or parties have equal moral status, from the point of view of justice difference in power takes a secondary place. A country or corporation that exercises its power in forcing the conditions of trade is not negotiating ethically or acknowledging reciprocity. Paying the lowest possible wages, when the alternative for the worker is starvation, is not true negotiation and does not involve reciprocity, even if the wages are not physically forced on the workers, who remain technically free to work at the stated wages or to starve. Such supposed agreements involve exploitation.

What justice involves in trade, aid, defense, or other interactions and relations between rich and poor countries is not an issue that should be settled unilaterally, even though unilateral judgments are made and are appropriate for arriving at one's position and for deciding internal policies. When the judgments of parties differ, those differences are not properly resolved by expecting either side to adopt a different conception or theory of justice or by expecting the poor country to align itself politically with any particular country. Rather, a resolution should be the product of negotiation on the terms of the transaction. At its limits, negotiations between two states or among groups of states might evolve into a truly global system involving all states. However many countries are involved, reciprocity requires that all affected parties agree to the justice of the terms. A just resolution of the dispute over the rain forests of Brazil would be a resolution that all parties would agree to as just, whatever their perspective. In such complicated issues, agreement is not easy to reach, even if everyone is willing to compromise. Often, despite negotiations, no agreement is reached.

Negotiation and compromise are ingredients in the notion of transactional international justice. Negotiation in business sounds political and therefore many treat it as having little to do with justice. Nonetheless, negotiation is morally justifiable and is often the proper procedure to follow. To say that a transaction or practice is just if all those importantly affected by it freely agree to it as just is to characterize justice by a procedure rather than by a specific outcome determined by a set of substantive principles. This is in fact what we find taking place with respect both to trade between and among countries, and to attempts to settle disputes, whether they be about borders, security, international pollution control, or other issues.

A just compromise does not involve compromising one's principles. An agreement that compromises a party's principles, that goes against its notion of justice, cannot be characterized by that party as a just agreement or solution to a problem. Compromise with respect to justice does not mean acceding to what one perceives as unjust. That would be a violation of principle and hence would not preserve one's principles and integrity. Rather, justifiable compromise involves freely giving up something to which one is entitled according to one's theory of justice. This is not unethical or unjust. Being forced by others to give it up is a different matter.

A party can consistently act from its own conception of justice to resolve disputes, while realizing that others have different views of justice. In this way, negotiation and compromise on issues is compatible with steadfast adherence to its conception of justice. Negotiation, moreover, carried on in the spirit of reciprocity often yields insights into the other's position and allows one to broaden one's own view of justice so as to include the claims to justice of others made from a conflicting perspective. Such accommodation in appropriate cases can be seen as a closer approximation to an encompassing ideal of justice, mediated by actual conditions and states of affairs that are far from ideal.

Nonetheless, not all issues, practices, or policies are open to negotiation. Just as individuals cannot morally sell themselves into slavery, so, for instance, nations or corporations cannot morally trade for products that involve slavery. In the case of South Africa, companies of integrity could not negotiate on apartheid. Negotiation and compromise should not be seen as attempts to engage in unethical practices but as means of facilitating legitimate exchanges between parties coming from different countries and cultures, with differing interests.

It is easier to negotiate agreements when the parties have a great deal in common. Thus, negotiations within the European Community (EC) will be hammered out before agreements between the EC and the Arab nations. Similarly, Canada and the United States will achieve agreements more easily than the United States and Japan. Agreements can be thought of as taking place in concentric circles. In the inner circle are agreements between those countries or those businesses that have close links, ties, traditions, and history. Those serve as a basis for agreements with the next broader concentric circle. These in turn form the basis for negotiating with those in the next ring, and so on, until we arrive at the global level.

Even with global agreement, however, negotiation is essential to international business. The ethical requirement is to keep negotiation fair and just, however all the concerned and affected parties define justice.

Study Questions

1. What is apartheid? Is it morally justifiable? Why or why not?
2. What are the Sullivan Principles? What do they call for?
3. Did following the Sullivan Principles justify the operations of American multinationals in South Africa? Why or why not?
4. What four conditions made South Africa attractive to U.S. companies?
5. What is *divestment?* What is *disinvestment?*
6. Should U.S. universities have divested themselves of the stock of firms that operated in South Africa? Why or why not?
7. Should U.S. firms have disinvested their interests in South Africa?
8. What lessons about international business can we learn from international business operations in South Africa? Explain.
9. Is bribery ethically justifiable? Why or why not?
10. What is the Foreign Corrupt Practices Act? Is the Act itself ethically defensible?
11. To what extent have other countries adopted policies similar to those contained in the FCPA?
12. What was the status of small private enterprises in Russia after the 1991 demise of the communist regime there?
13. Under those conditions, could a local entrepreneur justify paying bribes? Why or why not?
14. Under those conditions, could extortion be justified? Why or why not?
15. Under those conditions, could a U.S. multinational justify paying bribes? Why or why not?
16. Under those conditions, do U.S. multinationals have any special ethical obligations? If so, what are they. If not, why not?
17. Is international industrial intelligence gathering ethically justifiable?
18. What forms of intelligence gathering are unethical?
19. What is required of U.S. companies operating in countries in which racial or gender discrimination is widely practiced?

20. Under what conditions, if any, is it ethically permissible for U.S. cigarette manufacturers to produce and market cigarettes in developing countries?

21. Under what conditions, if any, is it ethically permissible for U.S. arms manufacturers to produce and market arms to developing countries?

22. Are there any ethical restrictions on the manufacture and sale of guns? Explain.

23. May U.S. multinationals ethically operate in countries in which drug lords or other corrupt elements exercise great control? Why or why not?

24. What measures may such companies take to protect themselves? Do they have any obligation to cooperate with legitimate local authorities? Why or why not?

25. What is international outsourcing? Is it ethically legitimate? Why or why not?

26. May U.S. companies use foreign suppliers that employ children if the use of child labor is widely practiced in the country in which the supplier is located? Why or why not?

27. American companies do not have the same access to Japanese markets as Japanese firms have to American markets. Is this unfair? Does it show unethical practices on the part of the Japanese? Explain.

28. What is a cross-cultural judgment?

29. Are negotiation and compromise ethically justifiable? Why or why not?

30. How is it possible to engage in compromise and still preserve one's integrity and one's principles? Explain.

31. What is international transactional justice?

32. What is the role of reciprocity in international transactional justice?

33. You represent a large U.S. mail-order clothing firm that is interested in lightweight cotton shirts of good quality made at a highly competitive price. You are sent to investigate possible suppliers in various parts of the world. From an ethical point of view, what considerations do you raise? When it comes to negotiating terms, what are some of the ethical constraints you should keep in mind?

21

>-!-‹›-•-◊-•-‹›-!-‹

FAMINE, NATURAL
RESOURCES, AND
INTERNATIONAL
OBLIGATIONS

The Case of Merck and Costa Rica

The rain forests of the world have drawn increasing attention in recent years as they have started to disappear. They are being cleared for farmland by burning, or the trees are being harvested for their wood. One threatened result is global climatic change. With fewer trees to absorb carbon dioxide, as well as the large amounts of carbon dioxide released by burning trees, many scientists predict global warming that could prove disastrous for various parts of the world. Of chief concern, because it is the largest, has been the Brazilian rain forest. Critics have called for a stop to the deforestation, not only citing climatic changes but also arguing that the way the deforestation is taking place will leave the land unusable and will lead to floods and other natural disasters, especially desertification.

Those engaged in the cutting and burning reply that they are only doing what the developed countries did for centuries. Those countries cut their forests without concern for its effect on the climate. They burned coal and polluted the atmosphere to such an extent that now they want to impose curbs on what others can do, which in effect locks underdeveloped countries into their underdeveloped status. If the rich countries of the world want to prevent climatic changes that will adversely affect them, the argument goes, they can pay to stop the cutting and burning. They can buy up portions of the forest and preserve them. Or they can pay those interested in cutting the forests not to do so. Moreover, the destruction of the rain forests carries with it the destruction of hundreds of thousands of species of plants and animals that thrive in that environment. Those interested in preserving those species can pay to do so.

Who owns the various species found in nature? One drug company extracted the multimillion-dollar cancer drug, vincristine, from Madagascar rosy periwinkle, paying just a few dollars for the plant. The company made millions, and Madagascar received nothing. What should it have received? Are its plants and their potential for supplying new drugs a resource similar to oil or gold from which they should receive royalties or some other kind of return?

Merck & Company, Inc., the American pharmaceutical giant, has set an example of how multinationals might act with respect to tropical rain forests. Costa Rica has set aside a quarter of its tropical forests as nature preserves, but it can afford to do so only if those areas are in some way productive. In 1991 Merck agreed to give Costa Rica's National Biodiversity Institute (INBio), a nonprofit organization established to inventory the country's flora and fauna, a 5 percent share of royalties on any drug it develops from species obtained from Costa Rica's forests. It also agreed to pay $1 million dollars up front—a considerable amount for a country whose national budget is only $1 billion—for the right to prospect for usable species. Merck has purchased the right to search the forests for samples of plants, insects, and microorganisms from which it might derive a useful drug. Since any returns in the form of royalties are speculative and at best would take ten to twenty years to materialize, the immediate payment makes possible further research by INBio. A portion of the payments also goes to the Costa Rica Ministry of Natural Resources, Energy, and Mines to be used for conservation projects.

The agreement, though widely hailed, had some critics. No one in principle opposed Costa Rica's selling its natural resources, but questions were raised about whether INBio—a private institute—had the right to sell the species that they do not own, whether the price Merck was paying was adequate, and whether the deal should have been decided by the Costa Rican people, who were not informed and had no say in the agreement. Lacking in the deal is any public accountability, as well as any consideration of other social and ecological groups and the indigenous people who developed and use herbal medicine in Costa Rica.[1]

From an ethical point of view, we may ask, who owns species existing in a forest? Who should benefit from their commercialization? What are they worth? Do pharmaceutical companies have any ethical obligation to share profits with the country in which they find a useful plant that leads them to develop a profitable drug? Was the agreement between Merck and INBio ethically justifiable?

[1] For details of this case, see Christopher Joyce, "Prospectors for Tropical Medicines," *New Scientist*, 132, no. 1791 (October 19, 1991), pp. 36-40; and Diane Gershom, "If Biological Diversity Has a Price, Who Sets It and Who Should Benefit?," *Nature*, 359, no. 6396 (October 15, 1992), p. 565.

Global Issues

In evaluating economic systems, we argued that a wealthy society that allows some of its members to die of starvation could hardly be called a moral society. In the United States, government supplements the economic system to provide for those unable to contribute to the economy and unable to care for themselves. The American economy is intertwined with much of the rest of the world, yet when we move beyond our borders and look at the rest of the world, we see that many people die of starvation and that millions of people in the world suffer from chronic malnutrition. Is it just or moral for Americans to stockpile surplus food or to cut back on the acreage planted while people in other countries starve or live on the edge of starvation? Do our moral obligations stop at our borders? It is immoral to let people in our own country die of starvation; is it therefore immoral to let people in other countries die of starvation? Can our society be a moral society if it does not respond to the needs of others? Starvation and malnutrition present one set of problems; the use of natural resources presents a second set.

If we look at the world as a unit, can we morally evaluate its overall system? If we were to do an end-state analysis, could we correctly draw any valid moral conclusions? The analogy between our analysis of the moral justifiability of the American system and of the international situation falters precisely because there is no developed international system. We have already noted the absence of adequate and effective international background institutions, and we have argued that there is a moral obligation to help create such institutions. Can we go further than that?

The United States, as a nation, possesses great material wealth while some other countries of the world are pitifully poor. By what right do some countries and people have so much wealth and use so much of the world's resources, while others have so little? To whom do the natural resources of the earth belong? The sun, moon, and ocean belong to no one. By what right do land and the natural resources on or under it belong to those who happen to inhabit the land or who happen to find the resources? By an accident of birth, people born in an arid, barren country are doomed. They have no free access to better land, no equal opportunity for improvement, and no chance for a decent life. Is it fair that others who happen to be born in lands of rich soil and with minerals, oil, and gold enjoy the exclusive use of these natural resources? The people of "have-not" nations are saying—more clearly and more often—that it is not fair. They are calling more and more strongly for an international plan of redistribution.[2]

If once there seemed to be an inexhaustible supply of land and natural resources, this is now no longer the case. We can foresee the complete depletion of the world's oil supply, and we know other minerals are exhaustible.

---

[2] For example, see United Nations General Assembly, A/9556 (Part II) May 1, 1974, *Study of the Problems of Raw Materials and Development: Report of the Ad Hoc Committee of the Sixth Special Session,* "Declaration on the Establishment of a New International Economic Order."

This knowledge raises a third set of problems. Do those who are now alive have the right to use as much of these as we wish and in any way we desire? Do we have an obligation to save any of these resources for future generations? Do Americans owe more to the poor of other countries who are now alive or to their their own descendants, if they must choose between them?

All of these questions are extremely complex, controversial, and difficult to answer. The moral intuitions of most people falter when they are faced with questions of this scope. It is easier to ignore them than to face them. But both as a nation and as individuals, we would be immoral if we chose to ignore our moral obligations simply because they were difficult and new and concerned people who were far away in space or time. Because businesses, large and small, are the major users of resources—and, some claim, the perpetrators of exploitation—as well as the chief mediators between the economies of rich and poor nations, they are centrally involved in the moral issues.

Famine, Malnutrition, and Moral Obligation

The basic approaches of utilitarianism and deontology can be used to handle any type of moral problem. But it is also possible, using these approaches, to develop second-order principles or rules. These rules, we saw, are typically substantive rather than formal and thus have specific moral content. We can use them in solving complex moral problems. Frequently, the application of second-order principles is clearer than the application of the general, basic first-order moral rules or principles.

The most fruitful approach to complex moral problems is to divide them into smaller, more manageable parts. As we develop clarity in each of the parts, we develop greater clarity with respect to the problem as a whole. In dealing with the general problems of famine and malnutrition, therefore, we should see if we can reduce them to manageable pieces. We should also see if we can find some appropriate second-order moral principles that are applicable. Questions of famine and malnutrition concern our relations to food and to other human beings. We can start with ourselves. Each of us needs food in order to live. We need a certain amount and quality of food to do more than just survive—that is, to develop fully, maintain our health, and work and act efficiently. When there is food enough for all, it is morally permissible for me to satisfy my need for food. It is, moreover, a prima facie moral duty for me to preserve my health, under normal conditions, and so it is a prima facie moral duty for me to eat adequately.

What about an obligation to others with respect to food? Most people would readily agree that parents are morally obliged to feed their children if they are able to do so. Parents have a special responsibility with respect to their children because the children are theirs. It would be inappropriate in a family of meager means for the parents to eat well and let the children starve. They are not required, however, to feed the children well and to starve themselves. How, in the long run, would the parents' resulting death benefit the children? As a general principle, no one is obliged to sacrifice himself for others. To do so may be morally praiseworthy, but it is not morally required because, as a moral agent, each person is an end in himself, as worthy of respect as any other person. We can also argue that each person has a greater obligation to feed those for whom he is responsible than to feed those for whom he is not so responsible, because of this special relationship.

We can push this a step further. In general, anyone is obliged to help others in serious need if he can do so at little cost to himself. Suppose we are in a boat when we see another boat turn over. We see that the occupant of the other boat is drowning. We could easily extend an oar, let him grab it, and then climb to safety in our boat. Most people would readily admit that we have the obligation to do so, because to adopt this rule would be to promote the greatest good of all concerned. In the case of the overturned boat, the good the drowning man gains is weighed against the minimal effort required for us to extend an oar. It is equally clear that we, as rational beings, would all will such a principle to be a universal law; it can be universalized without contradiction and would show respect to people as valuable ends in themselves. When we apply the same principle, if one person has plenty of food and sees someone else starving and if he can save that person at little cost to himself, the person with food is obliged to do so.

We used similar reasoning to arrive at the collective obligation to help those in U.S. society who are in serious need. Each person has an obligation to help if they can do so at little cost to themselves. If all those who are able to do so contribute a little, those in dire need can be helped. As a society, Americans collectively organize to fulfill this as well as other common ends. They achieve the redistribution of income through taxation and welfare programs.

But why help the needy in one's own society rather than those in other societies? Are they not all people and therefore have equal claim on us? By following a line of reasoning analogous to that we just used, we find that people have a special relation to those with whom they form a society. They are bound to each other by common laws, share common burdens, and jointly pursue common goods within their society. Just as they have a greater obligation to feed those for whom they are responsible, so they have a greater obligation to feed the hungry in their own society than they do the hungry of other societies if the need of each group is equal.

Suppose that as a nation all Americans are adequately fed and that they have surplus food or resources to produce it. There are starving people in other countries. Do Americans have a moral obligation to feed them? We saw that all persons have an obligation to help someone in serious need if they can do so at little cost to themselves. Is the principle applicable here? Starvation constitutes dire need. Individually, someone in the United States can do little to help someone starving in a remote area of Africa. But collectively, that is, through a united effort or through governmental action, one may be able to do a great deal. If this is the case, then the principle applies and the person has a moral obligation. An individual discharges this obligation by paying taxes or donating to CARE, the Red Cross, or some other relief fund. Obviously, those within our country who have barely enough for themselves cannot help others without significant cost and sacrifice to themselves. But those who can do so have the obligation to help others. They can discharge their obligation through the government, which acts for them and uses the money they pay in taxes in the way they authorize. The obligation of the government is to act as the people authorize; the obligation of the people is to help those in need. The distinction is an important one.

Thus far, we have argued using a weak second-order moral principle. Can we justify a stronger principle—for example, that each person has an obligation to help another seriously in need, even at considerable cost to himself? We argued that no one is morally obliged to sacrifice himself for another. But if we consider that principle as being at one end of a continuum and, at the other end, the obligation of helping another at little cost to oneself, we see there are many alternatives between the extremes. Where do we draw the line of obligation? How much cost must we bear in order to help others in dire need? Rather than attempt to answer that question directly, we can answer it indirectly. We can join our weak second-order principle to this principle: To those for whom we are directly responsible we owe more than others; and we owe more to those with whom we have a special relation than we owe to those with whom we have no special relation. Therefore, no matter where we draw the line concerning the trade-off of the other's good and one's own cost, we have greater obligations and should be willing to suffer a greater loss to benefit those with whom we have special relations and ties.

Up to now, we have been dealing with the responsibility of Americans, assuming that on the whole Americans have enough to eat and the wherewithal to help others. The argument, however, can be applied equally well to all other people. It can apply to the Japanese, the Germans, the people of the former Soviet Union, and many others as well. This consideration leads to two questions. Does each individual have an obligation to help up to a certain point, or do individuals have an obligation equal only to the total amount necessary do relieve starvation, divided by the total number of people on earth able to help? Are people in countries that are not organized for such purposes relieved of their responsibility?

In answer to the first question, our principle assigns an obligation to help if one can do so at little cost. What is little cost to someone who is rich is different from what is little cost to someone of very modest means. Hence, the obligation is proportional. If people choose to have the government discharge their obligations, they equalize the burden if the government taxes people in proportion to their income. If the people of some countries of the world do not fulfill their obligations with respect to starving peoples of other countries, does that affect the obligations of people of other countries? The first obligation is to help if it costs one little. The amount is initially determined by dividing what is required by all those capable of giving. The failure of some to give what they ought increases the amount the others must give if the lives of those in need are to be saved. These others are obliged to give that greater amount if they are able to give it at little cost.

The reply to the second question is that people are not relieved of their responsibility if their countries are not organized to serve these ends. The obligation remains, even if it cannot be directly discharged. It then leads to the obligation to so organize that they can discharge their obligations. But the situation is by no means simple. People who do not know of the starvation of others may be excused from fulfilling their obligation to the starving if they are invincibly ignorant or can satisfy some other excusing condition. For instance, at little cost to themselves, they may not be able to organize the country to satisfy this obligation.

How moral responsibility and blame for failure to fulfill one's responsibility should be assigned in all these cases is far from clear. The starving people of other countries are to us unknown, unseen people whose presence and plight do not impress themselves upon us as do the needy of our own society. If we feel an obligation to help the starving in other lands, it is usually an obligation that is not first and foremost on the list of other pressing obligations we have. If the share of each of us is 10 cents, it does not seem to be a major moral obligation, even if the 10 cents is part of the $2 million required to save the lives of the people in question. If no one helps and thousands die, is each of us responsible for the death of all these people or for only a very small part of the death of one person? In the latter case, is a small part of the death of one person a reasonable concept, or is each of us, together with some others, fully responsible for that one death? The answer, though not clear, is worth pondering.

There is a difference between a country suffering from a temporary famine because of an unusual and devastating drought and a country whose people suffer from chronic malnutrition. Are the obligations of those able to help the same in both cases? Many argue that they are not, and we can consider the cases separately.

People live in countries; they are organized into societies within certain geographical boundaries. Each of these nation-states has a government that, with only periodic exceptions, other governments recognize as exercising sovereignty within their domain. Recognition of sovereignty demands that no state physically violate the territorial integrity of another state. Each government rules its own people and represents them in the international arena. This in some ways simplifies and in other ways complicates our problem. If the people of one country are starving, the system of nation-states makes it possible for other countries to learn of their plight. The governments of these other countries can in turn respond with food or aid.

Suppose, however, that some people of a country are starving. The government of the country does not wish foreign aid and would prefer to have some of its people die; or suppose the starving people are a dissident, rebellious sect who are being starved into submission by the government; or suppose food delivered free to the government of a country is not freely given to the starving but sold by the government to those able to purchase it. Or suppose that the government wishes to distribute the food it received from abroad to the starving, but because of inefficiency on its part, it is unable to deliver the food to those needing it, and the food rots on the docks.

Is the moral obligation to help the starving greater than the obligation to respect national sovereignty? As with many cases that involve the clash of prima facie obligations, the question cannot be answered a priori. Because we are using the weak principle of little cost, if the violation of sovereignty might lead to war, to a break in diplomatic relations, or to something else that may be viewed as more than a little cost, the principle does not apply. The fact that such difficulties frequently arise, moreover, makes it difficult for individuals to know what the actual situation is and whether they actually have a moral obligation to supply aid.

What is the difference between cases of famine and cases of chronic malnutrition? We can distinguish cases: famine through no fault of the people versus famine through the fault of the people; and malnutrition through no fault of the people versus malnutrition through fault of the people. Does it make any difference whether people starve through no fault of their own or through their own fault? We might get a better perspective by making the fault versus no-fault distinction with respect to people in our own country. Suppose someone is able to work, work is available, but he prefers not to work; he chooses to sleep and idle away the hours. He runs out of money and still refuses to work. He comes close to starvation, announces that he is starving, and claims it is the obligation of others to feed him. Do they have this obligation? Each person has the obligation to care for himself if he is able to do so. If he does not, must others care for him? Several principles seem to apply here, in addition to the one concerning helping others. One is that it is not unjust to let people suffer the evil consequences of their freely chosen deliberate actions. A solution to the problem, which can satisfy both principles, would be not to feed the person indefinitely but to make it possible for him to work and to make his receiving food contingent on his working. Suppose he has children. Assuming they are starving through the fault of their father and no fault of their own, theirs is a no-fault case, which is governed by our weak principle concerning aid to the needy.

Let us now return to a starving country. Suppose a people were warned not to denude their forests and they did so nonetheless. This resulted in floods, loss of topsoil, and destruction of their farmlands. They are now starving and ask for help. By analogy with the prior case, only some of the people are at fault—those who cut the forests. The others suffer as a consequence of the actions of a few. Help should be given in accordance with earlier principles. But because the land is barren, help might appropriately include not only food but also fertilizer, saplings for planting, and technical aid necessary to prevent future failure. As in the case of the individual, the willingness of a country to help itself is an appropriate condition for continued aid.

The cases of malnutrition are in some ways parallel to the cases of starvation, and in some ways different. Let us assume the malnutrition is serious, and so the harm to those who suffer it is serious. Though the harm is less than in the cases of starvation, the same principles apply. We have not yet considered one principle, however, which some people claim is applicable—viz., we should not help others if giving such help will produce more harm than not giving it. This is a simple application of the general principle of utility. It can also be defended from a deontological perspective.[3]

Suppose that by supplying food to a country whose people chronically suffer from malnutrition we alleviate that malnutrition for a given year. If we did not supply them with food, some of them would die from their inability to fight off disease, but some children would still be born and the population would remain on the whole stable. If for one year we supply them with food, fewer people would die. Let us further suppose that being healthier, the population increases faster than it would otherwise. The result is a larger population than before. If there was not enough food for the smaller population, there will be even less food per person with the increase in population. By giving aid we thus render a larger number worse off than the number of people that would originally suffer without our help. In fact, our help produces more harm than good. If we alleviate the harm that would follow by helping them a second year, we postpone, but multiply, the harm of not helping them the third year and so on. If they can be helped to become nutritionally self-sufficient through technological aid, then that is our moral obligation. But if despite advanced agricultural techniques the land is unable to support their numbers, then the numbers must be reduced by decreasing the fertility rate. This, however, may not be what they choose to do. Then the principle of accepting the consequences of their freely chosen actions is applicable. A difficulty, of course, is that frequently the people involved do not freely and knowingly choose a course of action, and the situation is unclear.

We have argued thus far from the weak principle of help at little cost. We did not attempt to draw the line at some greater cost, except that it is higher for those for whom we are responsible and with whom we have special relations. If we defend and adopt a stronger principle, the analysis will proceed in much the same way: Our moral responsibility for helping those in need will increase in direct proportion to the increase in cost we are able to bear and inversely as the need of the other is less serious.

We did not claim that governments have the obligation to help people in foreign countries except insofar as government is the medium through which

---

[3] A good collection of papers on international redistribution and hunger is William Aiken and Hugh La Follette (Eds.), *World Hunger and Moral Obligation*, 2nd ed. (Upper Saddle River, N.J.: Prentice Hall, 1995). See also Lee A. Tavis (Ed.), *Multinational Managers and Poverty in the Third World* (Notre Dame, Ind.: University of Notre Dame Press, 1982), and P. T. Bauer, *Reality and Rhetoric: Studies in the Economics of Development* (Cambridge, Mass.: Harvard University Press, 1984), which rebuts critics' claims about the dependency of LDCs on more developed countries.

the people of a country discharge their obligations. The reason for making this distinction is that the government of a country has obligations to the people of the country which it governs. Its obligations to feed the hungry of its own country are a result of the structure of the society. The members of the society contribute to the government and, as members of that society, receive benefits and bear obligations. We are not subject to governments other than our own. We owe no duties to them and deserve no benefits from them. Our government properly takes the initiative in helping the starving in other countries, to the extent that that action is one that has been authorized by the people through their representatives.

Nation-states are not moral beings. The international arena is not one of total anarchy because there is cooperation and there are some agreed-upon rules of interaction. And although all peoples of the earth form a moral human community, the nations of the world form an ambiguous moral community. Although each of us has the obligation to help people in dire need, governments come and go and national boundaries change. Agreements may obligate one nation to help another. Nations per se do not starve, however; people do. The moral obligation to help the starving is an obligation to people, and so the obligation is not dependent on the type of government under which a people live. Nonetheless, we have a special relation to the people of those other countries with which our country forms special communities; we have a greater obligation to help them than to help those with whom we do not form a community. The absence of a world government precludes the kind of redistribution—through taxation, for instance—possible within a nation-state. This often makes it difficult to give effective and equitable aid to people in need in other countries.

Although individually we have some obligation to answer the legitimate claims of people to subsistence, when their governments are unable to satisfy this right, there are many impediments to our individually fulfilling this obligation. There are fewer impediments to people fulfilling an obligation collectively, however, through their governments. The major responsibility, therefore, falls on government. People can rightly demand that their government take an active role in helping them collectively meet their obligations. They can legitimately demand that their government take an active role in developing and supporting effective international structures capable of meeting these obligations. If their government so acts, it will mean increased taxation and possibly some loss of sovereignty. But as participants in a world economy, people cannot morally refuse to bear these costs.

What of businesses? Do they have obligations with respect to the starving in other lands? Do farmers and those in the food industry have special obligations? On the basis of the second-order principles we have been using, the answer is that businesses in this regard have no special obligations, providing they have no special relations to the country in question. But they have the obligation to bear their fair share of taxes, including their fair share of increased taxes.

A U.S.-based multinational corporation has increased obligations because of its international activity. It is more closely tied to foreign peoples and nations than are businesses that operate only in the United States. Multinationals are citizens of more than one country and hence have obligations to the people of all the countries in which they operate. The obligation to pay their fair share of taxes in each country is clear. The obligation not to harm is also clear. Agricultural multinationals have the obligation not to contribute to starvation and malnutrition by buying up farmland for export crops with no concern for the effect of this action on the local population. The general principles of morality will require different specific actions by particular corporations in particular countries. But the obligations of these corporations directly involved in a foreign country are greater to that country than are the obligations of corporations not so involved.

American farmers and businesses in the food industry, on the other hand, do not have greater obligations to feed the starving simply because they are food producers or processors. Because the food for starving people in other lands is paid for by the people of the nation giving the food, the burden should be equitably borne. No special responsibility falls on any group. The decision to increase crop production or to grow enough to produce a surplus for the needy of other countries is a decision to be made within our system. Production can be increased in response to the government's placing orders for food. Farmers have no special obligation to help others, though it would be immoral for them purposely to hinder others from providing such help by refusing to increase production. Hindering others from doing what they ought to do is wrong for everyone, and farmers in this instance come under the general rule.

The foregoing analysis of starvation and malnutrition has assumed certain background conditions. It has assumed, for instance, that it is possible to feed all the people of the world at a level above that of malnutrition and that each country is capable of doing so. If we change these background assumptions, we shall have to modify the analysis accordingly. Assume, for instance, that the world is not capable of supporting the number of people in it at a decent level of life. We might then argue either that the number of people should be reduced or that those with more than enough should change their diet, sharing more of what is available with others. The demand to share is already being pressed with respect to natural resources.

Property and Allocation of the World's Resources

In speaking of the resources of the world and asking to whom they belong, we imply that the resources are property. But there is a good deal of ambiguity in the term *resources*. We can categorize resources in several ways. In one category we can place natural resources—air, water, minerals, land, trees. In a second category we can include natural but developed resources—cultivated fruits and vegetables, domesticated animals and their products (milk, meat, wool, eggs, etc.). In a third category we can place manufactured goods, and in a fourth, social, nonmanufactured goods—knowledge, technology, organization, talents, skills, and perhaps even language. People, of course, inhabit the earth. Should they be considered as part of its resources? A country with a large labor force, for instance, has an important resource that a country with few people does not have. A country with a skilled labor force or with an industrious people or with a cooperative, productive population has a resource other countries may lack. People, however, are not property. Are their properties (their intelligence, their skill, their strength) their own, or are they simply bearers of these characteristics, which should be used for the benefit not only of themselves but for the benefit of humankind or at least of their fellow citizens?

In answer to the question of ownership of the resources of the world, three answers are often given. One is the common-sense answer of business: The resources of the world have already been divided up. Corporations, governments, and individuals own them. This is the status quo position. The second reply acknowledges that the resources of the earth have in fact been divided up, but claims that *by right* the resources of the world belong to all the people or to all the people of a given state or country or society. The third reply also acknowledges the fact that the division of resources has already taken place, but, like the second reply, it denies that the de facto division is necessarily morally justifiable. However, rather than claiming common ownership, it claims a universal right of access to the resources of the earth.

The Status Quo View of Resources

The common-sense view of natural resources is that we must start from where we are. The resources of the earth have already been divided up. It is futile to inquire about the original allocation of resources or to deny the reality of present ownership. However resources are defined, property comes into existence only within a framework of recognized rights—typically, the right to use, the right to exclude others from use, the right to dispose of an object, and sometimes the right to benefit from that which is owned. It makes no sense to speak of property or ownership in the abstract. Property is the result of a social practice and is always defined within a social context.

The world is divided into countries, each of which makes territorial claims. Most of these are not challenged by others, even though a few areas and borders are in dispute. Each of the countries has within it a government and an economic order. Ownership means different things in different societies, and claims and rights are treated differently in different countries. In some, individuals or groups are allowed to own land, minerals, factories; in others, only the government owns these. In all systems, however, some food and some goods are produced and distributed; some services are available and enjoyed. Each system has a mechanism for deciding when the ownership rights it recognizes have been violated and has procedures for deciding how to allocate them when there is a dispute. Fairness, according to this view, means abiding by the rules and procedures governing those within the system. This is usually equated with legality.

Instead of asking who by right owns the resources of the earth, suppose we ask who owns the large deposits of oil that have been discovered in Mexico? We know that the oil belongs to the human race because it is of no interest to the other species on earth. All of humankind is richer because of the discoveries because that much more oil is now available for human consumption. However, we refer quite properly to the oil as Mexican oil because it is in Mexico. The Mexican government has control of it, and hence the oil properly belongs to Mexico, where that means, ambiguously, to the government and to the people of Mexico. Within that country, the laws of the land determine to whom it belongs more specifically. It belongs in part to those who discovered it, to those who own the land under which it lies, to those who extract it, to those who process it, and to those who buy rights to it. Mexico is richer because of the new-found oil. But the oil is not apportioned to each Mexican citizen, much less to all people of the world. Most of them would have no use for a certain quantity of crude oil. After it is processed, the oil is used by Mexicans, who no longer have to import oil. But it is also sold to other countries. Mexico is richer because it sells oil to other countries. If a glut on the market diminishes the foreign demand for its oil, Mexico is no longer able to profit from its oil as it did before.

Any attempt to claim that the oil did not belong to Mexico but to all the people of the earth would be met with immediate, fierce, and legitimate resistance, for according to the rules by which Mexico and the rest of the world abide, the oil is Mexico's. Notice, moreover, that the natural resources of a country are valuable to a country not only because they are available for the direct use of the population. They are also important because of the possibility of selling (e.g., the oil) to others who want the resources and are willing to pay for them. Therefore, those who make simplistic charges that some people use too much oil or other resources because they buy them from other countries fail to understand that natural resources constitute economic riches only to the extent that they are usable and desired by someone. This is compatible with an obligation not to waste natural resources, even if one can afford to do so.

In the United States, the allocation and use of resources are determined by the market within limits set by the law. Individual firms buy the raw materials they need to produce their goods and services. Individual consumers buy what they need and want in order to achieve their own ends. Defenders of the system argue that this allocation of resources is more efficient and entails less waste than allocation by government. The same is true, they claim, on a worldwide scale.

The reality of sovereignty is of significance, not only for how much any one country can do for another, but also for any discussion of the rights of countries with respect to the allocation of resources. The status quo view resists any claims by resource-poor countries on the resources of other countries.

The Universal-Ownership View

The status quo view is attacked, however, by those who claim that the present division of the world's resources is unjust. The distribution of resources is arbitrary; some countries have very few resources, and others have many. From a moral point of view, the natural distribution can be taken as the starting point; but it must be corrected so that the resources serve the good of all people, not only the good of the lucky and rich. Originally, the goods of the earth belonged in common to all, and all people retain a claim on the earth's resources, despite arbitrary divisions and allocations that some people have introduced.

But what does it mean, when one says that the resources of the earth belong to everyone? In one sense, something can belong to everyone if each person has a right to its use, and no one has a right to exclude anyone else from its use. Thus, a public park might be said to belong to all the people. Anyone who wants to may use the park as a park; but there are limits on the use one can make of it, and the obligation to maintain it must somehow be assigned.

A second sense in which all land, resources, and productive property may belong to everyone is this: Each has the equal right to appropriate and use (and in the process, consume) the item in question. If everyone in the society owns the wheat grown in the country, then everyone has a claim on an equal or fair share of the grain. The grain does not belong to the farmers who grow it or to the people who process it or to those who distribute it. It belongs to all, and all are entitled to a fair and—other things being the same—an equal share. This would also be true of the mineral resources of land.

Yet it would be a vacuous right or type of ownership if the iron in the ground belonged to everyone, and this meant that everyone had the right to go to where it is, dig it up, and use it. Most people do not live near iron deposits and do not need iron ore. What they need and want are products made from iron. Then, to be effective, their ownership of the iron in the ground must mean a right or claim on that iron such that they eventually get the iron products they need. In practice, this would mean that some people would have the right and obligation to mine the ore, to smelt it, to process it, and to turn it into goods. At each stage, only certain people would have the right to access and to work on the material. It is unlikely that anyone, anywhere along the line, would be allowed to take what he or she wanted because everything belongs to everyone. Because there is scarcity, although everything would belong to everyone in the society, it would have to be apportioned so that each would get his or her fair share. To allow anyone to take anything at any time would interfere with the fair allocation. In this sense, saying that everything belongs to everyone means that each of us has a certain claim on a certain portion of what is available.

Clearly, if we were to have a society of any complexity, there would have to be rules and regulations about allocation, production, work, and the distribution of goods. How allocation, production, and distribution would be carried out in a society in which all property is socially owned is far from clear; thus far, socially owned property has been more or less equal to government-owned property. Whether, on a large scale, there would be any alternative, such as true social ownership without government, is at best problematic. But even if it were achieved, individuals would still have different bundles of rights with respect to different goods.

Defenders of the universal-ownership view have no clear plan for world-wide redistribution, but they defend the need for this redistribution nonetheless.

The existing division of humankind into sovereign states, each of which claims control of the natural resources within its borders, effectively divides up the resources of the earth. To a poor country it makes little difference whether the goods within some other country are privately or socially (government) owned. If a country has no oil and it needs oil for the development that it desires, it has as little claim on Mexican oil whether the oil is owned by the Mexican government or the Mexican people, as it has on United States oil, whether the oil is owned by corporations or individuals. The internal structures of these societies, and the internal property relations in these countries result, in both cases, in outside countries having no independent claim on their resources.

Proponents of the universal-ownership view maintain that because every person has a legitimate claim on goods of the earth and because national sovereignty prevents the exercise of that claim, national sovereignty stands in the way of a worldwide just distribution of natural resources. Hence, sovereignty is to this extent morally arbitrary and should be superseded.

The argument, even if it could be made out to be valid, is not soon to be accepted by the people of any country today. Nor is it clear what would replace national sovereignty and how a just allocation of natural resources would be accomplished.

The Right to Universal Access

Although the natural distribution of resources is arbitrary from a moral point of view, what is done with the resources is not arbitrary. According to the proponents of the right to universal access, the riches of the earth should be used for the benefit of all. To this extent this third view agrees with the second, that of universal ownership. But the heart of the dispute between rich and poor countries, they claim, does not hinge on the ownership of land or resources. Basically, the moral concern of most people is related to the standard of living of those within a country, or in the world. Asking whether each has a right to a certain standard of living is more important than asking whether each has the right to a certain amount of land or resources.

The right to a certain standard of living is in turn linked with the right of development. The right of development is a right that is properly and primarily ascribed to individuals. But because individuals can develop fully only in society with others and because their level of personal development is a function of the level of development of society, we can also speak of the right of nations to develop. Therefore, it makes sense to speak of the right of underdeveloped nations to develop. Such development may require access to and use of natural resources; but the question of the right to development can and should be kept distinct from the question of the ownership of the natural resources. The two issues are related, but they are not identical.

Because nations are not persons, a nation's rights—to the extent that it has any—are different from individual rights. Nations, for instance, have no right to continuance simply because they happen to have been established; but people have a right to at least subsistence.

What is being claimed when claiming the right of a nation to develop? There are three different, though related, components or three different subclaims. First, by the right to develop is meant the freedom to develop—that is, the right to be allowed to develop and not be prevented from developing by other nations. To speak this way is to envisage each nation as a sovereign entity, claiming for itself the freedom each individual has in virtue of his or her personhood. Although nations are not human persons, the right to develop as they wish without being kept from their development by other nations is a right easily defended if the nation is seen as the collection of people within it. Each nation legitimately exercises this right, providing it does not violate a similar right of other nations and providing it does not violate the rights of the persons who make it up. This claim raises no special problems and is generally acknowledged in principle, if not always in fact, by proponents even of the status quo view.

Second, the claim to development may be a claim of one nation to receive from those nations that have them the wealth and resources that the first country needs in order to develop as it wishes. But this will clearly conflict with the right those others will claim to what they have justly appropriated, produced, or in other ways obtained. Although there is a generally acknowledged obligation to keep people alive and at least minimally nourished, the obligation to go beyond that is not generally recognized and needs more defense. The obligation within a given community or state may arise from the agreement among the members of that community or state, which leads to a certain amount of redistribution. This obligation does not clearly exist in the international arena, either with respect to individuals or with respect to nations. Proponents of the third view acknowledge this. What they claim nations can morally demand is equal access to what they need to develop. But without the money or resources to buy what they need, the right of equal access is vacuous.

The developed nations do not deny the right of all nations to equal access, and they have in fact developed institutions (e.g., the International Monetary Fund and the World Bank) that assist nations in their development through capital loans. These are funded by developed nations. As the less developed nations develop and their people achieve higher standards of living, they increase the market for more and more goods. The development of the less developed countries is thus in the interest of the more developed countries. Multinational corporations can assist in the development of many less developed countries and can do so on conditions favorable to both the countries and the corporations. But none of these institutions or practices recognizes a *right* of less developed nations to loans, assistance from other governments, or help from multinationals. The third view insists on the right of access and the concomitant right to aid from developed nations. What is now done in the name of self-interest or charity, the view holds, should be recognized as a right.

In a previous chapter we noted the enormous external debt under which many Latin American nations are struggling. A country that pays up to 70 percent of the money it receives from its exports simply to pay the interest on its debt has no hope of development. The International Monetary Fund and the World Bank mandate austerity measures that these countries must take in order to qualify for additional loans. While there is some justification for this, the burden falls primarily on the bulk of the population of those countries, who never benefited from the earlier loans. The burden should rightly fall on those who benefited from the loans—the rich within the country, sometimes the leaders of the country, some local and some multinational corporations, and the banks that made the loans, among others. As we noted in Chapter 17, American banks are slowly writing off some of the debt as uncollectable. Even more important is for them to reduce the interest rate and to wipe out the interest on those parts of the loans that they write off as uncollectable. The well-to-do countries of the world, including many of the oil-rich countries (whose actions contributed to the current situation) should all bear a share of the cost of eliminating the debt burden and of making development in and of those countries possible.

The third component of the claim to development is the right to the knowledge—technological, scientific, social, and organizational—necessary for development. No one owns knowledge. It is no one's exclusive possession, with certain small exceptions—for instance, when, for a short period of time some proprietary or other right might protect the use and dissemination of certain types of information. Because knowledge is not used up by consumption and is infinitely sharable, sharing does not diminish the amount anyone has—although it may decrease the power of those who have it over those who do not. By its nature, knowledge is also social. It has been developed by humankind as a whole and does not belong to any particular people or tradition or society or set of societies. The knowledge of high technology builds on centuries of earlier work; this knowledge properly belongs to all human beings and is the common property of all. In this sense, it is the true common property from which no one can be excluded. And it does not fall prey to the tragedy of the commons, because all can cultivate it freely and fully without using it up or destroying it.

To some degree, the developed nations have raised the expectations of people in less developed countries and so bear some responsibility for helping them realize these expectations. This is especially true of the multinational corporations that have led the way in supplying the televisions, transistor radios, communication equipment, automobiles, airplanes, and other fruits of technology to the peoples of underdeveloped countries. Such corporations say that they have simply satisfied a demand, not created it; that on the whole they have helped such countries rather than hurt them, and that their responsibility ends with supplying the product paid for. In a situation in which a government provides adequate background institutions to keep the market fair, such a claim is plausible. In many developing countries this is not the case, and defenders of the universal-access view press on multinationals the obligation not only to refrain from causing harm as they pursue their profit but also to contribute actively in helping countries develop.

Of the resources necessary for development, the most important is an educated, skilled, industrious work force. Governments wishing to educate their people can use the present communications networks already available. But even more can and should be done. Multinational corporations can provide an important means of transferring technical knowledge and training to workers of less developed countries. The obligation on the part of firms to help educate local populations, train workers, and transfer technological and organizational knowledge is one that we have seen can be made contractual, assuming that a government is interested in the development of the country and of the people, and not just in its own power, wealth, and survival. If education and training cannot be carried on profitably by a company, such training might be underwritten through tax incentives or subsidies from either the host country or the United States and other developed countries. The justification for such action would be self-interest, the morally justifiable aim of helping others, and the fulfilling of the rights of the people and of less developed nations to socially developed knowledge. Little along these lines is now done.

Through prudence, rather than through moral obligation, the nations of the world already share their knowledge to some extent. The developed nations through the UN and other agencies send teams to help apply their knowledge to local problems; universities accept students from abroad, even though such programs run the risk of acculturating the students to the way of life of the host country and may make them reluctant to return to their own lands. Both activities could be multiplied considerably.

Although knowledge is the key to development for underdeveloped countries, they also need capital to finance the substructure—roads, railroads, telephone lines, schools, hospitals, electric power plants and lines, and so on—and the development of home industries. Adam Smith (1723–1790) spoke of the wealth of nations. There is also the wealth of the world as a whole. Just as knowledge was not developed by any one person or people and belongs to all human beings, so there is a sense in which the wealth of nations is not the result only of individual enterprise and work but is the result of the contributions of people as a whole. And each nation has some claim on that general world wealth. The universal-access view does not press these claims as strongly as the universal-ownership view does. But the right to access is not only a negative right. It is also a positive one that involves a right to aid on the part of those needing it.

Whether or not a fully defended moral claim can be made out for transferring some wealth to underdeveloped countries to provide capital for local development, it is prudent to extend aid. For extremes of wealth and poverty cause social disruption, and social disruption tends to hurt the well-to-do as well as the impoverished, who have less to lose. Such help can be made on terms acceptable to both sides, and not simply on terms dictated or demanded by either side. A match between what one country has to offer and what another country needs or desires might be made through individual negotiations or through the mechanisms provided by the United Nations and other international organizations. Individual firms can play a significant role here. Multinationals have not entered the poorest countries, for they offer few markets and fewer resources. Government subsidies or government guarantees against loss for firms that enter marginal, unstable, or unprofitable markets would often be a better use of money than government attempts at direct aid. This presupposes more planning and thought than has sometimes been the case with the giving of aid in the past. Aid seldom involves simply the giving of money to be used in any way the receiver wishes. For the most part, developmental aid should consist not only of supplying goods but also of transferring appropriate technology and building substructural or productive facilities. The ideal is to help each nation achieve productive development.

The claim of equal access to the goods one needs individually or as a nation can be justified in terms of justice or of the right to life and development. But the wherewithal to secure those goods separates those people who get the goods from those who do not. And the obligation to provide the wherewithal is a disputed one. The realization that all nations form part of an increasingly interwoven network, making each nation in some way dependent on a great many others, is slowly coming to the consciousness not only of world leaders but also of ordinary citizens in many lands. If this perception is correct, then the ultimate justification for the transfer not only of knowledge but also of wealth among nations is the same as that among people of the same nation, namely, the promotion of the common good. The difficulty is that we still lack the necessary structures to make the analogy hold, nor is it clear that even the recipient developing nations would be willing to give up the autonomy and sovereignty that such structures would demand.

We do not yet have a world society or even the necessary background institutions for the common sharing of goods and benefits and for implementing global distributive justice. We have, however, an obligation to attempt to establish such structures. Multinational corporations have an opportunity to play a significant role in helping the developed nations meet these obligations.

Global Common Goods

The question of who owns the resources of the world elicits one set of answers. The question of who owns the seas or the ozone cover, so necessary for life as we know it on earth, elicits another set of answers, the most common of which is no one. The use of the seas has been decided at least in part by various international agreements. The situation with respect to the global ozone cover poses a different set of problems. Clearly, the ozone cover belongs to no business, nation, or set of nations, and clearly, it is essential to all nations. But unlike resources that can be used up, the problem with respect to the ozone cover is not that of using it up but of preserving it. Whose responsibility is it to preserve it?

The ozone layer in the stratosphere absorbs ultraviolet radiation, which in too large quantities causes damage to plants and animals, including cancer, blindness, and other damage. The ozone layer is being depleted by atoms from a group of manufactured chemicals called chlorofluorocarbons (CFCs). CFCs are used principally as a coolant in refrigerators and as a propellant in spray cans. As these escape into the air, they rise and eventually react with ozone (O_3), changing it to oxygen (O_2). The result has been a serious thinning of the ozone level, or a hole, over the area of the South Pole. The hole is growing as a result of the CFCs produced and used by a variety of businesses. From an economic point of view, the depletion of the ozone level is what economists call an externality. It was a result of a business activity, the cost of which was not internalized by the producing firm. Were the companies that produced and used CFCs responsible for the harm done? Could the cost be internalized?

The problem is clearly an international one that can be adequately handled only on an international level. In 1985 an international conference in Vienna led the United States, Canada, and some European countries to call for a ban on aerosol cans—an action that the United States had already taken unilaterally. But each country had to take action to ban their use, and few did. The problem of the depletion of the ozone level is one that results from the wide use of CFCs by many companies throughout the world. To stop the damage means that all companies must stop producing and using them. Does one company have the obligation to stop when others do not? Does one country have the obligation to stop when other countries do not?

Chemical companies began a hunt for a substitute coolant to be used in refrigerators. Clearly, however, changing over to any new system of refrigeration, with all the refrigerators and air conditioners already in place, would be a costly and slow process.

By 1991 a substitute coolant had been developed, but it was more expensive than using CFCs. Poorer countries argued that it was unfair of the richer and more developed countries to demand that poorer countries adopt the more expensive means of refrigeration without help or subsidies from the richer countries. The poorer countries maintained that the developed countries had developed using cheaper technology, which has caused global harm, and that they now wanted to impose safe but costly alternatives on the poorer countries, which would mean delaying or preventing their development.

DuPont and other chemical companies have been urging a total ban on CFCs. But even these companies have been reluctant to abandon their use in favor of the more expensive alternatives unless their competitors do so as well. The issue is one that individual companies cannot solve alone, even when they realize that they are part of the problem and must be part of the solution. Since the problem is one that arises from many producers and many users, individual action is insufficient. Although companies that produce CFCs are responsible for finding substitutes and promoting the switch from the use of CFCs, the answer from a competitive point of view requires actions by nations, each agreeing to ban CFCs and then actually doing so. Since the developed countries are the major producers and users, they have the obligation to ban CFCs as soon as possible, even if less developed nations do not do so at the same time. It is in the self-interest of the developed countries, as well as their moral obligation, to help less developed countries implement similar bans through the transfer of technology.

The problem of ozone depletion demonstrates that global problems require global solutions. Those countries that are best placed to take action have the moral obligation to do so, even if others do not. But the same obligation to act when others do not cannot be placed on individual firms within a country. In that instance, firms have an obligation to develop the needed alternatives, to produce them to the extent competition makes feasible, to promote their use, and to foster rather than impede legislation that promotes the use of the alternative technology while keeping the competitive playing field level and fair for all.

Oil and the Depletion of Natural Resources

For many centuries, the goods of the earth seemed inexhaustible. Only in recent times have people come to realize that at our present rate of consumption and growth we can conceivably use up certain nonrenewable resources within the foreseeable future. This realization has raised many questions relating to the use of resources, to growth, to alternative means of producing energy, and to similar issues. For purposes of simplicity and illustration, we shall address only a few of the moral issues involved in our use of oil. How do we balance the present need for oil against that of future generations?

The Morally Justifiable Use of Oil

The United States today has approximately 6 percent of the world's population but collectively uses approximately 30 percent of the world's refined oil. Is the American use of so much oil just?

Until very recent times human beings lived without oil. Oil is not necessary for life as such, but it is essential to many aspects of modern life. Oil is used in the manufacture of gas for automobiles and of fuel for airplanes. Oil is widely used to heat homes and to run factories. Oil produces 43 percent of U.S. energy. In a modern society such as that of the United States, oil is a present and practical necessity. Oil is also important for underdeveloped nations if they are to achieve a standard of living that will approach that of the United States. And countries that produce no oil, such as Japan, are heavily dependent on it.

If we take the view that oil belongs to those who happen to own the oil fields or to those who produce the oil, a number of questions arise. Can those who own the oil do with it whatever they choose? Can they morally choose to produce it or not? Can they morally refuse either to pump it out of the ground or to sell it? Can they morally charge any price they wish for it? The traditional free-market approach to all these questions would be yes, providing that the market is truly free. The oil belongs to those who find and develop it. They can do with it what they choose. They will be induced to develop and sell it by others who want the oil, and it will be in the interests of both parties for them to do so. Competition and the market mechanism will determine the price of oil and its use. When the price becomes too high, alternatives will be used. The answer is straightforward and simple: The transaction is fair, providing both parties enter into it freely and with adequate knowledge.

Many people, however, will say that the situation is not that simple. Saudi Arabia is one of the largest oil producers in the world. Suppose that tomorrow it decided to terminate its oil production. Even worse, suppose that the Organization of Petroleum Exporting Countries (OPEC) decided to stop producing oil. The effect on the oil-importing countries would be devastating. It would be devastating to many of the highly industrialized countries, and it would also be devastating to oil-poor less developed countries. Can a producer, from a moral point of view, terminate its production in this way? It cannot if it has a contract that it has an obligation to honor. But suppose it honors those contracts but does not renew them and does not sell what it has not contracted to sell? The results will still be disastrous. A scenario that would have almost as serious consequences involves the OPEC countries raising their prices so that the poorer importing nations cannot afford to import the oil they need. Is this moral?

A defender of free enterprise might argue that it is moral but that neither scenario is likely to develop because both fail to take into account that it is in the interest of the oil-producing countries to sell oil. This is their chief source of wealth and income. If they do not produce and sell oil, they deprive themselves of the wealth they can use to modernize their countries and improve the standard of living of their people. If they wreck the economies of the industrialized countries, they kill off their markets, to their own detriment. But the assumption behind this reply is that the oil proceeds go to the country and not to individuals within the country, those who may have more money than they know what to do with and who therefore have no incentive to continue to produce and get more money. If they have reasons of their own for not producing oil, are they morally obliged to?

A utilitarian approach to this question considers the action and its consequences. Whereas the stopping of oil would produce very damaging results for large numbers of people, the action can be morally justified only if the damage is outweighed in the long run by advantages. One of the consequences to consider is the reaction of the industrialized countries to such a shut-off of oil. They would undoubtedly see the action as seriously detrimental to their life and not merely to their life-style. If this were in fact so, they could argue that they are justified in taking military action to secure for themselves the oil they need to survive and thereby preserve themselves. It is difficult to imagine the positive benefits of terminating the production of oil or to imagine them to be so great as to outweigh the evils that would result from such termination. To the extent that the action produces more harm than good, it is immoral.

Does the same line of reasoning hold with respect to raising the price of oil? Or to one country rather than all of the OPEC countries terminating the production of oil? Clearly, the consequences of one country's terminating its oil production would not be as serious as all of them doing so. Utilitarianism requires that we investigate the consequences of that particular action or, if it is an action based on a rule, that we investigate that rule in terms of its consequences.

The free-market approach to prices depends on the market's being truly free. Within the confines of the United States, the political mechanism operates to preclude collusion and monopolistic action. Internationally, we have no such mechanism. Hence, the setting of prices by an international cartel is possible. If users are dependent on the product, they are forced to purchase it on the terms of the seller or not to purchase it at all.

Within the United States, the price of oil is dependent not only on the cost of oil imported into the country but also on the cost of domestically produced oil. If the free market is allowed to operate, American oil companies will find it profitable to charge the same prices as foreign producers. American producers could compete against one another. But if the supply is less than the demand, they have no incentive to do so. One result of letting the market set the price of oil is that it may price oil out of the reach of the poor. For instance, if the poor need oil to heat their homes but cannot afford it, they suffer extreme consequences. The earlier principle of helping those in our society through taxes and governmental redistribution of income would have to come into play. The money that is redistributed might come from the well-to-do, but many would argue that it should come from the profits of the oil producers if they reap unusually high profits as a result of the operation of OPEC.

What of the poor countries of the world? We have no international mechanism to protect them from the effects of the rise in prices of oil owing to cartel action. If they are just beginning industrialization, they will be prevented from developing industrially and will be condemned to being poor and underdeveloped for the indefinite future. As we noted, there is a mechanism for redistribution from the oil companies to the poor in the United States; there is no similar mechanism for redistribution from the oil producers to the poor countries in the world. To the extent that their continued plight is a result of the cost of oil, they have a moral claim on the oil producers, a claim that the producers should weigh against the uses to which they put their profits. The moral claim of the poor countries is one, however, that they cannot presently press either by law, war, or economic sanctions.

If we start from the moral legitimacy of certain people owning and controlling the production of oil, then those who have a right to it are those who are able to purchase it. We adopt this general approach with nonessential as well as with essential resources. Because the people of the industrialized countries are dependent for their well-being on a continuing supply of oil, it would cause serious harm, and so be morally improper, for all oil producers to suddenly stop producing and selling oil. The price for oil is determined by the market, just as the price for other goods is determined. But when oil becomes very expensive, those who depend on it and cannot afford it must be taken care of by others.

The Needs of Developing Countries

The foregoing solution is plausible if oil is inexhaustible. We did not consider the fact, however, that the world's oil supply is not inexhaustible. Does this throw some special light on the fact that 6 percent of the people of the world use 30 percent of the oil? Does the fact that a portion of the human race can afford to buy up nonrenewable resources make it morally permissible to do so? We cannot find the answer by looking at statistics but by attempting to uncover the relevant second-order moral principles. Is there any reason to think that a principle is justifiable if it says that n percent of the people of the world should use n percent of the nonrenewable resources of the world? Might we derive it from a principle of equity, and might we defend that principle by saying that everyone has a right to an equal amount of the resources of the world? Is such a principle of equity reasonable? Suppose, for instance, we consider people in the sixteenth century. Did they have the right to the oil in the ground? It would have been a vacuous right, for they did not know about the vast deposits of oil, nor did they know what to do with oil. They had no need or use for it, given their knowledge and technological development. It only makes sense to talk about the equal right of people to oil if by that we mean equal right of access to the oil they need. If someone does not need oil, it is hard to understand what his or her right to it means.

Suppose we adopt the principle that each person has an equal right of access to the oil that he or she needs. Suppose, too, that Americans, for a variety of historical reasons, have built their houses in the suburbs, have not developed their public transportation systems, and hence need far more gasoline than do their German or Japanese counterparts. They also need much more gasoline than do countries with very few roads and automobiles, or small countries in which the need to travel great distances is much less than in the United States. People who live in cold climates need fuel oil to heat their homes and also need more oil than people who live in warm climates. There are a great many variables. If we consider need, therefore, the simple quotation of statistics is not necessarily morally significant.

There are several other principles, however, that are appropriate and that we can apply to the case of the use of oil. The amount of oil is limited. Oil is a natural resource available for the good of people. If we approach the use of oil either from a utilitarian point of view or from a deontological one, we can defend the principle that, other things being equal, we should not waste natural resources and hence should not waste oil. Stated positively, this is a principle of conservation. We should conserve natural resources to the extent possible, consistent with our needs.

Had Americans known that oil was limited and that they might exhaust it in the foreseeable future, they would not have built their cities as they did. But they did not, and perhaps could not, foresee the consequences of their actions. Therefore, as a nation, Americans can plausibly argue nonculpable ignorance. However, they can no longer make the same excuse. They are now morally obliged to conserve oil. This is a prima facie obligation to be weighed against their other obligations. It is an obligation not only of individuals but also of those in a position to make it possible to conserve oil—automobile manufacturers, those who build factories, and others appropriately placed.

If, so far, this argument has been correct, there is no set amount of oil which, in principle, has to be saved for some particular people. If Americans use more oil per capita than other nations, this is justifiable, providing the Americans do not waste it. They should make efforts to conserve it, and, as the cost grows higher, they are now becoming motivated to save it. They are also now motivated to develop alternative energy sources.

Poor countries, according to this analysis, have as much right to the available oil to satisfy their needs as do industrialized countries. As less developed countries develop, they will need more and more oil. This fact does not justify the industrialized nations preventing the development of the less developed countries. Nor does it justify an arbitrary limit being placed on the use of oil by industrialized nations, on the grounds that a certain amount must be saved for use by developing countries after they develop. Once oil is no longer available, no one has any right to it. To have a right to what does not exist is to have a vacuous right.

The Needs of Future Generations

We have argued that people have a right to equal access to the oil they need. But how are we to deal with the needs of future generations?[4] Do they have a right to oil? Do we have a moral responsibility to consider their future needs as well as our present needs? There are those who claim that future peoples have an equal right to the world's oil. This argument can be reduced to an absurdity. Consider the amount of oil that is in the ground. Call it x. If each person has a right to a certain amount of oil, then the amount to which each has proper claim is x divided by the number of people with a basic claim, however that is measured. The question, then, is how many people in the future we wish to count. The denominator of the equation increases as we add more and more generations. The amount each person has a right to gets proportionately smaller as the number we consider increases. Each of us has a right to a barrel, a gallon, or a thimbleful of gasoline, depending on how far into the future we extend our calculations.

We do not know the needs of all generations in the future, but there are some things we do know, assuming there will be future generations. They will have certain needs, some of which will be similar to our own. We also know that generations overlap. One obligation that every generation has to the next generation is to pass on to it the common goods that it has received. The goods of knowledge, virtue, and culture do not belong to individuals; they are not used up, and they should be passed along, at a higher level, if possible, than that at which they were received. The passage normally takes place by one generation teaching the next. In this way each generation maximizes good, and each fulfills an obligation to the next generation.

What of goods that can be used up? There is no obligation to pass on these goods at the same level at which they were received. Such an obligation could not be discharged. Because each generation uses part of the nonrenewable resources available, it necessarily leaves less to later generations. If such resources are needed by one generation, the people of that generation have the right to use them. They also have an obligation not to waste them. They have no obligation to make sure that those who come after them will enjoy a higher standard of living than they enjoy. Because the good of each person is as important as the good of any other, no sacrifice of one's good for another is required. No particular generation must sacrifice so that the next generation will have a higher standard of living than it had. It may do so out of love, but it is not morally required to do so.

Yet this does not mean that generations have no obligations to take into consideration the needs of those who come after them. No generation has the right to endanger future people any more than it has the right to endanger present people. It should not, for instance, bury nuclear waste in such a way that it will not affect people of the present, but will be dangerous five hundred years from now to people who live where it is buried. This obligation is one

---

[4] On obligations to future generations, see R. I. Sikora and Brian Barry (Eds.), *Obligations to Future Generations* (Philadelphia: Temple University Press, 1978); and K. E. Goodpaster and K. M. Sayre (Eds.), *Ethics and Problems of the 21st Century* (Notre Dame, Ind.: University of Notre Dame Press, 1979).

that applies not only to generations but also to individuals, governments, and businesses because it is through their agency that generations act.

Optimally, each generation should make it possible for all succeeding generations to live at a decent level of life, well above that of subsistence. But practically, we can only foresee a certain distance into the future and can only provide for a few generations beyond us, if that far. Nor can we guarantee that some later generation will not selfishly endanger the good of later generations.

How does this relate to oil? One suggested conclusion is that, collectively, we have no obligation to save oil that we can profitably use. Our resources are not so low as to demand that. Nor would there be any justification for Americans, for instance, to try to guarantee future Americans access to oil by preventing developing countries from developing and using more oil than they now do. Moreover, alternative sources of energy are not only imaginable, they are also already being developed. As oil resources are more and more depleted, we can expect the price of oil to rise. When the price rises it will become economical to turn to alternative sources of energy that are now marginally too expensive. Solar and wind power, natural gas to run cars, electric cars, nuclear power plants, liquefied coal, and other alternatives are all possible replacements for oil and will be more and more developed and used as the cost of oil increases.

People are sometimes spoken of as stewards of the earth. If we are stewards, we should use the resources of the earth wisely. But such stewardship cannot justify any group's preventing any other group from legitimate access to fulfill its needs. Nor does it demand that we not use what we need, so that we may pass it on to those who come after us.

In discussing these broad questions, the moral obligations of each individual are difficult to pinpoint. Individuals should not consider the small amount of resources they waste as inconsequential; their combined waste mounts up to a great deal. Businesses also should not waste, even if they can afford to do so—nor should governments. The difficulty, of course, comes in trying to specify exactly what constitutes waste and what constitutes need. There are clear cases of each, and there are gray areas. People may genuinely differ on these questions. But rational debate and discussion of the issues can help to clarify them, and an organized effort in these areas will make an important difference. By trying to think through the issues in moral terms, we may arrive at a course of action that will be just and maximally beneficial.

The problems of famine, of our obligations to people in foreign countries, and of our obligations to future generations to a large extent fall outside of the socioeconomic structures of any country. In our political process, future generations of Americans are represented only through those in the present who have an interest in representing and planning for them. The problems relating to people outside of our system are difficult to solve because of the absence of international structures necessary to make all the people of the world into a true community. Without a world community and without structures for redistributing wealth, redistribution is haphazard, inequitably assigned, and skewed by a host of barriers. A truly worldwide application of moral principles requires a truly worldwide community.

Whether such a community can be formed while preserving national sovereignty and differing economic systems is a basic question to which we have no clear answer. Without a true international community, however, it is difficult to form a clear idea of the extent of our duty—individually or collectively—to people of other countries, and it is even more difficult to fulfill our obligations. Paradoxically, the rise of multinational corporations, the targets of so much moral condemnation, may pave the way for increased contact and community and so lay the basis for developing the structures we need if we are to relate morally to peoples throughout the world. We should be aware of this possibility, even while we help prevent such companies from exploiting other peoples. We have argued that our government has no direct obligation to other peoples, but we as individuals do. It is up to us to make known to our government our desire to fulfill these obligations collectively through government action. We can come up with many rationalizations to ignore our moral obligations to the people of other nations. But we have no valid excuse for not attempting to determine our obligations in this area and then do what we can to fulfill these obligations.

Study Questions

1. Who, if anyone, owns the many species found in nature? Do they belong to the people who own the land or water on or in which they are found? If so, may they do with them what they wish?
2. Do you think Merck's deal with INBio was ethically defensible? Why or why not?
3. What second-order principles are helpful in deciding our obligations toward people of other nations?
4. Why help the needy in our own society first rather than those in other societies?
5. How can individuals help the starving in remote lands?
6. Is the obligation to help the starving greater than the obligation to respect national sovereignty? Why or why not?
7. Is there a difference between cases of famine and malnutrition through the fault of the people so affected and through no fault of theirs? Explain.
8. Does the American government have an obligation to help people in other lands? Why or why not? If yes, to what extent?
9. Are nation-states moral beings? Explain.
10. Do businesses and farmers in the United States have a greater obligation than other sectors to help the starving in other lands? Why or why not?

11. To whom do the resources of the world belong? Describe the status-quo answer; the universal-ownership view answer; the right to universal access answer.

12. Ozone depletion is a global problem. What is the ethical obligation of individuals, businesses, and nations with respect to this problem?

13. What does the right to development mean? How might such a right be justified?

14. How is the right to development linked with the international debt of less developed countries?

15. Would it be morally justifiable for all producers of oil to stop production? Why or why not?

16. What right does each person have with respect to oil?

17. Do future people have a right to oil? If so, to how much?

18. What obligation with respect to resources does any generation have to generations that come after it?

19. Is a worldwide moral community necessary for the full application worldwide of moral principles? Why or why not?

20. ABC Industries, an American-based company, operated profitably for many years in Brazil. As the Brazilian economy has deteriorated under the burden of its international debt, ABC Industries (Brazil) has become less and less profitable. If ABC Industries decides to close its Brazilian operation, does it have any moral obligations to its Brazilian operations, to its Brazilian employees, to the local communities in which it operated, or to the country? If so, what are they? If not, why not?

21. An African nation is systematically forcing dissident minority tribes, numbering in the millions, into barren areas of the country in which they will be unable to sustain themselves. Each month we receive reports of increasing numbers of deaths by starvation, especially among children. What obligations, if any, do we individually, do American firms, or does the United States have toward those starving people?

CONCLUSION

22

>─┼─◆〉─◆─○─◆─〈◆〉─┼─◄

THE NEW MORAL
IMPERATIVE
FOR BUSINESS

IBM: A Case Study

In 1983 *Fortune* started publishing an annual list of "America's Most Admired Corporations." Number one on the list that year was IBM, which reigned in that spot for the next three years. The list ranks slightly over three hundred of the largest American corporations and is based on a poll taken of over eight thousand senior executives, outside directors, and financial analysts. As we might expect given that group of judges, profitability is important and a *sine qua non* for scoring well. Perhaps surprisingly, however, profitability is not the only criterion and often not the most important one in a company's reputation.

In 1987 the then unthinkable happened. IBM slipped to number seven, with Merck & Company garnering the first position and holding it for a seven-year run thereafter. In 1994 Merck was replaced by Rubbermaid as number one, and IBM had fallen to number 354.[1] Finally, in 1998 it made a comeback.

What happened to IBM, and is there any correlation between being admired and being ethical? The answer to the latter question is yes. But being ethical is not enough to be admired in the workplace, at least by those highly placed therein. On financial grounds alone, we would have expected the tobacco company UST to be in second place in 1993. In fact, it ended up in number 94, and the tobacco industry in general ranked low.

---

[1] *Fortune*, February 7, 1994, pp. 68-69.

What makes a company's reputation? In *Fortune's* survey over the years, the qualities have been long-term (ten-year) annual return to stockholders, the quality of a firm's management, the quality of its products or services, the quality of its work force, and its perceived responsibility to the community and to the environment. The leaders rank high on all counts.

We can, of course, use other measures. Robert Levering, Milton Moskowitz, and Michael Katz in the 1985 edition of *The 100 Best Companies to Work for in America*[2] consider pay, benefits, job security, the chance to move up, and ambiance as the key factors in rating companies. IBM easily made the list. Employees took pride in their work, and the founder Thomas J. Watson established a "no-layoff" policy during the depression of the 1930s. Workers received high pay, generous pensions, health classes, physical examinations, adoption assistance, recreation facilities, and a wide range of employee assistance programs. They were expected to be ethical and to abide by the company's code of conduct. The company set an example and was a leader not only financially but also in its products and in the way it treated its employees and its customers. It was known for not giving bribes long before the Foreign Corrupt Practices Act was passed.

IBM received high marks in the Council on Economic Priorities' *Rating America's Corporate Conscience*.[3] The firm set up a job training program for disadvantaged youth, and by 1984 it was running forty-seven such programs around the United States. By 1984, 14 percent of its officials and managers were women, and 10.3 percent were minority members. It ranked among the top in its charitable contributions. Although it had operations in South Africa, it received the highest rating for compliance with the Sullivan Principles.

Yet in 1993 Robert J. Samuelson, writing in *Newsweek*, referred to the changing position of IBM as representing the "last rites for the 'good corporation'. This was our ideal of what all American companies might become. They would marry profit making and social responsibility, economic efficiency and enlightened labor relations. IBM was the model. It seemed to do everything right, and its present troubles (including its first layoffs) have shattered the vision with unmistakable finality."[4] What happened to IBM that so shook its image?

From 1985, when it employed 405,000 people worldwide, to 1994, when it employed 225,000, it had terminated 180,000 people, mostly through attrition, early retirement, and buyouts. IBM, which was known for its no-layoff policy, broke that policy in March 1993 with its first layoffs of 2,400 employees. In laying them off, it was more generous than other large companies, giving

[2] Robert Levering, Milton Moskowitz, and Michael Katz, *The 100 Best Companies to Work for in America* (New York: New American Library, 1985).

[3] Steven D. Lydenberg, Alice Tepper Marlin, Sean O'Brien Strub, and the Council on Economic Priorities, *Rating America's Corporate Conscience* (Reading, Mass.: Addison-Wesley Publishing Company, 1986).

[4] Robert J. Samuelson, "R.I.P.: The Good Corporation," *Newsweek*, July 5, 1993, p. 41.

them sizable severance pay, medical insurance, and help in finding new jobs. But this, too, diminished in the next round of cuts. The major difficulty was that IBM's profits plummeted. In 1992 the firm, with $65 billion in annual revenue, lost $4.97 billion, which was the largest loss by any U.S. company in history. Its charitable contributions declined, but it maintained many of its perks for its executive and top salespeople.[5] IBM cut $1 billion from its R&D budget. Its stock fell from $100.375 a share in July 1992 to a low of $40.625 in 1993—a loss of 60 percent of its value. This was accompanied by the loss of its AAA bond rating and by a 79 percent cut in its dividends, which had been the staple of many retirement portfolios.

The reasons for its fall from grace have been variously cited as fear of new risk, inept management at the top, a bureaucratic mentality, inability to adapt to changing times, overreliance on its lucrative mainframe computers, and somewhere along the line, its failure to live up to one of the cornerstones of its beliefs: respect for the individual.[6]

The disappointment that so many felt about IBM is an indication of the high ideals it exemplified. It was seen as a leader and as an example of what good companies should be. Did it act unethically in the actions it took? Was it unethical for IBM to lay off workers when it was losing money, even if it had had a history and a policy of not doing so? Was it unethical for it to cut its dividends, even though it had never done so in the past? Was IBM held to a higher standard than other companies, and if so was that fair?

The Changing Business Mandate

"There is no free lunch." This adage, often quoted in certain business circles, means that for everything we get, we pay a certain price. The price is sometimes in money, sometimes in time, sometimes in convenience, and sometimes in opportunities lost.

Business met the original mandate of the American people to grow, produce a rich variety of goods at as low a price as possible, provide employment, and help society achieve the good life. It met this mandate at a certain cost, which has varied with the times. As the service industries began to employ more people than did factories, the possibility of expanding output to cover increased wages diminished. Wage increases without increased productivity led to inflation. America's use of oil was profligate. People counted on this cheap energy source for inexpensive transportation, heating in winter, and industrial use. As the cost of oil rose dramatically, Americans faced, and will continue to face, decisions about the use of oil and of energy in general. Cost must be traded off against comfort.

---

[5] Michael W. Miller, "Vestiges of Success: As IBM Loses Mount, So Do the Complaints About Company Perks,: *Wall Street Journal*, October 27, 1993, p. A1.

[6] For one account of IBM's decline see Paul Carroll, *Big Blues: The Unmaking of IBM* (New York: Crown Publishers, 1993).

The original American mandate to business has changed, as times and conditions have changed. The change in the mandate has been gradual, and it has not been sufficiently articulated. Many businesses still do not realize there is a new mandate and struggle to maintain their old ways of doing things. They see increasing legislative controls on business not as part of a changing mandate but as a personal affront and attack by antibusiness factions and minorities. The national concern with pollution provides an index of the new mandate. When industry was starting, a certain amount of pollution was tolerated as a necessary evil. As automobiles came into popular use, again a certain level of pollution and smog was tolerated. But as industrial waste became more toxic, as lakes and rivers were threatened, as the air became dangerous to plants and humans, the general population came to see that something had to be done. Business was reluctant to change its ways and was slowly forced to do so by the Environmental Protection Agency. Car manufacturers were ordered to find ways to lower the pollution caused from car fumes. Once ordered, the industry responded. Unless ordered, it is unlikely that any manufacturer would have spent the money necessary to modify its engines because the increased cost would tend to make its cars uncompetitive. The cost of cleaner engines, of course, is ultimately borne by the consumer, who, although breathing cleaner air, pays for it through increased car costs. Electric power plants pay for antipollution devices and pass on the costs to their customers. But manufacturers are reluctant to incur expenses that force them to raise their prices, for fear of losing some customers who are no longer able to afford their products. Though the cost of controlling pollution might be handled through taxes, our society has favored the technique of making the user of the product bear the additional cost.

The American people have not operated according to a plan in changing the mandate of business. It has been changed through legislation, through collective bargaining, and through the rise of a powerful new force—consumerism.

American business started with the businessman in the dominant position. He set the pace, took the risks, invested his capital, and sometimes made a financial killing. The marketplace provided an opportunity for the poor to improve their lot. Social mobility was possible in the marketplace, and the stories of Horatio Alger inspired many workers to try to strike it rich. Some succeeded; most did not. Capitalism put the workers into a situation of inequality with respect to employers. The workers organized into unions to defend themselves and to advance their interests. Big labor soon matched big business; then big government became the third component of the system. A fourth component, the consumer, was long ignored, and has only recently gained the self-awareness necessary to organize. Consumers now fight for their rights; they lobby government, and they force management and labor to consider their interests.

The result is a new mix on the economic scene. Decisions are not as easy to make as they once were. Instead of aiming only at profits or at increasing production, managers must now weigh many factors and many interests. They must respect the rights of employees, consumers, and society in general. Respecting these rights has an economic as well as moral dimension. Faced with conflicting demands by different groups—some of which seem to be counter to the interests of business—many corporations have not known how to respond. Many of them do only what legislation forces them to do, evidently hoping that such things as consumerism and demands for social accounting will go away. Some corporations have indicated that they would like to comply with the new demands placed on them, but complain that the demands made on them by diverse groups are vague, sometimes at odds with one another, and not always clearly in the best interest of society as a whole. A few corporations have attempted to respond by taking positive action to preempt harsh legislation or by mounting public counterattacks, explaining and defending their views of the situation to all interested parties.

Frequently, a corporation has an outdated image of itself, that of an independent entity responding to the simple mandate of a former time, which precludes an effective response to current demands. We have seen that the attacks on the system of American free enterprise have not proven that capitalism is inherently immoral. But we have also seen that moral issues pervade business and society and that they cannot be ignored or dismissed as irrelevant to business.

The new moral mandate to business can be found not only in such movements as consumerism, environmentalism, and conservationism but also in public outcries over bribery and windfall profits, as well as in legislation. Business has opposed legislation dealing with environmental protection, worker safety, consumer protection, social welfare, affirmative action, truth-in-lending, fair packaging and labeling, truth in advertising, child labor, workmen's compensation, minimum wages, and pension reform. Legislation has been passed in all these areas, over the objections of business. Why has business been opposed to such legislation? In most instances, the legislation seems progressive, socially desirable, and in the public good. In each case, business decried the encroachment of government, and government claimed that business was protecting its profits. Nevertheless, all this new legislation has not prevented business from prospering and from making profits. The legislation has expressed social demands; it embodies a view of business that, when taken as a whole, is clearly different from the view found in the writings of John Locke or in the Constitution. The present mandate is different from the simplistic mandate given to business in an earlier time.

The negative response of business to each such piece of legislation shows that it is less sensitive to popular demands than many people think it should be. As a result, the general public has labeled business self-seeking, narrowly self-interested, and socially blind. The fact that business has prospered despite such legislation demonstrates that it is more resilient and more able to face social demands than many of its leaders believe or would have us believe. There may be a limit beyond which business cannot respond. But as long as the costs of such demands can be shifted to the consumer, who is the ultimate beneficiary, the costs represent social decisions. For instance, if air bags in cars increase passenger safety, and if the degree of safety that such bags represent is desired by the general population, then the car buyer will have to pay the cost. It is difficult to know whether any particular piece of legislation represents the will of the people. If air bags are optional, car buyers have a choice. Many Americans did not, and do not, want to wear seat belts. Do they want air bags? Should this issue be left to public choice? The new mandate to business is more complex than it was in the past; but exactly what it includes and what it does not is still not completely clear.

What is clear in the new mandate is that business must now consider the worker, consumer, and the general public as well as the shareholder—and the views and demands of all four—in making decisions. The good of all must be considered. The key to responding positively to this moral requirement is to develop a mechanism for assuming moral responsibility. Business must find structures for doing so.

The solution to handling competing demands is not to be found in ethical codes, although these are important, nor is it to be found in any other set of substantive guidelines. Sometimes the demands of workers will carry greater weight than the interests of shareholders, sometimes the opposite will be the case, and sometimes both will have to give way to environmental needs. And the demands cannot all be expressed in cost-accounting terms. The solution to handling these sometimes conflicting demands lies not so much in substantive as in procedural guidelines. This approach leaves the ultimate decisions concerning a business in the hands of management. But management can and should be held responsible for the decisions it makes and for its mistakes, making management more vulnerable than it was under an older view of the corporation and of business. More importantly, this approach requires a restructuring of business and of the corporate organization itself. Codes and substantive guidelines superimposed on an organization will not significantly change the way the organization functions. Procedural guidelines call for internal modifications. Therefore, in some ways, the corporation will no longer function as it did before.

By what right can anyone require such changes? The reply is that only organizational changes can enable the corporation to handle the many demands placed upon it and survive in anything like its present form. If corporations adhere to the traditional model, refuse to consider the social dimensions of a corporation's activities, and refuse to take positive action except when forced to, they invite increasingly harsh and restrictive legislation. Such legislation may eventually replace management of the corporation with governmental control and may lead, finally, to government ownership. The creative genius of American business, if put to the test, can undoubtedly come up with better solutions to many problems than those forced on it by procrustean legislation. But business must be willing to respond and willing to change.

In the past, consumers interested in buying a car have not been given the opportunity to vote on how much styling, as opposed to safety, they wanted to pay for. Car manufacturers assumed that the public was interested in styling. The automobile industry decided what would sell and what would not, and how much emphasis to put on safety. American car dealers until recently have not usually emphasized safety features when selling their cars. Despite market surveys, American drivers have had little voice in the decisions. Typical surveys ask about the consumer preferences among what the manufacturers wish to offer; they do not attempt to find out what consumers want.

In the preceding chapters, we have seen a variety of suggestions for change, including ways of increasing input by those employees with moral reservations about a company's policy or product, ways of making the board more responsive to the shareholders whom it represents, and ways of assigning responsibility. A bill that has been proposed in Congress requires company managers to disclose the existence of life-threatening defects in their products to the appropriate federal agency. Failure to do so, and attempts to conceal defects, could result in a fine of $50,000, or imprisonment for a minimum of two years, or both. The fine, in corporate terms, is negligible, but a prison term for corporate managers is not. The possibility of going to jail for one's corporate actions would make managers more careful of their decisions. The president of a corporation could be held criminally responsible for life-threatening defects, unless he or she could show who in the company was causally responsible for the decision to proceed with a product known to be dangerous. This would supply strong outside pressure to reorganize the corporation so that responsibility would be individually assigned and assumed. Such a law would provide an incentive for corporations to listen to complaints by their employees about defective and dangerous products.

We must have moral persons if we are to have moral businesses. The virtue theorists are correct about that. But that is only half the truth. We must also have structures that reinforce rather than hinder moral action.

In 1991 the new Federal Sentencing Guidelines[7] provided an added incentive to building ethics into corporate structures. According to this law, when an employee breaks a law in the course of acting for the corporation, a firm can reduce its culpability if it can demonstrate that it took action to develop a moral framework for its employees. It can potentially have its fine reduced by millions of dollars. This federal mandate has motivated companies to develop codes of conduct, to designate high-level personnel (often called corporate ethics officers) to oversee compliance, to establish ethics auditing and monitoring systems, and to enforce discipline in a consistent manner. Congress reasoned that if firms institute ethics into their structures in this

---

[7] See United States Sentencing Commission, *Guidelines Manual*, 1993, Chapter Eight: Sentencing of Organizations.

way, employees will be less likely to break the law for the company's benefit; and that companies that have acted in this way should not be penalized as harshly as those that have not. The guidelines are a response to the public's desire to hold companies to a higher standard and to impose on white-collar criminals heavier penalties than previously.

Business ethics has as much to do with business as with ethics. The Myth of Amoral Business with which we began this book has not yet been put to rest in the business world. Many still believe business has no moral responsibility. The myth stands in the way of suggested changes that would reinforce moral action. Showing it to be a myth is not enough. Corporate organization must be changed so that it can respond to moral mandates and so that those in business can act morally by design rather than by accident. Before concluding, we will briefly consider three topics: the role of government, corporate democracy, and the role of business ethics in building a good society.

The Role of Government

The government is involved with business at many levels. It is itself an employer and a purchaser of goods. It controls interest rates, regulates the money supply, and performs a great many other functions. Our central concern with respect to the new moral mandate is in government's relation to business through its regulatory agencies or through legislation. The question may therefore be asked: What is the proper role of government?

From a moral point of view, no government has the right to demand, through legislation, that which is immoral. And its proper function is not the legislation of morality. Through its courts, it settles disputes. Through its tax structure and social welfare programs, it provides for a redistribution of wealth and takes care of those for whom the market system does not provide. In supplementing the economic system of free enterprise, we saw that government fulfills a moral need.

A prime requisite for a moral government is that it act justly. It should treat its citizens as equals before the law, provide the conditions in which they can interact safely, and prevent gross injury by any individual or group against any other individual or group. It does this through its laws and its law-enforcement system. Beyond this, its primary moral obligation is not to harm or cause harm to any of its citizens. This obligation is stronger and more important than the moral obligation to provide for the welfare of its citizens. The first is a demand of justice, and the second a demand of welfare. A government has no right to harm its citizens. It has an obligation to help them to the extent possible. The first is an imperative by which it is bound; the second is a task that it should try to fulfill. As a result, it should not attempt to weigh the harm it does to some and the benefits it brings to others—it should not simply act so as to produce the greatest amount of good on the whole. The government is not an individual. It is a servant of all the people who have equal rights before it and who have the right not to be harmed by it. If its laws do harm or are unjust to any citizen, its laws cannot be morally justified on utilitarian grounds.

Let us consider the income tax, which some say is stealing from the rich for the benefit of the poor. If it were stealing, it would indeed be immoral. We have already seen the moral obligation of people within the same society to help those in need. The justification for taxation, moreover, goes beyond that. It is the result of legislation, which represents the majority will. The government has the moral as well as the legal right to take those actions that it is empowered to under the Constitution, with the consent of the majority, providing it violates no one's rights. The practice of majority rule is bounded by respect for the rights of the minority. But within that restriction, majority rule can be justified as productive of the greatest amount of good for all—even for those in the minority, assuming that the same group is not always in the minority on all issues.

If we follow this line of reasoning, the American government can protect the consumer through truth in advertising and labeling laws, through actions of the FDA and the FTC, and in many other ways, some of which we have discussed. The government is not morally obliged to interfere or to protect people in all their transactions, but it is entitled to do so to the extent that it is authorized to do so by the people. Hence, legislation that controls various aspects of business and places demands of one kind or another on it is morally justifiable, providing the laws represent the will of the people and do not violate the rights of any citizen. In this sense, legislation represents the people's mandate to business. A tendency for legislation to move in the direction of greater free enterprise is in itself no more or less moral than the tendency for it to move in the direction of socialism. Both are morally justifiable, providing that neither violates the rights of any citizen or infringes on norms of justice. We have seen no argument that satisfactorily concludes that one direction rather than another is morally preferable. How far we should go in either direction is therefore a matter for public debate.

Because the direction that government takes with respect to the control or lack of control of business is a matter for the public to decide, it is called *a public policy issue*. Such issues should be fully and publicly debated, even though frequently they are not. One of the difficulties of big government, however, is that decisions are often taken by agencies with limited vision. No one takes the time or has the capacity to see how all the different regulations impinge on those affected by them. Many small businesses, for instance, claim that there are so many government regulations with which they must now contend that they must hire more people than they can afford simply to fill out the required government forms and keep up with the government requirements. When requirements become so burdensome that they force people out of businesses, there should be some mechanism by which government and the people can see if legislation and regulation are becoming counterproductive. The tendency of Congress to form administrative units to carry out supervision has also led to such units passing regulations that seem, to some, to go well beyond what Congress originally intended. These units are not carefully overseen and therefore become self-perpetuating bureaucracies.

Issues that deserve careful scrutiny are the complaints about inefficient government regulation, about regulators being partial to the industries they regulate, about people moving back and forth between the regulating agencies and the industries that are regulated, and about overregulation. To the extent that these complaints are well founded, government tends to harm some of its citizens or treats some of them unjustly, and it thereby violates its primary obligation.

Immoral practices in business can be eliminated if those involved want to change. Governmental regulation and legislation have been used more and more frequently and now have become the favorite and usual means of reform. Self-regulation and self-reform are possible alternatives. But unless they are used, increased governmental control is the direction in which the public mandate will continue to move.

Corporate Democracy

We have already seen that workers own a large part of industry because of their pension plans and insurance policies and that workers have rights that should be respected. We have also discussed the need for greater disclosure to shareholders by and about the boards of directors. The corporation is now being looked at in a fresh light; there is more public debate about its future and concern about its power than in previous decades. But we are still a very long way from corporate democracy.

Worker self-management was an experiment that was tried with some success in the former Yugoslavia. Other forms of it have succeeded in Sweden. A few experiments, such as informing employees about a firm's entire operation and using teams instead of individual stations on an assembly line, have proved to be moderately successful. As possible models for future development, they deserve careful study. But most American workers do not want to take over management or to run their own corporations. Legislation has been suggested that would require a company to offer to sell to its employees a plant that it intended to close. But the point of the legislation is not clear. If the corporation feels the plant is unprofitable, why should the workers feel any differently? And why should anyone assume that the workers could run it successfully if management could not? Workers have even been reluctant to have union representatives sit on boards of directors of corporations because they feel that their representatives would take on management's view rather than that of the workers. Yet, the placing of union leaders on corporate boards, which has already taken place, may presage a direction that will be followed in the future. The practice of naming a majority of outside members to boards of directors is already in place.

The claim that political democracy demands economic democracy is ambiguous. In one sense, the freedom of individuals to form productive or service units and to work together to carry out an enterprise is democracy in the marketplace. The existence of private corporations, therefore, can be seen as an exercise of freedom in the economic realm. But when those corporations become giants, with a gross income as large as the gross national product of some nations, critics claim that they should be subject to the same kinds of controls citizens have over governments. The argument is reasonable if the shareholder is considered comparable to the citizen. It is less clear if the claim is that each person should have the right to some say in the operation of large corporations because such corporations influence all of our lives.

The movement toward some form of corporate democracy may be taking place, but if it is, it is taking place slowly and in a piecemeal fashion. No head-on movement for corporate democracy has as yet caught the conscience or the consciousness of the public at large. In a typically American way, the corporation is changing slowly as it meets new situations and encounters new problems. If our earlier analysis is correct and if corporations are beginning to perceive the new moral mandate more clearly, they could move more quickly to accommodate themselves to that mandate. But where there are still too little consensus and too little articulation of the mandate, the corporation will develop together with the mandate until, one day, some observer will bring to public consciousness what will then be readily perceived: That business has changed and that the corporation has responded willy-nilly to a new mandate.

Building a Good Society

A society without justice, at least without justice in its basic institutions, cannot be a good society. A good society must also have a sufficient amount of wealth, distributed in such a way that all its people have their basic needs satisfied and enough in addition for them to enjoy some of the goods of life. Beyond this, there is no single morally preferable mix of other goods in a good society.

One good society may have a certain amount of security for its people, together with a large amount of freedom of economic activity. Another good society may have less economic freedom and more security. Any good society probably has both freedom and security. But there is no one proper place to draw the line between them. Some societies desire and require a great deal of paternalism on the part of their leaders and government; some prosper with less.

And it is not necessary that a good society have no evil in it. A society that tolerates a limited amount of drunkenness among its citizens, for instance, might be preferable to one that has no drunkenness but that achieves this through periodic governmental searches and a lack of privacy. The totalitarian society depicted in Orwell's *Nineteen Eighty-Four* is hardly the notion of what most Americans think of as a good society, but neither are the societies portrayed in More's *Utopia* or in Plato's *Republic*.

The freedom of the individual to choose his or her own life-style, to develop those talents the individual wishes, to engage in one type of labor or occupation rather than another—all of these are part of what most Americans would expect to be available in a good society. A welfare state is not the kind of society that Americans want; nor do they want a society run by and for big business. Equality of opportunity, rather than equality of results, has long been treasured. But the opportunity must be truly equal and truly available to all.

We can describe no one best society. For each one we imagine we can always add more happiness, virtue, beauty, or knowledge. One of the tasks of ethics is to describe the goods worth seeking in life. Paramount among them is virtue, but it is not the only good. Happiness ranks a close second, and, for some people, happiness may be the same as virtue. A society whose people value virtue, respect each human individual, and think not only of themselves but of all whom their actions affect is a good society, even if it does not enjoy luxury and ease. One of the greatest gifts any generation can give to the next generation is the wisdom to make the best of what is available and the fortitude to overcome adversity.

Business is an activity in which human beings associate with one another to exchange goods and services for their mutual advantage. It is not an end in itself. It is a means by which people endeavor to attain a good life for themselves and their loved ones. Business is a central activity of society and a type of human association. Too often it is seen in terms of dollars and cents rather than in terms of people. Although a firm may be established for profit, the profit earned is simply a means to an end and not an end in itself. When this fact is obscured and profit becomes an end, then people are poorly served because they are forgotten and ignored in the business process.

This volume has been a long argument in defense of the thesis that the Myth of Amoral Business should be seen for what it truly is—a myth. Ethics and morality have an important part to play in business. If morality is to pervade the marketplace, management must come to acknowledge the role of ethics and morality, openly and vocally. The central moral obligation of business is not to cause harm to any of those affected by its actions. This is the heart of the new moral mandate. The obligation of business is not to reform society but to reform that part of society which is business. Business has no mandate to take on government's responsibility for promoting the general good, for providing welfare programs, or for redistributing income. These are properly public policy matters to be decided by the people. Business does have the obligation, however, to treat its workers and customers fairly, to give them adequate information, to control its toxic wastes, to provide reasonable safety in its products commensurate with the state of the engineering art, and to give due weight to those with whom it interacts.

There are three stages in the process of overcoming the Myth of Amoral Business. The first is to see it as a myth. The second is to raise the moral consciousness of those engaged in any aspect of business—managers, workers, shareholders, consumers, or simply people affected by what happens generally in business. The third is to change the structures that have been built under the guise of being value-neutral. The processes of business are all value-laden. The need for moral heroes in business is an indication of immoral structures in business. Moral heroes will appear from time to time, and they are to be applauded, but we cannot and should not expect ordinary people to be moral heroes. They cannot be trained in school or made heroic by courses in business ethics.

In recent years, we have had more moral heroes in the marketplace than we have had for many decades. Their appearance is an indication both of the changing times and of the need to change some of our social and corporate structures. Business ethics should have as a goal not only the teaching of moral reasoning and the presenting of moral arguments in defense of moral practices; it should also encourage thought among those in business, as well as among legislators and the general public, about the changes that are needed to promote morality. We have no moral blueprint for what has to be done, no panacea waiting in the wings, and no full-blown alternative system waiting to be adopted. But we are faced every day with moral problems, with immoral and unethical conduct and injustice. If we look carefully, we can see what needs change and improvement, what will increase justice and fairness, and what will motivate people to act so as to benefit rather than harm others. This requires moral imagination. A better life, a better society, and a more moral society will not be achieved by a few people developing and presenting such a society to others. A moral society is the product of a joint endeavor and can only be achieved jointly.

Business can cling tenaciously to the Myth of Amoral Business and can refuse to respond to the new moral mandate. If it does, it will convince the public that business is business, that it condones and fosters immorality and injustice, and that it puts profit above people. Some businesses and some businesspeople act in this way; but not all businesses do. Most are ethical. Some go beyond what ethics demands and strive toward and implement moral ideals. Such companies set an example for the rest and help raise the level of popular expectation with respect to business activity. Business will enjoy the moral respect of society only when it earns it. It can show that business ethics is not a contradiction in terms, not a myth, and not merely a body of theory. Ethics and morality can be a part of business. When they are built into its structure, when business lives up to its new moral mandate, it will deserve the public respect it will once again enjoy.

Study Questions

1. How do you define a "good corporation"?
2. Do you agree with Samuelson that changes in IBM mark the end of the notion of a good corporation? Why or why not?

3. What was the original mandate of the American people to business? Was it realistic for its time?

4. How has the original mandate been changed?

5. Under the new mandate, whom must business consider?

6. What is the solution to handling conflicting claims or demands?

7. What do procedural guidelines call for?

8. How might the Federal Sentencing Guidelines for Organizations promote ethical actions on the part of business? Might the guidelines be counterproductive from an ethical point of view? Explain.

9. Which is a stronger obligation of government: not to harm its citizens, or to provide for their welfare? Why?

10. How should public policy be decided?

11. What does *corporate democracy* mean? What is its status in the United States?

12. What is meant by a *good society*?

13. What are the three stages in the process of overcoming the Myth of Amoral Business?

14. How can business enjoy the moral respect of society?

15. Advanced Automotive invents an automatic braking system that will dramatically reduce accidents. The system will raise the cost of its automobiles several hundred dollars, which it is reluctant to do in the face of competition. May it ethically lobby government to pass legislation requiring the use of its system which it will license to all automakers? Is there some preferable, alternative course of action for it to follow? Explain.

INDEX